The Modernization of
Rural France

The Modernization of Rural France

Communications networks and agricultural market structures in nineteenth-century France

Roger Price

Hutchinson

London   Melbourne   Sydney   Auckland   Johannesburg

Hutchinson & Co. (Publishers) Ltd

An imprint of the Hutchinson Publishing Group

17–21 Conway Street, London W1P 6JD

Hutchinson Group (Australia) Pty Ltd
30–32 Cremorne Street, Richmond South, Victoria 3121
PO Box 151, Broadway, New South Wales 2007

Hutchinson Group (NZ) Ltd
32–34 View Road, PO Box 40–086, Glenfield, Auckland 10

Hutchinson Group (SA) (Pty) Ltd
PO Box 337, Bergvlei 2012, South Africa

First published 1983

Photoset in 10 on 12 Times Roman by
Kelly Typesetting Limited
Bradford-on-Avon, Wiltshire

Printed in Great Britain by The Anchor Press Ltd
and bound by Wm Brendon & Son Ltd
both of Tiptree, Essex

British Library Cataloguing in Publication Data

Price, Roger
    The modernization of rural France.
    1. France—Economic conditions—19th century
    2. France—Economic conditions—20th century
    3. France—Social conditions—19th century
    4. France—Social conditions—20th century
I. Title
944.06   HN336

ISBN 0 09 145180 9

Contents

Figures

Tables

Acknowledgements

A great many people helped in the preparation of this book. I would like in particular to express my gratitude to the British Academy, the Leverhulme Trust, the Twenty-Seven Foundation, the Wolfson Foundation and to the Overseas Studies Committee and the School of Modern Languages and European History of the University of East Anglia for the financial aid which made research possible; to the archivists and librarians of the Archives nationales, Bibliothèque nationale, Archives historiques du Ministère de la Guerre, of the Centre de Documentation of the Société nationale des chemins de fer français and of the University of East Anglia and in particular Barry Taylor and Ann Wood at the latter.

Christopher Johnson of Wayne State University, Detroit, John Merriman of Yale University, Madeleine Tearse of the University of Strathclyde and Jim Simpson of the University of East Anglia read and commented upon parts of the manuscript. Colin Heywood of Loughborough University, my colleague David Barrass and Heather Price read it all. I am especially grateful to all of them for their advice.

Richard Johnson, of the Audio-Visual Centre at the University of East Anglia drew the maps, Marjan Bhavsar took on the difficult task of preparing a typescript from my hand-written manuscript.

My publishers Claire L'Enfant, Pippa Driscoll and Sarah Conibear have given constant encouragement and their advice together with that of the readers whose comments they invited has been invaluable. Once again I would like to record my great debt to Robert and Jane Frugère of Bois Colombes for their many kindnesses. Above all I want to thank Heather, Richard, Siân and Emily who make life such a pleasure.

Roger Price
Norwich
1982

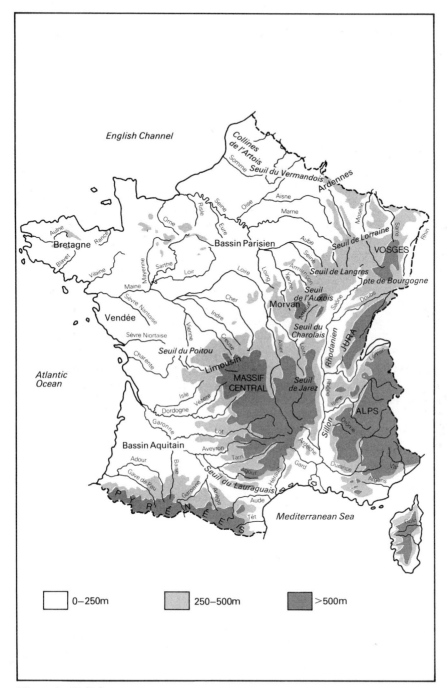

Figure 1 *Relief map*

1	Pas-de-Calais	15	Terr de Belfort	25	Seine-et-Oise
2	Nord	16	Haute-Saône	26	Seine
3	Somme	17	Doubs	27	Eure-et-Loir
4	Aisne	18	Haute-Marne	28	Eure
5	Ardennes	19	Cote-d'Or	29	Orne
6	Seine-Maritime	20	Aube	30	Calvados
7	Oise	21	Yonne	31	Manche
8	Marne	22	Nièvre	32	Mayenne
9	Meuse	23	Seine-et-Marne	33	Ille-et-Vilaine
10	Meurthe-et-Moselle	24	Loiret		
11	Moselle				
12	Bas-Rhin				
13	Vosges				
14	Haut-Rhin				

34	Côtes-du-Nord	62	Aveyron	76	Tarn-et-Garonne
35	Finistère	63	Cantal	77	Hautes-Pyrénées
36	Morbihan	64	Creuse	78	Haute-Garonne
37	Loire-Inférieure	65	Corrèze	79	Tarn
38	Vendée	66	Lot	80	Ariège
39	Maine-et-Loire	67	Haute-Vienne	81	Aude
40	Deux-Sèvres	68	Charente	82	Pyrénées-Orientales
41	Sarthe	69	Dordogne	83	Hérault
42	Indre-et-Loire	70	Lot-et-Garonne	84	Gard
43	Vienne	71	Charente Inférieure	85	Bouches-du-Rhône
44	Loir-et-Cher	72	Gironde	86	Vaucluse
45	Indre	73	Landes	87	Basses-Alpes
46	Cher	74	Basses-Pyrénées	88	Var
47	Allier	75	Gers	89	Alpes-Martimes
48	Saône-et-Loire				
49	Jura				
50	Ain				
51	Haute-Savoie				
52	Savoie				
53	Isère				
54	Hautes-Alpes				
55	Drôme				
56	Rhône				
57	Ardèche				
58	Loire				
59	Haute-Loire				
60	Puy-de-Dôme				
61	Lozère				

Figure 2 *Departments and their capitals*

Introduction

In recent years, as the New Economic Historians have turned their attention to the railways, traditional assessments of their importance for economic development have been challenged. It has been assumed that in the absence of railways 'the economy would have devised and constructed substitutes',[1]* that thereby its overall development would have been somewhat different and its rates of growth slowed, but that the development of industrial economies would have continued nevertheless. Such assumptions might seem reasonable enough but are, of course, impossible to prove conclusively.

The process of questioning accepted truths has, however, been of considerable value. It has stimulated more profound assessments of the importance of railways by reference to their advantages over existing alternatives. It has reinforced emphasis on the complexity of economic growth and has thus facilitated more realistic efforts to set the railway within particular developmental contexts. Moreover, the use of economic theory and systematic attempts to quantify have added increased rigour to the analysis.

My aim in this book is to contribute to an assessment of the importance of rail construction, and of communications more generally, to the development of the rural economy in France. Britain, the first industrial nation, has been described as 'a small country with integrated commodity markets adequately served by water-borne transport into the major centres of population'.[2] As the French economist Léonce de Lavergne observed in 1856, France was different[3] – she was a bigger country in which the development of waterways might integrate regional markets in the north and provide links between distinct regions but was insufficient to end basic market fragmentation. It was the complex of changes in the transport system associated with the development of the railway and its effects on market structure that finally brought the end of traditional French rural civilization. With the extension of commercialization and the widening of horizons, whatever the remaining obstacles to change and regardless of continuities, new economic and social structures and changed attitudes rapidly came into being.

* Superior figures refer to Notes and references on pages 399–476.

My intention is to go beyond the traditional topics of railway finance and the institutional character of railway companies, and to take up Hartwell's valid criticism that historians have 'failed to place railways in the context of essential structural change, and to relate them operationally to the process of economic change'.[4] Railways will be considered as part of a broader study of *circulation* – of the spatial flows of men, materials and of information – and of the way in which, in the historical past, the 'restrictive impact of distance . . . one of the basic factors affecting progress in the less-developed countries'[5] was overcome. I will seek to relate the communications systems of nineteenth-century France to the economic structures they connected by means of an analysis of commodity flows and changes in the spatial distribution of agricultural activity.

Part of the interest of the study lies in its concentration on the period of transition from the *ancien régime économique* to more recognizably modern economic structures – from a society characterized by population pressure on resources, restricted migration from the countryside, traditional forms of transport and semi-autarky to one with mechanized transport, extended commercial circuits, rural exodus and a growing need to adapt the structures of agriculture in order to increase productivity.

In this process consideration of regional variations in the development of communications and of agricultural economies is important. This study involves the identification of differences in resource structures and in subsequent paths of development. The significance for change of any given variable is determined largely by the pre-existing structure into which it is inserted. In the most general terms, it is likely that within any national economy a certain dualism will become evident between the most modern and the more traditional areas of the economy and society, and that transport improvement, while permitting spatial integration, will allow the survival and continued differentiation of advanced and backward areas. Certainly, no national economy can be understood without considering the difference and relationships between its regional subsystems.

Equally it is true that study of a regional economy reveals a multiplicity of interrelated causal factors. Nowhere is this more evident than in agriculture. A major purpose of this work is to analyse decision-making in the agricultural sector, to explain patterns of responses to changing market opportunities and to the diffusion of knowledge concerning possible innovations.

Economic decisions are fundamentally influenced by a range of social norms, rules of organization and conduct, which are intelligible only if examined within the framework of a given culture. They 'cannot be divorced from their political, social, institutional and cultural context'.[6] Above all it has to be accepted that 'the framework within which a response is made to a technical improvement is behavioural, not deterministic'.[7] Transport development itself has a 'permissive' rather than a 'causal' significance.[8] There might be a substantial time lag between awareness of an opportunity and response to it or there may be no positive response at all, for a wealth of both individual and collective reasons.

Some kind of theoretical background is obviously essential to provide a framework for analysis. In this respect I have tried to develop an inter-disciplinary approach, adopting a great deal from the other social sciences. The hypotheses of the economist or sociologist and particularly the geographer have provided a useful starting-point for an analysis of the 'real world'. This is not to say that it has been my intention to write either economic or sociological history *per se*. My own approach is that of the social historian, an approach which will, it is hoped, have much in common with that favoured by the social anthropologist I. M. Lewis, being – as far as the information available will allow, a 'holistic, comprehensive . . . approach', whose 'abiding concern is with the interconnectedness of things'.[9] 'Economic relationships are part of an overall system of social relation-ships',[10] and certainly economic history is seen not as an end in itself but as a means of understanding society better.

This work is concerned primarily to relate innovations in the means of transport to structural change in the agricultural economy. In part this is achieved through a 'before' and 'after' approach. Part I examines the state of communications and agricultural market structures in France prior to the development of a railway system. Taking demand and the available 'factor mix' as the basis of an explanation of development in agriculture, it considers the character and scale of change during a period when, primarily because of inadequate communications, the *ancien régime économique* survived. Part II considers the significance of the survival of a low-productivity agricultural system and a compartmentalized economic system in terms of living standards and social relationships. In this way I have tried to avoid some of the more obvious inadequacies of the 'new economic history', which, with its measurement of 'social saving' in abstract economic terms, fails to consider the alleviation of human misery that is contingent on structural change in the economy. Part III examines the development of railway networks and the modernization of communications in general, the effects this had on the organization of the market, the stimulus provided to agriculture by improved access to urban markets and the increasing com-petition to satisfy those markets.

Alexander Gerschenkron has pointed out: 'Modern discussion of economic development, vast as it is, has raised few problems that were not raised in one form or another in the course of European industrialization of the nineteenth century.' He warns, though: 'No past experience, however thorough, can save the living generations the creative task of finding their own answers.'[11] The point is well taken, but it is hoped that this study of the developmental problems and potential of a relatively backward economy in the historical past will at least offer some insights into the developmental process and lend confirmation to the necessity of development as a means of reducing human misery.

Above all, this is the story of how France, in the recent historical past, escaped from the fear of famine.

Part One

Food Production and Supply prior to Railway Construction

An analysis of the trade in agricultural commodities prior to the transport revolution is an essential prerequisite to an assessment of its significance. This first section of the book will consider relationships between demand and supply of foodstuffs, between communications networks and the organization of commerce mainly in the first half of the nineteenth century. The basic question to be considered is that of the effectiveness of the prevailing methods of food production and distribution.

1 Agriculture before the railway

Toutain has calculated that domestic agricultural production increased by 1.2 per cent per year through the period 1815–24 and 1865–74,[1] and Newell that the output of seven major cereal crops and of potatoes increased by 1.1 per cent per annum during the same period.[2] The most optimistic estimates of progress in the first half of the nineteenth century are probably those of Lévy-Leboyer, who calculates an increase in production between 1815 and 1852 of the order of 78 per cent, made up of a 72 per cent increase in the value of vegetable production and a 131 per cent increase in that of animal production.[3] One can have misgivings about such calculations, based as they are on flimsy statistical foundations, but they are the best indicators we have and suggest that agricultural productivity was more than keeping pace with population growth. By the mid nineteenth century yields were generally above levels recorded for the late eighteenth century. In the case of cereals, for example, it was generally assumed that except in mountain areas production in most years sufficed to meet local demand and also to allow the feeding of a growing number of animals and the production of beer and spirits. Yet in spite of this progress the fragility of the system was clearly revealed by repeated subsistence crises.

Limitations on technical innovation

Other than in the north (and even there progress was limited), technical innovation was localized and exceptional. In spite of the growth of commercial activity, the absence or difficulty of access to urban markets meant limited revenue and capital for investment and a lack of incentive. The limited degree to which regional specialization occurred is indicative of the continued dominance of subsistence production. Although farmers were to some extent responsive to the price variation of different crops, fear of food shortage limited the degree to which they could reduce the area under cereals. In Calvados, in spite of a fall in cereal prices of around 20 per cent in the first half of the century, the extension of pasture was slow. On the plains of Languedoc the vine was excluded from the best lands by cereals, even though wheat yields were as low as between 9.5 and 10 *quintaux* per hectare.[4]

The relative absence of specialization often meant cultivation of basic foodstuffs in unsuitable natural conditions which combined with technical backwardness to keep yields low (in many regions they hardly increased at all in the first half of the century) and extremely variable both between regions and, in the same region, between years. Total wheat production in 1840 was just over 60 million hectolitres and that of rye 27.8 million. The average yields were respectively 12.69 hectolitres and 10.03 per hectare.[5] Land-use statistics are indicative of this basic conservatism (see Table 1).

Land use reflects a complex of factors, not only environmental but also demographic and socio-legal in the shape of landownership and tenancy. Historical survivals continue to influence the potential of an agricultural region centuries after the system of which they originally formed part came into existence. This was especially the case in northern areas of open fields, in which the exercise of individual initiative depended on the transformation of agricultural systems through the abolition of *vaine pâture* and through enclosure. The survival of collective restrictions on land use was also symptomatic of overpopulation, which particularly in the north-east appears to have been a significant restraint on innovation.

Attitudes towards innovation should be seen as a part of an ensemble of social and mental attitudes in a given community. Economic systems engender a variety of goals, which might include the maximization of profit or a search for security. The foremost concern of the vast majority of peasant farmers remained the need to ensure the subsistence of their families.

Table 1   *Land use in the mid nineteenth century (1000s hectares)*

	1821	1840	1852
Land fit for tillage	25,500	25,227	26,139
of which:			
fallow	6,763	6,763	5,148
wheat	4,753	5,532	6,985
oats	2,498	2,899	3,263
rye	2,574	2,725	2,454
barley	1,073	1,188	1,040
maize	566	632	602
potatoes	564	922	829
sugar beet		58	111
flax		98	80
hemp		176	125
oils		174	
pasture	5,159	4,198	5,057
vineyards	2,088	1,972	2,191
wastelands and uncultivated	7,138	9,191	6,580
woods	7,688	8,805	

Prudence enjoined an effort to meet subsistence needs as a first priority. The reduction of risks, rather than profitability, was of prime concern. Innovation occurred, normally by means of a slow accumulation of experience, usually gained in the first instance by the larger farmers who possessed sufficient land and capital to take risks. Lullin de Châteauvieux, in his *Voyages agronomiques en France* published in 1843 stressed the significance of this essential empiricism and the gradualness of change.[6] Only in exceptional circumstances the pressure of need forced farmers into rapid innovation (the spread of the potato in response to harvest failure around the turn of the century appears to have been one such case),[7] and only when peasant farmers felt certain that they could provide for family needs more effectively by specialized production would the balance in agriculture move towards production for the market. Relative isolation, due to poor communications and the limited demands of urban markets, severely restricted this development in the first half of the nineteenth century, although everywhere commercialization of farm products increased as communications networks and commercial systems were gradually improved. The diversity of product within French agriculture is partially revealed by the estimates in Table 2.[8]

To some extent both contemporaries and historians have exaggerated the shortcomings of agriculture by concentrating on the production of basic foodstuffs and especially wheat, rye and potatoes. In societies where much of the food grown was for self-consumption no genuine record of its volume remains or ever existed. This is especially true of a mass of secondary products such as vegetables or chestnuts and the produce of numerous domestic gardens.

If subsistence polyculture prevailed in most areas, with cereals as its dominant element, variations in physical conditions inevitably resulted in nuances and in contrasts. These were infinitely varied and can be considered here only at the very broadest level. Thus the polyculture of northern France tended to be typified by the triennial rotation of crops, with an autumn cereal (such as winter wheat) followed by a spring-sown cereal (such as oats, barley or rye) and this by a year of fallow. Spring cereals could be sown because of the relatively high humidity of early summer.

Climate and rich soils were the primary natural advantages of the north, along with access to major urban markets. Population densities tended to be higher in northern France and communications better. The two major causes of change within traditional agricultural systems are increasing population and growing participation in commerce, and both stimuli were more effective in the north. In response, market-orientated agricultural systems had gradually developed over centuries with the establishment of relatively large farms, whose occupiers and/or owners possessed the capital to finance technical innovation. This was especially the case in the Paris Basin and the north. Here productivity increased substantially in the first half of the century. Yields varied with productive methods as well as natural conditions

Table 2 *Agriculture: annual average production, 1815–1914*

Period	Cereals (millions of quintaux)	Potatoes (millions of quintaux)	Wine (millions of hectolitres)	Natural and artificial meadows (millions of quintaux)	Fodder roots (millions of quintaux)	Oils (thousands of quintaux)	Flax and hemp (grains) (thousands of quintaux)	Flax and hemp (tow) (thousands of quintaux)	Beetroots (millions of quintaux)	Meat (millions of tonnes)	Milk (millions of hectolitres)	Butter and cheese (millions of tonnes)	
1815–24	86.44	25.30	37.24	—	—	—	—	—	—	548	43	113	
1825–34	97.02	42.16	40.17	—	—	—	—	—	—	602	47	127	
1835–44	111.60	63.26	38.65	178	(50)	1596	1385	1044	16	685	58	153	
1845–54	126.08	49.79	47.92	268	50	2590	859	978	18	823	63	167	
1855–64	138.89	68.77	48.42	313	52	2941	1077	1097	44	972	73	193	
1865–74	140.89	80.26	60.44	360	90	2274	753	1032	77	1091	74	200	
1875–84	142.92	92.99	46.01	408	128	1643	571	914	78	1251	74	200	
1885–94	147.39	118.04	30.70	418	143	886	352	613	64	1374	87	132	137
1895–1904	153.73	106.22	45.05	458	250	623	220	395	75	1464	81	150	154
1905–14	154.92	117.85	52.79	604	370	521	216	327	77	1535	109	170	174

– for example, in good land the effects of dryness or humidity might be attenuated by deep ploughing, manuring, drainage, etc. Nothing indicates the significance of this better than the contrasts in the net value of the product per hectare revealed by the agricultural census of 1852: in the Nord 393 francs, Seine-et-Oise 302 francs, Seine Inférieure and Pas-de-Calais 257 francs and in the southern departments such as Landes 47 francs, Basses-Alpes 50 francs, Lozère 51 francs. The west, centre and south suffered contrasting disadvantages, save exceptionally in the broad river valleys and on areas of plain. The polycultural systems of the south tended to include a greater variety of plants, but spring sowing was impossible, or very risky, due to the dryness of the summer months, so that in general only a biennial rotation, of cereals and fallow, was possible, although vegetables or fodder were often grown in the latter, particularly as population pressure grew. Practices varied with soils. On better soils in the south-west maize might be cultivated in what otherwise would have been the fallow year, or else a triennial rotation of wheat, maize and fallow introduced. But on the acidic or granite soils of much of the Massif Central or the Breton interior low yields meant misery.

Another major contrast was that in the north about 71 per cent of the land was cultivable, in the south only 29 per cent.[9] In compensation the south had large areas of poor-quality grazing and land for the cultivation of valuable supplementary foodstuffs like chestnuts. In spite of their relative technical backwardness, the varied nature of southern polycultures provided a greater guarantee against crop failure. This was important, for in the first half of the nineteenth century there were clear signs in most regions that in spite of overall improvements in supply the population remained extremely susceptible to food shortage in the event of a poor harvest. Low-productivity, technically backward agricultural systems are especially liable to yield fluctuation.

Among the symptoms of overpopulation were the increasing cultivation of marginal land and the use of a growing proportion of the land to produce basic foodstuffs. In a primarily subsistence economy price depression, from 1817 to 1851, did little to alter the balance between products. The cultivation of fodder did increase and allowed the maintenance of increased numbers of animals and an increasing supply of manure. But generally basic human subsistence needs continued to determine land use. Animals were often tolerated only as providers of draught power and manure but, because of inadequate care and feeding, were inefficient at both. Another symptom was the underemployment of the rural population, as population levels reached historical maxima in most agricultural regions without a commensurate increase in employment opportunities in either town or country. The development of rural industry and of temporary migration, while alleviating misery, was evidence of a desperate struggle to make ends meet.

Clearly, living conditions varied between places, depending upon agricultural productivity, population density and the social division of the products of labour. Living conditions were probably at their worst in upland areas,[10] but if conditions in the mountains were the most extreme, it does not appear as if anywhere in France the mass of the population had escaped from a situation in which misery was the normal state, intensified to chronic distress during the frequent periods of crisis caused by poor harvests. Thus an undernourished labour force producing relatively little sought to maintain a precarious balance between food resources and population by extending the area under cultivation, where a reserve of cultivable land still existed, or else by reducing the extent of fallow. Nationally fallow was estimated to have declined from about 10 million hectares in 1789 to about 6,700,000 by 1840. The cultivated area, which is believed to have been around 16 million hectares in 1789, increased to 20,590,000 by 1840 and to 22,340,000 by 1852.[11] In many areas with only limited technical innovation the result was increased total production but at the cost of reducing the marginal productivity of labour.

Innovation required capital and a sense of future security. Thus the size of units of exploitation and the characteristics of tenure systems were of considerable importance in determining ability to innovate. Most of the land was farmed in small units by peasant proprietors or tenants. Innovation depended to a large degree on willingness to invest on the part of those with capital resources. But, except for a small minority, large landowners had little interest in farming. Most behaved as *rentiers*, quite satisfied with the tendency for revenue from farms or sharecropping to increase as population pressure grew on the land and competition for the privilege of becoming a tenant intensified. Reinvestment of profits was not necessary to maintain income. Instead of encouraging innovation, leases tended to forbid the modification of established canons of good practice in case change would cause the impoverishment of the soil.

The great mass of small farm units were capable of generating only a very limited investment surplus, painstakingly saved over a long period and usually used to purchase land rather than to increase productivity. Landownership brought about not only greater economic security but also higher social status. Thus it was often judged to be worth the risk of borrowing, even at usurious rates (the only means of borrowing open to most peasants). Most tenants were in a worse position than were peasant proprietors. After payment of rent they had an even smaller proportion of their income available for reinvestment. Save in the north leases were too short, rents too high and farms too small. Tenants remained primarily subsistence cultivators. Rent was primarily a drain on the earnings of agriculture.

Capital shortage and the pressure to employ available workers made any innovation labour- rather than capital-intensive. Rich and poor alike were aware of the need to avoid fracturing the precarious social equilibrium by innovations which might threaten dispossession or unemployment. Indeed, where shortage of capital prevailed, labour-intensive means of cultivation represented the 'appropriate technology'. Land and labour remained the principal inputs of a traditional agriculture. In such a situation the technical inferiority of the small peasant farms was often compensated for by a more substantial labour input, and productivity levels per hectare might well be superior to those of larger farms.[12] This ceased to be the case only when landowners or wealthier tenants were prepared to invest in innovation.

In spite of improvement, food supply remained precarious before the late 1850s. Meteorological conditions continued to be a matter of obsessive interest. Excessive humidity in the north or drought in the south were the main causes of concern, which frequently turned to panic.

Demand

Demand has been characterized as 'the initiating force in the development of economic systems'.[13] The structure of farming and the nature of innovation were to a large degree determined by the characteristics of the markets for agricultural products. It is worth considering the interrelationships between the patterns of demand and methods of production in agriculture. Demand for foodstuffs depends upon the size of the population and per capita food consumption. The French population grew by some 30 per cent between 1801 and 1851. This represented an annual average of 0.6 per cent between 1821 and 1851 – not a particularly fast rate of growth by comparison with contemporary Third World societies.

Global population figures, however, tell us very little. More needs to be known about the structure of demand – i.e. about the nature of diet and the way in which it changed over time. In a predominantly rural society with an archaic communications system it is likely that diet was slow to change and that because of this and a low rate of urbanization the overall structure of demand for foodstuffs changed only very gradually. Dietary conservatism imposed by narrow social and geographical horizons and by low disposable incomes thus represented an obstacle to innovation in agriculture because of the traditional patterns of demand which it preserved.

Toutain has pointed out that food consumption allows historians to make more significant judgements about the effectiveness of an agricultural system than do statistics on the volume or value of total production. He has estimated an average food intake of 2000 calories per day in 1830, increasing to about 2800 or 3000 by the 1870s. This was made up by the consumption of 200 kilograms of bread per person per year in 1789 (550 grams per day), increasing to 280–90 kilograms during the Second Empire (750–800 grams per day) and a maximum of 295–315 kilograms (800–50 grams per day) by 1880–90. Potato consumption rose from only 20 kilograms per head per annum at the beginning of the nineteenth century to 80 kilograms per head in 1840 and 1890. He estimated fruit and vegetable consumption at about 50 kilograms per person per year at the end of the eighteenth century, rising to 90–100 during the Second Empire. Meat consumption, which is a useful indicator of living standards, rose only very slowly until after the Second Empire. These figures give some idea of the dominance of cereals in diet, bread providing an estimated 80 per cent of calorific intake at the beginning of the century and 72 per cent in 1850. The supply and price of cereals and of bread remained the main determining factors of popular living standards.[14] Although inferences can be made on the basis of statistics of production and size of population, it has to be stressed that the statistics on production are of limited accuracy. They offer a precision which is more apparent than real. The salutary warning penned by R. Musset as long ago as 1933 ought to be better heeded.[15] He maintained that although they were a convenient short-hand method of expressing relative values, they should be used only when *other* evidence confirmed the trends they suggested. In other words, he condemned the process of inference on the basis of uncertain macro-economic data and stressed the value of direct evidence of the type often condemned or ignored by modern economic historians (i.e. particularly descriptions by contemporaries).

There exists an enormous quantity of descriptive evidence about diet,[16] which makes it clear that diet varied greatly between both social groups and regions and according to local conditions of production and commercial currents. The information we possess, however, makes it clear that in spite of a tendency towards dietary improvement most of the population, in both town and country, lived in precarious conditions sustained by diets which were often inadequate to maintain the health of people engaged in hard physical labour.[17]

Some clear distinctions can be made between different types of diet. In the first place, diet tended to be better where economic activity was most developed and enough money was available to allow people to buy food. Even the poor in these conditions were less dependent on an inevitably fluctuating local food production – providing, of course, that supplies from other areas were maintained and that the scale of earnings and employment opportunities were adequate to cope with prevailing price levels. Thus between towns and between rural areas variations in economic activity influenced diet.

In this connection another distinction ought to be made, and that is between rural and urban diets. The latter were influenced by the character of the agriculture of their rural hinterlands, but the functions of the town inevitably meant that its communications and range of supply were superior to those of most rural areas. Within the town if all social groups tended to eat better than their rural counterparts, the richer inevitably ate best, although the quality of diet did not exactly correspond to wealth. Estimates of bread consumption in Paris certainly suggest considerable variation between different social groups. Husson in 1853 estimated an average daily consumption of 493 grams per person, but he further refined this by assuming the following class and sex variation:[18]

Working-class man	about 1000 grams
Working-class woman	about 550 grams
Bourgeois man	about 500 grams
Bourgeois woman	about 400 grams

The lower down the social hierarchy, the more dependent people were on basic staples like bread. Even if dietary conditions in general seem to have been better in town than country, at the middle point of the nineteenth century the most striking feature of large towns remained the widespread poverty. The Prefect of the Seine estimated in 1848 that 65 per cent of the population of Paris was close to indigence.[19] The frequency of cholera epidemics and the prevalence of tuberculosis are perhaps indicators of a deterioration in the food situation, which was not reversed in the case of Paris until the 1850s. The period 1830–55 has similarly been described as a period of dietary regression in Normandy, preceded and followed by periods of improvement.[20] But it should be noted that improvements in purchasing power were not always accompanied by improvements in the nutritional quality of foods purchased. During the 1859 inquiry into baking, witnesses stressed the repugnance of the whole Parisian population for anything other than white bread, although the repeated milling necessary to purify the flour sufficiently both increased the cost of bread and, by lowering its gluten content, reduced its nutritional value. In Paris and increasingly in other towns and villages it was claimed that workers felt humiliated if they were seen eating rye bread.[21] Thus complex questions of taste and pride come into play in determining demand.

In rural areas in particular diet was essentially determined by local resources. The majority of the population subsisted on the most common and cheapest of products – inevitably a cereal or potato crop. Only a small minority had the financial means necessary to purchase a balanced diet in all seasons, and a larger minority had the means by which to obtain regularly a sufficient, if more monotonous diet. Most of the population remained susceptible to harvest fluctuations. The economist brother of the revolutionary Blanqui, presenting the results of an inquiry undertaken in 1850–1 on behalf of the Académie des Sciences Morales et Politiques maintained that, in spite of regional contrasts, 'the dominant fact characteristic of their situation [that of the rural population] is distress . . . the general inability to satisfy the first necessities of life'.[22] In general terms the information on meat consumption as well as other indicators suggest that diet was nutritionally better north of the line Granville (Manche) – Geneva than to the south, with the continental interior in a worse position than the Midi.[23]

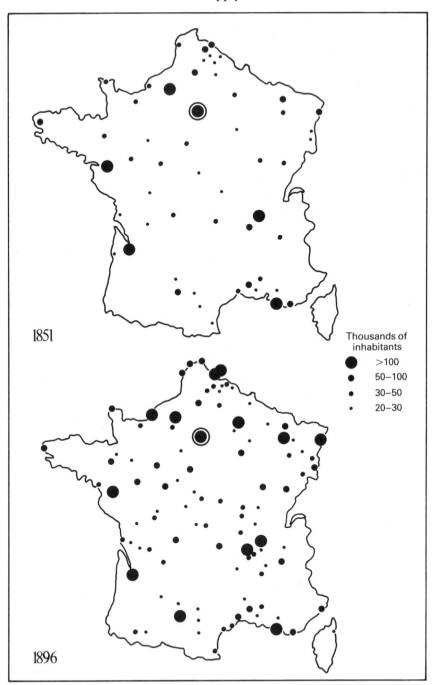

Figure 3   *Urban France 1851 and 1896*

There can be little doubt that the production of food was increasing and distribution improving in response both to the growth in demand as population rose and to the changing structure of demand. The growth of urban population provided a major stimulus to nearby agricultural regions. Figure 3, however, clearly indicates the limited degree of urbanization in the first half of the century. In most areas the bulk of production continued to be for subsistence or for local markets and was therefore barely affected by new demands or new incentives for farmers to alter their patterns of production. Such new stimuli had to await the development of communications and of commercial organization of the decades after 1850. Yet, despite their crucial importance to economic and social development, these are subjects which have been neglected by historians.

In the following chapters we shall try to follow the complicated chain of events that took agricultural products from the producer to the eventual consumer.

2 Pre-rail communication networks

The purpose of this chapter is to define the primary characteristics of the pre-rail transport system in France and to attempt to assess how effectively it met the transport needs of the economy in the first half of the nineteenth century.

In spite of its importance to our understanding of the economic and social history of France, this is a subject which has been strangely neglected by both geographers and historians. Even the regional studies which are an important product of both disciplines have, with some notable exceptions,[1] given limited space to the question of communications.

The most serious problem facing the historian is the absence of adequate bases for the construction of statistical series. J.-C. Toutain has very courageously used the various and variegated statistics which were collected (and have survived) to establish estimates of the traffic carried by the various modes of transport in the nineteenth century,[2] but these can be no more than indications of general trends (see Table 3).

There existed a functional division of labour between waterway and road transport. Historically the waterways and access to the sea were important determinants of urban location because of their capacity for bulk transport, which facilitated the feeding, warming and housing of relatively large populations and provided both fuel and raw materials and a means of marketing finished products. Road networks, because of shortcomings in their construction and reliance on animal power, provided a much more expensive alternative, which appears to have been employed for short-distance transport or the long-distance movement of goods of a value that was

Table 3 *Internal transport of merchandise, 1830–54*
        (milliard tonnes/kilometres)

Period	Road	Inland Waterways	Rail	Sea (coasters)
1830	2.0	0.5	—	0.6
1841–4	2.3	0.8	0.06	0.7
1845–54	2.6	1.2	0.46	0.7

relatively high in relation to bulk – except, of course, when there was no alternative, and goods had to bear the burden of road transport costs or remain at, or close to, their place of production. The improvement of communications in the eighteenth and the first part of the nineteenth century[3] did little to alter the fundamental pattern of relationships between the existing modes of transport.

Given these facts of economic life, one would have expected commercialization of the economy to be most highly developed near waterborne means of transport and, to an unmeasurable degree, for the growth of production in both industry and agriculture to be closely related to the efficiency of transport and the strength of commercial incentives. My first step will be to consider the economic effectiveness of the waterways.

Waterways

In the early nineteenth century

The most important parts of the French system of waterways were the rivers Loire, Rhône–Saône and Seine, and the networks of canals and rivers developed to create links between these river systems. Figure 4 illustrates this. It also indicates the existence of a system of waterways radiating from Paris and the concentration of navigable water in the economically more advanced and geographically better favoured north and north-east. Elsewhere, and particularly in central and southern France, natural conditions reduced the transport potential of rivers to a negligible level. Indeed, as will shortly become evident, natural conditions had adverse consequences for waterway users in all regions.

Assessment of the technical capacity and economic importance of the various waterways is not easy, again because of the shortcomings of the statistical sources. It is, however, generally assumed that in terms of volume carried, the Loire was the most important of the rivers. One estimate claims that as late as the 1840s traffic on the Loire was double that on the Seine and 20 per cent above that on the Rhône.[4] This was in spite of its notorious sandbanks and the interruption of movement caused by seasonal low water, which made navigation uncertain and sometimes perilous. Although from Nantes to Tours it was navigable for the whole of the year, it was navigable with certainty for only some six months from Tours to Orléans.[5] That the river continued to be so extensively used in spite of such difficulties is revealing of the high cost and inadequacies of road transport. It alone provided a relatively cheap link with the Atlantic seaboard for much of the Paris region and central France.

The Rhône corridor from Marseille was prolonged by the Saône to Gray and the Doubs and Canal du Rhône au Rhin to Strasbourg, but it provided

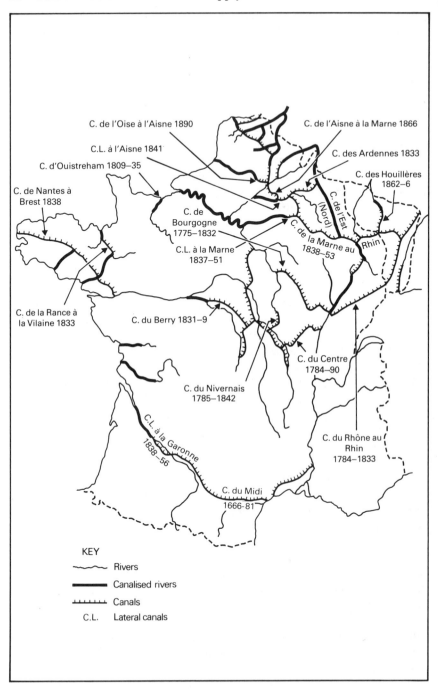

C. de l'Oise à l'Aisne 1890

C. de l'Aisne à la Marne 1866

C.L. à l'Aisne 1841

C. des Ardennes 1833

C. d'Ouistreham 1809–35

C. des Houillères 1862–6

C. de Nantes à Brest 1838

C. de l'Est (Nord)

C. de Bourgogne 1775–1832

C. de la Marne au Rhin 1838–53

C.L. à la Marne 1837–51

C. de la Rance à la Vilaine 1833

C. du Berry 1831–9

C. du Centre 1784–90

C. du Nivernais 1785–1842

C.L. à la Garonne 1838–56

C. du Rhône au Rhin 1784–1833

C. du Midi 1666–81

KEY

∼∼∼∼ Rivers

━━━━ Canalised rivers

⊥⊥⊥⊥ Canals

C.L.   Lateral canals

Figure 4   *Waterways in the nineteenth century*

Marseille with only very poor links with its hinterland. Even in the later 1840s navigation was still interrupted for something like three to four months a year, due to either excessively high or low water. In the most favourable conditions Lyon to Arles took three days down-river, and twenty days up-river hauled by horses, and these conditions lasted for only about three months. A bridge of boats at Arles made transshipment necessary before goods could proceed to or from Marseille.

Economic development, the improvement of water links with other regions, the growing importance of the port of Marseille and the intro-duction of steam boats from the late 1820s all contributed to the growth in importance of the Rhône. But even steamers could not offer regularity, security or cheapness, while their competition, having driven many of the carters out of the Rhône valley, during the periods of interrupted navigation left it less adequately provided with transport facilities than previously.[6] The problems of navigation on the Rhône were compounded by the fact that most of its tributaries were not navigable, so that movement from its banks depended on a network of feeder roads, frequently in a poor state of repair.[7] Moreover, the problem of the isolation of the Rhône valley from the rest of France was not easy to solve. Traffic to the north-east and north was interrupted on the Saône by ice in winter and by low water in summer. To the north-east, although completion of the Rhône–Rhine canal improved communications, two transshipments were still necessary en route for Mulhouse or Strasbourg, while traffic on the canal itself was liable to interruption for as much as three months in winter and one month in the summer.[8] Links with Paris and the north were provided by the Saône and the Canal du Centre and from 1832 the Canal du Bourgogne. Initially use was restricted by the interruption of movement on the Canal du Centre, caused by low water levels, and by the poor state of navigation of parts of the Saône. Subsequent improvements were financed by an increase in tolls, but these led to a transfer of traffic to the Canal du Bourgogne in spite of its ninety-five locks, which made movement very slow, and interruptions caused by adverse weather conditions.[9] Other factors hindering the development of links between the Midi and north, and Lyon and Paris included interruptions of traffic on the upper Seine for about two months each year,[10] and the general inadequacy of such essential features as towpaths. This reduced the pulling capacity of horses, which frequently found themselves in the water, and also the working lives of animals whose purchase represented a con-siderable investment.[11]

The problems of navigation on the Seine were various – including passage under the bridges (especially those of Paris) – and inadequate water levels. The most serious difficulty was that of propulsion; the meanders of the river made the use of sail difficult, while animal power was expensive and made up-river movement slow.[12] More intensive use of the Seine could occur only with the development of steam. Previously, because its orientation and lack of meanders had facilitated the use of sail, the Loire had been preferred. Now the situation was reversed. Steamers tended to draw too much water to be used extensively on the Loire.

A large number of other rivers were used for transport, at least in periods when water levels were suitable, even if this was limited in the case of some of the more torrential to the floating of wood. Among them were the Garonne and the Tarn, whose strong currents and irregular flows made up-river movement possible only for empty boats.[13] Conditions on the Allier were a little better, but even there navigation was interrupted for 180 to 200 days each year.[14] On the Dordogne down-river navigation alone was possible, and this only in spring and autumn, in between periods of summer low water and winter floods. The boats moved in the current at the speed of a trotting horse. Frequently they were unable to avoid rocks.[15] On reaching their destination boats were broken up, and their timber was sold for construction or firewood.

Attempts at improvement of the waterways

Awareness of the importance of the waterways for the transport of bulky commodities stimulated efforts to improve conditions for navigation on both natural waterways and canals. There were two main objectives: first, to mitigate the disruption caused by seasonal interruption of traffic and, second, to link the major river systems and to foster inter-regional trade through the construction and improvement of canals.

The only solution to the problem of seasonal disruption was substantial investment to improve water supply by means of barrages or reservoirs, to deepen canals and widen locks. The whole system needed to be brought up to the standards already prevailing on some of the northern canals, to take barges with a draught of 1.20–2 metres.[16] With this aim, from 1821 to the end of 1853, 535,448,759 francs were spent by the state and a further 100,560,000 francs by concessionary companies.[17] This work was concentrated especially on the economically more important waterways, in order to secure the maximum possible return in terms of the generation of economic activity and traffic.[18] Thus in the five departments of northern France the average annual investment between 1815 and 1830 was 835,869 francs and between 1830 and 1848 306,742 francs.[19] Here too favourable natural conditions reduced engineering costs. This concentration of effort led to constant complaints, especially from groups involved in navigation on the Loire, who increasingly felt that their interests were being neglected. This was in fact the case, because engineers judged that there was little chance of radical improvement and advised against the dispersal of limited financial resources.[20]

With the exception of the north, where the network possessed greater cohesion, the economic and engineering results of much of the work undertaken were sufficiently disappointing effectively to reduce subsequent investment. Thus although by 1847 there were some 3750 kilometres of canal in use, in addition to rivers, the movement of traffic was still obstructed by gaps and the unequal quality of component parts of the network which resulted in frequent transshipments and small-sized average consignments. In the centre, for example, the Canal du Berry, begun in 1823, took eighteen years to complete and then, due to inadequate water supply, could function for only around 240 days per annum.[21] This prevented the network from realizing much of its potential utility. Everywhere transport was slow, particularly where it was moving against the flow of the water. The locks constituted bottlenecks. Traffic was limited to the number of barges which could pass through them per day – on the Canal du Berry a maximum of forty – and was slow in proportion to the number of locks.[22] In April 1847, in a situation of localized grain shortage, the Prefect of Pas-de-Calais was forced to order that priority at locks be given to barges carrying grain,[23] with adverse effects on the carriage of other commodities.

Water-borne traffic and its costs

The available statistical information on the canals is very unsatisfactory. It has not been possible to make reasonable estimates of the particular kinds of merchandise carried. Another problem is our inability to account for the mass of localized movements.[24] Operating costs and freight rates were very variable over time and between places. Costs varied according to the price of boats, of horses and fodder and of course, wage levels. But the key factor determining the cost was the flow and depth of water, which affected the rapidity of movement and the carrying capacity. Freight rates were in addition determined by the scale of demand from users and the intensity of competition between transporters.[25]

The coincidence of adverse natural conditions and increased demand could cause substantial rises in charges. A major cause of short-term fluctuations in demand for transport facilities and in freight charges remained the variations in the level of inter-regional and international food transports, reflecting the success or failure of regional and national harvests. After the poor harvest of 1846 the combination of low water and increased imports of cereals through Marseille and their passage inland led to a doubling of transport tariffs on the Rhône. The efforts of merchants to guarantee themselves transport facilities in what could safely be predicted to be a difficult year ahead led them, in the autumn of 1846, to negotiate contracts with transport companies as quickly as possible, causing an increase in tariffs out of all proportion to the real increase in need at that stage of the year.[26] Even so, this was a wise move because within months barges which had not been contracted were charging far higher rates, and some merchants who had been unable to obtain space in barges were forced to pay even higher rates for transport by land.[27] Government instructions to steamer companies to load cereals in preference to other commodities appear to have had little effect.[28] The companies were operating in a sellers' market.

On the Loire and its affluents there were similar high costs and irregularity.[29] Moreover, the reduction of costs during the first half of the century was less marked than on the Seine, so that the relative economic significance of these two waterways underwent a major change. Given the importance of the Seine to the supply of Paris, it is worth looking in some detail at the evolution of its transport tariffs over time. In 1817 the administration responsible for the provisioning of Paris agreed to pay 34 francs per tonne for the transport of imported cereals from Rouen, which appears to have been quite a reasonable rate at a time of high demand for transport.[30] By 1844 rates as low as 14 francs per tonne were being quoted for a transit from Rouen greatly accelerated by the use of steam tugs – taking sixty hours compared with up to five days for barges pulled by horses.[31] But in periods of increased demand tariffs still rose rapidly.[32]

A useful breakdown of costs on the Seine above Paris was prepared in 1842 by Ponts et Chaussées engineers.[33] These clearly indicate the large variation over the course of a year in which there were no abnormal demands on facilities. They reveal also the decline in unit tariffs with increase in distance covered and the substantially higher cost of movement up-river compared with down. The frequent need to tow empty barges up-river was a key element in the establishment of transport costs. A report on movements under the bridge at Montereau on the Yonne during 1842 revealed that if the number of boats moving up- and down-stream were roughly similar, there was an enormous difference between the tonnages carried. While 3648 barges moved down-stream carrying 200,958 tonnes, 3740 barges came up-stream transporting only 30,763 tonnes.[34]

On the Canal du Midi, over the period 1836 to 1846, the cost of movement Toulouse–Bordeaux was calculated to average 12 francs per hectolitre down-stream (0.0418 francs per tonne kilometre) and 20 francs per hectolitre up-stream (0.0697 francs).[35] This was economically the most important waterway in southern France after the Rhône, linking Toulouse, an area of cereal surplus, directly with lower Languedoc, an area of deficit, and with Bordeaux by means of the Garonne.

Coastal shipping

In addition to inland waterways, substantial use was made of coastal shipping. Toutain's statistics clearly indicate the importance of this means of transport. Again, most of the traffic was made up of bulky commodities. For some areas, Brittany in particular, the sea provided the main link with other parts of France. There seems, in addition, to have been a growing tendency to use the Canal du Midi and its extensions and then the sea, rather than the

Rhône valley, for export from the south to the north and west. By the 1840s it took about twenty days in summer but perhaps forty in winter, and cost 42 francs per tonne, to reach Le Havre from Bordeaux. The journey could be abridged to eight days by a transit Bordeaux–Nantes and then up the Loire and its adjuncts to Paris. The cost then, however, was over 55 francs.[36]

The problem with sea-borne transport was its unreliability. In winter especially, winds were liable to delay movement to such an extent that land transport might be preferred. In periods of food shortage delays to the arrival of coastal or oceanic ships caused the authorities great concern.[37] During such periods the cost of both coastal and oceanic transport rose substantially because of increased international demand.[38] In 1853, for example, the basic freight charge from Odessa to Marseille was 1.25 francs per hectolitre. By 1854 it had reached 5 francs.[39]

Seaborne movement was further slowed by the inadequacies of port facilities. Little progress had been made in techniques of shipbuilding or in the size of vessels, and thus expansion of trade occurred without a corresponding increase in the capacity of ships and caused problems of overcrowding in ports. This was clearly the case at Marseille, in spite of the reconstruction of the old port from 1836 to 1844, and it was through Marseille that most cereal imports were directed – 71 per cent of the total in 1840. A poor harvest and increased imports caused severe handling problems.[40]

In 1844 an estimated 75,192 ships, grossing 2,596,160 tonnes and employing 309,497 men,[41] were engaged in coastal trade, using a multitude of ports, mostly small and degraded. There does seem to have been a tendency, however, for this traffic (and, to a far greater extent, ocean-going traffic) to concentrate on the larger, better equipped ports.[42]

Shortcomings of waterways

There can be no doubt about the importance of water-borne transport prior to the development of the railway network. Its economic significance can in large part be grasped in terms of the structure and location of industry and the development of specialized production in agriculture. Access to markets and to supplies of raw materials was heavily dependent upon location near waterways. This facilitated the development of large-scale mining and metallurgy in the Nord and Loire basin, the growth of commercial agriculture in much of northern France and the cultivation of the vine in the Loire valley and Bordelais. Conversely, the shortcomings of this form of transport were to a large degree responsible for the dispersal of industrial production close to raw materials and markets and for the survival of a semi-subsistence polyculture in most regions until the second part of the nineteenth century. The high cost of movement of most commodities in relation to their value and the fragmentation of markets which ensued limited the stimulating effects of access to large markets and of competition.

In France, unlike Britain, water transport did not provide a means of market integration other than on a limited regional basis. This was due primarily to differences in geographical structure between an island penetrated by numerous stretches of navigable water and a much larger continental land mass within which upland zones obstructed inter-regional transportation.

Given the limited effectiveness of waterway communications, economic activity in France was to a far greater extent than in Britain dependent upon road communication. This was of crucial importance for movement from waterside locations to those at a distance, for intra-regional transport, even in areas with a relatively high density of waterways, and for inter-regional movements into areas with negligible facilities for water-borne transport. It has been estimated that prior to the establishment of a railway network some 60 per cent of the tonnage kilometric (i.e. number of tonnes carried, multiplied by the number of kilometres covered) was carried by road, and 40 per cent by water.[43] Our next step is to consider the efficiency of road transport.

Roads

Major roads

The first traffic census in 1856 provided estimates of the annual tonnage transported on the *routes nationales* of the various departments. This provides no more than a general impression of regional variations in traffic density. It is not likely that the existence of a railway network had changed these very much by this date. It reveals, not unexpectedly, a close correlation between demographic densities, levels of economic activity and the volume of goods transported. Traffic density was heavier in the departments of the north, the Normandy and Paris regions and those of the Loire, Rhône, Puy-de-Dôme and the Marseille region than in the east, Brittany, Alpes, Pyrénées and most parts of the Massif Central.[44] Again not surprisingly, given the importance of waterways in determining the initial location of urban centres, and the subsequent generation of economic activity, road traffic was heaviest in precisely those areas with effective waterways. In effect, over the centuries those relatively efficient communications networks that existed stimulated economic activity, which in its turn encouraged efforts to improve communications.

The period of Revolution and Empire, through neglect of other than strategic roads, had seen a general deterioration in transport conditions. The work of improvement, so characteristic of the eighteenth century, was interrupted, to be resumed once more during the Restoration and, even more actively, during the July Monarchy. There was clearly a growing appreciation of their economic importance. An official report in 1824 observed that although transport by water offered a cheap means of movement, 'time is a value that is more appreciated today than it used to be: it enters into all the calculations of speculators'.[45] Delays could be expensive in terms of capital tied up, the deterioration of goods in transit[46] and changes in relative price levels while they were *en route* to their destination.

Attention was first concentrated on the main arteries linking Paris with other major urban centres, the *routes nationales*,* and secondarily upon the major roads, those of regional administrative and economic significance, the *routes départementales*.[47] Table 4 shows clearly the scale and chronology of achievement.[48] Assessment of the quality of work carried out is more difficult. In addition to new construction, substantial improvement of existing roads was necessary. A report presented to the king in 1824 stressed this. It observed that three factors contributed most to the deterioration of road surfaces: the action of wheels, the accumulation of rainwater, particularly where lack of any camber and potholes permitted water to settle, and the alternate action of freezing and thawing. Only improved construction techniques – lessons from MacAdam were suggested – and regular maintenance would prevent deterioration.[49] In many cases in the past roads had been constructed high on valley sides to avoid the problems of drainage and bridging that were likely to arise in valley bottoms. As traffic increased and loads grew heavier, the gradients to be climbed were increasingly regarded as burdensome and economically wasteful. In general, roads were also too narrow. For various reasons it was concluded that in very many cases the work of repair would cost as much as new construction. This highlighted the major problem faced by engineers, financial stringency limiting the amount of work allowed, in spite of the general awareness of the shortcomings of communications which existed in government circles.[50]

This partly explains the attempts made to reduce deterioration by orders like that of 1806, limiting the weight of carts and requiring minimum width

Table 4 *Road networks, 1800–54 (thousands kilometres)*

Year	Routes nationales	Routes départementales	Total
1800	25.7	17.3	43.0
1814	27.2	18.8	46.0
1830	28.9	23.8	52.7
1840	34.2	—	—
1847–54	35.6	41.8	77.4

* Their exact title varies with the regime. For consistency's sake, *routes nationales* will be used instead of *routes royales* or *routes impériales*.

for wheel rims – it had been calculated that narrow wheels were more likely to make furrows than broader ones. Insufficient surveillance and lack of weighbridges made implementation difficult, as did economic circumstances.[51] Thus an ordinance of 2 October 1846, fixing allowable summer and winter weights for carts, was declared inapplicable on the Marseille–Lyon road before the end of the year because carters were increasing tariffs to compensate for lighter loads, and merchandise was rapidly piling up.[52]

In response to an inquiry initiated by the Napoleonic administration, substantial evidence of poor communications and its economic consequences had been gathered. Quantifiable conclusions are not possible, but the inquiry illustrates the scale of the problem and also the variations in conditions. Thus the road from the important manufacturing town of St-Etienne to Rive-de-Gier was good in all seasons because paved, but on the road from Rive-de-Gier to Lyon the surface was bad enough to necessitate reducing cartloads by one half in winter. Men on horse or foot were said to abandon the road entirely and to follow ancient tracks. The St-Etienne to Montbrison road, frequented by large numbers of coal carts, was even worse.[53] There were many such examples.

The available statistics indicate substantial achievements by the middle of the century, both in the establishment of roads and in their improvement. Even in relatively isolated and neglected regions like the Limousin, the network of *routes nationales* had been given the basic configuration it would subsequently retain.[54] Most roads were provided with surfaces which allowed carts to carry heavy loads at higher speeds and with less wear and tear on animals and equipment.[55] Paradoxically, the condition of *routes nationales* and *départementales* was reported to have been especially good in departments like Loir-et-Cher, where they were relatively little used[56] – indicative of the fact that in some areas at least roads were adequate to the levels of traffic they had to bear. Elsewhere the engineers of the Corps des Ponts-et-Chaussées continued to report that insufficient funds prevented adequate maintenance, with inevitable results for those roads bearing the heaviest traffic,[57] so that even on major roads and in spite of improvements which in many areas transformed transport conditions, movement was often difficult. Furthermore, horse traction inevitably limited both the volume of merchandise carried and the speed of movement.

There were, of course, degrees of 'impracticability' of roads. Conditions depended upon soils, gradients, field patterns and willingness to improve them. The utility of improvement was most obvious and the capital most readily available in economically advanced areas – in the north and north-east, in the Paris region, on the plains of Flanders, northern Lorraine and Alsace – and those with relatively intense currents of movement like the 'sills' of Poitou (Paris–Bordeaux) and the Lauragais (Bordeaux–Cette), of Bourgogne (Paris–Lyon) and in the Rhône corridor. The important role of Paris as a commercial centre and market was particularly marked.

Traffic was sparse elsewhere, and even in these favoured regions the inadequacy of secondary roads made movement over vast areas difficult and reduced the volume of traffic fed on to major roads.

Secondary roads

Local roads (*chemins vicinaux*) were only very slowly improved. Again, the statistics available are not particularly helpful. But prior to the law of 1836 and for a considerable time afterwards the general opinion of all concerned seems to have been that the condition of these roads was poor and that they constituted a severe handicap to economic development.

The authorities were clearly aware of the problem. The responsible minister, the Comte Decazes, reported in 1820: 'The poor state of our *chemins vicinaux* is the subject of unanimous complaint. The relevant legislation is imperfect, since for the last thirty years it has been ineffective.'[58] This was a reference to the law of 1 December 1798, which had made the *chemins vicinaux* a charge on communes. This and the law of 28 July 1824 both lacked effective sanctions. Thus the financial resources available for expenditure on these minor roads were proportionately even less adequate than those expended on major roads.[59] A ministerial circular to the prefects on 15 February 1832 pointed out the inadequacies of resources allowed for local road works by the law of 28 July 1824 and asked the departmental *conseils généraux* for advice on revision of the law.[60] In the light of this advice a further circular on 5 December 1835 observed that responsibility for the maintenance of the local road network could no longer be left to the communes where these roads were in practice of more than local importance. Neither could the expenditure of large sums of money on road improvement be left to local bodies without proper supervision by agencies of the central government. Legislation was therefore to be introduced which would lay down general regulations for the raising and expenditure of money.[61]

The law of 21 May 1836 sought to transform the situation by clearly defining local responsibilities for the care of roads. It provided for an addition to the four main direct taxes of up to 5 per cent for expenditure on local roads, with the option for each head of family of providing up to three days' work (*prestation*) himself, for each male member of his household aged 18 to 60, and for each cart he possessed.[62] Abolition of labour service in 1818 had only led to a reduction in road maintenance where individuals and communes were unwilling to part with scarce cash resources. The 1824 law had restored the right to choose to meet one's obligation with labour or cash.[63] Under the terms of the new law, local roads of particular importance were to be classified as *chemins de grande communication* or *chemins d'intérêt commun* by the departmental *conseils généraux* on the advice of the municipalities or *conseils d'arrondissement*, to be transmitted by the prefect, who would determine the contribution of each commune to the maintenance of a particular stretch of road.[64]

What was probably the most significant innovation was reaffirmed in a circular of 24 June 1836 advising on the implementation of the new legislation. In the past the inability or unwillingness of communes to co-operate had constituted the major obstacle in the way of the establishment of local road networks. In establishing the responsibilities of communes for road maintenance, earlier legislation had provided no powers of coercion to ensure that these responsibilities were observed. Henceforth communes were to be obliged to maintain roads classified as *chemins vicinaux* to standards laid down by government engineers. Prefects were invested with the right of supervision and with the necessary coercive powers to overcome local indifference or inertia. In exceptional circumstances departmental financial aid might be provided, but the funds available for this remained very limited.[65]

The size of the task of improving local roads can be judged from an official description of the aims of the new law. These were to create, as a complement to 35,000 kilometres of *routes nationales* and 37,000 of *routes départementales*, over 48,000 kilometres of *chemins vicinaux de grande communication* and to 'repair, as well as maintain constantly viable' 677,000 kilometres of *chemins vicinaux de petite communication*, 'the state of absolute degradation of which strikes at the heart of our agriculture'.[66]

There clearly existed considerable local good will towards these intentions and growing awareness of the economic importance of road improvement. Road construction, improvement and maintenance, and the means by which work might be carried out, were frequently subjects of discussion by municipal authorities.[67] The Prefect of Hautes-Pyrénées highlighted the major continuing obstacle to progress, namely, 'the slenderness of the resources applicable to the *service vicinal*'. He added: 'It should not be concluded that municipal councils are opposed to the execution of the law; they understand the advantage of good roads, but they prefer not to take the responsibility of imposing sacrifices' (i.e. taxes or labour service).[68] Table 5 provides estimates of expenditure.[69]

Progress was slow. Only in some western areas, from fear of renewed rebellions in support of the Legitimist pretender, were substantial government funds available for the rapid construction of strategic roads.[70] Besides financial difficulties there was a shortage of trained engineers. In 1839 in seventy departments the engineers of the Corps des Ponts-et-Chaussées were not involved in the service of *chemins vicinaux*, the work being left to the largely untrained *agents voyeurs*. Resources continued to be wasted as a result of imperfect administration – particularly the difficulty of supervising labour.[71]

Although in most regions little was achieved in respect of the ordinary *chemins vicinaux* before the Second Empire and much even of the work on

Table 5   *Estimates of expenditure on* chemins vicinaux, *1837–66*

Period	Prestation* (estimated value in millions francs)	Cash Expenditure	Total
1837–41	109.4	133.6	243.0
1842–6	163.6	133.8	297.4
1847–51	179.0	171.6	350.6
1852–6	188.7	200.1	388.8
1857–61	218.4	219.5	437.9
1862–6	251.0	289.8	540.8

* Labour service or cash in lieu; the value of the former is clearly impossible to estimate accurately.

chemins vicinaux de grande communication remained to be completed in this later period, the 1836 law was of considerable significance, as the evolution of overall expenditure on *chemins vicinaux* clearly reveals.

The difficulties faced in carrying out improvements were greatest where isolation made improvements the most necessary. Thus an engineer reported from the Landes that even roads receiving particular attention as a consequence of their importance remained unpaved 'because of the expense of transporting the materials necessary for their establishment and maintenance from a considerable distance'.[72] Only the coming of the railway would permit the economical transport of road-building materials. In east Aquitaine at mid century even outside the mountains only *routes nationales* and *départementales* were passable in all seasons. On other roads the lack of bridges made even small streams impassable after rain.[73] Similar assessments can be quoted for most regions. In Bas- and Haut-Rhin in 1847 'half the villages were almost inaccessible during the winter; agricultural work was obstructed by the difficulty of carting fertilizer; the harvest only arrived at neighbouring markets due to a substantial reinforcement of teams of horses'.[74]

Complaints were frequent even from areas with relatively good communications. Thus in the canton of Maubeuge (Nord) in 1848 many villages remained quite isolated.[75] In the department of the Rhône the local road network remained a confused pattern of tracks, established over the centuries to meet the changing needs of population and economy, on which circulation was made difficult by steep gradients and rapid deterioration after rain.[76]

Although everywhere improvements were occurring, and more rapidly than ever before,[77] by comparison with later periods progress remained slow. In many areas carts replaced pack animals and horses replaced oxen in order that heavier loads could be pulled more rapidly than had been possible previously. The density of relations between communities increased.

Comparison with the pattern and mode of relations, as described by respondents to the transport inquiry of 1811, is instructive: a certain transformation had clearly occurred. But except for relations between town and town (via *routes nationales*) and between the larger markets or *bourgs* (usually by *routes départementales* or *chemins vicinaux de grande communication*), communications in most areas remained difficult in summer and often impossible in winter. Most communities continued to experience isolation because of poor links with major roads. Movement remained slow and expensive, particularly off the plains and major river valleys.

Balzac, in the *Médecin de Campagne*, described the transformation of a mountain commune by the opening of a road. This permitted the replacement of pack animals by carts. In general, mountain areas were the last to receive adequate roads. In the Pyrénées, Alpes and highland areas of central France mule transport survived into the third quarter of the nineteenth century, and even where movement of carts was possible, the gradients made it difficult.[78] In the Limousin by the late 1840s, if the improvement of *routes nationales* had opened up west–east, north–east and south–west axes, there were few north–south links, and the traffic in the mountains and the south-eastern plateau remained particularly light.[79] Winter snows were likely to interrupt movement for months and to make communications, even along valleys, hazardous.[80] Flooding was another frequent danger in valleys. Those of late 1846, for example, had dire consequences for food supplies.[81]

Another region of particular difficulty was the *bocage* of western France. Here sunken roads, encroached upon by hedges, turned to mud after rain. The dispersal of habitat necessitated the existence of numerous little-used tracks which communes with limited financial resources could not hope to maintain satisfactorily. The journey to church or market or from farm to field was thus rendered particularly extravagant of time and effort.[82]

Although aware of the problems of farm roads (*chemins ruraux*),[83] successive governments and local administrations felt unable to do anything about them. The work of improving *chemins vicinaux* more than absorbed available resources. The amount of time that a farmer spent on the road depended obviously on the scale of his farm, on its structure (frequently land holdings were accumulations of dispersed parcels) on the crops grown, on the techniques used and on the frequency of journeys to markets. With slow means of transport, the time taken up must always have been substantial.[84] This concerned large farmers, but for the peasant it was a normal part of his life; hence it is not likely that he, at least, conceived of it as time lost.[85]

The speed and costs of road transport

Transport by road thus remained slow and expensive, in spite of substantial improvements. In respect of both travelling times and tariffs, averages merely concealed infinite variation. It seems better therefore, while referring to calculations of averages, to list also specific examples (bearing in mind that these too tend to be averages or estimates) for particular places.

The two basic sources of information concerning the time taken to transport goods by road between two places are the transport inquiries of 1811 and 1870,[86] the latter providing information for as far back as the 1840s. Comparison is not easy because the information obtained from these inquiries (both, unfortunately, incomplete) rarely refers to the same places and because in the case of the first it is normally given in terms of the number of days taken to move from point A to point B, while in the second it specifies the distance covered in a given time – usually twenty-four hours. However, for want of anything better. . . .

In 1811 goods took twenty days to go from Lyon to Rouen or Lille, five to Grenoble and nine to Marseille.[87] Nantes to Paris took eighteen to twenty-two days, to Rennes eight to ten days, to Orléans ten to twenty-two, to Lyon thirty-six to forty.[88] Mont-de-Marson (Landes) to Bordeaux took three days using horse traction, seven to eight using oxen.[89]

By 1845 it might still take fifteen days for a cart to travel from La Rochelle to Paris,[90] eight days to travel the 100 kilometres from Marseille to Forcalquier (Basses-Alpes)[91] or sixteen from Le Puy to Paris,[92] although much faster times were possible by *roulage accéléré* at a cost, however, too high for commodities of low value in relation to bulk.

By *roulage ordinaire* by 1845 the kinds of speed recorded were 25 kilometres per day by carts from Ste-Menehould (Marne),[93] 33 kilometres per day by those of Sens (Yonne),[94] 40 kilometres by those of Beauvais (Oise),[95] 40 to 50 from Ferté-Macé (Orne).[96] By this time an ordinary goods train might well cover similar distances in an hour.

Freight rates depended on a multiplicity of factors, including, obviously, the time taken – which varied with the seasons and weather and with the nature of the road – and its effects on wage and fodder costs, the availability of return loads, the capacity of carts (in itself determined by road conditions and that of the draught animals available) and the formal organization of transport. These factors varied enormously, and as a result so did tariffs, creating a large margin of uncertainty in the profit calculations of merchants.[97]

In addition to specialized transport organizations, mainly small in scale and normally active in long- or medium-distance transport, many farmers hired out their carts during quiet periods on the farms, in order to earn some ready cash. The rewards were not great, but carting was one among a great variety of means of supplementing income from agriculture.[98] Their activity served to keep freight rates down. For short-distance movement of agricultural products the farmer, of course, depended upon his own means, and although the volume cannot be measured, it is likely that this constituted the bulk of actual commodity transport.

Another major factor influencing freight rates was the supply of, and demand for, transport facilities. Fluctuations were especially marked along the key route through the Rhône valley. Following large grain imports in 1816, at a time when flooding of the Rhône threw all the normal traffic on to the roads, the cost between Marseille and Lyon rose from the normal 80 francs per cart to 200 francs.[99] In 1846–7 a similar situation prevailed, and in both cases road tariffs were further increased by the deterioration of road surfaces caused both by the greater volume of traffic[100] and by the direct threat of pillaging of loads and damage to carts from hungry crowds after poor harvests.[101] Charges also increased with steeper gradients. Thus at mid century rates per kilogram were twice as high on the transit Moutiers–Albertville (Savoie) as on the itinerary Albertville–Chambéry.[102] In most areas tariffs always increased in winter because of the added difficulty of movement along muddy roads. At Lyon in 1811 the rates doubled;[103] at St-Etienne they normally increased by 20 or 30 per cent.[104] Tariffs also increased in various areas during the harvest, seeding or grape gathering, when peasants who normally sought part-time employment as carters were involved in agriculture. At Vinça (Pyrénées-Orientales) in 1812 the increased cost of transport during June, July, October and November because of this was of the order of one-third.[105]

In general, freight rates tended to fall in the first half of the nineteenth century as a result of generalized price depression. This was particularly the case in northern France, where there existed a relatively well developed network of roads, more intense economic activity (which encouraged better organization of transport) and the competition of waterways. However, even in this favoured region transport remained expensive and tariffs unstable.

Comparisons over time are difficult because of the diversity of the information available. In most small localities it was necessary first to find someone willing to cart commodities and then to negotiate the price. Prices were not likely to be fixed,[106] but it appears that the cost of *roulage ordinaire* was frequently around 40 centimes per tonne kilometre early in the nineteenth century,[107] although examples of both higher and lower rates are easy to find, and that by the mid 1840s rates of 25 centimes were common (but again so were higher and lower rates).[108] It ought further to be observed that these rates were for transport on *routes nationales* and *départementales* and that movement on other roads could be considerably more expensive. According to one experienced contemporary observer writing in the 1840s, on a good road transport might cost 30 centimes per tonne kilometre and on the typical *chemin vicinal* 80 centimes.[109]

It has been suggested that the main reduction in tariffs occurred before 1830 and that subsequently, in spite of improvements to roads, the growing demand for transport facilities permitted carters to maintain the level of their charges.[110] It might be affirmed with more confidence that rates were lowest in relatively flat areas and where competition from waterway or coastal traffic was possible – in general, in those areas already more advanced economically and particularly in the north. Everywhere, however, the cost of road transport remained a substantial economic burden.

Conclusion

The capacity of the pre-rail communications system to cope with the growth of traffic, in the absence of major technological innovations, was limited by geographical conditions and by dependence on animal power. The crisis caused by increased demand for transport facilities following the poor harvest of 1846 was indicative of this. Nothing more clearly illustrates this relative impermeability of economic space than the existence of major price differentials between markets. Although these clearly declined as transport conditions improved, they remained substantial. Improvement of conditions on the waterways had proved, with the limited geographical exception of the far north of the country, to be only a palliative for the inadequacies of road transport. Minard, a senior Ponts et Chaussées engineer, acknowledged this in observing: 'the utility of canals is recognized along their length but extends itself for only short distances from their banks. Immediately the merchandise transported by boats has to be reloaded into carts, the unloading, the reloading and carting eliminates the economies offered by water transport'.[111]

A transport system provides 'a facility for the movement of goods and people' and 'just as the flows create this network, the very form of the network conditions the nature of the traffic movements that can be accommodated'.[112] Until the middle of the nineteenth century, and in spite of substantial improvements, the 'form' of the communications network in France was such that movement was expensive and slow, and the result was that economic compartmentalization set a severe limitation on the 'flows' of traffic. Thus the *ancien régime économique* survived until the middle of the nineteenth century. It was characterized by the predominance of agriculture, artisanal forms of industrial production and slow and expensive modes of transport. The hallmarks of this society were isolation and localism. The economy was far from stagnant, but the volume of trade, and in consequence the incentives to innovation in both agriculture and industry, were restricted by the costs of transport. The potential for dynamic action was limited.

3 Agricultural market structures before the coming of the railway

The gradual improvement of communications in the eighteenth and the first half of the nineteenth century led to the enlargement of economic circuits and to increased economic activity, but without transforming the basic characteristics of the pre-industrial commodity market. This was shaped essentially by expensive transport, compartmentalization, limited specialization and low levels of purchasing power, and by differences in population densities and in natural environments, leading to variations in crop patterns between localities – the bases for trade in agricultural commodities.

Obviously, either production is orientated towards a consumer, who might be the farmer and his dependants (in which case production is for self-subsistence), or it is a commodity, an element in an economic system based upon exchange. In this latter case there must be a geographical separation between the functions of production and consumption, which are linked by the stage of distribution. This chapter is concerned primarily with the spatial characteristics of the distribution stage. It will concentrate broadly on the trade in cereals, and in particular wheat, as the most important agricultural commodity and the one on which we have most information.

Contemporary economists are able to use far more reliable statistics than are historians. The statistics available on agricultural production, although they gradually improved throughout the last century, are particularly unreliable. Prefects were to a large extent forced to take on trust whatever local mayors served up to them.[1] Warnings were proffered about the 'lack of sincerity', the arbitrary *confection d'une statistique* by local notables afraid that the information they supplied would serve as the basis for new tax assessments.[2] As a result, governments remained more interested in the results of general inquiries, whose wide range of information provided an insight into structural change in the economy, than in the inaccurate series of production statistics.[3] Historians ought to follow this example. Nineteenth-century market place sales statistics similarly have to be used with care, particularly given the large and increasing volume of trade which occurred off the market. Equally serious is the fact that information on the transport of commodities is notable mainly by its absence and, where it exists, gives only limited geographical coverage. The only reasonably reliable series of statistics available are those concerned with the prices of the range of commodities, particularly foodstuffs, listed in the *mercuriales*. These were of vital interest to officials concerned first and foremost with the preservation of public order because the price of bread, the main item in popular diet, was based on them. In spite of their shortcomings,[4] they reveal short-term movements in supply–demand relationships, and analysis of them can show something of the workings of price mechanisms and of the degree of permeability of the national market.

It would seem sensible to accept the limitations set on the analysis of market structure by the inadequacy of the statistical data rather than to aim for the apparent certainty of a statistical analysis based on flimsy foundations. I prefer to begin by exploring the possibilities suggested by the geographer who wrote: 'When inadequacies of the historical data entirely preclude their mathematical *analysis*, the alternative of a mathematical *approach* should prove of value. This involves determining the relationships between phenomena rather than being concerned with the particular characteristics of the phenomena themselves.'[5]

Market structures

The existence of numerous fairs and markets reveals the dispersed character of commercial activity, as well as the importance of exchange in communities, whose ideal nevertheless remained self-subsistence. At these fairs and markets people sold their cereals, poultry and eggs and bought draught animals or young cattle for fattening, sometimes clothes and farm or domestic equipment. This exchange of a surplus for necessities appears to have been the prime function of most local markets. In the marketing of this surplus the farm, and also the hamlet or village (conceived of as a collection of farms), can be identified as the first stage, 'the point to which all the produce . . . is brought either for consumption . . . or for onward shipment to the local dealer or market'. The farm, hamlet or village served as 'a collecting and clearing centre'.[6] In effect, consideration of the distribution of agricultural products involves two aspects: distribution within rural society and movement from country to town. In addition to consumption by the farmer and his family, there were a mass of unrecorded sales in which local consumers simply bought or exchanged goods and services with a local producer – a direct purchase eliminating expensive intermediaries. Sale by a farmer at a local market place had the same effect but was more onerous in its demands on his time. Much of the trade in rural society was based on small local markets performing commercial functions primarily for their immediate region. Villages, *bourgs* and small towns themselves consumed a great part of the food marketed locally. Exchanges of goods and services occurred there between peasants, artisans and notables, while the volume of external trade was limited and in the hands of a few merchants and artisans.

This level – that of farm to local market – might be perceived as the weakest link in the marketing chain, at which prices were established on the basis of inadequate information about supply and prices elsewhere in the region. When they wanted to sell surpluses not needed locally, farmers were very much subject to pressures from the few commercial intermediaries that were likely to be present. Most farmers lived within restricted economic horizons bounded by poor communications, limited literacy and the risk of straying into markets where their own reputations and those of the people with whom they dealt were unknown.[7] Furthermore, pressing financial needs – especially rents – frequently forced them into the market place to sell during periods of the year when prices were not at their highest.[8]

The local market place might be conceived of as the second stage in the marketing process. Organized long-distance trade was the exception, but intra-regional trade was relatively intense. The inquiry into transport of 1811–12 indicated that every little town or market village possessed either one or two carters, if it had serviceable roads, or else (and especially in mountainous areas) perhaps six or seven mule drivers.[9]

Since road transport was not capable of moving bulky agricultural commodities over long distances at sufficiently low cost, in most cases the only areas which could play much of a role in inter-regional trade were those close to waterways or the sea. The area served by most market places was thus normally a restricted one. It was determined by the practical distance over which farmers could transport their produce in order to arrive at market at the normal hour and then return home.[10] The essential criterion was accessibility. In the Gers at mid century there were 430 villages with less than 1500 inhabitants, regularly spaced every 4 or 5 kilometres, and, in addition, 37 *bourgs* or towns (higher-order marketing centres) with populations above 1500, each dominating a radius of 20 to 30 kilometres. These were little towns all located on valley roads, such as Lectoure, Fleurence, Auch, Mirande in the Gers valley, or Condom, Valence, Malauze in the valley of the Baise.[11] In economically more advanced departments, like Calvados, grain markets rarely served farmers outside a radius of 15 kilometres and, in the case of most secondary markets, less than 10 kilometres. In the 1830s the major cereal markets were at Falaise, Argences, St-Pierre-sur-Dives and Caen. The last owed its importance to its position in the centre of the grain-producing plain and to the size of its population. The other three were in the zone of contact between the plain, an area of relatively specialized grain production, and the Pays d'Auge, increasingly concentrating on cattle and dairy products.[12]

The areal limits served by a particular market might change over time as transport conditions changed, but the basic characteristics of the pre-industrial rural marketing system were not transformed prior to the railway era. A hierarchy among market places did, however, clearly evolve according to the varying functions of specific market centres. These functions included simple consumption but also retail and wholesale activities or transshipment where one form of transport linked with another. The importance of a market place thus depended on its geographical location as a route centre, the size of the region it was able to serve by collecting and redistributing commodities and its own size and significance as a centre of consumption. In some circumstances marketing centres were simply juxtaposed rather than hierarchically organized. The southern Alps seem to have been a case in point.[13] There topography intensified transport problems and increased the number of isolated market centres, each with its own zone of activity. In terms of compartmentalization of the market, such upland areas differed only in degree rather than in basic structure from lowland areas blessed with relative ease of communication. Everywhere the high cost of the movement of goods remained a massive disincentive to production for sale.

In terms of functional hierarchy, marketing centres might be divided into three groups: those of national importance, those of regional importance and those of only local importance. Most numerous were those centres forming the last group. Slowness of movement, and hence the limited distance a man could cover in one day, provided a *raison d'être* for the commercial activities of a large number of small markets.

Every village wanted its fair or market, not only in hope of increasing economic activity and prosperity but also as a mark of status and because regular gatherings had obvious socializing and entertainment functions. Not only the market villages, the *bourgs*, but also most of the small towns were dominated by rural activity. Many of their inhabitants worked the land, and often their merchants and professional men were also landowners.

A town with regional importance was distinguished from a *bourg* by the lesser degree of its attachment to its rural surroundings and the greater significance of its secondary and tertiary functions. Thus alongside the middle Loire not only major centres like Tours, Orléans and Blois but also smaller places like Chinon, Loches and Amboise in Indre-et-Loire, Vendôme and Romorantin in Loir-et-Cher and Gien and Pithiviers in Loiret could be readily distinguished in this way from the mass of smaller centres.[14] Their importance illustrates the limited scale of economic regions. They served as principal markets for the surrounding areas, collecting commodities from, and redistributing to, the networks of minor market places, but on the basis of a variously circumscribed choice of routes and range of contacts with centres outside their region.

Some centres were of national importance because of their greater commercial activity. This was usually a consequence of their role as entrepôts. Paris was obviously an exceptional case. Most, if not all, such centres were sea or river ports (Marseille, Bordeaux, Strasbourg, Toulouse) or were at the confluence of major waterways and roads. Limoges, for instance, at the intersection of the east–west routes with roads to the south, was the only significant centre in the Limousin and performed entrepôt functions for the whole centre-west. That the evident tendency towards concentration of commercial activity continued to be restrained by the slowness and cost of transport is suggested by the case of Dijon, which, although the major place of passage between the centre of the Paris Basin, Champagne, Lorraine and the Saône valley, still shared the regional grain trade with such places as Auxonne, Pontailler, St-Jean-de-Losne and especially Gray.

This was only one of the technical conditions restricting the commercialization of foodstuffs; another was the limited degree to which urbanization and the establishment of concentrations of population completely freed from connections with the land had occurred. The most urbanized regions of France in 1851 were the north, part of Languedoc (Montauban, Toulouse, Castres, Carcassonne), a region which might be defined as that of the lower Rhône enclosed in a triangle whose three points are Avignon, Montpellier and Toulon, the towns along the Loire from Orléans to Nantes, the Lyon–St-Etienne area and, of course, Paris. Urban France constituted a very diffuse network with only fifty-eight towns of over 20,000 inhabitants, including twenty-four with 20,000–30,000 and six with over 100,000. Normandy, Maine, Brittany, the south-east and east of the Paris Basin, the south-west and Alpes all had only a small share of urban population. Concentration of population had important consequences for the development of agricultural specialization. Given high transport costs, development tended to be determined largely by distance from market.

In general, every market place assumed dual functions: it permitted the local population to provision itself, and it acted as one element within a wider commercial circuit. In Côte-d'Or, given the lack of economic means of transport, even the most important markets – Beaune, Auxonne, Seurre, St-Jean-de-Losne, Pontailler, Nolay, Saulieu, Semur, Montbard, Châtillon – provided a means of direct contact between farmer and consumer in the form of a series of small transactions.[15] Although these markets had a dual function, local transactions overwhelmingly predominated. These were typical of what one economic journalist subsequently described as 'markets which are provisioned only with great difficulty by farmers who make the foodstuffs bear the cost of very expensive transport'.[16] The carting of grain to numerous small mills and marketing centres meant a continuous circulation of large numbers of carts – a movement relatively intense in terms of volume of traffic and of commodities carried, and occurring in all directions, but impossible to estimate or trace; it served to balance production and consumption at a local level, but with only intermittent links with extra-local trade.

In contrast were markets, again characterized by dual functions, where extra-local needs predominated. These might be centres draining the surplus above local needs from some dozens of small markets. Georges Frêche has examined in especially close detail the market structures of the important grain-producing region around Toulouse in the late eighteenth and early nineteenth century.[17] He has described a spatial hierarchy with, of greatest importance, centres like Toulouse, Montauban and Castelnaudary, which engaged in inter-regional trade, then an inferior group composed of two different kinds of centre. The first of these were 'markets of contact', such as Albi, supplying the Rouergue; Castres, the Montagne Noire; Limoux, the Roussillon; Pamiers, the Foix area; St-Gaudens and Montréjeau, the Central Pyrénées; and Auch and Condom, the Landes. The others were secondary river and canal ports like Auterive on the Ariège, Cazères and Castelsarrasin on the Garonne, Lectoure on the Gers, Beaumont on the Gimone, and Villefranche de Lauragais and Carcassonne on the Canal du Midi. These, and markets devoid of waterways like Revel, Mirande, Lombez and Lavaur, served as concentration centres for some dozens of surrounding villages and to them came merchants and their representatives from the main marketing centres.[18]

Paris was the most significant urban centre in terms of its dominance of regional agricultural and commodity flows. Within a radius of some 50 kilometres merchants and millers supplying the city were able to purchase directly from farmers. Beyond this market places still tended to function as points of concentration and relay. At Pont-Ste-Maxence, Etampes and Chartres were concentrated the production of the Valois, Soissonnais and Picardy, as well as of the Vexin, Beauce and parts of the Brie. Early in the century transactions concerning 200,000–400,000 hectolitres might occur annually at each of these three places, involving well over half of the grain destined for Paris.

In closer proximity to the capital, dealing with only 20,000–40,000 hectolitres per annum, were the markets of Montereau, Bray-sur-Seine, Melun, Nemours, Pontoise, Clermont-sur-Oise and Beaumont-sur-Oise, Fontainebleau, Meaux and Provins. The organization of these markets in space and also in time served to regularize supply. Thus in the Brie the most significant were markets held at Brie-Comte-Robert, Tournus, Donnemarie, Egreville and Rebais on Mondays; at Coulommiers and Nangis on Wednesdays; at Dammartin and La Ferté-Gauche on Thursdays; at Lagny, Fontainebleau, Bray, La Ferté-sous-Jouarre and Lizy on Fridays; and at Melun, Provins, Rozay, Montereau, Nemours and Meaux on Saturdays.[19]

As the century progressed and sales by sample became more common, however, cereals were increasingly turned into flour before transport to market – especially in the mills of the Marne and Ourcq valleys, at Corbeil, Coulommiers and in the Provins area.[20] Lyon also drew its supplies from a wide area, but particularly from regions adjacent to the Rhône and Saône, and imports moved up-river from Marseille.[21] Similarly, grain brought by the rivers Somme and Scarpe was concentrated at Arras, both for local consumption and for onward shipment to Lille and other urban centres in the Nord.[22] The pattern was repeated in the provisioning of all major population centres.

Geographical complementarity as a *raison d'être* for marketing centres was most obvious in the relationships between mountain and plain. In the Toulouse region, from around Albi, Castres and Pamiers, grain was moved to the highland areas of Rouergue and Foix, frequently causing a local deficit, which was then filled by purchases in areas closer to Toulouse itself. In the Ariège the major markets situated at valley crossroads or points of contact between plain and mountain served principally as redistribution centres for innumerable and unmeasurable currents of trade – wheat and maize from the lowlands being exchanged for iron, wool and potatoes from the mountains. Price variation between lowland and highland markets illustrates the frequent shortage of grains in the latter and their attractive pull on lowland surpluses. Thus in June 1821 (the moment of annual price maxima) prices in the Ariège varied between 14 francs per hectolitre of wheat at St-Ybars in the plain, increasing as one moved into the mountains to 14.50 francs at Mas-d'Azil, 17.55 francs at Foix, 17.96 francs at Tarascon and 18.75 francs at Castillon.[23]

Such price variation over relatively small distances gives one some idea of the impermeability of market space.

The survival of the *crise de subsistence* provides the clearest indicator of market imperfection. Although the frequency of crises and their violence tended to decline as agricultural productivity increased and communications and commercial organization were improved, the years 1802–3, 1810–13, 1816–17, 1828–30, 1839–40, 1846–7, 1854–6 could all be regarded as periods of subsistence crisis, when prices for basic foodstuffs, and especially cereals, rose to abnormally high levels following poor harvests. Periods of high prices were often followed by the collapse of prices to levels which were unremunerative to commercial farmers, although the bumper harvests which caused this were welcomed by the mass of subsistence cultivators. In many areas the price of wheat in 1818 and 1819 fell to half that of 1817, and this was again true in 1848 and 1850 in comparison with 1847. The years 1821–7 and 1834–8 were also periods of good harvests and low prices. In the first half of the century there appear to have been only short periods free of prices that were either excessively high or low.

In situations of both rising and of falling prices, if local price movements were linked to regional prices, they clearly possessed considerable autonomy, depending primarily upon local conditions of both production and supply. In 1846–7 prices were highest in the north and east, especially in Alsace, declining towards the south-west, the Massif Central and the south. In normal years prices in the south tended to be higher, while large surpluses were produced in the north. In a crisis year the south and south-east, especially the Rhône corridor, were favoured by imports through Marseille and Cette and benefited from the gradual improvement of access to these ports. For this reason, and because of a lesser degree of dependence on single crops, the Alpine region experienced a far less brutal crisis in 1846–7 than did the rich alluvial plains of the north. Whereas in the Nord in May 1847 the price of wheat rose above 44 francs per hectolitre, the maximum prices reached in the Isère and Vaucluse were 37.05 and 32.13 francs respectively. In the Vaucluse prices rose from the cyclical maximum of 1846 by some 25 per cent to a peak in 1847. In the relatively less accessible Isère the rise was of the order of 59 per cent.[24] Further along the Rhône–Saône corridor, in the Côte-d'Or additional transport costs pushed this maximum up to 38.90 francs in the second half of March 1847, at which time prices varied considerably between the different markets in the department, again illustrating the imperfections of the market – 42.50 francs at Beaune, 42 at Nolay, 40.25 at Châtillon, 39.59 at Dijon, 39 at Montbard, 30.12 at Semur and 34.87 at Auxonne.[25]

After a poor harvest in northern France it was likely that departments which normally purchased part of the surplus produced there would now go short, and, due to the relatively high degree of specialization in wheat production, local prices themselves would rise to high levels in the absence of alternative crops. Furthermore, the continued operations of commerce would contribute to the maintenance of anxiety and hence a high level of consumer demand.[26] In effect, three kinds of area were likely to be severely affected by harvest failure – areas heavily involved in commercial agriculture with a *tendency* towards monoculture and usually high population densities, most obviously Picardy, Beauce, Brie, Champagne, the northeast; areas with a large proportion of their land given over to fodder, forest or vines, which in normal times depended upon the first for their supplies – the Paris region, for example;[27] and, finally, isolated areas like the Massif Central, the Alpes and the Pyrénées, where poor soil meant that yields were low and in which local harvest failure could only be slowly compensated for by importations and then at high cost.[28]

As one would expect, price variations between markets were greatest where communications were most difficult, and especially in upland areas. In the Ardèche cereals production was never, even in the most abundant years, equal to consumption. Prices were consequently higher than those in neighbouring departments, especially in the south of the department. Official reports stressed the variation in prices even between markets separated by only short distances. Towards the end of the Second Empire this difference was 1.50 francs between Villeneuve-de-Berg and Aubenas, 16 kilometres distant along the same *route nationale*, rising to 3 francs between Barjac (Gard) and Vin, 24 kilometres distant.[29] Cultivators in Haut-Rhin, separated by a chain of mountains from Lorraine, Bourgogne and Franche-Comté, enjoyed a virtual monopoly in normal times because of the cost of transport from those places, so there too prices normally tended to be rather high.[30] In most of the departments of the north-east, on the contrary, prices in years of good harvests were the lowest in France because supply usually exceeded demand. Following poor harvests, however, these were the areas with the highest prices because they were farthest from the port areas in which imports provided a stimulus to price reduction. Here more than anywhere else the tendency for the traditional cereals market to range between glut and shortage could be observed.[31]

Transport costs, even in normal periods, remained high despite the improvements in conditions. Poor harvests, resulting in an increase in the traffic in cereals, increased price variations between markets because of both the alteration in the relation of supply and demand and the general increase in transport costs. Even along the Loire variations were substantial, and they rose rapidly with distance from the river: at markets held between 19 and 23 January 1847 average prices varied between 31.33 francs at Tours, 30 at Chinon, 29 at Azay-le-Rideau and 43 at Bourgueil.[32] Similar variations were recorded in markets in the Rhône–Saône corridor. According to a report written on 8 November 1846, a hectolitre of wheat had sold at an average price of 29.90 francs at the last market held at Lyon. On the same day the average price at Roanne and Belleville had been 35 francs, at Bourg 33.20 and at Mâcon and St-Laurent 36.[33] The poorer the transport links between markets, the less did information concerning price differentials spread, the higher was the actual cost of responding to them and the slower the response. One interesting survey of road movements towards the important grain marketing centre at Gray (Haute-Saône) in 1853 calculates a gap of one month between peaks in price movements and corresponding movements (the appropriate commercial response) in the volume of traffic.[34]

In the type of pre-industrial market situation we are discussing, with poor communications, 'equilibrium between the price of foodstuffs on various markets becomes impossible, and everywhere we are exposed to a perpetual variation between misery, born of need, and misery, born of abundance'.[35] In these words a government report in 1824 contrasted situations of shortage and glut occurring in the same place at different times because of the high cost of corrective action. Nothing more forcefully illustrated the limited effectiveness of market mechanisms, though the existence of major price differentials between markets provided an opportunity for substantial profit making through buying on one market and transporting for sale at another.

Clearly, poor communications represented a major obstacle to efficient commercial activity even in northern France, where communications were most developed.[36] This was true in 'normal' periods as well as in those of crisis, when obviously the consequences were much more serious.

In the first place, the shortcomings of available transport led to substantial variations in costs, according both to the season of the year and to the supply of, and demand for, transport facilities. The large margin of uncertainty that this left for the profit calculations of the individual merchant discouraged long-distance activity. Second, in general economic information circulated badly. Although news of the relative size of crops spread quite quickly, exact information was lacking, even to the government, while newspapers carried only limited information on prices. Personal contacts might allow the creation of a network of reliable correspondents, but extensive networks were the prerogative of the large merchants rather than the mass of small traders. Poor communications and the slow diffusion of information resulted in slow and imperfect reactions to changing market conditions.

This can be better appreciated with the aid of a fuller analysis of commodity flows.

Commodity flows

In spite of geographical diversity, the overwhelming factor, even as late as the 1850s, was the uniformity of agricultural systems. No wide region possessed a characteristic specialized agriculture. Due to the inadequacies of roads and river links, entire departments remained without economic links to major routes. The difficulty with which cereals filtered across large land areas in periods of shortage was an easily comprehensible reason for the reluctance to abandon subsistence polyculture. Wherever possible, products were exchanged between neighbouring complementary regions producing more or less regular surpluses of cereals, wines, animals, etc. Commodity flows were limited and resulted in most areas from an often simply coincidental deficit or surplus. External purchase tended to occur from what was regarded as unfortunate necessity rather than choice. The exceptions to this were those areas in the north and in Upper Languedoc where relatively specialist wheat production had gradually developed.

As we have seen, the scale of activity at particular market places was determined by several interrelated factors, including the characteristics of the surrounding agricultural area, the structure of communications and the size of the agglomerated population. A market might function primarily either as a centre for redistribution or as a centre for consumption. Inter-regional trade flows were determined by the changing relationships between demand and supply of foodstuffs – reflected in price differences – in the various regions and the facility of transport between them. Major urban centres acted as nodal points, stimulating and controlling inter-regional flows through the activity of their merchants. This was the sphere of the *négociant* rather than of the small-scale trader or farmer.

It would be a mistake to minimize the complexity of trade flows. Their direction fluctuated with relative prices and local levels of production and demand. In general local harvest failure or the inability of habitual suppliers to provide at any time resulted in the necessary extension of the zone of supply of a particular centre of consumption. This was very clear in the case of major centres – above all, Paris. In years like 1846–7 its merchants were forced to look far beyond usual markets in the Beauce, Champagne and Picardy. Conversely, farmers and merchants in Seine-et-Marne primarily supplied Paris but could also sell to Alsace, particularly when the natural suppliers of that region in Lorraine were attracted by higher prices in the Midi.[37] It was profitable for farmers and merchants at Langres (Haute-Marne) to sell wheat to the *négociants* of Gray at one moment, while consumer demand at Langres itself would have to be met soon afterwards by means of purchases made along the river line of the Saône.[38] In January 1847 merchants from Charente and the Vendée who normally sold grains for the supply of Bordeaux were making purchases in the better supplied market of the port city to compensate for poor local harvests.[39] Although a specific area might in a given year produce a surplus for sale in other regions, it might be found at a particular time during that same year, for a variety of reasons – the lateness of the harvest, the lack of water at mills – that purchases elsewhere of grain or flour became necessary. This frequently happened in the Caen region, which consequently purchased in Maine-et-Loire or Mayenne.[40] It would not be possible to describe all these complex flows of grains or flour. It is particularly difficult to monitor inter-regional exchanges within a single country. There are no statistics comparable with those based upon imports.

Everywhere although the cereals trade was dispersed between a multitude of markets, and prices varied significantly within regions whose scale varied with the cost of communications, major marketing centres assumed a degree of domination over supply/demand conditions and price movements. Given this dominance one would expect prices to fluctuate more widely on markets of lesser importance, within limits ultimately set by the range of variation on major markets and the cost of transport between secondary markets and those drawing on extra-regional supplies. In northern France such major markets as Paris and Amiens assumed dominant positions. Towards the end of the 1840s small-scale merchants in the surrounding regions had recourse to the *négociants en gros* of such centres in order to provision themselves.[41] Similarly prices at Toulouse essentially determined those within a radius of 50–100 kilometres, depending upon the direction.[42]

The normal zone of provisioning of Paris, the largest single market, extended over the departments of Aisne, Oise, Seine-et-Marne, Seine-et-Oise, Eure-et-Loir, Eure, and beyond, especially to the north. The stimulus afforded by proximity to Paris and other urban centres of the north and north-east led to increases in agricultural productivity and encouraged extension in both the volume and range of commercial activity.[43] Paris itself was claimed to be the best provisioned and the most competitive grain market in France.[44]

By means of a radial network of roads and especially waterways – the upper and lower Seine, its affluents, the Aube, Yonne, Canal d'Orléans, Loing, Marne – cereals were sent to Paris, or increasingly to the large mills at

Nogent and Corbeil, from which flour was subsequently sent to Paris and many other places.[45] The production and trade in cereals and flour for the supply of Paris in effect influenced economic activity and price levels over a considerable area of France.

The north-east, as well as the Paris region, was relatively heavily engaged in inter-regional cereals trade. Although Alsace, and especially the Haut-Rhin, was rather isolated by mountains and expensive communications,[46] trade was more active in Lorraine, Champagne and Bourgogne. The department of Moselle might be taken as a case in point. Normally an area of relatively low prices, attracting purchasers from such areas as Meurthe, Vosges and Alsace,[47] in years like 1846 it drew trade from as far afield as Valence (Drôme),[48] usually supplied from Bourgogne.

The Toulouse region constituted the main cereal-producing area of southern France. Grain entering inter-regional trade was concentrated primarily at Castelnaudary and Toulouse for export.[49] In the years between 1837 and 1852 when statistics were for the first time adequate, 70 per cent of the exports of cereals and vegetables on the Canal du Midi originated in Toulouse, 28 per cent in Castelnaudary and the remaining 2 per cent at Carcassonne. The trend seems to have been towards concentration at Toulouse.[50] The main markets were lower Languedoc and Provence, attained by the Canal du Midi and the Mediterranean.[51] The second major current was down the Tarn and Garonne towards Bordeaux, but the combination of higher transport costs and competition with sea-borne arrivals of grain from Brittany and Picardy meant low and uncertain levels of profit. The gap between prices at Toulouse and Bordeaux was frequently insufficient to cover transport costs between these two points. Grain from the Toulouse region was usually uncompetitive in the Bordeaux region, unless first milled, usually somewhere between Montauban and Agen.[52] Bordeaux was normally well supplied by sea and by producers in its hinterland, extending over a considerable area in the departments of Garonne, Lot, Lot-et-Garonne and Dordogne; large areas of land in the more immediate hinterland were thus freed for the cultivation of the vine. Towns like Moissac served as intermediary collecting points.[53]

On the markets of lower Languedoc and Provence, in contrast, competition from sea-borne cereals, originating in North Africa, Sicily or Syria, could be supported. The normal gap between prices at Toulouse and Marseille was more than adequate to cover transport costs.[54] Competition was not, however, entirely absent from these markets, although it was restrained by the cost of transport from other inland areas. When harvests in upper Languedoc were poor and prices rose, wheat from Bourgogne, coming down the Saône and Rhône entered southern markets, while sea-borne imports also tended to increase.[55]

Toulouse, as a marketing centre, remained dependent upon the capital and purchases made by merchants from Marseille, Montpellier and, to a lesser degree, Bordeaux. Price movements in these its major markets were followed after an interval by local prices.[56] The problem for merchants operating in and around Toulouse and for the farmers of the region was that not infrequently prices at the sea-ports were affected by imports from and exports to other regions. Thus in March 1847, following receipt by MM. Courtois, bankers at Toulouse, of the news that wheat had fallen by 2.50 francs per hectolitre at Marseille, it was regarded as highly likely that prices at Toulouse would also fall.[57] Slightly later in the same month reports of large-scale purchases at Marseille by merchants from Bordeaux, Le Havre, Rouen and Paris, leading to substantial price increases there, were thought bound to lead to similar increases in prices in the Toulouse area, which at that moment were relatively low by comparison.[58] By a kind of wave-like movement changes in prices were transferred from one market to another, with declining intensity as distance increased transport costs and reduced the degree of interaction between markets.

Just as there were areas of habitual surplus, so there were those normally in deficit, most notably the whole area of the Massif Central. Within the Massif the trade in grains was restricted. There more than anywhere else, the aim of cultivators was self-sufficiency. In good years surplus rye produced in Haute-Vienne might be sold in Creuse, Corrèze, Cantal or Aveyron, but more often shortages led to purchases of grain from surrounding regions. In effect the Massif Central, due to its geological structure, lacked internal unity. Trade tended to be with complementary areas in the surrounding plains rather than with other parts of a basically similar economic region. Thus the northern Massif was orientated towards the plains of Berry and the Paris region, the west towards the Charentes, the south and south-west towards Périgord and the Midi.[59]

Whenever possible, deficits were made up by purchases in the nearest markets with a surplus at a satisfactory price. Habitually, merchants from the Allier made purchases in Cher,[60] those from Lot in Lot-et-Garonne,[61] those from Creuse in Indre and in Cher.[62] But in periods of generalized shortage these areas of habitual deficit found themselves in especially difficult situations. The prefect of Creuse complained in February 1847 that in years of abundance the cultivators of Indre and Cher were glad to sell on the markets of his department, but when shortages occurred elsewhere they were attracted away by the greater convenience of supplying the larger towns, served as they were by easier communications and better-organized commerce.[63] Returning to the subject on 8 March 1847 he stressed the difficult position of areas in the interior, which received supplies of imported grains and foodstuffs produced in the plains only after more accessible areas.[64] If commodities appear to have moved with a wave-like motion, the amplitude of the last wave, striking the Massif Central, was the smallest of all.

The main axes for the movement of grain were the river valleys and particularly the Seine, Loire and the Rhône, with its continuation on the Saône. In functional terms (that is, in allowing for the penetration of the landmass) the Rhône–Saône axis was probably of greatest importance.

Although prolonged by the Doubs and the Rhône–Rhin canal to Strasbourg, the most significant stretch of water on the Rhône–Saône axis was that between Gray on the Saône and Marseille, with Arles serving as the terminus for most river traffic and acting as a link between the seaport and the interior.

At both extremes of this waterway were major grain-marketing centres, attracting supplies from their hinterlands and, in the case of Marseille, from overseas and by means of coastal shipping. Along the line of the waterway merchants competed to maintain existing markets and to extend their normal zone of supply. Competition was, however, restricted by transport difficulties and more especially by the cost of transport entering into the final selling price of the marketable commodity. Nevertheless, there existed somewhere between these two extreme points a zone in which price competition was possible – a zone whose position fluctuated with basic cereal prices and transport costs, but which could at various times extend the competition of cereals brought to market initially at, or in the region of, Gray, into the hinterland of Marseille, particularly when local supplies or sea-borne imports were inadequate at the latter.[65] Similarly, when supply conditions in Bourgogne made it feasible, cereals from Marseille became competitive there.[66]

Gray reached its apogee as a river port in the 1840s, serving particularly as an entrepôt for the Midi.[67] Surpluses produced in Champagne, Lorraine, Franche-Comté and especially Bourgogne were gathered there,[68] and at other river ports, like Dijon, St-Jean-de-Losne, Auxonne, Semur, Pontailler-sur-Saône, Verdun-sur-le-Doubs and Châlon,[69] for transport to Lyon and other places along the Saône and Rhône as far as Marseille.[70] In most years, providing that the harvest had been reasonably good, wheat from Bourgogne could be sold at prices competitive with those of imported wheat in Marseille itself.[71] The whole of Provence, rarely able to achieve self-sufficiency, depended for the period immediately prior to the harvest on imports from Bourgogne and abroad.[72]

Producers and merchants in departments like Côte-d'Or, although selling large quantities on local markets and for the supply of the neighbouring departments of Saône-et-Loire, Jura, Doubs and Haute-Saône, in most years depended for remunerative price levels in all these markets on a sufficient volume of sales to the Midi. Without this the result would be a glut and falling prices.[73] The movement of sales and prices at Gray was followed with keen interest by cultivators, especially during the key period from November to February, when an estimated 80 per cent of any farmer's surplus available would arrive at Gray.[74]

Poor harvests in Bourgogne caused problems for areas normally

dependent on the region for grain. So too did harvest failure further north –
in Haut- and Bas-Rhin, for example. In 1846 both situations existed, and
increased demand from Alsace for wheat at Gray increased prices there and
further reduced supplies available for purchasers along the Rhône–Saône
axis.[75] In fact, there seems to have been a general, if gradual, tendency
throughout the first half of the century for imports from Marseille rather
than from Bourgogne to assume greater importance in the supply of the river
line.[76] This was, of course, especially marked in years of generally poor
harvests, when the volume of sea-borne imports increased.

The unreliability of river transport and its fluctuating costs caused great
concern to both merchants and administrators. Marseille's links with its
hinterland were poor; movement on the Canal de Bouc, linking it with
Arles, was slow, the Rhône unusable for long periods of the year. M. Vaisse,
Prefect at Lyon, which depended heavily on supplies from Marseille,
remembered in the late 1850s the concern caused by irregularity of supply
prior to the construction of the rail network,[77] while prefectoral corres-
pondence during 1846 and 1847, when extraordinary demands were being
placed on supplies at Marseille from all areas between the city and
Strasbourg, reveals a constant concern with the state of navigation on the
Rhône.[78] According to the Prefect of Saône-et-Loire in November 1846,
transport difficulties on the Rhône were causing an increase at Lyon of 10
francs per sack of flour.[79]

This kind of effect was especially significant, given the predominant
position of a large city like Lyon in the market network. The size of its
population attracted suppliers, and the activity of its merchants made it a
centre for redistribution, partly determining supplies and prices in other
markets over a wide region.[80] In respect of up-Rhône movement from
Marseille, it tended to block movements further up-river until its own needs
were satisfied. The Prefect of Côte-d'Or complained in January 1847 that
only when Lyon was provisioned would prices in north-eastern France fall.[81]

In short, population centres along the Rhône–Saône axis were more or
less favoured in respect of supply conditions according to their position
vis-à-vis marketing centres, whether these were entrepôts like Gray or
Marseille, or centres of demand like Lyon. Proximity to the river line was a
considerable advantage to departments like the Ardèche, which even in the
most abundant years did not produce sufficient cereals for the needs of its
population;[82] Drôme, which was self-sufficient only in exceptional years and
normally imported from both the north-east and Marseille[83] to satisfy its
needs, and those of the large mills at Peyras, Etoile, Chabeuil and Valence,
which provided flour for less accessible places in the Drôme itself and also in
Ardèche and Isère;[84] or Rhône, which, according to a prefectoral report
made in 1850, 'produces only part of the foodstuffs necessary for its consumption, and receives each year from neighbouring departments, either as
wheat or flour, its needs for the months of August, September, October and

part of November, and completes this provisioning with considerable quantities brought by the Canal de la Bourgogne and the Rhône–Rhine Canal, by the Saône, and more rarely the Rhône'.[85]

In some areas access to relatively assured water-borne food supplies encouraged agricultural specialization, although this remained hazardous, as the problems of vine-growing areas of Saône-et-Loire, normally dependent on wheat from Haute-Saône, showed following the poor harvest of 1846.[86] In parts of Vaucluse wheat imported from Marseille or Bourgogne was cheaper than local wheat[87] – an incentive to innovation. In general, however, markets remained permeable only with difficulty, and the problem increased with distance from water. Customs tariffs and transport costs combined to limit competition between imported cereals and local production even in periods of local shortage, when the degree to which price increases attracted merchants was limited by the effects of increased transport costs on their profit margins.[88] The basic consequence was that noted by the Minister of Agriculture in a letter of 16 January 1847 – 'grains derived from imports from abroad have arrived in departments bordering the Rhône and Saône, but have not penetrated into the Loire basin'[89] (i.e. further inland) – and by the Prefect of Lozère, who on 19 June 1847 complained that the situation of his isolated department, with no large centres of population, was desperate.[90]

The Loire provided another major means of entry into the interior of the country. Entrepôt functions were particularly important at Nantes, near its mouth, and at Orléans, the crossroads for three major national routes.

Nantes served both as a centre for import by sea and as a collecting point for exports, again primarily by sea. The size of individual transactions engaged in by its merchants seems to have been smaller than those typical of ports such as Paris, Le Havre or Marseille. According to M. Banchau, a representative of the Chambre Syndicale des Courtiers at Nantes, grain arrived in small boats the loads of which rarely exceeded 150–200 hecto-litres.[91]

Orléans played a more significant role as a market centre. As a focal point for both the upper and lower Loire and on a major road to the north, it linked the Mediterranean and Atlantic coasts of France with the centre and north.[92] In normal years the bakers and merchants of towns like Montluçon or Moulins took part of their grain and flour supplies from Orléans and other ports on the Loire and its affluents. In years like 1846 this dependence was greatly reinforced, and the threat that floods might interrupt traffic caused consternation.[93]

The river system of which the Loire was the central feature provided an extensive network for the movement of grains. Some departments in Brittany and the Vendée were furthermore blessed with a network of good-quality strategic roads, constructed after the 1830 revolution. Grain producers in Mayenne and also Ille-et-Vilaine, who habitually produced a large surplus, were thus able to market this with relative ease, the roads giving access to the rivers Mayenne and Sarthe or directly to the Loire. In January 1847 the routes Laval–Sablé-sur-Sarthe, Laval–le Mans and Vitsé, and Fougères–Laval were reported to be carrying substantial quantities of grains.[94] According to the Minister of the Interior, Sablé was one of the most important grain markets in western France. It attracted most of its grains from Sarthe, Mayenne and part of Maine-et-Loire, and as close to the period of harvest as November and in 1846, a poor year, was already dealing with 10,000 hectolitres per week.[95] Angers, near the confluence of the rivers Mayenne and Sarthe with the Loire, also with relatively good links with its hinterland, was another important collecting centre in this region,[96] as in normal years, on a lesser scale, were a mass of minor river ports involved in the grain trade – for example, such places along the Loire as Calonne, St-Florent, Chamtoceaux.[97]

Imports through Nantes represented an element of insecurity for merchants engaged in these regional and inter-regional transactions. Imports affecting supply conditions and price levels were a constant threat to profitability, especially when imports increased following a poor domestic harvest. As long as uncertainty prevailed merchants tended, even if for some time they continued to make purchases, to lay up stocks while waiting for prices to stabilize rather than attempting to dispatch cereals along the river for sale.[98]

Normally, and especially in years of shortage, grains produced in the departments of Mayenne and Sarthe, as well as those brought by sea, either directly from overseas or from Marseille, provided an important source of supply for much of central France, even if the cost of transport from Marseille to Nantes added significantly to costs. At the beginning of 1847, for example, rates of 44 francs per *tonneau* of 15 hectolitres were being quoted.[99] The value of the river link was clear.[100]

So also must have been the utility of coastal traffic. Just as in the case of inland movement, it involved large numbers of entrepreneurs and activity whose direction varied significantly over time. Movement by sea facilitated the marketing of surpluses produced in coastal regions like Brittany, especially where their direct penetration inland was obstructed by high transport costs[101] or blocked in particular directions by competitors.

Marseille was the major point of import from overseas and of subsequent redistribution, feeding both inland and coastal traffic, with a range of operation which varied according to supply and price levels in various regions. Following poor harvests, merchants in areas on the Atlantic coast, such as those of St-Jean-d'Angély (Charente-Inférieure), in Brittany, in the Loire region and in the centre would place orders for cereals at Marseille.[102]

Other than the export of maize from the Pyrenean region, especially through the port of Bayonne (Basses-Pyrénées),[103] the remainder of the coastal traffic seems to have taken essentially a north-to-south direction.

Coastal shipping transported foodstuffs from numerous small ports along the Breton and Norman coasts.[104] Wheat remained, in much of Brittany, a necessary cash crop, exported in the absence of any alternative means of obtaining the essential minimum supply of money[105] and in spite of the poverty of diet of most of the local population. In most years there seems to have been a gap of about 5 to 8 francs between wheat prices in the major producing areas of northern France and the Midi[106] – enough of a difference to maintain a certain current of trade between northern ports and Marseille by way of the Straits of Gibraltar. The volume of this might be increased by poor harvests in the south, although shortage in the north itself and a high level of overseas imports into Marseille sometimes narrowed the price difference. The port of Cette, along with Marseille, played an important part in this trade. By June 1845, for example, its mills had for four years been occupied in milling grain from Brittany and Flanders, purchased to cover successive poor harvests in upper Languedoc.[107] In the same circumstances mills along the River Lez, owned and rented mainly by inhabitants of Montpellier, ground wheat imported from a variety of sources and produced flour for a wide area, including Hérault, Gard, Ardèche, Aveyron, Lozère, Vaucluse and parts of Aude.[108]

One interesting but probably unanswerable question, given the paucity of information, concerns the cash flows between regions which accompanied those of commodities. It seems clear that the less market-orientated areas suffered from a shortage of cash, which inhibited purchasing from other regions, but it is not possible to determine how extensive and how significant such balance of payments difficulties were. Inevitably merchants were attracted towards markets which promised relatively easy sales and ready cash. The newspaper *La Presse* highlighted the problems that this behaviour often caused in an article of 10 November 1845, which admitted that 'the difficulties of the grain trade are immense when occurring in the interior due to the obstacles hindering the transport of bulky and perishable foodstuffs'. It conceded that these difficulties were minimized by movement by sea but felt obliged to reject demands for freedom of trade in the interests of national food supply and security and because the seaports in England were far more accessible and attractive to merchants in the grain-producing areas of the north than were the ports of southern France, much less the mountainous areas of the centre.

International flows

International movements caused anxiety among consumers, who were concerned that they might result in local and regional shortages through the diversion of foodstuffs to foreign markets which promised to be profitable, and also among producers anxious that imports might cause a fall in prices. In every decade from 1815 there was a net surplus of imports over exports,[109] but although this might have exaggerated effects on supply and prices in particular regions, the effects on national supply conditions were limited by the relatively small volume of imports in relation to internal production.

Prior to 1846 imports of wheat were below 2,000,000 hectolitres per annum, except in 1832. The exceptional gravity of the supply situation in 1846–7 was clearly revealed by the high level of imports, as also was the severity of the crisis caused by poor harvests in 1853 and 1855. In general, during the period 1836–51 imports made up a very small proportion of total consumption:[110]

Total imports 1836–51	41,769,126 hectolitres
Total exports 1836–51	24,315,223
Excess of imports	17,453,903
Average per annum	872,695 = 0.01 per cent of national production
National production, annual average	77,764,936
Average annual consumption	78,337,631

The use of customs statistics allows import figures to be accepted as relatively accurate, especially by comparison with estimates of production. Even so, documents like that sent by the Minister of the Interior to the Director General of Customs in January 1829, complaining that little confidence could be placed in the customs statistics, must make the historian cautious.[111]

Statistics on exports are more suspect. Imports tended to go to big ports; exports occurred in addition from a mass of small ports, especially along the coast of Brittany and Normandy. They usually attracted little official attention because they were not normally subject to the customs tariffs charged on imports. They occurred even in years of high domestic prices, with England, Belgium and Holland as the main destinations. In 1847, although taxes on the export of wheat, rye and maize made export prohibitive, no taxes were levied on buckwheat and potato, which were important in the popular diet in these regions of export. The overall effect on food prices was out of all proportion to the volume exported because such exports increased consumer anxiety.[112]

In spite of low volumes of imports, domestic producers remained afraid of competition. The protection afforded to most of them by high transport costs and relative isolation gave insufficient security. In 1816 limited imports of Russian cereals to cover a domestic deficit had caused discontent, which influential landowners had voiced and turned into a demand for a ban on imports.[113] With the benefit of hindsight we can say that this move was unjustified. Only in some coastal regions, especially in the south, were imported grains a constant threat to producers; in lower Languedoc, for example, they were one of the factors permitting the gradual replacement of cereals by vines.[114] However, this kind of experience and more general, if less rational, feelings of insecurity promoted the establishment in the Chamber of Deputies of an alliance representing both agricultural and industrial interests which worked to block proposals for reductions of tariffs.[115]

Legislation of 2 December 1814 and 28 April 1816, modified on 16 July 1819, 4 July 1821, 20 October 1830, 15 April 1832 and 26 July 1833, established a sliding scale of tariffs on imports of cereals and flour. In its basic features this survived until 1861.[116] The intention of the legislation was to relate customs tariffs to the price of grain on internal regulating markets in order to ensure remunerative prices to producers in times of abundance and to safeguard consumers from excessive prices in times of shortage, while at the same time increasing price stability and the security of merchants.[117]

The most important legislative act, that of 28 April 1816, established a tariff of 1.25 francs per hectolitre of grain and 2.50 francs per metric *quintal* of flour when domestic wheat reached prices varying from 20 to 24 francs[118] in three geographical zones determined by proximity to the coast or land frontiers, the highest level being that of coastal areas. The tariffs were, however, reduced by 0.25 francs for wheat and 0.50 francs for flour if these commodities were carried on a French ship. Each reduction of 1 franc in domestic prices below the 20–4 franc level was followed by a corresponding increase of 1 franc in the tariff on wheat and 3 francs in that on flour. When domestic prices fell below a range from 16 to 20 francs a total ban on imports came into force. Similar dispositions applied to rye and maize.

To protect consumers, when domestic prices rose above 20–4 francs per hectolitre, tariffs were reduced until, when prices reached 32 francs, they fell to a nominal 0.25 francs. If prices rose above 26 francs, a ban on exports could be introduced.[119] Perhaps indicative of the limited effectiveness of this legislation was its suspension in difficult years, as, for example, in 1846–7.

Some flexibility was provided by a system of *acquits à caution*, a licensing system by which exports from one region – usually the north – of a specified quantity of grain could be balanced by the import against nominal tariffs of an equivalent quantity into a distant region in the south. This reduced the cost of obtaining cereals in sea-coast areas of the south and facilitated the sale of grain by areas which frequently had large surpluses. Complaints by agricultural interests about abuses of the system were frequent in spite of efforts to restrict its scope (in the case of imports) to specific towns and mills within 2 kilometres of them.[120]

Imports were derived from a variety of sources. The great days of the North American Plains were yet to come, although in years of poor harvests growing competition was evident from that continent, as well as from traditional zones of supply in Russia and Prussia. Especially significant were movements from the Black Sea, and secondarily from North Africa and Sicily, arriving in southern ports, particularly Marseille.[121] The degree of dependence on Russian exports to supplement domestic shortage was clearly revealed when in 1854 the Crimean War interrupted trade and increased transport rates by tying up shipping as military transports.[122] From the Baltic imports might be received via Holland and the Rhine to Strasbourg,[123] or else via Belgium and the Meuse. Even before the development of steam navigation the tendency for oceanic freight rates to fall was leading to a growing internationalization of trade.[124]

Dependence on imports was generally frowned upon – such sources were too unreliable.[125] In the first place, accurate information about the state of harvests in foreign countries was very difficult to obtain,[126] and in the second place, when France needed to import the same was true of other countries, and competition on international markets increased. Moreover, other states were liable to resort to prohibition of exports to protect domestic supplies. Thus the Chamber of Commerce at La Rochelle complained in March 1847 that purchases negotiated at Santander were effected by a ban on exports imposed by the Spanish government.[127] In January the Prefect of the Moselle had explained increased demand in the markets of his department by the action of the Prussian government, which by imposing a tax of 25 per cent on exports of cereals, had effectively prohibited them.[128]

Even when cereals were available from abroad it took time to complete the arrangements for purchase and then to transport them.[129] In 1846, with domestic cereals production estimated to be as low as 60 million hectolitres, it was claimed by some experts to be necessary to import as much as 40 million hectolitres to cover this deficit. According to a more reliable Ministry of Commerce internal memorandum, the deficit of wheat alone was 9,269,474 hectolitres in 1846, and in practice during the agricultural year 1846–7 6,695,431 hectolitres were actually imported. Commerce reacted far more slowly than it would in 1853, when considerable modification to both transport and tariff systems had occurred. In the last five months of 1853 imports were almost double those in the same period of 1846.[130]

The existence of the sliding scale of tariffs was a major element of uncertainty for merchants engaged in estimating potential profitability by relating domestic and external price levels. A fall in domestic price levels during a period in which grains purchased abroad were being transported towards the French frontier might lead to an increase in tariffs and turn a potentially profitable operation into a loss-making one.[131] It was felt by many observers that this situation resulted in excessive caution on the part of merchants and a slowness to act throughout periods of domestic shortage or surplus, which caused far larger price fluctuations, lasting much longer than might otherwise have been the case.[132] An article in the *Journal des chemins de fer* on 3 April 1847 maintained that for international operations to reduce prices more effectively in France, it was essential that merchants be secured against tariff fluctuations, especially such major changes as the ending of the period of suspension of the sliding scale. The favoured alternative to a sliding scale was fixed tariffs at a moderate level in order to eliminate the element of uncertainty. It was furthermore maintained that if this situation of moderate fixed tariffs prevailed, in periods of shortage purchases abroad would begin sooner and would be spread over a longer period, thus not only limiting price increases by a quicker response but also easing the pressure on scarce transport facilities and limiting the increase in transport costs.[133] The emergency measure of suspending the sliding scale was maintained to have an undesirable effect in that it provided clear notice to foreign suppliers of the scale of the French deficit and caused them to increase their prices.[134]

Each crisis, due to all the uncertainties faced by merchants, led to substantial business failures, which served to remind others of the need for caution.[135] Even without the problems of the sliding scale, merchants would have been cautious. For the 1866 agricultural inquiry the *rapporteur* for the Alsatian Departments, Eugène Tisserand, observed that:

the uncertain evaluation of crops over a vast area, the prudence of commerce in presence of an imprecise demand, in regard of bulky foodstuffs, susceptible to fairly substantial price fluctuations and finally the necessity to go great distances to find the wherewithal to satisfy this demand meant that it would be only in the case of large deficits, and in consequence when prices were sufficiently high that commerce would take the risk and that long-distance purchases would occur.[136]

In other words, import of foodstuffs would be considered only after internal prices reached abnormal levels, after which it was likely to take three months for grain to reach Le Havre from the Baltic or Marseille from Odessa and five months to reach Le Havre from the United States.[137] French merchants tended to begin to make purchases in overseas markets at a later date than many of their competitors, particularly the British, who maintained more permanent relations with foreign suppliers. The French entered the international market when price levels for cereals and freight rates were already rising.[138] Frequently, particularly for imports into northern France, overseas grains had to be purchased through intermediaries at Antwerp or London.[139] Ports like Le Havre were involved in the grain trade only after domestic harvest failure.[140] Marseille was exceptional in its continuous involvement in the international grain market.[141] Thus imports would affect price levels only after a considerable time lag, a lag which increased in length with distance from the point of import.

Only the small minority of large-scale operators were likely to possess a reasonably accurate picture of the international supply situation and to be in a position to act rapidly. They too would be in the best position to profit from high domestic prices.[142] Those who followed them were likely to buy abroad at higher prices and sell at home at lower ones.[143] Profitable operations in the winter of 1846–7 are known to have stimulated the ambitions and activity of merchants in the spring and summer of 1847. When it became increasingly clear that a good domestic harvest was likely, prices fell and large losses were incurred on remaining stocks.[144]

The effect of imports on price levels has to be considered in relation to a multiplicity of factors. In the first place, the cost of imported grains at their point of arrival in France. In the 1840s Baltic grains arriving at Le Havre and Dunkirk cost at least 23–4 francs. These were prices paid in years of plentiful supply. In December 1846 a hectolitre of wheat cost around 18.90 francs at Koenigsberg, 16.90 at Danzig, 19.40 at Hamburg, to which had to be added freight rates of 3.20 francs per hectolitre, 3.50 and 2.30 respectively, plus further handling and storage charges. Black Sea grains costing in December 1846 12 francs per hectolitre in Odessa sold for at least 18–23 francs after arrival at Marseille. American grain at Le Havre, Nantes or Bordeaux cost some 20 francs. In New York at the end of 1846 wheat cost 16.80 francs and transport to Le Havre cost 5.25 francs, and at New Orleans a hectolitre cost 13.70 francs, while the cost of transport was roughly the same.[145] Black Sea grains and those arriving from the United States were to a large extent sold in different markets, given the high cost of transporting Black Sea cereals from the Mediterranean area to northern France.

Movement of imported grains or flour inland would obviously tend to increase their price through the accumulation of transport costs. It seems doubtful, therefore (and the relatively low levels of imports confirm this), whether imports could in most years have competed successfully in the domestic market, particularly outside the narrow area accessible by water. Even in years in which high prices compensated for high transport costs, penetration inland was slow.[146] Furthermore, government policy tended to confuse the issue. Although consular agents in foreign countries collected information on behalf of French merchants on harvests, price levels, freight rates and the possibility of purchases,[147] official efforts to reassure domestic consumers with optimistic statements about the state of the harvest helped to dissuade merchants from commencing overseas operations.[148] The *Journal d'agriculture pratique* had already warned its readers about the 'incredible optimism' of the Ministry of Agriculture and Commerce in its commercial review for August 1846, but the Ministry in a circular to prefects dated 16 November 1846 continued to err on the side of optimism, blaming rising prices on temporary transport difficulties rather than on a poor harvest.[149] Officials at least learned their lesson on this occasion and, following the poor harvest of 1853, attempted to provide more accurate estimates of domestic supplies, rapidly suspended the sliding scale and sought to encourage imports.[150]

Rather than the volume of imports, it was probably the psychological effect of the first imports in reassuring consumers and persuading domestic suppliers with stocks to release them, that had the most dramatic effect on domestic price levels.

Although merchants sought to sell imports at prices close to previously prevailing domestic market prices,[151] the news of arrivals of foreign grains in the ports was often enough to cause a fall in prices further inland.[152] Farmers as well as merchants were hypersensitive to changing supply conditions.[153] Imports thus had the dual effect of directly increasing supply and, by the anxiety they caused concerning price levels, of encouraging the release of stocks.

In short, imports were more than a palliative in a situation of domestic shortage but, through their influence on the behaviour of internal suppliers, had consequences for domestic supply and price levels out of all proportion to their own volume. In spite of transportation difficulties, imports had some influence on prices in all regions, whether directly or indirectly. No one market was entirely isolated from others, so that changes in supply and price levels in more accessible areas necessarily, although with a time lag, had effects on related markets in less accessible areas. However intermittent the relationship between markets, in periods of shortage the range over which such interrelationships were established was extended. Nevertheless, as the statistics on volume indicate, it was not until after the 1850s that imports substantially reduced dependence upon domestic supplies and that transport of commodities and information was sufficiently rapid and cheap to establish an international market as opposed to an interlocking network of regional compartments. The effects of this would be seen in the more direct influence of international prices on those in the various localities. Prior to the transport revolution prices responded relatively quickly to international supply where large-scale merchants served large urban markets. These were the merchants with international networks of contacts and good access to information.[154] Even so, the response was sluggish compared with that of later periods, and it was only slowly that price equilibrium was established between major and secondary markets. In effect, if one can limit the mechanisms by which spatial variation of prices is established to three – namely, the direct influence of transport costs, the indirect influence of transport costs (especially on consumer behaviour) and the related mechanism of imitation – it is evident that because of the significance of the second factor, price variation tends to be of greater amplitude than transport costs would suggest. Furthermore, the effects of inter-market processes of imitation on supplier–consumer interaction and on price levels were restricted by the poor diffusion of information and consumer anxiety.

It should be clear that there was no simple relationship between imports and price levels. The existence of international frontiers and varying liability to customs tariffs obviously affected the scale of the zone of provisioning and the effectiveness of international commerce in stabilizing national prices. This was one complex variable in the situation, but the most complex was the psychology of merchants and consumers, which meant that the relationship between imports and prices was an indirect one, in that the *threat* of international competition resulted in a *tendency* for national prices to align themselves with international prices, but that high transport costs, inefficient diffusion of information and consumer over-reaction meant that in this period the relationship was only a very loose one in any particular place at any given time.

Actors in the market place

Merchants and farmers

Poor communications resulted in the geographical fragmentation of agricultural markets and in the restriction of the bulk of trading activity to local or regional levels. Most of the product, in the case of cereals, was either consumed on the farm or sold at local markets, in large part directly to consumers. The degree to which individual farmers were orientated towards production for the market depended upon the size of their marketable surplus, the opportunities for commercialization and their own awareness of these. The latter tended to vary with the scale of operation and proximity to major urban centres, but abundant examples exist of the slowness with which even those with a high degree of involvement in commerce responded to new opportunities, either because the diffusion of information was inadequate or simply because their *expectations* about supply and demand were too much dominated by past experience.

The overwhelming predominance of small-scale operations was reinforced by the weakness of the financial system. The banking system, like the structure of exchange of physical commodities, was archaic. Capital circulated slowly, and this contributed to its relative scarcity. The system was evolving in the first half of the nineteenth century as the economy developed, but it too remained geographically fragmented, slowing the development of inter-regional trade and limiting its volume. The defects of the banking system were felt particularly in the economically more backward regions. Thus the Prefect of the Nièvre complained after the poor harvests of 1846: 'the trade in grain is absolutely nil. . . . I have tried to persuade our main merchants to make purchases in the ports. I do not believe I succeeded. Capital is rare in our region, where there are no major credit institutions'.[155] The activity of individual merchants was limited by the lack of credit facilities, and the large numbers engaged in the grain trade served to restrict the possibilities for capital accumulation.[156]

Traditionally, there were two kinds of cereal merchants – those who dealt with the large proprietors (labelled *négociants en gros*) and engaged in the supply of large towns and inter-regional trade, and the mass of *blatiers*, small-scale merchants buying grain from small farmers and amassing only small quantities for local sale.[157] Large-scale mercantile activity tended to be characteristic of port areas and major centres of population. Dealing in large quantities, with accumulated capital and networks of correspondents, merchants were able to buy in areas where prices were relatively low and so make profits in spite of transport costs.[158] This was evident on the northern plains, where relatively large-scale farming activity coexisted with relatively large-scale trade to supply the urban populations of northern France.[159]

The number of large operators must have been relatively small in relation to the total number engaged in the grain trade. The economist Gosset observed in 1851 that because of this the commercial response to a harvest deficit was slow and, in the case of imports, tended to be made by financiers interested in speculative profits rather than by regular grain merchants.[160] M. Labaume, a grain merchant in Paris, complained in 1847 of the lack of enterprise of his fellow merchants by comparison with their English competitors in the Russian market. They were too afraid of losing from price fluctuations on the internal market.[161] As the preceding section has tried to show, this anxiety was reinforced both by uncertainty concerning transport rates and by customs tariffs which fluctuated with internal prices.

Complaints about the timidity of merchants were frequently expressed in periods of shortage. Their caution was quite natural in the circumstances, but the results were often unfortunate. In November 1846 the Prefect of the Côte-d'Or reported the exhaustion of merchants' stocks in the department. They had hesitated too long before ordering grains from other regions. Transport problems subsequently delayed the arrival of these grains and rendered them expensive, while local farmers with reserves, taking advantage of the situation, refused to sell to merchants except at very high prices.[162]

In general, prices at an under-supplied market tended to rise until sufficient outside supplies were attracted to satisfy consumer demand. High prices in one place tended to result in the appearance in its market places of outside merchants attracted by the prospect of greater profit. Prices would then tend to fall to an extent which depended on the volume of the supplies attracted and consumer appreciation of future prospects.[163] The Prefect of Saône-et-Loire reported on 7 April 1817 a significant fall in prices at markets held on 5 April: 'the high price of previous markets had attracted to this last one considerable quantities of grain of all kinds' but 'purchasers, without doubt reassured by this abundance, were not pressed to provision themselves'.[164] Prices fell on the 5th, and the Prefect thought that the probable result would be a reduction of supply to the next market unless sellers believed that a longer-term fall in prices was likely and rushed to sell before prices fell too far. Thus the commercial response to high prices might have the effect of equalizing price levels between geographically distinct places as a result of movements from areas of relatively low price to those of relatively high price. It might also increase instability and price fluctuations as a result of unpredicted consumer behaviour.

Following poor harvests, the zone of operation of merchants in many areas necessarily increased because of the need to search beyond more or less denuded normal areas of supply or because they were encouraged by the possibility of making large profits on the often substantial price variation between places frequently not very distant from each other. Areas in which supplies were relatively good and prices relatively low were invaded by merchants from areas in which prevailing price levels were higher – high enough to cover transport costs between the two and to ensure profitability. Thus at the end of 1846 and in 1847 the Toulouse region, departments in the west like Mayenne, Sarthe, Maine-et-Loire, Finistère, Morbihan and Côtes-du-Nord and in the east like Côte-d'Or experienced commercial operations which, by increasing demand, reduced local supplies and increased prices and, with these, local resentment.[165]

In general, the marketing decisions taken by farmers and merchants were the product of a complex of factors reflecting individual needs and local circumstances, or rather personal perceptions of these influenced by discussions around the market place, in the fields or village squares.

One consequence of the small scale of activity was that reserves of grain held from year to year in order to speculate on annual price variation were limited, and so therefore was the ability of commerce to even out price fluctuations. Reserves were expensive to maintain, in terms of both the capital tied up and the cost of storage facilities essential to prevent excessive spoilage. The combined cost of storage and losses in storage was estimated at 1 franc per *quintal* per annum, which only the comparatively prosperous could afford.[166] The problem of loss was serious enough to lead to a ministerial circular in October 1854 asking prefects to place posters in every commune asking for information on preservative methods.[167] The building up of reserves depended also upon the possession of financial reserves which allowed the farmer to forgo a more immediate return on his harvest and ensured his economic survival in the event of an unsuccessful speculation resulting in financial loss. The ability of farmers in relatively rich agricultural areas (like Picardy, Brie or the Nord) to lay up stocks was exceptional.[168] Paradoxically, it was precisely in years of good harvests and low prices, when the building up of reserves would have cost relatively little and would have reduced the tendency of prices to fall, that the income of many farmers selling in the market tended to drop to its lowest levels and that lack of capital forced sales even at low prices,[169] particularly in order to pay rents.[170]

Paris and the major ports of import were exceptional in the number of granaries provided by private enterprise to facilitate profitable market operations. Cultivators throughout the Paris region were able to store their own grain at such establishments as the Entrepôts Mouillard for varying periods, to await a rise in prices.[171] This, of course, represented a tying up of capital and was something that only the better-off could afford.

Legislation on bakers' stocks applied in Paris and similar measures taken in many towns also had the effect of attenuating price movements. Prior to 1854 bakers in Paris were collectively required to maintain a reserve of 81,280 sacks or 127,609 metric *quintals* – sufficient for thirty-five days' normal consumption – to be stored partly in municipal granaries, partly by the individual baker.[172] In periods when shortage seemed in prospect municipal authorities were likely to begin to increase the size of stocks. However, the timing of this tended to push up prices. The rush by consumers to build up their own stocks had a similar effect, as well as subsequently accelerating the fall in prices when part of these stocks were sold. Rather than reducing the amplitude of price fluctuation, these were actions which tended to increase them.[173]

Besides capital resources and stocking facilities, the other decisive influence on levels of reserve was weather conditions during the growing period of the cereal. Grain harvested during dry years was normally of a better quality and deteriorated far less rapidly in storage than did grain harvested during a wet spring or summer. Even so, dry grain became humid all too easily and needed to be stored carefully and turned regularly to prevent fermentation. In good conditions and with adequate care grains might be conserved for two, three or even four years. Flour was also extremely susceptible to dampness. The other major causes of losses in storage were the activities of rodents and insects. Proportionately, losses in storage were highest among low-income farmers who possessed the least adequate storage facilities.[174]

In spite of these limiting factors, the level of stocks was clearly of some importance in determining price movements. The relationship between the size of the harvest and prices was not a direct one. The latter were determined in large part by commercial activity in which stocking was of considerable significance. The effect of stocks on prices varied considerably, depending on whether they were placed on the market following a good or a bad harvest. In a period of shortage this obviously restrained the tendency for prices to rise.

Successive poor harvests were, however, likely to exhaust stocks. In many departments the crisis of 1846–7 was especially severe, coming after a series of mediocre harvests which had not allowed the building up of reserves.[175] The Prefect of Dordogne reported as early as September 1846 that 'farmers hold no stocks; all have profited from the rise in prices prior to the harvest to get rid of the old grains they possessed, and they did this all the more energetically because this year's harvest appeared as if it might be a rich one'.[176] The decision about whether or not to release reserves needed to be carefully judged but was, as we have seen, frequently based on ill-informed or badly conceived estimates of present situations. Thus, following the bad harvest of 1846 in central France, large quantities of cereals were attracted on to the market by high prices and also as a result of the farmers' fears of rapid deterioration due to the presence of large numbers of butterflies. For some time the rise in prices was limited, but the precipitant sale of current harvest production and of stocks resulted by early 1847 in serious shortage and substantially higher prices, especially in the Nièvre, Cher, Allier, Vienne, Indre and Creuse.[177] Decisions as to when to release stocks might then exaggerate short-term price fluctuations, as once stocks were exhausted or consumers feared this to be the case, the psychological pressure for prices to rise would be all the more intense.

Providing storage facilities were not already encumbered with the product of previous harvests, they made it possible, following a good harvest, to restrain the fall in prices. In the case of a series of good harvests, an effort would be made to sell old stocks prior to the harvest, although this would depend in part on assessments of the humidity and the potential for storage of new grains.[178] Inadequate facilities restricted the extent to which stocking could prevent the development of a market glut and a collapse of price levels. After a good harvest the existence of stocks from a previous year, particularly when they needed to be sold in order to limit deterioration, might aggravate a tendency for prices to fall. In the Landes in March 1847 the appearance of imported grains on local markets led local proprietors to sell their stocks before prevailing high prices fell too drastically, action which led, of course, to a further rapid decline in prices.[179]

The effects of stocks on prices was complex, therefore. In some years they had the beneficial effect claimed by economists and merchants, in that they did serve to even out price fluctuations and added stability to the market, but at other times – and in a shorter term – they exaggerated the amplitude of price movement. The facilities for storage were too inadequate, information about marketing possibilities too inaccurate and dependence upon local supply/demand conditions too great to allow the holding of reserves to act as an efficient stabilizing mechanism.

Inevitably, decision-making was frequently erratic.[180] The price levels prevailing at a given moment were important but by no means the sole determining factor. Among other things, the routines imposed by the calendar of agricultural activities had their effect in determining the level of supply and, consequently, prices. Each year there was a time lag between the harvest and the appearance of new grain on the market, which was the consequence not only of the time necessary to thresh the harvest but also of the postponement of this while more pressing tasks, like sowing, were performed.[181] Moreover, until threshing began it was impossible to be certain about yields and supply for the coming year. If, following the harvest, markets remained poorly supplied, this often led to popular suspicion of attempts by speculators to maintain prices at their high pre-harvest levels.[182]

In contrast, various factors served to promote sales, to increase supply and reduce prices at particular moments in the year. Most notable of these was the need of tenant farmers to pay rents, in many areas around St Martin's Day in November.[183] Immediately prior to this sales occurred whatever the prevailing price levels. Poor farmers were usually forced to sell their surpluses as soon as possible after the harvest to meet pressing needs.[184] If, because of the sale of other farm produce or savings after a period of prosperity they had no need to sell grain immediately, they too might profit from a rise in prices, especially the seasonal rise occurring before the next harvest was brought in.[185] To facilitate this, farmers would often ask landowners to accept a postponement of the payment of rent in periods of low prices so that they could sell instead when prices rose.[186] As stocks from the previous harvest declined and/or if prospects for the coming harvest looked bleak, farmers tended to limit sales in the local market place, aware that purchasers, finding their habitual place of purchase under-supplied, would address themselves directly to the farmer. On the farm they escaped from the competitive situation of the market place and were likely to obtain higher prices.[187]

Speculation – the ability to buy cheaply at one point and sell at a profit elsewhere – was then, and now, the basis of commercial activity. However, the scale of price fluctuations, due to the relative isolation of markets, encouraged particular forms of speculative activity which at times reached a scale and intensity that had significant short-term effects on price levels in particular places. The effect of popular fears and the rush to purchase foodstuffs after a poor harvest was to arouse the hope of quick and substantial profits among those holding reserves. Small traders and bakers, peasants, merchants and landowners were all anxious to share in the rewards. Rising prices provided great opportunities for profit for enterprising men with capital to spare. Thus in January 1847 it was reported from central France that 'all the cereals purchased at the moment by the different communes originate on boats which belong in part to M. Darblay, deputy, and which are stationed on the Loire in the department of Indre-et-Loire'.[188] But for every Darblay there were numerous active small traders, their numbers increased in periods of high price by the opportunities for making a speculative profit in cash or in kind, for sometimes desperate peasants, short of food and unable to pay current market prices, were forced to commit themselves to heavy repayments in kind – twice or threefold – after the harvest.[189] The Prefect of Côtes-du-Nord complained in October 1855 that in spite of his efforts to restrain the number of speculators by requiring that everyone engaged in trade, however trivial, should pay the proper *patente* tax, better-off peasants were speculating on cereals and reducing supplies by holding on to stocks in the hope of further price rises.[190] The number of commercial intermediaries increased, and so did their feverish desire to enrich themselves.[191]

Speculation on seasonal and cyclical price movements was an important source of revenue for many large merchants and landowners. This was a legitimate and valuable activity to the extent that it helped to even out fluctuations, but there must have been an ever-present temptation to provoke or sustain potentially profitable fluctuations, while the compartmentalization of market structures made this a practical possibility in the short term and over relatively restricted areas.[192] This was especially true of the period immediately prior to a harvest, when stocks tended to be at their lowest, particularly when the prospects for the coming harvest were judged to be poor. In periods of high prices consumers, and in general agents of the administration too, expressed resentment at what they regarded as 'fraudulent manoeuvres', designed to maintain prices at high levels. The administration was torn between its responsibility to repress fraud and its fear of obstructing legitimate commercial activity.

Close watch was kept on market places, especially by the *gendarmerie*. Their reports reveal the anxiety of consumers rushing to buy, the greater calm of merchants waiting until the first rush was over and paying less for their purchases.[193] They reveal the reluctance of sellers to part with grains for anything less than the highest prevailing prices and their essential optimism during periods when prices were rising.[194] They condemn the efforts of so-called speculators to buy up supplies at prices above those previously prevailing on the market.

Speculation often led to the sale of the same sacks of grain or flour at higher prices within hours of their initial purchase. This was especially easy on markets where grains were sold primarily by sample. The *gendarmerie* of Loir-et-Cher observed in August 1855 the 'repeated sales of grains which occur without ever these grains appearing on the markets and a large number of individuals, small-scale unlicensed purchasers, who unceasingly buy and sell'.[195] Bakers were often suspected of participating in such activities, for by causing increases or attempting to prevent falls in the *mercuriales* they might benefit from a rising *taxe du pain*. Small merchants were frequently suspected of acting as their agents.[196]

The simplest and probably the most common method of acting to maintain rising prices was to withhold supplies from the market until prices reached what was expected to be their highest level.[197] For this reason among others, the initial effect of an increase in prices was frequently to cause a reduction in supplies.[198] This was the kind of situation described by the *procureur-impérial* at Châteaubriant (Loire-Inférieure) in 1856: 'It is generally recognized that those who engage in this kind of activity need only buy the crops of small proprietors and farmers who lack the means of storing them, and who are forced to sell, to render themselves masters of the market. After they have filled their granaries they agree to buy in three months, six months, all the grain remaining in the countryside, thus procuring for themselves a monopoly in the sale of grain.' If during these operations prices began to fall, 'they rush to the markets to buy grains at any price without bargaining . . . and then the grain finds itself withering in the hands of the large proprietors and rich farmers who have no pressing need to sell and await the most favourable opportunities, or else in the granaries of the hoarders [*accapareurs*] which it will not leave unless a new rise in prices is in prospect'. The distinction implicit between landowners who speculated and merchants who hoarded is revealing of the bounds of morally legitimate action and of a contempt for commercial activity and those engaged in it.[199]

Speculators were frequently described as *accapareurs*, and high prices were explained in terms solely of their activities.[200] A baker named Corbian, actually sentenced to three months in prison for fraudulent manoeuvres, claimed in his appeal against sentence: 'You know that people distraught with fear of the hoarding of cereals believe they see hoarders in all those whose profession obliges them to engage in speculation, or simply, as in my case, the purchase of cereals.'[201] For the younger Darblay, a major industrial miller and president of the *comice agricole* of Seine-et-Oise, the belief in hoarders was an absolute prejudice. Prices simply reflected supply conditions.[202] However, M. Girardière, a miller at Melun (Seine-et-Marne), appearing before the same inquiry was equally certain that when prices were high hoarders did engage in activities designed to keep them high. This, he felt, ought to be prohibited.[203] Each of these gentlemen was perhaps correct in his analysis, at least in relation to the level of trade at which each operated. Hoarding was likely to have some effect on the minor local market, relatively isolated and supplied by a small number of farmers or merchants.

Even when administrators seem to have accepted that speculation was a normal and healthy element in the market mechanism, they generally believed that it should be restrained within strict limits. The holding back of grain to stimulate price increases or to preserve existing high levels was immoral in causing suffering among the poor and represented a danger to public order.[204]

The *procureur-impérial* at Châteaubriant (Loire-Inférieure) expressed more widely held views, and especially the doubts of those responsible for enforcing the law, when, as late as July 1856, he observed:

far be it for me to wish to reduce the liberty of commerce, but these two words *commerce* and *liberty* ought never to be separated, thus perfect liberty for merchants to purchase to resell, sell and buy, but on condition that the grains are never retired from commerce and that they are not heaped up in stores, from which they emerge only at the instant one succeeds in causing an artificial increase in prices, shortage in the midst of abundance; this, I believe, is how one should define cornering [*l'accaparement*] which is an abuse of the liberty of commerce.[205]

Other abuses likely to influence price levels were also criticized – for example, the transfer of many transactions from the market place to the farm or even the roads leading to market. From Finistère it was reported in March 1847 that merchants were sending their agents to buy at farms. These were paying high prices, and in consequence supplies to the local markets were inadequate and prices on them continued to rise.[206] In Bas-Rhin the involvement of local Jews in intermediary activities led to their being blamed for high prices and to the intensification of anti-Semitic sentiments in all classes.[207] Frequently it was rumoured that these merchants were buying up not only stocks but even standing crops, which, if true, would seem likely to extend the period of high prices beyond even the coming harvest.[208] Usually such rumours proved to be unfounded or at least impossible to prove. The authorities at any rate kept on looking,[209] although their investigations usually did not lead to prosecution. The *procureur-général* at Rennes, who in May 1847 set in course investigations of press rumours concerning the sale of standing crops, concluded:

it happens too often that legal and serious transactions are claimed to be punishable manoeuvres because of exaggerated fears about the next crop. These forward sales are . . . not illegal. They involve not . . . particular standing crops but cereals to be delivered at more or less distant periods, and if it is true that such transactions have an unfortunate influence on the price of cereals, it is almost impossible to establish that they have been the determining cause of the increase and that the purchasers had the intention of causing an increase. Prosecutions based on such cases would then only attack the liberty of trade.[210]

In a circular to his subordinates the *procureur-général* warned them against excessive zeal in the application of the law of *messidor* year III,[211] a course of action which the Minister of Justice subsequently warmly approved.[212]

Administrators, however, remained unclear as to the interpretation of the law. In May 1856 the Prefect of Maine-et-Loire asked for the prosecution of merchants and others dealing in futures, claiming that such activity was only a species of fraud.[213] The Minister of Justice agreed that such speculation was indeed reprehensible but pointed out that it was not illegal.[214]

It is probable that growing government reluctance to prosecute encouraged speculation. Although the significance of hoarding of the kind described above cannot be estimated by analysis of price movements, it seems probable that it was important, given the structure of the market and the relative isolation of its various units of activity. For, as M. Boitelle, the Paris prefect of police, observed with the benefit of hindsight: 'If hoarding occurred previously, it was because the reasons which prevent it today did not exist. When grain was lacking at one point, when one was not able to import it because of the state of the roads . . . it was possible for the merchants, for those who held it, producers or intermediaries, to establish a sort of agreement *vis-à-vis* consumers.'[215]

Speculation on grain could be a hazardous activity, as even the Rothschilds – who were relatively well informed about developments in the market – found out to their cost in 1847.[216] At a more mundane level the Mayor of Auxonne (Côte-d'Or) reported that market prices there for wheat had fallen from 40–2 francs per hectolitre on 22 January 1847 to 33–7 francs on the 29th. The drop was, he believed, due to a combination of factors, including the absence of merchants from the Jura on the second date and especially the rumour, which spread towards the end of the market, that between 12,000 and 14,000 sacks of grain were *en route* from Marseille. This suddenly made farmers very anxious to sell.[217]

Heavy losses could be made on stocks in hand at the moment when prices began to fall, as stocks represented immobilized capital which deteriorated more or less rapidly. The potential profits of such enterprise needed to be large both to attract speculators in the first instance and to balance possible losses. This in part explains the reluctance to sell at anything below what was felt to be the highest obtainable price and also the species of panic which afflicted markets when prices showed a clear tendency to fall. The first impulse in the latter situation was likely to be an effort to prevent the fall by withholding supplies or even purchasing small quantities in an effort to reverse the decline in prices.[218] If this failed, according to the Prefect of Côte-d'Or, those with stocks would carry these to market *avec empressement*. It would, he affirmed, require the appearance of imports on local markets to produce this result.[219] Then, 'at the moment when the fall begins, the producers release what they have: the consumers eat their reserves; there are commercial disasters. . .'.[220]

All this reveals something of the archaic structure of the grain trade, which was especially evident in periods following poor harvests. There were, however, clear signs, in some regions from at least the beginning of the century, of the reorganization of mercantile activity and of the emergence of new patterns of behaviour in the market place. In the Paris region merchants tended increasingly to purchase supplies directly from farms rather than at markets; otherwise, given that market places remained very active as centres of concentration – particularly outside a radius of 50 kilometres of Paris – purchases were increasingly made on the basis of samples of their cereals carried in a small bag by farmers and bought by merchants on a promise of future delivery of the amounts desired.[221] This had a clear advantage for the farmer in that it economized on transport costs, and in the absence of agreed categories of wheat and means of arbitration in case of conflict which a more highly organized marketing system might have provided, it was the most efficient alternative to the traditional bulk sale in the market place.

M. Georges, a farmer at Orgival (Aisne) and vice-president of the agricultural committee at St-Quentin, giving evidence before the 1859 inquiry, explained that sale by sample assured greater regularity in price movements, whereas 'the display of sacks allowed purchasers to appreciate in an instant the amount offered for sale, so that purchasers held back, if there was an abundance, and vied with each other to buy in the contrary case' – thus intensifying price fluctuations.[222] The adoption of these new procedures was gradual and not everyone was happy with them. If farmers and merchants tended to appreciate the greater flexibility of sale by sample, administrators and consumers greeted all changes in commercial methods with suspicion, particularly where they conflicted with a desire that all trade in essentials be 'open' and subject to surveillance. In 1846 the Prefect of Bas-Rhin actually ordered the Mayor of Strasbourg to take measures to ensure that all cereals were sold on the market place,[223] and many municipalities continued to exclude merchants from the market place for the first hour or so after it opened and tried to prevent sale by sample,[224] with what success it is impossible to judge.

In spite of continued interference, it was, and had been in general from the eighteenth century, government policy to ensure the freedom of trade, but as long as poor communications prevented the efficient workings of the economic mechanism official policy remained difficult to implement.

Millers

In addition to farmers and grain merchants, millers were another very active group operating in the cereals market, and they played an important role in the popular demonology.

In rural areas the most numerous industrial establishments were flour mills. The geographical distribution of mills reflected three main factors – the density of the river network, local needs for flour and the structure of commerce. Poor communications justified the existence of large numbers of mills. According to an inquiry conducted in the early 1840s, there were 1126 millers in Saône-et-Loire employing over 2000 workers.[225] In Haute-Loire in 1846 there were 801 mills – 81.4 per cent of all industrial establishments.[226] Almost everywhere mills were small and powered by wind or especially water. Their productive capacity varied, primarily in relation to the nature of the market they served. In Haute-Loire the mill at St-Préjet-d'Allier ground only 120 kilograms of rye flour per day, while that at Le Puy produced the same quantity of wheat flour each hour.[227] Water mills generally had a greater capacity than wind mills.[228]

Typically, people took their grain to a miller, who was paid in kind for his troubles (between 5 and 10 per cent of the grain, plus an additional 1 per cent if he supplied transport),[229] but the constant decline in the number of people making their own bread led to a gradual concentration of milling, to the intensification of competition and to the disappearance of many small mills, especially in areas of large-scale wheat production[230] and where access to large markets encouraged the establishment of mills. This development was especially evident in the second half of the century, but even in its first decade the large mills of Toulouse, for example, milling in two cases over 140,000 hectolitres per annum, were causing problems for small mills in that region.[231]

According to one estimate, by the 1850s the profit margins of millers in the Paris area had been reduced to what was regarded as an excessively low sum – 1 franc per sack.[232] Large outputs were necessary to produce a reasonable income for the miller, but for this substantial investments of capital were essential in order to meet the costs of equipment, which usually included dressed millstones and machinery and a steam engine as well as a water-wheel, for the large-scale miller could not afford to rely on water power, which was frequently reduced by seasonal fluctuation in river levels – with the result, according to M. Labiche-Baudoin, who had operated a mill at Maintenon (Eure-et-Loir), that in a dry year the cost of milling a sack of flour could increase by as much as two or three times the normal cost.[233] Requirements for working capital were also substantial, both to cover the time lag between payments for cereals (usually immediate) and receipt of payment for flour (thirty to forty days were often allowed) and to pay wages to workers and agents employed in purchasing grain and selling flour.[234]

Where large-scale demand was assured such operations could be very profitable. The wealth of the Darblay family operating in the Paris region, was frequently cited as proof. The Paris market which consumed some 4000 sacks of flour per day (157 kilograms in each), was the mecca of millers and flour merchants; in the 1850s it was provisioned by about 500 millers, though, significantly, none supplied more than 150 sacks each day.[235] Large profits could be made from the sale not only of flour but also of bran as animal feed.[236] Many observers maintained, however, that the main source of profit was speculation on the price movement of cereals.[237] In contrast, the typical small miller does not seem to have been particularly prosperous. He often struggled, by diverse means, to make ends meet, particularly in years when water supply was poor or when prices rose so high as to force customers to ask for credit.[238] In dealing in basic foodstuffs the miller was inevitably subject to public pressure. His professional activity and the inexcusable fact that he apparently sought to profit from other men's difficulties by selling his flour as expensively as possible while purchasing grain as cheaply as possible – often at moments when he was aware of farmers' desperate need for money to pay rent, for example – inevitably caused resentment. This should not, however, allow us to forget the frequent praise of relationships with both farmers and consumers based on trust and mutual respect.[239] Significantly, Nogaret, the miller in Eugène Le Roy's novel *Le Moulin du Frau*, carefully explained to his young nephew the importance of establishing and maintaining a clientele by the performance of reciprocal services or purchase from artisans in other trades.[240]

The economic significance of such relationships was that the desire to maximize profit was muted and that, within limits, the inefficient operator was protected from the full effects of competition. Monsieur Laveux, a farmer in the commune of Charny (Seine-et-Marne), reported in 1859 that for the past ten years he had always sold around 2000 *quintaux* of wheat to the same miller: 'I send him my wheat, without specifying a price. He tells me a few days later that he received from me so many *quintaux* of wheat that week, at such and such a price, according to the market rate.' He stressed the fact that 'many farmers do the same; you can see with what honesty transactions occur in our area'.[241]

Apart from individuals who took their own grain to the mill whenever they needed flour (trying to avoid periods when conditions caused interruptions in milling),[242] the millers' customers were bakers.

Bakers

In some places bakers depended on particular millers or flour merchants who extended credit facilities, a fact obviously restricting their freedom of choice. This kind of dependence was most clear in the Paris market, where, in 1859, 484 of the 601 bakers had agreed *marches à cuisson* with their flour suppliers.[243] These were generally established for one year and constituted an agreement by the baker to accept delivery of a given quantity of flour per month, to be paid for not at a fixed rate but at a price established in relation to the fluctuating price that bakers were allowed to charge for bread, minus a sum of 10 francs per sack, which was estimated to cover the costs of baking. Bakers gained the advantage of a guaranteed relationship between the price of the flour that they purchased and that of the bread they sold, and they escaped the adverse effects of fluctuating cereal and flour prices. Moreover, they enjoyed a more or less guaranteed supply of flour at the date they required it and the possibility of profiting from the tacit acceptance by both parties that the costs of baking were in fact lower than those allowed in the convention established between them. The miller or merchant gained an assured market for his product.[244] The major complaint made was that bakers, through indebtedness to their particular suppliers, tended to become irreversibly attached to them,[245] so that a market mechanism theoretically based upon competition in price and quality broke down.

In the countryside and small towns many families continued to bake their own bread throughout the century, whenever possible using flour ground from cereals they had grown themselves or had received in payment for labour, but otherwise, especially after poor harvests, they were forced into the market place to purchase these cereals. They baked their bread in their own ovens, those of neighbours or that belonging to the commune. Another alternative to depending entirely on the baker was to obtain grain of one's own, see to its milling and prepare the dough before finally taking it to a baker's to be baked. There was also the possibility of taking flour to the baker and exchanging it for a given quantity of bread, to be baked over a specified period of time. The baker, as payment, received a proportion of the flour. This solved the problem of storage space for the consumer.

Domestic bread cannot have been very palatable. The dough frequently seems to have been badly prepared; the bread did not rise properly; and the crust was very thick. (It needed to be if the bread was to be kept for weeks or even months, as it normally was.) Outside the towns and larger villages there were hardly any bakers, so people had to do their own baking.[246] In the Creuse – admittedly, a rather backward region – it has been calculated that in 1859 thirty of the forty-six communes in the *arrondissement* of Boussac had no baker and seventy-two of the ninety-nine in the *arrondissement* of Aubusson. Only 10 per cent of the bread consumed is estimated to have been produced by a baker.[247]

Contemporary observers agreed on the growing importance of bakers, particularly in and around the towns but increasingly also in rural areas. A number of reasons might be suggested for this, among them the increased productivity of agriculture, which permitted foodstuffs such as potatoes or chestnuts to be replaced with bread in the popular diet; the gradual intensification of agriculture and the demands this made on the female members of a household, encouraging recourse to the baker to save the considerable time spent in preparing dough; the more rigid enforcement of legislation to prevent over-use of forest resources after 1827, which deprived many poor people of the wood they needed to heat their ovens; and the growing urbanization of population. Most significant was the slow rise in material standards, combined with, as a sign of these new conditions, a growing taste for something better, for bread of quality rather than the traditional loaf.[248] There were clear signs of this development in the first half of the century, but it should be stressed that the causes and the changing taste affected most rural areas only later in the century or not until the following century.

The published census statistics, by grouping bakers under the general heading 'food industries', make it impossible to give an accurate statistical picture of the numbers of bakers in France. Contemporaries, citing the examples of large towns, tended to complain that there were too many and that in consequence most bakers were unable to earn a satisfactory living. At Bordeaux there were 240 bakers for 110,000 inhabitants in 1854 (i.e. one for every 458 people); at Brest one for every 650–700 in 1859; at Lyon at the same time the proportion was as low as one to 350.[249] In Paris the official rate was one baker to 1800. M. Berger, a former *syndic de la boulangerie*, claimed that because many people left the city for months each year, one to 2400 should be the minimum.[250] There were 601 bakers in the city, plus around 100 market stalls occupied mainly by bakers from outside the city limits.[251] Here and elsewhere their numbers were limited in partial compensation for their inability to establish their own prices.

Bakers were divided into classes for the purpose of establishing the reserve of flour that each baker was legally obliged to maintain (see Table 6). These classes were based on daily consumption of flour and give some idea of the scale of operation of Parisian bakers.[252]

Bakers were, in fact, subject to a complex of regulations designed to safeguard bread supplies and to limit prices. In most localities mayors acted according to the laws of 1790–1, which instituted the so-called *taxe du pain* – that is, the establishment of maximum bread prices in relation to the fluctuating market price for cereals. In 165 towns the system of regulation was more complete; an *arrêt* of 19 *vendémaire an X* (11 October 1801) affecting Paris and the general decrees of 4 and 8 May 1812 following a period of severe food shortage, re-established the corporations of the *Ancien Régime* for bakers, such was official concern that absence of regulation might lead to popular unrest. It was stipulated that the mayor of each of these towns must convoke a meeting of ten of the most reputable and prosperous bakers, who should designate a *syndic* and his assistants responsible for the co-ordination of the bakers of the locality. Their main task was to classify bakeries according to their scale of operation and to establish the size of the reserve of flour that each would be expected to maintain. The *syndic* and his assistants would subsequently be required to ensure that these stocks were maintained at the stipulated level and to check bakers' weights. In Paris the *taxe du pain* was established on the basis of flour prices, on the supposition that 100 kilograms of flour gave 130 kilograms of bread and on the estimate that the costs of production and sale of this quantity amounted to 7 francs. The finest-quality bread (*pains de fantaisie* and *petits pains*) were not subject to *taxe*. The growth in the consumption of such bread was a sign of prosperity and of changing taste, and in 1854 56 million of that year's total consumption of 158 million kilograms of bread was in this form.[253] Elsewhere the *taxe* was usually based on cereal prices in the regulating market rather than on flour prices. In Paris, in addition, a *caisse de la boulangerie* was established, from which, in time of high prices, advances were paid to bakers to allow them to maintain the price of bread below the level which otherwise would have been charged. These advances were recuperated by a *sur-taxe* on bread

Table 6   *Classification of Parisian bakers, 1853*

Classes	Daily consumption	Number of bakers per category
1	5 sacks* and above	86
2	4–5 sacks	150
3	3–4 sacks	244
4	2–3 sacks	116
5	below 2 sacks	5

* A sack contained 157 kilograms of flour.

during periods of low prices. This system and the maintenance of adequate reserves were designed to reduce the scale of price fluctuation.[254] For the bakers concerned, however, there was an obvious disadvantage in the immobilization of capital in stocks and storage space. In practice, the capital requirement for entry into the trade was such that the number of bakers in towns was frequently below the number established as the maximum permissible.[255] Although in Paris it was difficult to avoid the commitment, because two-thirds of the reserve had to be stored in municipal warehouses, elsewhere less close supervision allowed bakers to avoid their legal commitments. A spot check at Lyon in 1853 revealed reserves adequate for eight days' baking in place of the legally required fifteen.[256]

Bakers were subject to the control not only of their *syndic* but also of the administrative police authorities. This involved the occasional checking of weights (especially after public complaints), increasingly frequent chemical analysis of samples of flour[257] and powers to establish bread prices, to ensure that each baker provided daily the amount of bread he was expected to bake and to ascertain that no baker closed his business without due notice and the provision of an alternative supply. The authorities regarded the question of bread supply as an essential aspect of policing. They were made aware of popular anxiety frequently enough to pay it strict attention.

In general, they showed little sympathy for the economic difficulties in which bakers might find themselves. In periods when cereal prices were rising as a consequence of the free play of market forces, the price of bread could be increased only following two or three consecutive increases in cereal prices, and then only if the municipal authorities thought that this was warranted. It was too easy for mayors to try to avoid popular unrest and personal unpopularity by refusing to allow justifiable increases.[258] Thus the Minister of the Interior was forced to remind the Prefect of the Meurthe in 1854 that bakers could not be forced to sell at a loss.[259] Incidents of this kind were frequent,[260] as also were protests against what bakers felt to be unjustified reductions in bread prices.[261] In reply officials commonly accused them of attempting to manipulate the market price of cereals in order to cause an increase, which would then lead to an increase in bread prices.[262] Moreover, problems were caused for bakers not only by the unsympathetic attitude of many officials but also by the fact that, as the *procureur-général* at Orléans complained in 1855, the legislation was excessively complicated.[263] Neither the bakers nor the minor officials who usually interfered with their business were in a position to comprehend fully its ramifications.[264]

Obviously, the bakers were not operating in a free-market situation. According to M. Gauldrée-Boilleau, chief of the section of the Ministry of War charged with provisioning the army, bakers, especially in Paris, were required to invest a large amount of capital in premises, ovens, stocks and operating expenses in the hope of only a precarious return. He estimated the capital needs to vary between 20,000 francs for a baker in the fourth class to 60,000 francs for one in the first class.[265]

The larger his scale of operations, the more secure the position of the baker tended to be. For one thing, he was more likely to be able to negotiate favourable purchasing arrangements with flour millers and merchants. Bakers to whom millers were unwilling to accord credit or negotiate such arrangements as *marches à cuisson*, and who were forced to rely on day-to-day purchases on the markets, were fully liable to all the fluctuations of market prices and tended to pay substantially more for their flour.[266] Those who were unable to build up reserves of any kind but were legally obliged to furnish bread each day might thus find themselves in desperate straits, as increases in cereal and flour prices preceded, sometimes by a matter of weeks, increases in bread prices.[267]

This was not the end of bakers' problems. There was the relatively minor irritancy suffered by larger bakers who employed labour outside their immediate family of bakery workers who manifested a traditional spirit of association and a *compagnonnage* type of organization. This led to coalitions to increase wages in Paris in 1820, 1827, 1832, 1833 and 1840. However, these workers were subjected to especially close surveillance and rapid repression by the authorities.[268]

Then there was the great problem of relations with customers. Given fixed prices, and for as long as certain standards of quality were maintained, consumers tended to prefer the nearest shop,[269] but to retain them it was necessary to accord credit facilities. To some degree this assured a stable clientele and even gave the baker – through control over the extending of credit – a means of exercising pressure on a dependent clientele of debtors, who were unlikely to complain about cheating over weight or quality.[270] The cost was often excessive, however, in spite of the high rates of interest which might be charged on outstanding debts. One baker estimated that the average Parisian baker had 8000 francs in outstanding credit at any one time.[271] In a period of economic crisis as consumers became less able to pay, so credit facilities tended to decline.[272] Many small bakers went bankrupt,[273] and those who survived were forced 'to torment their clientele in order to be paid cash and risked losing customers'.[274]

The authorities were aware of the problems that bakers faced but generally chose to lend support to consumers' demands. It is therefore not surprising that in some places officials began to complain of the lack of new entrants to the bakery business.[275] Substantial profits might be possible for the larger-scale enterprise, but for the small baker the struggle to rise up the hierarchy meant years of hard labour, often rewarded only by bankruptcy.

To survive bakers were frequently reduced to such expedients as false measures. There was often administrative tolerance of small discrepancies in weight, although this declined with the establishment of the Second Empire.[276] Particularly outside Paris and other major cities, where surveillance was less close, the adulteration of bread (by mixing rice, potatoes, starch or beans with wheat flour) seems to have been a frequent practice. These methods all have the great advantage of retaining water and permitting the baker to achieve the legal weight requirement while using less wheat flour. M. Boussingault, a member of the Institut, who analysed the content of bread in Paris in 1847, reported that first-quality bread in the capital contained 34 to 39 per cent water, while in the provinces the water content was usually 43 to 46 per cent.[277] Even the cost of water might be reduced by using poor-quality water from the baker's well rather than paying for the installation of piped water where this was available.[278]

As a last resort bakers might associate to protest about their grievances, occasionally going so far as to threaten to stop baking unless they were permitted to increase their prices. This was a dangerous manoeuvre because it immediately heightened popular hostility and usually led to prosecution by the alarmed authorities, who would then compel bakers or else their employees to bake.[279]

The pressure to engage in some kind of fraudulent practice was especially marked when cereal prices, and therefore the cost of production, rose suddenly and massively. Whatever the cause of such transgressions – whether or not it was true, as one witness in 1859 claimed, that it was impossible to exercise the profession of baking in an honest manner[280] – the result was to establish a bad reputation for bakers in general. Consumers constantly complained about fraud and about coalitions designed to keep prices high. Feeling justifiably provoked when prices rose, they often resorted to smashing the offending bakers' windows.[281] Towards the end of the Second Empire, when conditions had changed, a baker wrote: 'When I was young, the doors of our bakeries were furnished with very strong iron bars; every bakery was a sort of fortress compared with other shops. This was due to the fact that bakers were obliged to defend themselves against sudden invasions by the people.'[282]

Consumers

Consumer behaviour was obviously a significant influence on that of bakers and millers or merchants and farmers operating in the market. This was particularly the case when substantial price increases occurred. In spite of official efforts, the effectiveness of the market mechanism in reducing and/or equalizing price levels was reduced by intimidation and disorders on the road and in the market places. M. Rabourdin, a grain and flour merchant at Paris, maintained, and with some justice, that commerce would be more active in periods of shortage if merchants were not afraid of having their carts pillaged by mobs.[283] In addition to this danger there was the likelihood that both physical and moral pressure to lower prices would be exerted in the market place. On 9 January 1847 the authorities suspended the market at

Laval because of the 'moral' pressure on sellers there. The crowd immediately resorted to physical assault instead.[284] A flour merchant from St-
Mesmin (Loire) claimed, and again with some justice, that popular attitudes
were the product of the fact that bread was a necessity and of the historical
tradition of a supposed *Pacte de Famine*. Memories of the official establishment of a price maximum during the Revolution served both to legitimize
and to encourage popular action, both directly against merchants and
farmers and indirectly by pleas for help from the government.[285] Numerous
examples could be quoted to reinforce a picture of continued market imperfection due to poor communications and to the emotions of the actors in the
market place.

Increases in the prices of basic necessities like bread caused severe hardship to much of the population. Even where bread was not actually in short
supply, a substantial increase in its price would deprive the poor of the
possibility of buying it in sufficient quantity. The result of the rigidity of
demand and the emotiveness of the market was to provoke price fluctuations
that were more than proportional to variations in the harvest. Price levels
were not simply products of the relationship between supply and demand
but were determined by, and had significance within, a 'complete political
and social reality',[286] which we hope to illuminate.

High prices bred social bitterness. The feeling was widespread in all
sections of the community, and no doubt with some justice, that, as the
gendarmerie commander in the department of Finistère put it, 'There is no
shortage, and no possibility of famine, because the farmers have grain', but
they would not bring it to market because they were speculating on further
price increases.[287] The deputy mayor of Nevers (Nièvre) complained in
March 1847 that part of the population was victim to another part, namely,
those with money to speculate or with reserves of foodstuffs to hoard.[288] The
economically better-off groups in society were able to satisfy their needs in
spite of increases in prices and, in so doing, intensified the shortage and the
rise in prices and the adverse consequences for the poor. Social divisions
were never as great as in times of high food prices.

Although food prices increased to compensate for the decline in marketable quantities, not every producer grew enough to make this profitable.
Only a minority, whose number varied in relation to the size of harvest but
tended to increase with time as productivity increased, was able, by waiting
for prices to rise, to make substantial profits. At some time during the
agricultural year many of those small producers, who in a good year would
have harvested sufficient for their own consumption and a small surplus to
sell, were drawn back into the market as consumers, at the very time when
supply was reduced.[289]

According to the *maire* of St-Ybars in the Ariège a poor harvest was an
inadequate explanation of the amplitude of the rise in prices: 'Everyone is
afraid of a coming shortage, and this fear prompts those who possess grains

to hold them in reserve.' A considerable amount of grain was thus taken out of circulation only to reappear when the danger of price rises had passed.[290] Moreover, 'the gravity [of the situation] creates needs. . . everyone anxiously searches for food and this abnormal movement causes price increases'.[291] In industrial areas a severe problem might occur on pay day, when workers rushed to provision themselves and so pushed up prices.[292] The market held at Château-la-Vallière (Indre-et-Loire), near Tours, on 23 November had attracted, it was estimated, three times as many purchasers as usual.[293] Not just the number of purchasers but the presence of onlookers, themselves anxious about prices, established an emotive market situation. A *gendarmerie* commander, writing in January 1847, maintained that 'everywhere in the department of Indre-et-Loire there exists a kind of panic; everyone provisions himself to the greatest extent possible; it is the same in all the other departments, everywhere; however well provisioned in grains the markets are, these are paid for in cash without any bargaining'. The ambience of the market place might be better understood if we quote the same officer's report of 'many women crying because they cannot buy any grain, saying that they do not know how they are going to feed their families'.[294]

Poor people in particular came to market frequently in order to make small purchases as and when their financial resources permitted. They were not likely to build up stocks, and for them the market place still fulfilled many of the functions which would shortly be taken over by shops. For women trying desperately to make ends meet every market day must have been a nightmare, their fears intensified by lack of knowledge about food resources outside their own immediate locality. At Villaines-la-Juhel (Mayenne) in November 1846 people finding the market less well provisioned than usual and 'already frightened by price increases at neighbouring markets' became alarmed and said to each other, 'the wheat is already so expensive, what will we do this winter, we'll starve to death'.[295] Their fears were exaggerated but nonetheless real to them. In some economically less advanced areas, especially in the Massif Central, the problem was already not only excessive demand but also lack of money, especially among the unemployed, and the consequent sheer inability to purchase sufficient food at inflated prices. Officials realized that provision would have to be made for such people.[296]

Anger against merchants and farmers was particularly intense in areas in which prices were increasing in spite of what seemed like an adequate local harvest. Even the normal operations of commerce lent themselves to criticism. Thus prices in the Toulouse region early in 1847 were influenced not only by levels at the port of Marseille but also by considerable purchases made on behalf of the merchants of Bordeaux, Le Havre, Rouen and Paris. This was recognized by local officials as inevitable; given the relatively low prices prevailing in the region, the problem for them was 'to make the lowest classes, the least enlightened in society, who are those who suffer most from this situation' understand and accept exports which substantially increased local prices.[297]

Alongside reports indicating simply that the market mechanism was levelling out prices, – for example, that of the Prefect of Morbihan of 25 January 1847, which noted that 'the considerable increase in prices of the week before last has called more grain into the market and there has been a slight fall'[298] – and the silence of many administrators, which leads one to presume that a not too abnormal situation prevailed in their departments, were those typified by the military commander in the Mayenne. He wrote:

the considerable exports of wheat made from the department . . . cause disquiet, rightly or wrongly, among the poor and the workers of the towns and countryside; they fear a shortage, in spite of the assurances to the contrary which have been given, and this disposition of spirits excited by malice . . . encourages them to obstruct exports of foodstuffs so that each locality wants to retain most of what it has produced and purchase it at a moderate price.[299]

According to the Prefect of the same department, 'every little village becomes an obstacle to the circulation of carts loaded with cereals'.[300]

The attitudes which caused such behaviour were shared by most of the population in regions of normal surplus. Even officials and notables, concerned about public order, sought to preserve local self-sufficiency at the expense of the areas which normally depended upon them for supply. Informal pressure might be brought to bear to limit or prevent sales.[301] Most significant were those exercised by public opinion in small communities. The typical consequence of this was reported by the Prefect of Allier in November 1846: 'The bakers of Moulins presented themselves at my residence to show me letters from proprietors in which these latter declared that they would not dare deliver them the grain that they had purchased for fear of being pillaged.'[302] In one of these letters a farmer called Renou wrote to a baker he normally supplied:

Monsieur, the present is to inform you that it will not be possible for me to deliver to you the wheat that I sold you at the last fair at Souvigny if I want to avoid the disfavour of the people. The workers I employ have been told to tell me that if I do deliver this, then I will regret it. I cannot go contrary to that; if you demand it, I will give you an indemnity. I would prefer the cost of that than to have people crying out after me and to expose myself to the fury of ill-intentioned men who would profit from that circumstance to do me ill.[303]

Living in a small community, Renou could not afford to offend too many of its members. Less cautious individuals are known not only to have suffered threats and insults but also to have been assaulted, had the windows of their houses broken, their sacks full of flour and cereals slashed with knives, their horses turned loose, their carts damaged.[304]

Old emotive labels were still used. Whoever seemed to be profiting from the grain trade in periods of distress – benefiting from the misery of others – was likely to be called an *accapareur*, a 'cornerer' or hoarder believed to be buying up supplies of a scarce commodity for speculative purposes. As M. Boitelle, prefect of police in Paris in the 1850s observed: 'As long as the populations believe in the possibility of cornering the supply of grains, they will want to struggle against this, and will hoard themselves for their own profit to avoid becoming dependent upon the hoarders.'[305] Merchants and farmers prepared to take the risk and go to market were exposed to danger from mobs along the roads and then to intimidation by crowds of angry consumers on the market place. It was no wonder that many of them stayed at home.

The *gendarmerie* commander in the *arrondissement* of Moissac reported on 2 February 1847:

this area . . . is far from lacking, and the true danger appears to me to consist in the momentary reduction in the activities . . . of the millers, proprietors and merchants who claim, in spite of the tranquillity of the region, not to dare to bring grain to the market from fear that they will be forced to sell it at arbitrarily fixed prices . . . or even that they will be pillaged.

He could not decide whether these fears were genuine or a manoeuvre designed to restrict supplies and force up prices.[306] Whether genuine or a pretext, their result was to reduce the volume of commercial activity below levels which might otherwise have prevailed and to ensure that 'commerce does not as effectively render the service it renders in ordinary times, of levelling out prices in transporting the surplus of one locality to a place where there is a shortage'.[307]

Conclusion

Until the middle of the nineteenth century, because of the slowness and cost of transport, most agricultural products were consumed in their region of origin. Cereals and, above all, wheat were a partial exception to this. The structure of the market for this commodity has been described as an 'interlocking web'[308] of local and regional markets, with interaction increasing in intensity and range following poor harvests which encouraged the development of long-distance links between markets along the axes of major rivers and wherever movement by sea was possible.

In years of good harvest trade was restricted. When local harvests were poor normal supplies failed, and prices increased as the zone of provisioning widened. As distance from the point of supply increased, so did the commodity's 'price' for the consumer. This fact limited the spatial range within which the commodity might find purchasers, and if that range tended to increase, often dramatically, in periods of general price rise, this effect was limited by changes in the supply/demand situation for transport. Because of poor communications compartmentalization of the market structure remained a profound reality. Difficulties of penetration from areas of surplus or ports of import to areas of shortage clearly reduced the effectiveness of the market mechanism in evening out price differences. As the newspaper *La Presse* complained on 26 April 1847, 'bread is expensive not only because of the inadequacy of the harvest, but also and especially due to poor communications'.

In 1847, even in a major producing department like Eure-et-Loir, with good communications, it was reported that 'imports, in spite of the efforts of millers, were so feeble that they had no influence on prices'.[309] The basic situation remained similar – characterized by the impermeability of space – to that described by M. de la Madeleine, Prefect of the Orne in the year IX: 'The lack of markets for the export of foodstuffs means that they are at a very low price at one place which is overflowing with them and very expensive in other places where they are lacking. Easy circulation extends prosperity everywhere, but this is far from having been established.'[310] Communications were improving, and commercial responses were becoming more effective, but the physical problems of distribution remained substantial.

The basic characteristic of the market, and a cause of substantial price fluctuation, continued to be the imperfect adjustment of supply to demand as a result of high transport costs and the slow diffusion of information. The latter indicates a limit to the validity of the general statement that 'the difference in price for the same merchandise between two markets cannot exceed transport costs between the two localities'.[311]

The situation prior to railway development was an evolving one. Reductions in transport costs occurred throughout the eighteenth and the nineteenth century and made a major contribution to reducing the fragmentation of the national market, to increasing the effectiveness of the supply/demand mechanism and to reducing the amplitude of price fluctuation. A more dynamic, commercially orientated market was gradually emerging. Indeed, an examination of the relationship between population and subsistence indicates that in most years local food production or normal channels of trade satisfied the normal levels of demand and even permitted the gradual improvement of diet.

But in spite of progress in agriculture and in the organization of commerce, it remained difficult to relate supply to the demand for basic foodstuffs in the still relatively frequent years of harvest failure. To varying degrees, according to fertility, social structure and agricultural techniques, the French countryside remained close to over-population. Although the rates of growth in agricultural produce that have been calculated for the first half of the nineteenth century are not very far below those of the second half, these show not so much dynamism as the maximum extension of traditional and labour-intensive techniques to produce a range of commodities dominated almost everywhere by cereals cultivated for local consumption. Subsistence remained the major preoccupation of farmers in most regions. The potentially dynamic interrelationship between agriculture and commerce could not be realized because of the restraints imposed on both by pressures for local self-sufficiency resulting from the under-developed character of the transport infrastructure and the inadequacies of inter-regional and international trade flows. Moreover, the amplitude of price fluctuations continued to be influenced by the fears, the psychology of people in the market place. As one contemporary observer noted: 'In times of high prices the principal cause of the extreme variation leading to an increase is the great multitude of purchasers who present themselves on the markets. When there is abundance . . . all is calm; then the farmers and millers find themselves alone in the market halls.'[312] These reactions are of interest not only because they directly affected prices but also because they reveal something of the mental constructs that men have about their environment, and this is crucial to our comprehension of economic behaviour.

Although there existed a significant degree of correlation between the harvest, the overall supply of food and market prices, the relationship was distorted by the consequence of rumour and fear. Market-place behaviour needs to be explained in large part in terms of social psychology. Price increases, which were the inevitable result of poor harvests when demand was relatively inelastic, were accelerated and exaggerated by fear of hunger. The state of continual insecurity in which much of the population lived, even in the economically more advanced regions, created a tension, a psychology of fear, which was the logical conclusion of an outlook on the environment which encouraged most cultivators to dream of self-sufficiency, of independence of the market place. For peasants and urban workers poor harvests and rising prices meant debt and economies on already tightly stretched budgets and, above all, the threat of hunger for themselves and their families.[313]

Part Two

Social Crisis

The traditional economic crisis associated with poor harvests and distribution difficulties had the effect of stimulating substantial increases in the prices of the basic necessities of diet at a time when more and more people were dependent on purchases in the market and when incomes of all kinds were under pressure. The consequence was widespread misery and suffering.

Misery led, in certain circumstances, to protest, as the deprived attempted to increase their influence in the market place through the use of intimidation and violence and to hit back against those they thought were to blame for their misery. A moral conception of economic relationships quite different from that of the long-developing capitalist system, frequently survived to provide justification for protest.

To contain protest, *notables* and administrators sought to alleviate misery through the traditional forms of charity and work relief. If these failed, they depended upon the rapid deployment of military force.

Study of the mid century subsistence crises thus not only provides us with insights into economic structures during the period of early industrialization and into the living conditions of the masses and the extreme insecurity of their existence, but also offers an important means of examining social relationships, social tensions, methods of protest and forms of social control and repression. The analysis of these crises – the last of the traditional subsistence crises – reveals both elements of continuity with the historical past and the beginnings of a rapid process of transition to a new and recognizably more modern economic system. The *ancien régime économique* was drawing to a close.

4 Subsistence crises and popular misery

Characteristics of crises

Increases in agricultural productivity and improvements in communications, and thereby the distribution of foodstuffs, had eliminated the possibility of famine from the early eighteenth century. Subsistence crises, however, continued to make life difficult for the mass of Frenchmen throughout the eighteenth century and until past the middle years of the nineteenth century. The purpose of this chapter is to consider some of the social consequences of this continued inability of agriculture and commerce to match supply with demand.

The classic mechanism of the pre-industrial economy has been described clearly by Labrousse.[1] A poor harvest had the effect of reducing incomes from agriculture and of forcing consumers to spend increasing proportions of their incomes upon basic foodstuffs as food prices rose. These two factors, together with a widespread crisis of confidence intensified by the disorder entailed by protest against high prices, had the effect of reducing demand for industrial products and causing a generalized economic crisis. As such crises were frequent in the first half of the nineteenth century – disaster struck in 1801–2, 1810–12, 1816–17, 1828–9, 1837–9, 1845–7 and 1853–6 – they occurred several times within the lifespan of most people and had both significant short-term effects on living standards and longer-term consequences for attitudes towards the natural and social worlds within which people lived.

The essential cause of crisis was low agricultural productivity, with yields highly susceptible to climatically induced fluctuation, compounded by distribution difficulties and the inefficient transmission of market-place information. Climatic causes of harvest failure varied between regions.

In the Mediterranean drought was the prime cause of failure of the grain crop, while further north rainy winters, cold and damp springs and summers were the likely causes. But a national subsistence crisis was possible even when harvest failure was not general, because imports into a zone of shortage caused shortage or fear of shortage elsewhere. The crisis years of 1845–7, and to a lesser extent 1853–6, are of particular interest because during them Frenchmen experienced, for the last time, the age-old phenomenon of dearth.

There are at least two good reasons for concentrating on the analysis of economic crises. In the first place, such analysis provides an insight into social relationships. Following a poor harvest, those who possessed sufficient stocks were able to profit from selling at high prices. A much larger proportion of both rural and urban populations suffered from under-nourishment and fear of starvation. Profit taking by the better-off, and resentment of this by the poor, led to an intensification of social hostilities and extensive, if short-lived, violence.

Secondly, crisis analysis provides an indicator of structural change in the economy. The frequency of crises indicated the susceptibility of even the most modern sectors of industry to crises beginning in agriculture. This was especially true of textiles. In this case demand was at all times restricted by low consumer incomes, while even a relatively limited increase in the price of basic necessities was enough to strain popular budgets. For the period of the July Monarchy the relatively modern, mechanized textile industry at Lille has been described as being in crisis from 1830 to early 1833, from the end of 1833 to 1834, from the end of 1836 to the end of 1838, from early 1839 to 1840, from the end of 1843 to the end of 1844, and again from the end of 1845 until at least 1849.[2] The relationship between poor harvests and industrial crises was strikingly obvious to contemporaries. As the report of the cantonal commission at Clary (Nord) to the 1848 inquiry explained: 'The high price of bread in 1846–7 was very harmful for trade. The poor, the working class, bought no clothing during these years.'[3]

The relationship between agriculture and industry was, then, one of the basic elements determining levels of demand and the pace of economic development. The continuing susceptibility of industry to subsistence crises until into the 1860s is revealing of the slowness of structural change in the French economy. The relationship should not be over-simplified, however. Increasingly, industrial crises became 'mixed' in character, due in large part to commercial and financial factors such as over-investment and consequent over-production and to shortages of working capital. This was especially the case in the more advanced economic regions and in the more capital-intensive heavy industries, which were not as dependent upon mass consumer demand as textiles. But structural change was increasingly effective everywhere, so that by the 1870s the economic crises of the *ancien régime économique* had essentially disappeared. Even in the case of the textile industry producing primarily for a mass consumer market, the traditional relationship between agricultural prices and demand was no longer dominant. Although the agricultural depression of the 1880s undoubtedly affected the demand for industrial products, this was far less marked than it would have been a few decades earlier.

Examination of successive crises shows their growing complexity as the process of industrialization gathered pace. The mid century crisis, while revealing again the extreme susceptibility of the whole economy to agricultural crises, makes this point clear.

As early as 1844 the relatively large numbers of business failures had indicated a malaise in commerce and industry, and indeed it is probable that a commercial and industrial crisis would have occurred around 1846–7 even without harvest failure. Although the subsequent crisis was to be of varying intensity for particular sectors of the economy, from the failure of the potato harvest in 1845 difficulties became more intense and more general. In 1846 the cereal harvest was also poor. Food prices varied by regions, but nationally the tendency was for a substantial rise. Some areas suffered more than others, particularly those which had experienced the failure of the potato as well as the cereal harvest. In east Aquitaine this was the culmination of a period of rising food prices, beginning in 1842. In the Nièvre this also continued a long period of difficulty, compounded there and in neighbouring departments by extensive flooding which interrupted communications, destroyed stocks and crops in the fields and damaged or destroyed many mills.[4]

Anxiety and speculation amplified the consequences of poor harvests. As demand for industrial products declined, so financial circles were affected by a crisis of confidence, clearly evident in the fall of railway company shares on the Bourse, the withdrawal of capital invested in railways and the decline in demand for metallurgical products. All sectors of the industrial economy, from textiles to metallurgy, were thus affected.

In terms of the size of the deficit and the consequent rise in food prices, the harvest failures of 1853 and 1855 were every bit as serious as those of 1846, but the effects on industry – short-lived stagnation in the second half of 1853, continuing into the early part of 1854 – were far less marked. In some regions there was a striking contrast between crisis affecting agriculture and high levels of industrial activity. Metallurgy in particular was protected by continued railway orders. This is indicative of the acceleration of structural change in the economy. Even so the industrial crisis at the end of 1857, which at first sight might appear to be linked to the international financial crisis, was in fact caused by reduced rural purchasing power following a series of poor harvests which the generally good harvest of that year was not sufficient to arrest.

Economic difficulties in the period 1862–5 were in part a consequence of an increase in grain prices in 1861–2 but were due primarily to other factors, especially the commercial effects of the American Civil War. Indeed, in 1863 for the first time harvest failure, which in unbalancing local supply/ demand conditions would normally have resulted in marked increases in prices, was followed by a period of depressed prices, another significant indicator of changing economic structures. In 1867–8 the traditional schema reasserted itself. The general crisis of that year, although a product largely of a crisis of confidence linked to the political situation, also to a considerable degree reflected harvest failure and high agricultural prices. The crisis was short-lived and was never to be repeated in such a form. In effect, the *ancien régime économique* had ended.

Diet and health

The main purpose of this brief reminder of the characteristics of pre-industrial economic crises is to preface a discussion of their social consequences. Our first consideration will be the effects of crisis on diet. What were the normal conditions, and to what extent did these decline in periods of crisis? Diet varied between areas mainly because of poor communications and dependence upon local production. Tradition also imposed a restraint upon adaptation. A geography of diet would reveal infinite variation between rural areas and more marked differences between rural and urban diets, although urban diets were far from uniform. Distinctions based upon socio-professional factors, and especially income levels, would also be evident.

At least into the middle of the nineteenth century cereals or potatoes provided the major part of the calorific intake of the vast majority of the population[5] – just to take one example, in 1848 it was reported from the Vienne that agricultural labourers subsisted on a diet of 'coarse bread, produced from the worst quality grains, never butcher's meat. . . . on feast days some vegetables, cheese in summer, some potatoes in winter'.[6] This is not typical but is as representative as any other example might be. Meat consumption appears to have been generally low. Normally, the poor ate home-killed pork or poultry rather than butcher's meat. Consumption of both meat and fish was more common in urban than in rural areas but remained low. In diets with a low meat content, alcohol often fulfilled the role of an energy-giving complement.[7]

Although the shortcomings in the information available make it difficult to assess dietary deficiencies accurately, levels of meat, vegetable and dairy-product intake were without doubt low enough to result in protein and vitamin deficiencies among large portions of the population of all areas. This under-nourishment, combined with contaminated water supplies and lack of hygiene, resulted in vulnerability to disease.

In spite of increases in food production, which made subsistence crises less frequent and generally less intense as time passed, the balance between population and resources remained precarious. Social and economic conditions maintained mortality rates at a high, if slowly diminishing, level. Infant mortality in particular reflects inadequacies of diet and hygiene, affecting both mother and children.

Continued improvement of diet was not assured. In Normandy, for example, following a period from 1810 to 1830 during which diet seemed to have improved, there were long years of regression from 1830 to 1855.[8] The difficulty and expense of supplying adequate quantities of food to Paris and other cities also seems to have caused deterioration in dietary standards until the late 1850s. The prevalence of tuberculosis is only one physical indicator of this.[9]

If one judges French agriculture in the 1840s in terms of its capacity to provide stable supplies of food and a nutritionally balanced diet, it seems reasonable to conclude that a situation of relative over-population prevailed. At the best of times the range of foodstuffs most people could afford to buy was limited in a manner likely to result in dietary deficiencies, while following harvest failure normal difficulties and their consequences were compounded.

Periodic deterioration of an already inadequate diet could only intensify the effects of otherwise permanent deficiencies. There was a clear relationship between high prices and high mortality. Certainly, men rarely, if ever, died of hunger. The demographic effect of food shortage was indirect – reduced physical resistance to disease. These consequences of crises can be easily traced until the end of the 1850s in an overall mortality rate of 239 per 10,000 in 1847, for example, compared with a more normal 220 in 1844. However, the direct effects of nineteenth-century subsistence crises, as opposed to habitual under-nourishment and especially the influence this had on infant mortality and on population growth, should not be exaggerated. Of far greater significance than the demographic consequences of crises were the effects they had on the conditions of the great mass of people who did not die but suffered and upon relationships between people in a society founded upon the exploitation and preservation of massive social inequalities. It is hardly surprising that many commentators, then as now, saw the evolution of food production and distribution as the fundamental factors influencing the lives of the mass of the population.

In town and countryside the problem of eating enough to maintain health and a level of energy permitting the worker or peasant to earn a living was faced by most of the population. Dr Antoine Dupoux and his colleague, the health officer of the canton of Pionsat (Puy-de-Dôme), reported in 1848 that the agricultural population was exposed to illness by 'excessive daily labour, the lack of a sufficiently fortifying diet, by its daily exposure to the elements and by the negligence which it generally effects in the care of its health'.[10] Such comments were far from uncommon.

Although, as one nutritionist has written, 'It is difficult to draw a precise line between good nutrition and malnutrition for there are many intermediate states between normal and pathological conditions',[11] and despite the absence of precise scientific analyses of human needs in terms of calories, protein and vitamins and of the physiological effects of nutritional deficiencies, some general points can safely be made.

In the first place it ought to be noted that under-nourishment and dietary deficiency due especially to inadequate consumption of meat and vegetables were considered to be normal throughout the first half of the nineteenth century. When cereal prices rose consumption of meat and vegetables would be even further reduced, as a larger portion of a family's budget was expended on basic necessities. Normal dietary deficiencies were thus intensified, with more or less long-lasting effects. The most obvious consequences were high mortality rates, especially among children, the aged and women, the prevalence of digestive and intestinal complaints and low resistance to disease. More generally, a widespread state of 'physiological misery' can be assumed to have prevailed among the urban and rural masses, which was evident in constitutional feebleness and limited work capacity, in dental deficiencies and the slowness with which ulcers healed. Rather than the more dramatic epidemics, it is this state of latent deficiency that should be stressed. A doctor's report on the canton of Lezoux (Puy-de-Dôme), written in 1848, perhaps illustrates the point by commenting:

the fruits of labour are not sufficient to allow the worker to live decently. Most of them are badly housed, badly clothed and badly fed. A rye bread . . . indigestible due to fermentation, potatoes, no meat or wine, except exceptionally, that is the basic diet of the population. . . . [It] is natural therefore that it must be pale, verminous, weak, with little resistance to fatigue, and less to illness.[12]

The *sous-préfet* at Châteaubriant (Maine-et-Loire) observed in 1856 that low levels of labour productivity were primarily due to under-nourishment and not laziness, as employers claimed.[13]

According to a Food and Agriculture Organization report on contemporary under-developed areas, 'the whole manner of life is adapted to an insufficient supply of calories, with results that are socially undesirable: lack of drive and initiative; avoidance of physical and mental effort; excessive rest'.[14] In France a national average intake of 1850 calories per day, estimated to have been achieved early in the nineteenth century,[15] might be viewed as an indispensable minimum permitting normal productive activity. When this increased not only would health improve and resistance to disease be increased but also an 'enormous reserve of human energy'[16] would be released. Until this happened sheer lack of energy would act as a major restraint on economic development.

Food needs vary between individuals according to height and weight, age and sex and also with intensity of work. But besides individual circumstances, 'nutrition must be seen in its medical, environmental, cultural and social milieu'.[17] Consideration of deficiencies should take into account effects on the height and weight of under-nourished children and also the possible retardation in 'psycho-motor, adaptive, language, and socio-personal behaviour'. Recent research suggests that general 'functional' lags can occur at only mild degrees of protein calorie shortage.[18] In effect, permanent psychological damage can result from relatively short-lived periods of deficiency.

Of course, all social groups do not experience such misery. In any society a series of social mechanisms determines access to goods and services. In part, malnutrition is a man-made disorder, reflecting the balance of economic and power relationships in a given society and the way in which resources are distributed.

In a pre-industrial society, at the risk of over-simplification, the population might be divided into two categories – those sheltered from need and those permanently or temporarily likely to be reduced to misery. The food of the better-off was always adequate, at least in quantity and often qualitatively as well. Possession of sufficient money permitted them to purchase foodstuffs from outside the restricted range of local production. In practice, of course, the hierarchy of diet was extremely complicated. A recent study of villages in the Limousin in the middle of the nineteenth century shows that among village artisans, millers, bakers, inn keepers, blacksmiths ate better than did masons, carpenters, cabinetmakers and weavers. Unskilled labourers, of course, did even worse.[19] Similar hierarchies, reflecting income and security of employment, existed among urban workers – wage differentials were frequently substantial – and amongst those working the land. However, the slowness with which dietary traditions changed maintained a certain structural uniformity in the content of diet between groups with markedly different incomes. Thus social differences were often expressed in terms of quantity. Increased purchasing power did not necessarily result in improvement in the nutritional quality of the food purchased.

The information available uniformly suggests the existence of large numbers of people in extremely miserable physiological conditions. According to the *Journal de la Société de Statistique* in 1856, 83 per cent of the population of Paris was at best close to want.[20] In 1858 the prefect of the Seine estimated that about 25 per cent of the population of Paris had access to adequate food at all times and a further 10 per cent except in periods of shortage, while the diet of the remainder of the population was always inadequate.[21] These estimates are not based on the kinds of statistical information which would satisfy modern surveys but represent, for the time, the views of the best-informed observers, all of whom stress the immense weight of poverty. In the countryside too, in proportions which varied according to economic conditions, population pressure and the social division of production, there were everywhere large numbers of desperately poor people – artisans, industrial workers, peasants and agricultural labourers – who lived from day to day in cramped and unhygienic conditions, in danger of infection from pollution of the air they breathed and the water they drank; their daily experiences are difficult for us to imagine.[22]

Industrial populations

In spite of substantial wage differentials, industrial workers in general faced constant insecurity. Normal wage levels varied between professions, localities and individuals. Statistical estimates of averages merely serve to conceal this behind an apparent clarity. A few examples will serve both to illustrate the variation and to give some idea of wage levels. The Paris Chamber of Commerce in 1846 and 1847 gathered information which indicated that workers in most professions in the capital were relatively well paid by comparison with workers elsewhere but that this was in large part a necessary response to higher living costs. The average male wage was estimated to be 3.80 francs per day, and it was calculated that about 80 per cent of all men earned between 3 and 5 francs. Wages appear to have stagnated at around these levels since the early 1820s.[23]

At Toulon in 1849 the daily wage of a blacksmith was 4 francs, of a stone cutter 3.50, of a mason 3. Most artisans – bakers, cabinetmakers, blacksmiths and carpenters – earned 2.50–3 francs and, at the bottom of the hierarchy, shoemakers, tanners, stevedores, soapmakers and labourers earned only 2 francs per day. By comparison with the élite of iron workers, other groups including tailors and shoemakers employed at piece rates under a putting-out system experienced real misery.[24] According to the response of the tailors of Rennes to the 1848 inquiry, 'in every profession there are some men advantageously enough placed, at least for the moment, to escape misery. . . . Those whom the scourge of misery affects most frequently are those employed in trades with the largest number of workers, who are in consequence the most exploited because they cannot refuse any wage, however minimal it may be'.[25]

This was as true of modern industrial establishments as it was of traditional artisanal workshops. At the iron works of Fourchambault (Nièvre) wages varied according to skills and to demand for them. In 1852 the daily wage for men working in the rolling mill and for steam-engine firemen was 2–2.75 francs, that for labourers of various kinds 1.50–1.75.[26]

A variety of dubious practices served to reduce wages further by taking advantage of the dependence of workers. At Amiens it was cheating on piece rates;[27] in the mines around St-Etienne, where extraction was relatively easy, miners were paid by the day, but where geological structures made it difficult piece rates were employed.[28] Such practices reduced costs but at the expense of hostility between master and men. The excuse offered by *patrons* – often with some justification – was competitive pressure. Urban workers suffered from the competition of producers using even lower-paid rural labour,[29] workers in one centre (e.g. Vienne) from the competition of workers in other towns where traditionally wages were low (in this case those of the Midi),[30] workers in artisanal industries from the development of mechanized production. More generally, the growth of population and of immigration from the countryside, while slow by some European standards, was sufficient to create labour-supply conditions that were unfavourable to wage demands. Only further reduction in birth rates, and above all the progress of industrialization and its effects on the labour market, could correct this situation.

Even worse were the conditions of most of the workers employed in rural industry. The reply to the 1848 inquiry in the canton of Mondoubleau (Loir-et-Cher) complained that local industry increasingly faced competition from mechanized producers, while 'to these causes of misery is joined that, not less powerful, of an excess of population'.[31] This could have been written of most rural areas in which population pressure on resources was reaching a level which condemned much of the population to an unceasing struggle to make ends meet.

Most adversely affected were those employed in the various branches of textiles, the major employer of rural labour. According to a report written in September 1846, some 50,000 workers depended on the linen industry in Maine-et-Loire centred at Cholet, Beaupréau, Montfaucon and Chemillé, and 20,000 others in neighbouring parts of the departments of Deux-Sèvres, Vendée and Loire-Inférieure. The prosperous period of this industry had been the First Empire, when wages had risen to 4–5 francs per day. Subsequently they had fallen to 1.50 francs by about 1830 for a ten- to twelve-hour day and to 0.90–1.20 francs for a fifteen- to sixteen-hour day in 1846. Women earned as little as 0.25–0.30 francs and children 0.20–0.25 francs. Unemployment was frequent, and at that moment although most of the workers in Cholet, the main centre of production, were employed, about one half of those in the countryside were not, save for what work they could find in agriculture.[32]

The consequence of the degrading of a profession depended on the degree of specialization of labour. Many peasants took on industrial work to supplement their earnings in agriculture,[33] and artisans were also far more mobile than we might expect,[34] but where earnings were already low any reduction caused considerable hardship. When substantial rises in basic foodstuff prices occurred at a time when wages were stable or, as was frequently the case, declining, then the problem of subsistence became, even for the workers still in employment, almost unmanageable.

Even where skills were not becoming technologically obsolete, artisans in town and country faced considerable difficulties when poor harvests reduced the demand for their products. Their problems were greatest in the most over-populated regions; for example, in the canton of Paimpol (Côtes-du-Nord) in 1853–5 the craftsmen – masons, carpenters, cabinetmakers, locksmiths, blacksmiths, charcoal burners – all earned 1.50 francs per day, while agricultural labourers earned 0.80 francs and hoped to supplement this by weaving.[35] But: 'When demand declines then each producer, in order to attract consumers to himself, offers a reduction on the price of finished goods or of work to execute. As the crisis worsens the worker forced by need to make further reductions each day to obtain work in the face of his competitors, ends by working at a price so low he is no longer able to support his family.'[36]

Employment opportunities and wage levels in many professions fluctuated seasonally as well as cyclically. In the canton of Mer (Loir-et-Cher), for example, building workers in the slack season sought employment in quarries, as woodcutters, etc.,[37] depressing wages in these professions, as did the agricultural labourers who also took up weaving. The longer inclement weather lasted, the more intense grew the problem of making ends meet.[38] Luxury trades such as the Lyon silk industry were affected by frequent changes in fashion and, in the Lyon case, by annual stoppages during which orders were placed with merchants and passed on to the weavers.[39]

Comment has already been made on the frequency of crises and upon their causes. The employer in a crisis must continue to seek profitability or at least to minimize losses. To some extent stocks of finished products might be accumulated, but as sales and receipts declined, it was necessary to reduce costs, and the most direct means of securing this was to reduce wages. Although strategies varied, the general pattern in factory industry was as follows. During the initial period of crisis there was a reduction in the piece rates and/or in the hours or days worked. Complete closure was avoided if at all possible, as fixed capital costs had to be met anyway. According to the *procureur-général* at Rouen, in December 1853, textile spinners were kept in employment for two or three days a week because of these general costs and the need to keep the machines active to avoid their degeneration into scrap iron. Employment was also frequently maintained out of a sense of responsibility towards employees. The same official accepted this when reporting that after three profitable years employers could sustain limited losses and stock temporarily unsaleable products.[40] The degree to which an employer could be humane reflected his financial solvency as well as his personality, competitive pressures and the behavioural norms of the social group to which he belonged.

The scale of wage reductions varied between industrial sectors in relation to the demand for their products and the concomitant demand for labour but also, if still to a limited degree, according to the capacity for resistance of labour. Unskilled workers with no organization were especially liable to dismissal, particularly the domestic workers in textiles and clothing in both town and country. Their dispersal made the organization of resistance especially difficult. Employers operating with minimal overhead costs simply stopped supplying workers with raw materials.[41]

Everywhere dismissals were selective. The best-qualified or best-disciplined were least likely to be dismissed. They constituted a minority in every group of workers and were relatively privileged because of their protected positions. Different degrees of security as well as wage differentials served to increase the heterogeneity of the working classes. Conversely, bachelors, strangers to a locality, the least productive and the troublemakers were all especially liable to dismissal.[42]

In 1846–7 commerce and industry generally were affected by the state of crisis, although the ports, and especially Marseille, benefited from the increased trade in grain.[43] The crisis was most marked in the textile industries, the major employers of industrial labour. As early as February 1846 the *procureur-royale* at Lille reported that many workers had been dismissed and the others were employed at reduced wages.[44] In May 1847 the *commissaire central de police* in the city reported that employed textile workers could hope for no more than three or four days' work per week. He believed that employers would use the excuse of a traditional holiday to close their establishments for at least a further week.[45] In Roubaix, of 13,000 textile workers resident in the town 4800 were estimated to be unemployed in February 1847, 8000 at the beginning of May. Most of the others were employed at reduced wages. Competition for employment from immigrant Belgian workers made the situation especially serious in the Nord and explains recurrent instances of xenophobia among French workers.[46] The prefect of Seine-Inférieure estimated that in his area by November 1847 the wages of those in employment had been reduced by about 30 per cent, with the male factory worker gaining 2.50 francs per day and the domestic worker generally 1.25 francs, but as little as 0.75 francs.[47]

Again in 1854 the *procureur-général* at Rouen reported the grave misery of unemployed and partially employed textile workers;[48] by January of 1855 one-fifth of the textile workers of Elbeuf were unemployed, and the remainder were earning only one third of their normal wage. The difficulty of generalizing about the situation of workers is illustrated by the fact that at nearby Louviers orders of cloth for the Army maintained employment at a high level.[49]

Diversity also existed in the extent to which unemployed workers could find temporary alternative employment. The effects of a crisis on the work force in any one locality depended to a considerable extent upon whether or not there were alternative sources of employment. A general crisis limited these opportunities, but they existed, and the extraordinary mobility of the labour force, compared with contemporary standards, should be stressed. Thus the *procureur-général* at Rouen reported in July 1853 that textile workers worked in the factories for three days a week and found additional employment in agriculture.[50] Many workers habitually sought alternatives to their main employment because of the annual slack periods which industries often experienced. But a severe crisis in a region like the Nord created too much unemployment for more than a small proportion to find alternatives, while reduced wages and rising prices caused suffering even among those still in employment.[51]

Besides the temporarily unemployed, one should not forget the 'perpetual' poor[52] – the aged, sick, widows and orphans. The poor, because of inadequate diets, inferior living standards and often harsh working conditions, were particularly susceptible to disease and to premature ageing.[53] The combination of poor working conditions and inadequate diet was frequently disastrous. Even where the conditions of particular industries did not lead to particular diseases – like the rheumatism and tuberculosis so common among the porcelain workers – physiological degeneration and premature death were likely consequences of the worker's struggle to earn his living. The insecurity caused by the frequent threat of unemployment was increased by the possibility of infirmity and inability to work. Groups like miners, who frequently suffered accidents at work, seem to have been especially, and not surprisingly, obsessed with this problem.[54] For those workers who survived into old age the best that could be hoped for was reduced earnings as working capacity declined or, if they had been extremely provident in earlier years – and few had the opportunity – a small pension of perhaps 50 francs per year from a mutual aid society.[55] The old and sick dragged themselves to work for as long as possible, unwilling or unable to become a drain on their families' resources, reluctant to throw themselves on the tender mercies of charity organizations. The sick, unwilling to stop work, unable to afford proper medical care, rarely took proper care of themselves.[56] Loss of earnings and the cost of medical care would rapidly eat up any savings. Even those who had been able to afford subscriptions to a mutual aid society received only an inadequate sum in aid – 7 francs per week in Marseille during the Second Empire.[57] The municipal *bureaux de bienfaisance* and private charity proved similarly inadequate due to the limited funds and rigorous definitions of who deserved help.[58]

Even in the most favourable circumstances the poor were extremely susceptible to seasonal and short-term cyclical movement in both employment opportunities and food prices. It was the adverse movement of both of these factors which made economic crises so severe prior to the transport revolution. Although by the late 1840s fluctuations in the price of basic cereals and also of bread prices were less violent than earlier in the century, growing population density and the progress of urbanization, together with the slowness of the increase in agricultural productivity and of the modernization of distribution networks, contributed to maintaining substantial price fluctuation.

As an example we can consider the evolution of bread prices at Douai, where between the cyclical low in February 1845 and the cyclical high in May 1847, the price of bread rose by a massive 108 per cent.[59] Such increases were not exceptional.[60] Between the establishment of one bread price and the next, increases of the order of 5–10 centimes per kilogram were common, and increases on such a scale did much to increase popular anxiety.[61] In Paris, by contrast with other towns, price increases were restrained largely by official action to 52.2 per cent between the low of 1845 and the high of 1847.[62]

The price of other basic foodstuffs rose with those of cereals, reflecting the overall food-supply position and popular anxiety. Potato prices were, moreover, affected by loss through disease. At Angers a rise from 0.45 to 0.98 francs per double decalitre was reported in autumn 1846.[63]

Although for a variety of reasons the crisis of 1853–6 was not as serious in its consequences as that of 1846–7, substantial increases in bread prices were recorded. In Rouen prices reached 55 centimes per kilogram in December 1855 and remained at a relatively high level, above 40 centimes, in December 1856.[64] In the mining community of Carmaux (Tarn), in contrast, the maximum increase for white bread was 104 per cent between 1852 and 1856 and for *pain bis* 115 per cent.[65]

Real income is normally calculated by the equation $RI = \dfrac{NI}{C}$, where NI is nominal income and C is cost of living. The information available on food prices alone – especially given the large proportion of total income necessarily spent on food – suggests violent fluctuations in the cost of living and therefore of real income. At least in the short term, standards of living depended less on nominal wages than on the cost of living, with periods of low prices and *relatively* good living conditions alternating with those of high prices and degradation.

Even when full employment and a subsistence crisis became compatible, as changes in the structure of the economy accelerated in the 1850s, real income remained susceptible to violent fluctuations. The *procureur-général* at Rouen commented in August 1855 that 'however hard-working and thrifty the worker may be, and even in the case of those who are never unemployed, it will always be difficult for him, with existing wage levels, to provide for his needs, and impossible, if he is married, to provide for those of his family'.[66] In part this was due to the continuing success of employers in maintaining wages at low levels. Labour had not yet organized effectively in self-defence. But since food supply and price fluctuations rather than wage levels continued to be the most important considerations determining living standards, it must have appeared to both employers and workers that they could do little to alleviate this.

Between June 1853 and February 1854 the increase in bread prices is estimated to have resulted in a reduction in the purchasing power of miners at Carmaux of the order of 35–6 per cent, and by July 1856 wages had been devalued by 41.9 per cent in the case of underground workers, 48.9 per cent for those on the surface.[67] The lower the level of wages, the higher the proportion devoted to the purchase of necessities.

In this particular case about 47 per cent of household expenditure was normally spent on bread alone. Situations varied enormously, but always a very large proportion of income had to be spent on food. Lille textile workers experienced hard times during the July Monarchy, when prices tended to rise and wages to fall. Families of the better-paid workers are estimated to have spent 51.56 per cent of their income on food and drink, while the poorer might spend up to 70–80 per cent. There remained 6 or even 10–12 per cent for rent, 13–21 per cent for clothing, 8–12 per cent for heating, lighting, furnishings, medical care, recreation, etc. In periods of crisis the structure of expenditure had to be adapted.[68] Reduction in wages or increases in the cost of particular elements enforced economies.

Variations in prices and wages were not the only causes of differences in the conditions of families. One needs to take account of the family budget rather than that of individuals, to pay attention to the natural history of the family. It was when the family included children, too young to work but having to be fed, that it was most vulnerable to subsistence crises. Old age, when earning capacity declined, could also be a period of considerable suffering, particularly if family members were unwilling or unable to provide for their aged parents. At some stage in its life cycle almost every worker family experienced considerable difficulty.

As children grew older, their contribution to the family's income would, of course, depend on the employment opportunities both for them and for their mother.

In textile towns there was usually the possibility of employment for all members of a family, including children, from a relatively early age. Estimates of daily wages in cotton-spinning factories at Lille before and during the 1846–7 crisis are shown in Table 7.[69] They reveal a slight decline in the nominal wage when in practice, due to short-time working and increased food prices, a substantial reduction in income and purchasing power had occurred. The single male, at least in terms of balancing his budget, was in the easiest position. In the canton of Soissons (Aisne) it was estimated that an unmarried labourer could manage on an income of 200–300 francs per annum, while a household with two young children required 500–600 francs.[70] Even at the best of times, low family income made it essential for married women to work – often with deleterious effects on young children.[71] Provision for child minding (preferably by a relative) had to be made if at all possible. Difficult situations often arose in isolated communities whose economic life was based on a single industry like iron or coal, in which the

Table 7   *Estimates of daily wages in Lille cotton-spinning factories, 1845 and 1847 (francs)*

	1845	1847
Male workers	2.25–2.60	2.40
Female workers	1.50	1.30
Children	0.75	0.85

employment of women was limited, thus enforcing dependence on a single breadwinner until male children were in their early teens. However, a large family at least offered substantial future compensation in the shape of greater ability to share the burden of caring for an aged or sick parent.[72]

It is also obvious that an individual or family's economic position would depend upon the skills that its members could offer in the labour market and the existing level of demand for those skills. Artisans were normally far better off than the unskilled or those, like domestic weavers, for whose skills demand continually fell. This tends to be borne out by Husson's statistics on the professions of those in need of assistance. Armand Husson, a senior official at the Préfecture de la Seine, in a work published in 1856, provides us with some interesting information about the provision of assistance in Paris (see Table 8).[73] The professions of adult paupers in 1853 are listed as follows:[74]

Male		Female	
Ragpickers	428	Washerwomen	675
Coachmen	165	Ragpickers	348
Shoemakers	861	Servants	313
Servants	135	Charwomen	1,140
Clerks	150	Child minders	224
Small traders	741	Sick-nurses	217
Building workers	1,875	Small traders	811
Labourers	3,452	Needlewomen	2,574
Water carriers	112	Unskilled female labourers	4,379
Porters	1,283	Water carriers	30
Cobblers	118	Porters	754
Tailors	537	Without profession	3,168
Without profession	1,652		

Table 8 *Provision of assistance in Paris, 1835–53*

Year	Number of people aided	Proportion
1835	62,539	1 pauper per 12.30 inhabitants
1838	58,500	14.55
1841	66,487	13.71
1844	68,148	13.78
1847	73,901	13.93
1850	63,133	16.30
1853	65,264	15.65

In all there were 29,142 people, while some 33,000 people, including most of the above, also received private charity.[75]

Husson felt that this was a relatively small number of paupers for a city the size of Paris. Many of this group were simply too old to work. The major problem of public assistance was that caused by economic crises, which rapidly inflated the numbers requiring aid well above that constituted by the habitually deprived.[76] Nothing better illustrates the precarious situation of most of the capital's population.

According to Husson, in 1846–7 25,177 people were registered as paupers, while a further 299,387 (about two-fifths of the total population) received bread coupons.[77] A report to the Prefect of the Seine on the distribution of bread coupons in 1846–7, however, claimed that 231,000 households in Paris (about 610,000 people, to which total ought to be added some 25,000 workers living in furnished rooms) could be described as being in a 'dangerous' situation. In all 475,000 of these had been aided in 1846–7[78], a much higher figure than Husson's.

Husson's statistics allow comparison of the occupations of paupers with those of recipients of temporary aid in this period of crisis.[79] The latter includes a far higher proportion of skilled workers, normally able to manage on their wages but now affected by high prices and unemployment.

Shoemakers	12,391	Coal men	2,510
Carpenters	4,135	Coachmen	4,228
Cabinetmakers	18,847	Messengers	8,480
Blacksmiths	5,011	Porters	21,092
Printers	12,293	Servants	5,319
Masons	16,840	Clerks	3,216
Painters	7,376	Day labourers	40,676
Saddlers	2,265	Ragpickers	8,218
Locksmiths	10,490	Small traders	6,048
Tailors	13,498	Charwomen	3,345
		Females (no other details)	17,346

Without profession	72,282

Unemployment, of course, greatly intensified the problem of making ends meet, and, as we have seen, it was a constant threat. Better-paid workers subscribed to friendly societies, but these possessed insufficient funds to provide real help in periods of crisis. In Marseille ministerial circulars of 1850 and 1852 which forbade friendly societies to give help to the unemployed, on the grounds that this would encourage laziness and strikes, were generally observed, indicating perhaps the weak financial position of these societies. For many people there was no alternative, when income levels fell, to dependence upon public and private charity – in the form of work relief and handouts – although often individuals were too proud to seek this, and in any case during a crisis these resources were rarely adequate. At such times misery proved to be a major cause of crime, particularly of petty theft and prostitution.[80]

Paradoxically for many workers, the under-developed character of the economy and the limits to occupational specialization served as safeguards. Many remained close to the soil. While recognizing that living conditions varied according to the sobriety of life, the size of the family, regularity of employment and wage levels, the cantonal commission at Bavay (Nord) in 1848 divided workers into four groups: (1) those possessing a small house and a little field; (2) those with a house; (3) those with neither; (4) paupers dependent upon charity. The first two categories, whose expenditure was limited by the ability to grow at least some of their own food and/or their freedom from rent payments, were regarded as living in satisfactory conditions. Particularly in developing industrial centres, immigration tended to push up rents, and even where workers attempted to moderate this burden by accepting atrocious living conditions, the payment took up a not inconsiderable portion of their income. The third group was made up of those too proud to ask for charity and was in the worst situation.[81]

The ability of workers to cope materially with a crisis obviously depended upon its duration and intensity, in terms of the effects both on wages and on prices. Each crisis had its own particular characteristics. Thus during the period 1852–6, when cereal prices were high, unemployment was not in general as severe as it had been in 1846–7, for a variety of reasons, including the structural modification of the economy and accidental factors such as the mildness of most of the winters in this period;[82] moreover, the food supply situation was easier, at least initially, because of the stocks that had been accumulated during the long period of agricultural depression from 1847–51. Only after at least three years of budgetary difficulty did the authorities begin to become alarmed about the situation of industrial workers.[83] In the initial stages of a crisis many workers could no doubt subsist on savings and credit or with help from relations and friends, but the ability of these to give aid must have declined as the crisis was prolonged. The degree to which the entire community was affected by unemployment (i.e. its occupational structure) was also a significant factor.[84]

High prices, unemployment, illness, young children – all were likely to lead to debt.[85] For most workers dependence on short-term credit at local food shops was a natural fact of life, tying them to particular shops.[86] At Amiens, as elsewhere, the poor, who needed credit were 'not able to change their baker'.[87] In bad periods they obtained credit, and in good periods they paid off their debts. Repayment of debts often required the poor to borrow money at the *mont-de-piété*, the municipal pawnshop, if they were lucky and had something to pawn. Here at least the interest rates were limited – 7 per cent at Marseille, 9 per cent at Paris, 10 per cent at Lyon, 12 per cent at

Lille.[88] In the case of loans from private individuals, rates of interest could be astronomical.

According to Husson, in Paris in 1849 seven-tenths of the borrowers from the municipal pawnshop were workers, but many small businessmen short of working capital also made use of these facilities,[89] as the number of loans made in that year, and those to whom they were made, indicate:

Merchants and manufacturers	96,094
Rentiers and proprietors	71,104
Liberal professions	35,542
Clerks	46,638
Soldiers	2,557
Workers	577,809

Besides workers, a subsistence crisis threw other urban groups into difficulties. The police *commissaire central* at Lille in May 1847 stressed the adverse effects of economic stagnation on small shopkeepers, due both to the decline of trade and often also to the tying up of capital by the extension of credit.[90] In January 1855 the *procureur-général* at Rennes reported that 'food prices are so high that the paupers of the working class are not the only ones to suffer. The small *rentier*, petty businessmen and minor officials find it difficult to produce the resources necessary to cope with the material needs of life'.[91] These groups, burdened by the need to keep up appearances and normally enjoying a superior diet to that of the mass of workers, were likely to find their misery especially intolerable.[92] In the 1850s the salaries paid to minor officials tended to stagnate, while most prices, including rents, were tending to increase, thus creating growing long-term difficulties.[93]

Rural population

Among the rural population conditions of existence varied significantly from year to year and from place to place, primarily as a result of the success or failure of the harvest. Generalizations are difficult. Adolphe Blanqui, making inquiries on behalf of the Académie des Sciences Morales et Politiques in 1850 wrote that regardless of 'what diversity exists in the soil occupied by these populations, in their customs, in their aptitudes, the dominant fact characteristic of their situation is their distress . . . the general inability to satisfy the basic needs of life'. The overwhelming impression was one of 'mediocrity, which became misery in years of shortage'.[94] Only a minority of peasants and farmers were likely to produce enough to be able to profit from the high prices following a poor harvest.

There was a great diversity of circumstances, both between regions and within the population of one area. The key differentiating factor was whether a land holding was productive enough to ensure economic independence for those who farmed it or whether they were obliged to supplement their income with work outside the farm. This was determined by the amount of land farmed and by its productivity. In any society the proportion of independent landowners depended on the historical evolution of the patterns of landownership and use and on the size and viability of farm units, bearing in mind variations in soil fertility.

Especially when considering the small peasant proprietor and farmer – in general, those farming fewer than 10 hectares – one should not forget the relatively closed character of the agricultural economy until the middle of the nineteenth century. Family subsistence was the motive for production and polyculture offered a degree of protection against the failure of single crops. The production of a surplus, or else a supplementary occupation, was obligatory in order to pay taxes and purchase necessities that could not be produced on the farm and, in the case of the tenant farmer, to pay rents, either in kind or in cash. However, neither in terms of motivation nor in terms of size of surplus were most small producers orientated towards speculative activities in the market place.

Fluctuations in production affected the ability of peasant farmers to feed themselves and/or earn enough from sales to purchase necessary supplements to domestic production. The effects of variations in the size of crops obviously depended on the scale of these variations. The cash income of the farmer depended on the proportion of his crop which he was able to market and on prevailing price levels. A simple example prepared by the respondents to the 1848 inquiry in the canton of Morlaix (Finistère) will clarify this point (see Table 9).[95] No account is taken here of fluctuations in costs with the scale of harvest which would affect profitability. Certainly, this example should not be taken as revealing an invariable relationship between quantity, price and revenue; for example, very abundant production over a large area could lead to a glut and collapse of price levels. It should simply be noted that the relationship between production and revenue was a complex one.

In determining the proportion of the rural population likely to suffer from

Table 9 *Production, price and revenue from wheat under varying conditions, mid nineteenth century*

Conditions	Production (hectolitres)	Price (francs)	Revenue (francs)
In a very abundant year	100	15	1500
In a less abundant year	80	17	1360
In a year *assez bonne*	60	19	1140
In a bad year	40	30	1200
In a very bad year	20	45	900

a poor harvest – in the sense that high prices did not offer sufficient compensation for the limited quantity produced – the basic factors were the structures of landownership and use, the average size of the farm, and crop yields, all of which varied considerably between regions. Hippolyte Passy recorded that in 1846 in the Eure areas with light soil produced very poor wheat harvests, but those with heavy soils had a good crop. He knew of two contiguous farms, one of which had experienced a disastrous year, the other an extremely profitable one.[96]

When arable harvests failed only a small minority of peasants and farmers were likely to have produced enough to be able to maintain a normal income due to the compensating effect of high prices, although the tendency for productivity to grow gradually increased the size of this minority, especially in regions of more progressive farming. In 1846–7, however, it remained the case that only the relatively well-off were able to produce in sufficient quantity, and to manipulate stocks in such a manner, as to maintain profitability.[97] This was the situation enjoyed by most of the tenant farmers exploiting medium-sized farms and probably by all those with large farms, as well as by landowners directly exploiting medium- or large-sized properties.

The ability of the larger landowners to profit from high prices depended on the proportion of their incomes normally derived from direct cultivation of crops for sale as opposed to rents. In a crisis caused by one of the two extreme situations of shortage or glut, tenants found it difficult to accumulate the wherewithal to pay rents. This was the case in 1847, even in an area of capitalist farming like the Beauce, and much more so in less dynamic agricultural regions. The example provided by the budget of a small tenant farmer in the valley of the Clairie (Vosges) in the 1850s will provide an illustration of the precarious situation of many tenants.[98]

Expenditure (francs)

Rent of a farmhouse and 5 hectares of meadow and field	330
Interest at 5 per cent on the cost of three cows	40
Taxes	15
Primary school fees for two children	15
Clothing and shoes for five people	100
Repairs, furniture	70
Lighting, soap, oil, vinegar, salt, bread, sugar, coffee, pepper and other necessities	90
Wine and liqueurs	50
Cattle feed	240
Losses of cattle, or due to frost, hail, etc.	50
TOTAL	1000 francs

Receipts (francs)
Produce of three cows:

Cheese and butter	800
Veal	75
TOTAL	875 francs

This is the not untypical case, particularly in upland areas, of a farmer providing for his cash needs with the income derived from his cows, able to produce most of the food his family needed, but farming only 5 hectares and obliged to supplement his income by industrial work and susceptible, in consequence, to poor harvests affecting both his food production and the demand for industrial labour, to shortages of fodder which might force him to purchase animal feed at high prices or else to sell animals at a moment when many other farmers were forced to do the same, and to the vagaries of cattle disease or poor weather.

Landowners' incomes suffered because of their tenants' problems and also from the decline in revenue from other sources, including interest on loans or stocks and shares. Thus although substantial speculative profits could be made in a period of shortage by landowners, large farmers and merchants, and although during such periods there was a certain concentration of wealth in their hands, one should not forget that the incomes of the wealthy were susceptible to reduction and that for this and other reasons no one escaped from the sense of malaise created by a harvest failure.[99]

Small peasant farmers were, far more obviously, among the victims of agricultural crises. The poorer the family, the more dependent it was on a uniform basic diet of cereals, the less food it was capable of producing for itself and the more susceptible it was to crises.

In a situation in which income fell one would expect to see the small peasant landowner in a better position than the small-scale tenant because the former was unburdened by the need to pay rent.

The weakness of the small-scale producer was that a poor harvest was likely to leave him with nothing to sell, and indeed might result in his entering the market as a purchaser of essential foodstuffs. He produced a marketable surplus only when yields were relatively high. For such men the rise in prices was unlikely to compensate for the decline in production. Many of those small producers who normally enjoyed economic independence now found themselves in the position of having insufficient money to meet the needs of their families; tenants among them were unable to pay their rents. Even medium-sized producers employing some labour found that this ate up a large proportion of the potential surplus in years of bad harvest. Even worse off, of course, were those farmers who in the best of years could not produce enough for their own needs. After a bad harvest they entered the market place to purchase earlier in the year than normally, at a time when, in all likelihood, the sources of income on which they habitually relied to supplement the produce of their land had also been affected by the crisis.[100]

The mass of small vine cultivators was subject not only to the irregularity of production and the instability of prices of their own crops but also to fluctuations in the price of foodstuffs that they needed to purchase. For them the most adverse situation was one in which food prices were high and their own revenue low. The good wine harvest in Bourgogne in 1846 was reported to have considerably eased the difficulties caused by high food prices.[101] For the *vignerons* of Loir-et-Cher the years of greatest economic difficulty appear to have been 1849–51, a period of over-production and glut in both the cereal and wine markets, rather than 1846–7.[102] In the second quarter of 1854, by contrast, it was reported that wine-producing regions were experiencing general misery because of the coincidence of high cereal prices and low revenues, although this is partially contradicted by reports from the Paris region.[103]

When family budgets would not balance and savings had been exhausted, farmers were unable to pay their rents, sharecroppers were forced to borrow from their landowners and peasant proprietors from anyone who would advance them the cash, thus giving birth to a mass of often officially unrecorded loans at varying (but normally high) rates of interest. A loan system existed, with both customary and legal sanctions against recalcitrant debtors, which might be a potential cause of resentment but at least helped many families over the most difficult periods of crisis.

Resentment at money lending was most likely to become apparent when the time for repayment arrived. After the distressing period of harvest failure had ended with the good harvest of 1847 cultivators of both wheat and wine found themselves from 1848 to 1852 coping with well supplied markets and depressed prices. Small producers with only limited quantities to sell often found it difficult to obtain enough money to meet pressing demands, including those for the repayment of debts, and were frequently brought face to face with the realities or, more likely, the threat of expropriation.[104]

Land remained the major source of status and economic security, but it was expensive because of this and because of the increasing demand for it as rural population densities reached their maxima. Expropriation for debt threatened the loss of land acquired often only after long years of hard work and deprivation. The threat of proletarianization must have been difficult to bear.[105] This was a major problem in all regions of small-scale exploitation and property, where debts were usually incurred when peasants borrowed to buy land or else were unable to meet their commitments to landlords.

Those with capital – landowners, notaries, but also better-off artisans and peasants – could hope to make substantially greater profits from lending than they could expect from agriculture. The return on agricultural capital in the Limousin, for example, has been estimated at about 3 per cent per annum.[106] According to an inquiry in the region in 1843–4 a well-off proprietor whose land was previously unmortgaged could hope to borrow from a bank at a rate of interest around 5 per cent, plus 0.5–1 per cent commission. This might easily be renewed four or five times, although any doubts arising about the debtor's ability to pay would cause the rate to be increased. More commonly, mortgages were obtained through notaries, who invested their own or their clients' money. In general, it was estimated that the rate would be about 6 per cent for one year but with substantial costs raising the effective interest on a one-year loan to about 25 per cent. The rate would be more moderate if these costs were spread over a longer period. Small landowners with relatively little security were forced to have recourse to loans carrying much higher rates of interest, often with very complicated terms of repayment, in kind as well as in money.[107]

The poor often preferred to borrow from their *patrons* rather than from a notary. They gained some protection from social conventions which made liberality on the part of a creditor a virtue as long as the intention of the debtor to repay as soon as the situation allowed was not in doubt. But even in this case an unenviable relationship of dependence was created which might easily become humiliating for the debtor. Debt dependency served to reinforce social hierarchy.[108]

Once in debt, peasants found it difficult to escape. To acquire land they took a risk, hoping that in subsequent years they would produce a surplus above subsistence needs which would enable them to earn money and repay their debts, or at the very least the interest on them. Any kind of crisis which affected budgeting, whether personal (as in the case of illness) or general, obviously made debt repayment more difficult. Interest accrued; the size of the debt increased; and the possibility of ever achieving their ambition of securely owning land disappeared. At best it might take years to repay the debts incurred during a subsistence crisis, especially for those who had no savings to live on at the onset of crisis. In the Auxois in 1847 wage earners were mortgaging their wages for months or even years to come by borrowing grain from those who still held stocks.[109] In the upland areas of the Alpine region complaints about the consequences of 1846–7 continued for years afterwards.[110]

Even a good harvest could in some circumstances bring disaster. Its effects on revenue depended on the complex relationships between volume and selling price. The success of the cereal and wine harvests in France from 1847 to 1851 and the fall in prices due to a market glut intensified the problems of all those who needed to maintain their cash incomes in order to meet debt repayments or pay rents. Subsistence might be easier, but this did not necessarily bring more security. The commercial crisis meant a shortage of cash for all those who were forced to sell their produce at low prices – if they could sell at all – or who found that their various sources of supplementary income in rural industry or seasonal migration were less rewarding because of the general depression.[111] For those who employed labour the proportion of gross revenue paid out in wages increased – in the Auxois from an estimated 50 to 62 per cent and in the Dijon plain from 50 to 76 per cent.[112] As far as possible, such farmers would try to reduce their labour forces.

Thus depression due to either poor harvests or excellent harvests brought for many the threat of expropriation and created grave disquiet in rural communities. Of fifty-two cantonal reports to the 1848 inquiry from the departments of Haute-Vienne and Corrèze, forty-two stressed the problems caused by the lack of cheap credit.[113] Vigier has stressed the significance of the problem in the Isère in creating political unrest. In seventeen out of forty-five cantons peasants lived in fear of expropriation and were easily attracted by the promise of cheap credit made by radical democrats during the Second Republic.[114]

Official statistics greatly under-estimated both the burden of debt and the threat of expropriation. Contracts often stipulated the right of the lender to sell property if a loan was not repaid, allowing him to avoid the slow legal procedures; many small debts were not even recorded in legal form.[115]

Provided sufficient cash could be raised to meet external demands, most small producers engaged in primarily subsistence agriculture were satisfied by abundance. It was those most heavily engaged in production for the market, cultivators of the vine and various industrial crops, together with farmers who paid rents in cash or debtors, who faced renewed difficulties in the period 1848–52.

A large part of the rural population grew a proportion of the food it consumed, but for most this was not enough to maintain a family without some supplement gained by wage labour. High prices had particularly serious consequences for that part of the rural population which was wage-earning and not fed on the farm.

The twin causes of rural misery were levels of productivity in agriculture, which remained low in spite of substantial advances, and high population density, which determined individual shares in what was produced both directly and indirectly by influencing the negotiating position of the various social groups. The supply of potential tenants and labourers was in most places too high in relation to the demand for both categories. This resulted in high rents and low wages – thus the tenant farmer, 'pressured by the landowner and by taxes of all kinds, is able to give only a minimal wage to the workers whom he periodically employs, otherwise he would be unable to pay his rent'.[116]

The highest wage levels appear to have occurred in two kinds of area – those in which changes in agricultural methods required more labour (for example, in the Beauce[117] or on the northern plains, although even then it seems likely that labour supply was excessive save at harvests)[118] or else where industrial development was setting up a competitive demand for labour. In 1857 a clear contrast was drawn between the *arrondissements* of Neufchâtel and Louviers in Normandy. In the latter industrial competition for labour was causing an increase in general wage levels. In the former not only was industry lacking but also the transfer of land from arable to pasture led to a reduction in the labour needs of farmers and in wages. Here farmers also took advantage of their strong negotiating positions to replace traditional payments in kind by a money wage – a considerable advantage to them in a period of rising food prices.[119] The basic fact remained, as the response to the 1848 inquiry from the canton of Ay (Marne) put it, that 'the price of labour, like the price of everything else which has a value, is determined by the balance between supply and demand'.[120] It was the product of the relationship between population growth and economic development. Only the general relaxation in demographic pressure from the 1850s and a long-term tendency for agricultural prices and profits to rise would ease the situation.

Among agricultural labourers, *domestiques* or farm servants were normally recognized as enjoying better material conditions, and certainly greater security of employment, than the day labourers. They were generally employed for special tasks, while day labourers took on the work of harvesting and threshing. François-Luc Barrault, farming in the canton of Pithiviers (Loiret), part of the rich Beauce plain, reported in 1848 that he employed a master carter at 310 francs per annum, while a good shepherd could earn slightly more. Other *domestiques* were employed at 155 francs from St John's Day to All Saints' and then at threshing on piece rates. Additionally, they were fed on the farm. Hired for long periods – usually a full year – *domestiques* thus gained significant advantages, but at the price of loss of personal independence, being continually under the farmer's eye, and of long hours of hard work.[121]

A great deal of information exists on the level of wages of the agricultural day labourer. It concurs to reveal a situation of intense misery, the result not simply of low wages, but also of frequent unemployment, which reduced families to beggary. In general, wages allowed only a bare subsistence and did not permit labourers to accumulate savings to tide them over periods of unemployment.[122] Désert's calculations for the department of Calvados reveal averages of 1.40–1.60 francs per day unfed,[123] but elsewhere wages were often far lower. Thus in the canton of Chaussin (Jura) in 1848 male agricultural labourers received 1 franc per day, females 0.60 francs;[124] at Lezoux (Puy-de-Dôme) men were paid 1 franc per day, women 0.55 franc and children 0.50 franc. Work was available on average for 260 days per annum, so that annual earnings amounted to 260, 143 and 130 francs respectively.[125]

Traditions varied, but in many areas labourers were still fed on the farm. On the plateau between the rivers Seine and Oise they received 0.75 franc per day in addition to their meals.[126] In the Basses-Pyrénées it was estimated that they received a meal worth around 0.50 franc per day plus 1 franc in cash, although this last sum was reduced when food prices increased.[127] Frequently, part of the cash wage was paid in kind, which had the dual advantage of cushioning labourers against price fluctuations and minimizing the farmers' need for cash.[128]

Harvest earnings were of crucial importance to the agricultural labourer. In return for working all the daylight hours, higher daily rewards could be expected, as well as employment for the whole family. In the canton of Paimpol (Côtes-du-Nord), for example, harvest wages were one-third above normal rates,[129] and in the canton of Guillon (Somme) wages were doubled to 2.80 francs for the harvest of 1854.[130] Moreover, it was customary in most areas for part of this payment, as well as that for threshing, to be made in kind, providing at least something of a reserve for the period of under-employment in winter. Thus for the agricultural labourer a poor harvest, whether of cereals or grapes, had especially severe consequences. Less labour was needed for harvesting and subsequently for threshing which, using the flail, provided much of the work normally available in winter.[131] This made the agricultural labourer one of the great victims of subsistence crises, his earning capacity substantially reduced at the moment when prices rose.

His main problem was subsistence during the winter months, when weather conditions, especially in the north and upland areas, limited outdoor work. Under-employment and seasonal unemployment compounded the effects of low wages. A mild winter would substantially alleviate the situation. A cold winter could be disastrous. Guy Thuillier quotes a 'Mémoire' written in 1844 by A. de Bourgoing:

If tomorrow snow covers the ground, [the labourers] will be without wages for a week. By what miracle will these men without work and without savings live? We'll tell you! After having made the repairs necessary to their tools at home, these men . . . will pass their days in their beds, huddled together to keep warm and eat less. They will voluntarily weaken themselves so as to be able to refuse food to their bodies, which do not appear to them to merit any, since they are inactive.[132]

People who were used to misery were instinctively economical. During a period of crisis, when proprietors and farmers found themselves short of money, they were likely to postpone jobs like hedging, ditching or repairs to buildings and tools which might otherwise provide work in winter.[133] Even those in employment normally worked for a lower wage than in summer – in the canton of Gençay (Vienne), for example, for 1 franc per day compared with 1.50–2 francs.[134] Particularly for those with large families, the arrival of winter constituted a repeated menace, alleviated for the unemployed by charity or work relief on local roads where communes could afford this.[135]

Their lives involved continued insecurity and hardship. Their great ambition was normally to acquire a small plot of land, and this might be achieved by constantly stinting themselves of all but the bare necessities and saving every spare penny. Many agricultural labourers envied the greater security of the factory worker.[136]

Again, however, it should be borne in mind that 'making a living was a family affair rather than a matter for the man of the house alone'.[137] On the Caen plain a male labourer earned about 450–500 francs per annum at a time when the living expenses of a family of four were estimated at 800 francs. The difference was made up by the earnings of women and children, in this case usually in lace manufacture.[138] Children needed to be set to work from as early an age as possible – guarding animals, for example. Even if they received only their keep, it eased the burden on their family. In the *arrondissement* of Troyes (Aube) the supplement to income came from hosiery, in the *arrondissement* of Avallon (Yonne) from seasonal migration by the men and wet-nursing by the women. This latter occupation paid 6–8 francs per month per child for infants from the orphanages of Paris and Melun and up to 12–15 francs for the children of Parisian workers.[139] It had the advantage of being less susceptible than the others to the economic consequences of a poor harvest.

Families sought to increase their incomes by whatever opportunities offered themselves. Thus considerable variation occurred in the structure of incomes, rendering suspect the value of many statistical averages. Clearly, those with nothing to sell but their labour suffered most, but it ought to be remembered that the day labourer living uniquely off the proceeds of his nominal profession must have been a rarity compared with those who mixed this labour with the activities of small proprietor, sharecropper, farmer, artisan or industrial labourer, while additional income might be obtained from grazing, wood gathering and hunting rights in forests (although legislation to prevent degradation of forests increasingly limited such possibilities),[140] gleaning, employment on public works projects or straightforward charity.

When employment opportunities in a community fell below acceptable limits recourse to temporary migration was a normal solution.[141] This might occur from one agricultural region to another (for example, from the Perche to help with the harvest in the Beauce),[142] or it might take the form of the employment of agricultural workers in the urban building industry. This had the dual advantage of reducing pressure on local resources and providing a cash income. Parts of the Limousin thus depended for their continuing prosperity on that of the Paris and Lyon building industries. An estimated 35,000–36,000 workers left the Creuse each year in the 1840s.[143]

Due to the over-supply of labour, even such a range of activities and constant hard work could not raise living standards above very mediocre levels, but they did provide the means by which the inhabitants of an over-populated countryside were able to subsist. If this whole range of possibilities proved inadequate in a particularly bad year, no one was as well practised in economy, even to the brink of starvation.

Given normal living standards barely above subsistence level, substantial increases in the price of basic necessities made life difficult even for those whose incomes did not decline. The basic problem of subsistence for the mass of labourers, during a period of high food prices, was to obtain money (the means of obtaining food). The Prefect of Creuse reported:

if we have nothing to fear concerning the provisioning of our markets, we have at least to concern ourselves with the absence of work during the winter, making money extremely rare in our mountains, and perhaps making it impossible for the workers to purchase the grain necessary for their food. The absence of work and the high cost of cereals is equivalent for this class . . . to a real *disette*.[144]

In such a situation for the poorest there was no alternative to dependence on relief given by municipal authorities or by their better-off neighbours. The degree to which charity alleviated suffering varied greatly between areas, depending on their resources and the attitudes of those who were relatively well-off. In the *arrondissement* of Melun (Seine-et-Marne) it was observed that 'all the commune are protected in difficult moments by the charity of the numerous *châtelains* who live there'.[145] Few areas can have been as fortunate as this appears to have been. Far more frequent were complaints concerning the inadequacy of relief, especially in the countryside.[146] This absence of adequate relief contributed to the survival of situations of extreme misery among the rural poor.

Descriptions of appalling conditions abound. In at least one case, that of upland areas in the department of Côtes-du-Nord, it was claimed that in October 1846 people were literally starving to death,[147] and even as late as June 1854 it was being reported from Alsace that in the countryside people were eating grass and rotten meat.[148] Yet a consideration of the development of agricultural productivity would suggest that conditions during the first half of the nineteenth century should have improved in normal years with reasonably good harvests and that even the crises were less intense. One should not minimize the importance of even marginal improvements for populations living around subsistence level. Most contemporary observers appear to have been conscious of this, although there were some exceptions, particularly in such areas of intense population pressure on resources as the Pyrénées.[149]

The traditional subsistence crisis disappeared after the 1850s as farm productivity continued to increase and the development of communications transformed national and international markets. The crises of the 1850s themselves were not as severe in their effects as those of the previous decade: wine prices were high; industrial employment kept up; market structures were adapting to the improvement in communications. A new era began in which for the first time the threat of dearth and the extremes of misery which it caused was lifted. But before we can consider these changes, we must continue our analysis of the traditional crisis and consider how men perceived their misery and how their perceptions conditioned their behaviour.

5 Subsistence crises and popular protest

Richard Cobb, writing of the beginning of the nineteenth century, maintained that dearth was

the problem to which the country people, at all times, devoted the most attention; no other topic took up so much time in popular debate, no other could inspire fiercer passions, greater fears, more hysteria, more envy, more violence and more unreason. One can find no better illustration of the processes of myth and rumour and the attitudes to dearth conditioned popular attitudes to everything else – the government, the countryside, life and death, inequality, deprivation, mortality, riot, humiliation, self-esteem. It is the central theme in all forms of popular political expression.[1]

It is the purpose of this chapter to examine 'popular political expression' half a century later, during the subsistence crises of 1845–7 and 1853–5, and to analyse change and continuity in people's attitudes towards the social and natural environments within which they lived. Our first concern will be with popular understanding and explanation of subsistence crises. Our primary source of information, besides the usual administrative and police reports, will be the words of the poor – graffiti, *placards* and conversations.

Explanations of crisis

Action or inaction, protest about or acceptance of conditions prevailing in the market place, depended initially upon how these conditions were understood, upon explanations of how the market worked and of the roles of the various participants in commerce.

The most widely shared explanation of high prices laid the blame on speculation. The major grain merchant Darblay the younger observed rather loftily to the 1859 inquiry that the masses still did not understand the causes of price increases, the processes of the market, which were to him 'so simple and obvious'. They were blinded by 'the most absurd prejudices',[2] which led them to believe in manoeuvres designed to increase prices, which existed only in their collective imaginations.[3] M. Rabourdin, a large farmer at Villacoubley (Seine-et-Oise), maintained rather indignantly that 'the population persists in thinking that wheat and flour are not merchandise with which one is able to dispose as one wishes'.[4]

Throughout the 1850s similar complaints were frequently made. The *procureur-général* at Agen in August 1855 doubted if more than one in one hundred workers blamed the prevailing high prices on the effects of bad weather rather than on the greed of landowners.[5] One major reason for this in most areas was the lack of access to information about harvests and supplies outside the immediate locality. The economist Gosset observed that even merchants found it difficult to obtain accurate information about the food resources of other regions, and because of this there was always 'surprise, uncertainty, ignorance about our real situation', which explained 'the facility with which fears arise, whether these are serious or imaginary'.[6] Others, indeed most of the population, were even less well informed.

According to the *procureur-général* at Poitiers, writing in September 1853, each successive crisis contributed by strengthening the folk memory of suffering and misery.[7] Few people alive in the first two-thirds of the century would not have experienced food shortage and price rises. At the very least their parents had. This experience and their awareness of history, however truncated and distorted, contributed to the construction of both an individual and a collective vision of the world and of human relationships. Among the villains it identified were those who profited from the misery of their fellows and particularly those who took away food belonging to the community. This sense of history helped to confirm the rumours of hoarding and speculation and to maintain the hyper-sensitivity of public opinion. Even if crises were not as intense as in the past, it appears evident that psychological mechanisms did not evolve as rapidly as those of the economy, and it was the popular conception of reality, rather than objective conditions, that determined attitudes and actions.

Normally low living standards exposed much of the population to continual insecurity. The fear of hunger was always with them, resulting in a constant preoccupation in rural areas with the state of the harvest,[8] particularly in those areas of relative monoculture which lacked a range of alternative foodstuffs.[9] To the anxiety caused by hunger were added the threats of unemployment and of indebtedness.

Most adversely affected by a subsistence crisis were those unable to supply themselves with all or part of the food they consumed. The poor spent such a large proportion of their income on food that once they depended on purchasing their needs in the market, their whole standard of living was dominated by the movement of food prices there. It became likely as prices rose that the poor would not 'earn enough to nourish themselves properly'.[10]

Thus it was that for much of the population 'the important question of subsistence dominates all others'.[11] When normal living standards were so low the problem could rarely be forgotten. Comfort at home was not expected by the poor; heating was appreciated only during sedentary periods. The way they dressed, as a source of status, had not yet come to be a matter for concern. As long as they ate enough not to be hungry, they were likely to be content. The real concern of workers and peasants, particularly in periods of high prices, was the question of what they and their families would have to eat for their next meal or on the next day. Insecurity of supply, rumours of shortage, legends of famine, the sheer misery experienced by the hungry all contributed to the creation of an obsessive and frequently hysterical attitude.[12]

'Misery reasons badly.'[13] This fact, together with the limited understanding of the market by the masses (or, indeed, of many apparently well educated people) and the restricted nature of the overall world view of individuals in most communities, made it hardly surprising that explanations of economic phenomena tended to be in personalized form. In large part they were based on experience. The opportunities for profitable speculation really did encourage fraud and efforts to manipulate market prices by farmers and merchants. Bakers, because of the reluctance of municipal authorities to allow bread prices to increase in relation to rising grain and flour prices, were often forced into fraudulent practices in an attempt to balance their accounts.[14] The masses were hardly capable, given the archaic character of the popular culture and education, of objectively relating their experience to the overall structure of the economy. Their understanding was based upon a constricted view of the world, informed by oral traditions which transmitted memories of the past in stories and proverbs. One cannot sufficiently stress the significance of enculturation within a specific 'cognitive frame'.[15]

The continued inability of agriculture and commerce to satisfy the demand for food had its effects not only on material conditions but also on individual intellectual development. Material conditions and psychology were directly and physiologically linked. As has been pointed out above, it seems to be accepted by medical experts that even mild and moderate degrees of protein calorie malnutrition have damaging consequences for the physical and mental development of adults as well as children. To this no doubt ought to be added the effects on the poor of overall social and environmental deprivation, also serving to reduce the capacity for intellectual development.[16] One distinguished medical observer has concluded that 'children who are malnourished in infancy, or who belong to families where food is not abundant, tend to develop anxiety about food'[17] – a not altogether surprising comment but one which might easily be overlooked by the historian concerned primarily with the observation of reported actions.

Anxiety, combined with low qualitative as well as quantitative levels of literacy and the predominance of an oral culture, combined to deform reality. Understanding of the present was based upon the more or less deformed reports of experiences in the past and thus to an important extent popular mentality fossilized this past, exhibiting a kind of functional lag in relation to the socio-economic structures of the present.

In a situation in which the dominant preoccupations of many individuals were food supply and price levels, it generally seems to have been the case that all kinds of apparently absurd explanations for high prices were credited. Rumours helped to maintain an atmosphere of fear and tension. According to the *procureur-impérial* at Châteaubriant (Loire-Inférieure) in 1856, 'because so many things exist which are difficult to explain, the population invents suppositions more extraordinary even than the things they want to explain'. He noted that in his area the people believed in sorcerers and ghosts as well as in plots to starve them.[18]

As a consequence of different cultural standards, rural areas generally proved more receptive to rumours than did urban centres. In the latter literacy levels were higher, access to information better and, as a result, the mental outlook different[19] – although it should not be forgotten that regional cultural levels varied considerably and that towns and their surrounding countryside were closely linked.

Individual mentality is closely dependent upon that of family and social group, upon their mode of life and daily preoccupations. Where complete or functional illiteracy dictates that group culture is formed in large part by an oral tradition, the dominance of the group over the individual is inevitably reinforced. There are simply no alternative sources of culture. In the basic French of the uneducated, particularly in *patois*, the range of vocabulary was limited. Remarks tended to be brief, sentences short. Few logical relationships were likely to be expressed. Even simple conceptualization was rendered difficult by the limited number of words available with which to express abstract ideas.

Closely interrelated with the question of levels of literacy and capacity for conceptualization and explanation is that of circulation of information. Individuals act on the basis of information received and their comprehension of it. Information spread through official announcements and the press, but also by word of mouth along the highways and roughly in proportion to the number of users. News from all these sources was concentrated where people gathered in greatest diversity, especially in market centres. The importance of the market place and *cabaret* should be stressed. In both these places people from various parts of the countryside met other rural dwellers as well as townsmen and strangers. They exchanged gossip and when they returned home or travelled further took their pieces of information with them.

Oral transmission of information, still so important when much of the population remained illiterate or did no regular reading, frequently led to successive deformation of news. This was a situation characterized by the inadequacy of the 'basic symbolic systems necessary to communication'.[20] Poor education and linguistic variations led to the haphazard accumulation of anecdotes without any overall conceptual framework, however simple, in which to fit them and give them meaning. The individual 'took his news selectively, paying attention solely to what affected him . . . and drawing his own conclusions'.[21] This 'primitive mentality', compounded by fear and anxiety, lent credence to all manner of absurdities, as for example when Agathe Lamarthe told her friends at Rennes that a local sailor had just written to his family that the sea was full of grain which had been thrown in by speculators. For effect she added that a ship lost recently had not run on to a sandbank, as was originally believed, but on to a great mound of grain thrown into the sea by these detestable *accapareurs*.[22] It was, however, likely to lead to disorder only when the fears and prejudices of the individual recipient of the information were confirmed by those of the wider social group of which he formed part.

Specific occurrences or incidents which gave them credibility can sometimes be pinpointed as the sources of particular rumours. In 1847 in Corrèze it was known that a law banning exports of foodstuffs had been introduced. Popular rumour enlarged this into a ban on movements between departments.[23] In December 1853 a law lifting customs tariffs on imports was transformed by the rumours circulating throughout fairs and markets in the Limoges region into a complete ban on imports introduced by the rich in order to increase prices.[24] In 1855, at a mill between Corbeil and Etampes (Seine-et-Oise), a delivery of wheat was made by a cart which also contained haricots and lentils. The news rapidly spread throughout the locality that the miller was mixing these with wheat, and a threatening crowd gathered.[25] Frequently a rise in prices following what had appeared to be a good harvest and due perhaps to a low wheat yield or a delay in threshing was something which demanded explanation, and in a tense situation the explanations offered were not often very objective and tended to reinforce the worst fears.[26] An already brittle social situation bred rumours which only served to heighten the tension. In the dry summer of 1846 fires in many areas, blamed on arsonists, further intensified the suspicion and fear caused by high food prices.[27] Rumours about plots to poison the poor were not uncommon. At Tours in 1856 the railway company laid out in a public square wheat which had spoiled in transit in order to assess liability for damages. This led to a rumour that spoilt grains were to be sold as part of a plot to poison the poor. The furious crowd which gathered had to be dispersed by a cavalry charge.[28] At Troyes (Aube) in September 1854 it was whispered that the cholera epidemic caused far higher mortality among the poor than among the rich because the poor were being poisoned.[29]

In such a situation careless or boastful words could easily cause trouble. On the market place at Plancoët (Côtes-du-Nord) in August 1854 Louise Chapelaine boasted that her brother Michel, supported by the nobles and the government, was going to buy up stocks to force up prices. She was saved by gendarmes from a crowd of exasperated women only with some difficulty.[30] In January 1847 a baker at Rennes complained that mobs were gathering nightly and throwing stones at his shop because someone had spread the rumour that he had said that two potatoes were enough for a worker.[31] This was precisely the sort of gossip which might be relayed over a drink or by women talking on their doorsteps.

In 1853 the *procureur-général* at Angers complained bitterly about popular credulity and ill-will and protested against the unfair accusations of hoarding directed against 'honourable men'.[32] Credulity is, however, easy to understand in men described by a defence lawyer as 'blinded by rumours, deranged by suffering and hunger'.[33] It also revealed how difficult it was for poor people caught up in the daily struggle for existence, and unlikely to be able to act from altruism themselves, to ascribe anything but the lowest motives to members of more fortunate social groups. The crisis which impoverished so many poor people was an opportunity for profit for others. Envy and their experience of exploitation at work or in the market place must have appeared to confirm pessimistic views of the motives of their fellow men. Contemporaries acted on the basis of their own understanding, their own perception of a crisis. However absurd some of these interpretations might seem in retrospect, within their own context they had a certain relevance and meaning. Reactions to crises quite clearly were not simple responses to varying material situations. They varied between social groups, between geographical areas and over time, depending largely upon 'pre-existing social psychologies' – upon ideologies and attitudes. Everywhere, however, fear of *disette* continued to be ingrained in the mentality of the masses and created 'a sentiment of envy which ferments in the inferior classes against those who possess, which manifests itself with more vehemence verbally in the day-to-day conversations between poor people, and through complaints and protests made to the authorities and to the wealthier members of society'.[34] A variety of forms of protest existed, from polite requests for the reduction of prices to violent demonstrations. I shall begin with the first stage of illicit protest – namely, *placards* or graffiti.

Verbal protest

As well as reporting on public opinion, police agents assiduously transcribed the sentiments expressed in *placards* and by means of graffiti. They provide a useful insight into the language of popular protest and into the social tensions prevailing in a society experiencing a serious crisis.

None of the questions one should ask of any historical document – who wrote it, for whom to read, with what purpose – can be answered with any certainty. Most of these *placards* were judged by the authorities to be genuine manifestations of popular discontent. Some, usually easily distinguishable by their content and/or orthography, were the work of political agitators. Even where a relatively educated person attempted to increase his anonymity by pretending, through spelling mistakes and clumsy hand-writing, to be poor and ignorant, it was likely that the kind of studied mistakes he introduced into his *placard* were not those which the semi-literate would have committed. The experienced police or judicial officer could detect such nuances.[35]

The most striking thing about the *placards* is the violence of the language used. Its savagery seems to express all the anguish of the poor, their lack of comprehension of events which had thrown them suddenly into a misery more intense even than that which they daily suffered and their bitter hatred of those who appeared to contravene the simplest morality by exploiting and deliberately worsening this misery. The phrases they used were intended to injure and abuse. They were not entirely spontaneous, in that they repro-duced the traditional phrases of verbal violence and represented age-old hostilities found in communities throughout France. But it is their stereo-typed character which increases their value to the historian, since it provides him with a genuine unrehearsed insight into popular psychology.

The *placards* varied in size and appearance. Usually they were written in large, badly formed letters and in a style and orthography which suggested semi-literacy. Sometimes the written message was replaced, or more frequently supplemented, by threatening symbols – a guillotine perhaps, or other reminders of an egalitarian republic and popular justice, or, as at Nancy on the night of 6–7 August 1856, the crayoned picture of a gallows with hanging figures taken to represent the prefect, the mayor and his deputy.[36] Demands and threats might be made in the words of a song or a poem.[37]

Placards were normally put in place during the night for obvious reasons, given their seditious character in law. Their total varied according to the energy and number of the writers and the number of places in which it was felt worthwhile to place them. Most frequently one or two would be found, but on 17 March 1847 at Metz *placards* were found in thirty different places,[38] while on two occasions in May–June 1847 at Beauvais first twenty-one *placards* and then twelve more were found.[39] Both incidents caused considerable alarm among the authorities because the large number of *placards* seemed to them to represent a more than usually determined effort to incite the populace to acts of violence.

In many communities, especially those with low levels of practical literacy, the written *placard* was assured more serious attention than verbal threats. Its written character gave it a semi-official character. Moreover, its layout and tone were often copied from those of official notices. The actual position selected for the *placard* was also of some significance. The most obvious place, when complaints were being made because of high food prices, was in the market place and especially on one of the pillars of the market hall.[40] There it would come to the attention of consumers, traders and the authorities. Another favourite public place was the wall or the fountain which still supplied public drinking water in most places and which was thus a common meeting place. At Metz on the nights of 26–7 and 28–9 September 1855 not only the fountains in the Place St-Louis and Rue des Allemands but also the *pissoirs* in the town were placarded.[41] When threats were combined with an appeal to public authorities or to particular farmers or merchants, the most obvious place to fix the *placard* was on the door of the person to whom the appeal or threat was addressed – on the door of the town hall or mayor's house,[42] on that of the church or lodgings of the parish priest,[43] or on that of a local landowner or merchant.[44]

The most striking and constant feature of the *placard* was the threats it contained. It is as if those who prepared them not only felt desperate but were convinced that the demands they made were more likely to be met if the alternative appeared to be death and destruction. Combined with the officialized language – indicative of the extent to which, particularly in the city, the popular classes in their daily life unavoidably made contact with elements of the élite culture – were expressions of popular resentment formulated in the archaic, badly constructed phrases of popular culture, reflecting as the representatives of the Rennes tanners accepted in 1848, 'the most absurd prejudices, the strangest ideas which maintain the worker's defiance against all those superior to him by position and education'.[45] It was these prejudices, this hostility, which gave the authorities particular cause for concern.

To upper-class justices, divorced from the masses by a major cultural gap, the violence of the language used to convey menace or injury must have appeared shocking. The limited vocabulary of the poor – those who spoke in French as well as those who employed dialect or *patois* – and the limited conceptualizing ability of the ill-educated, reduced their thoughts and expressions to the level of the concrete, everyday, and their abuse to the most basic level. Their bitterness and hatred of those who exploited them increased this verbal violence. That they had no real intention of carrying out their most vicious threats – at least, unless provoked at the moment of most intense anger – does not appear to have done much to ease the fears of those who felt threatened and who rarely understood the mentality of the crowd.

If *placards* calling for the poor to gather to protest about their condition or threatening violence were rarely followed by action, it was impossible to be certain that no action would ensue. Isolated cases in which such appeals apparently led to incidents – as at Nancy on 10 February 1847, when following a call to gather on the Place Stanislas, around a hundred people gathered in the snow in late evening before being dispersed[46] – intensified official concern. When, for example, a threatening *placard* on the door of the parish priest's house at Jouy (Eure-et-Loir) was followed two days later by a fire which destroyed seven houses, it was almost inevitable that the police should think that this was arson.[47]

One basic aim of the writers of *placards* was to make those with power aware of the plight and needs of the poor. This was why they were habitually directed at the local authorities or those who were believed to possess stocks of foodstuffs. Those *placards* concentrating on this aim were the most pathetic of all. Thus one found at Labersac (Corrèze) in February 1847 subordinated threats to the statement of need. Its author(s) maintained:

> we would prefer to die than see our poor children starving. . . . We want work, bread or money. We want one of these three things to be given to us by our fellow citizens or we will pay a visit to those who have grain . . . or money. It is impossible for us to eat bread at the present price, which is why the parish priest asked for a reduction. . . . We poor workers, what do you think we can do when we earn only 1.50 francs a day and have a large family?

It was claimed that this represented the views of seventy people. Three were arrested on suspicion of preparing the *placard*, a shoemaker and two tailors.[48]

Those who sought to profit from periods when food prices were high almost inevitably met with opprobrium. The grain merchant became the *accapareur*, the hoarder, guilty in the eyes of most of the population of the morally indefensible act of buying at a low price to sell at a high one. The process of purchasing in a region of relatively low price for export to one of higher prices, which had the socially advantageous result of levelling out prices, provoked particular hostility because it levelled prices in the first area and seemed to be the cause there of a deliberately manufactured shortage. Typically, the lieutenant of gendarmerie at Commercy (Meuse), reported on 24 February 1847: 'It should not be concealed that the rural population is beginning to grow concerned that the numerous purchases and transports of grain made on behalf of merchants is exhausting local resources; the granaries are empty, and if some farmers still possess grain, they are not disposed to sell it in the hope of benefiting from an increase in prices.' These factors were causing an 'effervescence amongst the people'.[49] When, especially after a relatively good local harvest, prices rose due to export, this appeared to confirm every prejudice. The population felt that it was being deprived of the food that it had itself grown by the greed of a small number of merchants.[50]

Placards at Nancy in mid August 1856 proposed that anyone who sold grains outside the market or sought to transport it elsewhere should be regarded as a 'traitor' and a 'scoundrel'.[51] This was restrained language indeed! More representative of the type was the *placard* found at Gondrecourt (Meuse) on 11 February 1847:

> I have the honour to inform you that if the grain merchants do not cease to take away grains by the 15th of the current month, then you, mayor, deputy-mayor and

councillors, if you let them pass through the town with their grains, I warn you that we are 150 men armed to the teeth; we will turn the town upside-down, beginning with you. We will go to your homes and cut your throats and those of the three bakers. We will hang you from the highest poplars around the lake. We'll arrive in tens until we are all gathered in the town, and then we will fight against you all, gendarmes and other employees of the town, and burn the whole place down.[52]

The first sentence follows polite forms with which everyone was familiar. It obviously became more difficult to formulate ideas once this model was dropped, so that writers borrowed from the everyday abuse of the street, and the councillors of Gondrecourt were faced with the prospect of dying several times over!

The threats made were frequently quite specific. In January 1847 the commune of Monsoche (Haute-Saône) was threatened with 'theft, pillage, murder',[53] while during March Warvilliers (Somme) was promised 'fire, blood and carnage' if bread prices were not reduced.[54] In the same month the Prefect at Chartres was promised that his face would be smashed in and that the grain market would be pillaged and the town and farms in the surrounding area burned to the ground.[55] The threat of fire was a favourite.

Most *placards* eschewed politics – their essential target was those individuals or local groups who could be seen to be directly exploiting the poor, particularly those dealing in basic foodstuffs. Landowners and farmers who held on to their stocks while awaiting a rise in prices were threatened, the offenders sometimes publicly named as objects of opprobrium. At Méru (Oise) in January 1847 a *placard* exhorted: 'People to Arms! Bread or death. . . . Wheat on Friday or the fire on Saturday for every farmer. Death to the traitors at Méru. Fire and Death to the homes of Baude, Petit, France, Bulard, the *curé* and the mayor.'[56] All those who traded in grain, flour or bread were 'vampires . . . who are fattening themselves on the people's substance'[57] and were exposed to threats. At Beauvais (Oise) in May 1847 the *placards* demanded death for the millers, farmers and bakers and marked the miller Warme for especial attention.[58]

Those who were believed to be attempting to corner food supplies and establish a monopoly position for themselves were especially feared and despised. Over a municipal announcement of an increase in the price of bread at Poitiers in August 1853 someone wrote: 'Find out who the *accapareurs* are, so that we can shoot them like mad dogs.'[59] At Corbeil (Seine-et-Oise) on 17 September 1854 a *placard* was found with a crude drawing of a scaffold from which hung three figures labelled 'Darblay Père, Darblay fils, Morel', three of the best-known grain merchants in France, who according to this *placard* 'deserve to be hung, those three pigs'.[60]

This establishment of a monopoly position was regarded as particularly dangerous when the monopolists determined to export their stocks. In February 1847 a *placard* found at Treignac (Corrèze) bemoaned the fact that 'the commerce of M. Pailler and so many others who buy grain in neighbouring communes to take it elsewhere' made it 'impossible for the poor people to live',[61] while at Lamballe (Côtes-du-Nord) on the night of 16–17 November 1845 a *placard* was nailed up reminding the citizens that 'every day you see your food and your children's taken away without asking where, if the next harvest fails, you will find food'. It called on them to 'annihilate' the merchants, to 'expel from your society all *accapareurs*, punish them for their vile trade'.[62] The rights of the community were affirmed against the freedom to make a profit demanded by individuals.

It seems evident also that the better-off members of a community were expected, wherever possible, to provide help, including work for the less fortunate. Slogans of the kind 'Work or Death' were not uncommon[63] and constituted a demand that the community provide for its own. Dismissals were particularly badly received by workers at moments when prices were rising. At Lannion (Côtes-du-Nord) in November 1845 a merchant who dismissed most of his sixty employees subsequently started to receive threats of death,[64] while at Tours (Indre-et-Loire) on 6 February 1847 a *placard* stressed the injustice of a relationship in which 'those pitiless Masters suck all our blood throughout the year' and then dismiss workers when demand falls, leaving them to depend on charity which 'degrades and humiliates the worker'.[65]

The belief was also frequently expressed that workers should receive a wage adequate for the subsistence of their families. In so many situations flagrant injustices appeared to be perpetrated. At Rennes on 5 September 1855 a *placard* informed the public that 'the entrepreneurs and master-architects have refused to increase wages by 0.50 francs a day, while the mayor and municipal councillors have increased the price of bread. . . . You want us to die of misery, but we will burn you alive unless you reduce the price of bread and pay the workers 0.50 francs more'.[66] That wages should either remain stable or, as frequently happened, be reduced at a moment when bread prices were being increased, was a threat to the living standards and even, it appeared, to the very existence of the poor.[67] Employers and municipal authorities appeared to be collaborating to increase their misery. They responded with individual complaints, *placards* and sometimes demonstrations or strikes against one or both of these agencies.

Ignorance of economic structures created a dilemma for the poor. To whom should they appeal? Against whom should threats be made? Frequently an obvious target offered itself in the shape of a particularly harsh employer or an especially greedy merchant, but their grievances could not always be so easily personified. Appeals and threats were as a result often made to and against the amorphous category of the 'rich'.

The poor were aware of their dependence on the 'rich' for both work and charity. It seemed obvious that they were the only ones who could do anything to provide work or reduce prices, and yet it often appeared that they did little or nothing to help: 'Haughty Rich . . . you have exhausted the patience of the worker. You have exhausted his means of existence, you have crushed him. . . .',[68] a fact which one *placard* emphasized would never be forgiven these 'enemies of humanity'.[69]

The characteristics of these 'enemies' varied according largely to pre-existing social tensions. Credence was far more easily given to descriptions of speculation and cornering where hostility already existed towards various individuals or social groups. A labourer at Neuville (Sarthe) was thus quite likely to blame nobles and clergy and to long for 'a revolution much more terrible than that of 1793'.[70] This was, after all, a region bitterly divided in 1793. Throughout the north-west similar accusations were made. A *placard* at Laval (Mayenne) in January 1847 appealed to its readers to burn a *château* belonging to nobles who bought up grains.[71] At Cherchigné (Mayenne) early in February a local landowner, the Marquis de Hautville, was publicly called a brigand and *Chouan*.[72] His political sentiments and economic activities were both condemned. Here and elsewhere the clergy as social and political collaborators of the nobles were attacked, in large part due to their choice of allies.[73]

Hostility was, however, hardly less marked against the wealthy bourgeoisie. In a *placard* found at La Châtaigneray (Vendée) in November 1846 it was recalled that the people had supported the bourgeoisie in overthrowing the Bourbons in 1830 but had gained nothing thereby.[74] The contempt of the workers for those who did not work but profited from their labours was clearly expressed in *placards* found at Lyon in July 1847, calling on the people to 'destroy this vermin which is the cause of the famine. . . '. It continued:

we see all these fat bourgeois, cigars between their fingers, going to the cafés or to the club and drinking, but at whose expense? Always that of the worker.

You see all those Big Wigs as soon as they show themselves out of doors, if it is the least bit hot, they are out of breath, at whose expense? Always that of the worker who has fattened them.

Just like the fat *Malazon*, isn't he too fat? Should we bleed him, like a fat pig?[75]

At Viva (Ariège) in March 1854 one among a group of workers maintained that the rich ought to be choked. He defined the rich as those who ate bread made from wheat, distinguished thereby from the poor who in that area could only afford bread made from maize.[76] Often the *placards* expressed the simple and understandable envy of the have-nots. A period of high food prices and general deprivation stimulated 'the sentiment of envy which ferments in the lower classes against those who possess',[77] as when at Metz in August 1853 a court sentenced two men to short periods of imprisonment for longingly discussing the day when they would take from the rich their food, wine and women.[78]

Measures taken by the local authorities to help the poor often did something to calm popular anxiety but could not entirely still feelings of resentment directed at both local and higher governmental authorities. Two kinds of mayor particularly annoyed the poor. In the first place there were those who appeared indifferent to their situation. Thus at Arras (Pas-de-Calais) on 10 October 1855 hundreds of workers gathered to complain about the price of bread and also at the mayor's absence during the summer months, which he had spent at his country house so that 'the people believes it has been forgotten'.[79] More despised was the mayor who clearly identified himself with the grain speculators and the interests of the 'rich'. A *placard* found at Rochefort (Charente-Inférieure) on 7 January 1839 – the product of a better education than were most *placards* – read: 'Workers and fathers, are we going to tolerate the authorities' support for the speculation which is occurring on grain and which serves only to enrich the proprietor and to expose the proletarian to death from starvation, and to failure in the most sacred of duties, that of giving bread to his children?' It called for revolt against these 'enemies of humanity'.[80] More typical was an anonymous letter to the mayor of the commune of Lacroix-sur-Meuse (Meuse) in April 1847, which demanded that the 'pigs of councillors', those 'brigands', instruct their tenants to sell grain to the poor at lower prices and promised that otherwise they would all die together.[81]

Governments which, without fail, claimed credit for prosperity could hardly expect to escape blame for crises. Whatever the limitations lack of means placed upon administrative action, the government appeared to the poor to possess an aura of omnipotence, and it was held responsible for everything.[82]

The *placards* with a political message certainly reveal something about the political conceptions and attitudes of the masses. At their simplest, they say something like 'Down with Louis-Philippe'.[83] In most of these *placards* the government and regime were personified by the king. The writers seem to have believed that if he wished he could improve their condition, so they demanded work or cheaper food or else 'a new king'.[84] In a *placard* found at Farschrisser (Moselle) it was observed that 'a dog takes care of his little ones, but our king does not care for his poor subjects'.[85] Only occasionally some other element of the government was denounced – at Senlis (Oise) on 27 December 1846, for example, the Chamber of Deputies.[86] At Châteaudun (Eure-et-Loir) in December 1846 a *placard* placed on the door of a landowner exemplified social hatred and the desire to bring down the government, together with a certain familiarity with political slogans:

Long live the Republic. People awaken, exterminate the race of kings. You will not be happy until you overthrow the bourgeoisie which governs us, which crushes us with taxes, and makes us die of hunger, overthrow this vile cowardly race which sells itself to every government. Rise, they have reigned; now we need the government of the people, by the people.[87]

A 'Chant National' found at the market hall of Cany (Seine-Inférieure) in April 1847 complained about the humiliation of workers forced to stand before the door of the bourgeois farmer to beg charity when the land should belong to everyone, and incited them to seize what they needed, to burn farms and factories, ending with 'Long live Robespierre'.[88] This and many other similar documents revived memories of 1793 and the myth of the *partageux*, as well as lending credence to contemporary rumours of communist agitation.[89] Alternatively, legitimist sentiments might be expressed. A *placard* at Mayenne on 2 February 1847 asked workers if sixteen years of the Orleanist monarchy had been long enough to convince them of the superior virtues of the previous government. Surely life had been better before 1830?[90] The basic point legitimist *placards* made was that life would only get better if the legitimate monarch was restored: 'Bread will be expensive as long as the usurper . . . occupies the throne.'[91] A *placard* found in the Vendée in 1847 asserted that 'our nobles have more humanity for the unfortunate than these bourgeois monsters' and called for revenge against 'those who seek to have us by means of famine'.[92]

Most venomous in their attacks on the king were the *placards* associating him with those who speculated on the misery of the poor. Most obviously, his were the soldiers who protected the grain merchants from popular justice.[93] He became, as the words of the song found in the market hall at Cony (Seine) expressed it, 'the monster who reigns over France', who allowed the starvation of children and forced the poor into a humiliating dependence upon the charity of the rich.[94] He was the monarch who betrayed France by sending soldiers to Africa to be massacred, who hoped that war would persuade the French to forget their misery, the 'inhuman monster' who could have prevented the export of grains but preferred to allow children to die of famine. This *placard*, found at Vitry-le-François on 28 March 1847, listed all manner of grievances against the regime, citing peers and deputies who had voted taxes twice as burdensome as those of the empire, the prefect and the mayor who failed to protect the poor, the nobles who gave charity only to good-for-nothings who attended mass and who sold their grain at 72 francs instead of 25 francs to the deserving poor.[95] Such a *placard* described the social system from the perspective of the poor on the basis of their everyday contacts with the military, officials and their social superiors.

The language of politicized protest changes more rapidly than that of social protest. A change of regime has obvious consequences, ranging from a new head of government to appeal to, or protest about, to more far-ranging modifications of political institutions which affect popular conceptions of the political system and the forms in which protest might be expressed.

The year 1848 brought universal suffrage and, briefly, substantial freedom of expression; then during the remaining years of the Second Republic, as repression grew, democratic socialists sought to attract electoral support and to increase membership of their organizations through attempts to link politics and ideology with the everyday concerns of the poor. Their press sought to identify the conservative republic with rich speculators,[96] reminding the poor of 'those sad times in all your lives' when the landowners had enriched themselves at their expense by charging high prices for grain. Thus the 'National d'Autun' justified its claim that 'the rich have too much and the poor not enough', and its simple, if vague, solution which was to take from the rich what they had in excess and to give it to the poor.[97] These were years in which there appeared to be 'institutional alternatives to violent dissent',[98] in which political modernization and mass politicization proceeded apace, in which men became susceptible to ideologies which explained their misery, condemned those responsible (the rich, and bad governments) and offered hope of better times through socialist electoral victory in 1852 or even a mass rising if reactionaries attempted to subvert the democratic process. The successful *coup d'état* mounted in December 1851 and the establishment of an authoritarian Empire a year later turned the masses away from institutionalized political protest once more.

The subsistence crisis of the early years of the Second Empire followed a period of exceptionally good harvests and low prices, which had caused difficulties for many farmers but had been appreciated by consumers. This period had largely coincided with that of the Second Republic, so that by dint of simple association in many minds the Republic was linked with cheap bread and the Empire, in spite of its relatively good popular image, with a high cost of living. This was the message conveyed by a *placard* found in the *faubourg* St-Antoine in Paris in October 1855, reminding people that 'under the Republic bread never cost more than 40 centimes'.[99]

The poor had to a large degree supported Louis-Napoléon Bonaparte with their votes, hoping that he would do something to relieve their misery. Now for some he was identified with high prices and profiteering grain merchants. Lemoine, a labourer at Massy (Seine-et-Oise), complained to other customers in a shop on 11 December 1853 that he had voted for the emperor in the past but would not do so in the future, because bread was too expensive. He received ten days in prison for making this association.[100] He was fortunate not to have drawn the further conclusion that the regime ought to be overthrown. At Rethel (Ardennes) in August 1853 a *cabaret* owner was sentenced to three months in prison and 150 francs fine for making that additional point.[101]

To many people the republic was a synonym for justice, a particular egalitarian concept of justice reflecting the popular obsession with food prices. A *placard* at Laval (Mayenne) on 31 August 1855 was addressed in revolutionary fashion to 'the Children of Glory, Long live the Red Republic' and then delivered its essential message: 'if wheat prices do not fall, the merchants will be hanged'.[102] During the July Monarchy Bonapartism had sometimes symbolized the same aspirations.[103] Appeals on these bases were fundamentally different from those with a legitimist content, which appealed to aristocrats and king as natural superiors and protectors. The language used is indicative of this difference, with demands for 'justice for the people',[104] or the affirmation of the dignity of labour found in the textile town of St-Pons (Hérault) in December 1867:

Bread is at 48 centimes per kilogram. No work! How are we going to feed our families? God alone knows! We are delivered to the greed of the speculators. Our resignation is shameful, our brows are downcast enough. It is time to look our enemies calmly in the face, calmness is the symbol of strength. Ours is the right, all laws, human and divine, say so. To live on charity is not worthy of us. To live by working or die fighting, that should be our motto.[105]

The language was that of workers on numerous other occasions, at least from the Lyon uprising of 1834.

The experience of revolution in 1848 must have made social change seem more than ever a practical possibility rather than a vague aspiration. Throughout the bad years of the 1850s there were frequent rumours of revolt in the major cities. At Blois (Loir-et-Cher) on 16 November 1854 it was said that the people of Lyon had risen in protest against high prices and that 1500 of them had been killed.[106] Those in need could dream of revolution as an immediate solution to their problems. A widow, Françoise Noel, gossiping in a field near Briey (Meurthe) in August 1853 about the high cost of bread, could tell her friends that in only a few days they would have the Republic and cheap bread.[107] In March 1855 the departure of the army to the Crimea had awakened the hopes of writer(s) of *placards* at Argèles-sur-Mer (Pyrénées-Orientales). It appeared to provide an ideal opportunity to kill the rich and the police and to establish the Red Republic. For this was what appeared to the writer(s) to be necessary – social revolution in every village – and this was the prospect which terrified conservatives.[108] However unlikely its realization might appear to us with the benefit of hindsight, the widespread disorders in 1846–7, followed by revolution, must have made it seem a not entirely impossible prospect.

Popular conceptions of politics were obviously not homogeneous. Although the regime as a whole inevitably suffered in public esteem from a period of high prices – as is clear from police reports on talk in market places and *cabarets* – it was possible to dissociate the emperor from the speculators blamed for high prices. Popular hatred was directed above all at local speculators and the local rich. It was maintained in a *placard* found in the commune of Moulins-le-Metz (Moselle) on 13 November 1853 that 'the emperor does not know everything that happens. Those who have elected him will know how to avenge him. Long live Napoléon III'.[109] The myth of the good-hearted monarch led astray by evil advisers was thus asserted, the personality of the emperor dissociated from the measures of his government. The poor could still hope for a better world once the emperor became aware of their misery and was able to escape from these advisers.

Interestingly enough, during the subsistence crises of the 1850s a number of senior administrators in the provinces agreed that, unlike in 1846–7, the government was not being blamed and that the measures it had taken to limit exports and stimulate imports, and the publicity these had received, had established for it a favourable popular image, so that in parts of the west the desire for direct action against speculators

with which the people is so lavish when it suffers, has had this year a completely different character from . . . 1846. Then it was the government which was attacked. It was it which starved the people, it was the bourgeoisie who hoarded grains and created the shortage. Today it is no longer the government, nor even the bourgeoisie they accuse. To the legitimists, to the religious orders, to the clergy are reputed all the harm. Absurd accusations today as then! But at least . . . the government is spared this time.[110]

The poor now explained high prices in terms of a plot by the legitimists and the clergy to render the government unpopular and to bring it down. Different areas, different social structures and different images of the central government.

The *placards* in all their variety represented a criticism of a society founded upon gross inequality. They called, often with considerable bravado, for revenge and sometimes for a period of anarchical violence in which to destroy society. In a bar at Chérioux (Indre) in March 1847 an egg merchant asserted: 'We must kill the King and take all the bourgeois to Paris to kill them'.[111] All marks of superiority should be extinguished and all superiors eliminated.[112] 'No more despots, no more bad Rich, no more hoarders of wheat.'[113] The day of 'deliverance' was at hand: 'Long live pillage, blood and death.'[114] The call was for vengeance: 'Knife in hand . . . Destroy, Destroy them all . . . those monsters. . . . the hand of God is ready to deliver us. . . . Death, death to the Brigands . . . for death will spare no one.'[115] At Beauvais (Oise) the call was to 'Burn down the château, turn over the altar, break the machines, pull up the iron rails'.[116] Expressions of hatred, threats and almost always sheer bravado, violence in language but not in fact – they reveal something of the powerlessness felt by the poor, the desire to act but with limited opportunity for translating this into reality, into 'death or work or food'. Frustration was thus expressed more often than not in purely verbal terms, using the most violent forms of everyday language. The threats represented wishful thinking on the part of some of the most deprived and miserable elements of society. More than this, however, they reflected in many areas a high degree of social tension which on occasion might be translated into violence.

Disorder

The forms of disorder we have to describe were typical of the pre-industrial world, of this *ancien régime économique* which survived until the coming of the railways. There were four main types: disorders in market places designed to secure the sale of food at a 'reasonable' price; protests about the high price of bread in the towns, often involving threats to bakers; efforts to prevent the transport of foodstuffs; and visits to the granaries of landowners and farmers believed to be holding stocks in order to assess the importance of these supplies and to persuade their owners to sell them to the local population. In practice these basic types were often confused. Furthermore, popular protest which began with a particular purpose in mind sometimes degenerated into incoherent violence, normally against property rather than persons, but nevertheless had the effect of punishing those who were condemned as transgressors by the demonstrators. Other related forms of protest will also need to be considered, including strikes, arson, begging with menaces and crime, primarily in the form of petty theft. All of these represented attempts by the rural and urban poor to alleviate their misery.

Although in most areas the poor were alarmed and agitated and the authorities and property owners had reason for anxiety, Figure 5 makes it clear that the propensity for violence varied between regions. One should stress, however, that it provides a general impression rather than a complete account of disorders. We are dependent on the uncertain reporting ability of officials and newspapers. Partly for the same reason, I have not attempted to follow Charles Tilly's lead and assess the significance of the various disorders in quantitative terms ('man-hours spent rioting').[117] 'Significance' can hardly be assessed in a straightforward, quantitative manner.

One thing which rapidly becomes obvious is that at no time was there a simple, direct relationship between the degree of economic deprivation and the likelihood of the occurrence of popular protest. This is not, of course, to deny the significance of poor harvests and of the severity and length of a period of crisis as the essential causes of discontent and of disorder, nor the frequent involvement of the most deprived social groups. Clearly there is a relationship between levels of misery and propensity to violent protest, as in the case of woodland and marsh dwellers, particularly the woodcutters, arguably the most deprived professional group in France, both in normal and in crisis years.[118] Even in this case, however, protest was likely because of a combination of factors, of which misery was only one. The key factor everywhere would appear to have been popular perceptions not only of material conditions but of the causes of misfortune and of the potential for, and likely results of, protest. The impulse to revolt 'is determined by men's

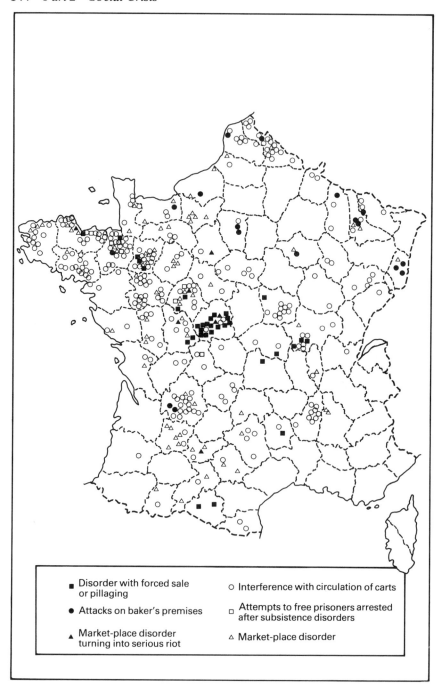

Figure 5   *Subsistence disorders, 1846–7*

beliefs about the sources of deprivation and about the normative and utilitarian justifiability of violent action directed at the agents responsible for it'.[119] As far as is possible, protest needs to be examined in relation to the social structure and traditions of local communities if it is to be fully comprehended.

The degree of social differentiation and the normal character of relationships between groups were obviously relevant factors. In the Limousin, for example, this produced hostility between sharecroppers and landowners in the lower Marche, in the *arrondissement* of Boussac between labourers and their employers in the chestnut woods, quarries and forges of the south-western plateau and generally between industrial workers and their *patrons*.[120] In the Alpine region, the one area seriously affected by disorders in 1846–7 was the wheat-growing area of the Isère, where landowners and merchants built up stocks for sale especially at Lyon and Grenoble. Their profits contrasted sharply with the misery of most of the population and especially that of the large number of day labourers.[121] Social tensions which were normally attenuated by community solidarity and feelings of dependence came to the fore when in periods of high prices the contrast between wealth and misery and the conflicting interests of rich and poor became more marked. In contrast, in areas where peasant farming remained dominant misery was spread fairly evenly throughout the community, and animosities born of envy and resentment at profit taking were less apparent. Division within the community was most likely where commercialization was most developed and economic and social distinctions were increasing.

The presence of professional groups dependent on purchases of food in the market place was a likely source of difficulties. Thus groups like peasant vine cultivators unable to build up more than a small stock of foodstuffs were especially sensitive to price movements, particularly in years when the vine produced little or wine prices were low. A close relationship was evident in Côte-d'Or, for example, from March 1829 to summer 1832 between the movement of wine prices and disorders.[122] Almost everywhere the number of impoverished industrial and agricultural labourers was growing. The presence of woodcutters, miners, quarrymen or textile workers at a market centre acted as a focus for discontent with which elements of the population of the surrounding countryside might associate themselves on market days.[123]

Protest was also frequent in areas with a commercial surplus of a particular foodstuff which, it appeared, was being bought up by merchants for transport to other regions with higher prices. It was, in addition, likely to occur along the routes linking regions in surplus with those in deficit. It can thus be closely related to the structure of communications networks, to the organization of commerce and to the distribution of major urban centres. In the department of Mayenne, for example, it was not the poorest area (in the *arrondissement* of Mayenne) which was the most seriously affected by

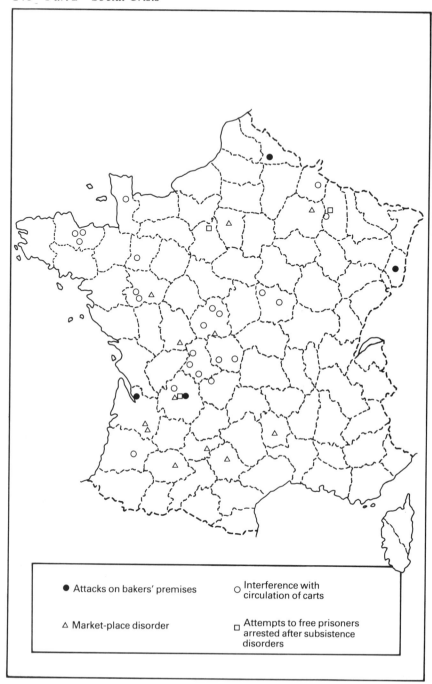

Figure 6 *Subsistence disorders, 1853–6*

Legend:
● Attacks on bakers' premises
△ Market-place disorder
○ Interference with circulation of carts
□ Attempts to free prisoners arrested after subsistence disorders

violence but rather communities in the more prosperous grain-producing *arrondissement* of Laval and on the roads heading away from it towards Brittany, Nantes, Paris and, secondarily, the local towns, Laval, Mayenne and Château-Gontier.[124] The movement of food out of an area tended to create fears of shortage within it. For this reason a marked concentration of incidents is evident throughout the west – in Brittany but particularly the departments of Ille-et-Vilaine, Mayenne and Maine-et-Loire, in Normandy, especially Seine-Inférieure, Eure and Eure-et-Loir, and in the centre-west in Indre-et-Loire, Indre, Vienne and Deux-Sèvres. Most notable in this case were the areas of *bocage*, zones of dispersed habitat, which themselves generated little commerce but were crossed by important roads used for the transport of foodstuffs. Particularist feelings in geographically and linguistically isolated communities were especially intense, making them all the more likely to act in defence of their food supplies and less willing to consider more general interests.

The link between social and economic conditions and popular protest was often a tenuous one because the 'location and timing [of disturbances] is often dictated by precipitating factors of a largely fortuitous nature',[125] and especially because the explanation of protest movements is 'not just a problem of calories and income but is a question of . . . conceptions of social justice, of rights and obligations, of reciprocity'.[126] Discontent, after all, only establishes the '*potential* for violence'.[127] It needs to be borne in mind that the 'symptoms of disorder' were frequently reported from places at which no significant violence was ever observed. People in many communities came close to violence but, for whatever reason, drew back.

Although disorders were probably more violent in communities in which firm divisions existed between rich and poor, they were more likely to occur in more cohesive societies and might then involve the quasi-unanimous participation or support of the population. This was an important *facilitating* factor. In relatively homogeneous communities it might easily be assumed by most of the local population that a 'just price' should prevail at a local market place or else that priority should be given to local consumers before transport to other markets became permissible. Often the better-off members of the community would accept this, sharing the moral outlook of their neighbours, aware that their social status depended on their 'reputation and moral standing in the community'.[128] Frequently they were willing to use their own surplus resources as a means of increasing their influence or because they were afraid of reprisals which were difficult to escape in the small community. A farmer called Gallotte, living near Semur (Côte-d'Or), described how in the autumn of 1846 his granary was carefully watched by all his neighbours. He had decided to distribute much of his grain without immediate payment – something he resented but felt he had to do.[129] His individual economic interests were clearly in conflict with the subsistence interests of the community, and this was a major cause of social tension as commercialization increased. Where individuals breached customary patterns of behaviour and rejected warnings, some form of protest was likely to occur and would have appeared to those involved to be fully justified. In the relatively homogeneous community, groups of demonstrators, large or small in size, could take action to enforce their will with little if any opposition from the rest of the population.[130] In a very real sense they were acting as representatives of the general will.

Clearly, there existed a widespread belief in the fundamental right to subsistence. Often this was expressed by means of appeals to the authorities either to enforce recognition of traditional restraints on the profit taking of those with food to sell or at least to provide aid to the poor. A crowd was likely to demand a reduction in prices and, with the experience of 1793 in mind, a legally established maximum.[131] Where a satisfactory response was not forthcoming, the result was sometimes a challenge to the legitimacy of the political system. The fact that many mayors and local councillors were also landowners or farmers interested in maximizing their profits frequently created for them a conflict of interests obvious to the entire community. They belonged to the 'greedy rich'. Thus at Quimperlé (Finistère), following the market of 7 May 1847, the houses of a municipal councillor, the mayor, the *commissaire de police* and other notables were surrounded successively by a crowd estimated at 600, which broke all the windows with a hail of stones.[132] The inactivity of the municipal authorities, while 'rich' farmers and merchants bought and sold the sustenance of the poor – appearing on the market place, according to the *commissaire de police* at Mondoubleau (Loir-et-Cher) in October 1858, for all the world like 'birds of prey'[133] – was likely therefore to be a direct cause of popular action. It is too much to describe the resultant violence as 'coherent political action', but it could fairly be viewed as 'the political tool of powerless people',[134] that is, of people conscious of the limited effectiveness of any action they might wish to take within the bounds of the established political-judicial system and who were able, by means of violence, to express their sense of grievance. It must, however, be stressed that there is a risk here of extending the use of the word 'political' to cover such a variety of circumstances as to render it almost meaningless. It has been used above to describe situations in which people apply pressure on the local authorities, but the crowds whose activities concern us, poor peasants and workers, were in general not politicized in the sense of acting in conscious adherence to a particular ideology, and protest was often compatible with a profound spiritual conformism and cultural traditionalism. It is worth stressing that although crowds registered a protest against the established political authorities and social notables, this was rarely extended to the established social order. Rarely, indeed, could they, except in the vaguest terms, conceive of a possible alternative to it.

Substantial evidence exists to justify an interpretation of popular behaviour in terms of defence of a 'moral economy',[135] of the right to subsistence at a 'just' price. This established expectations about the behaviour of others and also served to justify much of the resentment, and often physical violence, directed at individuals whose activities were judged in relation to the usages and norms of behaviour of the community within which they sought to operate. The individual who deliberately flaunted the traditions of the small community exposed himself to a variety of forms of reprisal. In this way the community was able to protect itself against action and especially innovations which were believed by all or some of its members to be harmful to their interests. The more firmly established the consensus, the greater the likelihood that the transgressor would be morally isolated and punished. In effect, the village or even the urban neighbourhood has to be regarded as 'a unit of moral obligation'[136] for as long that is as isolation (geographical and/or social) sets it apart from the wider society. When communications improve it ceases to be a distinct sphere of perception and information, and the small community gradually acquires alternative points of moral reference. However, an interpretation of crowd action based exclusively upon the notion of 'moral economy' as a mobilizing force would represent an over-simplification. The actions of many participants in disorder, driven by misery and fear and encouraged by the excitement generated by a crowd, were almost instinctive. Although there were many instances of prior organization, protest was frequently a response to the opportunity of the moment, offering relief from pent-up anger. Membership of a crowd led to the loss of a sense of individual responsibility. The course of action to be followed was obvious, the targets of the crowd's anger easily identifiable. The 'moral economy' argument, while representing an important truth and offering a vast improvement upon explanations of popular behaviour solely in terms of spontaneous aggression by hungry mobs, is not sufficient in itself. It is more satisfactory as a means of explaining general phenomena than as a tool for the analysis of the complex realities of particular incidents and individual motivation.

Particular incidents were frequently the product of purely fortuitous circumstances. In certain tense social situations consumers and sellers of foodstuffs interrelated in a manner which might lead from negotiation to threats and even to actual violence. If the potential consumer obtained material or psychological satisfaction at one of the earlier stages in this process – or if the seller was adequately protected by the authorities – violence would be avoided. Otherwise progression to the level of actual violence could occur. This was often an action of last resort on the part of the consumer, the last act in a system of intimidation, but it could represent a hasty response to a particular 'triggering' incident.

Such 'precipitating factors' might take a variety of forms once a situation of unrest and concern – a 'general predisposition to accept violent inspirations'[137] – existed. In the emotive atmosphere of the market place during a period of high prices disorders were easily born. An individual's violent language might excite the crowd. The exaggerated verbal expression of anger or grief was commonplace. Disagreements over prices often broke down into the exchange of gross invective. Invective frequently gave way to threats of violence, abusive gestures and attempts at intimidation. The whole range of inter-personal relationships within a community, about which we know so little, might come into play and either support or restrain protest. The presence of women, desperate to purchase sufficient for their families' needs, hungry themselves and in an intensely emotional state, was particularly frightening to observers.[138]

The expression of grievances could, and usually did, stop short of actual violence. Resigned acceptance of conditions was far more common than protest, although this often concealed the same kinds of social tension.

Whether or not action did occur depended on the particular circumstances of time and place but, more fundamentally, upon psychological, social and cultural factors which determined whether people – the historical actors – felt that it was an appropriate and viable strategy. In some archaic societies petty violence was often a fact of everyday life, and limited displays of aggression were socially sanctioned. Protest action was especially likely to occur where in the past it had resulted in the successful achievement of objectives.[139] Conversely, failure and the experience of military or judicial repression were likely to reduce the propensity to take potentially violent courses of action in the future.[140]

Although the importance of the social preconditions for protest action should be borne in mind, we also need to examine the causes of *particular* incidents. These are logically and practically distinct from a generalized potential for violence.

Disorder in the market place

The first prerequisite for disorder was obviously a gathering of people, and the primary role of a market was precisely that of bringing people together at regular intervals to conduct transactions. Of equal importance for us was its secondary role. People came to market to make purchases or sell goods but also to meet friends and acquaintances and also probably out of sheer curiosity, especially when prices were high and popular agitation intense. The potential size of the crowd must obviously have depended upon the economic importance of the market and the size of the population of the area it served. Present at the market would be not only the inhabitants of the town or village which sheltered it but also people from the surrounding countryside. The holding of a market provided a perfect occasion for the expression of dissatisfaction by people who could see both shortage and high prices around them and who were already gathered in a group within a limited space and were thus psychologically and physically relatively easy to mobilize. According to the military commander in the Indre, the result during a period of dearth was 'tumult' on each market day.[141] People in the crowd complained about prices they could ill afford or about the inadequacy of supplies. Women cried, and as the day proceeded, if prices continued to rise or failed to fall, tempers became more and more frayed. Hunger probably contributed to this. The afternoon was more likely to bring disorder than the morning.[142] From complaints people moved towards apportioning blame for their misery. Antoine Ceremaud, a plasterer arrested at Arbois (Jura) on 1 August 1856 after accusing sellers of wanting to starve the people, asserted that although the terms he had used might be reprehensible in the eyes of the law, in his heart he believed himself to be innocent.[143] We return again to this moral conception of commerce, in complete contradiction to the urge to maximize profits. It was such a feeling, combined with anger, which could lead individuals to tell their neighbours in the crowd that revolt was necessary,[144] to shout that prices must be reduced[145] or even suddenly to assault merchants physically.[146]

Words of anger or individual action led all too easily to riots. When at Chinon a woman called Sorneau, holding in her hand a crust of black bread, shouted to those around her, 'It's a month since I've had bread like this' and demanded wheat at 2 francs for one-eighth of a hectolitre, she contributed to the mounting anger,[147] as did the woman at Ry (Seine-Inférieure) on 13 March 1847 who complained that her children were starving to death.[148] Whatever the intentions of the speaker, there was always a potential for violence in such words and gestures, given the initial attitudes and hostilities of members of the crowd.

Bravado on the part of merchants might have a similar mobilizing effect, whether this bravado took the form of too obvious pleasure at the high prices obtained for the commodity on sale[149] or simply of greed, as in the case of the merchant at Bourges (Cher) on 16 January 1847 who bought at one end of the market hall for 4.50 francs a double decalitre and then sought to sell at 8 francs at the other end,[150] or the merchant at Trie (Hautes-Pyrénées) on 16 March 1847 who, seeing that supplies were exhausted, quickly brought more wheat to the market place and tried to sell it at 4 francs per hectolitre above the previously quoted price.[151] He was chased away by a crowd yelling that it wanted to tear him into little pieces. There was also the possibility of merchants responding in kind to bad-tempered customers and openly expressing contempt for the poor and their misery.[152]

As well as reacting to the words and actions of sellers, the crowd might also react to the civil authorities or police. Both inaction or over-energetic efforts at crowd control could have the same result, namely, disorder. Action was often difficult. The *procureur-général* at Bourges complained in 1854: 'In the markets of our small localities, to which flow the rural population, where the few representatives of authority lose themselves in the midst of the crowd, which gains a real sentiment of its power when repression is only a distant eventuality . . . there is an irresistible temptation to fail to recognize the respect due to property and to satisfy one's needs.'[153] The physical disposition of the market place could contribute to the creation of such a situation. Thus at Cluny (Saône-et-Loire), where the market was held in the cloisters of the former abbey, the gendarmes on duty on 30 January 1847 were unable to penetrate a compact mass of 3000–4000 people enforcing what it thought to be a reasonable price on sellers.[154] Action might have unwanted consequences. At Boulogne-sur-Gesse (Haute-Garonne) on 17 March 1847, in an effort to calm the crowd, the authorities felt obliged to arrest suspected *accapareurs* and attempted to persuade sellers to moderate their demands, but these actions were taken by members of the crowd to be confirmation of their own suspicions and served only to encourage further disorder.[155] Even action to prevent disorder by arresting troublemakers or to limit it by dispersing an agitated crowd could, at least initially, serve to intensify disorder through attempts to secure the release of those arrested or acts of self-defence against sabre-waving gendarmerie or troops, as at Châteauroux (Indre) in November 1846.[156]

The basic cause of disorder was fear, and the most obvious cause of fear was the real or apparent state of food supplies. When a market was badly provisioned after a poor harvest this usually led to a rush to purchase before supplies ran out, which, as we have seen, accelerated the rise in prices. Such behaviour was indicative of popular anxiety and served to intensify this, often, in the short term, to the level of hysteria. On a market place at Villaine-la-Juhel (Mayenne) in early November 1846 members of a crowd, finding the market less well provisioned than usual and already frightened by price increases at neighbouring markets, started asking, 'If grain is already at such a high price, how will we manage this winter? We'll die of hunger'.[157] The prospect of a long winter, high prices and frequently seasonal unemployment must have been a daunting one.

A sustained increase in prices, reflecting inadequate supply at a particular market place over a more or less lengthy period, heightened anxiety. At Bourges (Cher) by mid January 1847 supply was about one-third of normal levels, and a hectolitre of wheat cost as much as 40.50 francs.[158] Sudden and unexpected rises could stimulate similar fears.[159] Prices which were higher than consumers could afford were, if anything, more intolerable than the complete absence of supplies. The food was there, visible and yet unattainable. Thus people frequently left the market without being able to purchase basic necessities, returning home, as they did from the market held at Chartres (Eure-et-Loir) on the first Saturday of March 1847, 'desolate, sacks empty, unable to procure for themselves even with money in hand, the provisions which are necessary for them'. Prices on that Saturday were double their normal level.[160]

How infuriating it must have been in this kind of situation to see those with foodstuffs to sell raise their prices to levels beyond the reach of the poor consumer, to watch the grossest profiteering, to be forced to pay extortionate prices because markets were badly provisioned and one's family was hungry, to see quantities of grain left unsold because consumers were unable to pay the prices asked and merchants reloading their carts to take food away from those who desperately needed it. Such behaviour must have seemed inhuman. Such willingness to speculate on the misery and desperation of one's fellows was intolerable. Everywhere there was a 'normal' price for basic commodities, the price prevailing after an 'average' harvest. To sell at such a price did not result in excessive profits and was therefore 'just'. As one *gendarmerie* commander observed: 'There is no doubt that not one peasant, even landowners possessing four, ten, twenty or thirty thousand francs and more of goods, was not persuaded that one should force those with wheat to sell it at 16 francs per hectolitre'.[161] Indeed, in this particular area of the centre-west the demand for wheat at 2 francs per eighth of a hectolitre, or 15–16 francs per hectolitre, was frequently repeated.

Popular feeling was made evident in a variety of ways. In the first place, as we have seen already, the traditional device of the *placard* could be used to express discontent. These written threats were combined with verbal menaces, sometimes translated into violent action, as in a case at Bélâbre (Indre) in 1847, when physical intimidation was believed to have resulted in the murder of a grain merchant.[162] Such extreme action was very rare, but in many places from an atmosphere charged with emotion there emerged a variety of often horrendous threats intended to frighten those with food into selling it at what was judged to be a reasonable price.

If he ignored these threats, the farmer or merchant still had to brave the crowd at the market place. In periods of high prices crowds tended to gather in the market places and around the market halls. The authorities would be unable to determine initially whether they were there to make purchases or to intimidate sellers. In many cases, no doubt, those in the crowd had no clear objectives, but crowds like the 400 at Elbeuf (Seine-Inférieure) on 13 February 1847 or the several hundreds at Le Mans (Sarthe) on 21 March, complaining about their misery and blaming the prices asked by sellers, were hardly reassuring.[163] Prospective purchasers haggled over prices with sellers, and animated negotiation was all too likely to lead to threats on the part of the dissatisfied purchaser, as at Châteauroux (Indre) in November 1846, where at successive markets women abused sellers, protected by silent groups of their menfolk standing in the background.[164]

At Bray-sur-Seine (Seine-et-Marne) on 19 February 1847 negotiations over a price began, typically, with a woman asking how much a farmer wanted for a sack containing 1.5 hectolitres of mixed wheat and rye. He told her 45 francs. She lost her temper and began to insult him, and was soon joined by about thirty other women. Under this pressure the farmer took flight, leaving his wife to guard his grain until she also concluded that discretion might be the better part of valour.[165] The presence at some markets – for example, at Gacé on 22 March and Laigle (Orne) on 13 April 1847 – of groups of workers armed with large sticks[166] contributed quite forcefully to the moral pressure exerted by the crowd on sellers. Furthermore, the threat of violence was often realized. Haggling between two individuals frequently turned into a fist fight, in which one participant had the obvious support of the crowd.[167] In periods of high prices the market place became an arena of bitterness and barely repressed violence.

The clear hostility of purchasers was frequently sufficient to persuade sellers that they ought to reduce their prices, as at Laval (Mayenne) on 9 January 1847, when each merchant found himself surrounded by at least a dozen furious men and women.[168] At Chinon (Indre-et-Loire) on 26 November 1846 the market had barely opened when 'a thousand voices demanded grain at 2 francs per *huitième*' (i.e. 16 francs per hectolitre), and in the same week at nearby Azay-le-Rideau wheat estimated to be worth 27–8 francs per hectolitre was sold at the same figure of 16 francs.[169]

Such a reduction often appeared to merchants to be the obvious means of self-preservation. Even the presence of *gendarmes* and police was sometimes insufficient to establish an atmosphere of security in which transactions could freely take place.[170] They might be free in appearance, but intimidation and the threat of subsequent reprisals often had an effect.[171] In the face of a furious crowd many merchants seem to have decided to adopt the path of least resistance and accept whatever price they could get. Langeron, a miller, described how at a market at Chinon (Indre-et-Loire) towards the end of November 1846 he initially resisted intimidation but, after physically struggling with at least one purchaser to prevent him from simply taking away grain and paying whatever price he thought adequate, he became increasingly tired and frightened and just gave in.[172] Proclamations like that of the Prefect of Indre in January 1847, declaring null and void all agreements entered into under pressure, could do little in practice to change this.[173]

Once one seller had given in to pressure, it was difficult for others to hold out. A concession appeared both to confirm the crowd's belief that initial prices were unfair and to encourage further intimidation. At Revel (Haute-Garonne) on 20 March 1847 maize sold at 20 francs per hectolitre until crowd pressure forced one seller to sell at 18 francs. Other sellers realized that they had no alternative but to come down to this level. At this point pressure began to be exerted to force them to reduce their prices to 16 francs, and this too was soon conceded, first by one and then by the remainder. The crowd was estimated at 1200, and the ten *gendarmes* present had been incapable of controlling events.[174] Similar situations could evolve from the generous act of a wealthy seller prepared to part with his grain at a relatively low price in order to alleviate popular misery. Such action could lead to the establishment of a maximum price and its subsequent imposition upon all other sellers.[175]

In many places intimidation and its effects upon prices were but the first steps in a spiral of action within the market place intended to assure the supply of foodstuffs at 'fair' prices. Where sellers were determined to resist intimidation it was always likely (particularly in the west and centre) that elements of the crowd would seize the grain it wanted and pay what it believed to be a 'reasonable' price.

Although in such cases the crowd often evinced its respect for legal forms by actually paying for the grain taken, if only what it collectively thought the purchase to be worth, it is evident that this behaviour was illegal, whatever the poor and their sympathizers might have felt about their moral right to sustenance. It caused severe financial losses to sellers, both rich and poor. Thus at Quelaines (Mayenne) on 13 January 1847 wheat worth 40 francs per hectolitre at current market prices was sold at only half that price.[176] Even so, enforced sale must have seemed preferable to pillage without any payment for this is what agitation and intimidation might, in certain circumstances, turn into. At Lencloître (Vienne) on 4 January 1847, after a quiet morning, at 2 p.m. a large crowd suddenly entered the market place and began to threaten merchants. These, on the advice of the mayor, reduced their prices by 50 centimes per hectolitre to 24.50 francs, a not exceptionally high price, but this was not enough to satisfy the crowd. The mayor and the five *gendarmes* present rapidly lost control of the situation. Women, protected and encouraged by the men in the crowd, began to demand grain for nothing, and at this point a riot began. Sacks were ripped open with knives; those who offered opposition were beaten up with fists and sticks; and much of the grain was lost, trampled into the ground under the feet of the angry crowd. Only twelve National Guards dared to put in an appearance, and they were rapidly disarmed and their guns smashed. By 5 p.m. all the grain at the market had been pillaged. At that moment a cart was seen to be approaching the town. People left the market place and looted that too, then returned and forced the local bakers to sell their bread at 15 centimes per kilogram. After this the riot ended of its own accord. It was estimated that there had been around 2000 participants.[177]

Similarly, at Laval (Mayenne), on the 9th of the same month, a crowd of coalminers from outside the town, together with the local poor, invaded the market in a compact mass and pillaged the grain on display there and then the granaries of a local merchant.[178] Such disturbances were obviously most likely at market places which attracted large numbers of people. There, agitation, excitement and a sense of the power and security of the crowd were most likely to develop. Observers almost inevitably commented on the important role of the women. Moved by the needs of their families, they contributed significantly to the emotive atmosphere of many market places and were often the first to resort to violence.[179]

In addition to market disorders caused essentially by discontent over price levels, there were those due to the presence at a particular place of outsiders who intended to purchase foodstuffs and remove them to another place. The sheer presence of outsiders was enough to arouse suspicion and hostility, which was magnified by such acts as that of a young miller from Tabas (Haute-Garonne), who at L'Isle-en-Dodon in March 1847 offered 20 francs per hectolitre for grain when the prevailing market price was only 18 francs. This was immediately suspected to be a deliberate attempt to corner supplies.[180] The situation was likely to become particularly tense when strangers were seen to be loading their carts in preparation for departure.[181]

Failure on the part of outside purchasers to respond to warnings and threats frequently led to attempts by a crowd to impose its will through violent action directed against either individuals or their property. At Montsûrs (Mayenne) on 12 January 1847 a crowd threw a visiting merchant's cart into the river.[182] On 14 January 1847 two individuals from a neighbouring commune, arriving at the market of Saux (Lot), were greeted with a hail of stones and chased away by women shouting, 'Kill them!'.[183] A reputation as an *accapareur*, whether deserved or not, immediately put a merchant into a dangerous position. At St-Pois (Manche) on 4 March 1847 a group of people awaited the arrival of a miller from Vire who for the past two weeks had been buying up large quantities of grain in the neighbourhood. The miller failed to arrive, but another stranger appeared, so they beat him up instead.[184]

Thus far we have considered disorders which were essentially spontaneous in character. Some market-place riots were, however, concerted in advance. This was most likely to occur when an example had already been set. In November 1846 trouble at Chinon was clearly stimulated by previous disorders at Azay-le-Rideau, just as at Azay they had imitated events at Châteaurenault. Individuals arrived at Chinon with the news and a clear intention of intimidating sellers.[185] Prior consultation was especially obvious in cases where groups came to market armed with sticks. Their aim might be intimidation, but clearly they were prepared to go beyond this to physical violence. This was the case at Dieppe (Seine-Inférieure) on 30 November, when about sixty workers employed in constructing the port arrived at the market with obviously 'bad intentions'.[186] In such cases individual workers would not want to appear to be cowards or oppose the apparent unanimity of their comrades. When they did they could be brought into line by scorn or threats.[187]

The official response to the appearance of such groups was unambiguous. They were dispersed, if necessary by force, and as rapidly as possible. The authorities were all too easily ready to believe that disorders were 'the result of a movement of communists'[188] or whichever political opposition caused concern in a region. Strangers, sinister figures, whose dress and linguistic facility proved that they were from a class different from that of the mass of protesters whom they sought to lead astray, were often claimed to have been present, encouraging disorder for political ends.[189] Any appearance of prior organization tended to be seen as confirmation of the existence of a plot. Political animals themselves, unable to accept the criticism of the existing social order which popular protest against misery implied, conservatives found it easier to explain disorders in terms of the machinations of evil men who sought to lead astray the otherwise peaceful and obedient populace. An alternative view, equally self-excusatory, seems to have been based on an image of the poor as ignorant and brutalized, ready to use high prices as a pretext for revolt, looting and murder.[190]

In practice, where prior organization existed it seems to have been rudimentary in character. On occasion, by means of *placards* or word of mouth, someone took an initiative and arranged a *rendez-vous*. News of this was easily spread orally through family, neighbourhood and work relationships.[191] If those with personal authority in these groups lent support to action, then a crowd was likely to gather at the appointed time, although it is unlikely that all those present had clearly thought out their objectives or shared the same intentions.[192]

The lists of those arrested during or following market disorders provide us with a limited amount of information about crowd composition but do not necessarily supply a representative picture of the crowd as a whole. Police reports make it obvious that they arrested individuals believed to be 'leaders' and that at least one group – the women who played such a significant role in all the subsistence disorders – was substantially under-represented. After disturbances at Bléré in November 1846 those brought before the assizes of Indre-et-Loire were: one labourer, one vine cultivator, one farmer, two masons, one carpenter, one butcher and four women, including two laundresses, one labourer and the butcher's wife.[193] After a riot at Tours on 21 November 1846 those brought to trial were four day labourers, one vine cultivator, one gardener, two weavers, two stonecutters, one plasterer, one carpenter, three cabinetmakers, one locksmith, one painter, one old-clothes dealer, one baker and two inn keepers.[194] (In these and most other cases I have recorded those brought to trial represented almost a cross-section of the poorer inhabitants of market towns and villages.)

The place of residence of those who were at market would obviously depend upon the size of the area it served. Propensity to participate in disorders would vary according to the particular circumstances both of social groups living within the market towns and of those from the total area served. The *procureur-général* at Toulouse maintained that the rural poor were unlikely to be involved because they either had plots of land on which to grow their own food or else benefited from the custom of payment in kind.[195] In the Limousin also disorders were expected to involve urban rather than rural populations, because subdivision of the soil allowed much of the rural population to provide for its own subsistence. The *procureur-général* at Limoges contrasted this kind of situation with that prevailing in areas of Maine-et-Loire and Indre, where disorders had occurred and where relatively large-scale cereal cultivation rendered much of the rural population (which owned little or no land) dependent upon purchases in the market.[196]

The problem of maintaining order was especially difficult when a union between urban malcontents and those from the countryside was likely and the number of protesters was multiplied. At Ste-Maure (Indre-et-Loire) on 27 November 1846 a group of some forty workers from the town began a disturbance and were subsequently supported by an estimated 300 peasants.[197] Particularly serious was the arrival of a compact mass of people from a neighbouring commune, especially when, by a prior agreement, they came armed with sticks and stones. The more compact and united the incoming group, the more trouble it was likely to cause. Especially feared was the arrival of groups of forestry workers (woodcutters, charcoal burners and *sabot* makers) or of miners or quarry workers from outlying areas. Thus at St-Amand (Cher) on 12 January 1847 trouble was caused by miners and woodcutters from the communes of St-Baudel and Vittecelin.[198] In the Angers region the main threat to order was believed to come from the communities of quarry workers.[199] In 1847 a new threat became apparent in the shape of workers employed on railway construction.[200]

What all these occupational groups had in common was the fact that they lived in isolated communities with a developed sense of unity, had a deserved reputation for violence and were especially badly affected by crisis. It was such groups that were most likely to arrive *en masse* at a particular market. The community of interest among workers in towns dominated by particular professions, as in the case of textile workers in some towns in Calvados like Lisieux, could have similar results.[201]

Although market place crowds often succeeded in their immediate objective of securing a reduction in grain prices, in the longer term the effect of their actions was likely for some time to result in a reduction of supplies to a given market place, as merchants and farmers were frightened away. At Tours (Indre-et-Loire) on 5 December 1846 there were only 140 hectolitres of grain for sale compared with the normal 500–600 hectolitres at that time of year.[202] Relative shortages at a particular market, whatever its causes, had the obvious effect of stimulating increases in the price of grain in the market place or at the farm, and this in its turn had an effect on the price of bread. Numerically less significant than protests in the market place, those concerned with bread prices were likely to be more serious, mainly because they often occurred in major urban centres and involved large crowds.

Disorders provoked by the price of bread

Whether or not such disturbances would occur must obviously have depended on the extent to which populations had recourse to bakers. In most rural areas and in small towns much of the population bought grain and either prepared its own bread or supplied flour to a local baker. Substitutes like porridge or chestnuts also reduced dependence on bakers. However, the larger the urban settlement and the greater the degree of dependence upon industrial or commercial employment rather than on agriculture, the more likely was recourse to the baker for bread, the basic component of diet.

Relationships between bakers and their poorer clients were influenced to a substantial degree by the ability and willingness of the former to grant credit, both between one pay day and the next and during periods of hardship. Over-generous extension of credit could reduce a baker to bank-ruptcy, but credit was a useful means of maintaining a dependent clientele.[203] A sure sign of the severity of a crisis was the baker's decision that he could not afford to accord further credit. This and his demands for repayment must in many cases have embittered relations with his customers.

When the price of bread was high, credit unavailable and wages at best stagnant, and when informal approaches to bakers had failed, the obvious recourse for those in difficulty was an appeal to the local administration, which established the legal price of bread. Not unnaturally, given that the administration was responsible in this matter, there was always considerable popular feeling that mayors could and should act to reduce prices or at least to prevent further increases.[204] Usually a humble request was made, as at Pierrefonds (Oise) on 1 March 1847, where after work about 200 forestry workers gathered in front of the mayor's house. Three delegates were invited to enter and asked the mayor to fix the price of bread at 1.50 francs per 5 kilograms. On being told that he could do nothing to help them, the crowd quietly dispersed.[205]

Normally mayors refused to act on the grounds that the law obliged them to relate bread prices to the *mercuriales*. On hearing this, crowds usually dispersed and accepted their situation with resignation, but on occasion municipal inaction generated protest.[206] A particularly difficult moment for local officials came when increases in the price of bread had to be announced. On 13 May 1847, at the request of the Paris Prefect of Police, the military commander there ordered the special patrols mounted on 29 April when price increases had previously been announced to be repeated.[207] Descriptions of agitated crowds gathering in front of bakers' shops as new price levels came into force makes the reason for such precautions obvious.

The official bread price (*taxe du pain*) existed both as a means of prevent-ing excessive price increases, which might cause disorder, and to protect bakers from popular hostility by absolving them from responsibility for increases. For bakers there was the obvious disadvantage that these two aims were often in practice contradictory in the sense that mayors were frequently tempted to limit price increases and to minimize popular dis-content while forcing bakers to sell their bread at unremunerative prices.

After disorders at Nancy in June 1846 over an increase in the price of bread to 2.80 francs per 8 kilograms the Prefect of the Meurthe observed that the price should have been 3.10 francs if the bakers were to avoid losses.[208] The latter were so frequently placed in an unenviable situation that the Ministry of Agriculture was obliged to remind mayors in 1853 that they should not be compelled to sell at a loss.[209]

The bakers' lot in such a situation was generally not a very happy one, although it is not really possible to judge precisely how genuine their grievances were. They might, for example, have obtained grain or flour from alternative sources at lower prices than those prevailing at the local market and on the basis of which the *mercuriales* and *taxe du pain* were established.[210] But the volume of their complaints was such, and the action taken by many bakers when their complaints were ignored invited such severe administrative and popular reprisals, that it is probably safe to assume that most of the complainants were in severe financial difficulty, even if the tenor 'of their complaints was likely to be exaggerated.

One response of bakers to inadequate bread prices was a local agreement to threaten to cease baking. This, however, intensified popular fears about the security of food supply and increased hostility towards the bakers. At Cognac (Charente) in August 1854, when bakers refused to work, a crowd of around 1200 workers gathered and threatened to throw them into the river. The municipality fined two bakers and the other seventeen immediately agreed to resume baking, although they protested that this would mean financial loss.[211] The usual punishment for any concerted delay in baking seems to have been a small fine, provided the bakers involved heeded the warnings they received and recommenced work immediately.[212] Potentially more damaging for them and effective in ending their inactivity were threats of permanent closure,[213] of large fines[214] or of seizure of their stocks and premises and their use by municipal agents.[215] Although this kind of behaviour by bakers clearly damaged relationships with their clientele, it only rarely led to disorder because of rapid administrative action.

A far more common means employed by bakers in an effort to avoid financial loss was fraud. This took various forms but involved particularly the mixing into their flour of various varieties of relatively cheap vegetables.[216] Quite naturally, such frauds were most likely to be committed when the price of wheat and flour rose, at precisely that moment, in fact, when in order to reduce popular anxiety, and in the knowledge that such cheating was increasing, the public authorities sought rigorously to enforce various regulations and obligations imposed on bakers.[217] Even in rural communes, where continuous and frequent surveillance was hardly possible, numerous cases of fraud were detected,[218] while in urban centres more determined policing sometimes had quite startling effects. At Poitiers in the week ending 5 September 1853 fourteen bakers were condemned for the sale of bread below its proper weight and six for cheating on its content.[219] In the Dôle region of the Jura in 1854 large-scale fraud involving a miller and bakers was detected following cases of food poisoning. Chemical analysis revealed that the 'wheat' bread was in fact made from the flour of wheat, rye and oats, plus a mixture of plaster and alum to preserve its whiteness.[220] At Montpellier in April 1847 police, suspecting addition of haricots to flour, examined the accounts of all the city's bakers in order to determine who had purchased such adulterated flour. Payment of an excessively low price by a baker for what was supposed to be wheat flour was taken to reveal conspiracy with flour merchants.[221] The sudden change from a relatively tolerant attitude on the part of the authorities was bitterly resented by bakers, who often, as at Strasbourg, had tended to regard such tolerance as a right.[222] Moreover, as one former Parisian baker complained, when a shop was busy during the early part of the morning it was impossible to check the weight of every loaf. He had left baking because of the small profits it offered and the constant threat of being brought to court on charges of cheating on weight.[223]

There is no doubt that such incidents and also cases in which bakers engaging in the grain trade were convicted of fraudulent and speculative practices in the market places, appeared to confirm the worst public fears about bakers. At Lorient (Morbihan) in May 1847 the bread weighed too little, looked different and had a strange taste.[224] It seemed that bakers, in combination with speculators of all kinds, were determined to starve, and even poison the poor. In such situations popular hostility towards the bakers became intense.

At Nancy on 20 June 1847 crowds gathered in front of two bakers' premises in the *faubourg* St-Pierre. In anticipation of an expected price rise the following day, these bakers were believed to have hidden their bread and to be refusing to provide supplies to their normal clientele.[225] As was usually the case, the crowd did not proceed beyond threats. Such incidents were most common fairly late in a period of crisis, when bakers had already endured a long period of pressure on profit margins. They were not normally allowed to develop because local authorities acted rapidly in response to popular disquiet. Bakers restricting supplies were quite clearly threatening public order and acting in breach of a variety of ordinances and laws regulating their trade.[226] This was a battle the crowd could always be certain of winning.

In other cases, however, popular anger was not as easily assuaged. At Troyes (Aube) on 7 August 1847 a baker made a false declaration at the market hall – claiming to have paid more for grain that he had purchased than in fact he had – with the object of causing a rise in the *mercuriale* and the *taxe du pain*. This led to a short-lived disorder at the market, but when night fell a crowd gathered in front of his shop and smashed the windows. This crowd had to be dispersed by the military. On the 8th popular feeling remained inflamed. Troops and National Guardsmen stood-to from first light and were insulted and had stones thrown at them. Another baker had his windows smashed by members of a crowd of 200–300 people and had to distribute 400 kilograms of bread to the crowd before troops arrived. Then its members tried to attack a mill just outside the town, from which they were diverted by force. The rest of that day, however, crowds continued to form and had to be dispersed repeatedly.[227]

Bakers who engaged in the trade in grain and flour were likely to share in the general suspicion and fear of *accapareurs*. At Lisieux (Calvados) on 31 July 1847 a crowd variously estimated at 2000–3000, composed mainly of textile workers, many of whom were unemployed and in a state of extreme misery, pillaged the homes and premises of a baker and miller accused of 'illicit' speculation. It was subsequently claimed that fifty sacks of wheat and flour and 700 francs in cash had been stolen, as well as furnishings smashed. The fifty-eight people arrested included ten male and five female day labourers, seven female textile spinners, three dressmakers, two male textile workers, ten assorted artisans, five building workers, one bakery worker, two domestics and two beggars[228] – again a cross-section of urban misery.

The baker, in periods of crisis, was clearly not a popular person. He obviously needed to choose his words carefully to avoid giving the impression that he lacked sympathy for the suffering of the poor. If the contrary appeared to be the case, then at the very least he could expect to have insults shouted after him in the streets or his windows smashed at night.[229] In time of high prices it might – as at Douai (Nord) in May 1847 – become necessary to place an armed guard at the door of every baker,[230] while the premises needed to acquire some of the attributes of a fortress, with strong shutters and iron bars, to provide some security against the inroads of an angry crowd.[231]

Protests directed against bakers should be regarded as in many respects similar to the market-place riot, in that they occurred in towns and represented in the main a popular attempt to exert some control over prices. It was a matter of some significance, however, that this particular form of protest was likely to occur in the larger urban centres, in which the mass of consumers were already divorced from the market place as a source of supply for grain and purchased bread directly from bakers' shops. Just as the market place disorder was the typical form of protest in small country towns during a period of subsistence crisis, so the demonstration over the price of bread was typical of the large urban-industrial centre.

Of greatest concern to the central government was the possibility of disorder in Paris. A considerable effort was made to maintain bread prices there at comparatively low levels and with results which appeared to justify the expense. The only significant disorders recorded during the mid century crisis, the pillaging of bakers' shops, occurred in the working-class area of the *faubourg* St-Antoine in late September and early October 1846 and in May and June 1847. The last two affairs were insignificant and need not concern us. The first, beginning in the evening of 30 September, was more serious. During the 2–3 p.m. lunch break on that day, because of rumours that the price of bread was to be increased by 3 centimes per kilogram, many workers bought enough to last two or three days, with the result that others, going to the bakeries in the evening after work, found that many had sold out and that one had closed. Rioting actually began at this last shop when a crowd smashed the windows and tried to break down the door. Subsequently growing crowds rampaged through the streets, smashing windows and gas lights, and throwing stones at troops called out to control them. Similar incidents occurred on 3 October, this time spreading into the *quartier* St-Martin, and again on the 4th, and led to a large number of arrests. The professions of those brought to trial confirm that both the artisans and unskilled labourers of the city were experiencing some difficulty in making ends meet. Accused were three small traders, one inn keeper, one pedlar, one carpenter, eight cabinetmakers, one sawyer, one sculptor, one jewellery worker, one silversmith, one tinsmith, one mechanic, one worker in crystal, two shoemakers, one printing worker, one tapestry worker, four wallpaper printing workers, two textile workers, one carter, two shop boys and seven labourers. No women were brought to trial, which suggests that these riots represented primarily an expression of irritation with the general situation. The relative youthfulness of many of those arrested tends to confirm this (six were under 15, thirteen aged 15–20, three aged 20–5, nine aged 25–30, six aged 30–5, four aged 35–40), as does the commonly expressed excuse of drunkenness. The combination of food subsidies, charity and military patrols entirely prevented or limited the extension of subsequent disturbances.[232]

Far more serious disorders occurred at Lille in May 1847 and at Mulhouse in June. The first appears to have been caused by rumours of large-scale dismissals of workers following two markets, on 5 and 12 May, which were badly provisioned. On 12 May groups of hungry women and children gathered in the streets of the working-class quarter of St-Sauveur, to be joined around 7 p.m. by workers leaving the factories. An increasingly excited crowd began to demand 'bread at 5 *sols*'. One of the most excited members of these groups, a 24-year-old textile worker called Alexandre Delapaul, was reported to have been waving a red flag on the end of a stick to attract attention and to have loudly encouraged those around him to smash the windows of bakers' shops, break in and take whatever bread they could find. He subsequently admitted to having thrown perhaps a hundred stones at shutters and windows and to having climbed inside one shop and thrown out bread to the waiting crowd. This man had previously been sentenced to three months imprisonment for vagabondage and could expect little sympathy from the court. Indeed attention was drawn by the *commissaire central de police* to the 'hideous features' and ragged clothes which he used to attract sympathy and charity in order to avoid work.[233] He was in all likelihood a man with few inhibitions and, as such, quite likely to give a lead to an already excited crowd.

From their own quarter groups of 'young men and workers' ran through the town, smashing windows and street lights, pillaging bakers' shops, singing the 'Marseillaise' and throwing stones at National Guards and troops. In all, eighty-four bakers' shops were attacked. The authorities were especially struck by the unusual silence of the rampaging crowd. Often the first warning of trouble at a particular point was the sound of breaking glass. The large proportion of youths, aged around 10–16, was also striking, although in retrospect it should have been expected in a situation in which mobile groups were engaged in violent conflict with the guardians of order. At any rate, it took until midnight for the military to restore order.

On the following two days crowds again formed around 5 p.m., in spite of numerous patrols. They were able to profit from their superior knowledge of the streets and lanes of Lille to avoid contact. Stones were thrown once again at shop windows, but this time only three bakers were pillaged. The disturbances were far less serious and seem to have declined of their own volition.[234]

At Mulhouse trouble began on 26 June 1847. At 10 a.m. the mayor was surrounded on the square in front of the town hall by a crowd of 400–500 workers and their wives, who asked him to reduce the price of bread. He told them that before he would consider this they must disperse and then send delegates to see him. The crowd did disperse, but simultaneously in nearby streets the pillaging of bakers' premises began, and soon an estimated 3000 people were engaged in looting wine merchants and grocery shops as well. Troops were called to disperse the rioters but with little effect. Eventually the warnings stipulated by law were given to the stone-throwing crowd and the troops opened fire, killing four people outright and leaving four more to die subsequently of their wounds. Two hundred were arrested. By 8 p.m. the streets had been cleared. On 19 July, when a demonstration about the price of bread again occurred, it took only the appearance of the police to disperse the crowd.[235]

During the same week, on 19 June, potentially serious disturbances occurred in nearby Thann when workers met in the evening to demand a reduction in the price of bread. The mayor promised concessions and the crowd dispersed, smashing bakers' windows as it did. The authorities believed that more serious matters were planned for the following day, but large and obvious troop reinforcements probably served as an effective deterrent.[236] Again in the east, at Nancy on 20, 21 and 22 June, disorders took place in protest against the price of bread. Stones were thrown and, it was claimed, shots fired at a patrol of the 39th Infantry Regiment, which returned fire, killing one man and wounding several others.[237]

Disorders along the roads and waterways

Urban riots caused by the price of bread were in practice comparatively rare, although, as we have seen, they could be extremely serious. By far the most common forms of disorder in periods of high prices were the attempts to interfere with the free commercial circulation of foodstuffs. Such action reflected the popular fear that a particular area was being denuded of its food supplies and the conviction, which communities had traditionally sought to have respected, that local people had first right to locally grown food. Price increases were taken to be warnings of the danger of shortage and signs of the activities of speculators. The unexpected or increased presence of merchants in an area or at a market place always caused concern, and often with reason, as when at a market held at Chartres (Eure-et-Loir) on 8 March 1847 commercial millers bought up almost all the grain on sale, leaving insufficient for the needs of the local poor, even when they had enough money.[238] This situation often led to action contrary to the freedom of trade, to the interests of merchants and to their legal rights. In August 1846 women at Château-Chinon (Nièvre) rioted in protest. They had suffered from a poor harvest in 1845 and had hoped for a better life after that of 1846. Now this hope was being destroyed by the activities of the merchants.[239] Often when prices were high the widespread fear and belief that merchants were buying standing crops caused acute anxiety about the future, which intensified the psychological misery of the present.[240] Even where serious disorders were comparatively rare (in the Manche, for example) there was considerable hostility towards outside merchants buying up stocks and all those who sold to them.[241]

Commercial movements obviously tended to take place from areas with relatively low prices towards those with higher prices. The problem of convincing those who suffered from the consequent price increases that commerce which evened out supply and price variation was a good thing vexed the colonel commanding the 13th Legion of *gendarmerie* at Marseille in 1847.[242] There, as elsewhere, when carts went by 'the population, accessible to fear, due to its ignorance, and alarmed by the always increasing price of foodstuffs and their rarity' was too often tempted to stop them.[243] Each locality wished to hold on to whatever reserves it had. Official attempts to reassure people had little effect.

The rise in prices, the increase in activity of merchants purchasing local supplies and the growing intensity of long-distance traffic on the roads, all of them natural consequences of regional or national harvest failure, thus caused intense anxiety among the mass of consumers. Even where the normal volume of purchases by outside merchants was maintained, when this was from a smaller than usual stock purchasers who had previously been welcomed were now likely to meet with hostility. There was obviously less to share out.[244] In areas like Brittany, in which wheat was habitually grown for sale and rye, buckwheat and potatoes for local consumption, the export of wheat might be tolerated by popular opinion, but where merchants who were unable to purchase the richer cereal in sufficient quantity turned instead to the staples of popular diet, this caused agitation and often resistance.[245]

Popular reactions might be influenced by hunger or simply by the fear of hunger. At such times normally placid populations were likely to behave, according to one eye-witness, like 'furious beasts'.[246] Panic and hysteria spread quickly through the countryside, fed by the experience of poorly provisioned markets, high prices and rumours. The 'exultation' of the women is constantly stressed in reports. From the *arrondissement* of Beaupréau (Maine-et-Loire) in autumn 1846 it was reported that 'they are the first to make threats, the first to attack. In many localities they take guard on the roads throughout the night' to prevent carts leaving the area.[247]

Attempts to interfere with the circulation of foodstuffs were intended either to prevent the departure of carts carrying locally produced foodstuffs or else to halt carts passing through the town or village that were carrying food produced somewhere else to a more distant market. The majority of disturbances were caused by the first factor, but the second meant in effect that wherever prices were high and people were miserable there was the possibility of a disturbance. Figure 5 clearly indicates that action intended to obstruct the movement of foodstuffs was far more likely to occur in some regions than in others.

While it is possible to agree with Charles Tilly that such disturbances were most likely to occur either in 'an arc to the south and west of Paris', or in 'a series of smaller arcs around the Atlantic ports', it is not possible to accept his further contention that in 1846–7 rioting occurred largely in the first area. It appears from Figure 5 that a significant number of disturbances occurred in departments supplying the Atlantic ports, such as the Dordogne, Vendée, Haute-Vienne, Vienne, Maine-et-Loire, Deux-Sèvres, and also in those affected by demands from the Channel ports.

Tilly's contention that in the period 1853–6 riots were predominantly due to demand from the Atlantic ports is more firmly based. By this period both the structure of markets in the Paris region and popular attitudes had already been significantly transformed by the development of the railway network, and especially by links to the Channel ports. The Atlantic coast, on the other hand, had been relatively neglected by railway constructors, and fears concerning the security of supplies persisted there. Another valid point made by Tilly is that disturbances in the area to the south and west of Paris occurred 'beyond the intensely farmed areas which supplied it in normal years',[248] that is, in regions affected in periods of poor harvest by an abnormal level of demand from external purchasers.

Significantly, Figures 5 and 6 reveal changes in the location of disorders if compared with Richard Cobb's listing of places at which distribution tended to break down in times of dearth during the last decade of the eighteenth century. He includes such key marketing centres in close proximity to Paris as Pontoise, Beaumont, Conflans, Pont St-Maxence, Mantes and Vernon.[249] By 1846–7 the zone of disturbance had been pushed back towards secondary sources of supply, away from those areas which supplied the bulk of the city's food needs. As the non-agricultural population grew, so commercial activity developed, but popular attitudes towards this, and especially towards its moral legitimacy in periods of crisis, were slow to change. Disorders were especially likely in areas newly or not fully integrated into commercial circuits, as merchants were forced, after a poor harvest, to look further and to operate in areas which were unprepared economically and psychologically for an intensification of the scale of commercial operations. This was the case in departments as close to the capital as Loiret and Eure, but especially in departments like Mayenne and Ille-et-Vilaine, and indeed all those areas in proximity to the Loire and its confluents caught between the needs of ports like Nantes and Parisian demand.[250] Similar problems were caused in Côte-d'Or in autumn 1846, when merchants from Haut- and Bas-Rhin, Doubs and Jura appeared on markets there in unusual numbers.[251] The pattern was repeated in the extended zones of supply of a mass of other urban and marketing centres – around Bordeaux, for example, particularly in the Dordogne, Deux-Sèvres and Lot-et-Garonne,[252] and around much less important centres of consumption and trade like the marketing towns of Saverne (Bas-Rhin) and Sarrebourg (Moselle),[253] or around Ebreuil (Allier), a milling centre supplying Montluçon, Commentry and Montmarault and therefore a collecting point for grain,[254] or in proximity to the numerous ports of Finistère,[255] or on the Channel, as at Dinan (Côtes-du-Nord), where numerous ships were loading in January 1847, many of them destined for England.[256] All of these regions had traditions of disorder.

Within those secondary regions of supply to which merchants were most attracted incidents were most likely to occur in the more fertile areas of plain and river valley in which wheat cultivation predominated and communications were reasonably easy. Thus in the *arrondissement* of Beaupréau (Maine-et-Loire) the development of new roads during the 1830s, largely for strategic reasons, made the area for the first time accessible to outside merchants, with results in terms of external demand which caused intense disquiet in 1846. In Mayenne it was not the poorest areas in the *arrondissement* of Mayenne which experienced the most numerous disorders but the wheat-producing *arrondissement* of Laval and the roads leading from it.[257] Similarly, in the Limousin protest was most likely in the Basse-Marche, a relatively specialized cereal cultivating zone.[258] Attempts to move foodstuffs from areas of poor semi-subsistence farming could, however, cause conflict. Indeed, the more isolated the area, the more intense was likely to be the fear in case of shortage. In explanation of an incident at Bugny (Deux-Sèvres) on

25 August 1855, the *procureur-général* at Poitiers maintained that 'ill-informed women, inhabiting . . . a region in which the roads are almost impracticable in winter and seeing grain taken away from the commune . . . believed that in the following winter it would be necessary for them to go two or three leagues to buy grain and then to transport it with great difficulty and great cost'.[259] Frequently, and particularly in those regions in which communications were most difficult and communities most isolated, even the transfer of food to a neighbouring commune was opposed. In the area of Commentry (Allier) purchasers who were not resident in particular communes were simply being driven away in November 1846.[260] Similar problems arose in Burzet (Ardèche). People from the neighbouring mountains were forced to creep into the village after dark in order to buy chestnuts.[261] Even small-scale purchases by individuals for their own consumption were resented and opposed.

Initially, and prior to the creation of a national network, the railway was to worsen the situation in some areas by intensifying the commercial exploitation of their resources. At Tours in August 1847 it was estimated that the railway was transporting 500 hectolitres of wheat a day to the mills of MM. André at Etampes and of Darblay at Corbeil (Seine-et-Oise) for the supply of Paris. Grain was first concentrated at river ports along the Loire and then moved to the railhead at Tours. Local bakers complained about their inability to provision themselves in competition with the agents of such large-scale millers, while the poor muttered about this new method of 'starving' them, and the more violent promised themselves, in their cups, the pleasure of killing the drivers and firemen who were replacing the carters as servants of the speculators.[262]

The chronological development of disorders was obviously influenced by the volume of commercial traffic. The three peak periods appear, both in 1846–7 and 1853–6, to have been the difficult period of spring and early summer, immediately prior to the forthcoming harvest, although in the early summer the position might be relieved by the release of stocks in anticipation of a good harvest; in the autumn and early winter following a poor harvest, when merchants sought to buy up supplies; and also in January–February, in the depths of winter, by which time misery might be intense and populations were sufficiently incensed by speculators to overcome their initial reluctance to risk direct action.

As for the precipitants of disorder, according to the *procureur-général* at Angers:

the factors are everywhere identical; there are one or more carts loaded with grain or flour, stopped, usually while passing through some village, by a crowd composed in large part of women; the mayor intervenes but is ignored; in spite of his remonstrances and his efforts the crowd unloads the grain and it is sold at 4 francs per double decalitre, and even this is not paid in full or is often rejected by the carter.[263]

This is fine as far as it goes, but one problem with such official sources of information is that they tend to give popular demonstrations a coherence that they did not in fact always possess. A more detailed examination of particular incidents is called for.

In the first instance one might consider what could be called 'mobilizing ideas'. When a cart was stopped at Bresolles near Cholet (Maine-et-Loire) women told *gendarmes* who were called to the carter's aid that they did not want to die of hunger and that all they wanted was to be able to buy grain. The merchants had refused to sell, however, preferring to take their grain to a market at which they could obtain a higher price. The women asserted that for as long as this continued they would stop carts and assault the merchants.[264] Baptiste Bienvenue, a day labourer accused of being a member of a crowd which had stopped carts at Buzançais (Indre) in January 1847, claimed: 'everyone said that we could not get anything either with or without money; were we then to die of hunger?'[265] Such fears were painfully intense among the poorest members of the community including day labourers and non-agricultural workers living in the countryside. Among those involved in disturbances were miners at Blanzy (Saône-et-Loire),[266] quarry men at Renazé and St-Berthevin (Mayenne),[267] weavers as in the communes around Cholet[268] and woodcutters as in the *arrondissements* of Pithiviers and Orléans (Loiret), Châteaubriant (Loire-Inférieure) and Rennes (Ille-et-Vilaine).[269] These were employed in poorly paid professions, depended largely on purchases in the market place in order to provision themselves and resided in the main, especially in the case of the woodcutters, in unproductive agricultural areas.

On occasion protest action might be planned in advance. At Hennebont (Morbihan) in October 1846 news was received that the price of rye had increased by 3 francs per hectolitre at the market of Plouay. On Saturday and Sunday, the 17th and 18th, various individuals went around the village concerting action for the Monday to prevent further transport of rye from their commune. It was even rumoured that a list of those prepared to lend support had been drawn up, which sounds unlikely, but might indicate the concern of these leaders not to be left in the lurch. At any rate, on 19 October a riot did occur.[270] Plans might be made in the local café, a place for meeting, discussion and organization. *Placards* might be used to call on the people to act.[271]

More frequently disorders appear to have been essentially spontaneous in character. They were stimulated simply by the sight or sound of carts passing through a community. Because of this the Prefect of the Mayenne could report in January 1847 that 'every large village becomes an obstacle to the circulation of carts loaded with cereals'.[272] At Echalot (Côte-d'Or) in February 1847 all it took was the shouting of some excited women to mobilize half the village against passing carts.[273] At Lignac (Indre) in October 1855 a disturbance began after a carter *en route* with wheat from

Poitiers to mills at the Chute-d'Argentan stopped at an inn for refreshment. Men in the bar asked him what he carried and he told them oats, to which they were said to have responded, 'You're a liar, you thief; you have agreed with the others to starve us to death, but we're going to shave your head . . . and spread your guts along the roads, and by Sunday we'll have fixed a [price] maximum.' It was judged that in spite of these threats nothing might have happened if a stranger had not told those making them: 'You sound like women, it is necessary to act, not threaten. You are a crowd of fools who don't know your own strength. If it concerned me, the grain would not leave here; it should be divided up at 3 francs [per double decalitre].' The inn keeper persuaded his troublesome customers to leave, but they proceeded to gather a crowd of about a hundred men and returned to the inn to demand distribution of the grain. The inn keeper again persuaded them to leave, but by 10 p.m. the crowd had grown to between 400 and 500, and its members were increasingly aggressive. They demanded the municipal drum from the mayor, presumably to give the whole proceedings some kind of an air of legality, but in the end, faced with the determination of the inn keeper not to let them into the yard where the cart was being kept, they slowly drifted away as the night went on until at 10 a.m., when *gendarmes* arrived, only 80–100 remained, twelve of whom were arrested.[274] Disorders were easily born wherever violent expression of grief was a common feature of patterns of speech. In a small community with an intense social life, spontaneous agitation was the most natural beginning for popular protest.

Disorders were also common along the waterways, particularly those in the north, along which food supplies were being transported to major urban centres such as Lille and Paris. Thus on 22 February 1847 600–700 people from the communes of Beauvais (Nord) and Billy-Berdeau (Pas-de-Calais) pillaged a barge *en route* from Antwerp to Paris, excusing themselves to the boatman with the words, 'We do not want to die of hunger'.[275] On 16 March a barge carrying flour from Arques to Lille on the Canal d'Aire was subjected to three different attacks by a large crowd from the villages of Festubert, Givenchy, Annequin and Beuvry; seventy-five sacks containing 7575 kilograms were taken and only twenty subsequently recovered.[276] And the next day, at Grisolles (Tarn-et-Garonne), it was the sight of a barge on a nearby canal, loaded with the grain of a local proprietor, which sent some individuals scurrying back to town, to run from house to house telling people that all the grain in the area was being taken away and that they would all die of hunger. In this way a crowd of around 200 soon gathered.[277]

The most dangerous stretch of waterway of all seems to have been the Canal d'Orléans, an important link between the Loire valley and the Paris region, because of both the heavy traffic it carried and the extreme poverty and traditions of violence of the population living along its banks. Incidents in this area were especially serious in the period February–May 1847. By the end of March the Prefect of the Loiret claimed that barges would inevitably be pillaged if they lacked a military escort.[278] Although the military commander claimed that these fears were exaggerated, escorts were being provided, and barges by this time were travelling from Orléans to Briare on the Canal in convoys, watched from the banks by crowds of woodsmen and quarry workers.[279]

One of the most serious incidents on the Canal d'Orléans occurred at Chailly (Loiret) when on 14–15 March an estimated 1500 people from some fifteen communes gathered and took 350 barrels and 100 sacks of flour from one barge and twenty sacks from another, causing an estimated 40,000 francs loss to their owner. This incident occurred following a shortfall in supply and considerable increase in prices at the previous market held locally at Lorris. It was accepted by the authorities that the participants had simply responded to their hunger and fear and it was noted that they had carefully avoided violence,[280] but the incident, coming after a period of growing agitation among the local population, augured ill for the future. The crowds which watched the barges pass, followed them and shouted threats were likely to be encouraged by the successful looting at Chailly.

In fact, another serious incident occurred on 17 March at Sucy-en-Bois (Loiret). This involved a barge, which, because of earlier threats, was carrying thirty infantrymen. At Sucy a crowd of perhaps 1200 awaited it. In spite of the arrival of twenty-five hussars, members of this crowd, mainly women, with a sense of desperation tried to take hold of the barge's tow rope and were driven off only with great difficulty. The crowd then pulled up some of the planks of a bridge under which the barge had to pass and, in spite of the danger of being impaled on the upheld bayonets of the infantry, dropped on to the barge and succeeded in pillaging it despite the soldiers' resistance.[281] Subsequently, and in spite of continued threats, the military presence in this area appears to have been sufficient to overawe potential pillagers.

In other areas crowds showed a similar determination in attempting to prevent the movement of grain and flour on the waterways. The main danger points were river ports and lock gates. At Rennes on 9 January 1847 a crowd which had already expressed its hostility towards M. Lemichele, a local baker who traded in grain, by throwing stones at his shop, went to the canal to pillage a barge loaded with grain that he planned to sell at St-Severin. Not only was wheat stolen but sacks were emptied into the water or into the mud and trampled underfoot. Eventually the crowd, which, it was estimated, had grown to 3000, had to be dispersed by a cavalry charge.[282] Stones might be thrown into locks in order to delay or damage barges – at Gosselin (Morbihan) on 24–5 November 1845 the passage of grain barges to Nantes was obstructed.[283] Not only merchants but the barge owners were likely to lose heavily when, as at Blanzy (Saône-et-Loire) in November 1846, a crowd first pillaged a load of potatoes and then stove in the bottom of the barge.[284] Even when barges were able to keep in mid-stream, they were not entirely safe. Again at Gosselin on 24 November 1847, firebrands were thrown at barges and the sail of one was entirely burned.[285]

Movements by sea also caused great anxiety. In coastal areas it was merchants engaged in inter-regional and especially international trade who symbolized the threat of dearth to many communities. The roads to the ports and the ports themselves were almost inevitably plagued by disorder in periods of high prices. The export of food for the benefit of foreigners appears to have aroused even stronger passions than movements to other parts of France and continued to cause disturbances well into 1848 partly because of the xenophobic passions that had been aroused by the events of that year.[286]

The nature of the provocation is obvious. Foodstuffs from wide hinterlands were transported along a limited number of routes to be concentrated at specific points for subsequent export by sea. This caused disquiet at every point from that of origin to the port of embarkation. On the Channel coast, as late as 4 December 1848, a crowd at Dunkirk tried to prevent the loading of potatoes on to a ship, evidence of the persistence of popular misery and fear even after food prices had substantially declined. The port had previously experienced more serious trouble on 12 January 1847, again because of potato exports. These had been substantial (2,412,861 kilograms in the month 10 November–12 December 1846) and this was particularly significant after successive harvests had been reduced by disease.[287] Another troubled port was Boulogne, from which foodstuffs were exported to England in large quantities. The town saw intensive agitation and some disorder. On 25 November 1846, for example, cows waiting to be taken aboard a ship were driven into the water.[288]

In Normandy the situation was similar. At Yvetot on 21 January 1847 unemployed workers prevented the loading of potatoes on to an English ship and threw the boarding planks into the water. Only the distribution of 30 hectolitres of potatoes by the municipality prevented worse disorder.[289] On the 22nd and 23rd the port of Rouen was the scene of similar disorders,[290] and on the 19th at Carentan (Manche), a crowd barricaded the road from the town's granaries to the port. Only military intervention permitted loading to resume, and when the ship finally left along the canal to Rouen it was under heavy escort.[291]

Disorders were also common in both 1846–7 and 1853–6 in the ports of the Breton peninsula, as a consequence of both the poverty of its population and a tradition of taking action to block exports. At Pont-l'Abbé (Finistère) on 22 January 1847 the irritation of the local population, which had just watched the embarkation of 60,000 kilograms of potatoes for England, finally boiled over, and first the women and then the men began to pillage two carts. The mayor and *gendarmes* who sought to intervene were furiously attacked and had to be rescued by some influential local notables. The riot began at 10 a.m.; by eight o'clock that evening large groups, including many drunks, were still parading through the streets, as the alarm bell rang in a local church to call in people from neighbouring villages. To prevent the reinforcement of the rioters the *gendarmerie* removed the bell and guarded a bridge into the town. In spite of their eventual success in restoring order, the merchants involved decided not to continue with the loading of the ship, and the stevedores refused to work. They all maintained that they had to continue to live at Pont-l'Abbé and could not afford to risk further antagonizing their neighbours.[292] In October–November 1860 this same town was again the cause of grave concern to the authorities, and again because of the export of potatoes. By mid October of that year potatoes which in September had cost only 2–2.50 francs a hectolitre cost 3.50–4 francs, and on the 16th a dozen workers went to the mayor and warned him that unless he forbade further export the events of 1847 would be repeated.[293]

More or less serious incidents were reported from numerous large and small ports along the western coastline and rivers. At Château-Gontier (Mayenne) on 15 January 1847 port workers were so intimidated that they refused to work; a merchant was thrashed, stones were thrown at the authorities and the port offices were pillaged.[294] At Dinan (Côtes-du-Nord) on the 23rd a crowd actually unloaded two ships,[295] and at Vannes (Morbihan) in March another crowd was able to delay the loading of a ship for three days.[296]

These various forms of disorder should not be considered to be incidents of anarchical violence. They obviously had a purpose: directly to obtain food, indirectly to secure concessions from the authorities and/or merchants. Ideally, when carts or barges were stopped those in charge of them should agree to sell. They were most likely to do so when they were offered cash and a reasonable price. Unfortunately, if the crowd offered to purchase, it was usually at a price that *it* thought fair, and often the cash was promised rather than proffered.[297]

Another solution favoured by the crowd was intervention in their favour by the local authorities. Mayors might be induced to lend their unofficial support to efforts to persuade farmers and merchants not to transport food from a community. They might sympathize with the predicament of the local poor and might be afraid of disorder.[298] They were not likely to take quasi-official action in restraint of trade, although they often appealed to higher authority for bans on the export of food from their communities[299] and lent support to the demand that market sales should be regulated in order to give priority to local consumers.[300] The *procureur-général* at Dijon complained in 1847 that in the Auxois most notables supported such restrictions, although he explained that their motives were not entirely altruistic. Sale, on credit, to the local poor increased the social power of the notable and helped him to ensure the subservience of his labour force for as long as workers remained in his debt.[301] But whatever the motives, such attitudes and actions in obstruction of the commercial activities of merchants and farmers *within* particular communities helped to restrain the development of agricultural capitalism.

Disorder within the community

A great deal has been written about subsistence disorders in market places and along the highways. Much less is known about what might well have been the most effective means of exerting popular pressure on merchants and farmers – namely, its exercise within their communities of origin.

Over-population, poverty, the as yet far from complete integration of communities into a national market and a national society, closed horizons, suspicion of strangers – all contributed towards an extreme localism, towards unanimity in the belief that the subsistence of local inhabitants should be assured before sales to outsiders could be tolerated. In these respects the *bocage* of the west and south-west, a universe narrowed by hedges and muddy roads, could be contrasted with the more open country-side of the Paris basin and much of eastern France. Simple correlations should not, however, be drawn between ecology and the frequency of disorders. Besides isolation and *mentalité*, the pressure of poverty and the quality of inter-personal relationships in a community should obviously enter into the equation. Nevertheless, it remains the case that such relatively isolated communities were particularly likely to unite against both outsiders and members of the community who offended against the common interest.

A variety of methods might be used to persuade offending members of a community to curtail their commercial activities. Simple requests might be made[302] and these, on occasion, backed up by intimidation. At Langogne (Lozère), where on 5 January 1847 it was rumoured that a stranger had arrived to purchase grains, a crowd went successively to all the houses of those thought likely to sell to him, smashing their windows until eventually assured by the mayor that no grain would leave the commune.[303] Displeasure was clearly voiced and a warning given by such means.

The threat of arson was particularly frightening. At St-Aignon-sur-Roë (Mayenne) on 16 October 1853, while a merchant was negotiating with a farmer a mason said in a loud voice, 'I hope that the rich and those who sell grain to merchants have their granaries and shops burned down.' Later the merchant went into a bar in which the same mason and other workers were drinking. He was again threatened: 'You rich, and people who buy grain, you are all f— scoundrels. You want to make the workers die of hunger but don't bother yourselves; when your homes are burning, we won't come to put the flames out.'[304]

Such menaces – the threat of ostracism or worse by one's neighbours – must have reduced the commercial acquisitiveness of merchants and farmers. This explained the extreme reluctance in January 1847 of M. Beauquesne, the agent at Carentan (Manche) of a merchant at Rouen, to implement his employer's instructions to dispatch grain from his place of domicile, and the unwillingness of stevedores, also subject to community pressure, to load the waiting ship.[305] Failure to take heed of warnings could lead to such incidents as that at Faou (Finistère) at the end of the same month, when a merchant who had chosen to continue to trade attended a wedding and was beaten up by the other guests,[306] or that at La Metière (Mayenne) on 27 December 1846, when a miller, his wife and servants were stoned.[307] According to the military commander in the Sarthe in April 1847, popular hostility towards grain merchants was so great that they dared not go out after dark, although for him this situation had one advantage in that the merchants included some notable members of the republican opposition who had lost influence among the people because of their economic activities.[308]

Abuse and beatings were frequently dealt out to those involved in trade. On 23 December 1846 a carter on the Laval road was stopped by quarry men, asked if he was taking grain to Laval and, when he confirmed that he was, given a thrashing which resulted in two broken ribs.[309] At Brantôme (Dordogne) on 26 March 1847 the arrival of a M. Abrieux, who habitually made large purchases for the provisioning of Périgueux, had no sooner become known than a large and angry crowd formed outside his hotel. The hotelier managed to exclude its members from his premises, but the mayor was eventually forced to arrest Abrieux in order to calm them. They then proceeded to the village of Lambreau, 3 kilometres away, where a woman buying grain for her flour mill was known to be staying. She was forced to get out of bed, subjected to insults and dragged back to Brantôme to be incarcerated in the local prison for the next three days until *gendarmes* arrived to rescue her and the unfortunate M. Abrieux.[310] This was unusual. Far more common were fisticuffs, the throwing of stones or manure, insults and threats – and, most ominously perhaps, the threat to masculinity implied in the promise of an *honteuse mutilation*.[311]

Although the incident was exceptional, the murder of a landowner at Bélâbre (Indre) in January 1847, which appeared to the authorities to be linked to threats made on his life if he sold grain to a miller and the publicity given to this,[312] can only have confirmed the worst fears and increased the caution of many who might otherwise have energetically sought better markets than those in their immediate locality. It was not easy in a small rural community to engage in trade without this becoming rapidly known to all, and the consequences could be unpleasant for both seller and buyer. The threat of violence was very real.

Particularly resented was the apparent harshness of those who held on to their stocks in anticipation of a further price rise or who sold to outside merchants while refusing to sell small quantities to the local population to meet its daily needs. Such speculators might be prevented from leaving for market, as at Ardentes (Indre) on 22 January 1847, when a farmer driving his cart to market at Martizay was stopped by almost the whole population, including members of the National Guard, supposedly present to maintain order.[313] Even more provocative were the activities of a merchant called Charbonnier at La Bazoche-Gouet (Eure-et-Loir) in June 1847. On the morning of the 14th, when the market of the day appeared to be badly provisioned, he began taking delivery of cartloads of wheat and, within sight of the market hall, unloaded these into his granary. Women, unable to buy anything in the market place, were told that this wheat had already been sold, which only infuriated them the more. Eventually, and in spite of the protection of local *gendarmes*, Charbonnier saw the wisdom of selling small quantities at a low price to anyone who wanted to buy.[314]

The damage suffered from such incidents would vary from the loss of a potential sale because of the merchant's inability to reach a market to quite substantial amounts, as in the case of a proprietor *en route* from St-Pierre-la-Cour to La Gravelle (Mayenne), who was forced to sell his load, and then the stocks remaining at his farm, at a promised price of 4 francs per double decalitre when the prevailing market price at Laval was 5.75 francs. The contents of the cart alone were estimated to have been worth 500 francs, but he received in fact only 110.[315]

Farmers and merchants suffered financial loss in case of forced sales or pillage but also when crowds simply sought to punish them, as at Moulins in August 1856, when large quantities of fruit were systematically trampled into the mud,[316] or, on a less substantial scale, at Loches (Indre-et-Loire) on 17 December 1846, when individuals cut holes in the sacks on passing carts to cause wastage.[317] Carts themselves were also liable to be damaged. At Montignac (Dordogne) in February 1847, where two individuals had annoyed a crowd by purchasing 3 hectolitres of maize, the harness of their carts was cut and the crowd was on the point of throwing one cart into the river when prevented by *gendarmes*.[318] At Clinchamp (Haute-Marne) in November 1853 a merchant who had just sold grain to an inn keeper from Neufchâteau (Vosges) found that one wheel had been removed from his cart while it stood outside an inn in which he was eating.[319] All were minor incidents but an expensive burden for small merchants and a means of making popular hostility all the more obvious.

And it was not only merchants and farmers engaged in commerce who felt threatened but all those seen to be helping them as well. Carters were the most obvious targets,[320] along with the inn keepers who provided sustenance, beds for the night and yards in which to leave carts in some modicum of security and who often themselves trafficked in foodstuffs.[321] It cannot always have been easy for carters or merchants to find a bed for the night.

Administrative reports indicate that at least in some places and at particular moments violence and the threat of violence could induce commercial paralysis. At Mortagne (Vendée) in December 1846 a miller, M. Sionneau, had to suspend the movement of flour to Nantes because no carters dared to take that road;[322] while in Ille-et-Vilaine and Côtes-du-Nord it was observed in January 1847 that farmers in several communes were too afraid to take their grain to market.[323] In agitated periods like early 1847 military escorts were essential on some roads before merchants would set out at all.[324]

The problem for commercial farmers was that they had often previously contracted to supply a given quantity of cereals at a given date, and piecemeal sales necessitated by popular opposition to the movement of grain might prevent the fulfilment of such contracts. The authorities encouraged, and even put pressure on, farmers to meet their contractual obligations, but they often succumbed to intimidation, especially in under-policed rural communities, where, in spite of offers of protection, they were likely to persist with decisions to sell to local consumers which had initially been forced upon them.[325] By causing anxiety the masses were, in many areas, able to reduce the volume of commercial activity and to restrict the range of operation of individual farmers and merchants. As a result, the extent to which price variations between markets were reduced by commercial operations was limited because, as the general commanding the 4th Military Division from Tours explained:

from the beginning, farmers and merchants have been intimidated: because of this grain has only imperfectly circulated; a large number of those who engage in commerce cease their activities when they see that not only themselves but also their domestics, their horses and their carts are exposed to all kinds of violence. Thus commerce has been unable to render the services which it renders in ordinary times, of levelling prices by transporting the surplus of one locality to a place where there is shortage.[326]

From protest to insurrection

Of all the disorders which occurred those which naturally received the greatest publicity and which caused the greatest concern were the small number which got out of control and developed into minor insurrections and, as such, lasted longer and affected wider areas. These posed the threat of social revolution.

There were enough cases of protesting crowds pillaging property to cause considerable anxiety. The demands made by these crowds were almost always the same – food and an end to exporting. They were usually composed of people who felt desperate. At Varennes-sur-Teche (Allier) on 9 February 1847 members of a group of twenty-five which had gone to an isolated farm and taken wheat were even willing to give their names to the mayor and promised to pay for what they had taken when they were able. The motive for their action was the fact that at that moment they simply had no money with which to purchase food. In reply to the mayor's declaration that they were 'brigands' they had replied: 'No, we are hungry.' Their presumed leader, Jean Oblette, a *sabotier*, received a sentence of twenty years' hard labour for his part in this seemingly minor affair.[327] Even more than the pillage of carts, that of farms or their outbuildings was an act of last resort. Fixed property was even more sacred than mobile assets. It took a particularly angry crowd to interfere with it. Moreover, attempts to search farms and granaries (that is, enter private property) were far more likely to be resisted by their owners and the authorities than were other forms of popular action.

One of the solutions to the problem of subsistence suggested to the poor by memories of the not too distant past was the re-establishment of price maxima, first introduced by the Jacobin Republic in 1793, and, frequently linked to this demand, one for a ban on the maintenance of speculative stocks, combined with a census to establish the level of these. At Chauffailles (Saône-et-Loire), a textile and market centre, in August 1846 a crowd had alternately looted carts on roads in the commune and searched farms for hidden stocks, though without success in the latter respect.[328] In the days and weeks which followed there were repeated disturbances in the area, culminating in disorder at Génélard on 23 September, when hundreds of people armed with sticks gathered around a *château* and mill belonging to the Comtesse de Tournon demanding that she stop exporting grain. There was no alternative in such situations to the deployment of troops to preserve order.[329] In the troubled area of Bellac (Haute-Vienne) in January 1847 granaries were searched and account taken of the grains stored in them to ensure that none was moved to other areas. When these proceedings were opposed by the local authorities popular discontent increased, and on 30 January groups armed with forks and sticks and varying in number from ten, twenty, thirty to 200, and in one case 600–700, marched on Bellac. The local *gendarmes* attempted to maintain order but were eventually forced to barricade themselves in their barracks to escape injury at the hands of a crowd estimated to have grown to 1200.[330]

Small towns in the more troubled areas lived in fear of attack from the surrounding countryside. The desire of the populace to gain concessions from the municipal authorities and the merchants and landowners resident in these towns was frequently exaggerated by those who felt threatened into a nightmare vision of pillage and murder.[331] Occasionally incidents occurred which appeared to confirm these fears, as at Langogne (Lozère) in February 1847, when for two days, the 5th and 6th, a crowd seized control of the town, making threats and smashing the interior of two houses belonging to grain merchants.[332] As late as March 1858 a military commander was expressing concern about the intentions of the poor in and around Issoire (Puy-de-Dôme), who, he believed, were awaiting an opportunity to loot the place, which had, it is true, a tradition of violent protest.[333]

More striking from the point of view of conservative opinion were incidents like the pillaging of two *châteaux* in the Vendée in January 1847, one belonging to the Parisian banker Leroux,[334] and above all the series of disorders occurring in the Tours region and around Buzançais (Indre).

On Friday, 11 November 1846, following exports of wheat on the River Sarthe, disorders occurred in a number of communes around Tours (Indre-et-Loire). A crowd gathered first at Semblençay and marched towards Neuillé-Pont-Pierre, where it succeeded in stopping embarkations. From there it went to Sanzay, where it was joined by the local population. The enlarged crowd then proceeded to the villages of Souvigné, Couzeilles, Couirmen and Villiers-au-Bois, at every stage making obvious its attitude to merchants and the farmers who sold them grain. At Couesmes the mayor and his deputy were forced to join them. At Château-la-Vallière they seized the town drum in order to enhance the 'official' character of the procession. There too they demanded and obtained food for their immediate needs and seized flour at the local *château*, which was taken to the market *halle* to be sold at the Monday market. The crowd then dispersed after agreeing to meet at Charnay on the following day.

On 18 November a large crowd did, in fact, gather. In various villages in the neighbourhood the more committed had knocked on doors and, by a mixture of persuasion, taunts and threats, had encouraged the more reluctant to join them. At Charnay the crowd forced its way into the houses of an inn keeper and a grain merchant, refreshed itself and left for Château-la-Vallière with a quantity of wheat (again intended for the Monday market) and the mayor of Charnay and other notables who had been forced to join them. Arriving *en route* at Rillé, they forced its mayor, a rich landowner, to provide food and drink, taking him along to the next port of call, Souvigné, where about a hundred people joined them in marching to Cléré, where they had a last drink and finally dispersed. Although no acts of serious violence were committed, the fact that virtually the whole population of several communes could take part in what was to all intents and purposes an uprising – the assumption of at least temporary control over substantial areas of the countryside by the poor – combined with disorders in Tours itself on 21 November, caused great concern to the local administration and notables. The authorities, presumably because of lack of military personnel, did virtually nothing to stop the movement, which finally ended of its own accord, having, temporarily at least, achieved its aims. This official inactivity was perhaps fortunate in that a meeting between crowd and troops might well have led to violence. The rapidity with which the uprising occurred and then ended indicated the spontaneity, the localism and the lack of permanent organization for long-term aims among the discontented population.[335]

Very different in character, in terms of the violence involved and the social animosities which came to the fore were events in the Indre. These began on 13 January 1847 in Buzançais, a town of about 4000 inhabitants, in which social relationships were characterized, according to one senior

official, by the extreme misery of the poor and the uncharitable, unneces-
sarily harsh attitudes towards them of most of the middle-class citizens.[336]
There on 13 January six carts carrying grain were stopped by a crowd, and
the mayor was forced to accept its sale at what was considered to be a fair
price. Encouraged by their success, many poor people spent the night sitting
around camp fires in the town square, persuading themselves of the need to
take further revenge against those who had exploited them. They were
fortified against the cold by strong drink, some at least provided free by an
enthusiastic inn keeper.[337]

The following morning it was decided to punish the main object of popular
animosity, the proprietor of a mill just outside the town, who was guilty of
exporting large quantities of flour.[338] After devastating the mill, the crowd
returned to the town and forced the mayor, the justice of the peace and
finally over sixty of the town's more notable citizens to sign an engagement
to provide grain at a fixed price until the next harvest. The presence of a
large crowd – enlarged by the arrival of peasants from neighbouring
communes who were summoned by the ringing of the alarm bell – was
enough to persuade these notables of the wisdom of agreeing. Hesitation
resulted in the looting or smashing of the contents of nine houses. Only one
individual, a M. Chambert, refused to sign. Fearing ill treatment, he armed
himself with two pistols and fired at the crowd as it broke into his house. He
killed one rioter and wounded another, but this only infuriated the crowd.
Chambert was cut down by men armed with picks and axes. Subsequently,
François Arrouy, a *vigneron*, admitted that he alone had delivered two
blows against Chambert with his pitchfork, the first in the stomach, the
second in the face. When the fork had stuck in the unfortunate Chambert's
mouth he had needed to put one foot on the man's shoulder in order to gain
sufficient leverage to pull it out again.[339] Throughout all this the local
authorities, together with thirty dragoons who had just arrived, stood by,
afraid that intervention would compromise their own safety and that of the
peaceable inhabitants of the town.[340]

When order was finally restored retribution occurred. Those brought to
trial at the assizes were one clogmaker, one roadmender, one watchman,
one mason, two stonecutters, two carpenters, one wheelwright, one cabinet-
maker, one animal skinner, one vine cultivator and fourteen day
labourers,[341] once again representative of the poor of a small country town
and its neighbourhood. Jean Foigny, a 40-year-old agricultural labourer,
explained something of the predicament of the accused: 'It was misery which
made me do it. Do you believe that with 15 *sous* a day I can feed six people?
We can not live.' Prosecuting counsel asked if he had sought help at the
bureau de bienfaisance. The reply was, 'Yes, sir. They gave me 6 *livres* of
bread a week; and we were six people to live on 6 *livres* of bread a week and
15 *sous* a day!'

Etienne Billault, another labourer, claimed that he had been at first reluctant to leave his work and lose a day's pay in order to go to the mill, 'but even more I wanted the wheat to be less expensive'. He had also liked the idea of frightening M. Brillant, the miller, 'a hard man'. According to the correspondent of the *Gazette des Tribunaux*, with the exception of one 'dressed in the costume of the local artisans, all are dressed as agricultural labourers, in white or blue smocks . . . large hats or cotton caps, clogs or strong iron-shod shoes'. Their demeanour was that of 'dejected and frightened men; several were in tears'. As to their general appearance, 'the features of some indicated intelligence' but 'several have a physiognomy which appears to reveal a savage brutality'.[342] The relief of respectable citizens after the repression of such disorders was combined with the fear caused by an insight into a world of misery and degradation which had suddenly impinged on the lives of those of their own kind.

From Buzançais the revolt had spread. Local authorities without significant military support, in an area in which the National Guard existed only on paper, seem to have lacked all confidence and were largely inactive. On the morning of 15 January some of the rioters from Buzançais went along the road to Châteauroux until they reached Villedieu, where they were joined by part of the local population in ransacking the residence of a landowner involved in the grain trade, then a large commercial flour mill and finally the *château*. There they seem to have taken pains to smash those objects which symbolized the wealth of the owner – the doors and windows, the mirrors, the marble fireplace, every single piece of furniture, the contents of a picture gallery and of the library. All were systematically destroyed by a furious crowd. Even the ornate floors were broken up by men with axes. The authorities were clearly appalled by the degree of devastation, by the floors covered with glass, feathers from pillows and bits and pieces of precious objects of all kinds.

After leaving Villedieu the crowd committed further depredations in pillaging four other *châteaux*, though neither the mansions so treated nor their contents were apparently as impressive as those of the *château* at Villedieu[343] and the devastation was not as complete.

The main foci of trouble were to be the *arrondissements* of Châteauroux, in which Buzançais itself was situated, and that of Blanc to the south-west. Disturbances spread from Buzançais not only along the main road towards Châteauroux but also towards Vendoeuvres and Mézières on the road to Blanc, stimulated by the news carried both by active rioters and the pacific transmitters of information and rumour.

The object of most of the groups which marched through the countryside or of the crowds which formed in various villages in the area on the 15th seems to have been to increase the number of proprietors forced, as those of the town itself had been, to subscribe to a promise to supply wheat at around 15 francs per hectolitre. In cases, as at the *Château* de la Sauve, where the proprietor could not be found because he was either absent or in hiding, the mansion was pillaged and what could not be taken away was destroyed. When they were present proprietors appear to have been too frightened to resist the demands of groups of up to 500–600 armed 'peasants' and subscribed to the engagements demanded of them as well as providing food and drink.[344]

The *procureur-général* at Bourges was struck by what he described as 'a sort of instinct for legal forms' on the part of the people involved in these disorders, seen, for example, in their demands that proprietors should deliver grain to the municipal authorities of various communes, who would then distribute it among families according to need. In some communes rioters who had seized grain promised payment of a sum arbitrarily set by themselves, of course, but were prepared to recognize their debt by giving their names to the mayor or proprietor.[345]

The sense of power temporarily gained by the crowds often led them to make additional demands, some, such as that for the dismantling of the commercial flour mills along the River Indre, obviously in protest against the export of foodstuffs; others, such as that against the use of the labour-saving scythe at harvest or of threshing machines, were concerned with the reduction in employment which seemed to be one of the consequences of the growing commercialization of agriculture. Some proprietors were also asked to increase the wages they paid to compensate for the effects that their profit-seeking involvement in commerce had on prices.[346]

In the north of the *arrondissement* of Blanc the uprising began at Mézières, where the mayor was forced to order a search of the granaries and to ban the sale of grain to strangers on pain of death. The communes of Mige, Azay, Saulnay and Paulnay were reported to be in complete revolt.[347] Typically, in these communes agitators went from village to village and *cabaret* to *cabaret*, calling on the inhabitants to arm themselves and to meet at the *chef-lieu* of the commune to secure the reduction of grain prices and an increase in wages. In a *cabaret* at Chertoux an egg merchant claimed that it was necessary to kill the king and to take all the bourgeois to Paris to kill them too. He refused to pay for his drinks, claiming that from then on no-one anywhere would have to pay for anything. Here too the local authorities and notables were forced to sign written promises to provide grain at stipulated prices.[348] On 17 January, at Vandoeuvre, one proprietor avoided the devastation of his *château* by distributing 3000 francs among a threatening crowd.[349] At Bélâbre M. Robin Taillont, a 'rich' farmer and the mayor of his commune, was murdered apparently because he had ignored warnings and had sold grain to a merchant.[350]

Disorders, although on a smaller scale, also occurred in the *arrondissement* of La Châtre. To both notables and the authorities the whole department, given its agitated state, appeared insecure. *Placards*, threats and rumours in areas to the north of Buzançais – in places like Issoudun, which had a history of turbulence – raised difficult questions for those responsible for the deployment of repressive force.[351]

As late as 25 January it was reported from the Indre that 'the insurrectional movement still makes itself felt in communes which, by their isolation and the difficulty of communications, have been able to escape a prompt repression' but that 'these isolated movements are far from having the violent character of the first uprising', although the basic feature of crowd pressure on mayors and landowners survived.[352] Elsewhere, and soon enough in these isolated regions too, the combination of the organization of National Guard units formed by reliable citizens, military patrols and repression began to take effect.[353] Subsequent to the events at Buzançais itself three of those judged to be leading participants would receive death sentences, four hard labour for life and eighteen hard labour for varying terms of imprisonment, and many others lesser sentences.[354] The problem of choosing who to arrest when whole communities had participated in the various movements was one which caused the authorities some embarrassment.[355]

Even after numerous arrests and a proclamation by the prefect to remind landowners that engagements entered into under duress were not binding, many of them, made aware of the wisdom of conciliating the poor among whom they lived, continued to meet these engagements, at least in part, by providing relatively cheap food to local consumers,[356] while no doubt also resuming the commercial activity which was the *raison d'être* of their enterprise.

Both they and the authorities, on the basis of past experience, would have assumed that food riots were bound to recur. They could not be certain that events in the Indre did not signify the existence of more substantial ambitions among the poor. Much of the evidence collected after various incidents in 1847 appeared to point towards this conclusion.

Jeanne Petit, one of a group accused of pillage at Vieux-Moulin in the *arrondissement* of Cosne (Nièvre) was accused of advocating the sharing out of property. She told her interrogator that everyone had been talking about it for weeks, 'with the exception of you gentlemen who cannot, because you no doubt have grain to sell'. She maintained that projects of division were something the poor often talked about in a general sort of way, although not as a serious possibility, adding, perhaps a little ominously: 'I had no intention of causing harm to anyone, at least unless absolutely forced to by need.'[357] But the existence of need and of desperate misery was only too apparent. It was this which, according to the *procureur-général* at Bourges, had led in the Indre to 'an uprising of the poor classes against the rich classes',[358] which according to the commander of the 15th military division, gave to these movements an inescapably 'communist' character. It was not the existence of insurrectional bands in the countryside that really bothered him. These were easy to deal with from a military point of view. More frightening was the latent discontent of entire communities.[359]

It was their feeling of isolation in the midst of a desperate and furious populace which caused such fear among those who qualified as 'rich'. For them it was especially frightening when men whom they normally employed and who ate at their tables (and who, they felt, ought to be grateful for this) in return threatened them and destroyed their property. Faced with the prospect of a renewed peasant *jacquerie*, fear of the anarchic movements of old was combined with growing alarm at the supposed influence of the purveyors of communistic theories.[360] The *procureur-général*, better informed than most, insisted that this was not communism of a theoretical or political character. It was 'practical communism', involving the imposition of a *maximum* price by means of terror.[361] The distinction does not appear to have occurred to most local landowners. The Minister of Justice appeared convinced that the simultaneous uprising of a large number of communities was proof of the existence of an organized plot.[362] He shared the view expressed by the military commander at Tours that high food prices were being used as a pretext for revolt by 'rioters and assassins' and by undefined 'parties' whose character was evident from the shouts reported to him of 'War on the *Châteaux*! War on the Rich!'.[363]

With the benefit of hindsight it seems clear that these events were produced by widespread and intense misery. Neither the misery nor the disorder was ever to be experienced on such a scale again. Latent fear of hunger in the countryside influenced the development of politically motivated uprisings such as that of La Marianne, involving the slate workers of Trélazé who marched on Angers in 1855,[364] but this was exceptional and due to an extraordinary combination of factors. The year 1847 saw the last of the peasant *jacqueries* and the 1850s the last substantial wave of lesser disorders due to high food prices. Subsequently popular misery would be eased as a consequence of economic development.

Misery and crime

In addition to the more spectacular forms of protest against material deprivation, high prices generally resulted in significant increases in the number of cases of petty crime that were brought before the courts. Administrative reports continually stressed the multiplication of the number of thefts of small quantities of food and money. In effect, a causal relationship can be traced between criminal acts and seasonal as well as cyclical movements in the prices of basic necessities until at least the end of the Second Empire, although improving living standards increasingly made deprivation a more complex phenomenon than simply lack of bread.

'Men may steal because they are in need, but the assessment of need depends upon what they have been led to expect or desire.'[365] Need reflected community norms, and it should not be forgotten that the poor were hardened to a level of poverty that we should find intolerable. The practical definition of crime was also in part determined by communal norms, which might or might not accord with the legal definition; furthermore, there was a common reluctance to involve external authority in the affairs of a community. Crime was also a matter of opportunity. In the city expectations tended to be higher and opportunities greater, both because of the greater availability and display of material goods and because of the anonymity offered by the large population centre. Control depended far more on formal institutions than in the smaller community, where more informal relationships might be effective.

In many rural areas theft, and especially poaching and flouting of the forest regulations, were habitual methods not only of improving marginal material situations but also of protest against the 'rich' and the administration. In periods of economic crisis they simply became far more common. Theft of foodstuffs was a response to extreme poverty and often tended to be regarded in a sympathetic manner by both police and magistrates and to be dealt with leniently. It reflected 'needs that the working classes are unable to satisfy due to lack of resources'[366] and 'made delinquents of people who, in better times, would not have failed'.[367] This was also true of begging.

There was a degree of tolerance of beggars everywhere, providing that their need to beg was demonstrably proved – that is, that their incomes were otherwise insufficient to permit subsistence and that organized forms of public relief were lacking or inadequate; furthermore, they should be members of the community in which they begged and should not behave in a threatening manner. The responsibility of feeding one's own was generally accepted, but strangers, it was usually felt, ought to be forced to stay where they belonged. Unwillingness to share limited resources with them was combined with fear of strangers and the acts of desperation to which they might resort.[368]

The prevalence of begging not only reflected the severity of an economic crisis and its effects on incomes but also traditional social attitudes towards the beggar and the limited capacity of most communities to provide alternative forms of relief. The period of time for which begging might be tolerated by both civil authorities and public opinion again reflected local assessments of the necessity of the act. In most areas begging increased in 1846 at the start of winter and continued until employment opportunities, especially in agriculture, increased in the following spring.[369]

Particularly in the poorest regions and in communities with egalitarian structures the poor could be expected to share the little they had in case one day they might need reciprocal treatment. In Finistère poor peasants shared their bread and soup with those even worse off who knocked on their doors. But their resources were likely to be exhausted quickly, and the instinct to help was modified by a growing need to conserve what was left for their own families. This situation tended to increase social tension.[370] Another consequence of the exhaustion of charitable resources in one commune was to cause its poor to spread out over the countryside in search of aid. Thus the canton of Cloyes (Eure-et-Loir) was invaded in April 1847 by about 300 beggars from other communes in that department and from Loiret and Loir-et-Cher.[371] Now they appeared as strangers among people who feared them and were positively unwilling to help.

Although not entirely absent anywhere, begging appears to have been particularly intense in two kinds of region: first, those with a relatively advanced market-orientated agriculture and a large proportion of rural proletarians among their populations, employed both as agricultural labourers and in rural industry; second, the opposite extreme, the economically backward areas in which population densities were simply too high for resources. Those areas in which the level of resources, their variety and especially the prevalence of peasant smallholdings offered better protection against complete impoverishment had fewer beggars relative to their population and were better able to cope with these within the bounds of their community of origin.

Thus begging remained a problem in the advanced Ile-de-France and the rich agricultural areas of the Paris basin. Throughout the winter of 1846–7 the *gendarmerie* in these departments were forced to mount patrols both by day and especially by night to increase the security of farmers in areas as close to Paris as Chevreuse and Coignières (Seine-et-Oise).[372] Large groups of beggars were reported in the north in such departments as the Somme, Aisne, Pas-de-Calais and Nord.[373] In the canton of Cambrai (Nord) for example, there were 13,000 agricultural labourers. Of these normally about 5000 were employed for the whole year and were thus relatively secure. The others found work for eight months in agriculture and were then usually able to find alternative work for the remainder of the year or else lived off savings, but another group of about 500 was unable to do either and normally began to beg in November until agricultural work recommenced in March. In a bad year the size of this last group was considerably enlarged.[374] This problem was even greater in more industrial areas, such as that around Tourcoing (Nord), where the problems of the poor were intensified in years such as 1846 by the simultaneous decline of employment in agriculture and both rural and urban industry.[375] In the north-west numerous groups of beggars were recorded in some of the Norman departments, especially the relatively industrialized Seine-Inférieure and the Orne.[376]

Compared with periods of crisis during the Revolution, Empire and early Restoration, the problems caused by beggars do not appear to have been as serious in either the Paris region or the north. This suggests that these areas were better able than previously to provide employment and/or relief to their poor, in spite of the intense suffering they continued to experience.

Although meaningful statistics on the number of beggars are lacking, one obtains the clear impression that the problem was most intense in the west because of high population densities – in Brittany and especially in such departments as Mayenne, Sarthe, Maine-et-Loire, Deux-Sèvres and Vendée – and above all in areas of poor agriculture in which large numbers of people depended upon rural industry to subsist. In Mayenne the rural weavers in December 1846 were earning 50–60 centimes per day, and agricultural labourers, slightly better off, had earnings of between 90 centimes and 1 franc. Members of both groups were frequently unemployed, and it was they, not surprisingly, who made up the mass of beggars.[377] In 1848, in the canton of Montfort-le-Rotrou (Sarthe), of a population of 16,941, 12,000 were officially recognized as poor, living in hovels, sleeping on straw, clothed in rags, eating rye- or oat-bread and boiled potatoes. For the 600 who had recourse to begging life was 'a continual agony'.[378] In Deux-Sèvres it was the *arrondissements* of Bressuire and Parthenay, in which large numbers of people worked in textiles, which in 1846–7 and again in 1853–4 experienced the most extreme misery and widespread and often aggressive begging.[379]

Begging was also common throughout central France, above all in areas in which a multiplicity of methods of gaining a living did not exist – for example, among the agricultural labourers in areas of large-scale wheat production on the plains of the Isère or the lower Marche, which differed from other areas of the Limousin in the absence of substantial seasonal migration.[380] Although most of southern France was spared because of the less intense nature of the crises and the protection offered by the diversity of activity and landholding, the mountain areas of the Ariège exhibited more clearly than almost anywhere else the desperate situation of a population which had grown more rapidly than the resources it produced. Thus every crisis threw veritable armies of beggars on to the roads.[381]

It seems clear from the evidence considered that begging was primarily a problem for rural societies. In the towns it was contained by a mixture of public relief, private charity and repression, none of which was as well organized in the countryside.

Although in 1847 workers from the textile towns of Roubaix and Tourcoing (Nord) were reported to have gone into the surrounding countryside to beg,[382] this was relatively unusual and is perhaps explained by the severity of the problem of relief in such single-industry centres. Movement generally was in the opposite direction, from country to town, and this especially from the more impoverished rural areas like the Limousin or Pyrénées which had relatively few rich notables and were often denuded of even the meagre resources necessary for reciprocal aid.[383] An alternative to going to town was to move towards a richer agricultural area, where again occasional work or at least charity might be more forthcoming.[384]

Most of those who took to begging were giving in to their hunger. This surely was an activity of last resort, regarded as humiliating and degrading in all save the very poorest communities. But where these could not provide for their own and the law enforcement agencies did not compel the poor to stay in their communities of origin, it was inevitable that they should go wherever they might hope to gain and that, meeting resistance, their feelings of desperation should impel them to threaten violence to overcome this. In the rich agricultural area of the Beauce, which had a large population of labourers, it was observed in 1846–7 that beggars were more aggressive than they had been since the hard winter of 1816–17.[385] To reduce the risk of encountering the authorities and to increase the menace, begging frequently occurred at night.

Numerous such cases are recorded, normally involving socio-professional groups which habitually lived at bare subsistence level – rural weavers, woodsmen and agricultural labourers without other support. Usually a group, often with their faces blackened or covered with handkerchiefs, knocked at the door of an isolated farm or house, pleaded for help to feed starving women and children and, if help was denied them, proceeded to threats (most commonly to burn down the residence) while pretending that the band of which they were members was far larger than it in fact was. At a *château* in the commune of Faymoreau (Vendée) in April 1847 such a group, after frightening the caretaker into agreeing to provide bread, insisted that he impale the loaves on the end of a bayonet attached to a gun which was poked through an open window, something which no doubt added to the reality of their threats.[386]

Most desperate of all beggars were probably the foreigners, especially the Belgians attracted to the north, normally in search of better-paid work than was available in Belgium and, in time of crisis, by the prospect of charity. On both accounts their presence was bitterly resented. They took work and charity from the hands of native Frenchmen; they were thus particularly liable to dismissal when employers required less labour and to be refused charity by both public and private donors.[387]

Begging, especially by large bands or at night, caused considerable anxiety. Normal suspicion of strangers, about whose propensity for good or ill nothing was known and who in any case would never reciprocate in any way for the help they were given, was compounded by the threats made by beggars, by their appearance, both miserable and often disguised, and by the fact that they carried sticks or other potentially lethal instruments of violence. In the Sarthe, as the number of beggars increased early in 1847, many proprietors were reported to have deserted their homes for the towns from fear of marauding bands so numerous that it was impossible they could all be satisfied.[388]

Efforts had to be made to restrict and to control beggars. Traditionally there were two related ways in which the authorities attempted to control begging – by repressive police activity and by the provision of relief at a fixed point, either the community of habitual residence or a *dépôt de mendicité*, in which the stubborn beggar might be incarcerated.

These policies involved a ban on the movement of those in need outside their commune of habitual residence and, most significant, the provision in the communes of funds for relief. Where these funds were adequate to permit a tolerable existence, such measures were effective.[389] During the early 1850s the central government clearly encouraged such developments, and in many areas these years of crisis were unusual in that bands of beggars were far less common and social fears and tensions in rural areas less intense as a result.[390]

Generally, however, the construction of *dépôts de mendicité* was hindered by financial stringency. Too few were constructed, and these were too small to have a significant effect. The *dépôt* was a means of punishing sturdy professional beggars rather than of solving the problem of mass begging. Just like the other measures taken, it represented a response to the symptoms of poverty rather than their causes.

In economically backward areas and in some of the more advanced where low-paid wage labourers were numerous, the number of those in need in a period of crisis was likely to be too great a burden for the financial resources of many communes. There was simply no alternative in many areas but to allow begging while acting to prevent nocturnal begging in large groups and punishing those who made threats or who were armed. The judicial statistics in the period 1846–55 revealed growing numbers of prosecutions[391] (that is, more effective policing), which must have had something of a deterrent effect. Foreign beggars could be expelled from France[392] and natives returned to their communes, but if these could not feed them, it was clearly impossible to prevent them from going elsewhere.[393] *Gendarmes* often arrested beggars in departments in which a ban on their activities existed, but more often than not the local authorities had no alternative to releasing them and allowing them to return to their begging.[394]

In themselves administrative measures were insufficient to stop begging. It was inevitable for as long as much of the population lived on minimal incomes, in conditions of chronic insecurity and, in addition to their normal tribulations, had to face the problems of cyclical economic crises. Only the major structural changes in the economy which were increasingly evident from the 1850s and the easing of the problems of rural over-population by migration would reduce begging from a mass phenomenon to an activity involving a relatively small number of socially marginal individuals.

Another major problem for the authorities in many areas in these years of crisis was that of fire, often intimately connected by public opinion with begging. Although fires appear to have been less numerous and to have caused much less concern, at least to higher authority, than in 1829–30,[395] it is evident that especially in the north-west in the late summer and autumn of 1846 and 1847 and again in 1854 and 1857 frequent fires caused local concern. This was in large part because of the particular kind of explanation of the causes of fire, especially favoured in years of crisis and social tension –

in short, that many fires were started deliberately as an expression of grievance or from the desire for revenge.

There was considerable evidence to support such fears. Discontented crowds or individuals abusing or threatening those against whom they felt a grievance – merchants in the market place, farmers selling to merchants – habitually promised to burn them out unless they mended their ways. Beggars whose pleas were rejected were likely to utter the same time-honoured threat.[396] Ominous snatches of conversation might be heard in which the poor discussed with evident glee the possibility of burning out the objects of their hatred.[397] *Placards* and anonymous letters very often expressed these same threats and undoubtedly caused considerable alarm during periods when popular unrest was known and protests of various kinds were already being made.

It often appeared as if threats had been put into effect. When around Cholet (Maine-et-Loire) or in the *arrondissement* of Dreux (Eure-et-Loir) in the autumn of 1846 fires followed immediately after the appearance of *placards* and anonymous letters, the presumption that arsonists were at work did not seem too far-fetched.[398] The fire in the granary of an inn at Cholet on 29 August occurred on the same day as the inn keeper, who traded in grain, had been told that he would be punished by flames.[399] The assumption that arson had occurred was not surprising; nor was it surprising that those who were blamed were often strangers, without guarantees or protective solidarities within the community, and especially beggars who had been refused aid. Yet in most cases of suspected incendiarism there was little more than circumstantial evidence. Threats of arson were almost a natural tactic for beggars to employ, and one can be certain that more often than not action did not follow.[400] But that it did on occasion, and that arson was a traditional means of exacting vengeance and as such was especially likely during a period of crisis and social tensions, meant that the minority of deliberate fires created anxiety about the causes of all fires.

Whatever the causes, fires certainly frightened people, especially those living in relatively isolated settlements, who saw themselves at the mercy of beggars. It took only a few fires to set afoot rumours about plots by incendiarists.[401] On 17 January 1846 much of the town of Trouhans (Côte-d'Or) was burned to the ground. Among the population, already in a state of considerable anxiety about high food prices, talk of a band of *metteurs de feu* in the pay of the priests and nobles was easily accepted. Throughout the area travellers were stopped and questioned by armed groups searching for the incendiarists.[402] In the neighbouring Doubs the news of fires in Côte-d'Or caused alarm which appeared to be justified when the *Journal de Besançon* announced that the mayor of that town had received anonymous letters threatening to burn it down. Subsequently, and perhaps from a writer inspired by this false report, the mayor did receive such a letter promising that unless the members of the so-called Compagnie d'Incendiaires, supposedly imprisoned at Besançon, were immediately released, then this Compagnie would penetrate the town and blow up the local gunpowder manufactory. Even this absurd letter caused concern, and at the end of May nightly patrols were being mounted.[403] Early in 1853 the same pattern was repeated in the judicial *ressort* of Bourges. From the end of February to 25 April, sixty fires were reported.

The first idea that this scourge awoke among the masses was that of an association of evil-doers following a preconceived plan and acting as the agents of I know not what atrocious political system. It is always the same in the imagination of an easily agitated people; their already difficult conditions of existence contribute to the result that these fires cannot appear to be the results of natural causes, but have the character of evil-mindedness, analogous to the results which they have to suffer. Just as speculation presents itself to them initially as the cause of the shortage of cereals and their excessive prices, so the disasters they suffer from the fires must begin by appearing as the putting into practice of a system of destruction directed at them.[404]

There were obviously other potential causes of fire besides arson. Deliberate destruction designed to defraud insurance companies was one, often revealed by excessive valuations of properties by their owners.[405] Even the old red herring about insurance agents seeking to encourage owners to take out insurance policies by lighting some fires themselves appeared once again, although no proof was offered.[406] More likely causes were drought, internal combustion in hayricks and human carelessness.[407] Especially significant was the geographical correlation between frequency of fire and the prevalence of thatched roofing. According to an inquiry conducted in 1856, thatch was most commonly used in the north-west, from the Belgian frontier to Morbihan, where over 30 per cent of roofs were so covered, with maxima of 62 per cent in the department of Manche and 84 per cent in Calvados, and in a second zone from the Aube to Cantal and Cher to Doubs, in which 20–40 per cent of roofs had a thatched cover.[408]

Of fifty fires reported in the three departments composing his judicial *ressort* in the previous year, the *procureur-général* at Amiens in August 1853 attributed thirty to imprudence or accident and twenty to arson.[409] The latter figure is a high proportion of the total, and the *procureur-général* had seen all the evidence, but, given the suspicion prevalent at the time, who knows? His colleague at Bourges reported that of sixty fires occurring from the end of February to 25 April 1853, only ten were suspected of having been started deliberately.[410] Usually it was the more exposed parts of farms that burned. Although village fires were not uncommon, most reports on fires refer to hayricks, granaries and isolated farm buildings.

Whatever the exact role of arson, what is striking is the frequency of fire and the obvious fear of arson that prevailed. Flames propagated themselves with great rapidity, especially when the thatch was dry, and the lack of firepumps in most villages, the shortage of water in dry periods and the slowness with which help was organized in areas of dispersed habitat made fire difficult to stop. In short, to our description of popular sensibilities and social fear we must add the widespread sense of anxiety caused by fire in communities which were threatened by it to an extent which we find difficult to conceive.

Strikes: an example of the modernization of protest?

I have left until last a form of protest usually considered to be indicative of the modernization of social structures and of protest itself – the industrial strike. The withdrawal of labour had a long tradition, however, particularly among artisans, and strikes in the period of the mid century crisis must be understood in relation to this tradition rather than as a new, more modern form of protest. They would become recognizably modern only in succeeding decades with the beginnings of the organized trade union movement.

Economic crises brought a triple threat for workers – of high prices, unemployment and reduced wages. It seems likely that during both 1846–7 and 1853–6 most strikes occurred because of the increased difficulty of making a living. The *procureur-général* at Orléans complained in July 1855 that as usual high food prices raised 'the eternal question of wages'.[411] His colleague at Rouen observed that however hard-working most workers were in normal times, and even if they were never unemployed, they must have been finding it difficult to provide for their families. A subsistence crisis compounded all the normal difficulties.[412] It was in relation to these problems that they both explained the wave of strikes that they were reporting.

The relationship between economic conditions and propensity to strike was not, however, a simple one. Indeed, most of what we know about strikes confirms Labrousse's view that, at least until the 1860s, the combination of adverse circumstances which in the traditional economic crises served to increase food prices at the same time as wages and employment opportunities declined, made action in defence of wage levels appear less relevant than attempts to limit the increase in food prices. It appears as if for most workers the obsession with the price of food was dominant, and prices were determined by the sellers of grain, bread and the municipal authorities rather than by an employer.[413] Consequently, they were the most likely targets of protest. Such strikes that did occur were fundamentally defensive and not likely to be sustained beyond a day or two at most, given the poverty of the people involved.

Workers reacted to a crisis in diverse fashions, according to the varying situations of time and place, of particular occupations and occupational traditions. Some, and especially artisanal groups, tended to avoid striking in difficult periods when employer concessions were not likely, given declining levels of demand for products, and when it might seem advisable, in view of the rise in unemployment, for those still in work to make the best of this and to await more prosperous times to press for wage increases. This would not, of course, prevent them from attempting to persuade employers that their needs ought to be recognized or even from making threats after persuasion had failed, as in a *placard* found at Rennes in September 1855, which supported a request for an increase of 50 centimes per day for building workers.[414] Other groups, particularly among the lower-paid, living at best around subsistence level, were likely to find any further pressure on their margins of existence intolerable, and they reacted angrily in usually short-lived, unorganized but sometimes violent fashion, in marked contrast to their usual apathy.[415] At Roubaix (Nord) in February 1846 rampaging strikers threw stones at the windows of the homes of their employers, who had reduced the length of the working day and earnings. At Comines (Nord) in April 1847 workers went further and smashed the contents of the home of M. Remeaux, their employer.[416] On 1 July 1847 workers in the textile factories of Thann and Guebwiller (Haut-Rhin) went on strike, claiming that their wages were too low because of the rise in the cost of living. They returned to work on the following day without achieving anything.[417] In June 1855 textile workers in the same area were again involved in a short-lived strike against wage reductions.[418] Their colleagues at Rouen and Yvetot (Seine-Inférieure) were reported in August 1856 to have discussed the possibility of striking because there seemed to some of them little point in working if they could not earn enough to live on.[419]

Strikes among agricultural workers were especially rare. Occasionally, at periods of peak demand for labour such as harvest, brief stoppages might occur.[420] Rural strikes were more likely among forest workers who had a greater sense of cohesion and group solidarity, as a result of working together, than did agricultural labourers. In January and February 1847 woodcutters in the *arrondissements* of Orléans, Pithiviers and Montargis (Loiret) added strikes for higher wages (they earned around 80 centimes a day) to the action they were taking against the grain trade in market places and along roads and waterways.[421] Of all social groups perhaps, their material situation was the most desperate.

Among most occupational groups group solidarity was effectively limited by the needs of individual families. In the less skilled trades in particular there was always the threat of replacement of strikers by other workers recruited either from outside the community or from the ranks of its un-employed. Capacity to resist was limited, save in some artisanal trades, by lack of organization and funds. Strikes which occurred during general economic crises were especially difficult to maintain, given the pressures of competition among workers, the decline in the number of employment opportunities and the substantial rise in the cost of living.

Efforts to organize resistance to deteriorating working conditions were plagued by this lack of solidarity. Agreement was easier to establish and maintain in more prosperous periods, when families might subsist briefly from savings and employers could be expected to make concessions to avoid the loss of profitable orders, but in time of depression or crisis the outlook was very different. To many it must have seemed preferable to hang on to what they had rather than court dismissal by striking. Employers were aware of this. At Rive-de-Gier in February 1847 the Compagnie Générale des Mines de la Loire was able to break the solidarity of miners who had decided to demand an increase of 25 centimes a day by promising to supplement wages by the amount of further increases in bread prices. This, it was reported, satisfied married men with families but not unmarried workers, who continued to press for a permanent increase. The Company, however, succeeded in preventing a strike and at the cost of only a temporary increase in the workers' remuneration.[422] This method of making concessions was much preferred by employers to granting wage increases.

During the early phases of industrial development it was always difficult to organize workers to defend their interests. Too many were dispersed in small workshops; too many were illiterate and their horizons narrow; too many were recent immigrants to have much of a sense of collective interest with either workers in the same trade or workers generally. Moreover, the position of employers was overwhelmingly strong when labour was unorganized and, save in certain specialized trades, plentiful and when they could usually expect the wholehearted support of the administration against workers who broke the law, whether by associating together or by striking. In numerous cases threats from employers and officials were enough to prevent a strike.[423] Senior government officials were sometimes sympathetic towards workers, especially from the early years of the Second Empire, and on occasion sought to promote mutual concessions.[424] They were often hostile to employers who caused trouble by a harsh wages policy. The *procureur-général* at Rouen in August 1855 condemned the exclusive concern of employers with maximizing their profits. He claimed that a few were willing to grant higher wages, but that none would take the initiative for fear of losing a competitive advantage.[425] The primary responsibility of government officials was, however, the maintenance of order, and where they saw this to be threatened they normally blamed the lower classes. Typically, the *procureur-général* at Douai, although reporting in July 1855 a second successive harvest failure and high prices, maintained that the miners at Anzin and Le Cateau were on strike out of sheer perversity, given the paternalism of their employers.[426]

Conclusion

This long chapter will have made obvious the scale and intensity of the popular discontent caused by subsistence crises in mid nineteenth-century

France. The result was a general crisis as popular anxiety about food prices and the disorder that this caused intensified social tensions and created major problems for the authorities. During a period of dearth a wide panoply of measures was traditionally espoused by the authorities, by individual citizens and associations to alleviate popular misery. These included the provision of work in the appropriately named charity work-shops, established usually on the public highways, meals or bread at reduced prices and simple handouts. This activity was inspired both by humanitarian motives and by fear and the desire to prevent disorder. Misery should not be allowed to turn into despair.

These were essentially paternalistic measures. They did not involve the acceptance of any responsibility for the existence of poverty or any commitment to social reform. Just like any other ruling class, that of nineteenth-century France presented itself as the guardian of a moral code which supposedly represented the interests and sentiments of all social groups and served to explain and to justify social relationships based upon inequality and exploitation. Charity was a key element of this moral code.

Another vital element was order. If charity proved to be insufficient, repressive force was employed. Together charity and repression helped to maintain the mass of the population in a submissive state during a period of crisis. * That this could be achieved was symptomatic of the limited character of popular demands, of the limited capacity for organization in support of protest and of the survival of a traditional social and moral order as yet barely challenged by politicization and unionization. Rapidly, however, protest about dearth was to disappear with dearth itself, and new causes and forms of protest, together with new means for their containment, were to come to the fore.

* Charity and repression are analysed in two articles originally intended to be chapters in this book: 'Poor relief and social crisis in mid-nineteenth century France', *European Studies Review*, vol. 13 (1983); and 'Techniques of repression: the control of popular protest in mid-nineteenth century France', *The Historical Journal*, vol. 25 (1982), pp. 859–87.

6 An end to dearth

Subsistence crises caused considerable suffering and anxiety and led to serious and widespread disorder. The consequences of such social tension for the operation of the mechanisms of the food market were of crucial importance. Fear led to behaviour on the part of both consumers and suppliers which caused an increase in prices beyond the level which might have been expected simply from considering regional imbalances of supply and demand. Economic behaviour at all times is the product of complex decisions influenced by a variable range of individual and collective concerns. At no other time are collective mentalities as important in determining action within the market place as during subsistence crises.

Even during the first half of the nineteenth century the structure of economic crises was growing more complicated as industry developed and generated crises peculiar to itself as well as suffering the consequences of harvest fluctuations. From the 1850s structural change in the economy accelerated, largely in response to the impetus of improved communications, and with it the transformation of the economic cycle was completed by the 1880s.

The change can clearly be seen in the movement of agricultural prices. After 1856 there were no more cases of wheat prices doubling at times of shortage, and after 1867 no more increases of 50 per cent or more. Geographical variations were also evened out. Whereas in 1801 the maximum difference was between 11 francs per hectolitre in the Marne and 46 francs in Alpes-Maritimes, in 1817 between 36 francs in Côtes-du-Nord and an astronomical 81 francs in Haut-Rhin, and in 1847 there was still a difference of 28 francs, from 1860 it did not rise above 4 francs and was generally between 2 and 3 francs. The easing of cyclical variations and the levelling out of spatial variations were clear indications of a transformation of economic conditions. Contemporaries explained this in terms of both the transport revolution and/or the final abolition in 1861 of the sliding-scale tariffs which had eliminated a major element of uncertainty in the cost calculation of importers. Responses to the agricultural inquiries of 1866, 1870 and 1882 repeatedly expressed these views.

Tariff reform made France part of a worldwide agricultural market. Not only was importation easier; the decisive factor was that penetration of the interior of the country was now possible, and at relatively low cost. In 1846–7 imports still required eight months to reach French markets after the initial decision to place orders had been taken. Average annual prices on the regulating markets rose to 32.80 francs and real spot prices to 40 or even 45 francs per hectolitre. Transport facilities had been so inadequate that early in 1847 wheat was available in superfluity in and around the docks at Marseille, while a short distance inland there was a shortage. The municipal authorities of the city stressed that the problem was one of distribution and not supply, and that in future, once rail links with the interior had been completed, this problem would be greatly eased.[1]

The situation was indeed easier in 1855–6, but even then the average price of wheat reached 31.10 francs. Following the poor harvest of 1861, rail and telegraph and the abandonment of the sliding scale accelerated the process by which balance between demand and supply was achieved, so that before the end of the year supplies were adequate and prices remained below 30 francs per hectolitre.

Because of tariff reform, but above all because of improved communications, these changes involved a transformation of French economic life from isolation and the juxtaposition of local and regional agricultural economies to integration, and nowhere was this more clearly revealed than in the levelling out of regional price variations.

Gradually, but more rapidly and more widely than before, farmers would move from subsistence polyculture *towards* increased specialization. One should take care not to ignore the variations between regions and between different economic groups; but neither should one ignore the economic and psychological significance for the producer of vastly improved access to urban markets and for the consumer of an end to the threat of food shortage, from which Frenchmen had never previously succeeded in escaping.

In the 1850s people still spoke with a clear sense of relief about the eradication of this particular nightmare.[2] Publicists still needed to reassure the less well-informed. In an article in the *Journal d'agriculture pratique* in 1853 entitled 'Des moyens de prévenir les disettes', the influential economist Léonce de Lavergne saw fit carefully to explain the significance of the economic transformation that was under way; while in 1855, writing *De l'utilité des chemins de fer français pour les transports agricoles*, a senior engineer of the Corps des Ponts-et-Chaussées examined the lessons of the period following the harvest failure of 1853 and concluded with relief that, even with the incomplete state of the network, *disette* of the kind experienced in 1846–7 was impossible.

It was the attenuation of price fluctuations over time and from market to market, both seasonally and biennially, which was especially commented upon.[3] This had been evident in proximity to the railway lines even in 1847.[4] There followed in the 1850s and 1860s a complex period of transition as the communications network was transformed, during which the amplitude of fluctuation was again clearly reduced[5] – even if there were some difficult years, such as 1867–8.[6] The *procureur-général* at Bourges noted in 1859: 'We are experiencing something new. A slight increase in price occurs on our markets; and immediately there is an influx of reserves . . . and prices fall towards their previous levels.'[7] By the early 1870s the traditional subsistence crises of the pre-industrial economy had finally disappeared. If the amplitude of price variations tended to exceed those of production until the 1860s, subsequently variations in production tended to exceed those of price. This was symptomatic of increasing security, of a new market psychology, noted in the *Annales de l'agriculture française* in 1861, when its chronicler, recording evidence of a poor harvest, observed: 'The announcement of such a fact would once have caused grave disquiet.'[8] The stress is in the past tense. The *procureur-général* at Rouen reported in the same year that although local harvests had been poor, 'news spreads more rapidly than it used to, and there is not in the whole department of Seine-Inférieure a single worker who does not know that large provisions of cereals have arrived at Le Havre'.[9] This was a precondition for a less emotive market. Traditional villains such as *l'accapareur* all but disappeared from the public consciousness.[10] This was noted with great pleasure by the authorities in urban centres, which for the first time seemed to have guaranteed food supplies and were assured of protection against excessive price fluctuation. For them each advance in the construction of the rail network was 'a victory over . . . the causes of misery and of disorder'.[11]

The existence of the railway helped to establish a climate of confidence, so that a poor harvest no longer resulted in a panic rush to buy up foodstuffs. Now it became more nearly possible for the 'difference in the price of the same merchandise on two markets not to exceed the cost of transport between the two localities',[12] and, of course, this particular cost was being substantially reduced. Well might an economic journalist, contrasting the relative ease of provisioning Paris in the new railway age with the immense effort formerly required, conclude: '*La famine est désormais impossible en Europe!*'[13]

The crisis years from 1853 to 1856 already carried with them signs of the changes which were occurring. In terms of the scale of the deficit, the harvest failures of 1853 and 1855 were in most regions almost as serious as those of 1845–6, but the broad economic and social consequences were nowhere nearly as severe. This was in part because of the rapidity with which local and central administrations responded by providing employment on public works projects at a time when, besides temporary projects, substantial work of urban renewal and railway construction was under way. In addition to the image of itself as a strong authoritarian force, the imperial regime was creating something more positive through its evident concern for the poor and through its association with a new situation of prosperity in the midst of crisis in which much of the rural population now found itself.

For, despite poor harvest results, cereal yields in many regions remained sufficiently high for many small as well as large farmers to produce enough, after attending to the needs of their own families, to be able to profit from high market prices. With relatively few exceptions, contemporary reports indicate that a far wider section of the rural population had shared in the profits of shortage than in previous crises. Even from the impoverished region around Riom it was reported in January 1855 that 'the peasant has never been as rich; never has money been more abundant and circulated so easily'.[14] From Agen it was reported, at the same time, that three-quarters of the population were benefiting from the situation.[15] We might suspect the statistic while accepting the situation report. There were thus notably fewer discontented people in the countryside during these years than during the previous period of subsistence crisis. The unity of many communities in the face of dearth was broken.

The relative prosperity of cereal producers affected other sectors of the economy. Crisis contingent on harvest failure did not become generalized. For this and other reasons urban purchasing power was kept up. Continued sales of agricultural products, such as wine, livestock and dairy products, both reflected this and in turn increased the overall prosperity of the agricultural sector.[16] The sourest note was sounded by wine producers, affected by a poor harvest in 1854 and a rather mediocre one in 1855. The effects of *oidium* caused intense difficulty in many areas.[17]

Above all, it was the continuing activity of industry which should be quoted as evidence of a new situation. Although there were signs of depression in many regions and sectors of industry in 1853 and early 1854, in general from then on until the end of the crisis industry remained prosperous, in very marked contrast with the period 1845–7. Agricultural crises would henceforward no longer automatically cause industrial crises. In place of mass unemployment, reports from all over the country revealed that workers continued to find work, and often at a higher wage, which served to cushion them against the effects of increased food prices. There can be no doubt that high prices still meant considerable suffering, but this was greatly alleviated by the availability of work.[18]

Situations varied, of course, and so did perceptions of the economic situation. In the textile centres of Haut-Rhin workers complained about the low levels of their wages when their employers were making large profits – a fact which was sympathetically reported by the departmental *gendarmerie* commander.[19] In the Paris region it was reported that wages in the towns were adequate and that in the countryside the farm domestics, with security of employment and at least partial payment in kind, were well-off but that the labourers hired by the day were suffering.[20] In some areas labour supply continued to exceed demand, and employers as a result did not feel compelled to increase wages, as around Neufchâtel in Normandy, where the development of pasture reduced labour needs,[21] or economically backward areas with high birth rates, like the Breton departments.

In the more isolated regions, untouched as yet by the railways, the mechanisms of the traditional crisis continued to be effective. In Limousin agricultural and industrial workers seem to have suffered intense misery, but even here sharecroppers and small proprietors profited from the rise in cereal and livestock prices, while migrant workers found employment without any difficulty in the building industries of Paris and Lyon.[22] Mountain areas of Cantal and Haute-Loire, and especially the small urban centres like Mauriac, also suffered serious hardship after the harvest of 1854.[23]

The authorities remained concerned about the threat of disorder, especially in those areas most troubled in 1846-7, such as Indre.[24] Their experience conditioned them to expect it. The most obvious cause of disturbances (high prices) still existed, and many of the symptoms of agitation, especially rumours about *accapareurs* and *placards*, were heard and seen. The approach of winter, when outside work declined, always heralded difficulties. Perhaps it was just as well that the winter of 1855-6 was a mild one.[25] Even so, with bread reaching 55 centimes per kilogram in the Rouen area, for example, there was inevitably considerable misery and unrest, leading in this particular region to disturbances in December in the textile centres of Elbeuf and Bernay.[26]

In the months following the harvest of 1853 the large reserves left from the previous year limited the increase in prices. The *procureur-général* at Poitiers reported that the urban poor were far more agitated than the rural because the latter were aware of the existence of these stocks.[27] By 1856 successive years of high prices were reflected in a growing unrest in some industrial regions, most notably in the Nord, but even there the only disorders were those at Le Cateau in August.[28]

As Figures 5 and 6 (pages 144 and 146) clearly indicate, protest movements were far less likely to occur during the crises of the 1850s than in the previous decade. The *procureur-général* at Angers actually boasted in January 1856 that for the first time in history a year of shortage would pass without disorder.[29] Some of his colleagues also registered their astonishment at this new turn of events.[30] This relative absence of disorder might well have been because, as Dupeux suggests, the main victims of the crisis, the wage earners, found themselves isolated when a far larger proportion of the rural population shared in the profit taking.[31] We should not, however, forget the amelioration even in their situation brought about by the reduced burden of unemployment.

In many regions 1859 and 1861 were again years of poor harvest, but all social groups were sheltered by savings from previous more prosperous years, and again work existed in plenty.[32] In contrast, the period following the poor harvest of 1867 seemed almost to be a reversion to an earlier period. Even in Paris bread prices rose so high that they caused popular disquiet, leading to a rash of rumours and *placards* and to threats of violence against merchants and the Emperor which reminded the Prefect of Police of the situation in 1846–7.[33]

Again, it was the more backward and isolated agricultural areas which suffered most. Where agricultural productivity was particularly low, yields did not provide a surplus above subsistence needs, or even enough for subsistence, and peasants again went to market as consumers. Subsistence disorders occurred in March 1868 at the poorly supplied markets of Albi and Gaillac (Tarn) and also at Toulouse, a major marketing centre in a relatively backward region and thus liable to substantial increases in demand, which pushed up prices;[34] in April at Blancafort (Cher)[35] and at Le Cheylard (Ardèche),[36] both rather isolated from currents of trade; in June (involving textile workers) at Guebwiller (Bas-Rhin)[37] and July at Valognes (Manche).[38] In most areas the harsh winter of 1867–8 had contributed to the state of unrest by causing unemployment in the building industry and in agriculture at a time when uncertainty about the internal and external political situation had already caused a crisis of confidence, resulting in industrial and commercial depression.[39]

Previous prosperity helped many to endure the renewed crisis, but the agricultural crisis and its consequence for the spending power of the rural population and urban poor were sufficiently serious to reduce substantially the demand for manufactured goods. The age-old link between industrial and agricultural prosperity was clearly reaffirmed and the severity of the social crisis intensified by unemployment and wage reductions affecting industrial workers.[40]

This was, however, the last partial appearance of the traditional subsistence crisis. Not only had improved communications and distribution facilities levelled out price variations, but also an acceleration in the rate of increase of agricultural productivity, prompted by improved access to market, finally banished the fear of dearth. As one response to the 1866 agricultural inquiry expressed it, even if a community did not produce cereals in sufficient quantity to feed its inhabitants, the new means of communication would rapidly supply the desired quantities, and at relatively low price, 'so that the population is able to believe itself free from danger and is no longer preoccupied with the food which is the basis of its diet'.[41] Fear had been replaced by a sense of security. It is perhaps not without significance that the last wave of subsistence disorders in the Limousin occurred in the year prior to the opening of the first railway lines in the region. Alain Corbin suggests that with this the *ancien régime économique* was finally terminated and a major change in mass mentality effected, although a certain latent anxiety must have persisted for some time.[42] The date at which this termination occurred varies from place to place, but contemporary witnesses combine to support Corbin's point and the explanation he offers.[43] In most areas the period 1850–60 was a major historical turning point. Even in the many areas not directly touched until later by railway construction a different perception of the market emerged, a confidence in the security of supply which altered behaviour in the market place, made it less emotive and so contributed to the levelling out of price variations. In 1847, as we have noted, the normally calm people of Buzançais had behaved like 'wild beasts' out of fear of starvation; by the late 1850s a witness of this outburst was quite confident that it would not be repeated. The change was symbolized by the physical transformation of bakers' shops from fortresses protected by strong doors and iron bars to elegant shops with windows in place of grilles.[44] Although Victor Modeste's book *De la cherté des grains et des préjugés populaires*, written to prove to the masses that in spite of the folk memory there was no longer any need to be afraid of famine, went into its third edition in 1862, changed circumstances had already done its work.

Another sign of the times was the final extension of free trade to the bakers, with the suspension of age-old restrictions by a decree of 22 June 1863.[45] Regulation of bread prices (the *taxe du pain*) and controls over bakers had traditionally been key elements of police power. The ending of such regulations became acceptable only with the disappearance of massive price fluctuations and the reduction in the consumer emotiveness which had been so characteristic of the *ancien régime économique*. It was anticipated that liberation, accompanied by an end to limitations on the number of bakers, would increase competition and reduce price levels.

Even so, the government remained cautious. Local authorities were still required to establish a *taxe officieuse* and to publish it: this was to be the suggested selling price for bread. Furthermore, a list of bakers selling below this price was also to be published to encourage competition. These provisions were, of course, more likely to be effective in large towns with a substantial number of bakers than in small towns in which bakers could easily agree on a price and apply pressure to those who stepped out of line.[46] In 1863, after a good harvest, the price of bread in the thirty-eight departments for which information exists was estimated to be some 2 centimes higher than it would have been if the *taxe du pain* had been retained. In some predominantly rural departments, such as Allier, Ardèche and Calvados, it was 3–4 centimes higher.[47] There was thus widespread discontent with the new system. This noticeably increased after poor harvests in 1866 and 1867, when there were frequent requests for the re-establishment of the *taxe*.[48] In some localities the official *taxe* either was never abolished or was reintroduced as a result of these complaints.[49] Municipal authorities retained this right in law, even if they were discouraged from using it.[50] As late as the end of the 1870s many councils were resisting official persuasion, and the old complaints from bakers about municipalities maintaining bread prices at an excessively low level in order to curry favour with their constituents were often repeated.[51]

In general, consumers were not particularly happy with the new system, which they blamed for rising prices. Parisians, who had enjoyed special favour under the regulated system, now found their bread to be relatively expensive. In 1867, when bread cost 0.48 francs in the Aube and 0.50 francs in the Beauce, it cost 0.52 francs in Paris.[52] In spite of this, consumers were in a far better position than before because of the reduction in the amplitude and rapidity of price fluctuations. The length of price cycles for bread was extended; the average price of bread fell by 18.5 per cent between 1881–5, rose 22.8 per cent between 1886–9, fell 20.7 per cent in 1892–5, and then, exceptionally, rose rapidly by 24.8 per cent in 1897–8, a rise which led to some minor bread riots.[53] In Paris the average annual price of bread of prime quality exceeded 40 centimes per kilogram four times between 1854 and 1863, three times from 1864 to 1873 but only once between 1874 and 1883.[54] Consumers enjoyed considerably more budgetary security and thus improved living standards. One result of this was that employed workers increasingly realized that their standards of living depended on wage levels rather than on prices and exercised collective pressure to increase the former rather than reduce the latter.

The changes occurring in agriculture and in the overall economic structure led, according to most commentators, to improvements, unique in their amplitude, in living standards for most of the population from the early 1850s and especially in the 1860s. Wage levels rose, while the price of bread remained relatively stable, allowing a greater proportion of total income to be spent on other commodities, including a wider range of foodstuffs. A more diverse diet meant not only better nourishment but a further reduction in sensibility to the failure of cereal harvests. One should not exaggerate the pace of change, given the significance of dietary conservatism. One cannot ignore the continuing misery of so much of the population, but it is essential to stress the historical significance of this period. As France emerged from the *ancien régime économique*, so the physical misery of life markedly declined. In the countryside increasing productivity accompanied the appearance of labour shortage and stimulated increases in wages.[55] Migration from areas in which population density had weighed most heavily on food resources and on employment opportunities eased social problems and provided labour both for more dynamic agricultural regions and the growing urban centres.[56]

To what extent were the popular classes aware of these changes? This is really a question about the relationship between individuals and their environment, and it seems obvious that a variety of physical indicators of change were present and talked about, from railway lines to increased wages. The means of diffusing information, both formal and informal, must have become more effective as mass migration, large-circulation newspapers and schooling developed simultaneously to reinforce visual awareness. Whether better diffusion of information increased popular comprehension of economic processes might be doubted, but at the level of simple awareness of change something was achieved. People actually came to believe that higher prices might be due primarily to a poor harvest rather than to speculation. The absence of massive price variations between neighbouring markets or over short periods of time made this fact easier to accept.

To an important degree, the apparently enlightened attitude of the masses to the trade in foodstuffs was also the product of their image of the political regime. There does appear to have been a fairly general confidence, in rural areas in particular, in the imperial regime, not simply because of its aura of authority – although this was an important disincentive to protest – but also because of the assiduously cultivated belief that the government was actively seeking to prevent shortage and to stimulate prosperity,[57] a belief confirmed by the fortuitous circumstances of international economic growth.

The effectiveness of the means of social control was increased by prosperity. The improvement of communications in the widest sense, including education as well as roads and railways, accelerated the process of integration of local communities into the national society. It was intended that the primary schools should enlighten and, especially, moralize the masses. Education became, and with a considerable degree of success, a key element in the process of socialization designed by the ruling élite to facilitate control over the lower classes. Thus a complex combination of changes in market structures and the revised perception of their circumstances on the part of the popular classes led to the disappearance of traditional subsistence disorders. Modification of the material and moral economies of the poor had been caused by significant changes in the political, and especially the socio-economic, structures of France. The process of change was centuries old, but only from the 1850s, with railway development, could it culminate in a social and economic revolution.

Part Three

Transport Revolution and Agriculture

There are three chapters in this section. The first will examine the transport revolution in terms of the improvements in bulk carrying capacity, the speed of transport and the reductions in the cost of transport which it facilitated. The second will look at the effects of improved communications upon the structure of the markets for agricultural products. The third will consider the degree to which farmers were able and willing to respond to the new opportunities created by improved access to markets and to new problems caused by the intensification of competition on both internal and international markets. In effect, I intend to examine some key aspects of the role of transport in economic development.

There have been a number of studies of transport and others of market structures and of agriculture. By examining interrelationships I hope to throw some light on processes of social and economic change.

7 The transport revolution: railways, roads, waterways

A transport network 'provides a facility for the *movement* of goods and people'.[1] Our interest is both in the development of transport networks in France and, above all, in the changes introduced in the characteristics of commodity flows by modifications of these networks. In this context the traditional concerns of transport historians with the financing, construction and operation of the various technical forms can be relegated to a subsidiary place.

The effects of a particular form of transport on market structures depends upon a complex of factors: the characteristics of the technology applied, the efficiency with which it is employed and decisions taken about freight rates, which reflect operating costs, levels of competition and desired levels of profitability. Therefore we shall need to consider both the density and quality of transport networks and their constant evolution; the relationship between the various techniques used – rail, road and water; and the character of the reciprocal influences between evolving transport systems and regional and national economies.

The railway

The major new variable in the economy from the 1840s was, of course, the development of a railway network. This led to a massive acceleration in the pace of improvement of transport facilities by providing the means for the rapid and cheap movement of commodities.

Toutain has provided us with estimates of the growth in the transport of commodities of all kinds within France (see Table 10).[2] The pre-rail forms of transport continued to move similar or even slightly greater volumes, but their share of the carrying trade dropped considerably. Renouard has estimated that from 1851 to 1876, a period of especially rapid growth in the tonnage transported, the share of the railways increased by 1590 per cent (11.2 per cent per annum), while on the waterways and roads tonnage increased by only 18 and 19 per cent respectively (0.5 per cent per annum).[3]

The reduction in transport costs and the extension of the market area effected by railways stimulated a considerable increase in the volume of commodities transported. The economist Lavollée considered this to be 'the

Table 10   *Transport of commodities, 1830–1914 (milliard tonnes per kilometre)*

Period	Road	Canal	Rail	Sea (coaster)	Total
1830	2.0	0.5	—	0.6	3.5
1841–4	(2.3)	0.8	0.06	0.7	(3.9)
1845–54	2.6	1.2	0.46	0.7	5.0
1855–64	2.7	1.4	3.0	0.7	7.8
1865–74	2.8	1.3	6.3	0.6	11.0
1875–84	2.6	1.5	9.4	0.6	14.1
1885–94	2.7	2.3	10.9	0.8	16.7
1895–1904	2.8	3.2	14.9	1.1	22.0
1905–1914	2.9	3.8	21.0	1.1	28.8

most important achievement of our century'[4] and, judging by the obsession of his contemporaries (both economists and entrepreneurs) with transport problems, this view was shared generally. Transport was conceived of as the central problem of economic development and social modernization.

Rail construction

General evolution
Our immediate concern in this chapter will be to consider the development of the means of communication. One of the key factors of development in the modern world is the construction of more or less systematically conceived transport networks based upon advanced techniques. In France the initial plan for a railway network, prepared by the engineers of the Corps des Ponts-et-Chaussées and accepted after long debate by the Chamber of Deputies in 1842, was for a system radiating from Paris, linking the capital with the provinces. To a large extent, the directions taken by this network, as in the case of pre-existing technically inferior forms of transport, was determined by relief. Railway lines, like roads, tend to follow valleys and sills. They also tend to be constructed on the basis of existing information about trade flows; that is, priority will be given to the establishment of links between major and economically active centres of population, whose very existence was a consequence of a privileged position on what were previously relatively efficient axes of communication. Particularly noticeable in the early discussions was the concern to provide better communications for, and with, coal-producing areas and industrial regions generally, contrasting with a marked lack of interest in potential agricultural traffic. As a result, regions with already under-developed transport structures often

found this inferiority exacerbated by new developments. Thus initial modernization of communications, the establishment of the first 'lines of penetration',[5] was followed by demands for equal treatment from regional pressure groups in other areas. This helped to determine the shape of the developing networks as feeder routes and lateral links were constructed. The effectiveness of the overall transport system depended a great deal upon the scale of investment in secondary links and also on improvement of the efficiency of feeder routes using pre-existing techniques; for the railways this meant, above all, the improvement of road links.

The first important lines, from Paris to Orléans and from Paris to Rouen, were opened in 1843. They seemed to prove the claims being made for the economic potential of the new form of transport.[6] Further development was rather slow, not simply because of the complex technical and financial problems of the new enterprise but also because of the cumbersome nature of administrative and political decision-making. The economic crisis of 1846–7 led to the withdrawal of capital and a further slowing, so that by the end of 1847 only 1830 kilometres were being exploited and a further 2872 kilometres were under construction. The railway had reached Compiègne, Abbeville, Le Havre, Tours, Vierzon, Bourges and Châteauroux.[7] Political uncertainties and renewed economic dificulties throughout the Second Republic imposed further delays. Railway interests were therefore quick to welcome Louis-Napoléon Bonaparte's *coup d'état* in December 1851. As early as 7 December the financier Mirès, in an editorial in the *Journal des chemins de fer*, recorded his pleasure at the tangible signs of the dawning of a new era – the rise in railway shares – and at the fact that 'already important men are meeting to give force and support to the government, in the development of public works'.

Authoritarian government, with leaders committed to economic development and fully aware of the importance of communications, was able to reduce substantially the period of argument and hesitation. In place of long parliamentary debate, decisions tended to be taken by small groups of ministers, engineers and financiers, although these remained susceptible to the influence of a variety of pressure groups, particularly those from localities desiring rail links. At any rate, during the Second Empire the basic primary network was completed. Concessions for the construction of a total of 13,900 kilometres were distributed, and 13,600 kilometres were actually brought into operation.

A report to the Emperor from Rouher, the Minister of Public Works, in November 1856,[8] indicates the scale of the achievement during the early 1850s. 6500 kilometres were then in operation and 4750 under construction. The key Paris–Lyon–Marseille link had been completed in 1855 and a national network on an economically significant scale finally brought into being.

The regime was also able to promote the foundation of large and financially sound companies through the amalgamation of existing small ones. These would be better able to develop secondary lines and to increase the unity and homogeneity of service and thus to reduce overall transport costs. An internal Ministry of Public Works memorandum prepared for the Minister had already noted in 1849 that tariffs were lowest on the lines of the Nord Company, which had the advantage of a relatively large concession, on which the more profitable lines compensated for those with low returns. It had stressed the need to promote the amalgamation of the separate Paris–Lyon and Lyon–Avignon companies as a means of securing more economical transport.[9] By the end of 1853 fifteen companies had been reduced to four, each operating on a regional basis.

Another hallmark of the imperial years was a series of agreements between the government and the railway companies. Those of 1852 and 1859 extended the length of the concessions these companies possessed to ninety-nine years, allowing them to plan longer-term and more intensive investment programmes, relatively free from the burden of short-term debt redemption. The convention of 1859, by means of state guarantees of dividend payments, encouraged companies to proceed with the development of potentially less profitable secondary lines, which had previously been hindered by the reduction of receipts following a series of poor harvests and particularly by a financial crisis which had reduced the possibilities of borrowing.[10] As the demand for railway lines increased, even this was to be inadequate. An 1865 law designed to facilitate the construction of lines of local interest by local companies had little effect, so that to satisfy localized demand based on real economic needs, the government of the Third Republic in 1883 negotiated further conventions with the major companies, again guaranteeing their dividends in order to establish the financial conditions for the extension of the rail networks laid down in the Freycinet Plan approved by Parliament in 1878.[11]

A significant feature of these conventions, and of the development of railway legislation more generally, was the establishment of statutory controls over the companies in return for the concessions made to them. These affected matters such as safety and tariffs. In laying down obligations for the companies to fulfil, they developed a public-service conception of operations far removed from *laissez-faire* private interprise. The companies in return made a considerable effort through personal contacts and official representations and through the economic and financial press, to influence the administrative and judicial organs of the state to act in a manner favourable to company interests. They enjoyed a considerable degree of success, especially during the Second Empire, with a regime anxious to develop the economy and to support the efforts of large enterprises.[12]

The ultimate decision to favour one area over another, or to concede responsibility to one potential concessionary company rather than another, was a political one. The administration was, in effect, called upon to arbitrate between rival interest groups and to take decisions partly on the basis of technical advice from its own agents but also in response to the various kinds of influence exerted upon it. It goes without saying that prominent financiers and politicians exercised an influence commensurate with the economic and social power that they were presumed to exert, while other interest groups (e.g. the small carters and inn keepers whose enterprises were likely to be adversely affected by proposed railway developments) had neither much influence nor, indeed, the means to express their views effectively.

Official inquiries into proposed routes for lines were conducted by the engineers of the Ponts-et-Chaussées. They remain impressive, containing detailed descriptions of topography, estimates of the significance of this for rail construction and subsequent operating costs, as well as attempts to estimate traffic potential based upon studies of existing movement by road and water. Their key function was to offer advice on potential routes in relation to population centres and centres of production. While usually favouring the straightest possible line between termini for reasons of cost and speed of movement, engineers were clearly aware of the objective of serving the needs of the economy. Their views were typically expressed in the report of a commission of inquiry set up to examine a project for a line from Abbeville to Eu and Tréport and reporting in 1873. It made the point that:

in every railway study, the interests of the termini and those of intermediary localities must be conciliated; the former are in favour of the shortest possible route, the latter demand certain detours, increasing the costs of construction and operation, but one is able nevertheless to take into consideration the interests of important intermediary points without the termini having cause for complaint. [13]

The economic significance and potential of particular towns and regions had therefore to be assessed in relation to those which might be served by alternative routes. These inquiries provide the historian with a great deal of useful information on economic and, particularly, commercial activity. Their objectivity is not in doubt, which is more than can be said of the mass of brochures published by various interest groups while inquiries were under way, all seeking to prove to the government the wisdom of adopting a particular route, with stations at the town or village whose municipal council or Chamber of Commerce was responsible for the particular brochure. These do, however, clearly reveal the great public interest in rail construction, derived from a belief in its vital importance for economic development. Railway questions inevitably became important in local and regional politics, particularly as causes of conflict between localities. Bitter complaints came from the representatives of places judged to be of insufficient importance to justify an expensive detour or branch line, at least in the immediate future. [14]

Following numerous inquiries, the railway network grew in length and density. By 1913 the network of lines of general interest had grown from 3248 kilometres in 1851 to 40,770 kilometres,[15] while that of lines of local interest and tramways increased from 17 kilometres in 1867 to 7368 by 1906.[16] The increase in the number of railway workers to 27,900 in 1851, 86,300 in 1861, 113,000 in 1866, 172,000 in 1876, 222,800 in 1881, 308,000 in 1907 and 355,600 in 1913 is further illustration of a process of continual growth until the eve of the First World War.[17] The statistics published by Lévy-Leboyer on investment in railways illustrate the chronology and scale of expenditure (see Table 11).[18]

Until well into the 1840s the various technical journals reveal continuing uncertainty as to the utility of railways. In the early days it appears to have been generally believed that passengers would be the most profitable element of traffic. According to the annual report of the Orléans to Bordeaux Company for 1849, the transport of merchandise had been considered only as an accessory to this.[19] The administrators of the Chemin de fer de l'Ouest and of the Paris–Avignon admitted to the same error.[20] Nothing is more revealing of the mistaken estimates of the companies in respect of the development of goods traffic as the inadequacy of goods

Table 11   *Chronology and scale of expenditure on railways, 1830–1913 (millions of francs)*

a Infrastructure and construction (average annual expenditure)

Period	New expenditure	Maintenance costs	Total expenditure
1830–9	7.2	0.4	7.6
1840–9	84.5	2.6	87.1
1850–9	215.0	18.2	233.2
1860–9	227.5	45.0	272.5
1870–9	158.1	75.1	233.2
1880–9	262.3	92.2	354.5
1890–9	164.0	98.9	262.9
1900–9	214.3	124.2	338.5
1910–13	371.4	171.7	543.1

b Annual average investment in plant and equipment

Period	Investment	Period	Investment
1835–44	7	1875–84	140
1845–54	32	1885–94	121
1855–64	85	1895–1904	170
1865–74	86	1905–13	236

station facilities, which all companies soon experienced. The administration of the Compagnie de l'Est admitted in 1853 that goods traffic had 'increased . . . with such rapidity that our material has been found to be insufficient. We have found it necessary to refuse traffic'.[21] The administrators of the Compagnie du Nord felt that traffic 'exceeded all reasonable estimates'.[22]

The railway had in many quarters been thought to be unsuitable for the transport of bulky commodities like cereals, particularly where waterways were in existence.[23] Even as this view was modified, rail goods traffic still tended to be conceived of in terms of industrial rather than agricultural commodities.[24] We have already noted the priority given to industrial considerations in the planning of basic routes. The experience of the first major network to be exploited, that of the Nord, operating in the most industrialized region of the country and carrying large quantities of coal, seemed to confirm the wisdom of this. This attitude would lead subsequently to frequent complaints about neglect of the interests of agriculture, particularly as, from the end of the 1840s and in the early 1850s, public interest in railways and belief in their economic efficacy grew.

Whereas during discussions of railway development in the early 1840s considerable scepticism had been evident and disquiet expressed that it might upset the economic life of the various regions,[25] by the end of the decade the character of the discussion had changed. It was now not the possibility of a railway's being constructed that caused anxiety but the possibility that it might not or that construction might be delayed.[26] This growth in interest and appreciation of the economic utility of the railway accompanied and reflected the growth in traffic,[27] as nothing was to establish the value of railways or to stimulate pressure for their development more firmly. Table 12 shows the growth of traffic between 1841 and 1863.[28] From the early 1850s the changing pattern of receipts made clear to the companies the

Table 12   *Growth of railway traffic, 1841–1913 (millions kilometric tonnes)*

Year	Kilometric tonnage	Year	Kilometric tonnage	Year	Kilometric tonnage
1841	0.037	1865	5.12	1890	11.6
1842	0.044	1868	6.20	1893	11.9
1843	0.054	1870	5.06	1895	12.5
1845	0.102	1873	8.07	1898	14.5
1848	0.234	1875	8.03	1900	16.0
1850	0.423	1878	8.26	1903	16.1
1853	0.840	1880	10.20	1905	17.4
1855	1.53	1883	10.90	1908	20.0
1858	2.40	1885	9.48	1910	21.5
1863	4.06	1888	10.20	1913	25.2

financial importance of goods traffic and the need to improve neglected goods-handling facilities (see Table 13).[29]

Regional development
Most of rural France was to be penetrated by the railway only with the development of the minor local lines constructed from the 1880s. The process of development was to continue into the beginning of the era of motor transport. 1914 is both a convenient and realistic date to mark the end of the era of railway development in France.

At every stage of this process of network development voices could be heard complaining about the neglect of particular places and regions left without railways. The primary network completed in the 1850s certainly left vast areas untouched (as Figure 7 reveals). Each company faced pressure from both interest groups and government to construct more lines. Thus the senior Ponts-et-Chaussées official, Busche, reporting in 1860 on the Paris–Orléans network, observed that although it was the most extensive of all, 'the lines which form it are separated from each other by vast spaces entirely deprived of railways; the demands for new lines to fill these gaps in the network are . . . very numerous'.[30] From the Norman departments came complaints about the gulf between the line from Paris to Rouen in the Seine valley and that of the Ouest company, which left 'most localities so distant

Table 13   *Receipts from passenger and goods traffic, 1850–65*
            (percentage of total)

Year	Receipts from passenger traffic	Receipts from express goods (grande vitesse)	Receipts from ordinary goods traffic (petite vitesse)	Diverse
1850	64.74	8.14	27.12	—
1851	56.42	8.09	34.48	—
1852	53.37	9.15	37.48	—
1853	44.08	8.94	46.98	—
1854	41.16	8.45	50.39	—
1855	39.85	8.49	51.66	—
1856	37.07	8.13	54.80	—
1857	37.68	7.70	54.62	—
1858	35.12	7.03	57.85	—
1859	34.18	7.86	57.96	—
1860	33.96	6.93	59.11	—
1861	33.42	6.43	59.91	1.24
1862	33.27	6.69	58.32	1.72
1863	33.17	6.87	57.91	2.08
1864	31.27	6.28	60.46	1.99
1865	30.28	5.93	61.71	2.08

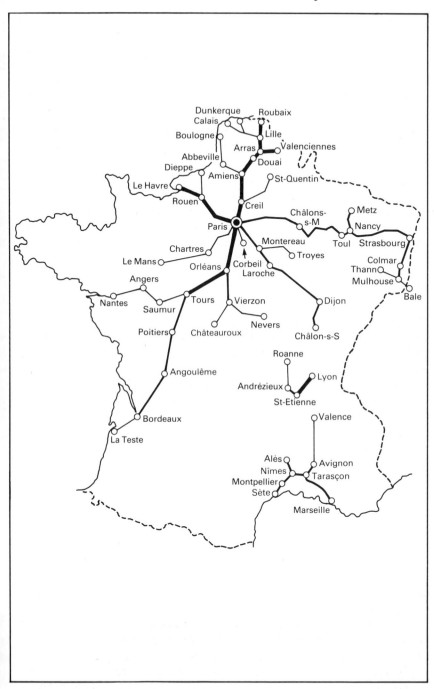

Figure 7 *Goods traffic by rail, 1854*

. . . that they find themselves outside of the zone of attraction'. A new line through the middle of the neglected area seemed to be the answer.[31] In 1855 a short-lived newspaper, the *Journal des chemins de fer départementaux*, was established to represent the interests of all those in similar situations.[32] This represented an attempt to co-ordinate the activities of numerous local pressure groups – a sign of the modernization of political processes. More effective pressures could, however, still be exerted by local notables, especially through their elected political representatives.[33] The companies themselves saw good economic reasons for further construction. According to the annual report of the *conseil d'administration de l'Est* in 1858:

at first we had thought only of linking Paris with the major towns or with the most distant parts of the country . . . [but] before even those lines had been completed, when each of them was only partially exploited, we were rapidly forced to recognize that if these lines remained isolated, they would be reduced to their own traffic and would be able to serve only the interests of localities situated on their routes; that if, on the contrary, we established branches from the main lines, we would extend their *zone d'action* and that traffic would increase. . . .

The policy of the company was therefore to develop branches wherever it seemed likely that the income from these would justify the expense, and to establish links with other networks in order to increase the volume of through traffic.[34]

The argument in favour of further construction was often based on equity. The case was put most succinctly by the mayor of Wasquehal (Nord), in a petition to the Emperor dated 23 September 1853, which observed that if communication had not been rapid in the past, at least it had been much the same for every locality in the region and none had been able to acquire a superiority over the others. The advent of the railway had destroyed this equality; now economic prosperity depended on 'more or less easy access to the railway'.[35]

Throughout the 1860s and in spite of the development of a secondary network (see Figure 8) the discussion continued in much the same terms.[36] Rural areas in particular complained that the construction of a network designed to serve the towns and industry meant that the interests of agriculture had been neglected.[37] Although almost everywhere roads had been, or were being, improved out of all recognition, this, although essential to continuing economic development, no longer seemed enough. Lack of easy access to the railway imposed extra costs of production and marketing on the farmer and merchant; a rail link would transform their situation.[38] In 1873 an official commission of inquiry admitted that the existing network needed improvement, particularly in regions without rail service or in those with an inadequate network, such as the Auvergne and Brittany.[39] Even relatively well endowed regions continued to feel dissatisfied. Thus the *conseil général*

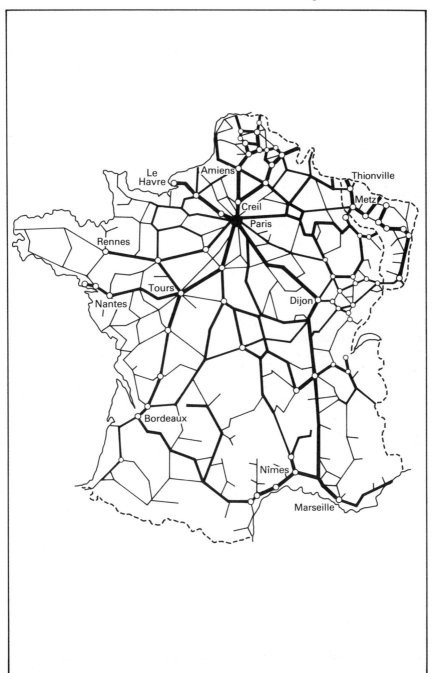

Figure 8 *Goods traffic by rail, 1878*

of the Nord complained that the density of the rail network in its department was inferior to that in neighbouring Belgium.[40]

Numerous proposals were made for rail links by departmental prefects anxious to improve the economic situation of the areas that they administered, by deputies or candidates seeking votes and by a variety of economic interest groups.[41] The strength of such pressure can be gauged from the concessions made to it by the Freycinet Plan and the earlier law (of 12 July 1865) on lines of local interest. Each act of legislation was immediately followed by a rush of proposals.

The 1865 law allowed the construction of lines of local interest, but the companies established tended to be too weak economically to maintain an efficient and competitive service.[42] Ministry of Public Works officials do not seem at any stage to have been particularly enthusiastic about such small companies and, by the mid 1870s, were clearly in favour of their absorption by the major networks. It was recognized to be in the 'general interest' to secure the profitability of the major companies against the activities of their small rivals in order to reduce the likelihood of their having to call upon state guarantees of dividends.[43] In spite of continuing anxiety about rail monopoly, the Chamber of Deputies was forced, in August 1867, to recognize that local companies were not viable – something their owners were generally prepared to concede by this time – and subsequently official encouragement was given to their amalgamation with existing major companies. In the case of the Vendée and Charente lines, which the Paris–Orléans was unwilling to acquire, the government itself repurchased the lines and constituted a new network, the Etat with 2615 kilometres of track, by a law of 18 May 1878.[44] Eventually this was to be followed by the repurchase of the Ouest (i.e. its effective nationalization) from 1 January 1909. The Ouest had been burdened by an excessive number of uneconomic lines and by financial problems which had affected the quality of its service.[45] The government thus felt obliged to secure control in order to safeguard the public interest. A new and more homogeneous Etat network was created by the amalgamation of the existing Etat company with the Ouest.[46]

The favour temporarily accorded to these *lignes d'intérêt local* constituted only a short interruption in a policy which, by a series of conventions between the government and the major companies, repeatedly provided for the construction of new lines by the latter. These recognized the capacity of large companies with profitable lines to bear the losses made by operating lines of secondary economic significance, and also their superior competence and operating experience. Reversal of the policy favouring small companies represented a return to the official aim of promoting the formation of large-scale integrated networks rather than a more fragmentary structure of more or less isolated lines.

By this means construction continued. Pressure from local interest groups for new lines had never abated, and was taken up by important national groups such as the Société des agriculteurs de France, which in 1873 pointed out the insufficient density of the networks, particularly in some regions, and also the lack of transversals which would have allowed more direct communications and considerable economy on transport costs.[47]

Charles Freycinet, a leading republican politician, wrote in the *Journal des économistes* in September 1872 that the Republic would succeed if it 'shows its true nature by the execution of useful projects; if it proves, as it shall, that it is a government of order, peace and industry'. The monarchist regime headed by MacMahon decided in January 1873 to establish *commissions régionales* (one for each network), including engineers, members of the *conseil d'état* and *conseils généraux*, to determine where lines were needed to complete the existing network by linking to it all the localities of some importance that were still deprived of a railway.[48] At each stage in the discussion process the number of lines proposed increased. The depressed economic conditions of the late 1870s and the evident popular demand for railways made them key vote catchers as well as an economically important measure. In a report of 2 and 16 January 1878 Freycinet, now Minister of Public Works, proposed a programme involving the spending of 3000 million francs on rail construction.[49] The detailed project presented on 4 June proposed the addition of 8700 kilometres to the network of 'general interest', including the reclassification of fifty-three lines previously conceded as lines of 'local interest' and the construction of 154 new lines. Subsequent discussion led to eventual proposals for the construction of 18,000 kilometres of railway – mainly transversals and branch lines[50] – at an estimated cost of 4500 million francs. The 1883 Convention with the railway companies made it clear that the construction of these lines was intended to take decades, but nevertheless a commitment to extend the network substantially had been taken and would to a large extent be implemented. By 1914 some 8000 kilometres had been added to the network of 'general interest' and 8000 more to that of 'local interest'.[51]

In his memoirs Freycinet appears to stress as the motive for extension of the network the importance of correcting regional inequalities in economic development rather than any potential profitability of the lines themselves. The government had in effect decided that all Frenchmen should, if possible, share the benefits to be gained from proximity to a railway by means of increasing the number of both lines and stations. In practice, priorities had once again to be painfully established. The immediate problem was to finance and secure the construction of new lines by railway companies and financial groups reluctant to assume new commitments. The Orléans had already failed to take up the construction of concessions made to it in 1862–5 and in 1875.[52] The Ouest was in financial difficulties because of the low revenue-earning capacity of many of its routes.[53] The network of 24,999 kilometres existing on 31 December 1881 already linked all major urban centres, and the relatively backward regions to be newly served were not likely to generate much traffic. The new commitments meant carrying small quantities of merchandise, often over short distances. They also entailed not just the construction of new lines but also an increase in the number of stations and halts on existing lines, so that on average there was one every 3–5 kilometres. These changes were very likely to cause an increase in operating costs that was proportionately higher than the increase in revenue generated. It was indeed claimed by one well-informed observer, at a meeting of a parliamentary committee in 1883, that as a consequence of this the companies were already actively discouraging the use of many secondary lines. He referred to the case of a line in Seine-Inférieure where trains were deliberately being run at 17 kilometres per hour with this intention.[54] However, the existing companies were favoured by the government as likely to be its most effective agents. To secure compliance and overcome doubts concerning the profitability of new lines, new conventions which guaranteed dividends were agreed with the companies and promulgated in November 1883. Subsequently, Millerand, as Minister of Public Works in 1910, recognized that the combination of lines with limited traffic and generalized economic depression from the 1880s had imposed severe financial burdens on the companies. However, he did not question the basic wisdom of the network extensions which had occurred since 1883.[55]

Both during the initial discussion and subsequently this new construction programme faced severe criticism because of the likely unprofitability of the lines and because it was presumed that political motives (vote catching) had been uppermost in the minds of the plan's proponents. There was a great deal of truth in these complaints. M. Raynal, Minister of Public Works, admitted as much before the parliamentary commission on railways on 19 June 1883 but added that in spite of financial difficulties and allowing 'that one can think what one wishes of M. Freycinet's plan . . . it is certain that the populations to which promises have been made and which think nothing of the financial difficulties involved, anticipate this network, and any halt or even serious delays in work on the third network would involve the greatest peril from the political, economic and social points of view'.[56]

In defence of the plan it could be said that prior to the development of motor transport the railway was of crucial economic and social importance to the regions newly served, and that indeed it would have been difficult politically to accept that large areas of France should be excluded from what was viewed as one of the major benefits of modern civilization. It might further be claimed that the new lines corresponded to the real needs of a society which remained profoundly rural. An article in the *Annales des Ponts-et-Chaussées* in 1894 on the 'utility of railway lines of local interest' made the point that only if the peasant had easy access to urban markets would he appreciate the potential for sale of his own products and purchase more of the products of industry.[57] The role of the new lines was thus both to satisfy and to stimulate local needs, and if many fond hopes concerning the generation of new traffic were not entirely realized, it remained the case that where lines were constructed market structures were radically transformed and the horizons of the rural population were greatly enlarged. The importance of these developments was not diminished by the fact that political influences were exercised and that senators, deputies and various pressure groups influenced the details of directions taken and the positioning of the stations. As a general point it might be observed that transport systems tend to develop to meet the needs of a particular period. Changing needs require further development. Hence the abandonment of so many minor railway lines in the twentieth century.

It should also be borne in mind that not all the new lines planned and constructed were of such doubtful economic value. Some were regarded as of considerable importance to the efficient operation of the existing primary network. Some major lines, particularly in the north-east and above all the Marseille–Lyon–Dijon–Paris link were overcrowded in spite of the laying of up to four tracks in places. The construction of alternative itineraries for use during periods of seasonal peak traffic was the essential means for the equalization of traffic over the network and for the limitation of delays caused by the accumulation of traffic.[58]

Another sound economic reason for the construction of additional lines of general interest was the establishment of more direct links between two points and the consequent reduction of transport costs. This involved a rather fine calculation as to whether the likely savings were worth the cost of construction plus the reductions in use of existing track.[59]

In large part, railway construction continued because of the survival of an optimistic belief in the potential for economic growth and of the role of the railway in this. The economic vitality of previously disinherited areas would be increased it was felt by their integration into the national economy. Traffic would be generated by the construction of the railway. Branch lines which served as feeders for the primary network would increase the volume of traffic on these, and this would at least partly offset any financial losses on the branch lines. This philosophy had been expressed for decades by every town or region which wanted a railway line and was so again in the debate on the Freycinet Plan and on its implementation.[60] No doubt in some cases it was true. Thus a senior Ponts-et-Chaussées engineer, M. Considère, studying the Morlaix–Roscoff line in 1885, calculated that its operating expenses were 133,000 francs and its receipts 77,500 francs, leaving an apparent loss of 55,500 francs, but that in providing traffic for other lines operated by the Ouest Company, it had increased overall receipts by 313,500 francs. After subtracting operating costs – estimated at 156,000 francs – this left 157,500 francs and a real profit of 102,000 francs.[61] These were the basic economic arguments and typical justifications for constantly extending the network. Clearly, M. Considère, arguing from one particular case to make a general point, was on shaky ground, but he had on his side a wave of enthusiasm for railways which had not yet moderated, which was supported by every locality still without a branch line, by their political representatives and by the powerful groups which supplied railway equipment.[62] The 1879 law had the effect, according to one calculation, of reducing the number of those without easy access to railways from 8,740,282 to 6,849,120 (17.4 per cent of the population),[63] a commendable but surprisingly limited consequence of such a considerable investment. It is also clear that the productivity of capital invested in railways was to be sharply reduced by the extension of the network. By 1906, for example, although making up 15.63 per cent of the total network, the 7368 kilometres classified as railway of local interest, or tramways, carried only 0.69 per cent of the total volume of traffic.[64]

Statistics on the density of track in 1907[65] by department indicate, and not surprisingly, that economically backward areas, which were generally areas of low population density, remained relatively neglected by rail constructors in spite of the developments associated with the Freycinet Plan (see Table 14). These statistics clearly reveal the extent of the concentration of railway

Table 14   *Density of rail network per square myriametre (10,000 m²)*
           by department, 1907

Department	Density of network	Department	Density of network
Ain	17.370	Loire-Inférieure	13.700
Aisne	17.644	Loiret	11.428
Allier	11.075	Lot	7.820
Basses-Alpes	3.903	Lot-et-Garonne	7.986
Hautes-Alpes	4.454	Lozère	4.614
Alpes-Maritimes	16.706	Maine-et-Loire	12.621
Ardèche	11.394	Manche	13.915
Ardennes	15.596	Marne	11.817
Ariège	4.270	Haute-Marne	9.704
Aube	7.768	Mayenne	9.494
Aude	10.503	Meurthe-et-Moselle	14.287
Aveyron	4.838	Meuse	11.747
Belfort	11.454	Morbihan	9.743
Bouches-du-Rhône	21.350	Nièvre	10.192
Calvados	14.825	Nord	33.716
Cantal	7.009	Oise	16.268
Charente	9.104	Orne	11.258
Charente-Inférieure	14.969	Pas-de-Calais	17.099
Cher	10.435	Puy-de-Dôme	7,094
Corrèze	9.335	Basses-Pyrénées	7.973
Corse	3.396	Hautes-Pyrénées	6.026
Côte-d'Or	10.859	Pyrénées-Orientales	8.092
Côtes-du-Nord	10.368	Rhône	26.851

Creuse	7.639	Haute-Saône	13.016
Dordogne	9.157	Saône-et-Loire	13.705
Doubs	10.046	Sarthe	13.984
Drôme	7.922	Savoie	6.038
Eure	13.131	Haute-Savoie	9.591
Eure-et-Loir	14.372	Seine	202.655
Finistère	10.142	Seine-Inférieure	15.744
Gard	12.647	Seine-et-Marne	15.692
Haute-Garonne	10.636	Seine-et-Oise	20.446
Gers	6.987	Deux-Sèvres	12.302
Gironde	12.094	Somme	15.647
Hérault	11.826	Tarn	9.918
Ille-et-Vilaine	15.802	Tarn-et-Garonne	6.889
Indre	9.361	Var	9.787
Indre-et-Loire	13.340	Vaucluse	9.667
Isère	13.767	Vendée	10.566
Jura	13.118	Vienne	8.940
Landes	10.318	Haute-Vienne	8.947
Loir-et-Cher	13.367	Vosges	11.250
Loire	14.313	Yonne	9.566
Haute-Loire	10.651		
		National average	11.585

development in the Paris region, north-east and centre-east. A calculation made in 1892 – which allowed a reduction in track length of 8–10 per cent to accommodate bifurcation – concluded that 40 per cent of the area of France remained outside the effective zone of attraction of the railway network.[66]

Rail operations

In considering the effects of railway development on the evolution of markets, operating efficiency is clearly a crucially important question. Transport networks evolve over time, in terms not only of area covered but also of efficiency. This was especially evident in the case of a technologically advanced system like the railway. Continuous investment was essential, both to replace worn equipment and to increase, or even maintain, operating efficiency through innovation.

Innovation was clearly a response to the linked problems of growing user demand, insufficient network density and lack or poor utilization of rolling stock. In analysing its form from the 1860s, Caron[67] has stressed the difficulty of synchronizing technical innovation in the various operational sectors; thus increases in the weight of trains made possible by more powerful locomotives depended, to be fully effective, on the introduction of heavier rails and improved braking systems, on the increased speed and frequency of trains, on the development of signalling systems adequate for their control. In the latter respect the development of the 'block system' and finally automatic signals substantially reduced the possibility of collision and allowed the safe reduction of gaps between trains. Hydraulic brakes and those with wooden blocks were inadequate from the point of view of safety and of the number of wagons which might be controlled. They imposed limits on the size of trains. The introduction of the Westinghouse system converted braking from a hand operation to one which could be operated from the engine and could control the whole train as a unit. It increased safety and facilitated increases in the length of the train. Innovations seem to have been introduced in clusters, influenced by a complex of factors including the interrelatedness of the various forms of technical change, the degree to which existing facilities met estimated needs and the capital available for investment. They occurred first where existing facilities were under pressure and were then gradually extended after their effectiveness had been empirically proven, although the process was slowed by the accounting procedures imposed on the companies by the Conseil d'Etat in the 1870s which did not allow sufficiently for amortization, and the additional fact that engineers favoured high-quality rolling stock, built to last, which was transferred to secondary lines once it had outlived its usefulness on main lines.[68]

Innovation occurred largely in order to lower, or at least to slow, the rate of increase of costs. These were made up both of economic and of social components, including wages and prices of materials used, particularly coal, and the cost of manufactured equipment. Companies seem to have been particularly adept at maintaining low wages but had limited control over the movement of general price levels. Innovation designed to reduce consumption of such expensive items as fuel and rails and to increase the capacity both of single trains and of the overall network was the major complement to a harsh labour relations policy.[69] Initially, increased running of trains could be effected by more intensive use of existing under-employed facilities, especially given that the supply of transport facilities on most routes tended at first to run ahead of the demand for them. Further improvement in carrying capacity was made possible by better use and improvement of rolling stock and station facilities. Thus the net revenue derived from various routes could be increased up to the point at which overcrowding occurred and costs rose sharply. Subsequently innovation had to take more expensive forms, with the development of alternative itineraries (that is, the construction of new lines) or a renewed cluster of technical innovations. This appears to have become necessary on major trunk routes by the closing years of the Second Empire. By this time the earning power of the networks and their capacity for innovation were already beginning to be threatened by the costs of construction and operation of lines of secondary importance, a burden which was to continue to grow.

By the end of the 1850s a contrast was already evident between the traffic density and revenue earned by the primary network largely completed by the mid 1850s and the less remunerative additions sanctioned subsequently. The effect of the exploitation of the latter was to reduce overall earnings per kilometre for the whole network (see Table 15).[70] Toutain's indices of the

Table 15 *Revenue per kilometre of track exploited, 1859–65 (francs)*

	1859	1860	1861	1862	1863	1864	1865
Primary networks	50,241	51,757	57,126	56,106	54,856	55,809	57,272
New networks	22,803	22,850	23,901	22,917	21,611	21,077	20,937

product per tonne/kilometre (i.e. excess of receipts over expenses) for goods traffic make the same point over a longer period (see Table 16).[71]

The effect of further additions of even less remunerative lines was gradually to reduce the product per kilometre. The tendency for this product to decline on both primary and new networks seems to have been a constant cause of concern for railway administrators from the mid 1850s, particularly

Table 16 *Goods traffic, product per tonne/kilometre, 1841–1913*

Index: 1913 = 100

Year	Product (per t/km)	Year	Product (per t/km)	Year	Product (per t/km)	Year	Product (per t/km)
1841	293	1860	168	1880	144	1900	115
1842	288	1861	163	1881	144	1901	115
1843	283	1862	163	1882	144	1902	115
1844	280	1863	161	1883	139	1903	112
1845	271	1864	151	1884	144	1904	112
1846	278	1865	149	1885	144	1905	110
1847	251	1866	146	1886	144	1906	110
1848	232	1867	149	1887	141	1907	107
1849	219	1868	149	1888	139	1908	105
1850	198	1869	151	1889	137	1909	105
1851	188	1870	149	1890	126	1910	105
1852	200	1871	154	1891	132	1911	102
1853	200	1872	144	1892	132	1912	102
1854	185	1873	144	1893	129	1913	100
1855	185	1874	146	1894	127		
1856	185	1875	149	1895	127		
1857	178	1876	146	1896	124		
1858	176	1877	146	1897	122		
1859	176	1878	146	1898	119		
		1879	146	1899	120		

as the most remunerative routes grew increasingly overcrowded in the late 1860s and their operating costs increased more rapidly than revenue.[72] The results for 1879 in terms of product per kilometre for each network illustrate both the continuation of this trend and the substantial variations between companies which reflected both their earning capacity and varying costs of operation (see Table 17).[73]

The Nord clearly benefited from its geographical situation, the plains of northern France making for low construction and amortization costs, lower operating costs and more intensive use due to operation in economically advanced regions – in short, relatively low cost and high revenue.[74]

Costs and income varied considerably according to the general layout of a network. The existence of competitive navigable waterways, and the level of demand for transport, were factors of fundamental importance. But, equally, each section of line had its own topographical characteristics which in large part determined its operation in terms of speed, weight and the spacing of trains (i.e. the capacity of the line) and inevitably influenced its costs and charges.[75]

Mountain areas presented particularly severe technical problems. These could be solved, although the costs of construction were substantially greater, but the difficulties of making operations profitable were insuperable. Gradients reduced the possible weights and speeds of trains while increasing their fuel consumption because the effective distance between two points was increased by the need to avoid the worst gradients and because frequent stops wasted time and fuel. All these factors increased operating costs above the levels which could be covered by operations in areas of low economic potential. This was to be the problem with many of the lines included in the 1883 Conventions.[76] As early as September 1887 when the *Journal officiel* published the results of the exploitation of some of the lines of local interest already completed, an editorial in the *Journal des chemins de fer*,[77] representing the interests of the major companies, reacted with horror to their low productivity and called for a revised appreciation of their worth, suggesting that narrow-gauge lines – which were cheaper to construct and operate – might be more appropriate than continuing standard gauge construction.

Table 17   *Company earnings per kilometre of track, 1879 (francs)*

Company	Revenue
Nord	35,532
Est	15,872
Ouest	16,439
Paris–Orléans	17,562
PLM	28,659
Midi	17,929

A new communications system, by definition, creates a range of unfamiliar problems in its operation, which take time to solve. Other inefficiencies are likely to be caused by the continuing processes of construction not only of track but also of superstructure, which are not always perfectly synchronized, and by the growth of traffic at a faster rate than the extension of handling facilities. French railways were plagued by such problems, most obviously during the earlier phases of development,[78] but also in later periods, when operating capacity and demand were out of line. Repeated crises – especially in the early 1870s and again in the early 1890s – were caused by shortages of rolling stock.[79]

The utility of rolling stock, like that of money, depends on the total stock and rapidity of circulation. It soon became obvious that users would employ railway wagons and station facilities for storing their goods if they were permitted to do so. In November 1846 it was agreed by the Minister that charges should be levied where goods were not collected within a limited period in order to discourage the immobilization of rolling stock,[80] which forced the companies to invest in a larger number of wagons than they might otherwise require.[81] Efficient use of equipment depended upon effective administration at the level of each station and on the co-operation of users. Tariffs sought to associate users with optimum use (i.e. maximum rotation of material) by a system of reductions encouraging rapid collection of goods and fines penalizing delays.[82] In 1869 the Est Company charged 5 francs per day per wagon for failure to collect goods within forty-eight hours of dispatch of the advice of arrival. This, however, represented only 20 centimes per tonne, and in certain circumstances – as, for example, in a year of large-scale grain imports – merchants whose own storage facilities were fully used still tended to use railway wagons as extensions of these, immobilizing considerable numbers.[83]

Annual and seasonal variations in traffic – in the case of agricultural traffic, with peaks following the wine or grain harvests – required the companies to maintain rolling stock in sufficient numbers to meet peak demand, although this meant excess capacity for most of the year.[84] The Orléans Company in the third quarter of 1847, for example, had to cope with the movement of 1,894,608 kilograms of cereals transported on the Orléans to Tours line in the direction of Tours. In the fourth quarter, following an abundant local crop, only 13,013 kilograms were transported.[85] Part of the problem was the difficulty of predicting the size of the crop, and of volumes to be transported, in any given year. In the last quarter of 1871 stations between Nîmes and Cette dispatched 205,689 tonnes of wines and spirits, which was already 20 per cent above the 1869 figure, but in the following year dispatches rose to 324,327 tonnes, a rise of a further 60 per cent.[86] The Ouest Company complained in 1899 about the special difficulties in areas of pastoral farming in Normandy, in which cattle fairs might require the use of 400 wagons on a given day at a small station some distance away from the large stations at which reserves of wagons were normally kept.[87] The companies had to be prepared for irregularities in demand for their facilities and to maintain in a state of readiness rolling stock and personnel which were rarely fully utilized. This had significant consequences for their operating costs. Repeated autumnal crises indicated that while recognizing this need, they sought to minimize the capital investment required, so that public complaints continued, becoming especially vocal in the regions worst affected by seasonal fluctuations and especially those in the south affected by the movement of wine and, in some years, cereal imports through Marseille.[88]

Company responses to such crises varied. The most obvious short-term solution to the problem was to reduce maintenance on rolling stock and increase its in-service time, making up for this neglect when demand for transport declined. This could not be prolonged for either locomotives or wagons. Moreover, such a response (and the obvious alternative, the ordering of new rolling stock) was likely to create a subsequent crisis in railway repair establishments. Following a period of relative tranquillity, when demand for rolling stock was high, these were likely to be overwhelmed by large numbers of neglected locomotives and wagons, as well as the responsibility for maintaining larger overall stock due to new purchases.[89] It was then likely, as the PLM reported in 1883, that operating efficiency would, for a considerable period, be affected by decisions taken in response to a short-lived crisis, and even that substantial investments in new workshop facilities would become necessary in order to cope with the increased number of wagons.[90]

In spite of the stop-go character of investment, the overall carrying capacity of the networks continued to increase. The number of locomotives also increased, from 1222 in 1853 to 14,344 by 1913, as did the average weight of locomotives and their power and durability.[91] This allowed more rapid circulation. In about 1850 a typical train included fourteen wagons and hauled 90 tonnes. By 1875 a train with twenty-four wagons hauled over 200 tonnes and by the 1880s trains of 300, 400 and even 500 tonnes were not uncommon.[92] With these changes calculations of operating costs had to be revised downwards and tariffs might be reduced.[93]

The size of wagons also increased, from the initial equipment with a capacity of 4–6 tonnes at the end of the 1840s and in the early 1850s, to the more usual 8–10 and even 12 tonnes by the late 1850s and early 1860s. Many of the smaller wagons, however, remained in use for a considerable period. The Nord, a leader in the move to larger wagons, was running 2550 of 6 tonnes, 6596 of 10, 150 of 12, and 83 of 15 tonnes in 1860 compared with 2728 of 6 tonnes and 627 of 10 in 1852.[94] By the beginning of the twentieth century the company was discussing with the Arras Société coopérative agricole the introduction of 40 tonne wagons similar to those used in the USA, which would move cereals from special sidings directly to granaries, docks or silos and then to mills or maltings as needed, eliminating the need for sacks and various commercial intermediaries.[95]

Another response designed to relate more effectively demand for, and supply of, transport facilities involved the maintenance of tariffs at a level which would discourage some potential users rather than seeking a level of tariff which would be more likely to maximize revenue. Caron believes this to have been a significant factor influencing the Nord's tariff policy in the 1880s. It permitted a slowing of the rate of increase in capital investment.[96] But reduced levels of investment were also possible because the increased purchases of rolling stock during the 1870s, designed to cope with an apparent shortage, had the result of creating excess capacity in the economically depressed 1880s.

More productive were improvements in the provision of station facilities and in the administrative control of traffic. In the first case, innovation was a response to shortcomings made all too evident by delays in transit and continual public criticism. Users complained about goods accumulating at stations instead of being transported immediately. Cases were frequently cited in which perishables had deteriorated in transit because of the excessive time taken.[97] The companies responded that it took time to weigh, classify and register the goods, that goods had to wait for the formation of trains heading in the correct direction and that at their destination the administrative processes had to be repeated.[98] Moreover, that there was insufficient staff and that station facilities generally were inadequate could in part be explained by the unexpectedly rapid growth of traffic.

As early as 1848 the Paris–Orléans admitted that it needed to triple or quadruple the size of its goods depots.[99] Because of competing demands for capital, it was slow to respond, and station facilities continued to be inadequate in terms of the area covered by platforms and marshalling yards, the material (such as small cranes) that they employed and the number of personnel. This resulted in congestion and bottlenecks at which the flow of traffic was slowed, reducing the carrying capacity of whole networks. Yet investment in more powerful locomotives and larger and more numerous wagons continued, while the stations, which, if improved, would have allowed the more productive utilization of rolling stock, were neglected. The Chamber of Commerce of Le Mans complained to the company in 1865 that, because of the lack of marshalling yards at Orléans, during periods of intense use wagons accumulated in their hundreds in sidings and delays became intolerable.[100] Sudden increases in traffic could cause chaos. In 1861 the movement of cereals from Marseille caused such problems that the Minister of Commerce, in order to secure the transport of essential foodstuffs, closed all the stations between Cette and Montpellier for the dispatch of wine between 5 and 15 November. Representatives of the wine trade, not unnaturally, felt aggrieved.[101]

The annual reports made by the companies to their shareholders continually mention the inadequacy of goods depots, but, save following especially severe handling crises, little improvement was effected. One such crisis occurred in 1871 as part of the post-war recovery. It stimulated public outcry and an official inquiry, during which the PLM in particular had to admit that not only its major stations at Marseille, Montpellier, Nîmes and Lyon but every station on the Cette–Tarascon line, one of the oldest in France, was grossly inadequate. The problems of this company were especially severe, particularly in years during which both the wine traffic from Languedoc and that in cereals from Marseille were heavy. In fact, it could not in any year guarantee a regular goods service from October, and in response to a commission of inquiry in 1872, actually admitted the 'impossibility of satisfying public needs'.[102] On the Nord the main bottlenecks were Boulogne, Calais, Dunkirk and Amiens, largely because of variations in international trade.[103] Increased traffic and inadequate station facilities forced the Paris–Orléans once again to admit in 1899 that substantial investment had become essential in order to enlarge goods stations and improve their equipment. Money was earmarked, but only for the most important stations.[104]

For all the networks with termini at Paris, the transport of agricultural produce to the capital was lucrative but presented particular problems of traffic control, due in large part to 'violent fluctuations' from season to season and geographical accumulation of traffic in producing and port areas. According to a Paris–Orléans Company report, in 1865 'a large part of our transport, notably of wines, had Paris for destination. The vendors, pressed to . . . realize the value of their merchandise, brought us very large quantities. The recipients collected the merchandise they had not yet paid for with far less energy. Because of this there was inevitable congestion at our arrivals station'. On 20 December 1865 the platforms and courtyards of the Paris–Orléans' Paris goods depot had been piled up with merchandise, while 1800 wagons waited entry in sidings all the way from Poitiers and Vierzon to Paris. The Company's inability to empty these wagons caused a severe shortage of rolling stock.[105]

The Nord reported in 1873 that similar problems were recurrent at its main Paris goods depot at La Chapelle, which dated from 1842 and had been extended in 1850 and again in 1856. The PLM had eased the difficulties it had suffered at its Paris depot at Bercy by constructing large facilities outside the city at Villeneuve-St-Georges, and this seemed to be the most practical solution to the problem. By 1913 the Nord had six goods stations serving Paris, not including those at nearby St-Denis and Aubervilliers. These new facilities soon suffered from the problems of the old. Increased traffic led to overcrowding, and, once a depot had been constructed, further extension was difficult, given that the establishment of a station led to the development of the neighbouring area and an increase in land values. New facilities might be provided, but always at a greater distance from the city centre unless the opportunity was taken to buy out existing companies, as did the Nord in the case of the Docks de St-Ouen in 1873. The construction of goods depots within existing urban areas, and their subsequent enlargement in response to pressing needs rather than on the basis of a long-term plan, meant that the organization of station facilities in large cities was always less than perfect and unfailingly constituted a restriction on rail operations and a factor increasing costs.[106] On this matter of delays in transit the points of view of users and companies were clearly irreconcilable. The meetings of the commissions of inquiry held in 1907 and 1912–13[107] heard the same arguments as had been used four decades earlier.

Other complaints were constantly being made about the handling charges levied by the companies, which were additional to the basic costs of transport. These were normally levied at a fixed rate of 1.50 francs whatever the distance transported. According to the Sedan Chamber of Commerce in September 1874 this charge increased the cost of transport by 28–30 per cent for a distance of less than 100 kilometres and by 8 per cent for over 300 kilometres.[108] Frequent criticism was also made of the system of fines imposed on rail users who failed to collect their goods from a station within a period of twenty-four to forty-eight hours of the dispatch of the note advising them of arrival. The interval was too short, especially when it was likely that advice notes would be delayed and when the recipients lived some distance from the station.[109]

The frequent repetition of these complaints engendered the belief that the railway companies were simply unwilling to do anything to meet them. This was explained in terms of their monopoly power and the bureaucratization of the administration at every level. It was claimed to be difficult for consumers to deal with station staff equipped with books of rules and regulations and massive tomes listing tariffs in all their countless variations. Staff lacked power of initiative and could not always individually be held responsible for mistakes, but they seemed to be indifferent to consumers' needs and took insufficient care with their goods.[110]

Successful operation of a railway company, like that of any large organization, depends upon the establishment of an efficient administration. It was necessary, for safe and efficient running, that central control be maintained over the various networks by means of a disciplined administrative hierarchy. The development of efficient administration was clearly a major problem when large organizations were created in a remarkably short time. Their primary functions included estimating the demand for transport facilities and calculating both the tariff levels which would maximize revenue and the technical innovations which would be most likely to reduce costs. They needed to control traffic flows in order to minimize the running of empty wagons or the likelihood of over-intensive working of particular routes, with the consequent danger of bottlenecks.

As regards goods traffic, the object of any company had to be to circulate fully loaded trains gaining the maximum revenue at minimum cost. This depended on such factors as the ability to form unmixed rather than mixed-merchandise trains and to avoid the immobilization of rolling stock. Experience taught that a combination of measures, including fines on those who failed to unload goods within the required time and the provision of more and larger marshalling yards, permitted increased success in the achievement of this aim.[111] The increased use of the telephone for traffic control towards the end of the century was another important factor.[112] Excessive flows of traffic in one direction rather than the other, which necessitated the return of large numbers of empty wagons, increased costs and caused concern. Thus the Paris–Rouen Company in 1847 sought to correct the imbalance in flows between Rouen and Paris by reducing the tariffs on movements from Paris in the hope of limiting the empty running of trains.[113]

As we have already seen, not all these administrative problems were dealt with satisfactorily. The administrators of the Nord stressed 'the difficulties and embarrassments inseparable from the beginnings of such a vast enterprise'.[114] The complex and often novel technical, commercial and financial problems that rail company officials at all levels had to deal with were rendered all the more difficult to solve by the possibility that innovation in one sector would result in unexpected difficulties because of lag in other sectors. Thus economizing on the cost of track infrastructure including signalling and station facilities, while investing heavily in locomotives clearly had adverse consequences for the company.[115]

Although administrative imperfection inevitably remained a constant problem – accounting techniques, for example, were so primitive that accurate costing of operations was impossible – experience did result in improvements in administrative methods and in the development of office routine.[116] Bureaucratization had advantages in this respect, as well as the disadvantages associated with inflexibility and administrative cumbersomeness, which were certainly evident from a fairly early date.

Advantage could also be seen in the regular meetings between representatives of the various networks which were organized from 1854 and which had as one of their aims the promotion of a united front *vis-à-vis* the Direction générale des chemins de fer instituted at the Ministry of Public Works on 6 November 1853. This followed the successful establishment in 1852 of an inter-company syndicate to construct a circular line around Paris linking the various networks. The line, brought into operation in 1854–6, allowed the passage of transit traffic without transshipment, which had involved carting through the city.[117] Other agreements on the movement of rolling stock between networks sought to reduce the delays in transport which frequently occurred when merchandise moved from one network to another.[118]

Complaints, however, continued to be made. Thus in 1870 the Chambre consultative des arts et manufactures de Bischwiller (Bas-Rhin) observed that movement between the networks of the Est and Nord was relatively easy, but that between the Est and PLM was very slow because a more distant working relationship existed between the two companies.[119] In addition, the major networks were accused of deliberately delaying the movement of goods using the track of independent local and regional companies.[120] It was claimed, and with some justification, that they preferred to give priority to goods originating on their own lines or on those of large companies from whom they hoped to get similar treatment.

Considerable benefits did, however, ensue from these closer links between companies. Through regular meetings and bilateral agreements common tariffs were promoted in order to increase traffic to the mutual profit of the companies involved.[121] These were especially evident from around 1860. Users were also likely to benefit from a reduction in the complexity of tariffs and through the application of long-distance differential tariffs across the lines of collaborating companies.

Users, in effect, benefited more from agreements between companies than from their competition. Agreements between companies by no means eliminated competition. Contracting companies clearly intended to maintain their future commercial freedom.[122] But competition was possible only in the small number of cases in which lines belonging to different networks actually took similar directions – most notably between the Midi and PLM for the traffic towards Paris and the east, and in the west between the Ouest, Paris–Orléans and the newly established Etat network from the 1870s. In the 1860s a certain amount of competitive construction occurred between the PLM and the Midi. For example, in the early 1860s the Midi's line from Agen gave wine producers in the Aude and Pyrénées-Orientales access to northern markets. Then, later in the decade, the PLM's Alais–Brioude link restored to it the advantage of the most direct link between lower Languedoc and Paris.[123] In general, the Ministry of Public Works and its officials sought both to limit competition, which might weaken the companies financially,[124] and to encourage agreement on common tariffs[125] and on greater uniformity of charges.[126]

Transport economies

The most obvious advantage the railways had to offer to commerce was cheap, rapid and regular transport of bulky commodities. This service both recognized, and increased awareness of, the importance of time in commercial activity.[127] A government inquiry in 1858 revealed that the average speed of goods trains on the Nord network was 20–8 kilometres per hour, on that of the PLM 20–30, on the Paris–Orléans 25 and on the Ouest 30.[128] Clearly, even at this relatively early stage in the technical development of locomotion the railway completely outclassed competitive forms of transport in terms of speed of movement. By 1885 the average speed of goods trains on the sixteen most heavily utilized lines of the Nord had risen to

34.1 kilometres per hour and by 1913 to 45.5.[129] Striking examples of economies in time have often been quoted; for example, for the movement of goods from Vierzon to Orléans in 1844, when the time for moving 1 tonne over 80 kilometres was reduced from sixty hours by cart to four hours by train.[130] It must, however, be borne in mind (and we will return to this point) that the time savings were not as great as might initially have appeared when delays in loading and delivery were taken into account. Complaints on this score became so numerous that the state felt bound to introduce legal limits on the delay in delivery which could be tolerated and to make companies responsible in law for the deterioration of goods in transit beyond the permissible time limits. It seized the opportunity of negotiations with the companies over financial guarantees in 1857 to fix at 125 kilometres per twenty-four hours the minimum obligation imposed on the companies, a figure revised in 1866 to 200 kilometres for most foodstuffs. Even so, delays continued to be frequent. The companies were accused of taking the legal maximum time for transit as their operational base time,[131] and indeed with the exception of the Nord and Paris–Orléans, the companies admitted as much in 1863, when even the Nord complained that the legal limits were too strict.[132]

We should therefore simply conclude that in general transport times were considerably reduced, particularly on long journeys, but that often the reductions were not as great as might have been expected. On some routes – for reasons ranging from temporary shortage of station facilities or rolling stock to the absence of a direct link between two points – transport times might be far longer than those suggested by average speeds.

The other obvious economy offered by use of rail transport was cost (see Table 18).[133] Clearly, there was a rapid fall in rail tariffs as the network developed, as operating costs were reduced and as commercial principles were reviewed. The reduction in rates was especially fast in the earlier period, when technical efficiency improved rapidly and the elasticity of demand for transport facilities was high. The statistical average, however, remained at a relatively high level for a considerable time because in many

Table 18   *Rail tariffs for goods, 1841–1913 (centimes per tonne/kilometre)*

Period	Tariff
1841–4	14.5
1845–54	10.6
1855–64	8.7
1865–74	7.5
1875–84	7.4
1885–94	6.8
1895–1904	6.0
1905–13	5.4

regions the absence of transversals between primary routes required the use of indirect routes and so increased costs and therefore tariffs. Further investment in technical innovation was encouraged by the possibility of long-term debt redemption opened up by the conventions of 1852 and 1859, which allowed such costs to be offset over a much longer period. Operating costs were reduced *directly* by the increased investment that this encouraged and *indirectly* by the reduction of the burden of debt repayment on annual costs. Limits to the reduction of tariffs were imposed only by the prevailing levels of technical efficiency and by the desire to maintain an adequate revenue. The stagnation evident in tariff levels from around 1865 to 1884 seems to have been the result of an assessment that tariffs had been reduced to such an extent that revenue was little more than the cost of operation.[134]

The initial problem for companies was to establish tariffs which were both competitive with other forms of transport and profitable. Inevitably, at a time when modern techniques of cost and revenue analysis were lacking, the complex procedures necessary for establishing a viable rate for each commodity were empirical and rather hit-or-miss. The pioneer Strasbourg–Bâle Company partly based its original tariffs on estimates of the maximum theoretical efficiency of its locomotives. In practice, of course, much of their power was wasted, and running costs proved substantially higher than first estimated.[135] Generally, companies based their tariffs on those already set by their road or waterway competitors and then reacted to the response of these and of users. In a letter to the Minister of Public Works dated 28 August 1843, the administrators of the Paris–Rouen line pointed out: 'we have no other means than to establish relationships with commerce, study its needs, its relationships with the old forms of transport and to try to find out by practice the conditions in which ours will be able to establish itself . . .'. Initially, they would, 'simply try to attract users at the legal tariffs [i.e. official maximum]. . . . We will experiment in the general interest . . . [and] attempt to reach by experiment and a few months' experience conclusions which we could not take *a priori* and without knowledge of these facts'. By February 1844, after operating the station at Paris–Batignolles for several months and having obtained 'a better appreciation of our operating costs', the company was prepared to offer tariff reductions.[136] The initial commercial objective of all companies had, of course, to be to break 'the established habits of commerce'.[137] The problem reaffirmed itself with the opening of every new station.[138]

Most of the major administrative and financial problems were evident at this early stage of development, and a whole range of major policy decisions were taken. The structures developed in these years included tariffs which were differential with distance and which varied in relation to the value of the merchandise sent and its volume. In effect, a simple proportional relationship between tariffs and distance provided an inadequate representation of costs. This was true of fixed costs in particular but also of operating costs, given that the labour and capital costs of particular movements were not proportional to distance transported. Moreover, for strictly commercial reasons – the need to attract traffic and to compete with other forms of transport – an elastic pricing policy was essential. This was something which the companies constantly struggled to maintain against official interference.

The costs of transport, however difficult to estimate, were obviously of considerable importance in determining tariffs. It should be stressed that technical, commercial and financial problems were closely interrelated. They were part of a complex range of variables affecting cost structures and pricing policies. The routes taken, profit levels of distinct lines, the location of stations and their operation, as well as the technical operation of the networks, including speed and number of trains, all influenced costs and tariff policy and all had to be taken into account when decisions about further innovations and their potential returns had to be taken. The estimates of the initial costs of establishment of the different primary networks suggested marked differences in eventual running costs. [139] Furthermore, the influence of tariff modifications on the levels of traffic and the use of rolling stock and station facilities – possibly causing disproportionate increases in costs – had to be carefully estimated. [140] The pioneer companies faced complex problems.

One basic principle determining tariff levels was that operating losses were normally to be avoided. Estimates of costs therefore set a lower limit below which the rate charged for the movement of a particular commodity, on a particular route, should not be allowed to fall. Above this the basic principle seems to have been to charge as much as the traffic could bear, taking into account, of course, the possible loss to competing forms of transport if rates were set too high. Rail transport had to be attractive to prospective clients, and the tariffs charged were subject to revision wherever it became evident that a competitive edge was being lost[141] or when it was believed that a reduction in tariffs might lead to an increase in net revenue. [142] Thus the Est in 1861, through reductions, sought to secure the transit trade in cereals originating in Germany and Hungary, [143] while the PLM in 1893 attempted by the same means to increase the competitiveness of grain imported through Marseille. [144]

It was an estimate of the marginal utility of rail transport for potential users which determined the possible upper levels of tariffs. This principle of tariffication *ad valorem* could the more easily be upheld in a general economic situation in which the demand for transport facilities by rail continued to expand. In respect of bulky products of low unit value – such as the agricultural products which particularly interest us here – low tariffs were essential in order to stimulate use. As their transport required relatively little care and manipulation at stations and variable operating costs were low, the cost factor and the commercial factor both facilitated and required low tariff charges. [145]

It rapidly became evident that the most rational pricing policy was not that based on general principles and worked out in the general *cahiers des charges* of each network but one which, while based on those same principles, took into account the particular costs and the commerical situations affecting the movement of given commodities on individual routes. Tariffs thus soon became characterized by extreme variability and complexity.

The principle of variability according to the burden of competition was acceptable to the Ministry of Public Works, although, as we shall see, restrictions were increasingly to be imposed in later years. On the part of the railway companies there was a clear and continuing awareness of the need to make tariff concessions on bulky goods previously carried by water. This was especially so for goods moving down-river, where waterway costs and charges were at their minimum levels.[146] Low tariffs attracted an increasing volume of goods and increased the return on capital; they also helped to overcome the inertia of canal users considering change. This was particularly clear in the case of the Nord Company, in whose region canal competition was most intense. Stress was laid upon the significance of canal competition in two undated memoranda, probably written in 1847 and originating with the commercial administration of the company. The first expressed dissatisfaction with the rate of growth of traffic. The second maintained: 'It should not be believed that commerce attracted by novelty will abandon its ordinary intermediaries from one day to the next . . . . we must also bear in mind all those people who live on the water from the movement of merchandise, and who will defend their existing position, only abandoning the competition after being submitted to the most intense commercial pressure . . .'. It recommended that the company should increase its competitiveness not only in respect of basic tariffs but also by reducing the costs of unloading and storage.[147] Efforts were also made to reduce competition by direct agreements with both users and competitors. Some of the latter agreed to act essentially as feeders to the railway; this was the case in an agreement dated 5 October 1847 between a group of master mariners and the Nord Company, in which the former agreed to renounce the transport of goods between places already served by the railway and instead to move goods from Reims and Soissons to what was then the railhead at Compiègne.[148] This particular agreement, by its very nature, was clearly a temporary measure, likely to be terminated once the railway progressed beyond Compiègne. An example of efforts to achieve a more lasting settlement can be seen in the case of negotiations between the Nord and a certain M. Leroy, a grain merchant and barge operator at Amiens. These continued for years. A first record, dated 17 June 1850, maintained that Leroy's barges were capturing most of the traffic in bulky commodities between Amiens and St-Quentin. The company had offered to purchase his barges and to take over contracts for the rental of barges that he had already signed with other owners. It was intended to use these acquisitions to drive independent barge owners out of business. Furthermore, providing Leroy would agree to dispatch a minimum of 2000 tonnes of flour and cereals by rail each year, it offered him a reduction of 1 franc per tonne on the normal cost of 8 francs for movement between St-Quentin and Amiens. By this one agreement the company would thus enjoy the dual advantage of reducing competition and attracting traffic. For reasons about which we have no information these negotiations broke down, and in a subsequent report of 2 May 1853 the company was proposing to reduce its tariffs to a level sufficient to combat Leroy's competition 'in attracting all this merchandise to the railway'.[149] Again we are not told whether this was successfully achieved. Few such reports survive among the railway company commercial records, but they do lend weight to what the bare information on tariffs suggests – in short, that the railway companies sought to maximize their competitive advantages.

Due in large part to this waterway competition, the tariffs levied by the Nord tended to be lower than those of other companies. Competition from canal transporters was a continual matter of concern for its administrators. Thus the lowering in canal tariffs following the reduction of the tax on waterway transport in 1860 required careful consideration of its own charges and in this case led to a further competitive reduction.[150] Indeed, by the later 1880s, as government measures to improve the efficiency and competitiveness of the waterways took effect, it was the turn of the railway company to complain about unfair competition[151] and to take further measures to increase competitiveness. Waterway tariffs influenced those of the railway not only along the major routes in northern France but also in the Seine valley,[152] along the Loire and its affluents,[153] the Rhône–Saône corridor[154] and some coastal routes.[155] In 1849 the administrators of the Paris–Avignon line had planned to charge 10–12 centimes per tonne/kilometre but were soon forced to the conclusion that in the face of the 'highly perfected navigation of the Saône and Rhône', this was unrealistic and that, although they might get away with a rate of 0.0980 francs on the transit Paris–Lyon with competition from the less perfect Canal du Bourgogne, 0.06 francs was likely to be the maximum possible between Lyon and Avignon.[156] The problem was a long-term one. In 1888, for example, Châlon-sur-Saône received 90,000 100 kilogram sacks of wheat from the ports of Marseille and Cette. The PLM carried only 4364 of these and sought to correct this imbalance by reducing its tariffs.[157] PLM tariffs on cereals moving as far inland as Dijon remained relatively low because of effective waterway competition. Furthermore, from the 1860s tariffs from Marseille to Paris had to be kept at a level low enough to allow competition in the Paris market with cereals imported along the Seine, in order to maintain traffic levels on that route. PLM tariffs remained highest for regions up-river from Dijon and those between the Rhône–Saône corridor and Paris in which waterway competition was less effective.[158]

The Midi Company was in the peculiar position of actually owning potentially competitive waterways on some of its most profitable routes – the lateral canal to the Garonne and the Canal du Midi. It maintained charges on these canals at an artificially high rate in order to force traffic on to its rails and then, in the absence of effective waterway competition, was able to maintain its railway tariffs at relatively high levels.[159] Because the company was anxious to attract traffic away from coastal shipping, its tariffs for coastal zones tended to be significantly lower than further inland.[160] It was not alone in this policy, and in 1898 the Minister of Marine, after expressing grave concern to the Minister of Public Works about the cumulative effects of rail tariff policies on coastal shipping, was able to exact a promise from the latter to try to limit such intense competition.[161] Efforts were also made by the companies, through tariff policy, to favour one port at the expense of others. This became a particularly important aspect of tariff policy as the volume of imported cereals increased. The Ouest sought, for example, from the 1850s to promote its ports at Le Havre and Dieppe, partly at the expense of Rouen.[162] It needed, furthermore, to attract traffic arriving at the ports which might otherwise have been transported inland along the Seine.[163] The tariff structures of the Nord sought to attract cereals destined for the provision of Paris to the ports of Boulogne, Calais and Dunkirk.[164] The PLM fought a losing battle to maintain the share of the French market once enjoyed by imports through Marseille.[165]

Not everyone was happy with the results. Such variation in charges inevitably meant that some regions were better treated than others. Moreover, the suspicion was continually voiced that the intention of the railway companies was to destroy waterway competition in order to achieve a monopoly position for themselves.[166] After competitors had been eliminated initially low rates might be substantially increased, as in the case referred to by the Valenciennes (Nord) agricultural society in 1850, in which, after driving out of business the barges which transported sugar to Paris with tariffs which fell as low as 21–5 francs per tonne, the Nord Company proceeded to raise its charges to 30–8 francs.[167] Certainly, the absence of such competition permitted the railway companies to charge higher rates and to increase the profitability of their operations.[168]

In relation to road transport the competitive position of the railways appeared much stronger. In spite of the improvement of road surfaces, in the absence of any technical advances in means of propulsion by road, costs were difficult to reduce, and competitive tariff reductions were necessarily limited. Toutain estimated an average road tariff of 25 centimes per tonne/kilometre throughout the second half of the century, at a time when the average rail tariff fell gradually from 10.6 centimes in 1845–54 to 5.4 centimes in 1905–13; Marqfoy's 1863 estimate suggested a similar relationship.[169]

The choice between competing forms of transport was not, however, made solely on the basis of cost. Regularity, convenience and habit were other factors which influenced decisions.

Even on the basis of cost in certain circumstances the railway might not be competitive. This was notably the case for short-distance movements. In comparison with water and road transport the railway has been said to be 'characterized by far higher terminal costs but lower line-haul costs.'[170] These terminal costs made up a lower percentage of total cost the farther commodities were transported. Indeed, basic to the ruling concepts of differential and special tariffs was the fact that unit costs fell with increasing distance and with higher volume. For shorter distance movements the addition of terminal costs to basic tariffs could easily result in an uneconomic charge for users. It was reported from Quimperlé (Finistère) in 1870, for example, that the effect of this for the transport of goods up to 20 kilometres was to double the basic tariff.[171] For such movements as those between farms and markets or mills, even where rail transport was available, road movement tended to be preferred, and indeed the railway companies seem often to have deliberately encouraged this. In the new *cahier des charges* it introduced in 1858 the Nord increased certain tariffs in an effort to discourage the number of short-distance movements of small quantities.[172] The Paris–Orléans Company determined in 1863 that it could provide satisfactory local services only by extending stations and increasing their staff and by putting on more trains while reducing their average load. The result would be increased costs and therefore tariffs, which the company felt would be contrary to the interests of commerce, which for short-distance movements was 'preoccupied more with the cheapness than the speed of transport', as well as being unprofitable to itself.[173]

Besides the fact that it was less expensive in these circumstances, short-distance road transport was often more convenient and even quicker. The millers of Pontoise in 1863 affirmed that they never used the railway to transport flour to Paris because the slowness and cost of carting to the station, of loading and unloading and then carting to destination outweighed any potential advantages from the speed of trains.[174] According to the Dieppe Chamber of Commerce, once the time taken to cart goods to and from the railway stations was taken into account, it became evident that movement by rail was quicker only for distances of over 100 kilometres.[175]

There was, however, a tendency (but only a tendency) for road competitiveness, even over shorter distances, to decline with time. The Ouest noted in 1889 that 'the opening of secondary lines tends each day to reduce the average distance travelled per tonne of merchandise'. In 1882 this had been 130 kilometres; by 1888 it had fallen to 122 kilometres.[176] Changing habits partly explained this, but more significant was the growing density of the rail network and the railway companies' desire in general to maximize utilization.[177] Thus where railway companies decided to attract the transport of a particular commodity to their tracks they were normally able to reduce their tariffs to a degree which outweighed the various disadvantages the use of rail might otherwise bring.[178] Tariff rates were far more flexible in the case of a large, technically innovatory company, able to compensate for losses made in one situation with profits made elsewhere, than they were for road hauliers working in a sector dominated by small businesses, with limited capital and in a situation of technical stagnation. From their earliest stages of development railway companies progressively sought not simply to undercut the rates charged by competing road hauliers but to establish tariff levels which offset any non-price advantages the hauliers might enjoy.[179]

Railways and agricultural marketing

The structure of agricultural traffic varied according to the crop patterns of various regions and their commercial habits. The major problem here is the sparsity of documentation on the transport of agricultural merchandise. I have not been able to find, among either official documentation or the railway company records, the kind of detailed information on quantities dispatched and received per station which I had hoped to be able to use. The most detailed statistics available[180] relate to quantities transported per network. The following discussion is based on these, although there is space here to record the national figures. These are inflated because of double counting due to the failure to distinguish between traffic originating along the network of a particular company and that coming from the lines of another company. There is no satisfactory method of eliminating this. Furthermore, there is no information on the average distances particular commodities were transported, so I cannot provide a tonne/kilometric figure.

Nevertheless, Tables 19–24 will provide a reasonably accurate indication of the importance of the railways in the carriage of agricultural commodities. In this chapter, which is concerned with the means of transport, I concentrate on recording statistics on quantities carried, leaving the analysis of marketing and agriculture for later chapters.

In each year from 1860 to 1866 the cereals and flour transported by the six main companies represented around one third of total consumption. If, in addition, one remembers that significant, if unmeasurable, quantities were consumed by the producers themselves or in close proximity to the place of production, then it becomes probable that well over half the cereals and flour traded were transported by rail.[181]

Within an overall tendency for the volume transported to increase quite considerably, as freight charges were reduced and as a result of the growing commercialization of the rural economy and increases in agricultural productivity, there occurred significant fluctuations from year to year. These were due to several factors. In the first place, the reduction of tariffs clearly stimulated an increase in traffic and in the average distance carried.

Table 19   *Tonnage of cereals and flour carried by the railways, 1854–1913*

Index: 1913 = 13,529,323 tonnes = 100

Year	Indexed tonnage	Year	Indexed tonnage	Year	Indexed tonnage
1854	0.61	1889	44	1909	81
1866	22	1890	46	1910	84
1867	24	1891	56	1911	93
1868	27	1892	52	1912	95
1869	23	1893	49	1913	100
1871	26*	1894	51		
1872	33	1895	53		
1873	34	1896	53		
1874	31	1897	53		
1875	32	1898	65†		
1876	35	1899	62		
1877	33	1900	64		
1878	38	1901	63		
1879	49†	1902	66		
1880	46†	1903	71		
1884	44	1904	71		
1885	39†	1905	72		
1886	41†	1906	74		
1887	40	1907	74		
1888	42	1908	77		

* Missing years mean that official statistics are not complete.
† Increase or decline exaggerated by changes in criteria for inclusion.

According to the Paris–Orléans company, for example, a reduction in tariffs for 1895 was the main cause of an increase of 178,586 tonnes in cereals and flour carried, which contrasted favourably with a decline of 105,000 tonnes in 1894.[182] But a range of other relevant factors should be cited. Good harvests throughout France were likely to have the effect of reducing the quantities of cereals and flour transported, whether between regions or from the ports. According to the directors of the Est, reporting in 1899, 'the general abundance of crops . . . facilitated local consumption and reduced exchange'.[183] Such general statements should not, however, be allowed to conceal the fact that in years of abundance traffic on lines supplying major centres of consumption such as Paris was likely to increase,[184] although within the ever narrower limits set by the increasing elasticity of demand for bread.

The failure of the harvest in only some regions generated inter-regional traffic – for example, in 1866 from Brittany, where the harvest had been good, to the Paris region after a poor harvest in the Beauce.[185] In 1891 the Paris–Orléans profited from the need to move foodstuffs to northern France and Belgium.[186] In its report on its operations in 1895 the PLM observed a substantial reduction in movements of cereals and flour from Marseille, down by 119,000 tonnes to 489,000 tonnes. Harvest failure in the south had been made up by movements from the north, east and west, which had all enjoyed a successful year, rather than by imports.[187]

In other years, there were other patterns. Years of more general harvest failure led to increased imports. The Est profited from overland imports from central and eastern Europe, but it was those companies with major ports on their networks, and especially the PLM, which particularly benefited. Although the development of imports from North America increased the importance of Le Havre, large scale imports from the Black Sea area continued to be moved inland from Marseille to other areas of France and Switzerland in years of shortage. In 1894 cereals imported through Marseille represented 38.7 per cent of the total cereals traffic of the PLM.[188] It should be noted that poor internal harvests did not necessarily lead to imports where adequate stocks existed, and that poor harvests might indeed be followed by reduced traffic. Thus in 1893, in spite of a poor harvest, cereals traffic at the railway stations of Le Havre and Rouen fell by 130,000 tonnes.[189]

The goods stations of Paris received large quantities of grain and flour each year. Tables 20[190] and 21[191] indicate the share of each railway company and that of the waterways in the total. Unfortunately, we have no information on the quantity of grain and flour entering the city by cart, the nominal *octroi* imposed to allow a census of traffic having been abolished in 1870.[192] The arrivals of flour are fairly stable, but the variation in quantities of grain carried by each line and even in the total quantities carried is striking. The fluctuations appear to reflect the state of the harvest in the regions served by the various networks, plus, of course, levels of imports and their port of arrival.

Table 20   *Arrival of grain in Paris, 1893–1900* (*thousands* quintaux)

Crops (millions of hectolitres)	Year	Est	Etat–Ouest	PLM	Nord	Orléans	Water	Total
97	1893	24	38	31	274	50	218	637
122	1894	21	57	161	157	178	237	793
119	1895	60	113	91	93	680	27	1,066
119	1896	61	366	104	166	435	87	1,223
86	1897	26	273	38	168	89	192	788
128	1898	71	377	78	143	129	248	1,048
128	1899	86	832	90	262	335	68	1,677
114	1900	119	640	112	335	347	89	1,644
Percentage over 8-year period		5.4	30.7	8.0	18.2	25.5	12.2	100.0

Table 21   *Arrival of flour in Paris, 1893–1900* (*thousands* quintaux)

		Railway companies					
Year	Est	Etat–Ouest	PLM	Nord	Orléans	Water	Total
1893	280	552	220	432	307	368	2,661
1894	262	574	231	455	270	390	2,185
1895	264	576	266	429	356	362	2,257
1896	247	513	287	394	493	330	2,268
1897	261	480	233	429	412	340	2,157
1898	229	476	198	461	351	349	2,067
1899	395	590	213	328	391	342	2,262
1900	209	721	232	354	500	345	2,375
Percentage over 8-year period	12.1	25.4	10.6	18.4	17.5	16.0	100.0

The Ouest brought flour milled from imported grain and from that of traditional suppliers of Paris like the Mayenne and Sarthe and, closer to the city, from the Beauce.[193] As a result of the configuration of the national railway network, a great deal of transit traffic flowed through or, more properly, around Paris. In 1879, for example, the Ouest, through its Paris depot at Batignolles, forwarded 34,000 tonnes of grain and flour on to the track of the Nord, 61,000 on to the lines of the Est and PLM and 48,000 tonnes on to the Paris–Orléans.[194]

The statistics in Table 22 indicate the importance of the railways in the transport of wines and spirits. They are marred, as are the other statistics dealing with volumes transported, by the same double counting. The relative importance of this particular element of traffic for the PLM, and especially the Midi company, should be noted. The most obvious feature of Table 22 is the tendency for volumes transported to grow, as a consequence of both the extension of the railway network and the growing production of wine. Traffic was extremely variable, depending as it did upon the size of the harvest. Thus in 1879 the traffic on the Midi was affected by a generally poor grape harvest. In compensation, shipments increased from the departments of Aude and Pyrénées-Orientales, which enjoyed exceptionally rich harvests, and also from Spain.[195] Phylloxera had surprisingly little effect on overall traffic because of increased imports, but the pattern of traffic was significantly affected, and receipts fell from about 1884. Reconstitution of the vineyards subsequently led to a substantial increase in the wine transported.[196]

The trade in livestock was also significantly influenced by the development of the railway network (see Table 23). Access to markets was improved and loss of weight due to movement on the hoof avoided. The overall increase reflects the growth in demand for meat as living standards

Table 22   *Transport of wines and spirits by rail, 1854–1913 (tonnes)*

Index: 1913 = 9,150,021 tonnes = 100

Year	Indexed tonnage	Year	Indexed tonnage	Year	Indexed tonnage
1854	4	1885	57†	1900	81
1866	32	1886	53	1901	85
1867	29	1887	51	1902	92
1868	33	1888	51	1903	87
1869	34	1889	54	1904	84
1871	34*	1890	57	1905	93
1872	46	1891	60	1906	94
1873	47	1892	60	1907	99
1874	45	1893	58	1908	104
1875	49	1894	63	1909	105
1876	48	1895	67	1910	101
1877	47	1896	63	1911	89
1878	47	1897	67	1912	105
1879	50	1898	78†	1913	100
1880	62	1899	78		
1884	63†				

* Territorial changes.
† Increase or decline exaggerated by changes in criteria for inclusion.

Table 23   *Carriage of livestock by rail, 1866–1913*

Index: 1913 = 12,763,846 head = 100

Year	Number (indexed)	Year	Number (indexed)	Year	Number (indexed)	Year	Number (indexed)
1866	39	1883	73	1899	87	1910	103
1867	42	1884	69	1900	88	1911	93
1868	39	1885	65	1901	89	1912	98
1869	42	1887	62	1902	93	1913	100
1871	32	1889	77	1903	92		
1872	40	1890	68	1904	92		
1873	42	1891	69	1905	88		
1874	43	1892	92	1906	80		
1875	54	1893	92	1907	95		
1876	52	1894	73	1908	94		
1877	53	1895	72	1909	97		
1878	57	1896	78				
1879	57	1897	81				
1880	60	1898	77*				

* Decline would have been more marked if criteria for inclusion had not been revised.

improved. Short-term fluctuations were caused by such factors as fodder supply, which influenced farmers' decisions about the possibility of retaining or selling livestock.

The official statistics on livestock divide animals into three categories: *gros* (oxen, bulls, cows), *moyen* (calves and pigs) and *petit* (sheep and goats). My original tables based on this division were simply too detailed for publication. It ought to be noted, however, that significant changes occurred in the balance between the various categories. Thus whereas the number of animals in the *petit* category increased by 138 per cent from 1866 to 1913 (2,514,900 to 5,984,421) and those in the *moyen* by 161 per cent (1,541,924 to 4,025,468), those in the *gros* grew by 209 per cent (889,861 to 2,753,957). This would seem to be another indicator of dietary change.

Similarly, the railway provided facilities for the rapid movement of perishables. For example, butter from Calvados took two days to reach Paris by fast cart in 1850 but only eight or nine hours once the Paris–Cherbourg railway had been opened, and with a reduction in cost of 65–75 per cent.[197] In the case of early vegetables the Compagnie de l'Est in 1870 established special low tariffs of 0.16 francs per tonne/kilometre for movements by fast train from Champagne and Lorraine to Paris and – far more significantly in terms of the potential traffic – of 0.28 francs per tonne/kilometre for fruit and vegetables brought as far as Paris by other companies for further movement towards eastern France and even Germany.[198] It was the south and west, and the lines serving these regions, which gained most from this facility.[199]

A more generally shared benefit came from the ease with which fertilizing agents could be moved (see Table 24). Particularly low tariffs favoured this. Those on the Nord had been reduced to between 0.035 and 0.06 francs per tonne/kilometre by 1866, from 0.10–0.16 francs in 1857.[200] The government encouraged the reduction of tariffs for the carriage of commodities so vital to agricultural improvement, and the railway companies themselves realized the potential for increased traffic not only from the shipment of fertilizers but also from the growth in agricultural production which would result. Thus in 1856 the Orléans Company introduced special tariffs as low as 0.02 francs per tonne/kilometre. It claimed that as a result the area between Orléans, Bourges and Châteauroux, which had provided it on average between 1855 and 1856 with only 11,100 tonnes of cereals per annum, by 1863–5 was shipping an average of 63,100 tonnes, in large part as a consequence of the increased application of fertilizers.[201] Nevertheless, the adoption of fertilizers was a relatively slow process.

In terms of the volume of agricultural commodities transported, the railway rapidly became the most important form of transport. Its tariffs clearly influenced those of its competitors, and access to it at reasonable cost was a crucial factor in determining the structure of the market for a particular commodity. In effect, the size of the market served by the agricultural

Table 24 *Carriage of fertilizers by rail, 1850–1913*

Index: 1913 = 9,812,080 tonnes = 100

Year	Indexed tonnage	Year	Indexed tonnage	Year	Indexed tonnage
1850	1	1884	20	1901	65
1866	5	1885	19	1902	66
1867	5	1887	23	1903	71
1868	6	1888	27	1904	72
1869	7	1889	32	1905	76
1871	5	1890	35	1906	76
1872	9	1891	40	1907	82
1873	10	1892	43	1908	84
1874	10	1893	46	1909	84
1875	10	1894	49	1910	88
1876	11	1895	46	1911	94
1877	12	1896	47	1912	100
1878	13*	1897	49	1913	100
1879	12	1898	58*		
1880	15	1899	61		
		1900	64		

* Increase or decrease exaggerated by changes in criteria for inclusion.

producers of a particular region depended not on distance but on the cost of transport. Reduction in transport tariffs, by reducing the cost of supplying a particular commodity to potential customers (its effective cost of production as far as they were concerned) was likely, other costs of production being favourable, to increase the size of the demand. Thus access to railways, and their tariffs, were questions of crucial importance to users and also to Government.

Relationships between the companies and their customers

Rail tariff policies effectively altered the economic geography of France. Changes in the relative position of producers and merchants, in terms of access to markets, threatened to have significant consequences for their respective competitive positions. Inevitably, constant concern was voiced about the principles on which tariffs were based and about the practical effects of tariff policy.

Criticism was made of the existence of a multiplicity of tariffs, general and special, varying according to commodity, station of departure and destination and between lines, and subject to frequent modification, which caused great confusion among users. The situation was particularly complicated where the transit of a commodity involved the use of several networks.[202] In the introduction to the *Album des tariffs généraux et spéciaux actuels*, published by the Ministry of Public Works in 1882, the failure to take into account *all* special tariffs was excused on the grounds of their number. Each special tariff listed in the general *cahier des charges* in reality represented several thousands of different charges, varying between stations. Thus the tariff No. 1 of the PLM Company, for the movement of cereals, covered 9500 possible tariffs, and No. 13, for wines, 11,200. It was simply impossible to list and represent diagrammatically all of these.[203] Complexity was in practice unavoidable where companies attempted both to stimulate traffic and to some degree to equate charges to costs which varied from line to line. Nevertheless, and although efforts were made in the direction of greater uniformity, users found it difficult to comprehend, and thus benefit to the extent that they might have, from special tariffs.[204]

As one would expect, complaints were also constantly made about tariffs judged to be too high. Here the need for reductions seemed only too obvious to users concerned to reduce what was in effect a cost of production. They were especially aggrieved where the rates charged by the railway company operating locally were higher than those charged by another company serving their competitors. This seemed to be providing the latter with an unfair advantage. In 1870 the representatives of the Mulhouse Chamber of Commerce complained that for the transport of cereals the Est Company charged 8 centimes per tonne/kilometre for distances below 200 kilometres, the PLM only 6 centimes; while for distances of over 500 kilometres rates weie 4 centimes and 3 centimes per tonne/kilometre respectively.[205] These differences were, as we have seen, usually explained by the pressure of waterway competition on particular routes.

So-called 'special' tariffs also provoked a variety of reactions from rail users. They tended to vary according to whether or not users could meet the various preconditions laid down by the companies. These normally included minimum amounts to be dispatched by rail in a given period. Thus the Nord in January 1847 offered a reduction of 4 per cent where the monthly amount sent from a given station amounted to 800 tonnes in the case of commodities listed in the third category of its *cahier des charges* or 1500 tonnes where listed in the fourth, 6 per cent where the minima per quarter were 3300 and 9000 tonnes respectively and 8 per cent where the annual minima were 16,000 and 50,000 tonnes respectively.[206] In April 1853 the Paris–Orléans announced the opportunity for users who agreed to send all their grain and flour by rail for a minimum of two years to benefit from special tariffs, but with the proviso that infractions of this agreement would render the user liable to a tariff double the standard rate for a volume of goods equal to those of whose transport the company had been deprived.[207]

These are typical of the special tariffs introduced by all companies. They were supplemented by additional agreements with individual users. Thus MM. J.-J. Legrand, miller at Persan (Seine-et-Oise), and A. Clerget, director-general of the La Parmentière Company of Paris, agreed in a document dated 31 July 1847 to give the Nord the exclusive right to transport all merchandise that these two enterprises would dispatch from, or receive at, Boran, Beaumont and Paris. The agreement provided for a rate of 0.80 francs per sack containing 159 kilograms sent from Beaumont to Paris, with an additional charge of 0.30 francs per sack for carting from the station to the La Parmentière Company. This amounted to a charge of 7 francs per tonne. Furthermore, empty sacks would be returned free.[208]

This was simply one of a number of agreements by which the company sought to capture the substantial traffic in flour originating in the Oise valley.[209] At the same time milk merchants were being persuaded by low tariffs to reach similar agreements. The company agreed in March to dispatch a train from Beaumont to Paris each evening to pick up milk, butter, cheese and eggs from stations *en route*, charging 50 francs for every three wagons loaded between Beaumont and Pontoise and 40.50 francs for those loaded between Pontoise and Paris. Each wagon had a capacity of 3600 litres or 4500 kilograms.[210]

Such agreements leading to special tariffs were to remain an important weapon in the railway companies' competitive armoury. They had the advantage of guaranteeing traffic for a certain period and of directly reducing operating costs. It was normally stipulated that the minimal requirement for taking advantage of special tariffs was the ability to use complete units (wagons or even trains). Tariffs and also fines sought to associate users with the optimum use (that is, rapid rotation) of material by reducing handling on stations to a minimum.[211] By 1905 the ideal means of transporting grain was in bulk in new wagons which permitted avoidance of the costly processes of en-sacking. Special reduced tariffs were introduced to encourage their use.[212]

Obviously, those who benefited from these reductions had to be able to send or receive the contents of the smallest basic unit, the wagon, and to do so over a given period. Rather than the small farmer, it was large-scale users, or the intermediaries who acted to group together the products of the individual producers, who profited. These latter operated primarily in the larger commercial centres. Among farmers it was livestock producers who were most likely to be able to benefit.[213]

The complaint that most farmers rarely had loads large enough to enjoy favourable treatment and were thus placed in an unfair competitive position *vis-à-vis* large producers was frequently made. For example, proposals by the Est in 1850 to reduce tariffs by 10 per cent in the case of merchants sending over 3600 tonnes of cereals or flour each year were criticized as benefiting only five or six large users.[214]

The Paris–Lyon Company responded to such complaints from merchants in the St-Florentin (Yonne) area in 1851 by pointing out that they could combine to meet the minimum requirement of 10,000 tonnes per annum, but the merchants were unable to agree on a course of action which would have limited individual freedom of action.[215]

However, the most frequent complaints were not about complexity or even high tariffs but rather about the workings of differential tariffs (i.e. tariffs digressive with distance), in effect about the basic rationale of railway tariff policy. A differential tariff structure had positive advantages for the railway companies. In the first place, it increased their competitiveness and could be deliberately manipulated to do so where competition was most severe. Second, differential tariffs attracted increased traffic. Given high initial construction costs and substantial fixed operating costs in respect of equipment and labour, it was important to use facilities to the maximum. Differential tariffs allowed the railway companies to relate tariffs more closely to operating costs, for, as we have already observed, fixed costs made up a smaller proportion of the total cost the farther the goods were transported, so that the actual cost of moving a commodity, while continuing to increase with distance, did so at a decreasing rate.[216]

Those transport users who were distant from a potential market were favoured by such a tariff system. Their costs of access were not as great as they might have been if a simple proportional system had been employed. There were, however, many anomalies – for example, for the movement of cereals from the Corrèze in 1870 for distances of up to 100 kilometres the charge per tonne/kilometre was 0.08 francs; for distances of 101–250 kilometres, 0.06 francs per tonne/kilometre; for 251–400 kilometres, 0.05 francs; for over 400 kilometres, 0.04 francs. In this case it would cost 800 francs to transport 100 tonnes for 100 kilometres; 1200 francs to move the same quantity 200 kilometres; 1500 francs for 300 kilometres; 2000 francs for 400 kilometres; but only 1604 francs for 401 kilometres.[217] Such anomalies were to be one cause of constant complaint, as were the grievances of all those who felt that unfair competition was being promoted by railway tariff policies. The reactions of users were to be an increasingly significant influence on these policies.

Particularly bitter complaints were made where such tariffs appeared to be favouring foreign at the expense of domestic producers. Differential tariffs which provided for particularly low charges on commodities transported for 500 kilometres or over seemed deliberately designed to benefit only those transporting for the maximum possible distances, that is, primarily importers. The tariff of 0.04 francs per tonne/kilometre for 500 kilometres or more, introduced by the Est in 1861, for example, served primarily German producers, who alone would send grain such a long distance on the network in order to reach the Paris market.[218] Domestic producers pressed for lower tariffs for their own products to preserve their competitiveness.[219] This was a clear case of difference of interests between railway companies, whose objective was to maximize traffic on their lines regardless of the origins of the commodities involved, and domestic agricultural interests.

The main burden of complaint was, however, the advantages given to particular places or regions within France at the expense of their competitors. It was usually felt by the disadvantaged that the benefits of reduced tariffs ought to be generalized rather than accorded by the arbitrary will of the railway companies.[220] One obvious result of the introduction of differential tariffs was that those charged for movements between the extreme points on a particular line were inevitably lower than those charged for movements from any intermediary point. Paris, situated at the termini of most lines benefited more than any other place from such differentials. However, areas which had once enjoyed a virtual monopoly of supply to the Paris market because of geographical proximity found that the very existence of the railway served to improve access from more distant areas, while the introduction of differential tariffs further reduced the value of proximity. This was true even within the restricted area of the Paris region. In 1866 it cost 2.60 francs to move a tonne of wheat 27 kilometres from Lagny to Paris, only 2.70 francs to move it the 35 kilometres from Esbly and the same from Meaux, 43 kilometres away.[221] It was asserted most vehemently that the effect of differential tariffs was to create uncertainty and disorder for commerce as relative cost advantages between localities were altered.[222]

Rail tariff structures affected the competitive position of various localities for bad or good, and every change in them constituted a renewed opportunity or threat. In 1850 the merchants of Orléans were complaining about tariffs which made it more economic for wine shippers in the Loire valley to send wine to the *entrepôt* at Paris-Bercy than to Orléans, destroying the traditional wine trade of the town. In 1893 the grain merchants of the same town, together with farmers from the surrounding area, were upset by tariffs which favoured the long-distance transport of imported cereals to Paris and threatened their established role in the supply of the capital. It was the threat to *situations acquises* which was particularly resented in this case.[223]

Initially doubts had been raised about the legality of differential tariffs because of the unequal treatment of transport users.[224] Final judicial sanction was only obtained from the Paris Appeal Court in May 1851.[225] Those who felt unfavourably treated by differential tariffs continued, nevertheless, to campaign against them. This pressure and growing government intervention made the railway companies increasingly cautious when considering tariff revisions for fear of the interests which might be alienated.[226] For the companies, however, the dominant factor remained the capacity of differential tariffs to stimulate traffic and increase revenue to offset high overhead costs. They were attracted above all by the prospect of securing the long-distance transport of large volumes of particular commodities and were always reluctant to extend the benefits of differential tariffs to undynamic economic regions, where traffic was limited and operating costs high. By 1901, for example, PLM tariff structures had evolved in a manner which favoured the transport of cereals and flour from the Mediterranean ports and also from stations within a vast triangle with Paris at its summit and its base some 200 kilometres away, on a line passing through Tonnerre, Auxerre, Clamecy and Nevers, which was also able to benefit from low tariffs. Charges from stations located outside this triangle were much higher, and as a consequence millers at places like Sens and Nemours made bitter complaints.[227]

The ability of the railway companies to engage in apparently arbitrary tariff policies was constantly blamed on their monopoly position. Railway monopoly became a bugbear of economic commentators even before the networks were established, and subsequently complaints only grew in intensity, particularly when it became evident that the railway companies were indeed using their cost and speed advantages in attempts to destroy road and water competition.[228] In the absence of competitors, it was believed by users and many government officials[229] (including in 1849 senior members of such organizations as the Commission centrale des chemins de fer, at that time the main advisory body on railways),[230] nothing would prevent the railways from abusing their monopoly. Every shortcoming in railway service tended to be blamed on the absence or decay of competition.

However, it made little economic sense on most routes to construct competing railway lines. The costs of construction were too high, and the volume of traffic would not have justified it. The concept of the network, the operation of lines on a regional basis by large, and financially powerful companies, involved the implicit rejection of the establishment of smaller companies competing for traffic within these regions.

The results of this policy which favoured the major networks were, nevertheless, according to most users, disastrous. A clear difference of interest existed between companies concerned to increase or at least to maintain revenue and users interested in cheap transport. For the latter tariffs were higher than they should have been, and the extension of trade was consequently limited. Feelings had become very strong by the 1870s. In the Nord an association of Chambers of Commerce and Chambres consultatives des arts et manufactures was formed in 1871 to organize regular meetings and to publish a news sheet whose object was made clear in the title of its first publication: 'Defence of commerce and industry against the railway companies'.[231]

Protesters against monopoly had positive suggestions to make as well as criticism. The most common proposal was that the government should act to encourage competition by coastal shipping and inland waterways,[232] but growing demands for government control over the railway companies were heard as well.

The state and the railway companies

The economic case for government control over railway operations (as opposed to considerations of safety) was summarized by a commission reporting in 1912. Railways providing cheap and regular transport were essential to economic development. Although nationalization had been rejected, it was the responsibility of the state, in the general interest, to ensure that lines were developed where needed and that they were run efficiently. It was also important, as a matter of equity, that railway companies be prevented from treating their clients unequally, that is, in a manner which might 'falsify' the conditions of competition between producers and merchants.[233] The organization for implementing the necessary controls had been established by a law of 15 July 1845 and an implementing order of 15 March 1846, which created *commissaires* to oversee the commercial operations of the companies and granted powers to engineers of the Ponts-et-Chaussées to supervise technical development. An *arrêt* of 20 March 1848 replaced the *commissaires* by *inspecteurs de l'exploitation commerciale*, and a law of 27 February 1850 created *commissaires de surveillance administrative* with more general duties. An *arrêt* of 15 April 1850 codified practice and more clearly defined responsibilities, organizing the system of surveillance by network. Besides further alterations in detail, the most significant subsequent change was the formation in 1855 of a permanent section of the advisory Comité consultatif des chemins de fer to make monthly and annual reports. This bureaucratic structure not only facilitated a degree of control of company activity but also served as an appeals mechanism through which transport users might register complaints and seek to influence company policy.[234]

A clear legal basis for statutory controls over company tariff policy was never firmly established. The initial agreements between companies and government and subsequent conventions established price maxima set out in a *cahier des charges*. Basic procedures allowing for government supervision were gradually established during the 1840s, when companies like the Mulhouse to Thann or Paris–Rouen in the earlier years of the decade or the Est at its end sought to avoid administrative control. They frequently changed tariffs as a means of competition with road hauliers without informing local prefects, as was legally required and protested vigorously about administrative interference, which restrained commercial enterprise.[235] It was laid down, as a direct result of disagreement with the administration of the Mulhouse to Thann Company in 1840, that tariffs, once established, should run for at least three months and that one month's notice of proposed changes should be given.[236]

Company proposals for the establishment of new tariffs or for changes had to be published before they could become effective to permit representations by the interested public. In addition, government officials consulted local notables and organizations such as Chambers of Commerce and agricultural societies.[237] Once interested views had been collected, the proposals together with company justifications went before the Comité consultatif or

the various commissions which preceded it and ultimately to the Minister of
Public Works for final confirmation or rejection.[238] General reductions in
tariffs were usually rapidly accepted by government officials as favouring the
extension of commerce, but careful consideration was essential because the
decisions taken often tended to establish precedents.[239]

The whole process of tariff revision involved cumbersome bureaucratic
procedures which allowed adequate time for organized pressure groups to
make their opinions known. It ought to be noted that the Comité consultatif
itself included the representatives of various interest groups, particularly
those of the ports, of industry and of agriculture. Above all, however, it
included the representatives of the railway companies, which tended to
weight its decisions in their favour.[240]

The Minister of Public Works had the legal right to accept or reject tariff
proposals but no authority, save in special circumstances, to secure changes
in tariffs. This seems to have been finally decided only in October 1849.[241] It
should however be stressed that the Minister had substantial potential for
exercising his authority through the right to reject tariff proposals, as well as
more informal means of influencing company administrations.[242] Certain
principles emerged which the companies were expected to respect in formu-
lating their tariffs. These included stipulations to the effect that the level of
tariffs should vary in relation to the value of the merchandise carried. This
meant, for example, that flour should never be transported at a lower rate
than grain.[243] It was required that users should be treated on an equal basis,
that no special favours should be offered to individual users which would
give them an unfair commercial advantage *vis-à-vis* their competitors. In
fact, once variations in rail operating costs were taken into account and the
whole complex range of special and differential tariffs evolved, it became
evident that anomalies between individuals and places were unavoidable,
however hard the authorities tried to eliminate them.

The main special circumstance in which the state was able to interfere with
tariffs was that of harvest failure, when governments felt obliged to take
action to reduce the cost of transporting foodstuffs. Thus the conventions
negotiated with the companies in the late 1850s included a provision according to which, 'when the price of a hectolitre of wheat on the regulating
market at Gray rises to 20 francs or above, the government is able to require
that the tariffs charged for the transport of wheat, grain, rice, maize, flour
and vegetables, tolls included, will not rise above a maximum of 0.07 francs
per tonne/kilometre'.[244] When this circumstance occurred a circular
requesting the necessary reduction was addressed to the companies by the
Minister of Agriculture. Prior to these conventions, and in practical accordance with prevailing liberal economic principles, the administration had felt
able only to request and not to require tariff reduction in times of dearth.
Nevertheless, the companies had felt bound to agree to the reductions
requested,[245] so that even before acquiring the legal right, the government

was interfering with tariff levels and, by doing so, clearly affirming the special public service responsibilities of the railway companies.

In practice, and for commercial reasons, tariffs for the transport of cereals were often, even in normal times, below the maximum of 7 centimes per tonne/kilometre which government regulations came to require after harvest failure.[246] Thus prior to the reduction demanded in November 1867, while tariffs charged for transits of less than 200 kilometres varied between 6 and 8 centimes per tonne/kilometre, at the other end of the scale for over 500 kilometres they were as low as 3–4 centimes. In this case the companies responded to the government initiative by introducing a minumum common tariff of 3.5 centimes.[247] In other circumstances, especially where rail tariffs were relatively high because of the absence of waterway competition, a reduction to 7 centimes might be extremely beneficial to users. Thus the Paris–Orléans rate in 1853 for the transport of cereals and flour towards the centre was 10 centimes per tonne/kilometre.[248] As late as 1897 the Minister of Public Works felt it worth urgently requiring companies to reduce tariffs following a poor harvest[249] in spite of the improvements in agricultural productivity and marketing techniques which had occurred by then.

Clearly, the railway permitted real savings in transport costs and allowed commercial interests to transport foodstuffs profitably over longer distances, so effecting an evening out of regional price variations. The value of these savings is revealed by comparison with transport costs by road or waterway in periods of dearth. As a result of increased demand for their services, these had habitually doubled, trebled, even quadrupled, whereas far from increasing their tariffs railway companies had introduced reductions.[250] According to Emile Pereire, reporting in the name of the Conseil d'administration of the Nord on its operations in 1847, the tariff reductions introduced in that year had effected an economy of at least 3 million francs on the normal tariffs charged by that company, and of at least 5 million francs on the charges which would have been made by road and water transporters.[251] On the Marseille–Lyon route in 1853–4, when the railway line was still incomplete, river transporters had charged rates varying from 40–90 francs per tonne according to the season. In 1856–7 the railway charged 17.50 francs per tonne, and the river companies were forced to reduce their rates to an unvarying 15–16 francs to remain competitive.[252] Rail tariff policies thus had favourable consequences for waterway users. A senior engineer of the Corps des Ponts-et-Chaussées, examining the 'utility of the railways for agriculture', estimated that in 1853, despite the far from complete nature of the railway networks, savings of the order of 33 per cent had been achieved in the transport of agricultural products. It was estimated that 58,467,616 francs would have been paid using pre-rail methods of transport, whereas 38,708,504 francs were in fact paid to the railway companies.[253]

Although the companies sought to co-operate, it was evident that they generally tried to do so on their own terms. Thus the reduction of tariffs when cereal prices rose, before the government even requested this, might be seen as an attempt to limit interference. Each occasion for government intervention created dangerous precedents which threatened their commercial independence and, when officials pressed for the retention of low tariffs for longer periods than the companies would have wished, also their profitability. The companies stressed the spontaneity of their tariff reductions and suggested that the legal powers taken by the government were not really necessary.[254] There was nevertheless a growing tendency towards government intervention in the interest of consumers.

Officials of the Ministry of Public Works felt obliged to seek to eliminate anomalies in tariff structures which appeared to give competitive advantages to particular areas. They faced complex problems. Typically, in 1890 an effort was made to satisfy the complaints of grain millers at Chartres.[255] If this and further modifications in 1910 did something to satisfy them, it also resulted in a weakening of the competitive position of millers in the Eure valley *vis-à-vis* those of Chartres.[256] The solution of one problem immediately created new ones.

From as early as 1847,[257] but especially from the end of the Second Empire, the administration had attempted to secure the generalized application of special tariffs to all those in analogous situations. The likelihood that this would occur inevitably reduced the number of special concessions made, particularly when the companies were obliged to construct new lines with limited traffic and higher operating costs, on which the generalized application of reduced tariffs would have been particularly unremunerative. It was not in the companies' interests to extend concessions to all stations regardless of the nature of the traffic they offered and the costs involved.[258]

This growing caution was the almost inevitable result of the conception many officials and members of the public had of the railways as providers of a public service, with obligations not only towards their own shareholders but towards the general public. This limited the strict application of commercial principles. It was an attitude which had always existed as a reaction to the quasi-monopoly position of the railways[259] and was only reinforced by the series of conventions negotiated between governments and companies. At a meeting of the Comité consultatif in May 1894 M. Cochery appears to have expressed a widely held view in affirming that 'in a country like France, where the rail networks have been established with substantial aid from the state', they were 'in reality its delegates for a great public service'.[260] As a logical consequence of this attitude, the government, influenced by pressure-group activities, sought from as early as the late 1860s to secure the establishment of a tariff structure deliberately designed to protect the economic interests of regions and, in effect, of relatively inefficient producers within them – in other words, to limit the potential for long-distance competitive penetration. This ran counter to the often stated objective of increasing market integration.

Ministry officials continued to favour reductions in tariffs, especially those for long-distance transport, but in the case of cereals one essential objective, particularly from the 1880s, was to improve the competitiveness of French cereals on internal markets. From this period the direct and indirect influence of government agencies was used to induce the railway companies to revise their overall tariff structures in a manner which lent support to the objective of establishing protective barriers for domestic agriculture.[261] In the conventions negotiated with the government in 1883 the companies agreed to suppress gradually tariffs which favoured imports, except where they were in competition with waterways.[262] In more positive vein, in 1892 the Orléans reduced cereal tariffs from 0.015 to 0.01 francs per tonne/kilometre for distances of over 400 kilometres, with the aim of extending the markets for grain grown in northern France and increasing its competitiveness with imports in the south. Its officials had made a careful study of transport costs from the north and centre to the south and were attempting to establish tariffs which ensured that transport costs between areas of habitual surplus and those of deficit did not exceed differences in the price of cereals, and that they were sufficiently low to ensure that minor price fluctuations did not eliminate the margin for profit. The aim was to establish a regular current of trade to benefit both farmers and the railway company.[263]

Tariff proposals were more likely to be rejected if they seemed likely to increase import penetration. A decision of the Comité consultatif regarding proposals made by the Ouest in May 1894 makes the point quite clearly. The *rapporteur* for the Comité explained the rejection of the company's proposals in the following manner:

The departments of Seine-et-Marne, Eure-et-Loir, Mayenne and Sarthe are major growers of wheat, which they produce in quantities well above their own needs. The cultivators have natural markets, and it would be an injustice to close these to them through the granting of considerable advantages to foreign cereals by the railways. It would be correct to consider the proposed reductions as likely to reduce the protection afforded by customs tariffs voted by parliament.

We understand that the Company needs to lower its charges to conserve its traffic or even to increase it in competition with the waterways, but equity commands that we maintain at least an equal balance between national products and foreign products. . . .[264]

In the same period tariffs were approved on the Midi which favoured the transportation of cereals and flour produced in southern departments such as Lot-et-Garonne, Gers, Tarn-et-Garonne, Haute-Garonne, Ariège and Tarn at the expense of imports through the ports of Bordeaux, Cette, Agde, La Nouvelle and Port-Vendres.[265] Proposals by the same company thought likely to favour imports were rejected.[266] The PLM in particular appears to have resented this policy. It had already seen its important traffic from

Marseille towards the north threatened by the development of imports through the Channel ports. Its administrators wanted to reduce 'tariffs to increase the competitive penetration inland of cereals along its tracks, but this ran contrary to government policy and was forbidden by government supervisory agencies. In January 1893 the Minister, acting on the advice of the Comité consultatif, rejected a proposed reduction from 28 to 22 francs per tonne in the charge for transporting cereals from Marseille to Paris because this would have represented 'in reality a *tarif de pénétration*', increasing foreign competition on the Paris market and threatening the 'natural markets' of producers in central France by allowing wheat at a cost of 2 francs per *quintal* to reach such places as Nevers, Dijon, Moulins, Tonnerre, Sens and Montereau. Similar proposals were again rejected in July 1895.[267]

Officials of the Ministry of Public Works showed a constant concern to avoid upsetting the *status quo*, the established economic position of particular enterprises. They were susceptible to requests which either limited the extension of differential and special tariffs and the favours accorded to large scale users or extended them more generally and eliminated particular advantages.[268] In some cases, however, they were reluctant to interfere with the privileged position within the railway system already built up by particular enterprises or places. For example, in a report prepared in 1889 it was recognized that low rail tariffs gave the industrial flour mills at Corbeil important competitive advantages, yet the report advised against changes which would cause difficulties for these mills.[269] It had to be recognized that 'tariffs existing for several years and considered [by] users to be definitive have become the base upon which all those who are involved in the grain trade . . . have based their calculations'.[270]

Besides the conflicting interests of users and differences of interest between them and the railway companies, government officials also had to resolve differences between the companies. In general, although the Ministry recognized that in regions served by more than one company tariff reductions might be legitimately used by one company to offset the advantages of another (in terms of distance, for example),[271] it generally frowned upon tariff combinations which sought to deprive one company of traffic for the benefit of another. The official view was clearly expressed in 1874: 'the administration. . . from the point of view of the general interest . . . as well as because of state guarantees [of dividends] cannot approve of competition likely to have disastrous results'.[272] As we shall see, competition between rail and waterways was even more deliberately limited. The basic policy in this respect was thus, again, one of caution.

Rouher, when Minister of Public Works, had insisted to Franqueville, the official responsible for the railway division of the Ministry, that his officials ought to be conciliatory by nature, particularly as they had to negotiate with railway company representatives, who were men of substance and importance.[273] This attitude might suggest that the companies, acting as pressure groups, were in a position to exercise an inordinate influence on official policy. During the initial phases of construction in the 1850s and 1860s their opinions in matters of tariffs were probably dominant. As costs were reduced, they were able to reduce tariffs, and this was what the government desired. Certainly, during these years close working relationships were built up between the parallel private and government bureaucracies. But subsequently other interests, such as the protection of agriculture, came to the fore, and the influence of the companies was reduced. In effect, they did not succeed in 'capturing' the officials of the Ministry.

The overall result of growing caution on the part of both companies and government was to restrain competition between the providers of transport facilities and between commercial users. The stagnation of tariff levels, particularly from the 1870s, was to have effects on the evolution of market structures which were to be one cause of a reduction in the dynamism of the French economy from the 1870s.

In assessing their importance for the development of the agricultural economy it is not possible to consider the railways in isolation. They functioned as one element of a transport network within which road, waterways and railways performed integrated as well as competitive functions. Most commodities were transported by road before they ever reached the railway. Consideration of the effectiveness with which road and waterways satisfied transportation needs is thus essential.

Road development

Transport conditions

The improvement of major roads persisted throughout the century. In the 1830s and 1840s in particular roads were straightened and gradients reduced, new bridges constructed and new construction techniques introduced to improve road surfaces. By the time railways came into operation substantial progress had occurred. This was to continue. Although, as we shall see, railway development affected the patterns of road use, many *routes nationales* continued to carry heavy volumes of traffic. As late as 1878 the length of these roads was still double that of the railway network, and many areas were still completely dependent on them for extra-local communications.[274] Consequently, the work of road improvement was carried on parallel to, and in association with, that of railway construction.

The objective of road building was clear – every settlement was to be linked to a major road network by roads which could be used by carts in all seasons.[275] Progress was inevitably slow for both technical and, especially, financial reasons. The chronology of development varied between regions; those with relatively dense existing networks giving access to markets – in short, the more economically advanced regions – tended to complete their local networks before backward regions plagued by lack of obvious incentives and of cash. Everywhere roads tended to be improved in order of their importance according to the official classification – first the *routes nationales*, then the *routes départementales*, then the *chemins de grande communication, chemins d'intérêt commun* and *chemins vicinaux ordinaires* and, finally, the lowest category, the *chemins ruraux*, linking individual hamlets and farms to other roads and to their fields.

Annual average expenditure on road works is estimated to have grown in the manner shown in Table 25.[276] In the early 1850s the central government provided only 34–5 million francs per annum for expenditure on roads and bridges. This rose to 40–5 million francs per annum during the 1860s.[277] The bulk of the funds available was therefore raised by local taxation.

Table 25   *Total annual expenditure on roads, 1815–1913 (millions francs)*

Period	Expenditure	Period	Expenditure
1815–19	58.2	1870–9	223.7
1820–9	65.0	1880–9	243.9
1830–9	110.3	1890–9	231.9
1840–9	170.6	1900–9	234.2
1850–9	176.8	1910–13	249.0
1860–9	220.7		

Both the general need for improvement and specific proposals were justified in terms of the necessity to stimulate economic activity and also in terms of social saving. Thus in the Minister of Public Works' report to the Emperor in 1860 it was estimated that a reduction in the cost of road transport of 0.01 franc per tonne/kilometre would result in an effective annual saving of 16 million francs on movement by *routes nationales* alone.[278] In 1878 it was estimated that the likely saving on a similar improvement was of the order of 17 millions.[279]

Analysis of the improvement of roads is a difficult problem, given the variety of types of road and regional variations in conditions. The simplest way to begin is to consider the significance of each class of road in the transport network and then to assess the importance of the work of improvement.

The length of the network of *routes nationales* changed relatively little (see Table 26).[280] Further improvements took much the same form as previous work, except that a new concern to establish links with railway stations became evident.[281] The report of Rouher, as Minister of Public Works, to the Emperor of 25 February 1860 instanced the survival of major

Table 26   *Extension of the* routes nationales, *1851–1913*
 (thousands kilometres)

Year	Extent of roads	Year	Extent of roads
1851–2	35.7	1882	37.5
1856–7	35.8	1888	37.7
1863–4	37.8	1894	37.9
1869	38.3	1903	38.1
1876	37.3	1913	38.3

gaps in the network amounting to 360 kilometres of a total of 36,150 kilometres and situated in eighteen departments, of which the most significant were in Hautes- and Basses-Alpes, Ardèche, Ariège, Isère, Lozère, Hautes- and Basses-Pyrénées and Pyrénées-Orientales.[282] It was upland areas which were most in need of substantial works of all kinds, but in these the complexity and cost of this work would be greatest and the economic returns least evident.

In economically more active regions, although road conditions were much better, new difficulties were caused by the growth of economic activity and of traffic. This led to the appearance or worsening of bottlenecks along major roads (for example, on access roads to Paris and other major markets), blocked from early morning on market days by large numbers of agricultural carts,[283] on narrow river bridges, such as those over the Loire at Nantes, which were only 10 metres wide,[284] or on the excessively narrow stretches of the roads passing through countless towns and villages.[285] These were all shortcomings which led to wastage of time and capital.

In departments in the Paris region and around other large cities the complaint was constantly made that maintenance did not keep pace with wear and tear.[286] Often this was because of a failure on the part of local authorities to realize that in spite of railways the *routes nationales* retained considerable importance and their unwillingness to increase credits at a time when the costs of material and labour were both increasing. The senior road engineer in another department with busy roads, the Pas-de-Calais, reported in 1866 that of a network of 684 kilometres of *routes nationales*, 521 were in a 'passable state' but with worn surfaces; 120 were mediocre in summer and pot-holed in winter; while on the remaining 43 kilometres the paved surfaces had been completely worn away.[287] The best road conditions seem to have been found in lowland areas with little traffic.[288]

Improvement of main roads had a significant effect on transport conditions and on the cost and speed of movement, but numerous imperfections survived. In spite of previous efforts, it was still felt necessary to include in the Freycinet Law of July 1881 provision for the expenditure of 120 million francs on the improvement of *routes nationales*. This included 30 millions to eliminate gaps, 40 millions for the rectification of gradients and 50 millions for the repair of road surfaces.[289] Even so, in 1888 there were still *routes nationales*, such as No. 125 in Haute-Garonne, between Bagnères-de-Luchon and the Spanish frontier, which were little better than mud tracks.[290]

As work continued to improve the networks of major roads, substantial efforts were made to improve the quality of local roads, which had previously suffered most from neglect. Among these the network of *routes départementales* performed important functions within particular regions, and the responsibility for their maintenance was placed upon the departmental authorities. As in the case of the *routes nationales*, changes in the length of the network (see Table 27)[291] were due primarily to reclassification. The complaints voiced about the *routes départementales* were also similar to those directed at the major roads. Again, it was the upland areas which suffered most. Thus the *routes départementales* Nos. 10, 11, 12, 13, in Basses-Alpes, all had numerous sections which were impassable to carts, were too narrow and frequently had precipitous cliffs alongside them and gradients which attained 14–18 per cent.[292]

Table 27   *Extension of the* routes départementales, *1851–1913* (*thousands kilometres*)

Year	Extent of roads	Year	Extent of roads
1851	42.3	1882	47.5
1856–7	45.2	1888	47.3
1863–4	45.9	1894	47.1
1869	47.0	1903	46.9
1876	47.7	1913	46.7

From the 1830s, for the first time, a substantial and growing proportion of the resources available was also devoted to the improvement of the *chemins vicinaux*, which previously had suffered almost complete neglect in many areas. Improvement of these roads was to be the major achievement of the second half of the century. The law of 21 May 1836 on local roads went a long way towards solving the problems of administrative and financial responsibility, which had previously hindered effective action. The aim of the law was declared to be the establishment of over 48,000 kilometres of *chemins vicinaux de grande communication*, to complement the existing maintained network of 35,000 kilometres of *routes nationales* and 37,000 of *routes départementales*, with, as a long-term objective, the surfacing of some 677,000 kilometres of *chemins vicinaux de petite communication*.[293] The realization of this last intention was to be slow, although more money and better administration brought improved standards of road construction and maintenance.[294] Expenditure on *chemins vicinaux* is shown in Table 28.[295] In 1865 an income made up of 40,956,089.90 francs derived from labour services plus 80,807,320.77 francs in money was used as follows:[296]

Table 28   *Average expenditure per annum on* chemins vicinaux, *1837–66 (millions francs)*

Period	Labour service (prestation) estimated value	Cash expenditure	Total
1837–41	27.35	33.4	60.75
1842–6	40.9	33.45	74.35
1847–51	44.75	42.9	87.65
1852–6	47.18	50.02	97.2
1857–61	54.6	54.88	109.48
1862–6	62.9	72.45	135.35

Payment of personnel	7,036,925.83 francs
Expenditure on *chemins de grande communication*	42,380,812.58 francs
Expenditure on *chemins d'intérêt commun*	31,847,228.76 francs
Expenditure on *chemins vicinaux ordinaires*	40,498,443.60 francs

The strictly limited nature of state aid for local roads is shown by a breakdown of the sources of finance for work on *chemins vicinaux* in the not untypical year 1879. The money came from:[297]

Communes	100,459,078 francs
Individual users	3,787,650 francs
Departments	61,880,987 francs
Government	5,968,969 francs

A further 75,021,507 francs remained unspent from the estimates for 1878.

Although the 1836 law accelerated the pace of development, this continued to be hindered above all by the financial difficulties experienced by the communal authorities responsible for these roads. It also took time to carry out inquiries and to agree on priorities. Inevitably, the initial effort was concentrated upon roads classified as *chemins de grande communication*, those establishing links between the more important population and economic centres.[298] Neglect of less important *chemins vicinaux* persisted, and complaints continued to be made for decades.[299] Moreover, the resources created by the 1836 law rapidly became inadequate as the tempo of economic activity increased.[300] It was reported from Mayenne in 1866 that 135,674 francs were available for the *chemins de moyenne et petite vicinalité*. After maintenance of the 435 kilometres of roads in those categories which had already been made up, only a pittance of 83,474 francs remained for new work. As the length of made-up roads grew, so the share of available monies necessary for their maintenance increased and the proportion for new works declined.[301] Attempts were therefore made to improve the financial provisions of the original Act. A decree of August 1861 provided 2 million francs and the law of July 1868 a further 100 million francs of state aid over ten years for urgent work which communes could not finance themselves.[302] The law of 12 March 1880 both intensified the mandatory character of earlier laws in respect of local responsibilities for road maintenance and provided 80 million francs.[303]

Government and departmental grants were made to communes of which the schemes were approved and the financial resources were judged to be inadequate and which agreed to contribute a sum which, normally at least, matched the grant from higher authority. In a relatively rich area like the Nord as early as 1862 only two communes were not linked to the primary road network because of their unwillingness to meet these conditions. Even so, the state of local roads in the department was still judged to be 'disastrous' as a result of poor original construction, heavy traffic and inadequate maintenance, and the *conseil général* was requested to provide 884,965 francs to meet the cost of the most urgent work in communes whose own financial resources were exhausted.[304] Elsewhere the combination of funds from all sources was much less adequate. The various extraordinary grants were spread too widely to alter the situation substantially. The members of *conseils généraux*, after long debates, divided out state and departmental subsidies in small amounts in order to maximize the political good will gained. The Gard's share in the subsidy of 1868 worked out at 111,000 francs, which were divided between 300 communes out of a total of 348. Only ten communes added significant sums themselves. It was estimated that 9 million francs needed to be spent to create a satisfactory network of local roads in the department.[305] The *chemins vicinaux* remained the main area of neglect in the communications system.

Even after roads had been improved, standards of maintenance were often very poor, particularly off the *routes nationales* and *départementales*, which were maintained at departmental expense. The condition of roads in a particular place thus depended a great deal on their classification. If a commune happened to be on the main route between two towns (usually connected by *routes nationales*) or between two *bourgs* (large market villages, usually linked by *routes départementales*) it would enjoy the benefits both of superior communications and a much reduced financial burden for itself. Those communes which were forced to finance road works mainly from their own resources were usually the less developed economically because of poor access to markets. It seemed to be a case of to those who have, more will be given.[306]

Where normal communal revenues were inadequate the 1836 law had provided for the levying of an additional tax of 5 per cent, or a *prestation* (labour service) for a maximum of three days per year. This was due from each head of family or enterprise, for himself and every male aged 18–60, whether member of his family or servant and also for every cart and draught animal. If desired, service could be commuted to a cash payment,[307] but in the Rhône during the Second Empire this was only 1.50 francs per day, at a time when a road labourer was paid between 2 and 3 francs.[308]

Controversy raged over this institution. According to the Comice agricole of the canton of Elven (Morbihan) in 1870, the work was badly done because the peasant did not understand the value and saw it only as 'a survival of the ancient *corvée*'.[309] There can be no doubt that the performance of the *prestation* was often bitterly resented,[310] and the resentment was compounded in some cases by the suspicion that mayors and municipal councillors were especially concerned to improve the roads leading to their own properties.[311] Local politics and rivalries were rarely absent from the discussion of road works. During the democratic period of the Second Republic the *prestation* had been condemned as feudal because, as every individual was equally liable, the poor who benefited least from road improvement bore an unfair share of the burden.[312] Then, as later, the official response tended to be that the poor would be happier to supply their labour than part with hard-earned money,[313] and even in 1912 the Congrès national des maires agreed that 'the peasant is more disposed to work for a day than to pay the tax collector even the smallest sum'.[314] The *prestation* was particularly important in the poorest regions in which subsistence farming predominated and hard cash was in short supply. Here it made some sense because of the seasonal underemployment of the work force – providing that this labour was effectively employed.

All too often local authorities lacked the personal authority and technical competence to make effective use of the labour available. The fact that much of the potential value of labour service was wasted in practice was the main criticism made of it. There was a lack of systematic organization and effective supervision.[315] The responsible official in the Vosges estimated in 1856 that of *prestations* theoretically worth about 290,000 francs, between 150,000 and 200,000 francs were wasted, and for France as a whole he calculated that since the 1836 law, 300 million francs worth of labour had been frittered away by incompetent or irresponsible communal authorities.[316] Yet in spite of such criticism, in response to a general inquiry in 1889 only the *conseils généraux* of Allier, Ardennes, Aube, Cher, Loire, Marne, Meuse, Pyrénées-Orientales, Saône-et-Loire and Seine-et-Oise were prepared to condemn the *prestation*.[317]

The responsibility was normally left in the hands of the local mayor, but efforts were made to recruit *agents voyers* who at least possessed technical training. Here too finance was the crucial factor, although it also seems to have been difficult to find suitably qualified personnel. The slow expansion of their numbers meant that road works were gradually better executed.[318] It was clearly essential, if available credits and labour were not to be wasted, that at the local level work should be supervised by individuals with at least elementary surveying and engineering skills.

The powers given to the prefectoral administration and, from 1871, to the *conseils généraux* and the departmental representatives of the *Ponts-et-Chaussées* imposed a certain degree of central control, but their interest still tended to be concentrated on the more important roads. Even when the economic importance of roads in a particular area changed, their reclassification and improvement was slow to occur.[319] However, the period 1840–80 saw everywhere growing efforts to improve the *chemins d'intérêt commun*, which linked communes, and the *chemins vicinaux ordinaires*, usually of interest to only a single commune, whose hamlets it linked together or to a more important road. At least these were attended to once superior categories had been improved.[320] The changing focus of road works can be illustrated by contrasting the proposed pattern of expenditure in 1879 with that for 1865 (in francs) (see Table 29).[321]

By contrast with the recent past, improvement was rapid, so that it became difficult to keep the representation of roads on maps up to date.[322] In Calvados, for example, in 1860 97 per cent of the *chemins de grande communication* were maintained (only 46 per cent in 1840); in 1870 93 per cent of the *chemins d'intérêt commun* (only 43 per cent in 1850), and in 1860 53 per cent of the *chemins vicinaux ordinaires*, a figure rising to 83 per cent in 1882 and 88 per cent in 1895.[323] This is not to deny that localized gaps in the maintained network were still to be found, especially along the *chemins vicinaux ordinaires*, and, more seriously, that improved roads had frequently not been made up to the standards judged to be necessary even at the time.[324] In addition, after they had been made up it was always difficult to maintain roads used by heavy traffic satisfactorily.[325] The achievement was considerable, yet much remained to be done. The state of the *chemins vicinaux* at the end of 1867 and then in 1881 illustrates both the magnitude of the achievement and the work which still needed to be undertaken (see Table 30).[326]

The economic effects of initial road works generally stimulated further interest in improvement and changed existing perceptions of what constituted an adequate road or a sufficiently dense network.[327] The representatives of areas without roads suitable for wheeled traffic complained that their economic development was being seriously hindered;[328] those of areas in which substantial capital had been invested in road works remained dissatisfied. Thus Count Martin, reporting on the development of *chemins vicinaux*

Table 29   *Expenditure on roads, 1865 (actual) and 1879 (proposed) (francs)*

Type of road	1865	1879
chemins de grande communication	42,380,813	50,575,627
chemins d'intérêt commun	31,847,229	38,876,348
chemins vicinaux ordinaires	40,498,444	138,602,482

Table 30 *Extent of maintained and unmaintained* chemins vicinaux, *1867 and 1881 (kilometres)*

	1867	1881
Maintained *chemins vicinaux*	265,504	362,200
practicable for traffic	62,470	63,359
under construction	35,269	28,132
Unmaintained (i.e. earth tracks)	185,260	139,292

to the *conseil général* of the Nord in 1862, observed that their development had helped to promote more rapid growth in industrial and agricultural output than anyone would have dared to hope but that this new level of activity had rendered many of the improved roads inadequate.[329]

The development of local roads transformed agricultural marketing, which was their primary purpose, but also improved access to the countryside for industrial products. Villages almost lost in the countryside were effectively connected with main roads built to link the towns, with consequences, above all perhaps for popular attitudes, which are difficult for us to imagine. According to the Agricultural Society of St-Pol (Pas-de-Calais), 'the old and the new situations are incomparable, the change total'.[330] This impression of an economic transformation is constantly repeated from the 1840s, while the complaints from places which felt neglected and isolated grew all the shriller, reflecting anxiety about their potential for development in competition with areas endowed with the facilities for cheaper bulk transport and especially with good road links to nearby railways.[331] In his report to the *conseil général* of the Nord, Count Martin insisted that the improvement of good roads ought to be accorded top priority because 'it is with good *chemins vicinaux* that progress, enlightenment and well-being spread through our countryside'.[332] These sound like the words of a colonial administrator. More prosaic was the appreciation of the senior Ponts-et-Chaussées engineer, Charté-Marsaines, in 1857 in stressing the importance of made-up roads in increasing the utility of horse traction. Horses could pull heavier loads at higher speeds and with less wear and tear on animals and carts.[333]

For many villages age-old isolation ended during the Second Empire or in the first two decades of the Third Republic. M. Baudart, the senior Ponts-et-Chaussées engineer in the Ain, reported in 1866 on the immense progress made since the 1836 law:

Before 1836 except for the *routes impériales et départementales* . . . none of the roads were paved in the Bresse or Dombes. It took a lot of time and powerful teams of oxen to take two or three sacks of grain to market because of the clay soils of these areas, and after rain the roads became impracticable. In the mountains, the roads offered other inconveniences, dangerous torrents, steep slopes, etc. . . . Today almost all roads are viable and all localities served. . . .[334]

In many upland regions it became possible to use carts for the first time in place of pack animals, while elsewhere improved roads allowed the use of bigger carts without requiring a commensurate increase in draught power.[335]

Throughout these years, however, important regional disparities survived. In general, it can be said that roads were still always better where they led to major markets in wide valleys and on the open plains than in areas of *bocage* or the uplands. Local road networks appear to have been in best condition in the Paris region as a result of the obvious advantages of improving access to the Paris market.[336] Similarly, around Lyon in the Rhône department by 1860 every commune had access to the roads leading into the city.[337] Further along the Rhône–Saône corridor, in Côte-d'Or, the best-maintained roads were those leading to the river in the first half of the century and, subsequently, those to railway stations.[338] An inquiry in 1867 revealed that in Côte-d'Or all the *chemins de grande communication*, 84 per cent of those of *intérêt commun* and 71 per cent of the *chemins vicinaux ordinaires* had been brought up to the proper standards and were being maintained. In Vienne, by contrast, the inquiry revealed that while all the *chemins de grande communication* were satisfactory and 82 per cent of the *chemins d'intérêt commun*, this was true of only 4 per cent of the *chemins ordinaires*,[339] indicative of the order of priorities when financial resources were limited. Thus it was still frequently claimed that poor roads were holding up agricultural progress.[340] According to the Société nationale d'agriculture de France in 1880, the effects of poor *chemins vicinaux* were felt most severely in upland areas and throughout the centre, west and south-west.[341] Steep gradients or mud reduced the weights which carts might transport. In Côtes-du-Nord the small light carts in common use at the end of the nineteenth century were well suited to uneven topography, steep gradients and rough and narrow roads,[342] but these conditions inevitably increased the cost (in money and time) of transport and remained a disincentive to the marketing of agricultural commodities.[343]

The situation was exacerbated by the limited funds available for the improvement of our last category of roads, simple rural roads (*chemins ruraux*) and private tracks leading from village or farm to fields.[344] Where farms were composed of dispersed plots, as they so often were, the daily problem of reaching these was compounded. Everywhere considerable time and energy was wasted and numerous disputes occurred over rights of access. Most peasant farmers took this for granted and preferred to use their energy, which cost them nothing, in this way rather than pay increased taxes for road improvement. It was those members of the rural population with capital to spare and who were orientated more completely towards market agriculture who were most prepared to accept the vital importance of better rural roads for agricultural improvement and to meet the cost.[345] Moreover, in areas where larger farm units predominated, dispersal of plots was less significant, fewer roads were needed and the problems were less severe. Yet the failure to improve these roads undoubtedly had deleterious effects for agriculture. According to reports from Normandy, the poor condition of the rural roads deprived the farmer in large measure of the benefits derived from improvement of other roads. The agricultural machinery in use, as well as the size of carts, was determined by the state of the roads, and draught teams were prematurely exhausted by the struggle to reach the fields and subsequently return to the farm. Equally serious was the inability to load carts fully and the requirement to make two or more journeys where one would have been sufficient on a paved road.[346] According to the inquiry conducted by the Société nationale d'agriculture de France in 1880, this particular problem of rural roads was especially serious in the west and south-west in areas of *bocage* and dispersed habitat where the road density was greatest, but complaints were common even from areas in close proximity to Paris. Poor conditions were particularly common in regions of heavy soil and poor drainage.[347]

Official awareness of the importance of these rural roads had been clearly expressed in a circular of 16 November 1839, which maintained that of every 2000 roads of importance for access to fields, perhaps only fifteen or twenty had been adopted as *chemins vicinaux*.[348] The problem was immense. In the Orne in 1866, for example, there were believed to be around 15,000 kilometres of rural roads, which it was estimated would cost around 50 million francs to improve.[349] The problem was essentially a financial one. Rather than increase taxation, communes preferred to do nothing, save perhaps to defend the rural roads from incorporation in neighbouring fields. Expenditure was concentrated on higher order roads, which seemed more important in economic terms and in relation to which prefectoral supervision was more demanding.[350] In law communes were permitted to spend money on rural roads only after work on classified roads had been satisfactorily completed.[351] Thus only isolated improvements were made to this vast network before the application of the law of 20 August 1881, which allowed 'recognition' of the more important rural roads. Even then, maintenance was not made obligatory, and progress was slow.[352] In terms of the efficiency of farm labour, access of inputs to farms and of produce to markets, the poor condition of rural road networks evidently remained a significant restraining factor.

Transport costs

It is clear that the cost of road transport (the cost in time even for those peasant farmers who did not count the cost in money) was influenced by road conditions. Poor road surfaces and gradients reduced the weight carts could carry, limited the size of carts and exhausted animals. Where it was a case of paying professional carters, all these things were taken into account, along with the basic cost of wages for men and the fluctuating cost of fodder for animals. Désert illustrates the significance of road improvements in Calvados by means of an evaluation of the average load pulled by one horse (see Table 31).[353] Besides, the speed of movement increased. Such

Table 31   *Average load pulled by one horse, c.1815–65 (kilograms)*

Year	Load
c.1815	c.650
1838	600–750
1843	750
1853	994
1865	1350

improvements obviously allowed for reductions in charges. Toutain's estimates of the evolution of tariffs (see Table 32)[354] are based on an immense variety of particular examples.[355] So many variables influenced tariffs, and variations around these averages are so substantial, that one is led to believe that they conceal as much as they reveal. The peasant hiring out his cart during quiet periods on the farm was likely to charge less than the professional carter, while the latter's rates were variable between places and over time. In the Nord in 1866 rates varied from 0.15–0.40 franc per tonne/kilometre, according to the season, which affected the availability of peasant carters (and the length of the working day), the state of the roads, which varied according to the direction taken, and whether or not return loads were available.[356]

The railways were, without doubt, strong competitors for traffic. They possessed obvious advantages in terms of both tariffs and speed, which tended to increase with operating efficiency. By 1871 the average charge per tonne/kilometre by rail was only 0.063 franc, and by 1913 this had fallen to 0.041 franc. In 1870 by *roulage accéléré*, the fastest form of transport for merchandise, it usually took one day to travel 60–80 kilometres, while by *roulage ordinaire*, the habitual form of transport for bulky commodities,

Table 32   *Carters' tariffs per tonne/kilometre* (roulage ordinaire),
1800–60 (francs)

Period	Tariff
1800–14	0.35
1815–24	0.30
1825–30	0.25
1830–45	0.20–0.25
1845–60	0.20

only 30–5 kilometres were normally covered.[357] An ordinary goods train could easily cover this distance in an hour and continued to move during the hours of darkness, unlike most carts.

In the period immediately after a railway began operating in a particular area the railway company had to break down established habits, create its own commercial agencies and station facilities and build up experience in dealing with users. This took time, although the employment of personnel with experience in road transport and the use, in large centres, of existing road hauliers as agents helped to abridge the transition period during which users began to transfer from one form of transport to another.[358] Fairly rapidly a dense network of well organized stations and commercial agencies was established, promising facilities for bulk transport at relatively fixed prices, a factor which offered the considerable advantage of reducing uncertainty for users.[359]

Competition from rail soon became effective for long-distance movements, for which tariffs per tonne/kilometre were substantially lower. In 1870 carters at Metz felt unable to charge less than 0.25 franc per tonne/kilometre over long distances and could not compete with the 0.08 franc charged by the Est railway company.[360] Even where efforts were made to reduce road tariffs to the absolute minimum, as for example the 0.18 franc per tonne/kilometre charged between Langres and Gray, this was still substantially higher than the 0.10 franc by rail.[361]

Competitive pressure on road hauliers continued to increase as rail networks were extended. The average distance goods were transported by road inevitably tended to fall, but it was in the sphere of short-distance transport that they remained price competitive because the fixed charges of the railway companies for station handling significantly increased the unit cost of short-distance movement.[362] The time taken to transship from road carts to railway wagons and then to form a whole train, plus the reverse procedure at destination, also made it possible to compete in terms of speed.[363] Users seem, in addition, to have felt frequently that merchandise transported by road was likely to have better care taken of it and was less likely to be damaged.[364] The road transporter, at least over short distances, continued to offer the advantages of 'flexibility in scheduling and door-to-door service'.[365]

In the long run road improvement reduced costs, as did improved breeding of horses, although the tendency for wages to rise from the 1840s partially counteracted this.[366] In the short term the fluctuation of fodder prices also affected costs. When these were low the competitiveness of road haulage might significantly increase. In 1850, mainly for this reason, hauliers competing with the Ouest reduced their charges per sack of flour from 3 francs to as low as 1.50 francs, forcing the railway company to take urgent measures to reduce its tariffs, and to offer long-term contracts at special low rates to some large users.[367]

Road traffic

It is not possible even to estimate the volume of agricultural produce carried by road, although Toutain has, very bravely, attempted to estimate the evolution of merchandise of all kinds that was carried (see Table 33).[368] Prior to 1913 the volume of merchandise moved by road appears to have stagnated or to have increased only very slowly. The volume carried by other forms of transport increased more rapidly, so that the share of road transport in the total reached its lowest point during 1905–13. The railway companies clearly established their tariffs in order to ensure that road competition on major long-distance routes would be destroyed, and in this they enjoyed a high degree of success.[369] Significantly, in 1856 the Paris–Caen road, parallel to the railway, carried an estimated 18,000 tonnes, while beyond Caen, where the railway had not been completed, the Caen–Cherbourg road carried over 50,000 tonnes. Similarly, the Lens–Douai and Cambrai–Douai roads, perpendicular to the rail links between Arras–Douai–Lille and Douai and Valenciennes, transported 113,000 tonnes and 95,000 tonnes respectively, whereas the Arras–Douai road, competing with the railway, carried only 24,000 tonnes.

Table 33   *Volume of merchandise transported by road, 1830–1913*
          (milliards tonnes/kilometres)

Period	Annual average volume of merchandise transported by road	Percentage of total merchandise transported
1830	2.0	53
1841–4	2.3	49
1845–54	2.6	43
1855–64	2.7	31
1865–74	2.8	24
1875–84	2.6	17
1885–94	2.7	15
1895–1904	2.8	12
1905–13	2.9	9

Rail construction was extended over a considerable period of time, so that the transformation of road use was gradual. The initial period of rail construction linked the more important population centres, and its lines tended to follow existing *routes impériales*. *Routes départementales* in this period were far less likely to meet direct rail competition, which explains why between 1851 and 1869 traffic on *routes impériales* increased only by an estimated 13 per cent, while that on *routes départementales* grew by 70 per cent.[370] Information on minor roads is more difficult to find. However, a report from Hérault in 1866 indicated an increase of about 40 per cent in traffic on the *chemins vicinaux de grande communication* between 1856 and 1864, adding that traffic had more than doubled on those roads which led to railway stations.[371]

Often it took time for those engaged in road transport to adapt to new conditions and to introduce regular new services.[372] The cost of reaching the nearest railway station remained quite high, particularly in regions like Brittany or the Massif Central, where the density of the railway network was relatively low. Figures prepared in 1870 on the cost of movement by road from the nearest railway station to various towns without rail connections revealed the disadvantages suffered by such centres in terms of road transport costs, which frequently rose as high as 50 centimes, 75 centimes or even 1 franc per tonne/kilometre.[373]

The basic effect of rail competition on road use was not to reduce the overall volume of traffic but rather to cause a displacement from routes parallel to railway lines on to those which served as feeders to them.[374] Railways were dependent upon carters to move goods to and from their stations and found it necessary in some instances to take a hand in the organization of such services.[375] The role of the road was, in fact, being transformed. It became an essentially subordinate element within the transport system, important for local movement and for linking communities without railway stations to the nearest railhead.[376]

Long-distance traffic by road declined, while local traffic, in particular that on roads leading to railway stations, increased, and overall traffic levels (measured in tonnes/kilometres) were maintained by the increase in economic activity. As the railway network was extended, so the average distance travelled by road declined. The opening of a line transformed local patterns of road use. As well as radiating out from and into major population centres, traffic tended increasingly to be drawn towards the nearest railway station, so the number of points of attraction increased greatly. Dependency on animal traction reinforced the attraction of the nearest station, whatever its size. The main consideration was to reduce the distance covered. Geographical position in relation to railway lines was a question of growing concern to local authorities, a factor affecting the economic potential and also the status of communities.[377]

In general, long-distance movement of agricultural commodities occurred by means of a combination of road and rail, and the costs of movement by road remained significant even in proximity to a railway station. An estimate of the cost of transport of cereals from a farm in the Mayenne to Paris in 1866 gives some indication of the relative significance of each form of transport.[378]

Transport from farm to market by farmers (cost not calculated)

Transport from market to the nearest station (average)	0.48 francs
Rail, from Laval to Gare Montparnasse (300 kilometres)	1.60 francs
Costs of loading and unloading	0.12 francs
Carting from station to grain markets or mill	0.24 francs
	2.44 francs per hectolitre

This estimate shows that road movement accounted for 29.5 per cent of the total cost of transport, without counting that from farm to market. The burden of movement by road grew with distance. According to the Comice agricole of Craon (Mayenne), in 1870 it cost as much to transport cereals by road to Laval (28 kilometres away) as it did for the rail transit Laval–Paris.[379]

It should be obvious, therefore, that everywhere road links continued to be of crucial economic significance. It was a matter of pressing concern to railway companies as well as to users that roads be improved. Complaints were constant, but significant improvement seems to have been rapidly undertaken. This had important effects on the costs of access to the developing rail network and to local and regional markets.

Waterways

Rail construction had significant consequences for the waterways, which had previously provided such a vital means of transporting bulky commodities. As the main routes of both tended to follow major valleys, they were in direct competition. The statistics[380] indicate that waterway traffic was maintained and even increased but also that this represented a substantially lower proportion of the total movement of commodities.

Transport conditions

The official ideal was always a division of labour between rail and water, with the latter specializing in the movement of bulky materials of low unit value.[381] Hence considerable effort was made to improve conditions for navigation and the operating efficiency of the waterways (see Table 34)[382] particularly during the 1840s and following acceptance of the Freycinet Plan, and partly as a result of this effort the waterways continued to provide an important facility for transport (see Table 35).[383] However, by comparison with the expenditure of 440 million francs on waterways between 1850 and 1870, 9000 million francs were invested in railways.[384] Railway construction

Table 34 *Average annual expenditure on waterways, 1815–1913*
(millions francs)

Period	Expenditure	Period	Expenditure
1815–19	5.0	1870–9	28.2
1820–9	19.1	1880–9	54.5
1830–9	28.5	1890–9	27.1
1840–9	40.7	1900–9	25.9
1850–9	19.0	1910–13	38.5
1860–9	30.0		

had far more effective supporters among pressure groups – its users, suppliers of materials, and the companies themselves – than did waterways.

Following the active period of the 1840s the years of the Second Empire saw little new construction but rather the continuation of improvements to existing waterways, together with studies for new works which came to fruition with the Freycinet Plan. The major achievements were improvements along the lines Le Havre–Marseille and Paris–Strasbourg and works on the tidal reaches of the Seine, Gironde and Loire which improved access for sea-going vessels to Rouen, Bordeaux and Nantes. Subsequently, although again the larger proportion of available funds was allocated to the railways, the Freycinet Plan contained provisions for canal construction and improvement as well as the continuation of work already under way. The Canal de l'Est, begun in 1878, was opened in 1887, the Marne–Saône link (which completed the Marne–Rhône) in 1878–9. Between 1880 and 1903 1300 kilometres of canal were constructed to establish a total of 12,240 kilometres of navigable waterways and 4000 kilometres were deepened to 2 metres. The essential aim was to increase the homogeneity of the main waterway network through the establishment of a minimum depth of 2 metres in order to make it entirely accessible to the *péniche flamande* of 300 tonnes, which could previously operate on only 1459 kilometres.[385]

Table 35 *Volume of traffic on navigable waterways, 1847–1913*
(millions tonnes/kilometres)

Index: 1905–13 = 100

Period	Tonnage kilometric	Index
1847–54	1706	31
1855–64	1965	36
1865–74	1896	35
1875–84	2126	39
1885–94	3262	59
1895–1904	4583	84
1905–13	5483	100

Throughout the second half of the century continued efforts were made to increase the depth and improve the continuity of flow of water by means of frequent dredging and deepening. On important rivers barrages were constructed to maintain water levels during periods of low water particularly on the Yonne, Marne, Oise, Saône, Meuse and especially the Seine; these proved to be unsuitable on the Rhône, Loire and Garonne. On the Rhône the most significant measures were those taken to clear the river bed of obstacles and the construction of dykes to prevent flooding. Wider and longer locks and the improvement of tow paths were other widely applied means of improvement.[386] This was a continuation of earlier work designed to reduce the costs of movement and to make the waterways more competitive. It reveals official concern to remedy the deficiencies of at least some waterways, essentially those which government engineers judged could be brought up to modern standards and whose development seemed economically worthwhile. However, at the turn of the century, and in spite of considerable improvement, the point frequently made in the past about the lack of homogeneity of the waterway network remained true. Improvement had always been piecemeal rather than part of a coherent overall plan.

In spite of considerable expenditure, even favoured routes generally continued to suffer from serious technical shortcomings. Typically, complaints were made about the inadequate depth of rivers and canals. Even in the north, the region with the best canals, this was often justified,[387] and although between 1879 and 1900 some 40 million francs were spent on improving the Rhône, it remained subject to variations in water levels and in the force of its current. Regularity of movement was impossible because of the effects of drought or flooding. The only real alternative was a lateral canal, a solution rejected in 1879 as too expensive.[388] Elsewhere – on the Loire in particular – far less was attempted, and conditions had deteriorated rather than improved. This was particularly serious in its effects over a wide area, given the length of the Loire's affluents. Transportation on an estimated 1321 kilometres of waterways joining the Loire, including the Nantes–Brest canal and the rivers Mayenne and Sarthe, was limited mainly to intra-regional activity because of the inadequacies of the main river. In spite of substantial expenditure on these waterways, they remained isolated from the major network.[389]

Particularly bitter complaints were made about the neglect of such waterways in the south as the Canal du Midi or the lateral canal to the Garonne[390] and of the Canal du Centre[391] and the Rhône–Rhine link.[392] The neglect of minor waterways like the Adour was even more apparent, and the effect was to destroy the carrying trade completely, to the advantage of the railway.[393] These regions felt that their waterways were being neglected by comparison with those of the north and east,[394] but even in these privileged zones concerned opinion complained that successive governments had deliberately neglected the waterways since the beginning of rail construction.[395]

The commercial value of waterways depended on the regularity with which circulation was possible, as indeed did transport costs, given that the flow of water affected the speed of movement and the carrying capacity of barges.[396] Insufficient depth made waterways all the more liable to the effects of drought or flooding and subject to long periods each year during which traffic was interrupted. The length of the period of crisis varied both between rivers and according to climatic conditions. Thus on the Loire, whatever the level of tariffs, competition with rail was at times simply impossible. At Tours in the 1860s interruptions of between twenty and twenty-five days were likely. In a particularly bad year like 1893 this period lasted for 200 days on the Loire and for 124 days on the Sarthe.[397] Even in the much better circumstances of the lower Seine, between June and November 1874 drought reduced water levels to 1–1.30 metres, which meant that for over five months barges were able to take only one-quarter of their normal loads, the large *chalands* loading with 80–90 tonnes instead of at least 320 and steamers with 45–50 instead of 200 tonnes. This, of course, caused a large increase in costs for boat operators who already found competition with the railways difficult.[398] Movement on the Rhône at Lyon was likely to be entirely interrupted for anything between three weeks and three months per annum.[399] At such times habitual waterway users transferred their goods to the railways, which could not always cope with the sudden increase in demand.[400] Interruptions and reductions in carrying capacity due to low water affected both the regularity of service and freight rates and constituted significant sources of uncertainty for users even when competition with rail led to efforts by operators to stabilize rates.[401]

Canals sometimes possessed advantages over rivers because their flow was more regular, but this was not always the case. Thus traffic on the canals of Bourgogne and Nivernais was regularly interrupted for thirty days each year.[402] Canals also possessed some of the most serious bottlenecks in the form of an excessive number of narrow locks. The 189 locks on the 242 kilometres of the Canal de Bourgogne constituted a major handicap, but complaints were general. The attraction of this particular canal was further weakened by its twists and turns, which meant that it traversed 213 kilometres between Laroche and Dijon, while the railway covered only 159 kilometres.[403]

The structure and organization of water transport provides further signs both of its archaism and of the efforts at adaptation. The first census of waterway barges in 1887 recorded the existence of 15,730 *bateaux ordinaires* with a capacity of 2,713,847 tonnes. The 5796 barges with a length of over 33 metres had a capacity of 1,758,847 tonnes, corresponding to two-thirds of the overall carrying capacity. Additionally, there were 673 steamers in operation (237 paddle- and 436 screw-powered, in all generating 55,932 horsepower) with a capacity of 45,865 tonnes. Of these 299 carried passengers, 120 merchandise only. The remainder towed or pushed barges.

The 1891 census provides a more detailed break-down of the types of *bateaux ordinaires*, of which there were then 15,925 (see Table 36.) By

Table 36   *Types of* bateaux ordinaires, *1891*

Tonnage	Number	Total capacity (tonnes)
Over 300	4191	1,477,860
300–200	3297	838,652
200–100	2459	391,733
100–50	2892	218,473
50–3	3086	69,512

comparison with 1887 the number of barges had increased by 1 per cent and their capacity by 10 per cent. In effect, the increase in number had been principally of barges of 38.50 metres in length and 5 metres width, of the type specified for trunk arteries by the law of 5 August 1879. These large barges were used primarily on the waterways of the north and east and to a lesser extent the centre and south-east (see Table 37). In the north and east the average load of barges varied between 130 and 235 tonnes by comparison with 40–95 tonnes in the regions of the centre and west and 10–35 tonnes in the Midi and the Garonne and Adour basins.

To a significant extent, waterway transport remained an artisanal industry in its organization. In 1891 there were 13,604 barge owners, including some large companies, one with 410 barges, but also 6381 owners of one barge each. This variation was reflected in the techniques of propulsion used.

Haulage, in fact, represented a considerable problem. The alternatives to steam power were sail, horse or even, in some cases, human power. Steam offered the advantages of speed and cost saving but required a substantial capital investment. It was not feasible on single barges because of the space needed for coal. Towing was practicable only on fairly straight stretches of water without frequent locks and occurred on the Dordogne below Libourne, the tidal stretches of the Garonne, the lower Loire, canalized stretches of the Meuse, the Rhône below Lyon, the Saône between

Table 37   *Distribution of barges, 1891*

Area	Number of French boats	Tonnage
North	3,553	936,843
Centre	4,403	803,897
East	1,347	295,296
South-east	802	118,494
Total	10,082	2,154,533
Other networks	3,522	196,726

St-Jean-de-Losne and Lyon and especially on the Seine between Montereau, Paris, Rouen and Le Havre.[404] The introduction of steam on the Rhône and lower Seine was of particular importance, given the strong currents of the former and meanders on the latter, which had caused serious difficulties for barges dependent on sail or haulage.

The use of sail was difficult on waterways which meandered and was likely to be hazardous on narrow waterways subject to gusts of wind.[405] Horses were thus the main source of power, and barges moved at their speed, helped or hindered by the force of the current. The horse as an item of capital investment in 1851 cost 800–1000 francs at the age of five and lasted about five years. Feed cost 2.75–3 francs per day. Horse-drawn barges could achieve a speed of 30–40 kilometres per day, which compared badly with the average speed of 35 kilometres per hour of the goods train in 1855. Thus down-river on the Yonne boats covered the 120 kilometres from Auxerre to Montereau in 30–6 hours. Up-river took six days, although this included only fifty-nine hours of effective movement.[406] Speed was an important competitive advantage possessed by the railway. Frequent complaints were made about the slowness of movement by water. In addition, it took time to accumulate a sufficient load for a large barge, and it took time to unload. Although only one day was necessary to move from Vertrieu (Isère) to Lyon, by the time loading and unloading and the return up-river were taken into account, the round journey lasted four days.[407] In some cases, however, slowness could be an advantage. Thus when after harvest millers made substantial purchases of grain, they often used the waterways because they were slower than the railways, and their storage costs were reduced for as long as their grain was in transit.[408]

Surprisingly, even as late as the mid 1870s instances of traction by men were recorded – on the Canal de Bourgogne, for example,[409] and more significantly through a large tunnel on the Canal de St-Quentin, where 250 hauliers possessed an established monopoly until the 1870s. This slowed movement to twenty-five barges per day and constituted a serious bottle-neck.[410] More serious because much more widespread was the obstacle represented by defective tow paths, which sometimes forced horses into the water, and the inadequate numbers of horses in many places. Again, this slowed movement and increased costs, and only in 1875 was legislation introduced to reorganize haulage.[411]

Transport costs

Tariffs varied significantly between places and over time, reflecting user demand, water levels which influenced speed of movement and carrying capacity, the wages paid, the cost of fodder for animals and capital costs. They were also obviously influenced by the intensity of competition.

State action was also important. From 1853, in an effort to reduce the cost of waterway transport and to promote its competitiveness, the government began to assume ownership of canals and to reduce or even, by a law of February 1880, to suppress tolls.[412] This, of course, led to complaints from the railway companies about unfair competition, in which the reduction of tolls was linked to the state's meeting the maintenance costs of waterways.[413] Regardless of these objections, the waterways were increasingly operated by the state as a public service. At the end of the Second Empire, of 4700 kilometres of canal only 569 remained in private ownership, including the lateral to the Garonne, Canal du Midi, lower Scarpe, Sambre to Oise and Canal de Beauclaire, and even on these the tolls were reduced.[414] For barge owners and canal companies, for users and government, the aim of improvement and reductions in charges was to attract traffic to the waterways by reductions in the cost of transport. Users and government were concerned to secure the survival of the only possible competitor for bulk transport with the railway, 'the only effective restraint on the power of the railways', according to the General Council of the Ponts-et-Chaussées, meeting in July 1855.[415]

In the initial period of development railway companies had certainly made determined efforts to destroy waterway competitors by means which included attempts to buy them off by compensation and agreements to share traffic. Inducements were offered to the larger waterway companies, and both those that rejected them and the host of small operators who were never given any alternative were faced with calculated tariff competition.[416]

Where barge operators were able to sustain this competition it undoubtedly had beneficial effects for users in the form of savings that were the result of competitive tariff reductions. Thus the cost of moving freight up-river between Rouen and Paris, which was 14 francs per tonne in 1844, was reduced to 8.50–9.20 francs by 1850 in response to rail competition. This it was claimed, was too low to allow the accumulation of the capital essential for the replacement of worn material, and even then the river was barely able to maintain the level of traffic that it carried and did not take a share in the increasing traffic moving in the Seine valley.[417] However, generalization about waterway tariffs is difficult. Individual barge owners were able to negotiate the price for particular jobs with individual users, a facility forbidden to railway companies. In an industry which still contained many owner-operators, these could choose to accept material deprivation in order to preserve their means of earning a living.[418] Moreover, in good conditions – on the Rhine or Seine or on the canals of the Nord, for example – waterways could compete with railways on tariffs, if not on speed. Inevitably, waterways more than ever specialized in the transport of bulky products with a low unit cost.

The use of tariffs as a means of competition is hardly surprising, but it nevertheless resulted in protests from waterway transporters[419] and those afraid of the creation of a rail monopoly,[420] which eventually had significant effects on government policy.

Efforts were, in fact, made to protect the waterways by limiting the intensity of rail tariff competition. In this latter respect it has not proved possible to fix a precise date to particular policy decisions, and most of the surviving evidence is in documents of the 1890s. It was, however, claimed that this had always been official policy,[421] and certainly by this period the Comité consultatif des chemins de fer and responsible officials in the Ministry of Public Works were rejecting what were judged to be excessive competitive tariff reductions by the railway companies. Thus, for example, on 5 January 1891 the committee maintained that rail tariffs should be at least 11–17 per cent higher than waterway tariffs between La Charité and Paris–Bercy. On 31 July 1895 proposals for a reduction in rail tariffs from 20 to 18.50 francs on the Marseille and Cette to Gray route were rejected because the difference between this and the waterway charge of 17.50 francs was inadequate. At the same time a reduction from 23 to 20 francs from the same ports to Belfort was accepted because the gap between this and the waterway charge of 17.75 francs was felt to be sufficient. It is clear that at this time considerable pressure was being exerted by various interested groups and by government engineers, who had already supervised substantial expenditure on the improvement of navigation on the river, to protect the interests of the one surviving steamer company on the Rhône.[422]

In a session of the Comité consultatif of 7 March 1895 it was affirmed that 'long experience' indicated the need for a difference of 20 per cent between rail and waterway tariffs on competing routes if the latter were to be able to compete on an 'equal' basis! As a result rail tariffs for cereals from the port of Dunkirk to Nancy were maintained at 15.45 francs compared with waterway charges which fluctuated between 8.50 and 11.50 francs according to the season.[423] In 1894 it had been claimed to be essential to maintain tariffs on the Ouest railway at a high level in order to permit the survival of competition on the extremely inefficient lower Loire waterway system.[424] The restrictions imposed on the reduction of rail tariff charges in such conditions were clearly likely to expose users to substantially higher charges than might otherwise have prevailed. The effectiveness of railway competition, and the social savings possible from competitive reductions in transport costs, were thus reduced by deliberate government action.

This 'protectionist' attitude *vis-à-vis* the waterways was a means of avoiding higher but economically more efficient expenditure on the technical improvement of the waterways. The overall result, however, was the maintenance of relatively high transport costs on both water and rail.

Coastal shipping

As well as waterways, efforts were made to improve port facilities to ease the movement of both coastal and long-distance shipping and again to reduce the costs of transport. This work tended to be increasingly concentrated upon the large ports rather than dispersed among a mass of tiny ports, both reflecting and helping to intensify the growing concentration of traffic. The small ports inevitably declined.[425] The structure of inland communications by water and rail, which tended to favour particular ports, had similar effects.

In spite of the modernization of port facilities, rail tariff competition and the speed, regularity and greater security of transport by rail had serious consequences for coastal traffic and led to repeated complaints from those who saw their interests being damaged.[426] The technical improvement of ocean-going and especially of coastal ships to meet competitive pressures was slow to occur because of the high percentage of family enterprises involved in shipping, with their limited capacity for investment and reluctance to accept external financing.[427]

The decline in the tonnage carried by coasters was initially substantial. Following the completion of direct rail links between Paris and Bordeaux, the coastal traffic entering Le Havre and Rouen fell by over 30 per cent between 1853 and 1855.[428] Subsequently, decline was more gradual but continuous from the 1850s into the 1890s, affecting in particular shorter-distance movements[429] (see Table 38).[430] The statistics available for 1888–93 give some indication of the significance of coastal shipping for agricultural products (see Table 39).[431] Comparison with the statistics on movement by rail during this period reveals how relatively insignificant coastal traffic had become.

Water-borne traffic

The first statistics on the carriage of agricultural commodities by inland waterways date from 1881, when it was estimated that 2,354,865 tonnes had

Table 38   *Coastal traffic, 1830–1913, annual average*
(milliard tonnes/kilometres)

Period	Volume of commodities carried
1830	1.1
1841–4	1.2
1845–54	1.3
1855–64	0.9
1865–74	0.8
1875–84	0.8
1885–94	1.4
1895–1904	1.9
1905–13	1.9

Table 39 *Coastal shipment of agricultural products, 1888–93 (tonnes)*

Year	Grain and flour	Wine	Fertilizers
1888	334,097	174,246	36,664
1889	369,048	199,516	54,492
1890	445,551	187,752	29,745
1891	384,146	201,675	27,671
1892	422,852	333,608	14,417
1893	468,190	308,356	22,194

been transported (some 11.9 per cent of the total movement of agricultural commodities).[432] The corresponding figures for 1886 and 1887 were 2,989,493 and 3,150,216 tonnes respectively, to which ought perhaps to be added the volume of fertilizing agents carried, amounting in these two years to 1,182,324 and 1,175,227 tonnes.[433]

The continuing significance of the major rivers for the carriage of agricultural products can be seen from Table 40, based on information collected in 1878.[434] Although there was significant variation in the volume of traffic from year to year, the proportions as between the different rivers remained roughly the same in subsequent years. Traffic on the major canals provides a clearer picture of concentration in the north-east and, to a lesser extent, in the centre-east.[435]

As early as 1860 three-quarters of the total waterway traffic in commodities of all kinds was concentrated on 1800 kilometres of water of a nominal navigable total of 9500 kilometres, and subsequently this concentration increased. By 1891 79 per cent of the merchandise transported was embarked on 5630 kilometres of waterways. In terms of tonnage kilometric, this rose to 92 per cent. The secondary network of 6832 kilometres received 21 per cent of the merchandise and accounted for 8 per cent of the tonnage kilometric.[436]

There were also clear indications of the declining relative importance of

Table 40 *Carriage of agricultural products by water, 1878 (tonnes)*

River	Tonnage carried up-river	Tonnage carried down-river
Garonne	29,654	27,935
Mayenne	28,803	12,288
Rhône	53,831	43,132
Saône	17,637	73,687
Upper Seine	97,965	98,645
Lower Seine	57,046	275,277
Yonne	14,725	3,323

the waterways. This could be deduced from the statistics on merchandise of all kinds transported between Paris and Rouen by rail and water during the initial period of rail operations (see Table 41).[437] The increased volumes in 1847 were explained by the subsistence crisis and the increase in the transport of cereals. Whereas prior to rail development almost all the extra-local transport of cereals and flour in the Seine valley was by water, subsequently a rapid decline occurred. In 1851 102,485 tonnes were carried (according to the official statistics) but only 53,049 in 1852 and 48,783 in 1853 in spite of a poor harvest.[438] By 1893–1900 in terms of the supply of grain and flour to Paris, the share of waterways had been reduced to 12.2 per cent and 16 per cent respectively of the combined totals transported by rail and water.[439] Water transport of agricultural commodities was of real significance only following poor domestic harvests, when the volume of grain imported through Le Havre and Rouen increased.[440]

This relative decline could also be measured in terms of the fall in the average distance travelled per tonne of merchandise on the waterways. On the Upper Seine it fell rapidly from 77 kilometres in 1851 to 70 in 1852 and 68 in 1853.[441] By 1887, however, this tendency appears to have been reversed. Taking all waterways into account, the average distance travelled per tonne was 133 kilometres, that per tonne of fertilizer 72 kilometres and of agricultural products 146 kilometres.[442] This was indicative of the continued competitiveness of the waterway networks of the north and east.

The effects of railway competition on the less efficient parts of the waterway network were more dramatic. There was grave concern over the decline of the river companies on the Rhône following the completion of the Paris–Lyon–Marseille railway in 1855.[443] Traffic on the river fell from 634,000 tonnes to 536,000 tonnes in 1856 and to 273,000 tonnes in 1859.[444] But the most marked decline was of the Loire and its affluents: from a peak of 400,000 tonnes carried on the section Orléans–Tours in the mid 1840s, the amount transported had fallen to 150,000 in 1853, 33,000 in 1877, 25,000 in 1880 and a mere 1000 tonnes in 1893.[445] Severe competition had been expected from a parallel railway line. The results had exceeded the most pessimistic expectations, especially for up-river movements.[446] Decline was even more marked on the upper reaches of the river in the Massif Central. In

Table 41   *Transport of merchandise by rail and water, 1844–9 (tonnes)*

Year	Rail	Water
1844	51,510	251,000
1845	90,000	281,000
1846	172,000	245,000
1847	253,000	248,000
1848	121,000	133,000
1849	157,000	166,000

the Loire-side towns the focus of commercial activity shifted from the river to the railway station.[447] Similarly, on the Canal de Bourgogne traffic fell from 179,000 tonnes in 1850 to only 80,000 in 1853 after the opening of the Laroche–Dijon section of the railway. Traffic in grain, which had made up a large portion of the total, was virtually eliminated, while wine traffic – 40,000 tonnes in 1846 – declined catastrophically to 2000 tonnes in 1856.[448] The Loire and various other waterways unable to compete effectively with railways were reduced to the status of local carriers with little transit traffic.

Traffic on some waterways was maintained by their relative efficiency as carriers or else their proximity to the location of users. The Seine was an example of the first category, its depth and the relative absence of obstacles allowing the use of large barges and comparative regularity of movement.[449] For the same reasons the canals of northern France continued to be useful in the carriage of bulky goods such as wheat or sugar beet and coal. Distilleries and sugar refineries tended to be constructed along their banks.[450] Local traffic in agricultural produce continued to be of some significance on the Rhône and Saône[451] and on the far less efficient Loire and its affluents, barges being able to move up-river on the Loire and Sarthe as far as Sablé, Le Suze and Le Mans and on the Mayenne as far as Château-Gontier, Laval and Mayenne, and by the Mayenne and Oudin to Segré. Again, in the west Redon and Rennes were linked by the Vilaine, St-Malo and Rennes by the Ille-et-Rance canal and the Vilaine.[452] The transport of grain was important on all of these. Grain millers used both rail and water according to season and changing cost and speed advantages, but only those with mills situated along waterways habitually favoured them.[453]

In general, after a breathing space during which the railway commercial agencies were organized and while the gaps in the railway network were being filled, waterways found it difficult to compete with the cost, speed and regularity offered by the new form of transport without some form of government aid, whether protective, as in the case of limits imposed on tariff competition, or more constructive attempts to reduce operating costs. As a result of this in the north and east at least along the axes of the canals of northern France, the Seine and Rhône–Saône, railway monopoly was avoided. Other areas were not as fortunate, and there costs of transport tended to be noticeably higher. The evolution of tariffs and the structure of the market for transport facilities was thus the product of the evolution of forces of supply and demand and reflected, in addition, official views of the 'general interest'. The state played a major part in shaping the structure of communications networks and of the commodity markets dependent upon these.

Conclusion

It is a mistake to consider the railway apart from other forms of transport.

These offered competition, but particularly in the case of roads were also essential to its successful operation. Our concern is thus with *communications networks*, and at a later stage something will have to be said about improvements in the transmission of information.

There can be no doubt that the effectiveness of all forms of communication, including the pre-rail forms, was substantially increased from the 1840s. The means were provided for the cheap and rapid transport of commodities, of people and, through the telegraph and press, of information. Progress had undoubtedly been made before the railway epoch, but the traditional forms of transport had constituted a major obstacle to the development of a more unified market. Comparisons might be instructive. Britain, a much smaller country, possessed the advantages of a relatively dense waterway system, which facilitated the easy establishment of integrated commodity markets. France had more in common with a large land mass like Russia, in which the railway played a major role in stimulating changes in market structures.

The 'new economic historians' have warned us against exaggerating the significance of railway development. It is impossible to prove that the railways were a necessary precondition for the substantial extension of markets which occurred in the nineteenth century. All sorts of counterfactual hypotheses can be developed which posit the possibility of the development of different modes of bulk transport, leading to economic growth based on alternative economic structures. But, clearly, if the establishment of the railway was not a necessary precondition for the growth of trade, the injection of a railway network into an already developing economy was likely to have important consequences. 'It is an incontrovertible fact that transport changes profoundly affected the spatial structure of economic change.'[454] Railway development occurred within the context of long-term economic development and contributed significantly to accelerating the process of development and determining its shape.

The new facilities for transport provided a stimulus to economic activity. Better communication was a key dynamic element promoting economic and social change. The posing of the counter-factual argument that this stimulus might somehow have been provided at this time in the absence of the railway is an interesting intellectual exercise but one of limited value for our understanding of the *actual development* of the nineteenth-century economy.

This depended on the spatial characteristics of the new transport networks. Railway companies were, as we have seen, understandably reluctant to construct potentially unprofitable lines. Following existing currents of traffic, the railway, in the first instance, linked the major political and economic centres to the more productive areas on the periphery, while largely ignoring the specific needs of the latter. Subsequently, while the primary network was extended into the less attractive regions, development of lines of local economic interest proceeded in those regions which already possessed their primary links. For the more backward regions there was always a time lag. This meant inevitably that the economically most backward regions tended to be provided with a modern transport system at a later date than more advanced regions, and even then with a lower density network. As a result of this, in part at least, their relative economic backwardness was confirmed. Subsequent development and adaptation to new market structures tended to be difficult and imperfect, although even in regions like Brittany and the Massif Central a vital stimulus to change was afforded.

We shall have to return to one key question. To what extent did shortages of modern transport facilities serve as a constraint on economic growth? Decisions taken about transport development had all sorts of consequences for the subsequent economic development of the regions and ultimately for their capacity to maintain established demographic densities and even their characteristic social structures. Contemporaries were clearly aware of this.

The railway companies were constantly criticized by chambers of commerce, *conseils généraux* and parliamentary commissions. In particular they were accused of maintaining their tariffs at excessively high levels. The Waddington Report in 1891, in condemning the failure of the companies to reduce tariffs significantly since 1865 and in comparing their charges adversely with those levied by foreign companies, was only the latest in a series of such utterances.[455] In spite of this it was generally agreed that substantial savings on transport costs had been achieved by means of the railway. The concept of social saving is not an invention of the proponents of the 'new economic history'. Louis Marchal, a senior Ponts-et-Chaussées engineer, calculated that in 1853 the cost of transporting 743,761 tonnes of cereals and flour by rail had been 8,443,679 francs at an average tariff of 0.132 franc per tonne/kilometre (the legal tariff would have been 0.162 franc). He estimated that the cost of moving this quantity in the absence of the railway would have been 12,687,242 francs.[456] This represented a saving of 33.5 per cent in a period when the rail network was far from complete. In a 'Note sur la question de l'utilité des chemins de fer' in the *Annales des ponts-et-chaussées* in 1896 M. Legay again stressed the need to compare the estimated economic results of the construction of a railway line with those which might have been expected from the use of the same capital to develop alternative forms of communication.[457] The problem was, and remains, the difficulty of achieving meaningful calculations of the savings achieved, given the inadequacies of the available statistics.

It is impossible to judge the accuracy of Marchal's statistics; nor is it possible to calculate the value of time savings and reduced spoilage in transit, or the levels that road and water tariffs might have reached in the absence of rail competition, or the significance of the more rapid diffusion of market information and the effects on commerce of new attitudes among both producers and consumers once their horizons had been enlarged by easier travel. We can, however, be certain that a large number of people came to assume that there was an advantage to be gained from the use of the railway and that as a result – as the various statistics have revealed – there was a substantial increase in the volume of commodities transported.

New traffic was generated both directly by railway development and indirectly by the stimulus to the improvement of road and waterway facilities that this afforded. The waterways were the main alternative means of cheap bulk transport, and rail competition led to substantial reductions in the charges for water-borne transport. In calculating the social saving that resulted from the establishment of railways, this would have to be taken into account. Conversely, the survival of waterway traffic, particularly in northern France, and the improvement of the waterways forced competitive reductions in tariffs on the railways – although the inefficiencies of the waterway system substantially reduced their competitive potential. More capital might have been invested in the improvement and construction of waterways. That it was not reflected decisions by engineers who estimated that, in general, this would not have been cost-effective. Inland waterways and coastal shipping could provide a cheap and effective service for only a relatively narrow strip of territory. The railway system was a far more flexible form of transport.[458]

In the case of France substantial cost savings were achieved by rail development and the effects of rail competition on the charges and effectiveness of other forms of transport. It cannot blithely be assumed that in the absence of railways, 'the economy would have devised and constructed substitutes'.[459] Another counter-factual hypothesis could be presented, according to which substitutes were not rapidly developed and the whole process of economic change, particularly of structural transformation, was slowed and substantially altered. Unfortunately, useful as our statistical sources are, they provide no easy answers to questions about the economic effects of railway development. The analytical problems are too complicated. We have to stress the great variety of rail, road and waterway operating costs and tariffs that had such important consequences for local and regional economic development. It is a major weakness of the case of the 'new economic historians' that they treat whatever statistics they are able to accumulate far too seriously, without sufficient consideration of their representativeness or accuracy.

In short, although the discussion of counter-factual situations can be a useful corrective to monocausal interpretations of development and to exaggerated emphasis on particular causal factors, it should not be forgotten that *in fact* it was the railway that provided a major stimulus to the development of communications in the nineteenth century. It was the railway that, prior to the development of the internal combustion engine, provided the cheapest and most flexible form of transport. It was the railway that accelerated the process of innovation in communications systems which led to substantial reductions in the cost of transport and a massive increase in the volume of merchandise transported.

The construction of new transport networks and their differential development in both time and space had complex effects on transport costs and upon the development of inter-regional and international currents of trade in agricultural commodities. It is the development of commodity marketing and the influence of new opportunities and competitive pressures upon merchants and farmers which will concern us in subsequent chapters.

8 Modernizing market structures

A great deal has been written about the subsistence crises of pre-industrial societies. Some of the most influential work, by Ernest Labrousse[1] and others, has dealt with this phenomenon in the French context, examining the changing characteristics of economic crises from the eighteenth century and the last great crises of the *ancien régime économique* that afflicted French society in the 1840s and 1850s.[2] Yet little has been written which deals *explicitly* with the disappearance of the traditional subsistence crisis.[3] It generally simply fades out of consideration. It is assumed – and no doubt correctly – that more rapid and low-cost bulk transport by rail and sea, together with the accelerated transmission of market-place information due to the telegraph, finally completed the centuries-old labour of creating a marketing system efficient enough to operate along the lines favoured by liberal economic theorists.

Surely though this is a subject of sufficient importance to merit more detailed consideration? What occurred, after all, was the rapid disappearance of an age-old threat to the living standards of the mass of the population, which had been a cause of permanent insecurity and often of disorder, the source of major problems of social control for both élites and governments.

This chapter considers the disappearance of these traditional crises as an aspect of a more general process of change in agricultural market structures, consequent upon improvements in communications networks; that is, it attempts to make explicit a process of structural change in the economy which was of momentous importance.

Improved communications meant an increase in the social capacity for transport, due both to new potential for bulk carriage and the increased rapidity of movement. In a period when the elasticity of demand for transport was high, railways were the main cause of a substantial increase in agricultural traffic. This in part resulted from the release of already existing regional surpluses of cereals and other produce, but also from the incentive to increasing production which was created by improved access to markets. The railway brought into existence a very different economic situation.[4]

The period which we are considering saw an acceleration of innovation in transport technology. Moreover, these were not once-and-for-all innovations but developments which, stimulated by constantly growing demand, were both extended spatially and subject to improvements which further increased efficiency and so affected transport costs. Gradually too the density of communications networks was increased, although differences in regional endowments and in the costs of providing a particular means of transport in physically varying environments, as well as the tariff policies of transport companies, inevitably meant continuing inequalities in transport costs over similar distances. Clearly, the analysis of evolving market structures is not easy. Transport innovation, continuous development, regional inequalities, differing user perceptions of opportunity, all represent unstable variables and suggest that market structures themselves must have been subject to frequent change.

In simplified terms, in this chapter we will need to consider the inter-relationship between three key factors: (1) transport networks, (2) the economic structure connected by these networks and (3) the flows of traffic generated by the economic structure and moved over the networks.

Market structures

The size of any marketed surplus depended upon the relative share of large and small-scale cultivators in production. At mid century in most regions, and particularly outside the Paris basin and northern plains, the balance remained heavily weighted in favour of the peasant farmer. The agricultural economy remained to a large degree pre-capitalist. It ought, however, to be stressed that almost all farmers sold some proportion of their crop or else their labour, so that even in the most under-developed regions, in which a major proportion of farm produce was consumed on the farm, agricultural systems should more accurately be described as semi-commercial. Substantial and increasingly voluminous currents of inter-regional trade existed before the advent of the railway, but the high cost of such trade limited its impact upon market structures. Markets remained compartmentalized as spatial variations in commodity prices clearly reveal.

The subsequent transformation of communications and the consequent changes in market structures were of decisive importance to the economic evolution of France, involving an acceleration in the transition from a relatively closed to a market economy, from an agricultural and artisanal economy producing for geographically restricted markets, to an industrial economy in which production occurred for substantially enlarged markets.

Modernization of the market structure had two essential bases – increased urban demand and the intensification of specialization and contraction of self-sufficiency in the countryside. The statistics on urban growth (see Table 42) give some indication of the growing importance of urban markets.

The rate of urbanization, if accelerating, was slow by comparison with

Table 42   *Growth of urban populations, 1851–1911*

Year	Urban population (millions)	Percentage of total population
1851	9.1	25.5
1861	10.8	28.9
1872	11.2	31.1
1881	13.1	34.8
1891	14.3	37.4
1901	15.9	40.9
1911	17.5	44.2

Britain, but nonetheless this redistribution of population was significant in its consequences. A smaller proportion of an increasing farm product was required for local consumption and a far larger proportion needed to be commercialized.

Urban growth had been general until the middle of the nineteenth century, but the concentration of urban functions engendered by the improvement of communications resulted in a differential urban development with the more rapid growth of the larger commercial and industrial centres (see p. 26). These were the towns which provided the most important stimulus to agriculture and whose growth, together with the more effective connection of rural and urban markets, resulted in the growing dominance of the town over the countryside.

The supply of urban centres is a basic determinant of the structures of agricultural markets. Commodities tend to flow towards markets along lines of communication which have the advantage of relative cheapness. In France the primary rail networks followed the existing major axes of communication. Their configuration was fundamentally unaltered. These remained the arteries around which commercial activity was organized. However, development of the railway implied greater concentration of commodity flows. Within the railway network the unit cost of transport tended to be lower on the heavily utilized main lines than on branch lines. This resulted in concentration of trade flows, as areas in proximity to those main lines were offered access to markets at relatively low cost and thus a greater incentive to commercialize their production. Improved transport, moreover, had the effect of increasing competition between regions and additionally of extending and intensifying the influence of the ports, so that in spite of directional continuity in the primary communications routes trade flows did not always take the same direction. Market structures were thus influenced by network structure and in addition, of course, by railway company tariff policies, changes in which might cause repeated alterations in market structures. In particular, the differential tariff policies favoured by railway companies had the effect of reducing the geographical disadvantages of distance or, conversely, of reducing the geographical advantage of proximity to particular markets. Above all they benefited Paris, the terminus for most lines, rather than intermediary points. They tended to favour departments distant from Paris or other major markets at the expense of those in close proximity, and in addition they favoured the penetration inland of imports from the ports. They were constantly criticized on these grounds.

In their response to the various inquiries, grain and flour producers in the Beauce, Brie and Picardy complained about tariff structures which increased competition on the Paris market, while producers in the Somme were concerned about tariffs which enabled farmers and merchants from the Beauce and Brie to compete with them in the markets of the Nord.[5] The market for wine was also affected. The tariffs of the PLM, particularly from the 1880s, tended to favour wine producers in the Midi at the expense of those of the Mâconnais, Bourgogne and the Beaujolais. Thus in the decade 1895–1905 it cost only 28 francs per tonne to transport wine from Cette to Paris–Bercy compared with 32 francs for the much shorter distance from Belleville (Rhône).[6]

Clearly, railway tariffs were encouraging long-distance movement and, given the characteristics of railway cost structures, which declined proportionately to distance travelled, it made good sense for the companies to encourage the regular development of long-distance and large-scale use of railway facilities. Repeated examples of tariff modifications with these ends in mind can be quoted.[7] Indeed, the Comité consultatif observed in 1896 that tariff proposals made jointly by the PLM and Midi showed 'no concern for economic conditions';[8] they were designed simply to improve the financial position of the two companies.[9]

Inevitably, given the existence of special and differential tariffs, some localities and some regions were favoured at the expense of others. It should not be forgotten, however, that there was considerable continuity in the shape of commodity flows, particularly of products of relatively low value in relation to bulk, like cereals, which continued to be cultivated in all regions. This element of continuity needs to be stressed. Short-distance movements, for the supply of local towns, and neighbouring areas of deficit, were by far the most common. Plain continued to supply neighbouring upland. High rural population densities necessitated the consumption of a substantial proportion of the product of agriculture in the countryside itself or in the mass of small market centres. Most farmers and merchants took the path of least resistance to traditional markets, sometimes responding to new opportunities but often only when forced to by competitive pressures. (An estimated 1,444,493 *quintaux* of wheat were produced in Côtes-du-Nord in 1903; only 340,000 *quintaux* were estimated to have entered commerce after producers had met their own needs.) Even in such highly productive departments as the Loiret, long engaged in commercial agriculture, most of the product was consumed within the department.[10] Large-scale producers who gave priority to large-scale merchants who resold either for consumption in regional metropolises or in more distant areas were the exceptions. In general, production which was not consumed on the farm was mainly marketed locally by the farmers, with merchants transporting to more distant markets any surplus to local needs.[11]

Although the zone of provisioning of Paris and other major urban centres was extended, a substantial proportion of their needs in foodstuffs continued to be met by the traditional zones of production – in the case of Paris by the farmers and millers of the Beauce, Brie, Vexin, Valois and the Picardy Plains. Elsewhere continuity was imposed on some of the less fortunate areas by their continued relative geographical isolation.[12] Members of the Comité consultatif, in discussions held in 1896, stressed that even on the railways movements occurred from a multiplicity of points and essentially over short distances. Oats and barley for animal feed tended to be moved over wider distances than cereals for human consumption because of the greater spatial variation in their price levels.[13] Movement of cereals from the Nord network on to the tracks of other companies represented only 6.5 per cent of the cereals transported in 1905 – and an abnormal 19.11 per cent in 1911 – although the tendency was increasingly towards long-distance transport.[14] Flour, of greater value in relation to weight, was transported over longer distances, but in general, although the reduction in transport costs was of great significance, particularly following poor harvests, it was not sufficiently large, relative to prices, to promote vast inter-regional flows over long distances in normal years.

Nevertheless, improved communications increasingly led to a functional reorganization of space, enhancing the strategic position of some areas, diminishing that of others. Planned to converge on Paris and to link regional centres to the capital, the rail network provided less effective links between the various regional centres and between each regional centre and second-order urban markets.

Secondary axes of communication were less competitive in price terms and were subject to adverse competitive pressures, at least in the short run, because of the differential development of the new means of communication. Thus producers in the Indre in the 1860s complained about the relative difficulty of access to both the south-east and north-west,[15] while the Massif Central was more firmly orientated towards the north because of the slow establishment of rail links with its traditional markets in the south-west and Languedoc. Only the opening of the Montluçon–Aurillac link in 1893 finally corrected this imbalance.[16]

Some regions were particularly disadvantaged by delays in initial construction and the continued effects of difficult natural conditions. In mountain areas steep gradients limited the efficiency of rail transport.

Modifications of transport networks thus had the basic effect of confirming existing disparities of importance within both the communications and the marketing systems. Many markets of secondary importance experienced rapid decline due to the growing spatial concentration of commerce, while with some significant exceptions existing regional centres experienced growth.[17] There were thus definite limits to the extent to which the hierarchy of markets was changed, but change nonetheless occurred, based upon modifications in the relative accessibility of markets to potential clients. Where the transport of goods was both slow and expensive, then markets were scattered. Changes in the distance–time equation allowed a growing concentration on central points which were more accessible and offered better services to users. As rail networks developed, the role of such primary centres of import from overseas as Le Havre and Marseille, or of consumption, such as Paris or Lyon, in determining commodity flows and influencing price levels on a wide range of secondary markets became all the greater.

The ease with which goods could be transported by rail from producer to the ultimate marketing point obviated the need to concentrate them initially at intermediary points. Improved roads provided farmers and merchants with easier access to primary markets at which commerce was more active and prices tended to be slightly higher. As a result they gradually deserted secondary markets. Trade on the mass of local markets increased until about 1840–50 and on the major markets until the late 1860s. In the last third of the century even the larger markets declined in significance as new methods of commercialization were adopted. A host of small towns which had expected prosperity with the coming of the railway found that the result was stagnation or decline. As marketing centres they might continue to function for local sales, especially of butter, cheese, eggs, vegetables, etc., for the distribution of a growing volume of industrial products and the provision of a range of services, but the volume of sales on the market for agricultural commodities declined. The statistics shown in Table 43, compiled by Désert,

Table 43 *Volume of market sales in four Calvados centres, 1819–89 (hectolitres)*

Year	Argences	Caen	Evrecy	Tilly
1819	33,580	31,490	12,132	4,580
1829	39,145	44,964	13,981	2,764
1839	44,298	62,288	14,052	3,443
1849	39,370	69,770	8,812	3,061
1859	39,192	90,867	11,371	3,786
1869	44,919	95,414	4,552	2,709
1879	22,061	60,362	832	1,325
1889	25,628	11,391	—	—

are based on wheat sales at two primary and two secondary markets in the department of Calvados.[18]

This decline and its chronology seems to have been general.[19] In the Nord and Paris region it can be seen in the dwindling importance, again in the last third of the century, of such traditional cereal marketing centres as Arras, Montreuil, and St-Pol and a concentration of commercial activity at Lille and Paris.[20] Especially notable was the decline of Orléans, which was the product not of its location *vis-à-vis* the railway but of the evolution of market structures and commercial practices. Orléans, at the junction of the Loire with major canal and road routes, had since time immemorial performed entrepôt functions in the marketing of a whole range of manufactured and agricultural products, particularly wine. The city declined in importance with the reduction in river traffic and the increased possibility for producers and merchants at the places of consumption to deal directly with each other. The entrepôt at Bercy, just outside Paris, appropriated its wine-marketing functions. The official response to the complaints made by the Orléans merchants was not very sympathetic. An internal Ministry of Public Works memorandum in October 1850 made the point that 'when merchandise can, without being transshipped, cover long distances to arrive at its destination, the intermediary is useless and must expect sooner or later to disappear'.[21]

Equally notable was the decline of such key centres of the grain trade as Châlon-sur-Saône and Gray. These two towns, but particularly Gray, had served as the heads of navigation in the Rhône–Saône corridor. At them grain cultivated in the east had been gathered for distribution and especially for movement down-river, while imported cereals moving up-stream had been directed towards the north and the Paris basin. Transshipment and entrepôt functions had made these towns major links between north and south. Within the new railway network they lost their privileged place. It was Dijon, which stood at the point at which the main railway lines from the north, Midi and east met, that assumed the functions of a regional crossroads. Because of this, and the growth of competition from imported cereals in traditional markets in the Midi, Gray rapidly lost some two-thirds of its trade.[22]

An initial distinction might be made between communes with and those without a railway station. In general, the latter tended to experience economic (and demographic) decline and to place all hope of arresting this in the improvement of their communications.[23] The former did not invariably experience substantial development as commercial centres – some railway centres were better located than others – but were better placed to market their own products and to develop economically, even though Le Mans developed at the expense of Alençon, for example, and Orléans, Besançon and Montpellier all lost some of their traditional regional importance in the wine trade, the last losing out to Béziers and Nîmes, which were at junctions in the railway network.[24] Position on main rather than on secondary rail routes and especially at crossroads in the network (nodal points) was an important factor for growth.

Although local food-supply functions and self-subsistence continued to be of importance, agricultural markets were becoming above all centres for the provisioning of rapidly growing cities. Local markets were integrated more and more closely into commercial systems, within which commodities flowed more easily as the friction offered by inadequate communications and slow transmission of information was reduced. The progress of integration is evinced most obviously by a growing concordance of price levels on the various markets, with levels on lower order markets being more closely determined by those of more important markets of concentration as the costs of movement between them were reduced.

Paris in particular assumed a dominant role not only as a market for consumption but also as a key centre for redistribution. According to the station master of the important goods station at La Chapelle, 'Parisian commerce does not limit its operation simply to local speculation; it draws supplies from the departments and from abroad and also sells to them . . . in order to profit from every favourable circumstance'. The consequence was to make 'merchandise much more mobile' and to establish Paris as 'the major regulating market for certain products, such as cereals, oil and alcohol'.[25] Its geographical position had, in effect, been improved. The alignment of the waterways had favoured trade with the north-west and south-east, whereas the new railway network radiated outwards from Paris in all directions; the hinterland of the city was thus greatly enlarged. The Paris market, because of the scale of its needs, increasingly dominated national price levels. In 1855 the *procureur-général* at Rouen explained general price movements in the local market primarily in relation to those prevailing in Paris, the market which 'serves as the regulator of our own'.[26] This growing dominance of Paris was the result of both direct influence on regional markets and also of the power of suggestion. M. Selz, a grain merchant at Strasbourg, spoke in 1859 of the influence of Parisian prices on 'merchants' spirits'.[27]

The cattle trade developed along similar lines, though more slowly, and even in the 1850s complaints were being made about the tendency for meat prices to rise in numerous provincial centres because of growing pressure of demand from Paris as communications improved.[28] By 1913, in part because of its superior commercial facilities and in part because of the structure of the rail network which tended to direct inter-regional traffic through Paris, 43 per cent of the *gros bétail*, 47 per cent of calves, 34 per cent of sheep and 56 per cent of pigs arriving at La Villette were subsequently transported out of the city.[29] The entrepôts at Bercy performed similar functions in the wine trade.[30]

On a lesser scale other regional centres experienced the same concentration of function – for example, Lille at the expense of Arras, Montreuil and

St-Pol (although Lille operated very much in the shadow of Paris)[31] and Lyon in relation to the upland areas of the Lyonnais and department of the Loire, and also for the important industrial centres of St-Etienne and the Loire basin.[32]

Merchants at Toulouse, which had owed its former importance in the cereals trade to its waterway links, were understandably nervous about the development of a new means of communication which threatened to 'throw [their] commercial relations into profound disorder'.[33] This was especially true in the anxious years before the opening of the Toulouse–Cette line in 1856, when normal commercial currents were interrupted. However, by the 1870s the city had become an important rail centre and retained its position as a major grain and flour market. During the 1880s, with the restoration of tariff protection, it resumed its role in the supply of lower Languedoc and Provence, which had been threatened from the early 1860s by imports through Marseille.[34]

The growth of imports and increasing importance of the ports, and particularly Marseille and Le Havre as market places and entrepôts, were significant features of the second half of the century. From mid century the increased size and carrying capacity of ships led to a growing concentration of traffic at the better-equipped ports. Furthermore, as the Paris Chamber of Commerce reported in 1852, 'when transport by water took a long time, it was important to have the merchandise at hand, but today, when the railways and electric telegraph provide rapid communications, there is on the contrary an interest in leaving merchandise in port entrepôts for as long as possible, since from there they can easily be sent to Paris or re-exported if necessary'.[35] The gradual introduction of steam milling also favoured concentration of milling either in proximity to major markets or more especially at the larger ports.[36]

This analysis of continuity and change in the basic structure of agricultural commodity markets, and particularly the identification of nodal points upon which trade was centred, should serve as a basis for the analysis of commodity flows within that structure.

Commodity flows

Increasing production due to increased yields meant the availability of larger surpluses to market at a time when imports were increasing and when demand elasticity was limited. (For a discussion of agricultural productivity, see Chapter 9.) This situation caused growing anxiety about sales and prices.

It was not easy for contemporaries,[37] nor is it easy for modern historians, to distinguish the effects of more efficient distribution on agricultural price levels from those of imports and from increased domestic production. Zolla's indices relating cereal supply, population and price (see Table 44)[38]

Table 44   *Cereal supply in relation to population and price, 1856–1905*

Index: 1856–65 = 100

Period	Total supply	Population	Price
1856–65	100	100	100
1866–75	104	101	114
1876–85	116	101.4	99.5
1886–95	122	103.6	83.3
1896–1905	119	104.5	74.2

do not make a decision concerning the relative importance of these variables any easier, but they do indicate that total supply was increasing more rapidly than population, and we know that per capita demand tended to stagnate.

Clearly, from the late 1870s decisive changes occurred. In particular, imports became more regular and increased substantially in quantity. Contemporaries were very conscious of, and often very anxious about, this development.

Throughout the first half of the century poor cereal harvests had been followed by the temporary suspension of the sliding scale of customs tariffs or at the very least by substantial reductions in the dues payable.[39] During the 1850s this had occurred following the harvests of 1853 and 1855. After the latter the sliding scale had not been restored until 12 May 1859, and it was then again suspended by a decree of 22–4 August 1860. Furthermore, a clear warning was delivered by Rouher, the responsible minister, that the government was thinking of more permanent changes in legislation,[40] a statement whose lack of precision had a considerable unsettling effect on markets.[41] On this occasion protective tariffs were not to be restored for twenty years, as suspension of the sliding scale was followed by a law of 15 June 1861 which reduced the tax on entry to a nominal 0.50 franc per *quintal* for cereals and flour carried in French ships and to 1 franc in foreign vessels. Tariffs on other agricultural products were also reduced.[42]

Abolition of the sliding scale had the considerable advantage of increasing security for merchants. It removed a fluctuating element from their cost and profit calculations. Its existence had additionally hindered the establishment of permanent relations with overseas suppliers, another factor limiting the speed of response to domestic shortage. In general, merchants involved in international trade seem to have favoured its replacement by a small fixed tax.[43] Those who relied on internal sources of grain and were linked to farming interests were, of course, less welcoming.[44]

The effects of new tariff legislation aided by telegraph and rail certainly included more rapid responses to domestic shortage.[45] This restrained the tendency for prices to rise after a poor harvest. Thus it took eight months after the poor harvest of 1855 to import the 10 million hectolitres of wheat necessary to supplement the domestic crop because of tariff legislation, the incompleteness of the railway network and uncertainty among merchants. Following the harvest of 1861, when 12 million hectolitres were imported, provisioning was completed before the end of the year.[46] If comparison is made with 1847, it should be noted that by 31 December in that year 3,800,000 hectolitres had arrived in French ports, whereas by 1 December 1861 the total was 7 million hectolitres.[47] This is not to deny that merchants could still be taken by surprise – as in 1867 when a good domestic harvest was anticipated, but yields fell far short of expectations. In this situation the mercantile response was rather slow, and prices remained at unusually high levels for some time.[48] It was also true that estimates of production could vary enormously between experts. The wheat harvest of 1888 was variously estimated at 96,480,002 hectolitres by the Ministry of Agriculture and 89,274,828 hectolitres by the *Bulletin des halles*, the journal of the grain merchants. The difference was explained by differing estimates of the area harvested, of yields per hectare and of weight. Ministry experts calculated that a deficit of 22 million hectolitres existed, the *Bulletin* 29 million hectolitres.[49] Such large variations exemplify the continued uncertainties and risks of the grain trade.

The railway was, of course, of decisive importance in facilitating the penetration of imports into the interior of the country. By land it made possible the transport of cereals from as far afield as Hungary, providing that the price differential between Hungarian and French markets was sufficiently large to cover a relatively high transport cost. The *procureur-général* at Metz recorded his great surprise at this development, which he believed occurred for the first time in the last quarter of 1861.[50]

However, it was the reduction in maritime freight rates and the extension of cultivation and/or commercialization in the United States, India and Russia that provided the main competitive threats to French farmers. At their peak from the mid 1880s, the main sources of wheat imports were as shown in Table 45.[51] The main traditional source of imports had been the Black Sea ports of southern Russia. American imports exceeded Russian from 1878, although there was a general tendency for imports from all sources to increase considerably from around this date. Even Australia contributed once the freight rate, which had amounted to 560 francs per tonne before the opening of the Suez Canal, had been reduced to 60 francs by 1880.[52] Although concern was frequently expressed about the growing dependence on foreign suppliers, particularly after the Crimean War interrupted supplies from Russia,[53] merchants continued to be attracted by competitive price levels whatever the source of the grain.

Imports of wheat grain and flour, which before 1845 had never risen above 3 million hectolitres in a year and rarely above 2 million, had risen to 5 million in 1846 and 10 million in 1847. Imports subsequently fell, then increased again after the poor harvests of 1853 and 1855 and reached 9

Table 45 *Principal sources of wheat imports, 1883–98 (metric* quintaux)

Year	USA	Russia	India	Algeria
1883	3,627,304	2,191,793	1,695,641	283,083
1884	2,969,077	2,621,662	1,621,387	414,601
1885	1,490,211	1,893,383	787,160	958,463
1886	2,508,769	1,736,600	960,967	1,182,947
1887	4,149,152	2,026,263	638,933	1,087,514
1888	1,759,034	4,074,655	970,727	775,956
1889	2,061,740	3,791,827	543,133	1,023,448
1890	1,810,087	2,993,146	465,567	1,454,504
1891	8,155,505	3,371,571	1,933,149	907,665
1892	10,062,892	2,423,020	1,674,421	780,746
1893	2,876,386	3,430,431	448,779	381,094
1894	3,233,230	5,003,554	367,100	786,085
1895	182,734	2,022,794	60,821	1,129,446
1896	770	479,244	885	538,887
1897	1,854,431	1,874,395	74	450,502
1898	9,433,771	4,880,940	1,267,923	485,995

million hectolitres in 1856, peaking again at 13.5 million hectolitres in 1861, 14 million in 1872 and an enormous 29,800,000 hectolitres in 1879 after a series of bad domestic harvests beginning in 1875.[54] The scale of the increase can also be seen in the rising value of cereal imports (see Table 46).[55]

The statistics on wheat production and on the balance between imports and exports combine to reveal a marked increase in total supply. They indicate a tendency towards stagnation in domestic production from the late 1860s but with consistently high levels of imports especially from 1878. The balance between imports and exports was constantly and increasingly in favour of the former (see Table 47).[56]

When cereal prices were low in northern France and at Marseille, exports of both grain and flour, especially to Britain and Belgium, became possible.

Table 46 *Value of cereal imports, 1827–96 (millions francs)*

Period	Imports (annual average)
1827–36	23
1837–46	31
1847–56	95
1857–66	91
1867–76	245
1877–86	467
1887–96	337

Table 47   *Wheat supply, 1831–91 (hectolitres)*

Year	Domestic production	Excess of imports	Excess of exports	Total available
1831	56,429,694	878,907		57,308,601
1832	80,089,016	4,240,088		84,329,104
1833	66,073,141		226,590	65,846,551
1834	61,981,226		263,701	61,717,525
1835	71,697,484		272,927	71,424,557
1836	63,583,725		90,052	63,493,673
1837	67,915,534		184,446	67,731,088
1838	67,743,571		549,885	67,193,686
1839	64,935,732	393,607		65,329,339
1840	80,880,431	2,035,642		82,916,073
1841	71,463,683		697,827	70,765,856
1842	71,314,220		295,927	71,018,293
1843	73,650,509	1,737,552		75,388,061
1844	82,454,845	2,098,211		84,553,056
1845	71,963,280	312,319		72,275,599
1846	60,696,968	4,669,683		65,366,651
1847	97,611,140	9,898,969		107,510,109
1848	87,994,435		674,839	87,319,596
1849	90,761,712		2,955,208	87,806,504
1850	87,986,788		4,345,044	83,641,744
1851	85,986,232		4,754,812	81,231,420
1852	86,065,386		2,091,526	83,973,860
1853	63,709,038	3,733,308		67,442,346
1854	97,194,271	5,318,304		102,512,575
1855	72,936,726	3,485,102		76,421,828
1856	85,308,953	8,604,711		93,913,664
1857	110,426,462	3,481,841		113,908,303
1858	109,989,747		4,626,287	105,363,460
1859	87,545,960		6,776,170	80,769,790
1860	101,573,625		4,093,765	97,479,860
1861	75,116,287	12,466,305		87,582,592
1862	99,292,224	5,725,863		105,018,087
1863	116,781,794	1,639,534		118,421,328
1864	111,274,018		1,243,310	110,030,708
1865	95,571,609		4,436,217	91,135,392
1866	85,131,455		6,022,293	79,109,162
1867	83,005,739	8,675,798		91,681,537
1868	116,783,000	10,392,565		127,175,565
1869	107,941,553	964,876		108,906,429
1870				
1871	69,276,419	13,770,933		83,047,352
1872	120,803,459	1,502,124		122,305,583
1873	81,892,667	3,951,869		85,844,536

1874	133,130,163	8,659,062		141,789,225
1875	100,634,861		1,843,109	98,791,752
1876	95,439,832	3,747,277		99,187,109
1877	100,145,651		524,526	99,621,125
1878	95,270,698	17,819,513		113,090,211
1879	79,355,866	29,349,390		108,705,256
1880	99,471,559	26,792,720		126,264,279
1881	96,810,356	17,151,735		113,962,091
1882	122,153,524	17,587,291		139,740,815
1883	103,753,426	13,938,868		117,692,294
1884	114,230,977	14,767,996		128,998,973
1885	109,861,862	8,915,219		118,777,081
1886	107,287,082	9,760,931		117,048,013
1887	112,456,107	12,214,914		124,671,021
1888	98,740,728	15,478,241		114,218,969
1889	108,319,771	15,574,552		123,894,323
1890	116,915,880	14,503,215		131,419,095
1891	77,265,828	17,413,250		94,679,078

This obviously had the advantage of limiting the fall in prices after a good crop and rapidly became a matter of importance particularly for grain and flour merchants in northern France.[57] However, it was generally believed that the level of exports was never sufficiently high to exert more than a marginal influence on domestic price levels. It took a considerable time to establish regular contacts and to overcome the usual reluctance to enter unknown markets. Moreover, the major British and Belgian markets soon became too competitive for French producers of cereals and flour. They were driven out by imports from America.[58]

As wheat supplies on the domestic market increased, so annual average consumption per head of population appears to have peaked in the decade 1881–90 and subsequently to have begun to decline (see Table 48). The initial increase in consumption might theoretically be explained by a reduction in transport costs which improved supply and reduced commodity prices, particularly on a regional basis following a poor harvest. In practice the extent to which reductions in the cost of production of particular commodities (including transport costs) widened their market depended, first, on the extent to which reductions were passed on to the consumers and, second, where retail prices were in fact reduced, on the elasticity of demand for the goods concerned.

Retail foodstuff prices, including those for bread, tended to rise until around 1858, then plateaued briefly before beginning a long period of continuous increase. This was due partly to increases in other costs and also because savings in transport costs do not always seem to have been passed on to the consumer by commercial intermediaries. However, food prices might well have increased more rapidly if transport costs had not been

Table 48   *Average annual supply of wheat and consumption per inhabitant, 1831–1910 (hectolitres)*

Period	Average annual supply	Average consumption per inhabitant
1831–40	68,932,000	2.06
1841–50	80,564,000	2.29
1851–60	90,302,000	2.49
1861–70	102,118,000	2.69
1871–80	107,865,000	2.93
1881–90	123,042,000	3.23
1891–1900	123,297,000	3.19
1901–10	118,786,000	3.04

reduced, and consumers did gain significantly from increased security of supply. Moreover, overall economic development permitted increases in real income for most social groups for most of the second part of the century. Increased purchasing power led to both quantitative and qualitative improvement in diet, the latter setting limits to the elasticity of demand for bread and wheat. Just as demand for the inferior cereals was affected by greater use of wheat in the first half of the century, so demand for wheat fell towards the end of the century as consumption of meat and vegetables increased.

Improved communications also had significant effects on the structure of livestock markets. Rail tariffs fell rapidly; from the centre, for example, early in December 1848 the reductions shown in Table 49 were introduced.[59] This was in all probability a response to the Ouest Company's tariff reductions for livestock from the Vendée, Loire-Inférieure and Maine-et-Loire, announced in the March of that year.[60] These were significant measures both in improving access to major markets for meat and in creating a more

Table 49   *Changes in rail tariffs for the carriage of livestock, December 1848 (francs)*

Route	Old tariffs per head for less than six head	Old tariffs per head for more than six head	New tariffs per head
Châteauroux–Paris	31.20	17	14
Issoudun–Paris	28.50	16	14
Bourges–Paris	27.80	16	13.50
Vierzon–Paris	24.80	14	13
Orléans–Paris	16.80	8	8

competitive market. The desire of the various railway companies to increase traffic by providing favourable transportation rates for livestock was clear, but even they seem to have been surprised by the volume of traffic generated.[61]

Improved access to the towns was especially significant because per capita consumption of meat remained far higher there than in the countryside,[62] but it also stimulated increased sales of a whole range of products, including those whose commercialization had formerly been neglected, such as dairy produce,[63] poultry[64] and eggs,[65] fruit (including everything from apples from Normandy to oranges from around Cannes and Grasse)[66] and vegetables.[67] Sale of such secondary products, even if they did not develop into specialities, diversified the commercialized produce of many farms, increased their cash income, and helped to offset the decline in cereal prices when that occurred.[68]

The zone of provisioning of Paris in fruit and vegetables expanded from 50 kilometres in 1830 to 250 kilometres by 1855;[69] that of milk expanded to some 150 kilometres by 1900 and annual consumption increased from 110 million litres in 1854 to 280 million in 1890 and 410 million by 1914.[70] Increasing sales of these 'secondary products' both reflected the growth of popular purchasing power and improvements in diet and stimulated further change in dietary habits. These were products with a relatively high elasticity of demand. The reduction in marketing costs and increase in price were incentives to both merchants and farmers.[71] The railway companies also shared in the benefits of this unexpected current of traffic and tried to encourage it by favourable tariffs.[72] However, the pace of change in eating habits and in commerce and agriculture should not be exaggerated. The lack of refrigerated wagons remained a major obstacle to the mobility of perishables until the twentieth century.

The relationship between reduced transport costs, reduction in retail prices and increased demand was most evident in the marketing of wines for mass consumption, of which estimated annual consumption increased from 55 litres per person in 1858 to 77 by 1872.[73] However, by the 1890s consumption of both wine and wheat had reached its peak. Demand elasticity for these commodities was subsequently limited by slow demographic growth, whereas that for vegetables and meat continued to be affected by changes in the structure of diet and improvements in the living standards of the mass of the population, which however still occurred slowly and at varying times in different social groups and regions. Even in Paris significant diversification of diet does not appear to have occurred among the lower classes until the mid 1870s.[74]

Exports did little to offset the growing saturation of the internal market for these two major products. The groups which benefited most from improved access to foreign markets were producers of quality wines[75] and dairy farmers exporting to Britain, primarily from Normandy and to a lesser extent from Brittany.[76] Before 1860 hardly any butter was exported to England from the port of St-Malo; by 1860–3 exports averaged 3,500,000 kilograms per annum and by 1866 had passed the 10 million kilogram mark.[77] But from the 1870s exports of dairy products were to suffer a marked decline.[78] Inferior wines tended to be excluded from most foreign markets by tariffs based on alcohol content rather than selling prices. Although these were reduced, they remained too high.[79] In effect the balance of trade in agricultural produce was not weighted in favour of French producers, heavily orientated as they remained towards the cultivation of basic cereals.

Market integration

Completion of the PLM in 1857 made it possible for grain and flour merchants in Marseille and Le Havre to compete for the supply of cereals to vast hinterlands. Initially their zone of competition extended as far as the Paris market; however, as the volume of imports from America became relatively more important, imports along the PLM were pushed further south. Purchase at Le Havre obviously meant lower transport costs for merchants operating in northern France.[80]

Here again rail tariff policy was of crucial importance. The movement of imports was an important source of revenue for the companies and increasingly so from the late 1860s. Differential tariff structures were devised to facilitate penetration inland and to maintain competitiveness.[81] Charges were designed in part to encourage import through ports which served their particular lines. Thus the Nord and Est were anxious to encourage import through Dunkirk, in competition with Antwerp,[82] the Nord through Boulogne and Calais,[83] the Ouest through Le Havre,[84] the Midi through Cette, Port Vendres, Bayonne and Bordeaux,[85] and the PLM through Marseille.[86] This policy was reinforced by a species of regional protectionism extended to the products of areas with access to the lines of particular companies when these faced competition from producers in regions served by other companies. The railway companies achieved this both by restrictions on application of low long-distance tariffs and by agreements with other companies to share traffic.[87] These restrictions on long-distance movement limited competitive pressures from outside the given 'zone of influence' of a particular company both from extra-regional and international producers.[88] Such measures were, of course, introduced only where the volume of imports was not sufficiently large and profitable to gain priority. The Comité consultatif, discussing such action in the early 1890s, accepted its legitimacy, although some of its members protested, as did M. Cochery on 30 May 1894, that 'in a country like France, where the railway networks were established with substantial aid from the state, where the companies are in reality its delegates for a great public service, it is not admissible that the regions served by each network should be treated as separate countries'.[89]

Imports had their most significant effect following poor domestic harvests. An official commission claimed in 1868 that France had been saved from famine prices in the previous year only by the combination of free trade, telegraph, steamers and railways.[90] Formerly poor harvests, necessitating large-scale movement of cereals, had strained transport facilities to the utmost and had led to substantial increases in tariffs. Now, with the railway, rapid and regular services were maintained, and tariffs, far from increasing, fell. It was during such years that the improved transport networks made their most significant contributions in assuring supply and evening out prices.[91] When domestic harvests were good, movements of both domestically produced and imported cereals and other foodstuffs were limited.[92]

Harvest fluctuations, both national and international, and predictive assessments of them continued to affect price variations. Seasonal fluctuations tended to remain relatively high in areas which increasingly specialized in non-cereal products like Calvados, in contrast with Loir-et-Cher, for example,[93] or in those regions most distant from ports of import or where communications remained relatively poor. They also continued to be influenced by farmers' needs to sell at particular periods (to raise cash to pay rents, for example) and by stocking procedures.

However, even in normal years, the improvement of supply to major markets led to heightened competition and a levelling of prices, particularly in the Paris basin and in the Rhône–Saône corridor, in both of which regions internal flows of cereals and flour had for some time past met with growing volumes of imports. The increase of supply in these two key areas had substantial direct and indirect effects on price levels and on commodity flows throughout the agricultural economy.

Direct effects were particularly evident in the case of cereal producers in northern France and those of the centre, centre-west and east. The former faced competition from imports, particularly those brought along the Seine,[94] and growing competition from domestic producers as production increased.[95] In the case of the latter by the late 1880s their wheat had been almost excluded from the Paris market by imports through Le Havre, while their zone of distribution towards the south was restricted by the direct and indirect consequences of imports through Marseille.[96]

Indirect effects were the consequence of the levelling of prices, which tended to occur initially between neighbouring zones[97] and then to proceed rapidly, as if by contagion, from zone to zone. Although new flows did not directly compete on every market, they had the effect of excluding some producers from traditional markets and 'imprisoning' their surpluses locally, that is, of cutting off flows and causing excessive local supply. This was the case in the Tarn in the late 1860s, with the loss of markets in the Alps and in Hérault.[98]

Prior to the establishment of the railway network, grains appear to have been moved mainly in a step-by-step manner, with, for example, in years of good domestic harvest some direct movements from the north to Marseille by sea but with the major flows taking place from north to centre, influencing supply and price levels in central France and generating flows from there towards the south.[99] After poor domestic harvests markets in the south were likely to be invaded by imports through the ports. This limited penetration from the centre and, indirectly, penetration of the centre from the north.[100]

By 1866 (that is, prior to the great period of import from North America) there were widespread complaints about the increased inability of grain marketed at Dijon, for example, to proceed as far down-river as Lyon, much less to reach Marseille,[101] about the decline of sea-borne traffic moving from the north towards the south[102] and, more generally, about the effects of imports on price levels along the Mediterranean coast as well as close to the axes of penetration.[103] Although Lyon appears to have remained the major point of contact between domestic produce moving south and imports, it seems that the competitive position of the former grew significantly weaker after the suspension of the sliding scale in October 1858.[104] Exclusion of the cereals of the east from the Midi caused an increase of supply in Lyon even when foreign grains did not penetrate as far as the city.[105] The responses to the 1866 inquiry from Ain, Côte-d'Or, Haute-Marne, Haute-Saône, Saône-et-Loire and the Vosges explained the decline in sales at Gray and in the Midi in terms of imports at Marseille 'driving back' cereals towards the north and also the establishment of new means of communication permitting areas which were closer to the Midi but had previously been isolated by inferior communications, to market more easily towards the south.[106] Some areas appear to have been caught in the middle – thus the Dauphiné Plains were increasingly excluded from markets further south by imports and found it difficult to sell further north because of the growing surplus produced in the north-east.[107]

If after good internal harvests grain would again flow down the Rhône–Saône corridor towards Marseille and levels of import decline, this was only because of the very low level of internal prices and the current was soon likely to be reversed.[108] Contemporaries were particularly concerned about the greater instability of the market which these various flows revealed. Nowhere did producers have guaranteed markets; improved communications and free trade had ended that. Farmers depended on merchants' assessments of the profit and loss potential of transactions conducted over increasingly wide areas. Merchants and millers bought grain with the object of maximizing profits; clearly, the interests of agriculture and those of commerce did not always coincide.[109] The origin of cereals was not of crucial importance to the latter. Typically, in 1890 mills along the line of the River Vilaine and the Ille-et-Rance canal were using cereals imported at St-Malo, which cost one-fifth less than locally grown wheat.[110] Of far greater importance was the similar policy of the major mills in the ports, especially Marseille and Le Havre, and at Corbeil for the supply of Paris[111] or those in Lot-et-Garonne, Gers and Tarn-et-Garonne, of using imported cereals purchased at Bordeaux to supply flour to the city and to Hérault and Pyrénées-Orientales as well as local consumers.[112]

In a particularly unfavourable position were producers in Isère or Basses-Alpes or in Haute-Garonne. Tarn, Lot-et-Garonne, Aude and Hautes-Pyrénées. They had to face competition on their traditional markets in lower Languedoc and Provence from cheaper cereals brought by rail from further north and from imports, while at the same time losing traditional markets in the Massif Central because of the priority given to the establishment of rail links between the Massif and the north.[113] The situation of producers in the second group of departments appears to have been made even more difficult by the relatively high tariffs of the Midi Company, on which they depended for access to markets, by comparison with those of the PLM serving competing regions.[114]

To some extent the growth of competition in particular markets was compensated for by the increased flexibility allowed by more rapid diffusion of information and improved transport. All commodities were claimed by M. Tisserand, *rapporteur* for the 1866 inquiry from Alsace, 'to have acquired more fluid properties'.[115] The declining significance of physical market places and the growing importance of direct purchase on the basis of samples further contributed to this fluidity, so that produce might be moved in directions which 'varied according to the circumstances and sometimes very briskly from one year to another'.[116] In spite of continued market imperfections and human hesitation, not altogether surprising in a period of rapid change, it became easier to transfer sales from one market to another.

This greater flexibility manifested itself both through sales in more distant markets without change of direction and through changes in the direction of commodity flows. The first development was likely to be a response to the production of growing surpluses and saturation of established markets,[117] the second to competition depriving sellers of traditional markets. Both might be responses to the attraction of markets with higher price levels.[118] But the shifts were extremely complicated and sometimes so gradual that contemporaries were hardly aware of them.[119] Moreover, accurate statistical measurement of internal commodity movements is impossible, given the number of distinct markets and the limited statistical information available. We have information on production levels of the various commodities and on prices. The effects of rail construction and of imports on market structures can thus be described only in general terms, with reference to specific examples and above all to relationships between prices on particular markets.

According to Renouard, France formed a single market by 1863, when the average distance travelled per tonne reached 197 kilometres, the same as in

1936.[120] By 1861–4 around 30 million hectolitres of cereals per annum were being transported by the six major railway companies, amounting to almost one-third of total consumption.[121] The wine trade and that in livestock were similarly affected. In 1863 the same companies transported over 6 million animals, including 1.5 million to the Paris market.[122] Substantial imperfections remained in the market system, due in part to the delay in providing some regions with modern transportation networks. Nevertheless, the period 1850–80/90 can be viewed as a key period of structural change resulting from improved access to markets and the creation of more or less integrated national and international markets.

Reduction in the cost of transport has two contradictory effects: by enlarging the market it tends to cause price increases, providing that demand is elastic, but by reducing marketing costs and by increasing competition it has the opposite effect – always providing, of course, that cost savings are passed on by producers, and especially wholesalers, to retailers and consumers. Thus improved distribution of products *tended* to reduce costs to consumers. But by increasing supply to a distant market it frequently had the opposite effect of increasing the cost at, or close to, the place of production, at least in the short term. This can be seen in the extension of the zone of provisioning of Paris in meat, dairy products, fruit and vegetables into Normandy and Touraine, for example,[123] or in the development of a mass market for wine.[124] The *procureur-général* at Agen complained in January 1857 about the 'cruel situation' of local consumers. Since the establishment of rail links with Paris, 'the price of everything is rising'.[125] Such a situation could bring increased prosperity to agriculture, providing farmers were able to meet changing patterns of demand and to increase their productivity to cover increasing costs of production.

Elsewhere, of course, and particularly where competition in local markets intensified, the tendency was for prices of particular commodities to fall to what were, by comparison with costs, often regarded as excessively low levels. This was the case with cereals, especially in regions in which productivity levels remained relatively low. The complaint was frequently made that the new economic structures favoured urban consumers at the expense of the countryside.[126]

The extent to which market integration has been achieved at any one time is revealed by the relationship between prices in various markets. The major new features of the market structure, as modified by rail construction, were the attenuation of price fluctuations over space and over time. The coefficient of variation for departmental cereal prices fell from 16 per cent in 1840 to 8 per cent in 1882.[127] On a regional basis the maximum difference between prices fell progressively, as the indices in Table 50 indicate.[128] The regions of the north, north-east, north-west, west and centre, in which prices had been below the national average in the first half of the century, were now much better placed to sell their surpluses. This had the dual effect of keeping up

Table 50   *Falls in cereal prices, 1849–90 (francs)*

Index: 1849 = 100

Year	Index	Maximum difference	Year	Index	Maximum difference
1849	100		1873	43	2.00f
1859		4.61f	1878	37	1.74f
1868	84	3.89f	1890	23	

their prices and limiting the rise of prices in other regions[129] – in the east, south-east, south-west and south. On the markets of the centre, which because of their isolation had tended to experience some of the most substantial price fluctuations in relation to the success or failure of regional harvests, prices rose in 1861 (a year of serious shortage) to only 24.09 francs per hectolitre, while in 1863, following an abundant harvest, they did not fall below 18.59 francs because of the facility for movement to other regions.[130] In all these regions price levels tended to converge on the national average.

The transport economist Jacqmin claimed in 1868 that all that was required was a rise of 1 franc in the price of wheat on a particular market for merchants within a 200–300-kilometre radius to respond. They were well informed by newspapers and telegraph, and 1 franc per hectolitre represented 13 francs per tonne; with prevailing rail tariffs, this covered the cost of transport over 200–300 kilometres.[131] This statement, while containing more than a grain of truth, is probably rather optimistic. According to a Comité consultatif report in July 1892, an additional margin was necessary to provide merchants with some sort of guarantee against price fluctuation.[132] The claim was to some extent justified because merchants' awareness of, and response to, similar opportunities did increase, and the mobility of commodities and scale of markets grew substantially.[133] 'No longer could one part of France suffer from shortage while another enjoyed abundance.'[134]

The decline in the difference between regional prices of a commodity was indicative of the gradual but accelerated formation of a national market. Market integration was, of course, not perfect. It never can be. Considerable imperfections remained in the working of the market mechanism. Prices must continue to differ between regions as long as transport costs have to be recouped, differences exist in their respective demand and supply potential and the diffusion of market place information is imperfect. Clearly, it is not possible in any market to eliminate added costs or to achieve perfect transmission of information. Furthermore, relatively high transport costs need not be the result of an inefficient transport system but may be simply the consequence of the distance between two markets. In spite of considerable improvement, late nineteenth-century commodity markets were still very far from perfection, and significant price variations still existed between distant markets, as Table 51, showing wheat prices from a range of different regions, indicates. This was in spite of the fact that railway companies, with official encouragement, had sought, and with some success, to facilitate long-distance movements through differential tariffs. Proportionately this was where the major cost reductions had occurred.

The scale of cost savings achieved by transport innovation depended on the significance of transport costs as a constituent element of total costs – that is, on the marketing margins of commodities which, in the case of cereals in normal years, do not seem to have been great enough to allow for major reductions in marketing costs. Rather than effecting a reduction in basic price levels, the primary contribution of the railway was to help effect an evening out in price fluctuations, thus reducing average prices measured over quinquennia or decades but not 'normal' prices determined essentially by costs of production.[135] This was the change repeatedly noted, with a mixture of surprise, pleasure and scepticism, in such periodicals as the *Journal d'agriculture pratique* throughout the 1850s.[136]

The effects of improved communications on price levels were more substantial in the case of agricultural produce which had traditionally cost more to market (as a proportion of final selling price) than had cereals, such as *vins ordinaires*, meat, dairy products and fruit and vegetables. In these cases substantial modifications were noted in the evolution of market structures. In the case of wine, as in that of wheat, in the past prices had moved in inverse relation to quantities produced, particularly in the markets for *vins ordinaires*, where variations in quality had little significance and markets were geographically circumscribed by the cost of communication. With access to wider markets and increasing demand the mechanism was altered. Prices tended to be set in a national market and were – until the development of over-production – stabilized at a relatively high level. Cycles of the type shortage = high price continued, but price increases were less marked because of more effective market integration; cycles of the type abundance = low price tended to disappear as a result of access to wider markets and increasing per capita demand.[137] This was a situation of great potential for profit.

In the long run, however, from the late 1870s and in the 1880s, but primarily in the 1890s, price levels were to be depressed as supply exceeded demand following the constitution of a national market and growing imports from Spain and Italy of wines which were often adulterated by the addition of alcohol to fortify them and artificially coloured to improve their appearance.[138] Subsequently, imports from Algeria worsened the situation. Again penetration was clearly facilitated by differential rail tariffs.[139] The increase in imports during the phylloxera crisis limited the rise in prices which should have compensated for the reduction in levels of production and thus represented a significant handicap to the process of capital accumulation which

Table 51 *Price per quintal of wheat in seven localities, 1884–1901 (francs)*

Locality	1884	1885	1886	1887	1888	1889	1890	1891	1892	1893
Ain	23.98	22.36	21.89	23.71	23.77	24.33	24.28	27.40	23.16	21.25
Bouches-du-Rhône	22.69	23.15	24.04	25.65	24.76	24.24	25.17	25.91	25.44	22.51
Cantal	25.06	23.15	22.99	21.50	24.0	24.37	23.70	25.40	23.62	20.72
Gironde	23.06	22.42	21.97	25.39	25.79	25.27	26.55	27.22	24.99	21.31
Ille-et-Vilaine	21.19	19.20	19.48	22.54	24.66	23.89	24.42	26.89	21.60	18.92
Meurthe-et-Moselle	22.93	21.52	21.56	22.52	24.51	22.21	23.96	28.42	21.89	20.55
Paris	23.0	21.03	21.05	23.01	24.07	23.04	25.01	27.05	23.01	20.09

Locality	1894	1895	1896	1897	1898	1899	1900	1901	Average
Ain	19.54	18.43	19.96	25.42	24.17	19.02	18.68	21.64	22.38
Bouches-du-Rhône	20.66	21.08	22.45	25.27	27.43	22.56	22.08	22.22	23.80
Cantal	20.33	17.96	19.54	27.06	28.22	22.55	21.18	20.96	22.90
Gironde	18.95	17.76	18.30	26.06	23.77	19.14	18.41	19.40	22.54
Ille-et-Vilaine	18.54	17.28	16.23	23.17	27.67	20.53	18.54	18.70	22.62
Meurthe-et-Moselle	18.85	17.76	18.62	24.77	24.21	19.07	17.74	18.92	22.77
Paris	19.04	18.08	19.0	25.02	25.07	19.09	19.08	20.05	22.37

was a necessary prelude to the reconstitution of French vineyards.[140] Subsequent reconstitution of the vineyards with high-yield plants led to domestic over-production. This was a case in which the response to the extension of the market and increased demand encouraged the entry of new producers and eventually led to substantial over-production.[141]

The changing relationship between regional price levels for meat over the previous twenty-five years are revealed in a report prepared by the Préfecture of the Seine in 1883 (see Table 52).[142] There was a tendency for the departmental average to equate increasingly to that of Paris and for prices to rise in accordance with dietary improvements and demand, which was growing at the same time as interrelationships between markets increased.

Meat prices were substantially influenced by those of fodder which continued to fluctuate much more widely than those of other agricultural products – sometimes by as much as 100 per cent.[143] Although it was easier to transport fodder, and this reduced the pressure to sell or slaughter livestock after localized drought, supply remained a problem. Thus in 1894, although the Midi was transporting large quantities of fodder from the Pyrenean valleys towards the west and north, the Paris–Orléans was at the same time recording the movement of increasing numbers of livestock to major markets for farmers unable to afford the cost of commercial feed.[144] A period in which the rate of slaughtering of livestock increased would, of course, be followed by one of relative shortage of animals and rising meat prices.

A complex of factors thus affected the degree of integration of national and international markets and led to substantial changes in the structure of agricultural marketing. This inevitably caused major problems of adaptation for those involved in farming and commerce. Improved communications evened out price fluctuations after poor harvests and stimulated increases in production by providing better access to markets. They were less satisfactory in increasing prices after abundant domestic harvests. Exports never attained the volumes achieved by imports. Internal demand was relatively inelastic in the short term. The continuance of a great deal of subsistence farming and the gradual nature of the transformation of diet meant that regional agricultural specialization was slow to develop. In such a situation good harvests meant that inter-regional flows declined, local glut prevailed and prices fell. The continuing increase in farm productivity made such situations increasingly frequent and largely explains the growing discontent in farming circles in the last third of the century.

A crise d'adaptation

This was a period in which most French rural communities experienced a major *crise d'adaptation*. The reduction of transport costs substantially

Table 52 *Average price per kilogram of meat of all kinds, 1860–73 (francs)*

Year	Paris	North	North-east	East	South	Centre	South-east	West	South-west	North-west	Average
1860	1.29	1.40	1.33	1.19	1.16	1.15	1.15	1.08	1.03	1.01	1.16
1865	1.27	1.40	1.31	1.18	1.22	1.18	1.20	1.09	1.08	1.06	1.19
1868	1.40	1.62	1.50	1.33	1.42	1.40	1.36	1.32	1.32	1.30	1.40
1869	1.37										1.38
1873	1.71										1.75

modified the conditions for economic activity. Every producer and merchant with easy access to a railway station and to the transport and commercial facilities it offered was able, with relative ease, to dispatch goods to countless destinations. But these new opportunities coexisted with the growing threat of competition.[145] At the very least they involved a loss of autonomy. External forces impinged upon the rural community to a far greater extent than before. The prices of locally produced commodities were henceforth dominated by prices on national markets.

Not all changes were welcomed. Producers of foodstuffs lost the quasi-monopoly they had often possessed in their localities. For some products they experienced an expansion of markets, while for others increased competition was more evident. The length of the period of rail construction meant repeated change. The Lyon municipal council explained its pre-occupation with the railway in 1845 by insisting that 'these new means of communication result in the complete transformation of social relation-ships', that their continued development threatened repeated and 'profound modifications' and 'displacement of interests', that in effect they engendered a massive degree of uncertainty.[146] As communications networks were constantly improved, further change was always possible, threatening the most prosperous market of the day with possible over-supply on the morrow.

The commodities most significantly affected at first were cereals and wine. Inadequate techniques limited the long-distance transport of perishables before the 1890s. The initial effect of improved communications, particu-larly in the earlier years of network development (perhaps into the 1860s) seems to have been the stimulation of trade in agricultural commodities rather than the intensification of competitive pressures, particularly as the first network had been constructed to provide links between major cities which were undergoing rapid population growth. However, as new commer-cial currents were organized and as the density of the network increased and more and more places were linked to it, the effects were more varied. Some regions, provided with improved access to markets, experienced a favour-able transformation of their competitive position, but others experienced the loss of the formerly privileged position ensured by geographical proximity to major markets or water-borne access to them.

This was most clearly evident in some of the areas supplying Paris. Calvados, for example, lost its pre-eminent role in the provision of meat throughout the Paris basin,[147] and in the south and east of the Paris basin farmers experienced a concurrent decline in the price of their two basic products, cereals and wool.[148] The social consequences were especially widespread in regions such as this, already orientated towards production for the market and thus susceptible to changes in the structure of that market. In the south and centre cereal producers with low yields, whose prices had previously been above the national average, evinced growing anxiety concerning competitive pressures. Indeed, in the 1860s imported cereals regularly appeared in the major market at Toulouse as well as competing with its merchants elsewhere.[149]

Vineyards on the climatic margins of production in northern France had formerly prospered because of their privileged access to major urban markets. These and especially the vineyards of the Ile-de-France, which had supplied Paris, declined rapidly once wine from Bourgogne, the Bordelais and Midi could be transported cheaply.[150] Elsewhere too local wines for popular consumption were unable to compete with southern vineyards in either quality or price – in parts of Puy-de-Dôme, Corrèze, Cher, Moselle or Alsace, for example.[151] It often came as a considerable shock. The *comice agricole* at Semur (Côte-d'Or) complained that sales 'of our wines of mediocre quality have greatly diminished since the establishment of the railway from Marseille to Lyon. The wines of the Midi offer disastrous competition'. The solution was either to improve the quality of their wine or to pull up the vines.[152] The wines of the Midi enjoyed advantages of quality, lower cost of production and, in addition, benefited from differential rail tariffs,[153] all of which contributed to the rapid extension of their markets. Legislation which allowed producers in seven southern departments to add alcohol to fortify their wines and to make them more portable, which increased their competitiveness, was frequently denounced.[154] In the north-centre and further south, in such departments as Aveyron, wine producers not only lost traditional markets but even found that their local consumers increasingly preferred the wines of such areas as Hérault, Aude and Tarn, with their higher alcoholic content.[155]

Change was not immediate. In the Nancy region the wines of the Midi had traditionally been mixed with the local vintage in order to fortify it when its quality was poor. By the early 1860s use of the railway was allowing the marketing of wine from the south at Nancy for the first time. However, it took time for consumers to develop a taste for this new product. It has been estimated that as late as 1869 only about one-fifth of the 75,000 hectolitres of wine consumed at Nancy came from the Midi. Although no statistics exist, it seems evident that it was only after 1874, when local vines were affected by both mildew and phylloxera, that Midi wines became truly competitive.[156] The chronology of the spread of phylloxera would have significant short-term effects on the geography of production and marketing.

Those regions with superior climatic conditions were favoured by a rapid expansion of their markets, which stimulated increased production. In the longer term this led to a generally more competitive market, affecting the major vine cultivating regions. Eventually the vineyards would be hit by over-production and price depression, but in the meantime a substantially larger market evolved in which the competitive advantages of southern *vins ordinaires* were quickly evident. Initially, in those areas which were provided with access to new markets in which their wines were competitive, the reaction was euphoric. From Bourg-de-Visa (Tarn-et-Garonne) it was reported in 1870 that 'thirty years ago there were no markets. Proprietors were forced to consume their wine themselves or sell it to local inn keepers. . . . Now merchants purchase it in the *caves* and send it to Bordeaux or Paris'. The construction of the railway and of a road to Valence were the decisive factors here.[157] In the Gard the railway stimulated increased planting of higher yield vines and ended the practice of distilling wines which were unmarketable because of the cost of transport.[158] The railway companies which profited from this lucrative traffic were naturally as enthusiastic as the vine growers and merchants.[159] The latter, of course, like entrepreneurs in any business, still complained constantly about rail tariff structures.[160]

The effects of improved communications on livestock markets brought similarly mixed reactions – in the case of lower Normandy the consequence was to neutralize a geographical privilege. Increasingly, the breeders of Berry, who had specialized previously in the supply of animals for fattening in Normandy and especially those from Poitou-Charente and the Nivernais-Charolais-Bourbonnais, sought a share of the lucrative Paris market. According to Désert, between 1845–52 and 1867–73 the share of the Paris basin in the supply of livestock to the Paris market fell from 65.9 to 49.4 per cent. Calvados, which had provided some 37 per cent of the total number of cows sold on the three great markets at Sceaux, Poissy and La Villette prior to rail development, provided only 25 per cent in 1860 and 20 per cent by 1880.[161] As early as 1849 the Prefect of the Manche had warned the departmental *conseil général* to prepare for increasing competition from Brittany and central France, stressing that previously when animals had been taken on the hoof to market relative proximity had been a major advantage, in that it had reduced weight loss and losses from the enforced sale of sick animals *en route*. Animals from the Manche took eight days to reach Paris, those of its competitors between ten and thirteen days.[162] This tremendous advantage would disappear once all these regions could use rail transport to reach Paris in a matter of hours.

In the worst situation were those areas which, because they were late in experiencing transport improvement, lost markets to producers provided more rapidly with improved communications. Thus the most bitter complaints came from areas which felt neglected. These were complaints about the lack of railways in a locality and about the relatively high cost of reaching the nearest station because of both distance and the poor quality of local roads from groups such as the farmers at Royère (Creuse) who had traditionally produced cereals for sale in the Auvergne. They found themselves in the 1880s in a less competitive situation as imports into the Auvergne by rail increased while they continued to depend on transport by ox cart.[163]

To be distant from a railway system meant additional difficulties in marketing produce which inevitably reduced the attractive forces of the market economy.[164] The Tarn in the mid 1860s was surrounded by areas served by railways, but because it still had none it was in danger of becoming a commercial void.[165] This meant that outside merchants rarely, and only as a last resort, approached these areas either to buy or sell because of the additional costs which resulted from activity there.[166] The deputy mayor of Semur-en-Brionnais (Saône-et-Loire) observed that the very facility with which other communes were able to export their wines by rail reduced the possibilities of sale for producers in his relatively isolated commune. Like many others, he called for a 're-establishment' of the equilibrium and insisted that this was only possible through the provision of a railway line.[167] According to an inquiry conducted by the Société nationale d'agriculture de France in 1879, such complaints were particularly frequent from the west and south-west.[168]

Throughout the period we are considering and beyond it commercially isolated regions with relatively closed economies survived, although their area constantly declined. This was a period marked by a gradual process of spatial integration. The entire countryside was gradually integrated into the market economy, and, as a parliamentary commission of inquiry in 1912 clearly recognized, the railway was the only means by which this could be achieved.[169]

By this means the markets were substantially transformed, providing new opportunities but in a more competitive situation. Ambitions might be developed, but insecurity increased as the feeling emerged that everything was in flux, that traditional assumptions were no longer valid. This nervousness was evident not only in backward, isolated areas but even in areas enjoying a unique prosperity due to improved communications because, as the economist Bineau had predicted in 1843, 'the railways are changing too quickly the conditions of well-being, of prosperity, of existence in those areas that they cross'.[170] Free trade intensified the problems of adaptation. It was difficult to comprehend and to adapt to the accelerated pace of change. Thus the response to new market opportunities by both merchants and farmers was often muted.[171] There was nothing inevitably positive about it.

Actors in the market place

Market structures were substantially transformed as transport costs declined, but the potential consequences were reduced because commercial practices changed more slowly. The small merchant, like the peasant, showed a remarkable capacity for survival. Because the essentially local orientation of commerce was only gradually broken down, the dates of change are inevitably imprecise. Traditional forms of commerce long managed to coexist with the most modern.

This time-lag in the process of adaptation to new conditions was inevitable and reduced the initial effects of improved communications on agricultural markets and on farmers. Past experience influenced the assumptions of all the actors in the market place and enjoined caution upon them. The commercial services of the Nord railway company stressed in 1847 that it 'shouldn't expect commerce to be carried away by novelty and abandon its usual relations from one day to the next'.[172] The importance of *expectations* about supply and demand was but one factor which helped to maintain existing imperfections in the market mechanism. It was not enough to establish physical links between town and country; merchants and farmers had to become aware of the potential offered by access to new markets and possess the desire and ability to respond. (This raises major questions about both the perception of opportunity and the 'rationality' of behaviour.)

If anything other than intermittent links were to be established, farmers and merchants needed to acquire a degree of certainty about the profitability of a particular crop or market, assurances about the stability of costs (e.g. rail tariffs) and price levels. The initial effect of innovation in the transportation infrastructure, as the Prefect of Haute-Vienne insisted in 1861, after completion of the Limoges–Périgueux line, was to cause uncertainty.[173] It took time for things to settle down. Moreover, it took time to establish new commercial circuits. Thus the Paris *banlieue*, benefiting from an existing commercial organization, was largely able to retain its monopoly in the supply of fruit and vegetables to the city for some thirty or forty years after the construction of the first railway networks.[174] The zone of provisioning grew only slowly.

The traditional system of compartmentalized markets based upon inefficient communications had provided a *raison d'être* for a tertiary sector which included a large number of small enterprises, a complex and, to our eyes, inefficient distribution system which to an important extent survived the coming of the railway because of inertia and the powers of resistance to change of vested interests, but also because agriculture based upon small and dispersed producers needed a similarly dispersed system of commercial intermediaries. The complexities of the marketing system and of price fluctuations were beyond the comprehension of most farmers, and active involvement in commerce was beyond their capital resources.[175] They lacked the necessary contacts in marketing centres. Moreover, large-scale merchants found it easier to deal with the smaller-scale merchants, or *courtiers*, who acted as their agents than with the even larger host of farmers.[176]

Only gradually did the number of commercial intermediaries decline and the network of intermediaries become less complex. The improvement of communications accelerated previous tendencies towards change in the organization of commerce. From Eceuillé (Indre) for example, by 1859 it was possible for farmers to deliver grain directly by rail to the mills at Etampes or Corbeil within forty-eight hours. This undertaking had formerly taken eight or ten days and had required the services of two or three intermediaries.[177]

The period was marked by the disappearance of many small-scale 'hoarders of grain' because of the declining opportunities for windfall profits and the existence of new investment opportunities in stocks and shares, but also, it seems, as a result of the tightening up of regulations for payment of the *patente*, the tax due from wholesale merchants.[178] In addition, better communications had the effect of facilitating monetization of the economy and the development of modern banking and credit networks.[179] Improved credit facilities, together with cheaper transport, increased the potential range of operation of individual merchants. This was especially evident in the case of merchants at major marketing centres such as Paris, Marseille or Le Havre. In the supply of flour to Paris it seems to have been the millers rather than the grain merchants who profited most. According to the younger Darblay, the major millers bought grain directly from large farmers. This required substantial capital resources, while the combination of milling and mercantile functions increased the element of risk – but also increased the potential for profit.[180] In areas distant from major urban markets both the grain and the flour trade were organized on a much smaller scale. There it was the grain trade which tended to be favoured as a form of activity because of its greater potential profitability,[181] even if the reduced amplitude of price fluctuations eliminated much of the traditional specu-lative activity and limited the opportunities for quick and substantial profit taking. Merchants had to be content with smaller but more assured profit margins.[182] Increasingly, they were obliged to avoid tying up capital in stocks and to increase turnover as a means of ensuring profitability.[183] Similarly, at Belleville-sur-Saône (Rhône), instead of sending wine to major markets at most twice a year, merchants dispatched a large number of small shipments spread throughout the year.[184] The reduction in stocks that this allowed led to substantial reductions in commercial costs, to be added to the savings on transport. The more secure environment in which merchants now operated, the links established with the railway bureaucracies and the imperatives of trade over longer distances all combined to encourage the application of more rational business methods. In more competitive markets those whose operating costs were lowest tended to expand their activities.

The most visible and obvious signs of change in the organization of commerce were, first, an acceleration in the tendency to abandon the *halles des grains* and, secondly, the process of concentration in flour milling. More and more often grain was not brought to market. Purchases were made on the basis of samples, and transactions occurred in buildings reserved for the grain trade or in cafés which constituted known meeting places.[185] In the Aisne in the early twentieth century specialized *agences* existed at Laon, La Fère, St-Quentin, Soissons, Marle, Guise, Chauny, Château-Thierry and Fère-en-Tardenois. The tendency in the department had been for the *courtiers* who bought on commission to disappear and for direct dealing to occur between farmers and merchants.[186] In Côte-d'Or sale by sample occurred during the weekly markets at Dijon, Beaune and Gray; transactions were especially active in autumn after the first threshing.[187] The grain merchants of the Paris region met in the Bourse off the rue Vivienne until 1863, when the *cercle commercial* in the Place du Louvre was established to provide them with more space. The advantages of not having to transport bulky grains to and from market are clear. With samples in their pockets, sellers tended to go to market more often, to become better informed about prices and to respond more rapidly to price movements. The process of sale by sample also facilitated the geographical concentration of commercial activity and the concentration of trade in fewer hands. The same effect was engendered by the growth of imports and the development of trade in futures.

Great concern was expressed by both officials and knowledgeable private individuals about the development of the latter form of speculation.[188] Clearly, the improvement in the means of communication, in its widest sense, eased the transformation of 'concrete markets . . . into abstract markets'.[189] Merchants entering into commitments could be reasonably certain of finding a commodity that they had agreed to buy or sell when the finalization of a transaction became due, although this was not always necessary. Thus at Marseille, as elsewhere,

the seller engages himself to deliver at the end of the current month or in two, three or four months a certain quantity of grain which he does not possess and often has no means of procuring. . . . If at the due date the grain is not delivered, which is usually the case, the transaction is concluded by a payment by the seller to the purchaser or vice versa, according to whether the price on the day the agreement was made was higher or lower than the price on the due date.[190]

In reply to demands for the prosecution of dealers in futures, the Minister of Justice agreed in June 1856 that such activities were reprehensible but concluded, to his deep regret, that Articles 421 and 422 of the 1810 Code limited the possibility of judicial action. The defenders of this activity maintained that it helped to even out price fluctuations.[191]

Besides meeting at commercial exchanges, merchants or their representatives also frequently made purchases at the farms, from which grain was carted directly to the merchants' granaries or to the mills.[192] It seems that large-scale transactions tended to occur at regular meeting places, lesser transactions at farms and small sales, particularly of seed or by small peasants in need of ready cash, immediately after the harvest in the market place.[193]

The practices of the mass of small farmers changed particularly slowly. It was they, and not the large or even medium-scale farmers, who continued to frequent the market places rather than selling directly to merchants. Inevitably, they were reluctant to cart their produce back home again if they did not sell and were thus more at the mercy of purchasers than those who sold by sample and who, moreover, were likely to have reserves of capital which would permit them to wait a little longer.

But the outlook even of the peasant farmer was subject to change as information about markets spread, and particularly during the inflationary period lasting from the early 1850s into the 1870s they were likely to respond to the growing demand for a wider range of produce, including formerly neglected commodities such as milk, fruit, vegetables and cereals. An important stimulus was provided by the increased availability of manufactured goods. To purchase these the peasant farmer had to sell more, even when his primary motive remained the subsistence of his family. Thus the peasant farmer was drawn more and more into the orbit of the market by a gradually accumulative process. It became increasingly important to produce a marketable surplus regularly. This, however, required larger capital inputs, on however small a scale.[194]

Everywhere there were problems of adaptation. The small peasant remained *relatively* ignorant of market opportunities. He could not comprehend the workings of price mechanisms which were largely independent of local supply and demand.[195] As many of the smaller markets rapidly declined in significance, farmers, large and small, became more dependent upon commercial intermediaries whether they chose to or not.[196] Although in theory the numerous railway stations established the opportunity for 'the humblest producer' to trade over distances of anything from 10 to 400 kilometres,[197] in practice it was the merchants rather than the mass of farmers who traded over longer distances, although both were affected by the consequences for demand and price levels.[198] It was the larger farmers especially who benefited from easier access to such markets as Amiens, Rouen or Paris and who transferred their activities from local market towns to these major centres, dealing with large merchants in them rather than with their agents or small-scale merchants in minor and declining markets.[199] This is not, of course, to deny that small-scale farmers were able to use railway commercial facilities to send their produce a little further – to use the lines of the Ouest Company, for example, to send their grains from Illiers or Beville-le-Comte (Eure-et-Loir) to Paris rather than (or as well as) to local mills.[200] But most would have been dealing in small surpluses and would have lacked both the experience and contacts which made such direct links possible. They tended to use local intermediaries, often working on a commission basis, if they did not sell on the market place or directly to a nearby mill. In every canton some hundreds of farmers depended upon a few merchants, themselves subordinate to the large-scale merchants of a major urban centre who were involved in inter-regional trade.[201]

After farmers and merchants, millers were the next link in the commercial chain. France contained an infinite number of small flour mills, which ground local cereals usually for local consumption unless proximity or ease of access to major urban markets offered an alternative. Statistics gathered towards the end of 1851 (see Table 53) sought to distinguish cereal mills from other types of mill. They are, unfortunately, incomplete but illustrate the small scale of production and the overwhelming prevalence of natural power sources.[202]

The most prosperous mills were those which enjoyed good communications. For the greater number it remained the case that, 'the costs of transport being considerable, their industry is of necessity limited'.[203] Most mills continued to grind grain brought to them by particular customers – farmers, agricultural workers paid partly in kind, bakers – and were paid with a certain proportion of the flour; most worked exclusively for local consumption. At Malesherbes (Loiret) these were known as *moulins . . . au petit sac*.[204] The village of Christal de Rodiéros (Gard), with a population of 251, was served by two mills in 1882, one worked by its proprietor on his own, the other by a tenant employing one worker. Both of these were unable

Table 53   *Flour mills in twenty-three departments, 1851*

Department	Total no. of mills	No. of workers	Water	Wind	Steam	Horse
Loire	509	1591	891		18	
Doubs	553	1093	553			
Aube	324	743	290	31	3	
Haut-Rhin	276	797	379		3	
Marne	665	1278	494	171		
Nord	1156	2676	88	959	8	
Pas-de-Calais	1250	2877	422	828		
Ardennes	580	954	484	90	6	
Meurthe	358	1105	382	3		
Seine-et-Marne	230	431	192	4	2	
Haute-Marne	236	523	210	10		
Vosges	718	975	713	2		
Rhône	412	813	394	15	8	3
Bas-Rhin	295		295			
Cher	689		469	114		106
Hautes-Pyrénées	283					
Moselle	593	973	589	1	3	
Gironde	1200	2538	771	531	2	3
Bouches-du-Rhône	243		176	52		15
Pyrénées-Orientales	343	728	342	1		
Oise	665					
Vaucluse	308					
Nièvre	c.600					

to operate for about three months of each year when water levels fell.[205] Often millers had to take on other work to earn a living – using water power to operate a sawmill perhaps or working on the land.[206] Even in the major grain-producing department of Eure-et-Loir in 1866 there were still 450 watermills and 160 windmills, the latter especially on the Beauce plain, which had little surface water.[207] But small mills were obviously declining in number as market conditions changed.

It is clear that improved communications led to the evolution of a more competitive flour market. It was soon appreciated that the range of supply to the larger urban markets had significantly increased.[208] This new facility benefited both consumers and also the larger mills capable of taking advantage of new opportunities.[209] In the case of the Paris market, mills in close proximity, and particularly those at Corbeil, possessed clear competitive advantages, including (because of easy import of cereals up-river and favourable rail tariffs) lower transport costs, technical efficiency and established commercial links.[210]

Investment in improving efficiency further increased the competitiveness of well situated large mills. Steam engines, although reluctantly adopted at first because of the large capital cost involved (perhaps 60,000 francs per pair of millstones) and the comparative cost of fuel when free-flowing water was the alternative, ensured regularity of milling at low unit cost. The introduction of steam was relatively slow and occurred especially near large population centres and ports of import. The last third of the century also saw the replacement of traditional millstones by rotating cylinders in the most modern mills.[211] These produced a whiter flour, in accord with consumer tastes. Improved processing reduced the amount of wastage and thus contributed to increasing the supply of flour. These new processes had spread westwards from Hungary, increasing at first the competitive pressure from imports and then, as French millers took up the innovation, creating even more intense pressures. This development was relatively expensive, and by 1882 there were only 130 modernized mills in France compared with perhaps 140,000 pairs of millstones.[212]

Large-scale millers were able to drive the small ones out of business through a combination of better quality, lower prices, the use of credit to secure clients and higher prices to attract sellers of grain.[213] In effect, the tendency for milling to be concentrated at larger mills resulted not only in economies of scale in processing but also in the development of a more efficient marketing system, which induced further concentration. Typically, in the Pontarlier area of Doubs by 1870 bakers were obtaining flour from large mills at Besançon and Gray instead of buying exclusively from small local mills.[214] Particular concentration points assumed a degree of dominance in the market. The Paris region was one, with major mills at Corbeil, Nogent, Pontoise and Etampes;[215] Marseille and Le Havre, with their large imports of cereals and milling, were others.[216] To these might be added the less important centres of Bar-le-Duc[217] and Dijon[218] because of their railway functions. In all these cases facilities for cheap bulk transport were obviously essential both for the concentration of the raw material and the distribution of the processed commodity. Millers at the ports or on major waterways had clear advantages in terms of the transport costs of both grain and flour. In addition, they could draw upon either imported or domestically produced grains, depending upon their relative price levels.[219]

The new mobility of flour created major problems for many small mills. In the Paris region the period 1878–81 appears to have brought the onset of particular difficulties. It was reported that rentals had fallen from 12,000 to 15,000 or even 22,000 to 4000, 5000, 7000 or 8000 francs and that formerly prosperous mills were entirely abandoned. One cause of this had been a series of poor harvests which had forced millers to provision themselves at the ports – mainly at Le Havre and Dunkirk – instead of locally and had thus added considerably to their transport costs. The second and more significant explanation offered was their technical backwardness.[220] Millers in the *arrondissement* of Albi (Tarn) were in financial difficulty by 1870 because of the loss of traditional markets in the Cévennes and lower Languedoc, such as Le Vignon and Lodève, which had been invaded by more competitively priced flour from Marseille. Furthermore, they feared the loss of St-Affrique and Millau – markets in which they were already facing competition – as soon as the branch line from Rodez to the main Cette–Marseille line was completed. In partial compensation for their losses all they had gained from better communications was an improved position for the supply of Aurillac, at the expense, of course, of its local millers.[221] Complaints from Castelnaudary (Aude) and Toulouse were almost an echo of those from Albi.[222] The growing predominance of the mills at Marseille throughout the Midi, because of their ability to employ relatively cheap imported cereals, was a major cause of complaint.

From the 1890s, however, government officials favoured rail tariff proposals designed to improve the competitive position of mills dependent upon domestic cereals. Proposals which, for example, would reduce the cost of receiving grains from the Beauce for millers at Etampes were warmly welcomed by the Comité consultatif des chemins de fer.[223] Tariff structures were introduced which helped mills throughout the south to compete with those at Marseille[224] and which facilitated the movement of flour from the north towards the south to compete with flour produced in Marseille using imported raw materials.[225]

In spite of substantial change, many relatively small mills managed to hang on to local markets. Old habits among consumers were modified only slowly. Productive facilities in which substantial capital had been invested would not be abandoned overnight. New commercial networks took time to become established. Flour production everywhere remained dispersed. Although the very small wind- or watermills rapidly declined in number, at the turn of the century a large number of the more efficient, medium-sized mills survived and even prospered, although subject to the price dominance of producers in the major centres. Even a department as close to Paris as the Oise had 174 significant mills. In Aude in the early years of this century, although windmills had lost all importance, there were still forty-seven *minoteries* (relatively large mills) employing mainly water power to produce daily 1600 metric *quintaux* of flour (twenty-one at Carcassonne, six at Castelnaudary, seven at Limoux and thirteen at Narbonne) and 148 *moulins* producing 900 metric *quintaux* per day. In Côte-d'Or at the same time there were some 350 mills, but only fifty-five of these were classified as 'industrial mills'. They used both steam and water power to produce an annual average of 850,000 metric *quintaux*.[226]

Small millers continued to supply a declining clientele of bakers and those consumers who persisted in baking their own bread especially in small villages and isolated hamlets and farms. Their numbers fell rapidly as communications improved. As early as 1855 a report on the *arrondissement* of Evreux (Eure) observed: 'On the one hand, the popular classes in the town and even in the villages no longer prepare their own bread; they all buy it at the baker's. On the other hand, the mills open to the public have almost entirely disappeared; the bakers furnish themselves with flour from the large mills.'[227] By the end of the 1850s in more advanced agricultural areas such as the Soissonnais and Beauce even the smallest villages had bakers.[228] Rising incomes were leading to a growing demand for specialized services, which by 1900 had affected all but the most isolated areas and the most recalcitrant individuals.[229]

Similarly, bakers increasingly relied upon the specialized services of millers. Rather than themselves purchasing grain and having it milled by a neighbouring miller, they tended to purchase flour from a large-scale commercial miller. According to the *procureur-général* at Besançon, by 1855 bakers in his area purchased seven-eighths of their needs in the form of flour and only one-eighth as cereals on the market place.[230] By the 1890s this process had gone much further. The 1893 inquiry into *La petite industrie* recorded the change: 'The time when the baker bought 100 sacks of wheat and had them ground by a nearby miller (*meunier*), is past. . . . An intermediary has appeared between him and the peasant producer, not a simple grain merchant . . . but an intermediate manufacturer, the large-scale miller (*minotier*).'[231] Bakers now had the advantage of being able to purchase flour from a number of millers located over a wide geographical area and of having the flour delivered relatively cheaply by rail. However, they were usually tied to particular millers by the extension of credit facilities.[232] Thus the trade in cereals and flour was increasingly controlled by a declining, though still large, number of miller merchants.

Another significant indicator of change in the organization of the market was the decline in the practice of stocking by the mass of farmers and

328 Part 3 Transport Revolution and Agriculture

merchants. This was in part a consequence of the improved facility of provisioning, which made the maintenance of merchants' stocks unnecessary. They could purchase as needed and reduce the amount of capital tied up in stocks.[233] More generally, it followed the realization that major price fluctuations were less likely. Thus the smaller farmers no longer kept stocks because they 'no longer feared either shortage or famine',[234] while the larger farmers 'no longer hoped for the very high prices of other times'. Thus, 'all, with very few exceptions, sell within the year of harvest'.[235] Frequently the lesson had to be learned the hard way. In 1862 merchants at Meung (Loiret), Chinon (Indre-et-Loire) and Vendôme (Loir-et-Cher) were reported to have bankrupted themselves by traditional speculative practices,[236] while a report from Marines (Seine-et-Oise) in 1870 claimed that farmers had made substantial losses before realizing that they needed to revise their commercial practices.[237]

By 1866 it was claimed that farmers in eastern France were 'beginning to understand' that the changing characteristics of price movements, and particularly the absence of the high prices of old, was not accidental but a product of the 'new economic regime'.[238] The change was often regretted. A landowner from Châteaumeillant (Cher) observed that formerly he could have expected to have made substantial windfall profits at least once or twice per decade.[239] Now improved communications left no place for those surprises which led to sudden price rises. By 1870 it appears that speculative stocking procedures still survived in only the most isolated areas.[240] Only when cereal prices fell too low – below 20 francs per hectolitre, according to a report from the Ardèche in 1870[241] – would a farmer lay in stocks and attempt to wait for an increase. To do so was 'to expose oneself to falling prices and to the weevil: a double risk of loss'.[242] This problem of falling prices was to become, in the last third of the century, the major concern of French farmers.

The demand for protection

Continuity and change coexisted in the structure of the market for agricultural commodities. Marketing efficiency appears to have increased, but within limits set by the high costs of operation of a declining but still large number of producers and intermediaries. This effectively limited the effects of transport innovation upon market structures, and yet during this period improved communications and changes in commercial practices occurred at a speed which shocked and concerned most contemporaries.

Changes in market structures were most strongly brought home to sellers by the clear tendency from the 1860s for agricultural prices to stagnate and by the complex effects this had on incomes.[243] The period between 1874 and 1895, that of the 'great depression', was to be particularly difficult due to the decline in the prices of most products of the farm. The crisis was especially marked for cereals, wine and wool producers but also affected, although far less severely, the producers of meat and dairy products. Farmers still producing primarily for subsistence were least affected, but even they needed to earn some cash.

Cereal prices began to decline in the 1870s and by 1895 were 27 per cent below the 1871–5 level. This was over 33 per cent in the case of wheat, 14 per cent for oats, 26 per cent for rye.[244] The decline in potato prices began later, falling by about 35 per cent from 1885. The decline in livestock prices was less marked and less regular – by 1895 it amounted to 19 per cent for beef and 10 per cent for veal. Butter fell by about 7 per cent, cheese by 15 per cent, while milk prices remained stable. Only sugar beet prices continued to increase, but this was because of the substantial increase in the sugar content of the beet. Wine prices were affected by phylloxera and rose until about 1881–5, then fell as domestic production recovered and imports increased. By the turn of the century glut was evident. The problems that this caused in the departments of Gard, Drôme, Ardèche and Vaucluse were intensified by the concurrent decline of silk production, the result of disease and of madder due to chemical competition.[245]

Estimates of the evolution of the value of production between 1871–5 and 1891–5 give a better impression of the gravity of the crisis:[246] wine −41.2 per cent, textile plants −60.2, cereals −22.7, potatoes +5.8, oil seeds −36.7 and industrial beet +4.7. The simultaneous decline in the prices of a range of products increased its severity, although it should be remembered, especially in the case of cereals, that a substantial proportion was not commercialized. Further proof of the intensity of crisis can be deduced from calculations of the annual rates of growth of agricultural production,[247] measured in terms of value of production: 1847–72 +1.8 per cent, 1872–88 −0.7, 1888–92 −0.7, 1892–8 +0.65 and 1898–1909 +2.7. The declining value of the land was yet another indicator of crisis, although this was due additionally to declining population densities in the countryside. From about 1879 to about 1913 land lost approximately one-third of its value, with substantial regional variations, for example, between 25 per cent in Landes, 18 per cent in Finistère and 40–50 per cent in departments such as Aube, Marne, Haute-Marne, Lot, Lot-et-Garonne, Dordogne, Tarn-et-Garonne and Aude.[248] Only the best-quality land escaped this trend. For similar reasons rents tended to fall, except in parts of Brittany, where population densities remained high, in the Nord because of the cultivation of industrial crops and in the Alpes-Maritimes, where horticulture experienced rapid development. In most areas as population fell, competition for farms declined. Furthermore, because income was reduced by price depression farmers were unable to pay existing rents. Landowners were forced to make concessions which reduced their own incomes and their ability and willingness to invest in agriculture. Even in rich departments like the Aisne farmers demanded longer leases and lower rents in order to facilitate investment in increasing productivity.[249] For all these reasons the last quarter of the century was a period of decline in the economic and social power of the landlord.

New attitudes were revealed by the decline in the cultivated area – although equally significant is the fact that this did not really begin until the 1890s. By 1912 a decline of some 9 per cent, from 26 million hectares in 1882 to 23.7 million, had occurred. The abandonment of marginal land was accompanied by the sale of some 'uneconomic' units. The number of small-scale proprietors declined in the Midi – especially in Var and Hérault after phylloxera, in the Paris basin, the north and Normandy. A minimal increase in the size of average units was made possible as the long process of parcellation came to an end.

The overall consequences of the crisis are not easy to estimate because the decline in prices varied between different products and was to some degree compensated for by transfer to alternative crops and especially by increased productivity. The significance of variation between social groups and regions should also be noted. Innumerable nuances could be identified, but whatever the real decline in agricultural incomes, there can be no doubt about the damaging psychological effects. Lack of confidence limited investment in agriculture, particularly as this period of price depression followed a period, beginning in the late 1850s, of increasing anxiety caused by the growth of imports, rapid changes in internal markets and rising costs of production.

Along with improved communications (and, indeed, made possible by them), increased imports had had positive effects in securing food supplies and stabilizing price movements. At the same time, however, they had greatly intensified the crisis of adaptation to new market structures, which improved communications would anyway have caused, and had provoked considerable criticism. It is difficult to be certain about the causes of opposition to free trade in the period prior to the depression. Was it based upon an objective appreciation of the competitive position of French agriculture? Was it the response of articulate and politically powerful interest groups, anxious to profit from high price levels without having to concern themselves with increasing productivity to internationally competitive levels by means of substantial capital inputs? Alternatively, it could be seen as a simple, emotional 'gut reaction', uniting large sections of the rural community. These attitudes are not, of course, mutually exclusive.

Contemporary assessments varied to a significant degree according to geographical location and the extent to which particular producers were exposed to imports. They varied over time and between places in terms of their perceptions of the actual effect of imports on prices. Increasingly, however, the conclusion was a pessimistic one. Only in a minority of cases was it felt that adequate compensation for the falling prices of basic products had been secured by improved access to markets or through the price movements of alternative products.

Grain producers and grain and flour merchants operating in close proximity to ports of entry or to the axes of penetration of imports were, not surprisingly, particularly anxious. In the earlier stages of change in market structures their perception of the situation of French agriculture might be very different from that in communities still enjoying a measure of protection because of relative isolation. Thus complaints during the 1850s, caused by the repeated suspension of the sliding scale after poor harvests, came particularly from the south and from areas along the Rhône and Saône, including the centre and north-east. Producers in the north-east were increasingly concerned in the 1850s and 1860s about the threat to their traditional markets along the Rhône–Saône corridor as far as Marseille as imports from Russia increased. In the following decades they were, moreover, to be directly challenged in their local markets as imports into the north and east through Le Havre and Dunkirk rose.[250] Comte Benoist d'Azy, a member of the departmental agricultural society of the Nièvre, complained that the wines of the Midi were being allowed to invade central France, while its cereals were now obliged to face competition in their old markets in the Midi. He bitterly resented this dual pressure.[251] He was echoed by the producers of *vins ordinaires* and cereals in Bourgogne and Lorraine. As free trade reduced the cost of imports and railways facilitated the wider distribution of imported commodities, discontent became more general.

By 1870 the traditional current of movement from Dijon and Gray down-river had greatly declined, and foreign cereals were being used in local mills.[252] Lyon seems to have remained the place at which movements down-river met with imports from Marseille, but in most years cereals produced above Lyon were largely excluded from the lower valley and the Midi.[253] Swiss purchasers also transferred their trade from Dijon to Marseille.[254] Prior to 1862 grain from such departments as Ain and Isère and areas further north, in Saône-et-Loire, Côte-d'Or, Haute-Saône and Haute-Marne, had substantially provisioned Lyon and, to a lesser extent, Marseille. From 1862 these supplies were increasingly excluded from Marseille; as a consequence, supplies and competition increased on the Lyon market, causing a fall in prices there. By the late 1860s regular and direct competition from imports appears to have become a major problem on the Lyon market itself.[255]

From the same period farmers and merchants in the Toulouse region complained that competition on their normal markets in Gard, Aude, Hérault and in Provence largely restricted sales to local consumers.[256] Similarly – although apparently less dramatically because of the lower volume of import and less ready penetration – imports through Bordeaux affected sales of grain produced in the Charentes, Deux-Sèvres and Vienne.[257] In both the Midi and the south-west the cultivation of cereals declined in coastal departments because of the reduction of sea-borne movements to Bordeaux and Marseille and under the pressure of imports.

The more fortunate areas obtained some compensation through the development of specialized vine cultivation and, to a lesser extent, the sale of fruit and vegetables.[258] Otherwise southern grain producers suffered more than others, not only because of their proximity to Marseille, for long the major port of import, but also because of the lower levels of productivity and higher costs of cultivation of cereals in what were often unsuitable natural conditions.[259]

Internal producers were not entirely uncompetitive. Good domestic harvests led to low prices, which reduced the volume of imports. In such periods, of course, it was the intensification of internal competition which largely reduced price levels. In addition, superior quality was claimed to be, in most years, a clear competitive advantage for home-grown cereals. In part this was a matter of taste, but it was also a question of the relative yields of flour per hectolitre of wheat. The question of quality was, however, secondary to that of price in increasingly competitive markets.[260]

On the eastern frontier imports by rail from Germany and Hungary caused growing concern. In Haut-Rhin in 1866 it was estimated that exports had continued until local prices had reached 23.50 francs per hectolitre and imports had occurred at 24.84 francs. The sum of 22 francs was set as the rough point of equilibrium. Up to this level prices were determined by local production; above it imports came into play. Penetration that far inland from Marseille was usually prevented by the excessive cost of transport.[261] However, even when imported cereals did not physically appear on such inland markets, their effects on price levels were nonetheless apparent in most regions. This was the case in Tarn in the mid 1860s because the surplus above local needs produced there was largely 'imprisoned' in the department as a result of the loss of external markets.[262]

Producers of grain in the north and west were also affected by competition, particularly on the Paris market and in English markets. Wool producers who experienced a collapse in prices as a consequence of imports from Argentina and Australia suffered dual pressure on their incomes. This was especially serious in such relatively advanced areas as the Beauce and Brie, where mixed farming had previously flourished.[263]

Initially at least, free trade had its supporters among the producers of wine, livestock and dairy products. They benefited from the extension of their markets, and once they were able to assume that their cereal supplies were secure, were more likely to specialize. In parts of the south as specialization in vine cultivation increased and consequently dependence on cereal imports grew, so too free trade was favoured for as long as imported wines were not a major competitive threat.[264] The security of residents of areas of habitual deficit in cereal production, particularly in the highland zones, was also increased.[265] More generally, it was difficult for anyone to deny the advantages of free trade following domestic harvest failure,[266] although farmers frequently regretted the fact that imports limited the rise in price levels after poor domestic harvests, which, it was claimed, did not allow the producer sufficient compensation for a low level of production.[267] Increasingly, agricultural interests claimed that low cereal prices were the product of the flooding of national markets with imports, in good years as well as bad, from countries which possessed 'unfair' competitive advantages in terms of low labour costs, lower taxes and lower transport costs, etc. Agricultural interests were bitterly critical of 'cosmopolitan' and 'Jew' merchants who bought the cheapest without concern for the 'national interest', as they defined it.[268]

To some extent the evidence presented to the agricultural inquiries varies according to whether it comes from consumer or producer interests. Thus in Gard in 1866 representatives of the *arrondissements* of Nîmes, Uzès and the south of Alais, where cereals were still extensively grown, favoured protection. Those of the north of Alais and the *arrondissement* of Vignon, where manufacture and silk production were more important, supported free trade in cereals.[269] In Hérault a similar distinction could be made between the mountain areas of the *arrondissements* of St-Pons and Lodève in which cereals were significant and the lower, vine-growing areas in these *arrondissements*, and in those of Montpellier and Béziers.[270] Similarly, further north in the area of Tours, where many small farmers grew wheat only for their own consumption and sold wine or livestock, the effect of imports on cereal prices did not cause too much concern.[271]

Until over-production occurred free trade tended to be viewed with favour by wine producers as likely to improve access to foreign markets. This, of course, did not deter them from complaining about the precise terms of the various commercial treaties. Most wine producers were more concerned about the restrictions imposed on the expansion of their internal market by municipal taxes on entry, the *octroi*. In 1870 the charge at Paris was 47.50 francs per *barrique* of *vin ordinaire* from the Rhône. On expensive wines worth perhaps 300 francs per *barrique* this represented some 15 per cent of their value, but in the case of ordinary wines worth 30–40 francs this was a massive 150 per cent.[272] Producers of meat and dairy products continued to escape overseas competition until refrigeration techniques were improved in the 1890s.

Regardless of realities, however, even within those sectors of agriculture relatively sheltered from competition there was often considerable anxiety. Thus alongside an appreciation by the *comice agricole* of Craon (Mayenne) in 1870 of the extension of the domestic market for livestock, complaints were heard about the appearance of animals from the Rhineland on the Paris market, and concern was expressed that one day a means of transporting fresh meat across the Atlantic would be devised.[273] Typically, the *comice* wanted all the advantages of free trade without the disadvantages of a more competitive market. This is only one of the countless similar expressions of anxiety as improved communications increased the penetration of imports. It was symptomatic of the general state of mind that in the 1850s, 1860s and 1870s, when import levels were still quite restrained, and in years when the low level of prices might have been explained by a good domestic harvest, substantial stocks, increasing productivity or the changing structure of the internal market, the tendency was always to blame imports rather than a complex of other factors.[274]

Rather than causing an overall decline in price levels, the primary effect of easier import and better internal distribution in the late 1850s and 1860s was the limitation of the increase in prices after poor domestic harvests. This represented the end of the age-old tendency for harvests and prices to move in inverse relation to each other. It came as a great surprise and was only slowly comprehended. Inquiry after inquiry into the 1870s, records the perplexity of farmers and their hope that the traditional situation would soon be restored. The peasant in particular was caught up in a complex market and was dominated by forces of supply and demand whose movement he could not easily understand: 'It takes time to achieve an understanding of this modification of our trade in grains, because to farmers who rarely leave their village it appears strange that after a poor harvest in their own region, the price of wheat immediately falls.'[275] Even senior and well informed government officials had found it difficult to appreciate fully the changes taking place, although most realized, as did the *procureur-général* at Bourges in 1859, that as soon as price rises occurred on a market improved communications would ensure that stocks flowed in from elsewhere.[276]

It is significant that in spite of the disquiet voiced by agricultural societies, few representatives of agricultural interests in the Corps législatif voted against the renewal of free-trade treaties in 1869.[277] Support for protection came especially from industrial interests. Prices had remained remunerative for many farmers; rents remained high for landlords. The interval since the ending of protection had been too short to permit a clear judgement, and, more significant, perceptions had been confused by a number of poor domestic harvests and the still relatively low average annual level of import.[278] High prices in the 1860s permitted the more influential large farmers and landowners to make substantial profits and reduced their anxiety about the new economic system.[279] In this decade at least it seems probable that the elasticity of demand for bread, cereals and certainly for animal feed kept pace with the increase in production.

Subsequently, the graph of wheat prices (see Figure 9) reveals the declining amplitude of price fluctuation and the clear tendency for lower price levels to prevail as both domestic production and import levels increased. Although low prices are evident in earlier periods, there is nothing to compare with the substantial depression from about 1873 to about 1896. Price movements from this period lent confirmation to anxieties about the likely movement of international prices that were expressed from the late 1850s, when the combination of rail and free trade first began to influence

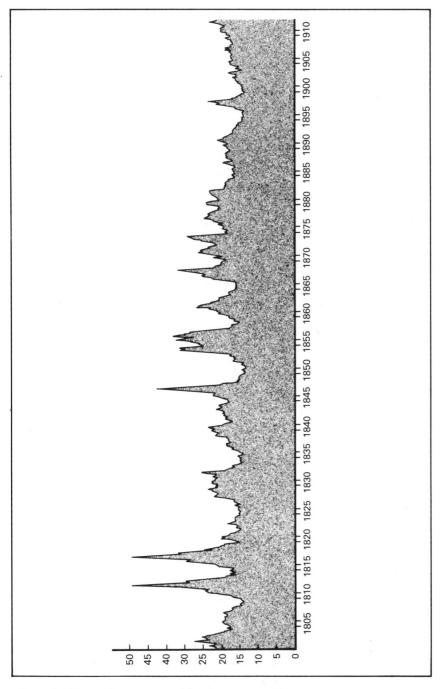

Figure 9   *National average monthly wheat prices, 1805–1910 (francs per hectolitre)*

internal prices. From this period, as the statistics clearly indicate, imports occurred on a more regular and more substantial basis and coincided with a tendency for internal prices to decline because of this, the growing productivity of agriculture and the modification of the internal market. By the 1880s it was generally accepted that 'with the existing means of transport the price of wheat will never rise very high'.[280]

French prices fell from the 1870s primarily because of the increase in supply, the consequence of both increased world production and the improvement of commercial organization, and the reduction in costs of both production and transport. Until the mid 1870s transatlantic shipping rates were still probably high enough to offer a substantial measure of protection to domestic agriculture. Only from this period does it seem likely that imports and, secondarily, the loss of export markets contributed to the establishment of a situation of over-supply, with marked effects on price levels. Earlier the traditional pattern of imports, which essentially covered only domestic deficits, had been largely maintained. Subsequently, although fluctuating wildly with variations in both domestic and world harvests, the level of imports showed a general tendency to increase at least until protection began to take effect in the 1890s.

There was no simple relationship between levels of import and prices. Besides important general factors like money supply and the overall movement of price levels in an inflationary or deflationary direction, price levels depended on the balance between total internal supply/demand conditions and continued to reflect a primary dependence on domestic production. Imports made up only a small proportion of total supply, but they had an effect on price levels, especially in a situation of free trade, which was more than commensurate with their volume in view of the fact that the threat of international competition tended to align national with international prices.

The effects on farmers were undoubtedly serious. In 1884 the Prefect of Gers calculated that it cost 19–20 francs per hectolitre to produce wheat at a time when its selling price had fallen to 16–17 francs.[281] It seems likely, however, that farmers frequently exaggerated their costs of production to strengthen their case for protection. In 1859 the *procureur-général* at Douai had confidently asserted that statistics presented at Lille to support the protectionist case were manifestly false. According to these, the average cost of production per hectare on local farms was 450 francs and the product only 432 francs. His own informed statistics were 397 francs and 792 francs respectively. He maintained that farmers were adequately compensated for the decline in cereal prices following suspension of the sliding scale by the high price of sugar beet, colza, meat and dairy produce, and that their obvious material prosperity made nonsense of their figures.[282] Moreover, given the continued high degree of consumption on the farm itself, the reduction in revenue should be calculated in relation only to the volumes entering commerce and not to total production. The attempts to isolate wheat and to calculate its particular costs of production rather than work on the basis of a complex of interdependent products was one typical and usually tendentious exercise. However, in a period when costs were undoubtedly rising and the prices of most products falling, although to varying extents, farmers' concern is understandable.

By 1879 the position taken by the agricultural interests represented in the National Assembly showed signs of change. In February a meeting of the Société d'agriculteurs, representative of large landowners, revealed a growing support for protection while meetings of departmental *conseils généraux* in the same year revealed similar attitudes in the north-west – in Eure, Nord, Seine-Inférieure – *conseils* in which the influence of industrialists was strong, and in the south-west, in Ariège and Cantal. In the centre and south, most *conseils* called for the renewal of treaties but also for higher tariffs.[283] Clearly, support for protection was growing and in politically influential circles.

The years 1879–82 brought a series of poor harvests, during which imports increased and served to hold down domestic price levels. The responses to the 1882 inquiry into agricultural conditions clearly reflected the worsening situation. They appear to represent a significant strengthening of the demand for protection. Explaining this development, the Mayor of Palaiseau (Seine-et-Oise) wrote: 'At first the crisis [caused by free trade] was imperceptible, though it was predicted by some serious thinkers, and this was because other nations did not know the French market, because communications . . . were less developed and, finally, because some of these countries produced much less than they do today.'[284] The ending of the American Civil War was noted as a major turning point.[285] M. Léfèbre, a large farmer in the *arrondissement* of Etampes (Seine-et-Oise), recorded his impressions of a long *crise d'adaptation* in the Paris region caused first by 'the competition of distant provinces after the creation of railways' and subsequently by American imports.[286] He was one of many who appeared fatigued by the struggle, the insecurity and low returns on capital invested. In the long run, M. Macarez, president of the Société des agriculteurs du Nord, told an emergency meeting of the society in October 1884, the commercial treaties and low transport costs had 'profoundly modified our economic system'.[287]

The accumulation of competitive pressures had been gradual but constant. To observers it seemed also to be spreading, affecting an ever greater range of agricultural products and thus reducing the possibilities of compensation. It was noted in 1882, for example, in a report from the Beauce, that sugar beet refineries were closing because of German competition.[288] The Prefect of the Gers in 1884 registered the growth of anxiety about possible competition from meat imports from the USA. Salted meats had already appeared, and he had received information about experiments with refrigeration. Over the past decades large investments had been made in order to create pasture; now the returns from this also appeared threatened.[289] Only the producers of quality wines, heavily engaged in the export market, appear to have continued to object to protection[290] as the essential means of escape from a deepening crisis. By 1882 most producers of mass consumption wines were already in the depths of a crisis caused by the heightening of internal and international competition and the effects of phylloxera.[291] Most farmers, short of capital and lacking confidence, either could not or would not invest in raising productivity to levels which would have made them competitive on international markets. This anyway would have taken time. They pressed instead for immediate measures, above all protection, but in addition for concessions which would help them reduce costs – lower taxes, better credit facilities, lower rail charges and better rural roads.[292] Essentially, they demanded an improved economic context within which to work.

This was a political quite as much as an economic question. Pressure on government was continuous, although not always effective. It could safely be said that the mass of farmers were attracted by the idea of 'protection' without really thinking about it or understanding it.[293] The word had favourable connotations.

The mass of the rural population tolerated rather than welcomed the commercial treaties of the Second Empire.[294] Subsequently, as the productivity of peasant farms gradually increased and they found themselves with growing surpluses to sell on increasingly competitive markets, discontent with falling prices became much more intense. A protectionist campaign backed by falling prices could have proved an attractive political weapon, and clearly the prospect of such campaigns was viewed with great concern by successive governments. In 1859 it was claimed that political opponents of the regime in the north were using the anxieties of farmers to develop 'the spirit of opposition'.[295] The Second Empire was accused repeatedly of sacrificing rural interests to those of the towns, both because it favoured urban consumers with *le pain à bon marché* and because the policy of urban renewal had to be paid for by rural taxpayers.[296]

The growing volume of complaints caused governments increasing anxiety as the economic depression deepened and eventually required concessions. In 1884 the Prefect of the Haute-Saône reported, 'there is almost unanimity in favour of protection'. He added a warning: 'In spite of the sincerely republican sentiments of the majority of the population, it is not likely that they will vote for anyone, however devoted to the republic he may be, who declared himself to be a partisan of free trade.' According to his colleague in the Moselle, 'regardless of the merits of protection, the government urgently needs to act in order to prove to the rural population that it is not indifferent to their interests as its enemies claim'.[297]

Once the rural élite had been won over, governments were faced with the united will of the rural population. The rural élite increasingly favoured protection not simply out of consideration of the profit margins of its agricultural enterprises or because these increasingly appeared too low by comparison with other forms of investment,[298] but also because of the effects of competition from imports and the possibility of the extension of such competition at some unspecified time in the future (from American wines, for example).[299] Such was the lack of confidence and feeling of malaise in French agriculture. The solution to every problem, the universal panacea, appeared to be protection rather than technical improvement. Even when substantial innovation occurred, as in Picardy, agriculturalists still complained about the absence of protection,[300] perhaps because their already high profit margins would be further increased in a domestic market from which their only genuine competitors (i.e. foreign producers) were excluded. According to one of the most active propagandists for protection, Auguste Mimerel, what agriculture needed above all if capital were to continue to be invested, was confidence – and this depended upon protection.[301] Rather than accepting the conditions created by new market structures, agricultural interests contrasted price levels with expectations based on past experience. Their perceptions of the present and their hopes for the future were shaped by these expectations and the idealized construction of the past upon which they were based.

The introduction of tariff protection by other nations, as the world agricultural depression deepened, was another powerful argument advanced by French protectionists.[302] The reintroduction of protection should thus be viewed as a part of a general European response.

February 1881 brought a first tariff on animals and meat. In May 1885 a tariff of 3 francs per hectolitre on cereals was introduced, increased to 5 francs in 1887 and 7 francs in 1894 as price levels continued to decline, although the government reserved the right to suspend tariffs in exceptional circumstances – a right it exercised in spring 1898, following a poor harvest. A tariff of 2 francs on imported wines introduced in 1881 was increased to a minimum of 7 francs in 1892, or 25 francs in the case of Italian wines, whose competition had become particularly intense.[303] Not surprisingly, the main opposition came from merchants interested in the import trade, representatives of the ports and of consumer interests, although to some extent port and milling interests were protected by the old established practice of issuing special licences (*acquits à caution*) which permitted the import against nominal tariffs of stipulated quantities of grain against future export of flour (not necessarily from the port of entry).[304]

The restoration of tariff protection did not entirely prevent imports, although it succeeded in its aim of increasing French price levels. At the end of January 1911, for example, a *quintal* of wheat was priced at 18.42 francs in Chicago, 18.84 francs in New York, 18.98 francs in London and 18.87 francs in Brussels, with price differentials explained almost solely by transport costs. On the Paris market the price quoted was 27.50 francs because of the existence of a customs tariff of 7 francs per *quintal*.[305] The mechanism is an obvious one. Domestic production influenced price levels, which in turn acted to promote or discourage imports. Protection did not change this but served to postpone the moment at which importation was a profitable response.

For grain merchants in the 1880s and 1890s transactions were once again subject to uncertainty as successive tariff increases or the prospect of suspension of protective legislation following domestic harvest failure distorted patterns of trade. Those in the ports of import in particular were extremely critical of legislation which reduced volumes of trade and altered the direction of commodity flows.[306] One corollary of protection was, however, to increase the number of profitable transactions which might be conducted internally by means of movement from north to south in particular. This involved the covering of regional deficit by the supply of French grains whose basic costs of production and of transport were higher than those of imports. As we have seen, the Ministry of Public Works made continued efforts to influence the railway companies in order to ensure that movement of domestic produce was eased by more favourable charges. Thus the return to protection was accompanied by the deliberate manipulation of railway tariffs in favour of domestic producers. To some extent at least, the commodity flows from the ports inland which had built up during the free trade years were reversed as the competitive position of domestic producers was improved by these measures,[307] but the mobility of grains and the effectiveness of international market mechanisms were reduced.

Protection seemed to many contemporaries to be a social as well as an economic necessity at a time of low cereal prices and when other sectors of farming, and particularly the vineyards, affected by phylloxera, were also in deep crisis. Farming groups of all kinds desperately needed to be reassured. Politically it was hardly possible to stand against the tide. It is an illusion to believe that politicians could have resisted and asserted the need for international competition as a means of stimulating long-term structural change in agriculture. In strictly economic terms, numerous small farming units no doubt needed to go to the wall. They were economically unviable; but socially the families which lived on them were people with a problem, and politically they were people with a vote. The return to protection was a rational response to the problems of French agriculture as it then existed, a result rather than a cause of its economic weaknesses. In effect, the transition to free trade had been too rapid, and once American production expanded after the Civil War, many French cereal producers had need of protection. Protection largely succeeded in its aim of helping to restore the confidence of farmers, but it also had the effect of reducing the pressures to innovate and the rate of structural change both in patterns of land use and farm size.

Conclusion

In spite of the policy reversal represented by the return to protectionism, market structures had been disrupted permanently not only by the improvement of communications and the increase in imports but also by the growth of regional specialization as farmers adapted to opportunities and pressures.

Within limits, the improvement of communications allowed the more efficient working of the market mechanisms desired by liberal economic theorists – the enlargement of markets, the levelling out of price variations, regional specialization in production, more rapid innovation. Previously specialization had been limited by the widespread need to provide basic foodstuffs and by poor access to markets and lack of incentives. Farmers could not be sure of obtaining necessities; neither could they be certain that there was a good prospect of selling surpluses. Thus their first priority had been to achieve basic household sufficiency regardless of the market prices for subsistence crops, and their aim to market any surpluses was secondary. Cash crops which were compatible with subsistence crops within an overall agricultural system might be cultivated to earn some extra money. The opening up of the countryside by improved communications led to the more rapid development of specialization. It was no longer essential to produce basic necessities everywhere. Regular supply could be assured. It therefore became possible to adapt agriculture more efficiently to the environment and to market pressures. The process was gradual but more rapid than ever before. The interrelated development of market structure and agriculture had fundamental effects on both.

New opportunities were an incentive to change, and competitive pressures forced change. The decline in the relative importance of transportation costs increased the significance of other factors. The cost of production, rather than the cost of access to market, became the basic determinant in areal specialization. Even before the 1850s and 1860s, imports of grain through Marseille were reducing cereals cultivation in departments such as Aude and Hérault. The latter department obtained about one-fifth to one-sixth of its needs from outside its own area in 1850, but by 1862 this had risen to three-quarters, and Hérault was well on the way to becoming a region of monoculture.[308] Improved communications and free trade accelerated previous development. In this case competitive pressures were compensated for by new opportunities. Here, and in other southern departments such as Gard, soils and climate were less suitable for cereals than for the vine. The interest of agriculture was clear; it was obliged to 'purchase elsewhere all the cereals needed' and cultivate more suitable crops,[309] identified both by local natural conditions, which determined the cost of production, and by those of the specific commodity market. Gradually, as in the Var and Alpes-Maritimes, 'easier and more frequent relationships between farmers and the main centres of consumption . . .

[helped] the former to understand which [were] the products whose sale would give them the most certain and advantageous benefits'.[310] Specialization and higher production stimulated commercialization and increased the integration of farmers into extra-regional markets, both to buy and to sell.

The provision of modern communications did not necessarily or inevitably produce a concurrent commercial or technical response in agriculture. Everywhere it took time to organize commercial links and, in the case of wine, for example, to overcome consumer resistance based on initial preference for local vintages.[311] It also took time to determine whether competitive pressures were temporary or permanent,[312] to accept the risks implicit in a long cycle of production, especially in the case of vines or fruit trees. The faculty for adaptation by agriculture in response to a growing market is less rapid than in the case of industry; supply was inevitably less elastic. With the exception of the Paris basin, where specialization in cereals production increased, the Mediterranean wine-producing areas and, to a lesser extent, the centre-west, which increasingly specialized in livestock and dairy produce, there were relatively few instances of regional specialization. Substantial change occurred almost everywhere, but it generally took the form of the minimum necessary to preserve the equilibrium of existing agricultural systems as competitive pressures built up, as migration reduced labour supply and as the need to increase productivity both increased the size of surpluses for sale and required a continuing increase in investment and earning capacity. But for most farmers this participation in the market remained partial. Only a minority of efficient cultivators were *primarily* orientated towards the market and were in a position to compete effectively on international markets. For the others price depression and protection reduced the incentives to sell on the market on the one hand and the pressure to innovate on the other. The potential for change was reduced and its progress notably slowed. Moreover, regional imbalances in development survived. The most backward areas were characterized by inferior transportation systems, but this was only one of the reasons for their continuing backwardness, and perhaps not the most important, if one bears in mind differences in natural endowment. Thus the opening up of the Lozère and Haute-Ardèche or the southern Alps was not favourable to the agriculture of areas which could not find a specialized production to exploit and whose traditional products faced growing competition.

Commerce serves as the mediating element between demand and supply. Demand might well be the vital initiating force in agriculture, stimulating efforts to increase productivity and to commercialize the product, but demand is a complex variable. If demand for a variety of agricultural products substantially increased in the second part of the nineteenth century, for others demand fell or stagnated. Supply too was complex, depending on decisions by a mass of farmers and merchants in France and abroad and on government decisions about customs tariffs.

This chapter has considered changes in agricultural market structures in the second half of the nineteenth century, caused essentially by improvements in the means of communication. In the next chapter we shall be more concerned with farmers' responses to modifications in the markets for their produce.

9 Agriculture in a changing market

The development of modern communications networks was the decisive stimulus to innovation in agriculture in the second half of the nineteenth century. The changes in market structures which resulted provided both incentives and the threat of competition. In response two main options were open to farmers: they could seek to increase productivity, both of the land and of labour, by technical innovation or modification of their crop mix, or they could continue to farm in the traditional manner. The capacity to innovate was determined in large part by the structure of pre-existing agricultural and social systems – natural conditions, structure of land holdings, access to capital, crop mix, social attitudes – and their spatial relationship with the new means of communication which provided access to market and to information and also facilitated the introduction of new inputs. The main problem for the historian is that of assessing the relative significance of each of these variables. Their very different characteristics make precise measurement impossible, although statistical indicators will be used below wherever possible.

The two prime inputs of traditional agriculture were land and labour. Productivity was thus limited by the quality of the land and the amount of labour. In a modern agriculture productivity is substantially increased by inputs of working capital in the form of fertilizer and mechanical power. This shift seems to have been determined by the evolution of three basic groups of variables – product prices, factor prices and development of the economic infrastructure (i.e. of transport and marketing facilities) – an evolution which intensified the commercialization of agriculture by means of a 'two-way tie'[1] to the market economy through both the sale of products and the purchase of inputs. We are particularly concerned with the changes which occurred in the balance between the three categories so cherished by classical economists – land, labour and capital.

The first step will be to consider the key indicators of change in French agricultural productivity. Then the context for change will be examined: the basic structural characteristics of French agriculture, particularly farm structure (i.e. land use) and labour supply.

Productivity

Productivity can be calculated in terms of yields per hectare or per seed, but labour productivity seems more appropriate in this period when labour ceased to be abundant and its cost increased. In theory it ought to be possible to calculate labour supply in terms of $N \times C \times E$, where N is the number of workers available, C the number of days' labour supplied by a given category and E a measure of labour efficiency. Unfortunately, we have too little information about the categories of part-time labour, while the measurement of efficiency is impossible. We shall simply take into account the active male labour force. Similarly, only a simplified calculation of production is possible – in terms of its cash value, the only viable method of adding together the diverse products of the farm. The calculation of labour productivity has therefore to be reduced to the simplest possible terms: value of production/number of active male workers.

One cannot be entirely happy about the statistics used. René Musset has pointed out that the decennial inquiries which are our major source of statistical information were the work of a large number of untrained individuals conducting a very complex operation.[2] The questionnaires with which they were equipped in 1882 included 1253 questions. Even in the 1880s these inquiries were often received with complete indifference by those who were expected to supply or collate the information,[3] and the information supplied was frequently inaccurate. The Prefect of Meurthe-et-Moselle in November 1884 bemoaned his inability to give reliable information on levels and costs of production. The obstacles here were both primitive accounting on the part of farmers[4] and deliberate efforts to mislead the authorities because of the belief that information might be used for tax assessment.[5]

The preparation of the decennial inquiries was nevertheless more thorough than that of the annual agricultural statistics. Musset concludes that these 'were prepared, in each commune, using a questionnaire which was much too complicated, by the mayor's secretary, who usually possessed neither the competence nor the interest for this task. They usually contented themselves with modifying by estimation the figures of the previous year'.[6] There is no way in which biases and errors in this data can be satisfactorily corrected. Musset warns historians not to use these statistical series as the basis of a study. They might conveniently supplement other information or be used for illustrative purposes as a convenient shorthand method of indicating trends, but only if other indicators confirmed these trends.

In spite of obvious ill will, it is likely that with experience the accuracy of the returns increased,[7] but for the historian this creates another problem, that of the validity of comparisons between inquiries. If the value of production was under-estimated because of concern about taxation, this under-estimation was likely to have been more marked in the first inquiry in the series, that of 1852, which would give us an exaggerated impression of the increase in productivity by 1882, by which time returns might be expected to have become more accurate. In short, the apparent certainty offered by statistics is a dangerous illusion. Statistical information has to be employed with care and in relation to information gathered from a wide range of sources, which alone permits *critical* use of statistics. There is no easy alternative to the slow accumulation of diverse forms of information and the intimate knowledge of a society favoured by traditional historians.

The value of production is not a very satisfactory basis for the calculation of productivity, linked as it is with fluctuating market prices for a diverse range of products. Thus to a significant extent the increase in labour productivity between 1852 and 1882 is an illusion provoked by prices which rose at least until 1873, when price depression set in, and continued until 1896. It has, in fact, been calculated that whereas the value of production increased by 80 per cent, from 6050 million to 10,920 million francs, between 1852 and 1882, the *real* increase in production was only 25 per cent.[8] Estimates of annual rates of growth of production measured in constant prices (those of Toutain[9] and Lévy-Leboyer[10] – see Table 54) indicate a less dramatic achievement. These vary according to the way in which the basic statistics have been 'corrected', the definition of what precisely agricultural production includes, the periods considered, etc., but the general statistical picture is of an acceleration in the rate of growth from the 1830–40s, maintained at a relatively high level into the 1860s but then clearly slowing. Most, if not all regions, exhibit the same basic tendencies.

Besides price inflation, an increase in the value of products could have been due to an extension of the cultivable area and/or increased productivity per hectare. The statistics on the extent of the cultivable area suggest a limited increase, so that most of the expansion in production must have been achieved by increased productivity – by an intensification of production rather than extensification. This can be confirmed by calculations of increases in the yields of particular crops. Thus, to take the example of wheat, the average national yield increased from an estimated 13.64

Table 54   *Two estimates of the annual rates of growth of production, 1815–1914 (percentage)*

Period	Toutain	Period	Lévy-Leboyer
1845–54	1.07	1815/19–1874/78	1.1
1855–64	1.39		
1865–74	0.81		
1875–84	−0.48	1874/78–1900/13	−0.5
1885–94	0.34		
1895–1904	1.04		
1905–14	1.11		

hectolitres per hectare in 1852 to 18 hectolitres in 1882. The latter was, however, an exceptionally good year, and although 1852 provided a good harvest, this tends to exaggerate the extent of improvement. On a quinquennial basis the increase in wheat yields was of the order of 8 per cent rather than the 18 per cent suggested by the inquiries.

The increase in yields of other cereals was higher; estimates vary between 15 and 30 per cent. Potato yields increased by 10–15 per cent, sugar beet by 27 per cent, vine yields by 38 per cent, while meat production per hectare rose by 12 per cent.[11] Production statistics are another indicator both of increased productivity and of the changing mixtures of crops (see Table 55).[12]

The size of the active agricultural population is also an obvious influence on the calculation of productivity. In the period of transition from pre-industrial to industrial social structures significant changes in labour supply/demand relationships were taking place. Of special significance was the fact that the rate of population growth was far below that of contemporary Third World countries and that agricultural productivity increased more rapidly than population. In 1852 there were 100 male agricultural workers for every 459 inhabitants of France. By 1882, in spite of improvements in diet, 100 were able to provide food for 590. Admittedly, imports had increased, but the basic fact remained that a break-out had occurred from a predominantly subsistence agriculture into a more productive, commercialized system.

Figures 10 and 11 illustrate both the increase in labour productivity and its regional variations. They reveal that the gross product per agricultural worker increased by something like two and a half times over the three decades considered, and also that although increased productivity in both monetary and real terms was general, the scale and rate of increase varied considerably between departments. It should be noted, furthermore, that in spite of some substantial variations in rates of growth between departments within regions, the major existing regional differences in productivity were maintained. North of a line very roughly linking St-Malo and Geneva levels of productivity were above the national average, while to the south they tended to be lower. The Lyon and Marseille areas were the most notable exceptions to the rule. The poorest regions remained the upland zones of the Massif Central, Alps and Pyrénées, and Brittany with its high population densities. Later in this chapter I shall offer some explanations both for the general increase in labour productivity and for the survival of basic differences between regions.

Simple comparison of the net agricultural product per department is not entirely satisfactory, given differences in area and in the proportion of cultivable land each contains. Comparisons should therefore be on the basis of what French economic historians have labelled *surface agricole utile* (SAU), but this only slightly attenuates regional contrasts based on the simpler calculation.[13]

Table 55   Agriculture: annual average production, 1815–1914

Period	Cereals (millions of quintaux)	Potatoes (millions of quintaux)	Wine (millions of hectolitres)	Natural and cultivated pasture (millions of quintaux)	Roots (millions of quintaux)	Sugar beet (millions of quintaux)	Meat (millions of tonnes)	Milk (millions of hectolitres)	Butter and cheese (millions of tonnes)	
1815–24	86.44	25.30	37.24	—	—	—	548	43	113	
1825–34	97.02	42.16	40.17	—	—	—	602	47	127	
1835–44	111.60	63.26	38.65	178	(50)	16	685	58	153	
1845–54	126.08	49.79	47.92	268	50	18	823	63	167	
1855–64	138.89	68.77	48.42	313	52	44	972	73	193	
1865–74	140.89	80.26	60.44	360	90	77	1091	74	200	
1875–84	142.92	92.99	46.01	408	128	78	1251	74	200	
1885–94	147.39	118.04	30.70	418	143	64	1374	87	132	137
1895–1904	153.73	106.22	45.05	458	250	75	1464	81	150	154
1905–14	154.92	117.35	52.79	604	370	77	1535	109	170	174

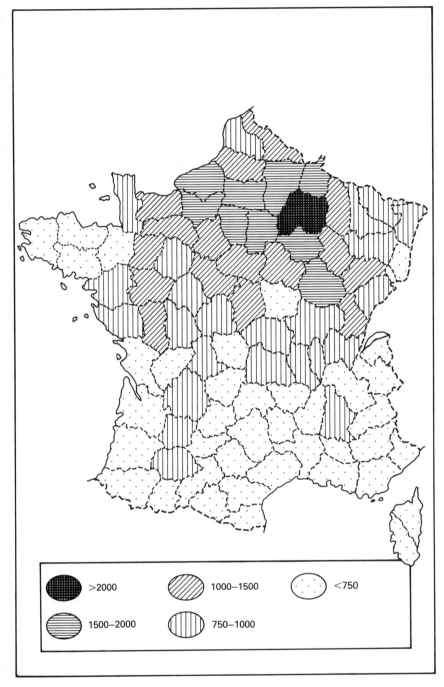

Figure 10   *Gross product per agricultural worker, 1852 (francs)*

The most favoured departments were those with relatively high rates of productivity per person and per hectare. Other departments had a high revenue per hectare, but demographic pressure resulted in a low average per worker – this was especially true of the west but also, to a lesser extent, of departments like the Pas-de-Calais, Seine-Inférieure and Rhône. The least favoured areas had low rates of productivity per hectare and per worker; these were, in particular, upland areas like the Ardèche, Lozère and Aveyron, where natural conditions limited the potential for improvement.

Agricultural structures and factors of production

Land

The question of farm size is of crucial importance to an understanding of the technical, financial and economic structure of farming in France. In effect, the mix of factors of production, labour and capital *tends* to be determined by the size of the farm.

Ideally, comparisons between the results of the 1852 and 1892 agricultural censuses would have provided us with a picture of structure and development from mid century, but differences in the categories preclude this. The 1862 and 1882 censuses have been used instead as a means of identifying trends. Comparison between the statistics of these two agricultural censuses is possible (see Table 56)[14] because the categories and definitions used are relatively homogeneous. These statistics combine to show a clear tendency towards parcellation – that is, a decline in the number of large farms and an increase in the number of smaller units which continued until the last decade of the century. Options varied between places and over time. The increase in the number of land holdings in consequence of parcellation tended to be a characteristic of areas in the south and west, regions of polyculture or else vine cultivation and market gardening. By contrast, in an area roughly north of the Loire subdivision of large farms was far less evident, with a clear

Table 56   *Number of farms by size, 1862 and 1882*

Hectares	1862	1882	Change	1882 as percentage of 1862
1–5	1,815,558	1,865,878	50,320	103
5–10	619,843	769,152	149,309	124
10–20	363,769	431,335	67,556	119
20–30	176,744	198,041	21,297	116
30–40	95,796	97,828	2,032	102
40 and above	154,167	142,088	12,979	92

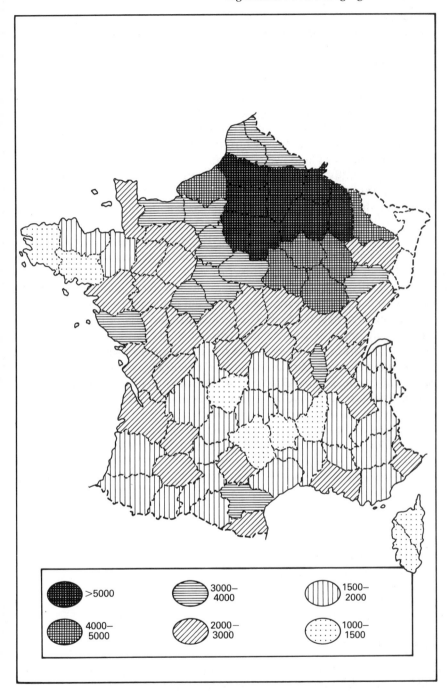

Figure 11 *Gross product per agricultural worker, 1882 (francs)*

tendency towards concentration in the centre of the Paris basin and especially in Valois and the Beauce. In lower Normandy the extension of cattle fattening encouraged an increase in the scale of farming. After phylloxera the expensive process of reconstitution of the vines reversed the process of parcellation in much of the south.

Large farms were the product of an old-established orientation to the market and the acceptance by both landowners and tenant farmers that income, whether in the form of rent or profit, could be maximized by an intensification of this capitalistic farming. Parcellation was the result of the growing tendency of landowners in many areas to transfer capital from the land to apparently more profitable investments. Division into small plots maximized returns from sales to peasants anxious to fulfil their dreams of landownership.[15] As George Grantham has pointed out, it was 'the rise of the wage that made large-scale farming less profitable [and] created the means for transferring its ownership to the peasants'.[16]

The coexistence of both market-orientated producers and those with a fundamental orientation towards provision for the subsistence of the peasant family constitutes a major analytical problem. Holdings below 10 hectares represented an estimated 68 per cent of the total in 1852, 85 per cent in 1882 and 84 per cent in 1908. The existence of such a large number of small units employing essentially family labour would have significant consequences for farm technology. However, the number of small farms should not be allowed to obscure the economic importance of larger units. Thus, according to the decennial inquiry of 1892 (and now excluding holdings of below 1 hectare, effectively gardens), holdings of over 40 hectares represented only 4 per cent of the total number but covered almost one half of the land farmed, with an average size of 162 hectares; those under 10 hectares included 76 per cent of the total number but covered only 23 per cent of the total area. The remaining 20 per cent of the total number and 30 per cent of area were held by medium farmers with 10–40 hectares.[17] Wage labour was employed essentially on the 24 per cent of farms above 10 hectares. As for forms of tenure, in 1892 75 per cent of the farms exploited were owned directly by those who worked them, but these covered only 53 per cent of agricultural land, with an average size of only 4.37 hectares; 6 per cent (mostly in the west and south) were sharecropped, covering 11 per cent of the farm land, with an average size of 10.70 hectares; and 19 per cent were rented, covering 36 per cent of the land and averaging 11.71 hectares.[18]

Labour

In analysing the factor labour we need to consider its supply conditions and subsequently labour as a social product which might be improved as a productive agent – in short, the changing significance of wages as a cost of production. It ought to be noted that labour as a factor of production (a complex variable) has to be considered as part of an evolving 'factor mix', which is itself determined by interaction with 'a multiplicity of variables of different types'.[19] Labour as a form of enterprise will be considered later.

Statistics are available on the structure of the agricultural labour force, but, like all the other agricultural statistics, they are not very accurate. Comparison between agricultural censuses, and between them and population censuses, is rendered difficult by the different categories used. Changes in these and uncertainty among enumerators as to which professions to include in particular categories mean that some apparent shifts in population or productivity might be mere statistical illusions caused by the revision of census categories.

A variety of forms of evidence, however, combine to suggest that whatever the statistical problems, certain basic changes in the balance between land and labour were occurring which resulted in a reduction in the supply of labour. This affected primarily those farms that were dependent for at least a part of the year on hired labour, but it also influenced family farms in so far as new crops were introduced into rotation systems and new demands thereby imposed on family members (see Table 57).[20] Stability in the overall size of the labour force should not be allowed to conceal intersectoral transfers, already evident in the 1850s, which had the effect of substantially

Table 57 *Agricultural labour force by status, 1862 and 1882*

| | 1862 | | 1882 | | |
	Number (thou-sands)	Per-centage	Number (thou-sands)	Per-centage	1882 as percentage of 1862
Landowners	1813	24.7	2151	31.2	119
Landowners who also rented land	649	8.8	500	7.3	77
Landowners who were also sharecroppers	204	2.8	147	2.1	72
Landowners who were also labourers	1134	15.4	727	10.5	64
Total landowners	3800	51.7	3525	51.1	93
Non-landowners					
tenant farmers	387	5.3	468	6.8	121
sharecroppers	202	2.7	194	2.8	96
labourers and domestics	2965	40.3	2707	39.2	91
Total non-landowners	3554	48.3	3369	48.8	95
Total employed in agriculture	7354		6894		94

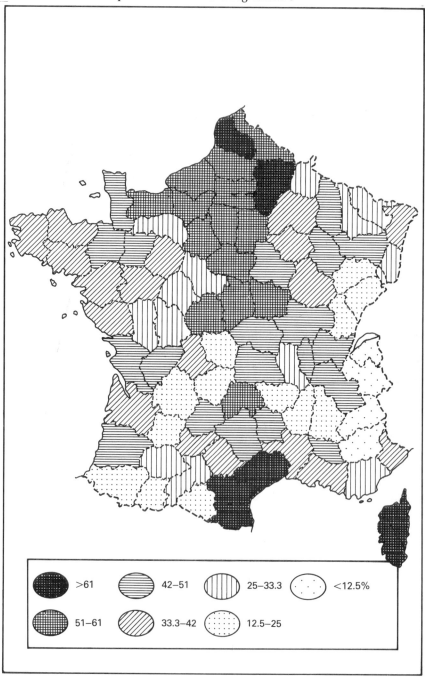

Figure 12   *Proportion of the agricultural population composed of wage labourers and their families, 1866*

reducing the numbers of labourers, both full-time and especially part-time. Many were able to purchase small farms during the prosperous 1850s and 1860s and became less dependent on hiring out their labour. Although comparison of the structure of the total agricultural labour force in 1852 with later years is difficult because of differences in the categories used, the censuses indicate a decline of some 1,172,000 male agricultural labourers between 1852 and 1862 due to migration and purchase of land.[21] During the following decades the same trends continued but at a slower pace. The result, during a period when agricultural labour needs were increasing, was a relative shortage of labour, especially during the seasonal peaks of demand.

Moreover, the available statistics do not take proper account of the reductions in supply consequent upon the withdrawal of part-time labourers who had previously also farmed some land or worked as artisans or in industry. This was especially serious because of the reliance on such marginal groups for work at the peak periods of demand such as harvest.[22] Such developments as the decline of the rural textile industry, the rapid closure of charcoal metallurgical establishments or the growing professionalization of the labour force in the mining industry had serious consequences for labour supply.[23] The availability of women and children as wage labour also began to decline gradually,[24] although again the significance of this is impossible to estimate accurately, given the paucity of statistics. On the small peasant farm intensification of cultivation often resulted in modifications in the division of labour and an exhausting accumulation of tasks by women.[25] During this period seasonal migratory labour flows were also disrupted, causing uncertainty for farmers in the Paris basin and especially Picardy, Ile-de-France, Brie and Beauce as well as in the south-east, which had been the major regions of influx.[26]

Most observers blamed labour shortage primarily on migration, and from the 1850s this was to be a matter of great concern to all those for whom urbanization represented the unwelcome death of the traditional rural civilization. Thus on such questions much of the evidence is emotive and unreasoned, coming as it does from the rural élite, who for a variety of reasons felt their economic situation and social authority to be under attack. Nevertheless, in this case other indicators, particularly information on wages, tend to confirm the existence of a growing shortage from the 1850s.

The labour-supply situation was influenced by the dual process of the intensification of agriculture (i.e. increasing labour needs) and reductions in the supply of labour. Migration from the countryside was a response both to the harsh work and miserable conditions of existence still prevailing for much of the population and above all – particularly among those with little or no land of their own, who faced the worst insecurity and unemployment – to an awareness of the possibility of a better life either in other rural areas or more especially in the towns.[27] The poorest migrated; the better-off sought material improvement by limiting the size of their families.[28] (Contraception was both consequence and cause of improving living standards.) The process of migration was stimulated by the long economic crisis of 1845–56, by the crisis of rural industry,[29] by the accelerated development of urban job opportunities,[30] and, in the 1870s and 1880s, by the crises affecting cereals, silk and vine cultivators.[31] Increases in wages in the countryside during the relatively prosperous 1850s and 1860s could do little to arrest it.[32] Respondents to the agricultural inquiries in 1866, 1870 and 1882 were aware of a fundamental change in the availability and cost of the primary agricultural input. Formerly the problem for employers of hired labour had been *l'embarras de choix*[33] in a situation of rural over-population. From the 1850s relative shortage was forcing increases in wages and thus substantially increasing costs.[34]

The significance of increased wages clearly varied greatly between the peasant holding and the large capitalist farms of the Ile-de-France. On the latter, to take the example of a farm with 225 hectares – 60 in beet, 80 in wheat, 40 in rye and 25 in lucerne – and with a small sugar refinery attached to the farm, the annual cost of labour might reach 50,000–60,000 francs per annum.[35] But if the problem was apparently more severe in such circumstances, superior capital resources made possible a response in the form of investment to increase yields and reduce unit costs of production.

Situations and attitudes varied among employers of labour. Most obviously, on the peasant farm labour was only a 'subjective cost', on the capitalist farm a 'monetary cost'[36] which had to be minimized if the enterprise was to survive at all. Some farmers were able to accept that increases in wages might be covered by higher productivity. Most, from the 1860s and particularly during the period of price depression, complained bitterly as their revenue was reduced and blamed the crisis on the absence of tariff protection and the failure of increases in productivity to keep pace with wages.[37] Wages were, without any doubt, the single most important item in costs, so that those who employed hired labour were faced with a major problem.

The rupture in the labour supply/demand equilibrium seems to have been most severe in the Paris basin, in the north and in departments near Marseille and Bordeaux. In spite of migration into these areas of relatively high wages, and although rural population densities in them remained relatively high, labour supply was nonetheless increasingly felt to be inadequate to needs. In these advanced regions although there remained little land worth clearing, the process of intensification continued. In Seine-et-Oise the spread of a four-year rotation system of wheat–oats–sugar beet–cultivated fodder is calculated to have doubled or even tripled labour needs in the second half of the century.[38] In southern France the extension of the vine significantly increased labour needs. Where a hectare of wheat might have required thirty days' labour a year, the same area under vines required

100 days.[39] The reduction of fallow – an estimated 6,700,000 hectares in 1840, 3,600,000 by 1882 – represented a substantial increase in the area under cultivation, as did clearance, especially in Brittany, the centre-west and Aquitaine. Furthermore, these processes tended to be accompanied by technical changes which increased yields and caused evident difficulties at harvest.

Although there is no comprehensive statistical basis for the analysis of wages, there is a great deal of fragmentary evidence which lends credibility to the suggestion that between 1851 and 1881 agricultural wages rose by over a half and generally by two-thirds to three-quarters. On the plateau between the Seine and the Oise, in the centre of the Paris basin, the average wage of the day labourer, fed on the farm, rose from 0.60 franc in 1820–30 to 0.75 franc in 1830–40, 1 franc in 1840–60 and 1.80 francs in 1860–75. In the Var wages for men rose from 1.50–1.75 francs in 1848 to 2.25–3 francs in 1866, and those for women from 0.50–0.60 franc to 0.75–1.25 francs.[40] Wage levels varied between places according to local relationships between the demand for and supply of labour, the extent of non-agricultural competition for labour resources, local foodstuff prices and local living standards and expectations.[41] But whatever the variation, the picture is one of an almost universal rise. This established a clear incentive to improve labour productivity.

In other regions the introduction of more intensive cultivation occurred more slowly, and the reduction in population levels had less serious consequences for labour supply. In practice, the continuing availability of labour would prove a disincentive to efforts to increase labour productivity. In the Nantes region, for example, social and cultural isolation reduced the desire to emigrate, preserved traditional sexual behaviour and high birth rates and kept people on the over-populated land. Rural population in most communes in the area continued to increase until the first decade of the twentieth century, reducing the pressure to improve tools and machinery and, because of the plentiful supply of labour, preserving a social situation marked by the dependence and subordination of labourers and tenants.[42]

Labour costs obviously presented more of a problem to employers of hired labour than to peasant farmers using essentially family labour. For the latter intensification meant increased hard work: the only limit was physical capacity and the desire for leisure. To some extent in the short term the problem of labour shortage was solved by the continuing parcellation of the land. Inter-sectoral shifts in labour, while worsening the situation for the larger farmers, also represented a response to labour shortage as larger labour-expensive units gave way to small peasant farms on which the cost of labour was hardly calculated. To some extent the problem was also lessened where increased real income led to improvement in the quality of labour through the improvement of diet. Although living conditions often remained 'deplorable', and a reply to the 1882 agricultural inquiry from La

Garnache (Vendée) could blame the continued prevalence of both rickets and apathy amongst peasants on this,[43] it does seem that dietary standards were improving generally and that increased robustness led to a greater capacity for work and to increased production, often in spite of a reduction in the number of hours worked.[44] Certainly, contemporary studies have indicated that a better diet reduces lethargy and inertia.[45] The improvement in productivity directly attributable to this is impossible to measure but was undoubtedly significant in that it involved the fuller realization of the physical potential of the labour force.

Contrasting views were put forward concerning the capacity of agricultural labour. Some observers maintained that higher incomes, together with the availability of more goods to purchase, stimulated ambitions. Workers were both encouraged, and physically able, to work harder.[46] Others maintained that the intelligent and energetic migrated to the towns, leaving only the less able workers in the countryside, but praise was also heard for the more intelligent performance of work by both farmers and labourers.[47] This development was usually associated with the growth of primary education.

Little is known about the effect of the acquisition of basic educational skills upon productivity in agriculture, but it is likely that as a shift occurs towards a more dynamic economic system, literacy acquires new value. It provides a means of access to technical and market information, facilitates book keeping and serves to demonstrate change as part of a general broadening of horizons. Literacy also encourages rationalization, stimulating the examination of alternatives and helping farmers to break with traditional modes of thought and action.[48] The Paris Chamber of Commerce in 1881 stressed the importance of book keeping for the selection of profitable techniques and products and asked that elementary accounting be taught in rural schools.[49] In the past, even on large farms like that of the Flahaut family, farming 100 hectares in the Béthune area, the accounts had been so badly kept as to make it extremely difficult to balance credit and debit,[50] while the accounting of the peasant farmer simply took the form of a constant effort to make ends meet.[51]

The circulation of information is necessarily the first step in any decision-making process, even if awareness does not guarantee action upon the basis of this information. The whole process of diffusion, of values and of technical knowledge, requires more detailed analysis. For some contemporaries ignorance, lack of education, was the major obstacle to change – 'the leprosy of our time'.[52] For as long as most of the population remained dependent upon the oral transmission of information, the process of change was slowed and contingent on restricted personal contacts based upon economic networks and, within communities, on those of 'opinion leaders'.[53] The establishment of a system of primary education provoked a major breach in the wall of custom, involving a systematic and sustained effort to inculcate a new outlook. This particularly benefited those who possessed land and capital but nonetheless also affected the aspirations and behaviour patterns of more deprived social groups.

It was indirectly, rather than through a specific orientation towards agriculture, that primary education affected productivity. There were, in fact, constant complaints about the uniform urban orientation given to teaching. If some efforts were made to provide the *instituteurs* with a useful knowledge of modern agricultural techniques, to encourage them to devote some time to the cultivation of the school garden and to provide them with textbooks,[54] these appear to have had little effect and to have remained at rather a theoretical level, incomprehensible to most pupils[55] and the object of contempt on the part of their fathers.[56]

Only for the rural élite of landowners and large farmers was some specialized education provided at the Institut national agronomique, the Ecole nationale d'agriculture and the various small *écoles d'agriculture*. These were expanding by 1880, but the number of places was pitifully small.[57] The secondary education provided by the *lycées* remained divorced from practical agriculture. The élite did, however, share in the significant form of informal education offered by the numerous agricultural societies, and the shows at which new techniques and equipment were demonstrated and prizes presented to successful farmers and long-serving labourers. There can be no doubt that these were an important method of diffusing information, but neither should it be forgotten that, controlled as they were by the rural élite, they sought primarily to cater for its interests rather than those of the peasant.[58]

The general lack of technical education must have slowed the process of adaptation to economic change. It meant that most farmers were primarily dependent upon the example of their fathers for technical instruction. Often the significance even of basic literacy was reduced by the poor quality of the education received and by widespread popular indifference. There was certainly substantial progress, as the statistics on school attendance reveal, but mere attendance does not produce functional literacy. The official statistics continue to conceal minimal standards of achievement. In the countryside attendance was often irregular and declined markedly in periods of peak agricultural activity, when children might be useful on the farms.[59] Regular school attendance was not made compulsory until 1882. The majority of children left school at 11 or 12 years of age, which was when most *instituteurs* seemed to feel that they were beginning to learn something.[60] Parents who offended against community norms by persisting in sending their children to school beyond this age were likely to find themselves accused of wanting to make them 'work-shy'. To many parents, illiterate themselves, learning appeared unnecessary.[61]

Popular attitudes towards education were, however, changing as part of the more general widening of horizons that saw the rapid capitulation of patois and regional languages in the face of French, regarded as the essential language of progress in a period in which the external world increasingly impinged upon the village community. They changed above all as the practical utility of education became evident, as farmers became involved more and more in commerce. This occurred first in the economically more advanced areas and among the better-off[62] and with the construction of the school network and the provision of more highly trained teachers by whom the younger generations were better educated than had been the older.[63] The relative prosperity of the 1850s and 1860s helped to accelerate this process and to create a generalized belief in the value of education which led to higher levels of literacy as a result of more regular attendance at school.[64] In effect, the development of primary education was an inseparable aspect of the process of economic development, of a change in values and outlook which called for a more calculating and critical attitude towards traditional farming methods. The creation of alternative sources of information challenged paternal authority based on traditional, empirically derived knowledge and community norms based on established practice.

Élite attitudes towards education for the poor remained ambivalent. They welcomed greater mental alertness, which resulted in productivity gains, but also frequently blamed the schools for migration and labour shortage, for a reduction in the employers' authority over hired labour and for the declining cohesion of the family group.[65] Employers everywhere appear to have been conscious of changes in their relationships with their workers, which amounted effectively to a reduction in their control over the labour force. This, it was claimed, was 'due especially to the certainty that the insufficient number of workers enables the former to find lucrative employment whatever their reputations and merit as workers'.[66] Employers always complain about their workers, but in this case a real change in relationships does seem to have been occurring. In practice, labour shortage improved the bargaining position of workers, and migration provided them with the opportunity for escape, enlarged their horizons and gave them new terms of reference. Workers were less submissive, revealing their distaste for past relationships which employers imagined they had freely accepted when in fact they had had no alternative where labour had exceeded demand and men had competed for employment. The change was swift and its consequences dramatic.[67]

Not only were there fewer workers, but many of those who remained had acquired some land of their own, were less available and could be more independent than in the past. Large farms in the Ile-de-France were forced into dependence upon Belgian and Breton harvest workers.[68] All these changes intensified the problems of supervision of the labour force. The growing frequency of disputes over wages exemplified the difficulties. These rarely took the form of strikes, and most passed unrecorded, but observers agreed that they were common.[69] Even when they judged that their employees worked as hard as in the past, employers felt that loyalty was more difficult to secure because workers no longer identified their interests with those of their 'masters', as it was presumed they had done previously. With incredulity and bitterness one respondent to the 1870 agricultural inquiry observed that now they worked only for money.[70] Thus more constant supervision became essential and piece work was introduced wherever possible, better organization of labour having positive effects on productivity.[71] Efforts continued to tie workers to particular farms in return for services such as the ploughing of their small plots or the provision of land for vegetable gardens or of tied cottages, especially for the more skilled.[72] Some employers pronounced themselves satisfied with the effects of these measures, but in general they were conscious of a growing distance between master and man.[73] This was due in part, as some admitted, to a growing gulf in life styles symbolized by the disappearance of shared meals at the 'patriarchal table' as the better-off farmers developed a taste for comfort and 'polite' company.[74] Both sides grew more conscious of class difference. The alarm that this caused, intensified by memories of 1848, encouraged a systematic national campaign to improve social control, particularly through the education system and the inculcation of Christian morality, discipline and respect for authority.[75]

This apparent digression is of importance because changed conditions affected not only wages and social relationships but also the attitude of mind of those who, through the provision of capital, could increase the productivity of agricultural labour. The persistent reluctance to invest was a consequence not only of the existence of competing investment opportunities but also of lack of confidence and a growing distaste for their social situation on the part of those landowners and farmers who possessed the bulk of the available capital.

Capital

Agricultural systems undergoing modernization require substantial capital inputs in spite of the fact that change is limited and relatively slow. In this respect the rate of innovation is determined partly by the availability of capital. Toutain has estimated that between 1851–3 and 1873–82 the value of capital invested in agriculture increased by between 34 and 41 per cent (or 14–26 per cent excluding land). The variations are mute comment on the shortcomings of agricultural statistics. While the value of buildings and of 'material' inexplicably stagnated, investment in livestock increased by 107 per cent. But even in 1878–82 the value of livestock + 'material', compared with land and buildings, was only about 9 per cent (9 milliard francs as against 98 milliard).[76] The distribution of capital between farm types and regions is unknown. Capital shortage, however, inevitably confined the more expensive innovations to the minority of commercial farmers – to some of the 800,000 or 900,000 who in 1882 habitually had a surplus to sell in the market. This meant that the other three-quarters of all *exploitants* who were less completely involved in commercial agriculture[77] were likely to be restricted to the less capital-intensive forms of innovation.

Increased productivity in the nineteenth century was thus founded essentially upon increase in the cultivable area, changes in rotation systems which replaced fallow with roots and cultivated fodder, increased numbers of livestock and improvements in the supply of manure and draught power, and the extension of liming and marling. These were changes which could be implemented on small farms and which accommodated themselves to regional situations in which abundant labour remained available. More expensive investment, particularly in machinery, was, as we shall see, especially slow to spread and, with the notable exceptions of improved ploughs and threshing machines, was restricted to large farms experiencing labour shortage.

While accepting that capital needs were restrained one should not make the mistake of under-estimating the problems faced by contemporaries in accumulating satisfactory amounts. More expensive and more intensive cultivation required more draught animals and more human labour. Fertilizing agents, tools, new buildings, selected livestock and seeds all cost money.[78] A clear statement of the new capital requirements of the commercial farmer was made by the Chambre d'agriculture of the *arrondissement* of Compiègne in 1879:[79]

The increased cost of labour, the development of industrial farming, specialization in livestock, the suppression of payment in kind have doubled, often tripled fixed capital needs and have increased working capital needs tenfold. In the old three-year rotation with fallow, cultivated partly in fodder and a small part in roots, there were few improvements to make to the soil; little additional fertilizer, little labour; the work proceeded regularly and had no need of supplementary teams of oxen which require large investments of capital each year. The sheepfold and the cow shed renewed themselves, labour was paid largely in kind . . . cash payments were made in two instalments and always after the harvest . . . the equipment – all very simple – lasted indefinitely and was repaired by the village wheelwright and blacksmith; in conclusion . . . one sold always and made purchases never; poor crops did not create financial crises; one postponed payment of rents – this was all the credit needed.

Today the need to produce more obliges us to make all kinds of investments in the land; the price of animals has doubled, and the need to specialize in . . . livestock breeding and fattening . . . requires numerous annual transactions which have to be completed rapidly; then draught animals from which we demand incessant work rapidly become exhausted and need frequent renewal, besides the need for extra teams which requires a large capital. . . The cost . . . of tools and machines has increased most and . . . together with the labour employed, makes up one-quarter to one-third of our capital, a proportion which varies in inverse proportion to the size of the farm.

This survey does not take account of the need to reconstruct and extend farm buildings to store increasingly large harvests and new equipment, and to provide stabling to reduce the wastage of manure.[80] According to an estimate for a farm of 150 hectares in the Beauce, the amount of capital employed had risen from 400 francs per hectare in 1865 (i.e. 60,000 francs in all) to 700 or 800 francs per hectare (a total capital of between 105,000 and 120,000 francs) in 1882.[81]

Even the peasant farmer was to some extent affected by this growing need to purchase inputs which he had formerly produced himself or had exchanged with neighbours. Furthermore, during the prosperous years of the Second Empire many had developed a taste for minor luxuries which they would subsequently find difficult to renounce. Goods like coffee or sugar or better clothes became necessities.[82]

Although peasant farmers continued to spend as little as possible and to rely on family labour rather than capital inputs, their situation had changed. A slow increase in the level of investment occurred as awareness of the new opportunities and competitive pressures built up and also in response to particular crises like that of phylloxera. French agriculture slowly entered a phase in which 'the modernization of traditional agriculture [was] closely associated with increase in the use of forms of capital which [were] produced off the farm'.[83] The rate at which innovation could occur was in large part determined by the availability of capital, and this to a considerable degree reflected pre-existing processes of profit earning and capital accumulation, together with the degree and speed with which farms could increase marketable output in order to finance new inputs. Given the farm structures of the period and the existence of a free market system, the process of accumulation and change was inevitably slow. Thus if in absolute terms capital needs might appear to have been small, in relative terms (i.e. in terms of the capacity of most farmers to accumulate) they were far from negligible.

Lack of capital was therefore a major obstacle to increasing productivity. The departmental *professeur d'agriculture* in the Ardennes, writing in 1884, claimed that shortage of capital was paralysing progress. The *comice agricole* at Lanmaur (Finistère) insisted that it 'condemned' local farmers to following traditional techniques.[84] Significantly, observers frequently linked this with the diminishing supply of labour. For many the problem was that neither the traditional means of increasing production through the intensive use of labour nor the new means, that of increasing capital inputs, appeared to be open to them.[85] Yet capital was not entirely lacking, so we need to consider to what degree that which was available was invested in agriculture and subsequently the effectiveness of this investment.

From Toutain's calculations it appears that during the period of prosperity in the 1850s, 1860s and 1870s, when the value of production increased rapidly and substantially, relatively little of the gain was reinvested in the means of increasing productivity. It was the will to invest as well as the lack of capital which limited technical advance in agriculture.[86] Investment behaviour was determined by a complex of factors including perceived opportunity, which varied between regions and social groups, and among which must be counted non-economic motives which affected 'the form in which savings are held and the goals towards which they are used'.[87] Thus although from the 1850s the price movements of agricultural commodities and the increased size of the marketable surplus accelerated the rate of capital accumulation, this did not necessarily entail a commensurate increase in investment. Certainly, by comparison with periods of low prices both before and after, the situation prevailing from the early 1850s into the 1870s was more encouraging to investors.[88] The overall tendency for prices to rise and the existence of favourable terms of trade with non-agricultural sectors did much to establish a climate of confidence. The investment process itself was cumulative. The cycle of modernization accelerated as investment increased production and sales at increasing prices provided capital for further investment. Technical change, by raising the marginal productivity of capital, tended to increase income and to encourage investment.[89] Subsequently, in the period of price depression, although farmers were encouraged to invest in increasing productivity to offset low prices, and no doubt many did, the usual picture is one of efforts to reduce expenditure to a minimum and so balance receipts and expenses.[90] Low rates of capital accumulation and an increasingly unfavourable price relationship with industry further contributed to the reduction of investment.[91]

This ignores the problem of farm structure, which had vital effects on the propensity to save and invest. Where the money earned was dispersed among a large number of farm enterprises, as it was in most regions, only piecemeal reinvestment could be generated. The peasant farmer faced with the problem of initial capital accumulation and with only a limited marketable surplus could hope to accumulate capital only very gradually even in the most favourable general market conditions. It was the large farms that accumulated capital in sufficient volume and with sufficient rapidity to make substantial innovation possible. Their very existence, of course, represented the prior accumulation of capital, from which process, in more favourable circumstances, they were able to enjoy considerable benefits. As a result, existing social and regional differences were confirmed, and these were to become especially marked in the succeeding period of price depression, when, on the basis of superior technology and capital resources, the gulf between 'efficient' and 'backward' producers became even more evident, and the latter entered a long period of technical stagnation.

A useful distinction might be made between capital-attractive and non-attractive sectors. The former would include the large commercial farms of Flanders, Picardy, the Paris basin and Normandy, but also farms in departments such as Mayenne, in which agriculture attracted capital from the declining textile industry, and the developing zones of vine cultivation especially in Languedoc prior to phylloxera, which attracted substantial peasant as well as noble and bourgeois investment, again including capital diverted from textiles.[92] It is safe to assume, however, that in general agriculture provided most of its own capital. This was certainly true of *petite culture*, which tended to follow traditional routines through ignorance but also because of lack of capital.

Peasants preferred to invest in land, the traditional source of security and status, rather than in means of increasing productivity, and they were likely to remain under-equipped in terms of tools and fertilizers.[93] This preference created unfavourable circumstances for capital formation. Productivity tended to be low and cash earnings limited. A vicious circle existed in which, for as long as cash earnings were low, the peasant was forced to grow the food his family needed. The resulting failure to specialize in conformity with soil and climate was a basic cause of low productivity and helped to maintain these earnings at a low level.

It is hardly possible to apply to the average peasant farm the forms of analysis that one would use normally to judge the economic performance of an enterprise. Economic rationale and the choice of techniques were subordinated to social criteria, that is, the provision of the family's basic needs. The peasant farmer was above all dominated by a short-term rationale. Although, significantly, assessments of what were minimal standards of living began to change markedly during this period, the land remained 'a means to live and not capital to make remunerative'.[94] Most peasant farmers continued to ignore such concepts as return on capital invested and rate of profit. As they employed essentially family labour, there was no need to assess the cost of work performed in terms of the wages paid.

Traditionally, time meant little to the peasant. There were tasks to perform on the land – the repair of tools, carting from field to farm and farm to market – and the farmer simply worked until these were completed. Thus there was far less pressure on the peasant farmer to introduce labour-saving innovations and a strong reason, given his lack of disposable capital, to minimize these.[95] Even when he sold much of his produce in the market these attitudes were slow to change.

Just like peasant proprietors, tenants and sharecroppers on small farms were under-capitalized. After paying their rents they normally retained only minimal profits and tended to save their money in the hope of purchasing land one day. Generally, leases were held to be too short to justify investments in increased productivity by the tenants themselves. According to the 1862 inquiry, of 568,688 farms 96,555 were tenanted on three-year leases, 142,632 on six-year leases, 288,390 on nine-year leases and 41,111 had longer leases.[96] Long leases were especially common in the north,[97] but large-scale farmers in the rich Beauce region complained that even nine years was too short to allow profitable investment.[98]

If tenants were to invest, a degree of confidence between proprietor and tenant was essential to guarantee the latter tenure for long enough to benefit from his investment and preserve him from rent increases which otherwise would threaten potential additions to his income. Customary practices gave the tenant some protection in many areas, but this did not eliminate insecurity or the temptation to exploit the natural fertility of the soil as much as possible just in case a lease was not renewed rather than, for example, investing in fertilizer.[99]

Without security the processes of capital accumulation and investment were seriously hindered. In most cases capital was anyway minimal and was likely to be rapidly exhausted by the initial costs of entry into a property.[100] Basic equipment, seeds, etc., were all relatively expensive.[101] The survival of sharecropping especially in the south and west, was indicative of capital starvation on the part of the tenant. In general, the contractual obligations and social relationships implied by this system severely constrained the tenant's own initiative, as a sharecropper at Castets (Landes) implied when he reported in 1882: 'I have undertaken to cultivate the land . . . following local usages.'[102] It should not be ignored, however, that there were cases where paternalistic landowners were interested in agricultural innovation and where their domination facilitated change. In Mayenne, for example, the north of the department was relatively backward, in part because landowners simply leased their land and behaved as *rentiers*. In the south, where sharecropping was common, landowners were interested far more in the activities of their tenants.[103]

Most tenants outside the rich cereal-growing plains were in fact subsistence farmers, often of the poorest kind. Payment of rents caused a significant depletion of their incomes. Peasants tended to rent (and to purchase) land at prices above those which might be paid by a capitalist farmer concerned with the potential rate of return on his investment. Their motives for purchase – especially the desire for security – were different. The payment of rents involving transfers of capital to landowners increased the significance of the latter's investment policy and made all the more obvious the importance of social structure for the development of the rural economy.

The investment behaviour of most large landowners was not such as to compensate for the lack of capital among peasant farmers. Generally, landlords continued to behave primarily as *rentiers* drawing income from their farms while reinvesting as little of it as possible and failing to provide an example of good husbandry. There is also evidence of considerable expenditure by resident landlords on the refurbishing of mansions and on such socially paternalistic measures as church building, both of which must have diverted considerable sums away from productive investment.[104] This serves as a reminder that the estate was conceived of traditionally by its owners more as a social entity than simply as an economic unit.

Ill-informed tenants and peasant proprietors in most areas required a lead from those better able to afford risks before they would innovate themselves. This was a key channel in the process of diffusion of technical innovation. The social prestige of the landowner often encouraged imitation. Thus in Haute-Saône during the Second Empire there were only some hundred farm units of over 50 hectares, but their real significance was their involvement in commerce and their aptitude for innovation.[105] In Calvados the introduction of colza into rotation systems from the 1840s began on the large farms, was encouraged by an élite of large-scale landowners and slowly spread.[106] In areas with large farms such as the Beauce rich tenant farmers usurped this traditional leading role of the proprietor.[107]

Many active farmers and landowners were, however, to be discouraged by unfortunate experiences of innovation. M. de Sauvage, an agronomist at the Institut national agronomique at Versailles, maintained in 1882 that many local farmers had recently spent, in addition to the normal 1400 francs per hectare, a further 1800 francs on manure and chemical fertilizer over a period of three years, when the returns over the same period had amounted to only 2900 francs. Careful accounting would have indicated that no more than 900 francs should have been spent on fertilizers if profitability were to be assured. Beyond this level the law of diminishing returns set in with a vengeance.[108] Optimistic investments made in the years prior to the period of price depression were rewarded often with disappointing returns as prices fell.[109] For a variety of reasons interest in agriculture on the part of those with capital seems to have been declining in the last three decades of the century. As population pressure and competition for the land fell, and particularly with the onset of price depression, income from rents tended to decline.[110] Landowners were forced to accord delays in payment, and subsequently reductions in rent, to tenants who could no longer afford to pay rents established in more prosperous periods.[111] Even in 1861, according to a report on the Nancy area, while landowners who cultivated their own land had gained a return on their capital of about 6 per cent, those who rented out their land earned only some 2.5 per cent.[112] Subsequently, the poorer the quality of the soil, the greater the dependence on cereals and the farther from market, the larger tended to be the reduction in both rents and the value of land.[113]

It became evident to many landowners that the sort of return likely from a tenanted farm was inadequate, given the rise in the cost of living and the comparison with the returns from alternative forms of investment. As most large landowners were not attracted by the prospect of farming their own land, this could lead only to a diversion of capital from agriculture, resulting both in the limitation of technical improvement and, in some situations, in regression as necessary maintenance was neglected.

Capital drainage occurred through the payment of rents to absentee landlords, much of the income from which was attracted by the growth of easily accessible and apparently secure investment alternatives in the form of public borrowing and railway and other shares. From the 1880s the development of branch banking made investment all the simpler. Life became a great deal easier for a former landowner freed from the difficulties of relationships with tenants and labourers or those caused by fluctuating harvests and revenue.[114] Increasingly it was the will to invest in agriculture, rather than the existence of spare capital, that was lacking. Landowners frequently stinted on investments or sold land, generally in small lots – the existing units of exploitation – in order to maximize returns.[115] Désert shows, however, that even at the end of the nineteenth century in Calvados 40 per cent of the land was owned by non-resident proprietors. Others, while technically resident, spent much of the year in their town houses, a form of dual residence which was expensive in terms of the outflow of capital.[116] In the long run the growing tendency to sell land would have the effect of reducing the outflow of capital caused by rent payments, but in the short term the act of purchasing increased this outflow.

Capital drainage should be analysed on a regional as well as on a social basis. An economically dynamic region would tend to drain the capital from less active areas in the form of both direct investments and payment for goods, causing internal 'balance of payment' difficulties. The Paris region, the north and for some time the Languedoc vineyards were obviously in a more favourable position and less likely to suffer from capital shortage. High rates of return on investment in agriculture, the product of previous technical development, allowed such regions to continue to attract capital and to maintain relatively high rates of investment. Everywhere, however, development in the non-agricultural sectors of the economy and new fashions in investment inevitably limited the amount of capital available for agriculture.

The obvious alternative to the investment of accumulated savings was to borrow. The problem was that those who possessed the kind of security which made them worthy credit risks were increasingly uninterested in investment in agriculture, while the mass of peasant farmers were not favoured by the existing credit institutions. For them the cost of borrowing remained high, although outright usury appears to have declined in significance as rural prosperity and savings increased. At Aunay in Calvados in 1870 interest rates were about 7 per cent per annum for the small proprietor and 8–9 per cent for the tenant farmer.[117] Most small farmers were reluctant to borrow at such rates because of the risk of future ruin which they implied – particularly when earnings might equal only 2.5–3 per cent on the capital invested.[118] In any case, in their obsessive rush to purchase land too many peasants were already over-extended.[119] Successive inquiries into the problems of agriculture highlighted the lack of cheap and easily accessible credit facilities. The Crédit agricole, a subsidiary of the Crédit foncier, established in 1860 specifically to lend to agriculture, in practice made loans available only to large-scale farmers.[120] During the same period many traditional sources of borrowing were drying up. The wealthy members of the communities whose knowledge of their neighbours had helped them to sort out good from bad risks were increasingly attracted to more secure investments in stocks and shares, which appeared to offer 'a better return for much less effort'.[121] As land values fell in many areas, and with them the security offered to the lender, the latter was less and less interested in what appeared to be a rapidly depreciating asset.[122]

The overall result of investment behaviour was to reduce the capital input into agriculture to peasant savings, plus the increment remaining after the transfer of landlord and capitalist farmer capital into non-agricultural sectors. Discussion of the nature of technical innovation and also its geographical variation will provide more detail about investment behaviour and its effects.

Innovation

Changes in land use

Innovation occurred in patterns of land use, through improvement of the soil and of hand tools and machinery. First we shall consider innovations in land use, which were essentially labour-intensive in character. As the statistics on land use in Table 58 indicate,[123] one of the few clear indications of change was the decline of fallow. This was the essential base for increased production in the first half of the nineteenth century.

It ought to be noted, however, that the designation 'fallow' is somewhat misleading. Far from being unproductive, the fallow provided pasture and in practice was often partially cultivated. By 1852 there was little left in the Paris basin. At the other extreme were departments like Cantal and Lozère, where intensive agriculture had hardly appeared. In the next three decades the decline was most marked in Brittany and the south-west. By 1882 the proportion of the arable in fallow varied between departments from 0.4 to 30.5 per cent, remaining most significant in the north-east, centre and south.[124]

Replacement of fallow by rotation systems which included cultivated grasses, nitrogen-fixing plants which regenerated the soil (particularly when residues were left *in situ*) and cleaning plants which substantially reduced the number of weeds, all had the effect of directly increasing yields. They had the added advantage of allowing the retention of increased numbers of livestock, which increased the supply of manure. These innovations had spread rapidly in the Paris basin in the first half of the century and into other areas subsequently. They not only increased the product of farms by allowing the cultivation of land formerly bare or carrying snatch crops but also substantially improved the returns from the crops which followed them in rotation. Moreover, the cultivation of fodder in areas of the centre, south and west allowed the clearance and cultivation of waste land which had served formerly as an essential source of pasture.[125]

Table 58   *Land use, c.1821–1910 (thousands hectares)*

Land use	c.1821	1840	1852	1862	1872	1882	1892	1902	1910
Arable land	25,500	25,227	26,139	26,569		25,588	25,387		23,679
Fallow	6,763	6,763	5,148				3,368		
Cultivated grass						2,730	2,549	3,322	4,051
Roots						297	360	533	980
Wheat	4,753	5,532	6,985	7,473	6,938	6,908	6,987	6,564	6,554
Oats	2,498	2,899	3,263	3,324	3,397	3,611	3,813	3,832	3,991
Rye	2,574	2,725	2,454	1,928	1,868	1,744	1,542	1,332	1,212
Barley	1,073	1,188	1,040	1,087	1,088	976	916	694	748
Maize	566	632	602	586	698	548	559	503	482
Potatoes	564	922	829	1,234	1,151	1,345	1,512	1,458	1,547
Sugar beet		58	111	136	253	237	254	253	247
Flax		98	80	105	83	54	27	22	22
Hemp		176	125	109	128	74	45	21	14
Oil seeds		174		290	226	158	90	48	42
Natural meadow					4,115	4,115	4,403		4,884
Pasture	5,159	4,198	5,057	5,021	1,422	1,421	1,517		1,568
Grazing									3,610
Vineyards	2,088	1,972	2,191	2,321		2,197	1,800		1,600
Wasteland and uncultivated	7,138	9,191	6,580	6,546		6,253	6,226		3,909
Forests	7,688	8,805		9,317		9,455	9,522		9,329

The cultivation of sugar beet in particular offered substantial advantages. It required large amounts of manure or fertilizer and needed deep and careful ploughing to eliminate weeds. Remunerative in itself because of its sugar content and the animal feed it provided, its cultivation improved the soil and substantially increased the yield of the cereal which followed it. In Flanders and Picardy it largely supplanted clover, lucerne and sainfoin in rotation systems in the second half of the century. Its introduction depended, however, on the availability of substantial capital for the purchase of seed and to cover the cost of large amounts of manure, deep ploughing, weeding and thinning out. It required a market in the shape of a sugar refinery, which in turn depended on cheap transport and cheap fuel. Cultivation of sugar beet appears to have been particularly profitable where sugar or alcohol refineries were established as an integral part of the farm complex. It was much less so, particularly in the market conditions of the last third of the century, where the beet was sold on the open market or was subject to long-term contracts.[126] All these reasons explain the tendency for sugar-beet cultivation to be concentrated in the north, gradually spreading into the centre of the Paris basin. In 1882 four-fifths of total production occurred in the five departments of Nord, Aisne, Pas-de-Calais, Somme and Oise. Fodder beet was spread more widely especially in the west and east, constituting 233,878 hectares of the total of 508,421 hectares under beet in 1884.[127]

For a variety of reasons, the introduction of new rotation systems and the elimination of fallow progressed slowly. Many small farmers could not afford the investment or were unprepared to take the risk. As late as 1861 the aristocratic Société d'agriculture of the department of Vienne questioned the value of cultivated fodders, considering that they might exhaust the soil.[128] More generally, on peasant farms products were selected on the basis of family needs, the obligation to produce a cash crop and in order to regularize and to space out the labour required. Thus any transformation of a rotation system required the introduction of a new crop which did not upset existing labour routines or threaten subsistence. Rotation systems were publicized which had been designed to suit the conditions of the rich northern plains. They were not suitable everywhere. There were enough false starts involving the introduction of rotation systems unsuitable for local conditions to confirm the wisdom of caution.[129]

Peasant agriculture was not merely an occupation or a source of income; it was a way of life. The theoretical concepts sometimes employed by economic historians, which tend to be borrowed largely from neo-classical economic theory, are not entirely appropriate to the analysis of peasant farming. Peasant farmers were not stupid or irrational. They were cautious. They responded to economic incentives and opportunities but their ability to respond was necessarily determined largely by the economic, social and natural environments within which they worked. Ill-informed, lacking capital, with little margin above basic subsistence needs in case of failure, it is hardly surprising what was so often castigated by outside observers as mindless routine tended to be viewed by its practitioners as respect for past experience. Within an authoritarian family structure the elders represented a repository of wisdom and practical knowledge which reinforced this commitment to the past.[130]

The kind of risk aversion deeply rooted in peasant tradition was difficult to overcome. The peasant did not require just empirical proof of the suitability of particular innovations; he tended to be sceptical about the necessity of change and suspicious of innovators. Within this context those alternatives which appeared to carry the least risk, which cost little and which involved minimal disturbance of existing crop systems were preferred. Caution meant that the innovators in a locality were followed only slowly by a majority of farmers.[131] This was especially true in those regions in which land was most subdivided, rural society most egalitarian and the influence of innovating landowners or large-scale farmers most restricted.[132] The presence of influential *notables* made it more likely that the norms of economic behaviour would change. They served as intermediaries, providing an orientation external to the village social system. Social structures and behavioural norms could otherwise act as major obstacles to change.

Caution meant the continuing and widespread survival of subsistence polyculture. The memory of subsistence crises within the lifetimes of many of the decision-makers of the later nineteenth century doubtless influenced their subsequent action.[133] The *Chambre d'agriculture* of the *arrondissement* of Argèles (Hautes-Pyrénées) claimed in 1870 that 'as for the choice of crops, the population is concerned to produce all the food it consumes and finds it difficult to understand the advantage of crops more suitable to the climate and grown with a speculative purpose'.[134] The cultivation of cereals for auto-consumption was gradually affected by the decline of cereal prices from the 1860s, but market price movements were not for most peasant farmers a sufficient reason for the replacement of one crop by another.[135]

Even though assuming a more significant place as cash needs increased, commercial crops continued to take second place to the peasants' concern with subsistence. Most peasant farmers sought to combine an assured supply of basic foodstuffs with increased sales by means of the continuous marginal improvement of their polycultural systems. But for as long as cereals remained the basis of these systems the margin for evolution was necessarily limited. As late as 1882, it is estimated, three-quarters of all *exploitants* were only marginally involved in production for the market.[136]

Peasant farmers introduced new plants once their success had been empirically proven. This was inevitably a slow, piecemeal process but gradually brought into existence a new, more intensive *petite culture*.[137] It made possible increased yields through modifications of land use. This was the primary means of increasing productivity. Most simply, and thus most often, it was achieved by improving existing polycultural systems rather than by their rapid transformation, through a process of selection between potential cash crops and a gradual move towards specialization.

The extension of the vine in southern France was, nevertheless, relatively rapid. Improved access to urban markets provided an immense stimulus to wine production. This was the essential causal factor. Production was increased by means of an extension of the area under vines and by increase in yields through the introduction of higher yield plants and more intensive cultivation. An assured supply of wheat from other regions and, with free trade, from international suppliers led to an acceleration in the replacement of cereals by vines.[138] This decline was not uniform either in time or in space. Wheat cultivation, for example, increased in the 1850s following poor harvests and again during the phylloxera crisis, when it replaced infected vines. Moreover, changes in the nature of production for the market in response to demand and price movements took time. They required capital and some assurance that perceived demand trends were more than short-term fluctuations.[139] Nevertheless, the end of the necessity to ensure self-subsistence in case of dearth allowed a wider margin for change, while the reduction of fallow permitted the farmer both to sell more and to provide for family subsistence. Relatively high wine prices until the 1870s, combined with barely profitable cereal prices in the south, to make cultivation of the vine a far more attractive prospect than a low yield cereal production.[140]

Small landowners and day labourers who were able to acquire land could hope to earn enough from their small plots to ensure better living standards for their families than the traditional polyculture had allowed. According to one estimate, even the sharecropper was enjoying prosperity and earning a return of 5–6 francs per day on his labour, when previously he had been lucky to make 1.5–2 francs.[141] Not surprisingly, in these conditions the cultivation of the vine became a popular craze. Small peasants grew enough cereals to meet their bare subsistence needs but nothing for sale.[142] Wine became their cash crop. Its initial success led to decisive shifts within traditional polycultural systems in the direction of increased dependence upon the market. This contrasted with the experience of the first part of the century, when the extension of the vine had been much more gradual, restrained both by lack of demand and by the need to preserve a subsistence polyculture. The cultivation of vines now spread from the hillsides and over the more fertile plains.[143] At the same time cultivation of the vine declined rapidly in regions at the climatic margin – in Oise, Seine, Seine-et-Oise and Aisne, for example – wherever low quality wine for popular consumption was now unable to compete with wine transported cheaply from the south.[144]

In much of the Midi, where soil and climate were unsuitable for cereal cultivation or for the introduction of fodder crops, the vine provided a means of modernization through better adaptation to the natural environment. Its extension was limited only by geographical conditions. Above 500 metres vine cultivation remained impossible, and extensive cereal cultivation survived. It did so also in other areas like upper Languedoc, where high humidity caused the development of parasitic fungi on the vines, which only expensive chemical treatment could prevent. The economy of upper Languedoc, formerly a region of commercial wheat production, now contracted as a result of competitive pressures, while that of lower Languedoc turned from subsistence polyculture towards specialized wine production.[145] New market conditions encouraged the rapid extension of specialization in the production of this one element of the traditional polyculture, and with it a marked tendency towards regional specialization. Table 59[146] makes clear the declining relative importance of the departments of the Atlantic seaboard – Gironde, Charente-Inférieure, Loire-Inférieure and Maine-et-Loire – which had previously possessed the advantage of easy access to markets by water.

The further development of specialization was slowed by phylloxera, which affected the south first. It restrained competitive pressures on northern producers and postponed the demise of *vin ordinaire* production in

Table 59   *Wine production, 1850–79*

Area	1870–9 production (millions of hectolitres)	1850–9 to 1870–9, increase in production (percentage)	1870–9, percentage of national production
France as a whole	51.7	71	—
Midi	16.3	152	31.4
South-west Aquitaine	8.0	89	15.4
Charentes	7.7	112	15.0
Middle Loire	4.3	137	8.3
Bourgogne– Lyonnais	2.8	94	5.5

departments like Côte-d'Or.[147] In the south itself areas affected relatively late by the disease (for example, Aude and Pyrénées-Orientales, infected a decade after Gard), were able to profit from high prices as total production fell.[148]

Land affected by phylloxera might be abandoned if farmers lacked capital either to replace or to reconstitute the vines. Both of these alternatives were expensive. Often the replacement of vines with traditional crops like cereals was a necessary prelude to reconstitution during the long period in which a solution to phylloxera was being sought.[149] Sometimes there was little alternative to the abandonment of the land. A proprietor at St-Sulpice et Cameyrac (Gironde) wrote in 1882 that it was impossible to return to cereal cultivation when wheat sold at 16–18 francs per hectolitre but cost 20 francs to produce. He added that local farms were too subdivided for livestock to be a feasible alternative.[150] In such circumstances farmers tended to continue to cultivate the vine for years, hoping for the best, without taking decisive measures towards reconstitution or replacement. The common treatment with sulphur or carbon substantially increased costs but had little effect.[151]

Replanting significantly accelerated changes already occurring in the structure of the vineyards. The combination of the capital costs of reconstituting the vines, and the higher costs of production as a consequence of the need to provide chemical protection for the plants and increased applications of manure, encouraged replanting on the plains where yields were high.[152] The earlier profitability had attracted large-scale investors, in part using capital transferred from the declining southern textile industry. Now reconstitution, because of its cost at perhaps 2000 francs per hectare and the temporary immobilization of capital while the plants matured, increased the tendency towards concentration and accentuated the capitalist character of part of the wine industry and the technical gulf between large-scale producers like the Compagnie des Salines du Midi and the mass of peasant producers.

Improved transport also encouraged the commercial production of other products formerly of secondary importance in a polyculture, especially fruit and vegetables.[153] The development of market gardening on the plains of the lower Rhône valley was one of the few examples of the rapid transformation of agricultural structures prompted by the better access to markets provided by rail.

The emergence in some regions of new specializations more suited to natural conditions and to new market structures was accompanied by a reduction in cereal cultivation, which was replaced especially by pasture or vines. Productivity per worker increased as the product mix shifted in favour of higher-value outputs. However, natural caution and the force of tradition, plus continued market imperfection, slowed the process of change. Cereals continued to be grown at high cost in unsuitable physical conditions,[154] especially where no immediate alternatives were obvious. In the Midi the combination of high costs, low yields, increased competition and low prices with a growing demand for wine created a situation favourable to innovation in crop patterns. Elsewhere, where negative factors were more evident, it took farmers longer to realize that fundamental transformation had occurred in the market for cereals. The establishment of international and inter-regional markets had created a more competitive situation and one in which lower prices generally prevailed.

The response to increased competition was often to continue with cereal cultivation, to innovate only very slowly and to see salvation in the restoration of tariff protection.[155] In 1882 France remained above all a cereals producer. However, the area given over to cereals had declined from 61 per cent of the arable in 1851–62 to 57 per cent in 1882, marking the end of the age-old effort to extend the area of cultivation. Increased yields and international supplies meant that a smaller percentage of the land needed to be given over to cereal production for human subsistence.

If a more competitive market often resulted in the reduction of cereal cultivation in areas in which conditions were unsuitable, it also stimulated more efficient wheat production by means of more complex rotation systems and intensive cultivation, which both increased the fertility of the land and provided additional marketable products in the form of fodder for animals or sugar beet, and thus reduced the overall cost of production.[156] As part of the development of regional specialization, a growing proportion of total production and even more of the total volume of grain entering the market, tended to be produced in the region of advanced agriculture in the north. With improved transport the farmers there were able to sell their grains more easily and to sustain local price levels. This tendency towards specialization in cereal production can be seen in the slow decline between 1852 and

1882 especially evident in the Mediterranean region and in the north-east, and to a lesser extent in the east and in Normandy. Conversely, cereal cultivation increased in some thirteen departments, including the plains of the Brie and Beauce and in Poitou-Limousin.[157]

The modifications considered so far constituted labour-intensive responses to new market opportunities. Increased specialization in livestock was a response which economized on an increasingly expensive resource for those who hired labour. An increase in the number of cows and horses[158] was advantageous in itself, providing increased supplies of manure and draught power and also marketable products. Where pasture was extended to replace arable it reduced farm labour needs. Thus the motives for change were varied, and their scale ranged from alterations in the polycultural balance to the development of a more specialized form of agriculture.

The provision of better access to major urban markets was everywhere the factor of crucial importance. Estimates of per capita meat consumption in 1882 indicate a Parisian average of 79.31 kilograms of meat per annum, a lower figure of 60.39 kilograms for other towns and a minimal 21.89 kilograms for the rural population.[159] The change in market conditions led to livestock being considered as a viable commercial proposition in many areas where formerly they had been viewed merely as necessary auxiliaries to arable farming.[160] From the mid 1850s a significant change had been evident in the relationship between cereal and meat prices. Particularly in the 1860s, as cereal prices levelled out and supplies were more assured, it was realized in some regions that livestock or livestock products might be more profitable,[161] although the amount of capital required remained a major obstacle.[162] In this respect the movement of relative costs and prices was of crucial importance.

In lower Normandy the tendency towards livestock specialization evident from the eighteenth century, particularly in the Pays d'Auge, had previously been restrained by the need to ensure self-subsistence. In the first half of the nineteenth century improved intra-regional communications had already encouraged local specialization, although it remained a secondary activity until the railway revolution.[163] Similarly, in coastal Brittany better transport, together with the commercial treaty with Britain, encouraged substantial exports of meat, poultry, eggs and butter from the 1860s.[164] Subsequently, from the 1870s, price depression was less marked for meat and dairy products than for cereals, a factor which to some degree accelerated the slow trend towards regional specialization.[165]

This growing interest in the commercial potential of livestock led to efforts to improve feeding and stabling conditions and to an increase in selective breeding, which, judging by the increase in average weights and the milk yields of cows, had some success.[166] The possibility of increased specialization in livestock was especially welcome in upland areas, where natural conditions were unsuitable for cereal cultivation and the yields exceptionally low. In parts of the Basses-Alpes, for example, wheat yields were as low as 8–10 hectolitres per hectare in the 1860s. The abandonment of cereal cultivation was, however, relatively slow to begin because of the delay in improving communications in the mountains.[167]

Sheep were integrated more easily than were cows into mountain agriculture, with its thin pasture, or into poor-quality pasture everywhere.[168] Elsewhere as the number of cows increased, the number of sheep declined because of the reduction of the area of pasture on fallow, the clearance of wasteland and especially the decline in wool prices caused by imports in spite of breeding designed to increase meat yields in order to compensate for this.[169]

The change to livestock was not always a wise one. A deposition by an instructor at the Institut national agronomique in 1882 complained about the conversion of excellent arable land into poor-quality pasture at great expense.[170] Agronomists frequently preached the need to increase cultivation of fodder, but this was possible on a substantial scale only where natural conditions were suitable, capital available and markets for animal products accessible. For most farmers, during the period of depression it could be only a palliative for their problems. Without capital or easy access to markets, many farmers still tended to keep the minimum number of animals that was consistent with requirements for manure, draught power and milk.[171]

The statistics on land use indicate how gradual the extension of cultivated fodder was in spite of substantial progress. There are basically three ways of providing feed to increase livestock numbers: allowing more land to lie under grass, increasing grass yields and the external purchase of fodder. The first tended to be favoured in France because it required the least capital or labour. This inevitably meant relatively low rates of yield and of labour productivity, even in a potentially rich area like Normandy. Productivity was still lower in the south, but for essentially climatic reasons rather than reluctance to invest. In spite of these shortcomings, concentration on livestock, obviously a speculative product, was indicative of the extension of commercial networks and a new, more capitalistic conception of the purpose of farming.

By 1882 there were five main areas which were, to some degree, specializing in livestock: one block including the Charolais, Nivernais and Bourbonnais, producing meat for Paris, Lyon, Dijon and the east; another composed of Maine, Poitou, Vendée and the Charentes, specializing both in the provision of young cattle for other regions and in fattening cattle for the Paris market; Brittany, selling young cattle to other regions; and south-west Aquitaine. The degree of specialization reflected the scale of local markets and ease of access to other regions. Possession of milk cows was widespread, but specialization in dairy produce was limited to Brittany and Normandy and upland areas of the Franche-Comté, spreading into Poitou and the Saintonge in the 1880s.

Improvement of the soil

Increase in the number of cows and the establishment of better land–animal relationships had significant effects on the supply of nutrients to the land. One major weakness of traditional cereal-based rotation systems had been their inability to maintain a number of livestock adequate to the manure needs of the fields. Traditionally attempts had been made to offset the shortage of manure resulting from an insufficient number of animals by the collection of dead leaves and other vegetable matter, of sand and of waste products from sugar-beet refining, oil mills, etc. Yet what was available was often wasted because of the lack of stabling, which resulted in the haphazard dispersal of manure in the fields and in the creation of dung heaps in the open where wind and rain could dry and wash away nutrients.[172] Although in the Paris region and Flanders farmers enjoyed the advantage of supplies of urban manure,[173] in most regions the normal insufficiency of natural fertilizers had made a period of fallow essential to avoid exhausting the soil. Cultivation of fodder permitted an increase in the numbers and weight of animals, particularly on the larger farms which had the space and could afford the investment. Moreover, from the 1850s those who could afford to supplemented manure with commercial fertilizer, especially guano. This and other fertilizing agents were inputs whose purchase represented a significant change in the character of agriculture. They symbolized its commercialization and required the application of some forms of cost-benefit analysis to innovation. Imports of guano rose from 14,000 tonnes in 1853 to 94,000 in 1874. It was used especially in the Paris basin and Normandy. Chemical phosphates, used especially in the north, were produced on a relatively large scale only from the 1870s, and in 1876 only some 60,000 tonnes were used.[174] A response to the 1882 inquiry from the canton of Frénouville (Seine-Inférieure) pointed out: 'chemical fertilizers are used on large farms, a little on medium-sized farms and not at all on small farms'.[175] This comment might be applied to the rest of France.

Of greater significance in increasing yields was the growing application of marl and lime. Most fodder crops depended on the presence of lime to do well, while its addition to acid soils permitted the cultivation of wheat in place of rye and encouraged land clearance. It could be adopted only gradually because of the problem of transport costs from lime deposits. In 1870, for example, a cubic metre of lime costing 6 francs at a kiln near Carmaux (Tarn) cost 7.50 francs at Albi railway station but 20 francs in more distant parts of the canton.[176] The cost of using marl, which in 1876 constituted 49.6 per cent by weight of the total *amendement* (lime represented 17.5 per cent) similarly varied with distance from the deposits and transport costs. In the 1860s it was estimated to be 75–100 francs per hectare in Seine-et-Marne, 140–250 in the Ardennes, 250–300 in Doubs and 300 in Basses-Pyrénées.[177]

Thus the use of fertilizing agents in large part reflected the degree of development of communications; isolated areas lacked not only the incentive of access to markets but also the ability to increase yields rapidly and substantially. Progress in this respect depended on the development of efficient distribution systems for fertilizers, using waterways and especially railways for long-distance transport and road networks for local distribution.[178] Innovation tended to follow the railway, entering the plains first and spreading along the valleys and the coast before penetrating the interior or plateaux and mountains. Those areas in the centre, south and south-west that had some of the poorest soils and were most in need of fertilizer were disadvantaged by comparison with areas in the north with both relatively fertile soils and easier access to the various kinds of fertilizers.[179]

In the west and in the Massif Central, Gâtinais, Vosges, Bresse and Landes improved access to lime and marl resulted in substantial changes in agriculture, and in particular in the reduction of the area of wasteland and increased wheat production. A report from the *arrondissement* of Dinan (Côtes-du-Nord) in 1870 claimed that in some communes 'the productivity of the soil had been doubled simply by the addition of calcareous sands and marl to the soil'. By making this possible, 'the completion of local roads had caused . . . a minor agricultural revolution'.[180] In the Sarthe it was estimated that the application of 50 hectolitres of lime per hectare might increase wheat yields by two-thirds. In practice this sort of volume was applied only rarely, and on average liming increased yields in the department by only 13 per cent in the first two-thirds of the century.[181]

Transport was the central facilitating factor. Observers repeatedly associated agricultural progress with better transport and with the improved access to markets and to fertilizers that this provided.[182] In 1883 the Conseil supérieur de l'agriculture claimed that above all agriculture required further reductions in rail tariffs for the transport of fertilizers.[183] Government agents frequently sought to persuade the railway companies to reduce their tariffs,[184] and to a large degree the rail companies co-operated. They reaped rewards both through the increasing transport of fertilizers and through the growing volume of agricultural produce which resulted.[185]

These particular innovations involved relatively low capital costs and could be varied in relation to fluctuations in income. Even then, peasants tended to be reluctant to purchase inputs of any kind. For many farmers this reluctance increased during the years of depression, for there are signs that in some regions at least the application of lime and marl temporarily declined.[186] Lack of capital was a major obstacle; so too was limited technical knowledge and lack of confidence in non-traditional fertilizers.[187] Empiricism often resulted in mistakes, usually the result of failure to adapt new methods to particular farms. In the case of fertilizers success depended in large part on prior analysis of the soil, otherwise the result might be excessive or, more often, inadequate applications. Such unfortunate experiences must have slowed the process of adaptation.[188]

Another factor increasing reluctance to innovate was the frequent falsification of the contents of fertilizers, especially guano, which led to an official inquiry in 1864.[189] Confidence in the efficacy of new methods was essential to their widespread adoption. One should also remember that agricultural improvement takes the form of a complex of associated changes rather than single, isolated and once-and-for-all innovations. In the Sologne, for example, the provision of marl at 4–5 francs per cubic metre rendered worthwhile further innovations such as the introduction of clover and wheat into the rotation, deeper ploughing and drainage.[190]

In many areas short leases made tenant farmers reluctant to invest capital even when they possessed it. Nevertheless, relatively low-cost innovations such as liming were far more likely to be introduced than were more expensive procedures like drainage or irrigation. This was true even in areas in the north, where heavy soils made drainage particularly important and where the advantages in terms of easier ploughing, the efficacy of liming, etc., were recognized.[191] In the second half of the nineteenth century it was estimated that only some 750,000 hectares had been drained – mainly in the richer departments like Seine-et-Marne, Oise, Aisne and Seine-et-Oise – and that this was only 7.5 per cent of the area estimated to need drainage. In this case the reduction of transport costs for the movement of drainage pipes had little effect, given the high overall cost of at least 250 francs per hectare in the 1860s.[192]

The desire for irrigation was constantly expressed, in replies to the agricultural inquiries, as a response to lack of water in the south.[193] Irrigation was an important means of increasing productivity in the Mediterranean area, with its low rainfall, but in addition to the cost, parcellation of property and the water rights of a host of often tiny mills remained fundamental obstacles.[194] Most significant, it was very expensive, and adequate returns were possible only when a market for high-value plants existed. The preconditions of capital and markets were combined only in the Comtat and Bouches-du-Rhône.[195] The traditional alternative, which was to choose plants according to their vegetative cycles and the length of their roots, generally remained dominant.

Even though French agriculture continued to suffer from inadequate efforts to improve soil fertility, the increased application of fertilizing agents seems to have been fairly general. Large-scale farmers with capital to spare inevitably benefited more than small from the increased availability of manure, marl and lime. Thus it was reported in 1859 from the Sologne that the cost of production of a hectolitre of wheat was 12–13 francs in the case of a large-scale farmer employing fertilizers of various kinds, and as high as 16–20 where they used only little.[196] However, fertilizers represented a relatively cheap means by which the productivity of the land – and existing resources – could be increased. This represented the addition of new inputs with a high marginal productivity; the same was true, as we shall see, of improved hand tools and some machinery.

Improvement of equipment

The least costly of all improvements was the modification of hand tools in order to increase their efficiency, usually through the replacement of wooden by iron spade blades, forks, etc.,[197] and the more widespread use of new tools. Reduction of the cost of iron and increased competition between local and extra-local producers, which further reduced the expense, made this low-cost innovation more generally acceptable. The scythe rapidly replaced the sickle for harvesting the major cereal crop. The scythe had not been unknown previously and might be used, as it was in the Beauce and Brie, for cutting meadow grass and barley and oats, but the sickle had offered the dual advantage of wasting fewer of the precious grains of wheat and of providing more employment. It was a technical form suitable for conditions of over-population. Whereas in 1848 the sickle had been in use through most of France, by the end of the 1870s it had been superseded generally.[198] The scythe substantially increased labour productivity (by 25–35 per cent)[199] while tiring the worker less. In the vineyards the concurrent replacement of the knife (*serpette*) by the pruning scissors (*sécateur*) had similar consequences.[200]

Somewhat more costly than the adoption of the scythe, but as widespread, was the introduction of new or improved ploughs. According to the agricultural inquiries, the numbers of ploughs increased as follows: in 1852 there were 2,577,000; in 1862, 3,206,000; in 1882, 3,267,000; in 1892, 3,669,000. It is not possible to distinguish between different types of ploughs. At its most dramatic this change involved the replacement of hand-tilling by horse-drawn implements such as the plough or the horse hoe.[201] At another level the *araire*, a plough without a mould-board, so common in the centre and south, was improved by the replacement of some wooden parts by iron or was replaced altogether by the *charrue* with mould-board and wheels, which permitted deeper ploughing. Throughout the century the *charrue* spread gradually from the north, along the Atlantic cost and Rhône valley into the south.[202]

In this case the availability of larger numbers of stronger draught animals would appear to have been a prerequisite, although the replacement of a wooden *araire* by an iron ploughshare, which penetrated the soil more easily, in fact limited the need for increased power. The *araire* had the advantage of being light and cheap and required few draught animals. It was particularly useful on hill slopes and thin soils, but its inability to do much more than break the surface of the soil required subsequent hand hoeing and clod breaking or the use of the spade to work the soil more deeply.[203] New ploughs, particularly of the Dombasle and the Brabant type, became wide-spread from the 1840s, as design improved and weight and cost were reduced. They were simple in design, heavy enough for heavy soils but light and manoeuvrable enough not to require large draught teams. Previously, even in the west, north and east and in the heavier soils of the southern river valleys, where wheeled ploughs had been dominant, most of these had not ploughed deeply. In the Ile-de-France the traditional *charrue* pulled by two horses ploughed to a depth of 12 centimetres, and repeated ploughings were necessary. The twin-share Brabant, entering general use around 1880, required three horses but ploughed a furrow 25–30 centimetres deep, so that only one ploughing was needed.[204]

More efficient ploughs should be considered as part of an innovation complex. Improvement was often the consequence of changes in rotation; in Normandy, for example, it accompanied the introduction of colza,[205] in the north that of sugar beet.[206] In the west and centre the Dombasle greatly facilitated the clearance of wasteland.[207] Everywhere better ploughs offered economies in time and labour but at the cost of increased investment in draught teams, especially in areas of heavy soil.[208] Deeper ploughing had the crucially important effect of improving the aeration of the soil while reducing the number of weeds, both of which substantially improved crop yields. Wheat yields were highly susceptible to weeds, and in terms of weed control the alternatives to deep ploughing were costly, involving the thick sowing of seeds to smother weeds or the intensive use of labour.

Improved ploughs were introduced in the north earlier than elsewhere, and especially from the 1830s and 1840s[209] but subsequently innovations became general. In the south and centre innovation followed the river valleys and plains but only slowly penetrated the uplands, where steep slopes and thin soils favoured the *araire*.[210] In Aveyron, where the Dombasle appeared first around 1845 and became common in the 1860s, it was only with the introduction of the Brabant in the 1880s that the *araire* was generally replaced.[211] Thus a continuing technical lag *vis-à-vis* the north was evident. However, even in relatively backward areas like Tarn-et-Garonne wooden ploughs were replaced by iron from the 1860s.[212] As one philo-sophical observer put it in 1870, 'the worst ploughs of today are much better than those of yesterday'.[213] As for the innovation process, Roger Thabault has described how the first Dombasle to reach the commune of Mazières-en-Gâtine (Deux-Sèvres) in 1856 was watched at work by a crowd of 200 people. Initially most farmers there believed that deeper ploughing would only bring the poor-quality subsoil to the surface, and it took a number of good harvests to convince them of its advantages. The new plough, in fact, got rid of the bracken which the old, wooden plough had failed to eradicate.[214]

In the vineyards by permitting the use of the plough planting in lines rather than haphazardly achieved considerable savings in the use of labour. The practice of growing other crops in between the vines also began to disappear from the 1850s, a change largely completed with the reconstitution of the vines after phylloxera.[215]

It was not so much increase in the number of ploughs which mattered as the widespread improvement in their efficiency. Whereas the old ploughs had left the land badly drained, poorly aerated and weed-infested and made bare fallow essential to clear the fields, the new ones prepared the land more adequately through deeper ploughing. Combined with improved fertilization and, probably more significant, given the continued insufficiency of the latter, better ploughing substantially increased agricultural productivity.[216] Other significant innovations in the preparation of the soil included the replacement of wooden with iron harrows and rollers and the use of horse hoes to break up the surface of the soil and often to replace hand hoeing.[217]

So far we have been concerned mainly with technically relatively simple innovations in the preparation of the soil and in harvesting procedures. Mechanization of cultivation, particularly at harvest, was a slower process. In 1862 there were 9000 mowers and reapers; by 1882 the number of mowers had risen to 19,000 and that of reapers to 16,000; ten years later there were 39,000 mowers and 23,000 reapers. In 1882 there were, by contrast, some 3,500,000 farms.

The obstacles to mechanization were numerous. They included reluctance on the part of the labour force to accept new and more complex techniques, which, moreover, they were afraid might displace them. Often higher wages were paid as an act of conciliation.[218] Farmers feared risk-taking not only because of possible financial loss but because failure would invite scorn from the rest of the community, an effective means of social control in a village society.[219] Although great interest was shown in machines exhibited at local and regional exhibitions, the mass of small farmers required a lengthier process of empirical proof of the value of new technology before they would even contemplate its adoption.[220] Early machines were often technically unreliable, so that improved construction was a vital prerequisite for widespread use. Obviously, disappointing results would discourage further innovation.[221] The contemporary press – full of advertisements for new machinery – can give a very false impression of technical progress. It and the cantonal and departmental agricultural societies influenced in the first place the large proprietors and farmers and then, through their example, the mass of small-scale farmers.[222] In the Ariège new ploughs were introduced first by notables belonging to the departmental agricultural society and were subsequently copied by local blacksmiths.[223] The role of local artisans in the adoption, the adaptation to meet local needs and in the diffusion of information about new techniques must have been considerable.

Inertia could be overcome with time, but lack of capital was often an even greater problem. The President of the *comice agricole* of Heuvec-sur-l'Isle

(Dordogne) in 1882 bemoaned the fact that twenty years of setting a good example had not persuaded the mass of peasant cultivators to abandon their traditional equipment.[224] In general, the more complex (and the more expensive) an innovation, the fewer the people who adopted it and the more gradual the process of adoption. This was partly because of cost but also because of the greater need for skills in its use and maintenance.[225]

There is no doubt that the spread of mechanization was hindered by its costs and by the fact that it was economically worthwhile only on relatively large farms. Where a sufficiency of family labour existed, the introduction of expensive labour-saving techniques would have seemed hardly appropriate.[226] Unfortunately, there is no statistical evidence which would allow a precise assessment of technical innovation in relation to farm size. The crucial relationship between farm structure and innovation, in terms of both capital accumulation and the scale of profitable innovation, is clear, however. Labour-saving innovations occurred everywhere, given the existence of a range of technological possibilities, some of which even the smallest farmer could afford and all of which proved of value to the large-scale farmer. Mechanization proper was, however, far more limited in its geographical spread, essentially to the Paris region and the north. There were not only broad regional differences but also variations within every region. According to M. Pagèzy, mayor of Montpellier in 1859, there were three types of farming in the Hérault – one using only hand tools, another the *araire* and a third using a plough (*charrue*) and various other types of machine.[227]

The tendency towards parcellation evident throughout the nineteenth century increased the significance of structural obstacles to change. According to M. de Lorière, representing the canton of Meslay on the departmental council of the Mayenne, 'the more subdivided the land, the fewer improvements are possible'.[228] Dispersal of plots had been an advantage in the traditional polyculture. In spite of the waste of time involved in moving from one plot to another, it gave the farmer access to a range of local soil types and exposures.[229] It came to be regarded as a disadvantage only as peasants became committed to changing their local agricultural systems.

Location on steep slopes further compounded the problems of innovation. At St-Maurice-sur-Chaloman (Ardèche) in 1882 continued dependence on hand tools for cultivation, and on panniers carried on human backs for the transport of manure to the fields, reflected the existence of terraces on steep hillsides.[230] The answer to low productivity here was abandonment rather than innovation. Only relatively high population densities permitted the cultivation of such land, but abandonment of marginal land, although evident in some regions as population declined – especially in the north-east and the south of the Massif Central – was slow.[231]

Another possible obstacle to innovation was the shortage of power. Steam was utilized to only a very limited extent, so that reliance on traditional animal sources continued. Contemporary estimates of the evolution of demand for power vary. According to some accounts, new ploughs required an increased number of draught animals – an expensive investment. According to others, because of improved design the new ploughs cut the soil more easily and required smaller draught teams.[232] The equipment used in the fields necessarily reflected the animal energy available, and there can be no doubt that the gradual increase in the number of ploughs and the introduction of reapers and threshers – in short, the tendency for animal power to replace human – must have required a substantial increase in draught power.

Increased animal power in the fields could be supplied in three ways: first, by the release of animals from alternative tasks; second, by an increase in the average strength of the animals; third, by an increase in their number. During this period all three developments were evident.

Improved roads and mechanical transport reduced the number of farm animals required for transport and the time and energy taken to perform particular tasks.[233] Breeding and better feeding and care of animals increased their vigour.[234] The gradual replacement of cows and oxen by horses and mules had similar consequences.[235] In the past the horse had been the draught animal of the north, the Paris basin and some departments of the north-east. In the west and other departments of the north-east oxen had shared the work, while in the centre and south cows, oxen and mules had been most common.[236]

Increases in the number of draught animals required an improvement in fodder supply, which occurred as crop rotations were altered, although less markedly on small farms than on large. Many small farms were unable to maintain the animals required for the introduction of heavier ploughs. The number of horses increased only slowly, at 0.5 per cent per annum between 1852 and 1882. Even so, there does seem to have been a very marked decline in the number of hectares of arable land per draught animal during this period.[237]

Mechanization of the harvest occurred first in the Paris region and the north, areas in which large-scale, capital intensive farms existed, adequate draught power was available and labour supply problems were causing considerable difficulties.[238] Another obvious attraction was a speeding up of the harvest, which rendered it less subject to adverse weather conditions. But for many this was offset by increased wastage and the cost of the labour needed to collect straw left in the field. Elsewhere replacement of the sickle by the scythe proved to be an adequate increase in labour productivity for most farmers. When the Vienne agricultural society experimented with machines in 1863 it found that because they cost 18.8 francs per hectare, it was cheaper to use the scythe (16.50 francs), though not the sickle (23.50 francs).[239] Reapers costing anywhere between 600 and 1250 francs[240] were a costly investment. In Haut-Rhin the first harvesting machines were introduced as late as 1880 and became common only after 1900.[241] Reaperbinders were particularly expensive and were hardly seen anywhere before the 1880s.[242] The application of steam power to harvesting was even slower. In 1870 a meeting of large farmers in the canton of Caumont-en-Vexin (Oise), where farmers had been experimenting with steam ploughs and harvesting machines, decided that in all probability these would never be more than objects of curiosity.[243]

The geography of mechanization can in large part be explained in terms of farm structure and labour shortage.[244] If one looks at the distribution of reaping machines in 1882, of around 16,000 machines, over half were used in twenty departments around Paris, areas of large farms and flat land, which were also suffering from labour shortage.[245] Chatelain has revealed how departments on the margins of the Paris Basin, which were more accessible to migrant labour from Belgium, Brittany and the Massif Central, were far less likely to have mechanized harvest processes.[246] Indeed, throughout the Paris region the availability of seasonal migrant labour for harvest slowed mechanization, while in the Cambrésis, Pas-de-Calais and the north of the department of the Somme migrant labour was reinforced by workers from the domestic textile industry, which survived into the 1880s. In the south the cereal harvest was mechanized in only a handful of departments with some similarities in farm structure and labour shortage.[247] Generally, the availability of substantial labour resources through the predominance of the family farm, in spite of migration, reduced the need to innovate beyond the level of the hand tool, plough and perhaps threshing machine.

The mechanization of post-harvest processes was of far greater significance. Threshing machines of varying capacities and degrees of technical complexity, using human, animal or steam power, were by far the most commonly accepted machines. Often they were the only real machines to be found on farms. Nationally in 1856 51,000 threshing machines had been counted; by 1862 there were 160,735 and by 1882 214,045. They were most common in the north-east, especially in Meuse, Haute-Marne, Meurthe, Côte-d'Or, Moselle, Vosges and Doubs, and least common in the south.[248] In Aude, where the flail was in general use until around 1860, it had completely disappeared by 1880–90.[249] The rate of innovation seems to have been second only to that of the plough. Most depended on human or animal power. The steam engine, requiring coal and water and good roads, was limited effectively to the plains. In 1852 there were 81 steam threshers in use, 2253 in 1858, 6000 in 1873 and over 9000 in 1882, generating 42,000 h.p., estimated to be the equivalent of 240,000 man hours.[250] Estimates vary, but a steam thresher serviced by six men might thresh 150 hectolitres per day, compared with 3 hectolitres per man using the flail. In Calvados in 1855 the typical horse-powered threshing machine with two men threshed 11 hectolitres; by 1880 a larger machine with five men threshed 55 hectolitres.[251] In southern departments, where threshing had often been done by the hooves of mules or horses, from the 1840s the introduction of machines was preceded, as an intermediary stage, by the use of stone rollers.[252]

Even in this case, however, farmers tended to be wary of machines which, even if relatively inexpensive, still cost money and were often unreliable in the early stages.[253] The flail continued to be used in some areas, even in the Paris region, into the twentieth century. This was especially true on small farms. In the Dordogne, for example, in the 1870s farmers threshed the crop in two or three weeks using the flail and the help of neighbours.[254] Increasingly, though, peasants saw the threshing machine as a means of escape from the massive physical effort demanded by the flail.[255] On larger farms it began to disappear in the 1860s, being retained only when it was felt to be an essential means of providing winter work for a labour force less willing than before to accept long seasonal unemployment.[256] It was increasingly considered to represent an extravagant use of labour.[257] Use of the machine might not always be cheaper, but it released workers who could be deployed more productively on other tasks.[258] Even small-scale farmers who could not afford to purchase a threshing machine, and the size of whose harvest would have made its use uneconomic, often found it worth while to hire a mobile thresher (although complaints were frequently made about the hire charges)[259] or, more rarely, to purchase a machine collectively.[260]

Explanations of innovation

Replies to the agricultural inquiries repeatedly explain innovation in hand tools and machines as a response to the intensification of cultivation and to the shortage of labour, its increasing costs and growing insubordination.[261] Employers have always been dissatisfied with the workers they employ for one reason or another, and one needs to consider the validity of their complaints with care. In this case, however, other indicators, including official reports, wage movements and the information available on the intensification and growing labour needs of agriculture and on the withdrawal of workers from the agricultural labour force all point in the same direction. They indicate that the landowners and large farmers who were the typical respondents to official inquiries presented a more or less accurate picture of their problems.

To a significant extent the pace of technical innovation in agriculture can be linked with changing relationships between factor costs and to factor availability. As long as the marginal cost of labour remained low, it was possible to use it intensively. The labour-intensive character of agriculture meant that any change in the balance between labour supply and demand, whether due to migration of population or intensification of cultivation, resulted in severe crisis. As labour became more expensive and its supply less reliable, increased capital was invested in items ranging from improved spades, scythes and ploughs to reapers and threshers, all of which in more or less dramatic fashion increased labour productivity. The major alternative to technical innovation, the more intensive use of labour, was practicable only on peasant family farms. Even there, physical capacity and new attitudes towards work were limiting factors. Moreover, the extension of market opportunities was an additional and growing incentive to innovation, even for the mass of peasants. It encouraged efforts to increase production, especially during the period of rising prices, when increased revenue provided the capital for limited innovation.

The gradualness with which population migration and the structural transformation of farms occurred slowed the impulse to change, particularly in the south, the Massif Central, Brittany and the north-east. In these areas, although labour productivity improved, it remained low. It was the regions of *grande culture*, mainly north of the Loire and especially in the Paris basin, which, by initiating more intensive rotation systems, first required more labour and then, when supply became less assured, had recourse to labour-saving equipment. They did so essentially to cope with the peak periods of labour use, the preparation of the soil, harvesting and threshing. More aware of trends in the markets, whether for labour, equipment or his products, the large farmer was better able to respond to change.[262] The need was not everywhere a pressing one, and even in this sector of farming not everyone had the specialist knowledge or the willingness to invest.

The importance of the 1851–73 period was that rising agricultural prices and the relative prosperity of the countryside accelerated the processes of capital accumulation, of investment, of increasing productivity and of participation in commercial agriculture[263] and, as an aspect of this, the farmers' dependence on purchased goods and services. Even the small-scale tenant farmer benefited from the tendency of rents to rise less rapidly than prices.

Awareness of opportunities increased as communications improved. Access to new markets encouraged efforts to increase production and to modify its structure. The gradual and accumulative response even of peasant farmers to growing urban demand reflected an exposure to new networks of communications and mechanisms of decision-taking external to the village community. A new, less fatalistic, mentality turned awareness of new techniques of cultivation into a desire to employ them. In the past change had become respectable once its virtues had been empirically proven, but now minds were more open to change than they had ever been. Once successful innovation commenced, the reluctant were forced to recognize that they also could 'do better'. Pressures for conformity in small communities were then as likely as not to promote emulation in the adoption of innovations.[264] The rapid disappearance of subsistence crises after the early 1850s and the increased reliability of basic food supplies encouraged a tendency towards specialization and away from subsistence polyculture, if only to the extent of growing grain sufficient for the average year rather than to cover the possibility of a poor crop. In some regions in the south, however, the opportunities presented by vine cultivation encouraged a more complete transition from subsistence to commercial agriculture.

Peasant communities responded to processes of cultural as well as economic and demographic change. Both seemed necessary before innovation could occur. Freed from fear of dearth, presented with increasing opportunities of earning money (but also with new ways of spending it), the peasant became concerned less with subsistence and more with prices.[265] The aims of the family farm underwent gradual revision. Families slowly acquired a desire for greater comfort and for more from life than hard work. In effect, new factors began to influence the decision-making process. Peasants began to look favourably upon labour-saving and cash-earning innovations. Migration, or the threat of migration, and a tendency for family size to decline helped to maintain this more positive outlook in individual cases. The intensification of competitive pressures as better communications changed market structures proved another stimulus as involvement in the market became inescapable.

Whatever the shape or scale of innovation, it was significant in that it involved the cultivator in new economic relationships. Even if these were limited to making use of the services of specialists in the modification and manufacture of ploughs and accompanying harness, this required more cash payments, and these had to be earned by greater commercialization.

Market-place participation and the purchase of inputs made it essential to balance cash earning and outlays. This enjoined constant caution upon the innovator and explains the attraction of small-scale and low-cost innovations, allowing the gradual accumulation of marginal increases in productivity.[266] One can only presume that individuals followed innovators to the degree that their economic situation, their financial means and their attitudes allowed, and that at a certain point particular innovations became the orthodox way of doing things. This helps explain the time lag between initial innovation, usually by the larger farmers more aware of change and for whom the penalty for introducing an uneconomic innovation was an acceptable risk, and its generalization among the less well-off. Only detailed community studies will permit answers to questions about actual adoption. It needs, however, to be borne constantly in mind that if all farmers were vitally concerned with the relationship agricultural prices/price of purchases, monetary costs were of reduced significance on the peasant farms and so, therefore, was the stimulus to commercialize their product.

The capitalist farm and that of the average peasant farmer represented two types of agriculture. The large farm was directed by a relatively well-educated and informed farmer with capital to spare for innovation, specializing in the production of a small number of products (usually vegetable) which suited natural conditions, responsive to changing market conditions and concerned to minimize costs by investment in increasing the productivity of both land and labour. The world of the small farmer was very different. It was only in the regions of advanced farming that he was systematically exposed to the influence of capitalist farmers and opportunities for profit. There many peasants, working as labourers on large farms, were ideally placed to assess the value of innovation. The large majority of peasant farmers only slowly extended their participation in commercial agriculture. Even where he kept accounts, the peasant farmer made no effort to account for his own labour and for that of his family. They received their keep and pocket money and could hope to inherit family property. In a society far less conscious of the passing of time than we are today, people expected to work all the daylight hours. Reliance on family labour and low living standards made possible economic survival, at least until the burden of labour became intolerable or the capacity of the peasant farm to earn sufficient income to finance even minimal outgoings became insufficient.[267]

Thus in the second half of the nineteenth century not all change was conducive to increasing labour productivity. Many larger landowners, and especially those whose properties were not large enough to produce returns adequate to meet either the payment of higher wages or mechanization, were attracted by alternative investment opportunities and sold land which peasants and labourers could afford to purchase in the prosperous 1860s and early 1870s.[268] In some regions this led to further parcellation, as the statistics on farm size reveal (see Table 56, p. 350). In favourable conditions the land farmed with minute care might produce a high yield per hectare, even if a low one in relation to the labour employed. This was particularly the case in the south, where the extension of the vine and high market prices allowed the family to sustain itself on as little as two hectares.[269] However, parcellation in southern France did not depend entirely on the extension of the vine. In Haute-Languedoc it involved in addition a reversion to subsistence polyculture and a move away from commercial wheat production.[270] Parcellation in the short term reduced the rate of migration and also diverted agricultural labour from large to small units. On these, in spite of hard and unremitting labour, much energy was wasted by inadequate tools and machinery and by the need to move from plot to plot.[271] In the long term it reinforced a major obstacle to structural change and improvement in labour productivity in agriculture.

North of the Loire, and especially in the Paris basin, parcellation was less common. Labour-intensive farming, other than market gardening, was less profitable and land more expensive.[272] In the centre of the Paris basin, in the Beauce and Valois, the tendency was the opposite – towards concentration of ownership and exploitation. By 1860–80 the largest farms covered about 200 hectares of arable and rented at 200–400 francs per hectare.[273] These called for a very different kind of enterprise from that of the mass of small peasant farms.

The differences were the logical outcome of a situation in which the peasant farmer had cheap labour, expensive credit and a strong incentive to economize in the use of capital and the capitalist dearer labour and cheaper credit and could choose to economize in the use of labour. This inevitably led to a technical dualism between regions and also within regions, but with future developments taking primarily one direction: in spite of the slowing effects of parcellation, phylloxera, price depression and protection, that was towards increased market participation under the fourfold pressure of the development of transport and commerce, the monetization of economic relations, technological change and the extension of labour shortage caused by migration and increased birth control.

Among these factors the development of transport, which provided an incentive to expansion through improved access to growing urban markets and also permitted specialization, ought to be seen as decisive.[274] In many cases growing uniformity of prices, and the consequent intensification of competition, encouraged the search for more remunerative cash crops. Improved transport had the effect of altering the relative prices of crops and farmers responded to these changes, although few regions showed such sensibility to changing relative prices as lower Normandy, which increasingly concentrated on livestock, or lower Languedoc, where the vines spread rapidly across the plains. Everywhere there were marked crises of adaptation. It took time to establish new commercial networks and to persuade farmers to adapt to them. Adaptation was also very much affected by the great variety of geographical locations, natural conditions, farm structures, social structures and mentalities.

When the statistics on production, and especially those on the value of the product per hectare of useful agricultural land for 1882, are compared with those of 1852, a general progress and overall enrichment is evident, but the regional differences existing at the earlier date were largely maintained. Similarly, Désert's statistics based on tax records indicate that while there was a narrowing of the gap between rich and poor regions in the rate of increase in revenue, due to the intensification of agriculture in the latter, there continued to be major differences (see Table 60).[275] In the north, Flanders and Picardy, the Paris basin and Normandy retained the advantages of richer soils, larger farms, accumulated capital and access to major urban markets. Here agriculture had become, in decisive fashion, a speculative activity, requiring capital investment and attracting capital by success measured in terms of profitability. This had affected the outlook of peasant family farmers as well as more obvious capitalists. Despite the family nature of their operations, peasants in the north had easier access to, and were more responsive to, urban markets than were peasant farmers in other regions. This distinction between traditional and market-orientated peasant farming is an important one, too easily forgotten.

Substantial improvements in productivity occurred in some areas of the west and centre-west as a result of the application of lime, the cultivation of

Table 60   *Increase in net taxable income in seven regions, 1851–79, and revenue per hectare, 1879*

Region	Increase 1851–79 (percentage)	Revenue per hectare, 1879 (francs)
Brittany	60.9	49.3
Garonne region	59.1	63.6
Midi	56.0	58.3
North	45.7	114.5
Massif Central	41.4	33.0
Centre of Paris basin	23.8	77.0
East-north-east	18.0	42.4

wheat in place of inferior cereals and, in some upland areas of the Doubs and Jura, increased specialization in livestock. In these areas the handicaps imposed by natural environment were reduced by technical change.

It has been suggested that the failure of the 1882 census to account adequately for cattle bred for fattening led to a serious under-estimation of the value of agricultural production in much of south-central France.[276] The poor results recorded in this census should not therefore be allowed to conceal the considerable progress made in cattle raising, and in vine-growing areas prior to the onset of phylloxera, which represented a change from low-yield cereal production to the production of commodities more suited to natural conditions – a means of reducing the effects of inherent environmental constraints.

The poorest regions remained the upland zones of central France, the Aquitaine basin and the south-east, joined now by the north-east, which had experienced relative decline. In the north-east and Aquitaine this was due to the maintenance of an especially traditionalist polyculture in the absence of large population centres, and in the latter also to the loss of markets for cereals in the Midi as a more competitive grain market was established; in the south-east, to a series of crises affecting silk, madder and vine, often leading to the temporary replanting of cereals in unfavourable geographical conditions. In all these regions a far larger proportion of farmers than elsewhere remained fundamentally orientated towards family subsistence. By 1882, moreover, throughout much of southern France the onset of phylloxera had a marked effect on farm incomes, and more generally the onset of price depression had begun to affect incomes and attitudes.

Conclusions

Geographical and cultural factors in effect functioned to confine growth spatially to specific regions for long periods of time.[277] Investment patterns favoured already advanced regions and helped to maintain existing regional growth differences, highlighting one major economic problem of developing countries, the transmission of growth from dynamic to relatively stagnant regions.

In giving access to growing urban markets, improved communications created a situation encouraging development. In France by comparison with other European countries, the rate of urbanization was slow and the stimulus this provided inevitably more limited. Just as, inevitably, adaptation to changing market conditions was gradual. It took time to become fully aware of a new situation and to assess the potential for innovation. Moreover, the penetration of the countryside by improved means of communication was itself a gradual process and, although an essential precondition, in itself was not sufficient to ensure rapid commercialization. This required the organization of commerce to establish the necessary links between farms and market. There can be no doubt that because of gaps in communications systems, rail tariff structures and inadequate commercial organization, substantial imperfection remained in the market structure which both served to protect the inefficient producer and to offer extra profits to the efficient.

The slowness of structural change and of the increase in productivity and the survival of high-cost producers have often been blamed on the return to protection after the interlude of liberal trade policies from 1860. But by the 1880s no government could afford to ignore the social trauma and likely political consequences of the continuation of unrestrained imports of cereals and livestock in a period of generalized price depression. The Société des agriculteurs de France told a parliamentary commission in 1879 that only a minority, even of large-scale producers, could be expected to be able to reduce their costs of production significantly in the short term.[278] In most regions farmers had not adapted rapidly enough to the new marketing situations created by improved communications and free trade either to take advantage of new opportunities or to meet the problems caused by intensified inter-regional and international competition. In this situation tariff protection was a political as well as an economic necessity, the latter because of the inability of much of French agriculture to compete with overseas producers and also, and perhaps especially, because of the deep pessimism which awareness of this situation had created and which limited further investment. French agriculture, in effect, seems to have been suffering from a deep spiritual malaise, a major crisis of confidence reinforced by comparison with previous prosperity. It had experienced a continuing *crise d'adaptation* caused first by the need to respond to the changes in internal market structures as communications rapidly improved and then to the intensification of international trade. This appears to have caused a state of hyper-anxiety in the agricultural community.[279] The Prefect of Meurthe-et-Moselle stressed that protection was necessary, not because he believed in its economic value but because of its 'moral value'.[280] Protection seems to have been a necessary *interim* measure and was successful in inducing an increase in prices.

Its long-term consequences as a cause of technical and structural stagnation were less happy. It reinforced rigidity in the agricultural system by reducing the effects of international competition. It additionally reinforced regional disparities by allowing some areas, and the more efficient farmers within them, to make surplus profits from artificially high prices.[281] More significantly, by reducing competitive pressures it facilitated the survival of the traditional peasant farm. On such farms, given a lack of capital, it made sense to employ labour-intensive methods, but the consequence of this was relatively low productivity, low per capita incomes and harsh and increasingly intolerable living conditions.

Until the 1870s rising prices encouraged market participation and both stimulated and paid for innovation. Subsequently the pace of change slowed. Much of French agriculture stuck at the phase of biological innovation and was able to postpone implementation of the phase of mechanization beyond the introduction of the scythe and of improved ploughs. Most farmers were not prepared, or did not feel the need, to go beyond the labour-intensive phase of innovation. This was especially the case in economically backward regions characterized by a high density of labour relative to cultivable land and limited availability of capital.

By contrast with the best farms – the large rented units of the Nord and Aisne, for example – there survived a vast number of technically backward smallholdings. These were in contact with more dynamic sectors of the rural economy, but the process of adjustment to new conditions which they were undergoing was more gradual and depended ultimately upon migration to reduce labour supply, increase the size of farms and stimulate urban demand. The growing gulf in living conditions between advanced and backward regions, and increasing awareness of this, slowly brought about this adjustment. In the meantime the peasant farm constituted an element of rigidity in the economic system, preventing the more economic use of land and labour, limiting the consequences of the modernization of the economic infrastructure and contributing to the stagnation of labour productivity. There thus remained marked contrasts in French agriculture, based to a substantial extent on differing natural environments but also on contrasts in human opportunity and response.

In spite of substantial change, French agriculture remained labour-intensive. By comparison, for example, with Britain, investment in livestock and equipment in the second half of the nineteenth century was restrained, leaving agriculture under-capitalized. The survival of traditional peasant agriculture was to have significant consequences for the development of French society in the twentieth century. It was only after the Second World War that the advantages of mechanization and fertilization became sufficiently clear, and the exodus from the countryside sufficiently great, to overcome finally the economic and subjective 'cost advantages' of labour-intensive agriculture. Structural transformation in agriculture depended on a wider modernization of economic structures through the expansion of output and employment opportunities in non-agricultural sectors.

This somewhat negative judgement, however, should not be allowed to conceal the fact that a massive change did occur in the second half of the nineteenth century. It is easy to assess economic achievement in a particular country in the past on the basis of comparison with apparently more advanced neighbours or with its own later achievements, but this is to ignore the particular structures and problems, the conditioning influence, of time and place. However limited the consequences, it was during these years that the development of a modern communications network facilitated the creation of a market system which, if still in many respects imperfect, brought the traditional subsistence crises to an end. It was then that improved access to markets, together with the growth of competition, stimulated increased commercialization, improvements in productivity in all sectors of the farming community, and that town and country came to be, for better or worse, far more closely united than ever before. It marked the belated end of the *ancien régime* in the countryside.

Conclusion

Throughout the eighteenth and nineteenth centuries there developed a growing awareness of the economic costs of difficult communications. Considerable efforts were made to improve both roads and waterways. Substantial progress occurred but always within the limits imposed by inadequate financing, ineffective bureaucratic control and the frequent reluctance of many communities to meet the costs of maintenance or improvement. By the 1830s, as economic change became more rapid, so dissatisfaction with the state of communications grew. New legislation and increased expenditure were indicative of the desire of both central government and local administrations to respond to this. Discussion increasingly centred, however, on a new form of conveyance – the railway – which would allow transport to escape from the limitations imposed by horse traction. Once the capacity of the railway had been proved in Britain, it was probably inevitable that French engineers and financiers, with government support, should first hesitatingly, but then with increasing rapidity, seek to create a new transport network.

The construction of a railway network in France occurred in response to the demand of economic and political interest groups to enjoy the advantages of low-cost, large-scale and rapid transport. In most cases this demand was based on an interpretation of particular material interests, in others on a more lofty conception of progress and modernity.

This book has been concerned less with the development of the railway networks *per se* than with the consequences for economic activity and more especially with the effects on agriculture. The improvement of communications was a permissive factor in the development of commerce and of agriculture. Nothing inevitably followed, but the establishment of a rail network, and the improvement of road and waterway transport, transformed the context of economic activity by improving access to markets and intensifying competitive pressures.

Prior to these developments, and in spite of the almost continual work of improvement of communications throughout the eighteenth and nineteenth centuries, the *ancien régime économique* had survived, typified by the fragmentation of markets. The firmest evidence for this is the variation in market prices over relatively short distances and repeated subsistence crises.

Railway development increased the degree of spatial integration within France from the late 1840s. Subsequently, from the 1860s, reductions in customs tariffs and in oceanic freight rates, together with the use of the telegraph, created a more efficient international market. Thus, within a very short period, a massive acceleration occurred of the age-old trend towards market integration and the commercialization of production. The pace of change was sufficiently rapid to cause repeated *crises d'adaptation* for both merchants and farmers as the technical conditions for their activities changed. New opportunities existed but within far more competitive markets.

Commerce served as the mediating factor between the demand for, and the supply of, agricultural commodities. The responsiveness of farmers to new opportunities and to competitive forces has to be considered in relation to commercial activity.

The conditions for commercial activity were transformed through the development of both the capacity for bulk transport and the rapid transmission of information. These developments promoted changes in the day-to-day practices of merchants, the overall effects of which were to reduce the costs and complexity of commercial operations and to benefit consumers, particularly through increasing the security of food supply. The structure of commerce was far from totally transformed. The organization of agriculture, with its numerous small-scale producers, facilitated the survival of small-scale trade, as did the structure of the retail trade and the location of consumers. However, by comparison with the cultivator who could choose to accept material deprivation in return for family subsistence, the small merchant was more pressed to earn a cash profit. The process of concentration in commerce, slow as it undoubtedly was, was more rapid than the concurrent process in agriculture.

The rural responses to the growing pressures for change varied, largely according to the pre-existing structures of farms, the characteristics of labour supply, the availability of capital, geographical situation in relation to the means of communication and natural endowments. Previous regional inequalities tended to be preserved even at new levels of development. Nevertheless, a decisive shift in the direction of commercial agriculture occurred within a relatively short period.

This accelerated development caused severe strains and considerable anxiety, particularly as import penetration increased, and looked likely to continue to do so indefinitely. Political pressures built up which successfully demanded a return to tariff protection. This succeeded in its objective of reducing competitive pressures and also inevitably had the effect of slowing structural change in French agriculture. Protection was one of the factors which facilitated the survival of the small peasant farm. Inertia on the part of many farmers was no doubt another, as were deliberate decisions in favour of a particular way of life. Inefficient, high-cost producers were able to survive for as long as they were prepared to bear the cost in terms of hard physical labour, poor material conditions and minimal leisure. The technical dualism of French agriculture became increasingly pronounced both between and within regions. The large-scale commercial farmer and his peasant counterpart continued to operate on the basis of contrasting rationales – for the latter his farm constituted a way of life rather than a means of making money. More generally, as a consequence of the relaxation of competitive pressures, French agriculture remained labour- rather than capital-intensive; its capacity for structural change and its rates of growth in productivity were necessarily restrained.

Yet while reminding ourselves of the survival of important continuities with the past, the developments we have sought to describe and explain constituted an economic and social revolution. The disappearance of the subsistence crises so characteristic of the *ancien régime économique*, together with the widening of people's horizons and the growing commercialization of relationships between town and country, are clear evidence of a major transformation of the way of life of the people of France. A new world was being created.

Notes and references

Place of publication is either London or Paris unless otherwise stated.

Introduction

1   G. Gunderson, *A New Economic History of America*, New York, 1976, p. 325.
2   P. O'Brien, *The New Economic History of the Railways*, 1977, p. 89.
3   Quoted in *Journal des chemins de fer*, 15 March 1856.
4   R. M. Hartwell, *The Industrial Revolution and Economic Growth*, 1971, p. 208.
5   B. S. Hoyle (ed.), *Transport and Development*, 1973, p. 16.
6   M. P. Todara, *Economics for a Developing World*, 1977, p. 6.
7   E. Pawson, *Transport and Economy: The Turnpike Roads of Eighteenth Century Britain*, 1977, p. 303.
8   H. L. Gauthier, 'Geography, transportation and regional development', in B. S. Hoyle (ed.), *Transport and Development*, p. 21.
9   I. M. Lewis, *Social Anthropology in Perspective*, 1976, pp. 19–20.
10 R. Firth, in R. Firth and B. S. Yamey (eds.), *Capital Saving and Credit in Peasant Societies*, 1964, pp. 15–16.
11 A. Gerschenkron, *Continuity in History and Other Essays*, Cambridge, Mass. 1968, p. 7.

Chapter 1   Agriculture before the railway

1   J.-C. Toutain, *Le produit de l'agriculture française de 1700 à 1958*, 1961, p. 118f.
2   W. H. Newell, 'The agricultural revolution in nineteenth-century France', *Journal of Economic History*, 1973, p. 710.
3   M. Agulhon, G. Désert, and R. Specklin, *Histoire de la France rurale*, vol. 3, *Apogée et crise de la civilisation paysanne, 1789–1914* (1976), p. 137.
4   G. Désert, 'Les paysans du Calvados au 19ᵉ siècle', *Annales de Normandie*, 1979, p. 128.
5   M. Morineau, *Les faux-semblants d'un démarrage économique: agriculture et démographie en France au 18ᵉ siècle*, 1970, p. 24.
6   F. Lullin de Châteauvieux, *Voyages agronomiques en France*, 2 vols., 1843.
7   See e.g. B. Mazières, 'Etude géographique de l'alimentation dans le département du Lot entre 1840 et 1880', *Revue géographique des Pyrénées et du Sud-Ouest*, 1954, pp. 299ff.; G. Désert, *Une société rurale au 19ᵉ siècle. Les paysans du Calvados 1815–1895*, vol. 1, Lille, 1975, p. 607.

8   Toutain, *Le produit de l'agriculture française*, pp. 13–14.

9   M. Augé-Laribé, *La politique agricole de la France de 1880 à 1940*, 1950, p. 16.

10   See, for example, M. Chevalier, *La vie humaine dans les pyrénées ariègoises*, 1956, pp. 146–7.

11   J. Pautard, *Les disparités régionales dans la croissance de l'agriculture française*, 1965, p. 102.

12   See, for example, P. Goujon, *Le vignoble de Saône-et-Loire au 19ᵉ siècle (1815–70)*, Lyon, 1974, pp. 113–14; R. Fruit, *La croissance économique du pays de Saint-Amand (Nord)*, 1963, p. 149.

13   P. E. Lloyd, and P. Dickens, *Location in Space: A Theoretical Approach to Economic Geography*, New York, 1972, p. 110.

14   Toutain, *Le produit de l'agriculture française*, pp. 1920–36, 1997–2010. See also B. Benassar, and J. Gay, 'Contribution à l'histoire de la consommation alimentaire du 14ᵉ au 19ᵉ siècles', *Annales ESC*, 1975, p. 427.

15   R. Musset, 'Les statistiques agricoles officielles françaises: étude critique', *Annales d'histoire économique et sociale*, 1933, p. 427.

16   One notable example is the *Enquête sur le travail agricole et industriel* of 1848, a reading of which clearly reveals the survival of what M. Chevalier referred to as the *ancien régime alimentaire* among the mass of the population.

17   See also G. Thuillier, 'Note sur les sources de l'histoire régionale de l'alimentation au 19ᵉ siècle', *Annales ESC*, 1968, p. 1302; M. Aymard, 'Pour l'histoire de l'alimentation quelques remarques de méthode', *Annales ESC*, 1975, p. 40.

18   A. Husson, *Les consommations de Paris*, 1858, pp. 106–8. Husson was a senior official at the Préfecture of the Seine, with full access to official documents.

19   See Bonnain-Moerdyk, 'Sur la cuisine traditionnelle comme culte culinaire du passé', *Ethnologie française*, 1972, p. 290.

20   Benassar and Gay, 'Contribution à l'histoire de la consommation', p. 411.

21   See, for example, Conseil d'Etat, *Enquête sur la boulangerie du département de la Seine*, 1859, p. 56, evidence of M. Bethmont; p. 440, evidence of M. Leclerc-Fleureau, miller and director of the municipal bakery at Orléans.

22   A. Blanqui, *Journal des économistes*, 1851.

23   G. Désert, 'Viande et poisson dans l'alimentation des français au milieu du 19ᵉ siècle', *Annales ESC*, 1975, p. 519.

Chapter 2   Pre-rail communication networks

1   See, however, M. Wolkowitsch, *L'économie des transports dans le centre et le centre-ouest de la France*, n.d.; A. Corbin, *Archaïsme et modernité en Limousin au 19ᵉ siècle*, vol. 1, 1975.

2   J.-C. Toutain, 'Les transports en France', *Economie et Société*, 1967.

3   For a general survey see R. Price, *An Economic History of Modern France*, 1981, ch. 2, *passim*.

4   Wolkowitsch, *L'économie des transports*, p. 35.

5   R. Dion, 'Orléans et l'ancienne navigation de la Loire', *Annales de géographie*, 1938, pp. 146–7.

6   Report from Procureur-Impérial, Lyon, 8 October 1853, in Archives Nationales (hereafter AN), BB³⁰379.

7   D. Faucher, *L'Homme et le Rhône*, 1968, p. 198.

8   1870 *Enquête sur le transport*, reply from arrondissement of Schlestadt (Bas-Rhin), in AN C1161; F. Rivet, *La navigation à vapeur sur la Saône et le Rhône*, 1962, pp. 116, 150.

9   M. Comoy, 'Documents statistiques sur le mouvement commercial du Canal du Centre', *Annales des ponts-et-chaussées*, 3ᵉ série, vol. 5, 1853, p. 184.

10 M. Belgrand, 'Etudes hydrologiques dans le bassin de la Seine entre la limite des terrains jurassiques et Paris', ibid., vol. 3, 1852, p. 61.

11 M. Vignon, 'Etudes statistiques sur la navigation de la rivière d'Yonne', ibid., vol. 1, 1851, p. 365.

12 See, for example, *Préfet*, Seine, 29 June 1817, in AN F¹¹2741.

13 A. Armengaud, *Les populations de l'Est Aquitain au début de l'époque contemporaine*, 1961, p. 128.

14 Wolkowitsch, *L'économie des transports*, p. 35.

15 A. Corbin, 'Limousins migrants et Limousins sédentaires', unpublished Doctorat d'état, Clermont-Ferrand, 1973, pp. 146–7.

16 See, for example, Comoy, 'Documents statistiques', pp. 158–9.

17 Reported in *Annales des ponts-et-chaussées*, 3ᵉ série, vol. 2, 1856, p. 254.

18 Senior Ponts-et-Chaussées engineers show a frequent concern with economic viability; see, for example, M. Comoy, 'Observations sur les conditions dans lesquelles on doit mettre les canaux de navigation pour qu'ils puissent augmenter la fortune publique', *Annales des ponts-et-chaussées*, 2ᵉ série, vol. 14, 1847, pp. 166–7.

19 F. Caron, *Histoire de l'exploitation d'un grand réseau. La compagnie du chemin de fer du Nord, 1846–1937*, 1973, p. 56.

20 Dion, 'Orléans', p. 152.

21 ibid.

22 Comoy, 'Observations sur les conditions dans lesquelles on doit mettre les canaux de navigation pour qu'ils puissent augmenter la fortune publique'.

23 Reported by General Officer Commanding (hereafter GOC) 16th *Division militaire* (hereafter DM), 19 April 1847, in Archives historiques du Ministère de la Guerre (AHG), E⁵158.

24 Comoy, 'Documents statistiques', pp. 173–4.

25 See, for example, *Procureur-du-Roi* (PR) at Lyon, 21 November 1845, in AN BB¹⁹38.

26 Minister of Agriculture to Justice, 23 October 1846, in AN BB¹⁹38.

27 PG, Lyon, 7 November 1846, in AN BB¹⁹37.

28 PR, Lyon, 22 October 1846, in ibid.

29 Dion, 'Orléans'.

30 See, for example, contracts with Bruard, *commissaire de roulage* at Paris, and Lesseur fils for transport of cereals, in AN F¹¹1409–10.

31 L. Girard, *La politique des travaux publics du Second Empire*, 1952, pp. 17–18.

32 See, for example, Compagnie du chemin de fer du Nord, inspector's report to Comité du direction, 13 March 1846, in AN 48 AQ 3660.

33 M. Chanoine, 'Mémoire sur les tonnages de la Haute-Seine', *Annales des ponts-et-chaussées*, 2ᵉ série, vol. 8, 1854, p. 358; see also Chambre de Commerce de Paris, *Rapport sur les tarifs de navigation*, 1846, *passim*.

34 Vignon, 'Etudes statistiques sur la navigation de la rivière d'Yonne', p. 378.

35 Chanoine, 'Mémoire'.

36   Girard, *La politique des travaux publics*, pp. 22, 32; Rivet, *La navigation à vapeur*, p. 42.

37   See, for example, report to Nord Comité de direction, 13 March 1846, in AN 48 AQ 3660.

38   Evidence of M. Pommier, editor of *Echo agricole*, to Conseil d'Etat. *Enquête sur la révision de la législation des céréales*, vol. 1, 1859, pp. 128–9.

39   ibid., p. 439, evidence of M. Durand, merchant and landowner, deputy for Pyrénées-Orientales.

40   M. Lévy-Leboyer, *Les banques européennes et l'industrialisation internationale dans la première moitié du 19ᵉ siècle*, 1964, p. 280.

41   *Journal d'agriculture pratique*, 2ᵉ série, vol. 3, 1845–6, p. 378.

42   Girard, *La politique des travaux publics*, p. 30.

43   D. Renouard, *Les Transports de marchandises par fer, route, et eau depuis 1850*, 1960, p. 39; cf. Lévy-Leboyer, *Les banques européennes*, p. 290, who estimates that about two-thirds (i.e. 22,760 million tks) were carried by land.

44   The census is summarized in Renouard, *Les Transports de marchandises*, p. 69.

45   Ministère de l'Intérieur, *Statistique des routes royales de France . . . 1824*, p. vi.

46   Minister of Interior to Directeur de l'approvisionnement de réserve pour Paris, 22 October 1816, in AN F¹¹1409–10.

47   For a mass of details on road improvement by department see AN F¹⁴1444–1673 (1794–1850); F¹⁴1674–1756 (1840–95); F¹⁴1757–1878 (1820–50). I have only sampled these series.

48   Ministère des Travaux Publics, *Documents statistiques sur les routes et les ponts*, 1873; *Annuaire statistique de l'Insée*, 1952; see also Toutain, 'Les transports en France', p. 11.

49   Ministère de l'Intérieur, *Administration générale des ponts-et-chaussées . . . Statistique des routes royales de France*, 1824, in AN AD XIX i 147.

50   For detailed topographical descriptions, including road conditions throughout the century, see the reports in AHG series *Mémoires et reconnaissances* (MR).

51   On this legislation see Ponts-et-Chaussées, *Police du roulage, Rapport d'une commission . . .*, 9 August 1814, in AN AD XIX N51.

52   Petition to Minister of the Interior and Commerce, from *négociants* of Valence (Drôme), November 1846; Minister of Agriculture to Prefect of the Drôme, 23 November 1846, in AN F¹¹2758.

53   Undated reply of the Mayor of St-Etienne to the 1811 inquiry into transport, in AN F¹⁴1270.

54   Corbin, 'Limousins migrants et Limousins sédentaires', p. 141.

55   M. Charté-Marsaines, 'Mémoire sur la comparaison des chaussées pavées et empierrées et sur la force de traction du cheval', *Annales des ponts-et-chaussées*, 3ᵉ série, vol. 13, 1854, pp. 161f.

56   G. Dupeux, *Aspects de l'histoire sociale et politique du Loir-et-Cher*, 1962, pp. 217–18.

57   M. Bonamy, 'Note sur l'entretien des routes en empierrement', *Annales des ponts-et-chaussées*, 2ᵉ série, 1847, table 14, p. 114.

58   *Rapport au Roi par . . . M le Comte Decazes, Ministère de l'Intérieur sur les travaux du conseil d'agriculture pendant l'année 1819*, 1820, p. 38, in AN F¹⁰1482.

59 *Ministère de l'Intérieur . . . Statistique des routes royales de France,* 1824; see also Ministry of the Interior circular to Prefects of 20 April 1818 on the need to avoid burdening local taxpayers, in AN F²I 1027.

60 In AN F²I 1027.

61 ibid.

62 Ministère de l'Intérieur, *Direction des Ponts-et-Chaussées, Chemins vicinaux. Instruction pour l'exécution de la loi du 21 mai 1836,* article 2, in AN AD XIX N52.

63 *Enquête agricole 1866 Rapport . . . par le Directeur de l'agriculture, commissaire général de l'enquête,* vol. 1, 1867, pp. 147f., 324f. provides a survey of legislation.

64 *Chemins vicinaux. Instruction pour l'exécution de la loi du 21 mai 1836,* article 7, in AN AD XIX N52; and also Minister of Interior Circular to Prefects of 21 May 1836 on implementation, ibid.

65 ibid.

66 Ministère de l'Intérieur, *Rapport au roi sur l'exécution pendant l'année 1839, de la loi du 21 mai 1836 relative aux chemins vicinaux,* 1840, pp. vii–viii, in AN AD XIX N183.

67 See, for example, G. Garrier, *Paysans du Beaujolais et du Lyonnais,* vol. 1, Grenoble, 1973, p. 331.

68 *Rapport . . . sur l'exécution pendant l'année 1839, de la loi du 21 mai 1836,* p. 197.

69 *Enquête agricole,* 1866, vol. 1.

70 *Enquête agricole,* 1866, vol. 2, Maine-et-Loire, p. 269.

71 *Rapport . . . sur l'exécution pendant l'année 1839, de la loi du 21 mai 1836,* p. lii.

72 Ponts-et-Chaussées, *arrondissement* Bayonne (Basses-Pyrénées), report on projected railway line Toulouse–Bayonne, in AN F¹⁴9240.

73 Armengaud, *Les populations de l'Est,* p. 127.

74 1866 *Enquête,* vol. 13, Bas and Haut-Rhin, p. 97.

75 *Enquête,* 1848, Archives départementales (AD), Nord M 547/1.

76 *Rapport du commissaire extraordinaire du Gouvernement, Préfet du Rhône, au conseil général du département, Session de 1851–2,* Lyon, 1851, p. 8.

77 For awareness of this see, for example, report of the *comice agricole* at Fouesuant (Finistère), in AN C1157.

78 See, for example, M. Chevalier, *La vie humaine dans les pyrénées ariègeoises,* 1956, p. 280; P. Bozon, *La vie rurale en Vivarais,* 1963, pp. 120, 277.

79 Corbin, 'Limousins migrants et Limousins sédentaires', p. 142.

80 See, for example, report of *Préfet,* Doubs, 13 December 1846, in AN F¹¹2758.

81 See, for example, Minister of Agriculture to Minister of Public Works, 6 November 1846, in AN F¹¹2758; *Journal d'agriculture pratique,* vol. 4, 1846–7, p. 190.

82 M. Gautier, *Chemins et véhicules de nos campagnes,* St-Brieuc, 1971, p. 77.

83 See ministerial circular of 16 November 1839, quoted by R. Falaise, *Des chemins et sentiers d'exploitation,* 1907, p. 14.

84 See, for example, *Bulletin des séances de la Société royale d'agriculture,* 1845–6, p. 502; ibid., 1846–7, p. 53, speech of M. Berthereau de la Giraudière.

85 P. Richard, 'Les charges de transport dans les exploitations agricoles des divers types', *Economie rurale,* 1962, p. 14; E. Guillaumin, *La vie d'un simple,* 1904, p. 42, for the not untypical case of a farm in the Allier.

86   AN F^{14}1270 and AN C1161.
87   Report from the Mayor of Lyon, 24 September 1811, in AN F^{14}1270.
88   Reply of the Mayor of Nantes, 3 October 1811, in AN F^{14}1270.
89   Report from Mont-de-Marson (undated) 1812, ibid.
90   Reply of the Chamber of Commerce at La Rochelle (Charente-Inférieure) to the transport inquiry of 1870, in AN C1161.
91   Reply of the *comice agricole* of Forcalquier (Basses-Alpes), ibid.
92   Reply of the *Chambre consultative*, Le Puy, ibid.
93   Reply signed by a large number of businessmen at Ste-Menehould, ibid.
94   Chambre consultative de Sens (Yonne), ibid.
95   Reply from the secretary of the Chambre d'agriculture of the Somme, ibid.
96   Reply from the mayor of Ferté-Mace (Orne), ibid.
97   *Conseil général . . . de la Somme, Rapport de M Gaulthier de Rumilly sur la question des subsistances. Séance du 4 Septembre 1847*, p. 8.
98   See Report of Mayor of St-Symphorien (Gironde), undated (1811/12), in AN F^{14}1270.
99   Rivet, *La navigation à vapeur*, pp. 23–4.
100 Report from Mayor of Valence, 13 December 1846, in AN F^{11}2758.
101 M. de Courtais, deputy for Montluçon to Minister of War, 2 February 1847, in AHG E^{5}153.
102 Reply from M. le Flô, *arrondissement* de Moutiers (Savoie), in AN C1161.
103 Report from Mayor of Lyon, 24 September 1811, in AN F^{11}1270.
104 Reply from Mayor of St-Etienne, undated (1811/12), ibid.
105 Reply of Mayor of Vinça, 11 September 1812, ibid.
106 See, for example, Report of Mayors of St-Sever (Landes) and St-Rambert (Loire), undated (1811/12), in AN F^{14}1270.
107 See AN F^{14}1270.
108 See AN C1161.
109 L. Marchal, *Question des subsistances. Mémoire qui a obtenu la médaille d'or de M. Cormenin dans le concours ouvert par la société charitable*, 1849, p. 76.
110 P. Lévèque, 'La Bourgogne de la monarchie de juillet au Second Empire' unpublished Doctorat d'Etat, Université de Paris I, 1976, vol. 1, pp. 352–3.
111 M. Minard, 'Notions élémentaires d'économie politique appliquée aux travaux publics', *Annales des ponts-et-chaussées*, 2e série, vol. 19, 1850, p. 12.
112 M. Chisholm, *Human Geography: Evolution or Revolution?*, 1967, p. 94.

Chapter 3   Agricultural market structures before the coming of the railways

1   B. Gille, *Les sources statistiques de l'histoire de France*, Geneva, 1964, p. 158.
2   *Mémoire* written by L.-P. Desneubourg, *justice de paix*, and A. Profillet, *commissaire de police* of the canton of Montmarillon (Vienne), 1856, in AN F^{11}2752.
3   Gille, *Les sources statistiques*, pp. 13–14.
4   AN F^{11}2755, see especially report from Mayor of Metz, 28 July 1851.
5   A. R. H. Baker, 'Rethinking historical geography', in A. R. H. Baker (ed.), *Progress in Historical Geography*, Newton Abbot, 1972, p. 20.
6   M. Chisholm, *Human Geography: Evolution or Revolution?*, 1967, pp. 43–4.
7   Conseil d'Etat 1859, vol. 1, p. 157, evidence of M. Babille, *propriétaire-agriculteur* in Loiret.

8   See, for example, report from the *sous-préfet* at Bayeux for December 1853, in AN F¹CIII Calvados 9.

9   AN F¹⁴1270; see also M. Blanchard, 'L'enquête de 1811 sur le roulage', *Revue de géographie alpine*, 1920, pp. 588–9.

10 E. Fox, *History in Geographical Perspective: The Other France*, 1971, p. 25; see also E. le Roy, *Le Moulin de Frau*, n.d., pp. 118–19, for an elucidation of the practical problems.

11 J. Dagnan, *Le Gers sous la seconde république*, vol. 1, Auch, 1928, pp. xvi–xvii.

12 G. Désert, *Les Paysans du Calvados*, vol. 1, Lille, 1975, p. 149.

13 B. Barbier, *Villes et centres des Alpes du sud. Etude de réseau urbain*, Gap, n.d., pp. 16–20.

14 Y. Babonaux, *Villes et régions de la Loire moyenne*, 1966, p. 27.

15 R. Laurent, *L'agriculture en Côte-d'Or pendant la première moitié du 19ᵉ siècle*, Dijon, 1931, pp. 116–17.

16 *Journal des chemins de fer départementaux*, editorial of 30 June 1855.

17 G. Frêche, *Toulouse et la région Midi-Pyrénées au siècle des lumières*, Toulouse, 1974, pp. 700f.

18 ibid., pp. 777–84.

19 This follows closely M. Reinhard, 'La révolution en Ile-de-France', in M. Mollat (ed.) *Histoire de l'Ile-de-France et de Paris*, Toulouse, 1971, p. 411; see also reports from the mayors of Pont-Ste-Maxence, 26 November 1811, and of Crespy (Oise), 10 July 1812, in AN F¹⁴1270.

20 See, for example, Mayor, Provins, 20 November 1811, in AN F¹⁴1270.

21 PG, Dijon, 25 August 1846; PG, Lyon, 6 November 1846, in AN BB¹⁹38; *Journal d'agriculture pratique*, vol. 4, 1846–7, p. 218, *Revue commerciale* for January 1847. P. Lévèque, 'La Bourgogne de la monarchie de juillet au Second Empire', unpublished Doctorat d'état, Universite de Paris I, 1976, p. 295.

22 Commission of inquiry into proposed railway, meeting at Boulogne in 1842, papers in AN F¹⁴8821. See also 1811 *Enquête*, reply of mayor of Douai, in AN F¹⁴1270.

23 Frêche, *Toulouse*, pp. 818–19, who asserts that these currents changed little in the first half of the nineteenth century. M. Chevalier, *La vie humaine dans les pyrénées ariègeoises*, 1956, p. 628.

24 P. Vigier, *La Seconde République dans la région alpine*, vol. 1, 1963, pp. 72–3.

25 Laurent, *L'agriculture en Côte-d'Or*, pp. 118, 133–4.

26 See, for example, report from the PG, Paris, 4 March 1854, in AN BB³⁰432, for an analysis of the situation prevailing in the Beauce.

27 L. Chevalier, 'Les fondements économiques et sociaux de l'histoire politique de la région parisienne', unpublished Doctorat ès lettres, Université de Paris, 1950, pp. 175–6.

28 1866 *Enquête*, vol. 9, Allier, pp. 27–8, also makes this point.

29 ibid., vol. 23, Ardèche, p. 39.

30 ibid., vol. 13, Bas and Haut-Rhin, p. 134.

31 Chamber of commerce, Metz, *Rapport sur les travaux du conseil général de agriculture, des manufactures et du commerce*, Metz, 1850, pp. 33–4; Ministère de l'Agriculture to Minister des Travaux Publics (TP), 20 June 1851, in AN F¹⁴9389.

32   GOC 4th DM, 23 January 1847, in AHG E⁵155.

33   PR, Lyon, 8 November 1846, in AN BB¹⁹38.

34   P. Gonnet, 'Contribution à l'étude du trafic routier au milieu du 19ᵉ siècle', *Actes du 90ᵉ Congrès national des sociétés savantes*, vol. 3, 1966, p. 113.

35   *Ministère de l'Intérieur . . . Statistique des routes royales de France 1824*, p. ii, in AN AD XIX i 147.

36   *Journal d'agriculture pratique*, vol. 4, 1846–7, p. 189, *Revue commerciale* for December 1846.

37   Conseil d'Etat 1859, vol. 2, p. 85, evidence of General Yvelin, *propriétaire-agriculteur* and member of *comice agricole* de Provins (Seine-et-Marne).

38   PG, Dijon, 8 February 1847, in AN BB¹⁹38.

39   *Journal d'agriculture pratique*, vol. 4, 1846–7, p. 218, *Revue commerciale* for January 1847.

40   Conseil d'Etat 1859, vol. 1, p. 346, evidence of Marquis de Fontette, *propriétaire-agriculteur* in Calvados, president of the *Chambre consultative d'agriculture* de Caen.

41   See, for example, *Enquête sur la boulangerie* (1859 *Enquête*), p. 774, evidence of the Vicomte de Tocqueville.

42   Frêche, *Toulouse*.

43   For descriptions of some of the markets in the Paris region see, for example mayors of Pont-Ste-Maxence, of Crespy (Oise), of Provins (Seine-et-Marne), in AN F¹⁴1270; 1859 *Enquête*, p. 553, evidence of M. Gonnart, secretary of *comice agricole*, St-Quentin.

44   1859 *Enquête*, pp. 40–1, evidence of M. Bethmont.

45   M. Chanoine, 'Mémoire sur le tonnage de la Haute-Saône', *Annales des ponts-et-chaussées*, 3ᵉ série, vol. 8, 1854, p. 370.

46   1866 *Enquête*, vol. 13, Bas- and Haut-Rhin, p. 134.

47   *Préfet*, Moselle, 19 January 1847, in AN F¹¹2758.

48   Report from the Mayor of Valence to the *Préfet* of the Drôme of 13 December 1846, in AN F¹¹2758.

49   What follows depends heavily on Frêche, *Toulouse*, pp. 700f.

50   ibid., pp. 781–3.

51   Conseil d'Etat 1859, vol. 2, p. 772, evidence of M. Coste-Floret, mayor of Agde (Hérault); ibid., p. 358, of M. Pagenzy, landowner, Mayor of Montpellier, president of *comice agricole*, Castres.

52   Frêche, *Toulouse*, pp. 797, 800, 818–19; G. Jorré, 'Le commerce des grains et la minoterie à Toulouse', *Revue géographique des Pyrénées et du Sud-Ouest*, 1933, p. 44.

53   Report from OC 13 Legion *gendarmerie*, 2 February 1847, in AHG E⁵156. Conseil d'Etat 1859, vol. 2, p. 590, evidence of M. Blondeau, grain merchant, member of Bordeaux Chamber of Commerce.

54   1866 *Enquête*, vol. 21, Aude, p. 27.

55   Jorré, 'Le commerce des grains', pp. 47–8.

56   G. Frêche, 'Etudes statistiques sur le commerce céréalière de la France méridionale au 18ᵉ siècle', *Revue d'histoire économique et sociale*, 1971, p. 191.

57   Report from OC 13 Legion *gendarmerie*, 4 March 1847, in AHG E⁵156.

58   ibid., 17 March 1847.

59 A. Corbin, 'Limousins migrants et Limousins sédentaires. Contribution à l'histoire de la région limousine au 19ᵉ siècle', unpublished Doctorat d'état, Université de Clermont-Ferrand, 1973, pp. 151–7.

60 *Préfet*, Allier, 13 November 1846, in AN F¹¹2758; Conseil d'Etat 1859, vol. 2, p. 709, evidence of M. Lupin, *propriétaire-agriculteur* in Cher.

61 Report from the GOC 11 DM, 5 February 1847, in AHG E⁵156.

62 *Préfet*, Creuse, 27 February 1847, in AN F¹¹2758.

63 ibid.

64 In AN F¹¹2758.

65 Conseil d'Etat 1859, vol. 2, pp. 676–7, evidence of Baron Laugier de Chartroux, *propriétaire*, and deputy for Bouches-du-Rhône.

66 See, for example, ibid., vol. 1, p. 539, evidence of M. Rodet, president of the Société d'agriculture de l'Ain.

67 See, for example, Conseil d'Etat 1859, vol. 1, p. 5, evidence of Marquis d'Andellarre, vice-president, Société d'agriculture de la Haute-Saône. P. Gonnet, 'Contribution à l'étude du trafic routier au milieu du 19ᵉ siècle', p. 103; F. Rivet, *La navigation à vapeur sur la Saône et le Rhône*, 1962, p. 116.

68 1866 *Enquête*, vol. 26, Haute-Saône, p. 60.

69 Laurent, *L'agriculture en Côte-d'Or*, p. 135; G. Martin, 'Evolution de l'agriculture en Auxois de 1840 à 1939', *Cahiers de l'association interuniversitaire de l'Est*, 1966, p. 105; Lévèque, 'La Bourgogne', pp. 293–4.

70 Y. Nolle, 'Dijon au début du Second Empire (1851–8): Notes sur une crise de croissance économique', *Annales de Bourgogne*, 1952, p. 278.

71 Frêche, *Toulouse*, p. 695.

72 R. Livet, *Habitat rural et structures agraires en Basse-Provence*, Aix, 1962, p. 99.

73 Laurent, *L'agriculture en Côte-d'Or*, pp. 116–18, 135.

74 1866 *Enquête*, vol. 26, Haute-Saône, p. 70.

75 *Préfet*, Côte-d'Or, 4 November 1846, in AN F¹¹2758.

76 See, for example, P. Seignour, *La vie économique du Vaucluse de 1815 à 1848*, Aix, 1957, p. 161.

77 1859 *Enquête*, p. 271, evidence of M. Vaisse, Préfet of Rhône.

78 For example, *Préfet*, Doubs, 3 November 1846; Prefect, Drôme, 13 December 1846; *Préfet*, Côte-d'Or, 17 June 1847, in AN F¹¹2758.

79 Minister of Agriculture to War, 19 November 1846, in AHG E⁵159.

80 Conseil d'Etat 1859, vol. 1, pp. 410–11, evidence of M. Vachon, *négociant meunier*, member of Société de l'agriculture, des arts et de l'industrie, Lyon.

81 17 January 1847, in AN F¹¹2758. See also *Préfet*, Rhône, undated report (probably 1850), in AN F¹¹2758 on redistributive role.

82 1866 *Enquête*, vol. 23, Ardèche, p. 39; Ministry of War, internal note on Ardèche, in AHG E⁵156.

83 1866 *Enquête*, vol. 23, Drôme, p. 25.

84 Mayor Valence to *Préfet*, 13 December 1846, in AN F¹¹2758.

85 *Préfet*, Rhône, undated report (probably 1850).

86 GOC 18 DM, 9 February 1847, in AHG E⁵159.

87 Seignour, *La vie économique du Vaucluse*, p. 162.

88 A factor noted by the Mayor of Lyon, 24 September 1811, in AN F¹⁴1270.

89 In AHG E⁵155.

90   In AN F¹¹2758.

91   Conseil d'Etat, *Enquête sur le courtage*, 1864, pp. 259–60, in AN AD XIX D 167.

92   R. Dion, 'Orléans et l'ancienne navigation de la Loire', *Annales de géographie*, 1938, pp. 134–5.

93   *Préfet*, Allier, 13 November 1846; *sous-préfet*, Montluçon, 27 October 1846, in AN F¹¹2758.

94   GOC Mayenne, 24 January 1847, in AHG E⁵155. See also Commission municipale du Mans, *Chemin de fer de Paris à Rennes par le Mans*, Le Mans, 1846, p. 20.

95   Minister of Interior to War, 14 November 1846, in AHG E⁵154.

96   *Préfet*, Maine-et-Loire, 6 October 1846, in AN F¹¹2758; *Journal d'agriculture pratique*, vol. 4, 1846–7, p. 218, *Revue commerciale* for January 1847.

97   PG, Angers, 11 September 1846, in AHG E⁵157.

98   ibid.

99   Minister of Agriculture to War, 16 January 1847, in AHG E⁵155.

100   OC 7th Legion *gendarmerie*, 7 January 1847, ibid.

101   Conseil d'Etat 1859, vol. 2, p. 600, evidence of M. Piedvache, *négociant en grains* at St-Brieuc (Côtes-du-Nord).

102   *Préfet*, Charente-Inférieure, (?) March 1847, in AN F¹¹2758; GOC 13 DM, 4 February 1847, in AHG E⁵159; Minister of Agriculture to War, 16 January 1847, in AHG E⁵155.

103   OC 13th Legion *gendarmerie*, 8 February 1847, in AHG E⁵156.

104   Conseil d'Etat 1859, vol. 2, p. 358, evidence of M. Pagézy, mayor of Montpellier.

105   ibid., p. 431, M. Human, *négociant*, president, Tribunal de commerce, and vice-president, Chambre de Commerce of Morlaix.

106   1866 *Enquête*, vol. 22, Bouches-du-Rhône, p. 818, evidence of M. Gros.

107   GOC 13 DM, 14 June 1845, in AHG E⁵159, and for an earlier period report of Paris Prefect of Police, 18 October 1815, in AN F¹¹2741.

108   Extract from Registre des délibérations du conseil municipal de la ville de Montpellier, session 1 May 1849, in AN F¹¹2750; see also Prefect Lozère, 29 March 1847, in AN F¹¹2758.

109   J.-C. Toutain, *Le produit de l'agriculture française de 1700 à 1958*, 1961, p. 224.

110   Bureau des subsistances, *Récoltes de céréales*, p. xxiii.

111   In AN F¹¹2749.

112   See chapter 5.

113   P. Bairoch, 'Commerce extérieur et développement économique. Quelques enseignements de l'expérience libre-échangiste de la France au 19ᵉ siècle', *Revue économique*, 1970, p. 4.

114   P. Marres, 'La modernisation de l'économie du Bas-Languedoc et les Cévennes méridionales', *Société languedocienne de géographie: Bulletin*, 1954, pp. 126–7.

115   E. Levasseur, *Histoire du commerce de la France*, vol. 2, 1912, p. 161.

116   D. Zolla, *Le blé et les céréales*, 1909, p. 96.

117   Official orthodoxy well expressed by *Préfet*, Allier, in a circular to *sous-préfets* of 16 November 1846, in AN F¹¹2758.

118   Amendment of 1821 – previously 19–23 francs.

119 Zolla, *Le blé et les céréales*; Levasseur, *Histoire du commerce de la France*, vol. 2, pp. 180–1.

120 Conseil d'Etat 1859, vol. 3, pp. 26–7, *Rapport à S. M. l'Empereur sur la question de la révision de la législation sur les céréales*, for a description of the system.

121 Report commissioned by the Paris Préfecture de Police: *Les moyens de prévenir des fluctuations excessives du prix extrêmes du pain à Paris*, 1853, p. 25, in AN AD XIX S 7.

122 Jorré, *Le commerce des grains*, pp. 47–8; *sous-préfet*, Dunkirk, 31 October 1854, in AN F C III Nord 8.

123 *Préfet*, Bas-Rhin, 4 July 1817, in AN F^{11}2741.

124 P. Schöler, 'L'évolution séculaire des taux de fret et d'assurance maritimes, 1819–1940', *Bulletin de l'institut de recherches économiques et sociales* (Louvain), 1951, pp. 523f.

125 See, for example, *La Presse*, 10 November 1845.

126 1859 *Enquête*, p. 68, evidence of M. Gosset, economist.

127 Letter to Minister of Agriculture, 24 March 1847, in AN F^{11}2758.

128 11 January 1847, ibid.

129 See, for example, M. Jacqmin, 'Notes sur l'agriculture et les chemins de fer', *Annales des ponts-et-chaussées*, 4e série, vol. 10, pp. 325–6.

130 AN F^{11}2752.

131 Conseil d'Etat 1859, vol. 2, p. 626, evidence of M. Warner, shipowner and *négociant* at Le Havre; PG Dijon, 8 March 1847, in AN BB^{19}38.

132 See, for example, Chambre de commerce de Metz, *Rapport sur les travaux du conseil général de l'agriculture, des manufactures et du commerce*, Metz, 1850, p. 39.

133 See also 1859 *Enquête*, pp. 217–19, evidence of M. Pommier, editor-in-chief of the *Echo agricole*; ibid., p. 770, M. Joubert de Delord, municipal councillor at Marseille.

134 1859 *Enquête*, p. 758, evidence of M. Lenoir, director of the *manutention civile* at Lyon.

135 See, for example, *gendarmerie* commander Doubs, monthly report for January 1847, for fears concerning the solvency of several flour merchants at Gray, in AN F^{7}3985.

136 1866 *Enquête*, vol. 13, Bas- and Haut-Rhin, p. 138; see also letter from M. Labaume, grain merchant at Paris, to Minister of Commerce, 9 March 1847, in AN F^{11}2758.

137 M. Chevalier, *Des forces alimentaires des états et des devoirs du gouvernement dans la crise actuelle*, 1847, p. 44.

138 Conseil d'Etat 1859, vol. 3, p. 249, evidence of M. Hippolyte Passy; ibid., vol. 2, p. 598, of A. Léon, shipowner at Bordeaux.

139 ibid., vol. 2, p. 294, evidence of M. Schotsman, miller and grain merchant at Dun near Lille (Nord).

140 ibid., vol. 2, p. 458, evidence of H. Barbet, landowner and president of the Chambre consultative d'agriculture de Rouen.

141 Conseil d'Etat 1859, vol. 2, pp. 727–8, evidence of M. Lebeau, merchant and shipowner at Boulogne-sur-Mer.

142 B. Gille, *Histoire de la maison Rothschild*, vol. 1, Geneva, 1965, pp. 409–10.

143   1859 *Enquête*, p. 350, evidence of M. Payen, Professor at the Conservatoire des arts et des métiers, secretary-general of the Société impériale et centrale d'agriculture.

144   See, for example, *sous-préfet*, Dunkirk, 31 October 1854, in AN F¹C III Nord 8.

145   Préfecture de Police, *Les moyens de prévenir des fluctuations excessives du prix des blés*, p. 25.

146   See *Préfet*, Doubs, 6 November 1846, in AN F¹¹2758. Minister of Agriculture to War, 16 January 1847, in AHG E⁵155.

147   See, for example, *Céréales: Etat des récoltes à l'étranger 1846–59*, in AN F¹¹2751.

148   1859 *Enquête*, p. 786, evidence of M. Formant, former *syndic de la boulangerie* at Cambrai (Nord); *sous-préfet*, Provins, report for March–April 1854, in AN BB³⁰383.

149   Published in *Journal d'agriculture pratique*, vol. 4, 1846–7, p. 120.

150   *Journal d'agriculture pratique*, 4ᵉ série, vol. 2, 1854, p. 475, *Revue commerciale* for second half of November.

151   See Conseil d'Etat 1859, vol. 1, p. 432, evidence of M. Aynard, merchant at Lyon.

152   ibid., vol. 2, p. 684, evidence of Comte Benoît d'Azy, landowner in Nièvre, member of the departmental agricultural society.

153   *Préfet*, Côte-d'Or, 17 January 1847, in AN F¹¹2758.

154   1859 *Enquête*, pp. 40–1, evidence of M. Bethmont, *avocat*.

155   Report of 22 January 1847, quoted by A. Thuillier, *Economie et société nivernaise au début du 19ᵉ siècle*, 1976, p. 260.

156   1859 *Enquête*, p. 68, evidence of Gosset, economist.

157   See, for example, J. Letaconnoux, *Les subsistances et le commerce des grains en Bretagne au 18ᵉ siècle*, Rennes, 1909, pp. 40–9, 265, 342.

158   Ministre de l'agriculture internal memo, 'Observations extraites d'un rapport présenté après la crise [of 1812] par M. le Comte de Montalivet, Ministre de l'intérieur', undated (probably October–November 1853), in AN F¹¹2752.

159   1859 *Enquête*, p. 774, evidence of Vicomte de Tocqueville, President of Compiègne agricultural society.

160   1859 *Enquête*, p. 68.

161   Letter of 9 March 1847, in AN F¹¹2758.

162   4 November 1846, in AN F¹¹2758.

163   See, for example, 7th Legion *gendarmerie*, 5 January 1847, in AHG E⁵155, for a description of supply and price movements at Tours.

164   7 April 1817, in AN F¹¹2741.

165   GOC 10th DM, 22 February 1847; and GOC 11th DM, 5 February 1847, in AHG E⁵156; GOC 4 DM, 7 February in AHG E⁵155; GOC 12 DM, 5 October 1846, in AHG E⁵157; 13th Legion gend., 17 March 1847, in AHG E⁵156; *gendarmerie* commander in Finistère for November 1846, in AN F⁷4002.

166   G. Thuillier, *Aspects de l'économie nivernaise au 19ᵉ siècle*, 1966, p. 19.

167   In An F¹¹2752.

168   1859 *Enquête*, p. 197, evidence of Darblay the elder.

169   ibid., p. 445, evidence of M. Bella.

170   ibid., p. 674, evidence of A. de St-Léger.

171 ibid., pp. 442–3, evidence of M. Leclerc-Fleureau, director of *manutention civile* at Orléans.

172 A. Husson, *Les consommations de Paris*, 1856, p. 92. A decree of 1 November 1854 increased the quoted figure to 210,825 sacks or 330,995 quintals.

173 1859 *Enquête*, pp. 197–8, evidence of Darblay the elder. GOC 4th DM, 2 January 1847, in AHG E⁵155.

174 1859 *Enquête*, p. 68, evidence of M. Gosset; A. Boland, *Traité pratique de la boulangerie*, 1860, pp. 63–5.

175 See, for example, *Préfet* Creuse, 26 September 1846, in AN F¹¹2758; F. Ponteil, *La crise alimentaire dans le Bas-Rhin en 1847*, 1926, p. 11.

176 23 September 1846, in AN F¹¹2758.

177 Minister of Agriculture to War, 16 January 1847, in AHG E⁵155.

178 J. Meyer, *La noblesse bretonne au 18ᵉ siècle*, 1966, pp. 507–8.

179 GOC 20th DM, 31 March 1847, in AHG E⁵159.

180 See, for example, Conseil d'Etat 1859, vol. 1, p. 359, evidence of Marquis de Fontette, president de la Chambre consultative d'agriculture de Caen.

181 *Sous-préfet*, Provins, 3 November 1855, in AN F¹C III, Seine-et-Marne, 7; *Journal d'agriculture pratique*, 4ᵉ série, vol. 2, p. 475.

182 PG Rouen, 13 September 1854, in AN BB³⁰432.

183 See, for example, *Préfet*, Allier, 20 November 1846, in AN F¹¹2785.

184 See, for example, 1866 *Enquête*, vol. 26, Haute-Saône, p. 70.

185 See, for example, Société d'agriculture de l'arrondissement de Yvetot (Seine-Inférieure), session of 10 August 1851, in AN F¹⁰1482.

186 1859 *Enquête*, p. 196, evidence of M. Darblay *aîné, propriétaire-agriculteur*, retired miller, member of *comice agricole* of Melun and Provins (Seine-et-Marne).

187 1859 *Enquête*, pp. 686–7, evidence of M. Bazille, grain merchant and land-owner, deputy to the mayor of Rouen (Seine-Inférieure).

188 7th Legion *gendarmerie*, 23 January 1847, in AHG E⁵155.

189 R. Marlin, *La crise des subsistances de 1816–17 dans le Doubs*, Besançon, 1960, p. 21.

190 1 October 1858, in AN F¹C III, Côtes-du-Nord, 11.

191 See, for example, 1859 *Enquête*, pp. 744–5, evidence of M. Jozon, member of the *comice agricole*, Aude.

192 Meyer, *La noblesse bretonne*, pp. 504, 512–13.

193 For example, *Préfet*, Loir-et-Cher, 29 March 1847, in AN F¹¹2758.

194 For example, 7th Legion *gendarmerie*, 21 February 1847, in AHG E⁵155 on market of 20 February at Blois.

195 An F⁷4042.

196 For example, PG Poitiers, 31 January 1854, in AN BB³⁰385; GOC 4th DM, 18 July 1847, in AHG E⁵155.

197 1859 *Enquête*, pp. 686–7.

198 1859 *Enquête*, p. 505, evidence of M. Boitelle; L. Marchal, *Question des subsistances*, 1849, p. 67.

199 7 July 1856, in AN BB³⁰386.

200 GOC 4th DM, 29 July 1847, in AHG E⁵155.

201 Ministry of Justice, minute no. S3.4275, in AN BB²⁴327–47.

202 1859 *Enquête*, p. 693, evidence of Darblay *jeune*.

203 ibid., pp. 741–2.
204 See, for example, OC *gendarmerie* Haute-Marne, 26 March 1847, in AN F⁷4081.
205 ? July 1856, in AN BB³⁰386.
206 GOC 13th DM, 8 March 1847, in AHG E⁵157.
207 GOC 5th DM, ? February 1847, in AHG E⁵156.
208 See, for example, PG, Angers, 9 June 1847, in AN BB¹⁸1452; OC *gendarmerie* Cantal, monthly reports for September and October 1856, in AN F⁷3949.
209 See, for example, PG, Paris, 26 July 1856, in AN BB¹⁸1553.
210 25 May 1847, in AN BB¹⁸1452.
211 Circular of 25 May 1847, ibid.
212 Minister of Justice to PG, Rennes, 5 June 1847, in AN BB¹⁸1452.
213 Minister of the Interior to Justice, 15 May 1856, in AN BB¹⁸1553.
214 Justice to Interior, 6 June 1856, ibid.
215 1859 *Enquête*, p. 504.
216 Ministère des Finances et de l'Agriculture, du Commerce et des Travaux Publics, *Enquête sur les principes et les faits généraux qui régissent la circulation monétaire et fiduciaire*, 1867, p. 164, evidence of M. Ducuing, economist; Gille, *Histoire de la maison Rothschild*, vol. 1, p. 410.
217 *Préfet*, Côte-d'Or, 31 January 1847, in AN F⁷3928.
218 See, for example, OC *gendarmerie* Ardennes, monthly report for June 1847, in AN F⁷3928.
219 17 January 1847, in AN F¹¹2785.
220 1859 *Enquête*, p. 505, evidence of M. Boitelle.
221 M. Reinhard, 'Révolution démographique Restauration politique', in Mollat, *Histoire de l'Ile-de-France et de Paris*, p. 41.
222 1859 *Enquête*, p. 746.
223 1859 *Enquête*, p. 322, evidence of D. Lauth, member of Strasbourg Municipal Council.
224 1859 *Enquête*, p. 216, evidence of M. Pommier; ibid., p. 67, of M. Bethmont.
225 Lévèque, 'La Bourgogne', p. 296.
226 J. Merley, *L'industrie en Haute-Loire de la fin de la monarchie aux débuts de la 3ᵉ République*, Lyon, 1972, p. 377; see also *Statistique de la France*, 2ᵉ série, vol. 19, *Industrie. Résultats généraux de l'enquête effectuée dans les années 1861–65*, Nancy, 1873, p. lxx.
227 Merley, *L'industrie en Haute-Loire*, p. 377.
228 See, for example, E. Bougeâtre, *La vie rurale dans le mantois et le vexin au 19ᵉ siècle*, Meulan, 1971, p. 86; M. Gautier, 'Un type d'habitat rural à fonction "industrielle". Les moulins de Bretagne et de Vendée', in *Norois*, 1969, pp. 390–1.
229 S. Tardieu, *La vie domestique dans le Mâconnais rural préindustriel*, 1964, p. 188; G. Garrier, *Paysans du Beaujolais et du Lyonnais, 1800–1970*, vol. 1, Grenoble, 1973, p. 198.
230 1848 *Enquête*, report from the canton of Senlis (Oise), in AN C 961.
231 Jorré, *Le commerce des grains*, pp. 49–51.
232 1859 *Enquête*, p. 236, evidence of M. Pommier; see also ibid., p. 510, evidence of M. Boitelle.
233 1859 *Enquête*, p. 738; also ibid., p. 11, evidence of M. Doussaient-Péan.

234 1859 *Enquête*, p. 529, evidence of M. Ferrand, *inspecteur général des halles et marchés de Paris*; ibid., p. 708, evidence of Darblay *père*.

235 1859 *Enquête*, p. 9, the estimate by M. Doussaient-Péan, a flour merchant; it was not challenged, and I have not found anything to invalidate it. The figures are admittedly only rough estimates designed to give an impression of proportions.

236 1859 *Enquête*, p. 442, evidence of M. Leclerc-Fleaureau, miller, director of *manutention civile* at Orléans.

237 ibid., p. 509, evidence of M. Boitelle, Paris Prefect of Police.

238 Bougeâtre, *La vie rurale*, p. 86.

239 1858 *Enquête*, p. 457, evidence of Virgile Bauchart, landowner at St-Quentin (Nord).

240 E. le Roy, *Le Moulin de Frau*, n.d., p. 37.

241 1859 *Enquête*, p. 549.

242 Tardieu, *La vie domestique*, p. 187.

243 1859 *Enquête*, p. 421, evidence of Baron de Beauverger, deputy, member of *conseil général* of Seine-et-Marne; ibid., p. 274, evidence of M. Vaisse, Prefect of the Rhône, who insisted that such formalized relationships did not exist at Lyon.

244 ibid., p. 58, M. Bethmont; ibid., pp. 232–3, M. Pommier.

245 ibid., p. 140, evidence of M. Lamarre, *Syndic de la boulangerie* of the *arrondissement* of St-Denis.

246 J. Vidalenc, *Le peuple des villes et des bourgs*, 1972, pp. 241–2.

247 Corbin, 'Limousins migrants et Limousins sédentaires', p. 675.

248 1859 *Enquête*, pp. 197–8, evidence of M. Darblay *aîné*; Vidalenc, *Le peuple des villes*, p. 246.

249 1859 *Enquête*, p. 177, evidence of M. Burat, editor of the *Constitutionnel* and Professeur de l'Administration industrielle au Conservatoire des arts et des métiers; ibid., p. 102, of M. Doyère, member of Conseil de surveillance de la boulangerie de Sebastopol; ibid., p. 293, of M. Vaisse.

250 ibid., p. 114.

251 ibid., pp. 172–3, evidence of M. Burat.

252 Husson, *Les consommations de Paris*, p. 92.

253 ibid., pp. 172–5, evidence of M. Burat.

254 1859 *Enquête*, p. 797, evidence of M. Gaudrée-Boilleau, *chef de bureau des subsistances militaires au Ministère de le Guerre*; ibid., p. 713, evidence of M. Burat; ibid., pp. 139–40 of MM. Lamarre and Gautheron, *syndics de la boulangerie* of the *arrondissement* of St-Denis; J.-C. Devos, 'Les conséquences du décret du 22 Juin 1863 sur la liberté du commerce de la boulangerie', *Actes du 93ᵉ Congrès national des sociétés savantes, Tours 1968*, 1971, p. 359.

255 Vidalenc, *Le peuple des villes*, p. 243.

256 1859 *Enquête*, p. 279, evidence of M. Vaisse, Prefect of the Rhône.

257 See, for example, Y. Bergeron, 'La crise économique de 1846–48 à Toulouse et dans la Haute-Garonne', in J. Godechot (ed.), *La Révolution de 1848 à Toulouse et dans la Haute-Garonne*, 1948, p. 87.

258 Mayor of Caen, 2 July 1847, in AN F¹¹2752.

259 28 September 1854, in AN F¹¹2752.

260 See, for example, PG, Paris, August 1855, in AN BB³⁰383, and a number of reports in AHG G⁸9.

261 See, for example, GOC 9th DM, 1847, in AHG E^{5}156 *re* Beaucaire (Gard) – these were less common than protests against municipal refusals to increase prices.

262 PG, Poitiers, 31 January 1854, in AN BB^{30}385.

263 25 January 1855, in AN BB^{30}382.

264 See, for example, 1859 *Enquête*, p. 641, evidence of M. Decauville, *cultivateur* at Petit-Bourg (Seine-et-Oise).

265 1859 *Enquête*, p. 795.

266 ibid., p. 440, evidence of M. Leclerc-Fleaureau, miller and director of the *manutention civile* at Orléans.

267 GOC 13th DM, 8 March 1847, in AHG E^{5}157.

268 Vidalenc, *Le peuple des villes*, p. 247.

269 1859 *Enquête*, p. 627, evidence of M. Léger, director of La boulangerie dite de Sebastopol (a large bakery in Paris).

270 G. Thuillier, *Pour une histoire du quotidien au 19e siècle en Nivernais*, 1977, p. 382.

271 1859 *Enquête*, p. 122, evidence of M. Berger, former *syndic de la boulangerie de Paris*.

272 ibid., p. 470, evidence of M. Morel, assistant to the Mayor of Vernon (Eure).

273 See, for example, GOC 4th DM, 27 June 1847, in AHG E^{5}155.

274 1859 *Enquête*, p. 331, evidence of M. Vittecoq, miller at Beaumont-le-Roger (Eure).

275 For example, PG, Caen, 9 January 1867, in AHG E^{5}155.

276 1859 *Enquête*, pp. 72–3, evidence of Gosset; ibid., p. 322, of D. Lauth, member of Strasbourg municipal council.

277 ibid., pp. 767–8.

278 1859 *Enquête*, p. 796, evidence of M. Gauldrée-Bouilleau.

279 See, for example, GOC 14th DM, 10 March 1847, in AHG E^{5}157.

280 1859 *Enquête*, p. 641, evidence of M. Decauville, *cultivateur* at Petit-Bourg (Seine-et-Oise).

281 See, for example, GOC 18th DM, 10 August 1847, in AHG E^{5}159, on incident at Troyes (Aube).

282 Quoted by Vidalenc, *Le peuple des villes*, pp. 244–5.

283 1859 *Enquête*, p. 581.

284 OC *gendarmerie*, Mayenne, 10 January 1847, in AHG E^{5}155.

285 1859 *Enquête*, p. 13, evidence of M. Doussaient-Péan.

286 Frêche, *Toulouse*, pp. 667–8.

287 10 February 1847, in AHG E^{5}157.

288 Quoted by A. Thuillier, *Economie et société*, pp. 263–4.

289 GOC 15th DM, 15 February 1847, in AHG E^{5}158.

290 Quoted by P. Morère, 'Disette et vie chère en Ariège à la fin de la Monarchie de Juillet', *Bulletin de la société ariègeoise des sciences, lettres et arts*, 1922, p. 12.

291 *Préfet*, Loir-et-Cher, 29 March 1847, in AN F^{11}2758.

292 See, for example, OC *gendarmerie* Finistère, 10 February 1847, in AHG E^{5}157, *re* mines of Huelgouet.

293 OC 7th Legion *gendarmerie*, 24 November 1846, in AHG E^{5}155.

294 20 January 1845, ibid.

295 OC gendarmerie Mayenne, 4 November 1846, in AHG E^{5}155.

296   *Préfet*, Creuse, 26 September 1846, in AN F¹¹2758.

297   OC 13th Legion *gendarmerie*, 17 March 1847, in AHG E⁵156.

298   AN F¹¹2758.

299   GOC Mayenne, 24 January 1847, in AHG E⁵155.

300   12 January 1847, in AN F¹¹2758.

301   See, for example, PG, Caen, 20 November 1856, in AN BB³⁰433.

302   18 November 1846, in AN F¹¹2758.

303   Enclosed with report from *Préfet*, Allier, 18 November 1846, ibid.

304   See, for example, letter from a merchant at Morlaix to the Ministre de l'Agriculture et du Commerce, 28 January 1848, in AN F¹¹2758.

305   1859 *Enquête*, p. 508.

306   OC 13th Legion *gendarmerie*, 2 February 1847, in AHG E⁵156.

307   GOC 4th DM, 22 March 1847, in AHG E⁵155.

308   L. A. Tilly, 'The food riot as a form of political conflict in France', *Journal of Interdisciplinary History*, 1971, p. 45.

309   1866 *Enquête*, vol. 6, Eure-et-Loir, p. 43.

310   1866 *Enquête*, vol. 2, Orne, p. 51.

311   P. Froment, 'Les chemins de fer et l'agriculture', *L'année ferroviaire*, 1948, pp. 86–7.

312   1859 *Enquête*, p. 623, evidence of M. Léger, *directeur* of La boulangerie dite de Sebastopol at Paris.

313   See, for example, *Préfet*, Creuse, 13 March 1847, in AHG E⁵159; J. Bourdin, 'Psychosociologie de la famine', *Annales de démographie historique*, 1968.

Chapter 4   Subsistence crises and popular misery

1   See, for example, E. Labrousse, 'Panoramas de la crise', in E. Labrousse (ed.), *Aspects de la crise et de la dépression de l'économie française au milieu du 19ᵉ siècle*, 1956, p. vi.

2   M. Lévy-Leboyer, *Les banques européennes et l'industrialisation internationale dans la 1ᵉʳᵉ moitié du 19ᵉ siècle*, 1964, p. 519.

3   Archives départementales (hereafter AD) M547/1.

4   Labrousse, 'Panoramas', pp. iv–v, xv; A. Thuillier, 'La crise des subsistances dans la Nièvre en 1846–7', *Actes du 90ᵉ Congrès des sociétés savantes 1965*, vol. 3, 1966, pp. 227–8, 242; A. Armengaud, 'Les populations de l'est Aquitain au début de l'époque contemporaine', 1961, p. 171.

5   J.-C. Toutain, 'La consommation alimentaire en France de 1789 à 1964', *Economies et Sociétés*, 1971, p. 1996.

6   1848 *Enquête*, AN C 968.

7   G. Désert, 'Viande et poisson dans l'alimentation des français au milieu du 19ᵉ siècle', *Actes du 93ᵉ Congrès national des sociétés savantes, 1968*, 1971, pp. 519–26.

8   M. Aymard, 'Pour l'histoire de l'alimentation: quelques remarques de méthode', *Annales ESC*, 1975, p. 438.

9   ibid., p. 440.

10   AN C 962.

11   T. M. Bengoa, 'Significance of malnutrition and priorities for its prevention', in

B. Berg *et al.*, *Nutrition, National Development and Planning*, Cambridge, Mass., 1973, p. 104.

12   AN C 962.

13   Report of 29 February 1856 to Minister of Agriculture, in AN F[20]714.

14   Quoted by C. Clark, and M. Haswell, *The Economics of Subsistence Agriculture*, 1964, p. 21.

15   Toutain, 'La consommation alimentaire', p. 1910.

16   Aymard, 'Pour l'histoire de l'alimentation', pp. 441–2.

17   B. Berg, 'Nutrition and national development', in Berg *et al.*, *Nutrition*, p. 54.

18   J. Craviolo, and E. R. de Licardie, 'The effect of malnutrition on the individual', in ibid., p. 9.

19   A. Corbin, 'Limousins migrants et limousins sédentaires', unpublished Doctorat d'état, Clermont-Ferrand, 1973, pp. 74, 79–80.

20   A. Husson, *Les consommations de Paris*, 1856, pp. 36–8.

21   R. Bonnain-Moerdyk, 'Sur la cuisine traditionnelle comme culte culinaire du passé', *Ethnologie française*, 1972, p. 290.

22   See especially G. Thuillier, *Pour une histoire du quotidien au 19e siècle en Nivernais*, 1977, pp. 31–9.

23   *Statistique de l'industrie à Paris résultant de l'enquête faite par la Chambre de Commerce pour les années 1847–48*, 1851, vol. 1, pp. 49–50.

24   M. Agulhon, *Une ville ouvrière au temps du socialisme utopique. Toulon de 1815 à 1851*, 1971, p. 73.

25   AN C 954.

26   G. Thuillier, *Aspects de l'économie nivernaise au 19e siècle*, 1966, p. 283.

27   PI, Tours, 28 September 1858, in BB[30]382; his previous appointment had been at Amiens.

28   AN C 956.

29   See, for example, 1848 *Enquête*, reply of the cabinetmakers of the canton of Coucy (Yonne), in AN C 969.

30   1848 *Enquête*, cantons of Vienne-Nord and Sud (Isère), in AD Isère 162[m]1–2.

31   AN C 956.

32   PG, Angers, 11 September 1846, in AHG E[5]157.

33   See, for example, GOC 4th DM, 2 March 1847, in AHG E[5]155.

34   See, for example, Y. Lequin, *La Formation de la classe ouvrière régionale: les ouvriers de la région lyonnaise*, vol. 2, Lyon, 1977, p. 67.

35   E. Gautier, *Un siècle d'indigence*, 1950, p. 98.

36   1848 *Enquête*, canton Issoire (Puy-de-Dôme), in AN C 962.

37   AN C 956.

38   See, for example, PG, Bourges, 18 January 1847, in AN BB[19]37.

39   AN C 963.

40   24 December 1853, in AN BB[30]387.

41   ibid., 24 December 1853.

42   This paragraph owes much to M. Perrot, *Les ouvriers en grève*, vol. 1, 1974, pp. 153f.

43   PG, Aix, 12 February 1847, in AN BB[19]32; 1848 *Enquête*, canton Cette (Hérault), in AN C 954.

44   20 February 1846, in AN BB[18]1440.

45 Commissaire central de police at Lille to Prefect Nord, 7 May 1847, in AHG E⁵158.

46 A. Chanut *et al.*, 'Aspects industriels de la crise: le département du Nord', in Labrousse (ed.), *Aspects de la crise*, pp. 103–7.

47 P. Deyon, 'Aspects industriels de la crise: le cas de Rouen', ibid., p. 144.

48 23 September 1854, in AN BB³⁰432.

49 PG, Rouen, 31 January 1855, in AN BB³⁰387.

50 5 July 1853, ibid.

51 Chanut *et al.*, 'Aspects industriels', pp. 103–6.

52 O. Hufton, *The Poor of 18th Century France*, 1974, p. 18.

53 See, for example, medical report on textile workers of Faucogney (Haute-Saône), in AN C 963.

54 For example, 1848 *Enquête*, report of representatives of the miners of St-Etienne (Loire), in AN C 956.

55 L. Gaillard, 'La vie ouvrière et les mouvements ouvriers à Marseille de 1848 à 1879', unpublished Doctorat d'Etat, Université d'Aix, 1972, vol. 2, pp. 362–3.

56 See, for example, 1848 *Enquête*, canton Bavay (Nord), in AD M547/1.

57 Gaillard, 'La vie ouvrière, vol. 2, p. 371.

58 For example, ibid., p. 374.

59 Mayor, Douai, 29 March 1850, 'Relève des taxes du pain blanc', in AN F¹¹2756.

60 See, for example, OC *gendarmerie* Cher to colonel commanding 8th Legion *gendarmerie*, 16 January 1847, in AHG E⁵159; A. Thuillier, 'La crise des subsistances', pp. 228, 265.

61 For example, OC *gendarmerie* Eure-et-Loir, 17 March 1847, in AHG E⁵154; at Dreux bread prices had risen by 5 centimes to 0.59 francs per kilogram.

62 J. Singer-Kerel, *Le coût de la vie à Paris de 1840 à 1961*, 1961, p. 183.

63 PG, Angers, 11 September 1846, in AN F¹¹2758.

64 PG, Rouen, 2 February 1857, in AN BB³⁰387.

65 R. Trempé, *Les mineurs de Carmaux*, vol. 1, 1970, p. 386.

66 7 August 1855, in AN BB³⁰381.

67 Trempé, *Les mineurs*, pp. 388–91.

68 A. Lasserre, *La situation des ouvriers de l'industrie textile dans la région Lilloise sous la monarchie de juillet*, Lausanne, 1952, pp. 124–6; see also 1848 *Enquête*, cantons Lille nord and Tourcoing, on inadequacy of wages, in AD Nord M547/1.

69 P. Pierrard, *La vie ouvrière à Lille sous le Second Empire*, 1965, p. 208.

70 AN C 943.

71 See, for example, 1848 *Enquête*, canton Dunkirk (Nord), in AD Nord M547/1.

72 Pierrard, *La vie ouvrière*, p. 208.

73 Husson, *Les consommations de Paris*, p. 33.

74 ibid., p. 38.

75 ibid., p. 30.

76 ibid.

77 ibid., pp. 36–7.

78 'Rapport à M. le Préfet de la Seine sur le service de distribution des bons supplémentaires du pain délivrés aux indigènes et aux familles nécessiteuses de la ville de Paris en 1846 et en 1847', 1848, p. 8, in AN 45 AP 23, Rouher papers.

79   Husson, *Les consommations de Paris*, pp. 36–7.
80   Gaillard, 'La vie ouvrière', vol. 2, p. 487.
81   1848 *Enquête*, canton Bavay, in AD Nord M547/1.
82   On significance of weather conditions see, for example, PG, Rouen, 14 August 1855, in AN BB[30]387.
83   See, for example, PG, Rouen, 31 January 1855 and 2 February 1857, in AN BB[30]387.
84   *Conseil d'Etat. Enquête sur la révision de la législation des céréales*, 1859, vol. 2, p. 369, point made in evidence by M. Pagèzy, mayor of Montpellier.
85   See, for example, PG, Rouen, 31 January and 14 August 1855, in AN BB[30]387.
86   Perrot, *Les ouvriers en grève*, vol. 1, pp. 210–11.
87   J.-C. Devos, 'Les conséquences du décret du 22 Juin 1863 sur la liberté du commerce de la boulangerie', *Actes du 93ᵉ Congrès national des sociétés savantes, 1968,* 1971, pp. 357–8.
88   Gaillard, 'La vie ouvrière', vol. 2, p. 397.
89   Husson, *Les consommations de Paris*, p. 41.
90   Report to *Préfet*, Nord, 7 May 1847, in AHG E[5]158.
91   15 January 1855, in AN BB[30]386.
92   See, for example, PG, Nancy, 4 November 1859, in AN BB[30]381.
93   See, for example, PG, Aix, 16 July 1855, in AN BB[30]370.
94   A. Blanqui, 'Les populations rurales de la France en 1850', in *Annales provençales d'agriculture*, 1851, p. 210.
95   AN C 952.
96   Conseil d'Etat 1859, vol. 1, p. 262, evidence of M. Hippolyte Passy, landowner in Eure, former minister.
97   See, for example, 1859 *Enquête*, p. 473, evidence of A. de St-Léger.
98   Musée des Arts et Traditions Populaires (hereafter ATP) *Enquête*: ancienne agriculture, Vosges.
99   A. J. Tudesq, *Les Grands notables en France 1840–49*: étude historique d'une psychologie sociale, 1964, p. 932.
100 For example, 1848 *Enquête*, canton Buis (Drôme), in AN C 951.
101 GOC 18th DM, 22 January 1847, in AHG E[5]159; see also P. Lévèque, 'La Bourgogne de la monarchie de juillet au Second Empire', unpublished Doctorat d'Etat, Université de Paris I, 1976, p. 1066.
102 G. Dupeux, *Aspects de l'histoire sociale et politique du Loir-et-Cher*, 1962, p. 83.
103 PG, Paris, 4 March 1854, in AN BB[30]432.
104 See, for example, 1848 *Enquête*, canton Damartin (Seine-et-Marne), in AN C 965.
105 See, for example, report from canton of Bertincourt (Pas-de-Calais), AN C 961.
106 A. Corbin, *Archaïsme et modernité en Limousin au 19ᵉ siècle*, vol. 1, 1975, p. 165.
107 This follows closely ibid.
108 See, for example, PG Orléans, 26 January 1857, in AN BB[30]382.
109 PG, Dijon, 8 February 1847, in AN BB[19]38.
110 P. Vigier, *La Seconde République dans la région alpine*, vol. 1, 1963, p. 78.
111 See, for example, 1848 *Enquête*, canton Buis (Drôme), in AN C 951.

112 Lévêque, 'La Bourgogne', p. 1153.
113 Corbin, *Archaïsme et modernité*, vol. 1, pp. 165, 170–1.
114 Vigier, *La Seconde Republique*, vol. 1, p. 39.
115 See, for example, Corbin, *Archaïsme et modernité*, vol. 1, pp. 166–7; Lévêque, 'La Bourgogne', pp. 579–81.
116 1848 *Enquête*, canton Brest (Finistère), in AN C 952.
117 1848 *Enquête*, Nord and Sud cantons of Chartres (Eure-et-Loir), in AN C 952.
118 For example, 1848 *Enquête*, canton Serrier, in AD Nord M547/1.
119 PG, Rouen, 2 February 1857, in AN BB^{30}387.
120 AN C 958.
121 AN C 957.
122 See, for example, 1848 *Enquête*, canton St-Germain-les Belles (Haute-Vienne), in AN C 968.
123 G. Désert, *Une société rurale au 19ᵉ siècle: les paysans du Calvados 1815–95*, vol. 3, Lille, 1975, Annexe 43.
124 AN C 955.
125 AN C 962.
126 P. Brunet, *Structure agraire et économie rurale des plateaux tertiaires entre la Seine et l'Oise*, Caen, 1960, p. 371.
127 1848 *Enquête*, *résumé* of reports by JPs of Basses-Pyrénées, in AN C 962.
128 See, for example, M. Boullay, *Statistique agricole et industrielle . . . de Saône-et-Loire*, Mâcon, 1867, p. 38.
129 Gautier, *Un siècle d'indigence*, p. 98.
130 PG, Paris, 4 March 1854, in AN BB^{30}432.
131 See, for example, PG, Paris, 4 March 1854, in AN BB^{30}432.
132 G. Thuillier, *Pour une histoire du quotidien*, p. 206.
133 See, for example, *gendarmerie* Haute-Saône, report on April 1847, in AN F^{7}4150.
134 AN C 968.
135 See, for example, PG, Paris, 4 March 1854, re *arrondissement* Corbeil, in AN BB^{30}432.
136 See, for example, 1848 *Enquête*, canton Saillans (Drôme), in AN C 951.
137 G. Garrier, *Paysans du Beaujolais et du Lyonnais*, vol. 1, Grenoble, 1974, p. 297.
138 G. Désert, 'Aspects agricoles de la crise: la région de Caen', in Labrousse, *Aspects de la crise*, p. 61.
139 PG, Paris, 4 March 1854, in AN BB^{30}432.
140 See, for example, M. Goldberg, deputy for Bas-Rhin to Minister of Justice, 12 July 1849, in AN BB^{18}1460.
141 See especially A. Chatelain, *Les migrants temporaires en France de 1800 à 1914*, 2 vols., n.d., *passim*.
142 PG, Paris, 4 March 1854, in AN BB^{30}432.
143 *Préfet*, Creuse, 20 January 1847, in AN F^{11}2758.
144 26 September 1846, ibid.
145 PG, Paris, 4 March 1854, in AN BB^{30}432.
146 See, for example, PG, Poitiers, 31 January 1854, in AN BB^{30}385.
147 GOC 13th DM, 11 October 1846, in AHG E^{5}157.

148   PG, Colmar, 1 July 1854, in AN BB³⁰376.
149   AN C 945.

Chapter 5   Subsistence crises and popular protest

1   *The Police and the People*, 1970, pp. xvii–xviii.
2   1859 *Enquête*, pp. 693–4, evidence of Darblay *jeune, négociant meunier,* president of *comice agricole*, Seine-et-Oise, deputy.
3   See also 1859 *Enquête*, p. 768, evidence of M. Georges, *cultivateur* at Orgival (Aisne).
4   1859 *Enquête*, p. 735.
5   PG, Agen, 14 July 1855, in AN BB³⁰433.
6   1859 *Enquête*, p. 68.
7   PG, Poitiers, 1 September 1853, in AN BB³⁰432.
8   See, for example, GOC 20th DM, 25 April and 5 May 1847, in AHG E⁵159.
9   A. Corbin, 'Limousins migrants et Limousins sédentaires', Doctorat d'état, Clermont-Ferrand, 1973, pp. 80, 626.
10   OC *gendarmerie* Basses-Pyrénées, report on March 1847, in AN F⁷4126.
11   PG, Angers, 11 January 1857, in AN BB³⁰370.
12   See, for example, OC *gendarmerie* Nord, reports of March, May and June 1855, in AN F⁷4106.
13   PG, Angers, 11 January 1857, in AN BB³⁰370.
14   See, for example, five-day reports 2nd DM, 15–20 December 1853, re bakers at Ouistseham (Calvados) in AHG G⁸9.
15   E. C. Gamst, *Peasants in a Complex Society*, 1974, p. 34.
16   B. Berg, 'Nutrition and national development', and V. Ramalingaswami, 'The effect of malnutrition on the individual's cellular growth and development', in B. Berg *et al.*, *Nutrition, National Development and Planning*, Cambridge, Mass., 1973, pp. 50 and 38.
17   Cravioto, de Licardie, 'The effect of malnutrition on the individual', in Berg *et al.*, *Nutrition, National Development and Planning*, p. 17.
18   PI, Châteaubriant, 7 July 1856, in AN BB³⁰386.
19   Conclusions reached by PG, Orléans, 24 July 1855, in AN BB³⁰382.
20   C. S. Belshaw, *Traditional Exchange and Modern Markets*, Englewood Cliffs, NJ, 1965, p. 129.
21   E. Weber, *Peasants into Frenchmen*, 1976, p. 42.
22   PG, Rennes, 11 January 1854, in AN BB³⁰434.
23   OC *gendarmerie* Corrèze, 27 February 1847, in AHG E⁵159.
24   PG, Limoges, 4 January 1854, in AN BB³⁰378.
25   1859 *Enquête*, p. 588, evidence of M. Rabourdin, *négociant en grains et farines* at Paris.
26   Circular from PG, Angers (undated but autumn 1853) makes this point in AN BB³⁰432.
27   See, for example, GOC 15th DM, 24 August 1846, in AHG E⁵158.
28   GOC 18th DM, in AHG G⁸27.
29   PG, Paris, 21 February 1855, in AN BB³⁰432.
30   PG, Rennes, 11 August 1854, in AN BB³⁰434; she received six months' imprisonment and a fine of 150 francs for her boasting.

31 Report on assizes of Ille-et-Vilaine held on 21–2 May in *Gazette des Tribunaux*, 27 May 1847.

32 AN BB^{30}432.

33 Petition for pardon on behalf of Jean Oblette, *sabotier* at Barrais (Allier), sentenced in February 1847, in AN BB^{24}286–326.

34 GOC 15th DM, 15 February 1847 in AHG E^{5}158.

35 See, for example, PG, Poitiers, 1 September 1853, in AN BB^{30}432, for precisely this kind of case in a *placard* beginning 'Pauvre abitant . . . se le est donc fini. . .'.

36 Five-day report, 5th DM, 6–10 August 1856, in AHG G^{8}37.

37 See, for example, OC 3rd Legion *gendarmerie*, 15 April 1847, in AHG E^{5}157.

38 GOC 3rd DM, 17 March 1847, in AHG E^{5}154.

39 GOC 1st DM, 30 May and 4 June 1847, in AHG E^{5}154.

40 See, for example, OC *gendarmerie* Lot, on December 1856; on 26th two *placards* were found in the *halle aux blés* of the commune of La Capelle-Marival, in AN F^{7}4061.

41 GOC 5th DM, 5 October 1855, in AHG G^{8}27.

42 See, for example, *gendarmerie lieutenant* at Montdidier, 18 March 1847, in AHG E^{5}158, re *placard* found on door of house of Mayor of Warwillers (Somme).

43 See, for example, *gendarmerie lieutenant* at Sarreguemines, 12 February 1847, in AHG E^{5}154, re *placard* found on 8th on church door of commune of Farschrisser (Moselle).

44 See, for example, PG, Rennes, 15 November 1860, re *placard* found during the night of 11–12 on the walls of the *château* of Pont-l'Abbé, in AN BB^{18}1618.

45 AN C 954.

46 GOC 3rd DM, 13 February 1847, in AHG E^{5}154.

47 GOC 1st DM, 25 May 1847, in AHG E^{5}154.

48 OC *gendarmerie* Corrèze, 13 February 1847, in AHG E^{5}159.

49 In AHG E^{5}154.

50 See, for example, OC *gendarmerie* Eure-et-Loir, 11 December 1846, in AHG E^{5}159.

51 Five-day report 5th DM, 16–20 August 1856, in AHG G^{8}37.

52 OC 23rd Legion *gendarmerie*, 14 February 1847, in AHG E^{5}154.

53 OC *gendarmerie* Haute-Saône, 4 February 1847, in AHG E^{5}156.

54 *Gendarmerie lieutenant* Mondidier, 18 March 1847, in AHG E^{5}158.

55 OC *gendarmerie* Eure-et-Loir, 20 March 1847, in AHG E^{5}154.

56 OC *gendarmerie* Oise, 29 January 1847, in AHG E^{5}154.

57 GOC 13th DM, 23 May 1847, in AHG E^{5}157, re *placard* at Carhaix (Finistère).

58 GOC 1st DM, 30 May 1847, in AHG E^{5}154.

59 PG, Poitiers, 30 August 1853, in AN BB^{30}432.

60 PG, Paris, 23 September 1854, in AN BB^{30}432.

61 GOC 9th DM, 5 February 1847, in AHG E^{5}159.

62 PG, Rennes, 22 November 1845, in AN BB^{18}1436.

63 See, for example, GOC 12th DM, 24 January 1847, in AHG E^{5}157.

64 OC *gendarmerie* Côtes-du-Nord, on November 1845, in AN F^{7}3975.

65 OC 7th Legion, 6 February 1847, in AHG E^{5}155.

66 Five-day report 16th DM, 1–5 September 1855, in AHG G^{8}27.

67   See, for example, PG, Bourges, 19 May 1854, re arrest of one Robert, *chef mineur* at St-Hilaire-de-Gandilly (Cher), in AN BB³⁰434.

68   OC *gendarmerie* Vendée, 27 April 1847, in AHG E⁵157, re anonymous letters sent to municipal councillors and landowners at Pouzauges.

69   OC *gendarmerie* Maine-et-Loire, 16 April 1847, in AHG E⁵158, re *placard* found at Angers during the night of 14–15 April.

70   PG Angers, 30 January 1854, re case of Jean Jouveau, in AN BB³⁰434.

71   GOC 4th DM, 13 January 1847, in AHG E⁵153.

72   ibid., 9 February 1847, in AHG E⁵155.

73   See, for example, PG, Rennes, 24 November 1855, in AN BB³⁰435.

74   OC *gendarmerie* Vendée, 14 November 1846, in in AHG E⁵157.

75   PG, Lyon, July 1857, in AN BB³⁰379.

76   PG, Toulouse, 25 March 1854, in AN BB³⁰432.

77   GOC 15th DM, 15 February 1847, in AHG E⁵158.

78   PG, Metz, 28 September 1853, in AN BB³⁰434.

79   PG, Douai, 10 October 1855, in AN BB³⁰433.

80   GOC Charente-Inférieure, 7 January 1839, in AHG E⁵152.

81   *Gendarmerie lieutenant* Commercy, 4 May 1847, in AHG E⁵157.

82   See, for example, Conseil d'Etat 1859, vol. 2, p. 759, evidence of Baron Oudet, *propriétaire-agriculteur* in Charente-Inférieure; president, *comice agricole*, Saintes.

83   See, for example, *Gendarmerie lieutenant* Châteaudun (Eure-et-Loir), 15 December 1846, in AHG E⁵154.

84   OC *gendarmerie* Puy-de-Dôme, 9 March 1847, in AHG E⁵159.

85   *Gendarmerie lieutenant* Sarreguemines, 12 February 1847, in AHG E⁵154.

86   GOC 1st DM, 20 December 1846, in AHG E⁵154.

87   *Gendarmerie lieutenant* Châteaudun, 19 December 1846, in AHG E⁵154.

88   OC 3rd Legion *gendarmerie*, 15 April 1847, in AHG E⁵157.

89   See O. J. Hammon, 'The spectre of communism in the 1840s', *Journal of the History of Ideas*, 1953, *passim*.

90   GOC 4th DM, 7 February 1847, in AHG E⁵155.

91   PG, Grenoble, 24 February 1854, re *placard* found at Buis (Drôme) on 6 February, in AN BB³⁰378.

92   OC *gendarmerie* Vendée, 21 March 1847, in AHG E⁵157, re *placard* found at Estart.

93   GOC 12th DM, 3 February 1847; complaint of a *placard* found during the night of January 30–31 1847 at Châteaubriant, in AHG E⁵157.

94   OC 3rd Legion *gendarmerie*, 15 April 1847, in AHG E⁵157.

95   GOC 2nd DM, 2 April 1847, in AHG E⁵154.

96   See, for example, article entitled 'La comédie sociale – peuples et rois', a pastiche of the 'Paroles d'un croyant', published in *Le Bien du Peuple*, 2 November 1851, quoted in J. Dagnan, *Le Gers sous la Seconde République*, vol. 1, Auch, 1928, p. 395.

97   'Le National d'Autun' of 3 April 1850, quoted by P. Lévèque, 'La Bourgogne de la monarchie de juillet au Second Empire', Doctorat d'état, Université de Paris I, 1976, p. 1433.

98   T. R. Gurr, *Why Men Rebel*, Princeton, NJ, 1970, p. 272.

99   Prefect of Police, 1 November 1855, in AN BB³⁰366.

100 PG, Paris, 27 December 1853, in AN BB[30]366.

101 *Greffier* of the tribunal of Rethel (Ardennes), 20 September 1853, in AN BB[30]434.

102 Five-day report, 10th DM, 1–5 September 1855, in AHG G[8]27.

103 For example, in song found at Cany (Seine-Inférieure) on 11 April 1847; 3rd Legion *gendarmerie*, 15 April 1847, in AHG E[5]157.

104 OC 7th Legion, 19 January 1847, in AHG E[5]155, re *placard* found near La Châtre (Indre).

105 Quoted by G. Cholvy, *Religion et société au 19ᵉ siècle. Le diocèse de Montpellier*, vol. 1, Lille, 1973, p. 824.

106 PG, Orléans, 11 November 1854, in AN BB[30]382.

107 PG, Metz, 28 September 1853, in AN BB[30]434.

108 OC *gendarmerie* Pyrénées-Orientales, on March 1855, in AN F[7]4132.

109 Five-day report 5th DM, 11–15 November 1853, in AHG G[8]9.

110 PG, Rouen, 31 January 1855, in AN BB[30]387; see also PG Angers, 3 January 1853, in AN BB[30]370.

111 Report on Indre assizes in *Gazette des Tribunaux*, 25 March 1847.

112 OC *gendarmerie* Lot-et-Garonne, on March 1847, re *placard* found on 20th at Tonneins in AN F[7]4064.

113 OC *gendarmerie* Vendée, 20 June 1847, in AHG E[5]157, re *placards* found at Fontenay.

114 GOC 1st DM, 27 March 1847, in AHG E[8]154, re *placard* found at St-Ay (Loiret).

115 OC *gendarmerie* Lot-et-Garonne, 25 March 1847, in AHG E[5]156, re *placard* found at Tonneins.

116 GOC 1st DM, 30 May 1847, in AHG E[5]154.

117 C. Tilly, 'How protest modernized in France', in W. Aydelotte *et al.*, *The Dimensions of Quantitative Research in History*, 1972, p. 213.

118 See, for example, 1848 *Enquête*, canton Beaune-la-Rolande (Loiret), on misery of woodcutters and disorders in 1846–7, in AN C 957.

119 Gurr, *Why Men Rebel*, p. 13.

120 A. Corbin, *Archaïsme et modernité en Limousin au 19ᵉ siècle*, vol. 1, 1975, p. 495.

121 P. Vigier, *La Seconde République dans la région alpine*, vol. 1, 1963, p. 79.

122 P. Gonnet, 'Esquisse de la crise économique en France de 1827 à 1832', *Revue d'histoire économique et sociale*, 1975, p. 266.

123 See, for example, PG, Paris, 4 March 1854, in AN BB[30]432, re *arrondissement* of Nogent-le-Rotrou (Eure-et-Loir).

124 J. Suret-Canale, 'L'état économique et sociale de la Mayenne au milieu du 19ᵉ siècle', *Revue d'histoire économique et sociale*, 1958, p. 318.

125 R. Quinault, and J. Stevenson (eds.) *Popular Protest and Public Order*, 1974, pp. 26–7.

126 J. C. Scott, *The Moral Economy of the Peasants. Rebellion and Subsistence in South-East Asia*, 1976, p. vii.

127 Gurr, *Why Men Rebel*, p. 10.

128 Scott, *The Moral Economy of the Peasants*, p. 42.

129 Lévêque, 'La Bourgogne', p. 924.

130 See, for example, PG Bordeaux, 10 March 1857, re Mayor of Mouthiers, in AN BB^{18}1563.

131 See, for example, PG Angers, 23 April 1847, re anonymous letter to Mayor of Angers, in AN BB^{19}32.

132 PG, Rennes, 11 May 1847, in AN BB^{19}41.

133 Quoted by G. Dupeux, *Aspects de l'histoire sociale et politique du Loir-et-Cher*, 1962, p. 411.

134 C. Tilly, 'Food supply and public order in modern Europe', in *The Formation of National States in Western Europe*, 1975, p. 6.

135 See especially E. P. Thompson, 'The moral economy of the English crowd in the eighteenth century', *Past and Present*, 1971, pp. 76f.

136 J. C. Scott, 'Protest and profanation: agrarian revolt and the Little Tradition', *Theory and Society*, 1977, p. 213.

137 PG, Rouen, 20 September 1855, in AN BB^{30}433.

138 See, for example, PG, Bourges, 21 January 1854, in AN BB^{30}374.

139 See, for example, PG, Riom, 7 September 1830, in AN BB^{18}1186.

140 Point made by PG, Poitiers, 1 September 1853, in AN BB^{30}432.

141 GOC 15th DM, 27 January 1847, in AHG E^{5}158.

142 See, for example, *gendarmerie lieutenant* Civray (Vienne), 11 March 1847, in AHG E^{5}155.

143 PG, Besançon, 13 December 1856, in AN BB^{24}500–6.

144 See, for example, PG, Poitiers, 31 January 1854, re events at Mirabeau and Jauzens, in AN BB^{30}385.

145 For example, 7th Legion *gendarmerie*, 21 November 1847, in AHG E^{5}155, re market of 21st at Tours.

146 For example, PG, Bordeaux, 17 January 1854, in AN BB^{30}432.

147 Report on *tribunal correctionnel* of Chinon, 25–27 January 1847, in *Gazette des Tribunaux*, 11 February 1847.

148 OC 3rd Legion *gendarmerie*, 15 March 1847, in AHG E^{5}157.

149 See, for example, appeal for pardon from eight individuals involved in disorders at market of Boulogne-sur-Gesse on 17 March 1847, dated 7 April, in AN BB^{24}286–326.

150 OC *gendarmerie* Cher, 16 January 1847, in AHG E^{5}159.

151 OC *gendarmerie* Hautes-Pyrénées, 17 March 1847, in AHG E^{5}159.

152 See, for example, OC *gendarmerie* Eure, n.d., in AHG E^{5}157, re disorders at Breteuil on 27 January 1847.

153 PG, Bourges, 27 January 1854, in AN BB^{30}374.

154 PI, Mâcon, 6 February 1847, in AN BB^{19}38.

155 Appeal for pardon from eight individuals condemned by the *tribunal correctionnel* of St-Gaudens, 7 April 1847, in AN BB^{24}286–326.

156 GOC Indre, 16 November 1846, in AHG E^{5}158.

157 OC *gendarmerie* Mayenne, 4 November 1846, in AHG E^{5}155.

158 OC *gendarmerie* Cher, 16 January 1847, in AHG E^{5}159.

159 See, for example, PG, Bourges, 8 July 1853, in AN BB^{30}432.

160 GOC 1st DM, 8 March 1847, in AHG E^{5}154.

161 OC 7th Legion *gendarmerie*, 1 December 1846, in AHG E^{5}155.

162 Minister of Justice to Interior, 31 July 1847, in AN BB^{19}37.

163 OC 3rd Legion *gendarmerie*, 15 February 1847, in AHG E^{5}157.

164 GOC 15th DM, 25 and 28 November 1846, in AHG E^{5}158.

165 *Gendarmerie lieutenant* Provins, 20 February 1847, in AHG E^{5}154.

166 GOC 13th DM, 17 April 1847, in AHG E^{5}157; OC *gendarmerie* Orne, report on March 1847, in AN F^{7}4114.

167 See, for example, OC *gendarmerie* Orne, 17 February 1847, in AHG E^{5}157, re incident at market of Flers on 9th.

168 GOC 4th DM, 11 January 1847, in AHG E^{5}155.

169 GOC 4th DM, 27 November 1846, in AHG E^{5}155.

170 ibid., and PG Angers, 11 January 1847, in AN BB^{19}37.

171 See, for example, GOC 4th DM, 3 December 1846, in AHG E^{5}155, re markets at Bourgueil, Châteaurenault, Amboise, Loches, Azay-le-Rideau in Indre-et-Loire.

172 *Tribunal correctionnel de Chinon*, Session 25–27 January 1847, reported in *Gazette des Tribunaux*, 11 February 1847.

173 Proclamation of 20 January 1847, in AHG E^{5}155.

174 OC *gendarmerie* Haute-Garonne, 21 March 1847, in AHG E^{5}156.

175 See, for example, OC 7th Legion *gendarmerie*, 5 December 1846, in AHG E^{5}155, re markets at Ste-Maure and Bléré (Indre-et-Loire).

176 GOC 4th DM, 16 January 1847, in AHG E^{5}155.

177 *Gendarmerie lieutenant*, Lencloître, 5 January 1847, in AHG E^{5}159; PG Angers, 11 January 1847, in AN BB^{19}37.

178 OC *gendarmerie* Mayenne, 10 January 1847, in AHG E^{5}155.

179 See, for example, *gendarmerie* brigadier at Lencloître (see note 177).

180 OC 13th Legion *gendarmerie*, 27 March 1847, in AHG E^{5}155.

181 See, for example, *gendarmerie* Mayenne, 4 November 1846, in AHG E^{5}155, re incident at market of Villains-la-Juhel on 2nd.

182 GOC 4th DM, 16 January 1847, in AHG E^{5}155.

183 7th Legion *gendarmerie*, 19 January 1847, in AHG E^{5}157.

184 PG, Caen, 13 March 1847, in AN BB^{19}32.

185 Report on *tribunal correctionnel* of Chinon, 25–27 January 1847, in *Gazette des Tribunaux*, 11 February 1847.

186 OC 3rd Legion, 2 February 1847, in AHG E^{5}159.

187 PG, Amiens, 25 March 1847, in AN BB^{19}37.

188 GOC 18th DM, 1 February 1847, in AHG E^{5}159.

189 For example, ibid., five-day report 7th DM, 25–31 January 1852, re market at Luxeuil, in AHG F^{1}69.

190 See, for example, GOC 4th DM, 17 January 1847, in AHG E^{5}158.

191 See, for example, OC 7th Legion, 9 January 1847, in AHG E^{5}155, re *placard* posted in Châteauroux during night of 6–7.

192 See, for example, *gendarmerie lieutenant*, St-Amand (Cher), 21 December 1846, in AHG E^{5}158, re influence of a miner on his workmates.

193 Report on assizes of Indre-et-Loire in *Gazette des Tribunaux*, 22 January 1847.

194 OC 7th Legion *gendarmerie*, 5 January 1847, in AHG E^{5}159.

195 PG, Toulouse, 25 November 1853, in AN BB^{30}432.

196 PG, Limoges, 23 January 1847, in AN BB^{19}38.

197 OC 7th Legion *gendarmerie*, 28 November 1846, in AHG E^{5}157.

198 *Gendarmerie lieutenant*, St-Amand (Cher), 12 January 1847, in AHG E^{5}158.

199 PG, Angers, 11 January 1847, in AN BB^{19}37.

200   PG, Angers, 16 March 1847, in AN BB¹⁹37.
201   M. Perrot, 'Aspects industriels de la crise: Les régions textiles du Calvados', in E. Labrousse (ed.), *Aspects de la crise et de la dépression de l'économie française au milieu du 19ᵉ siècle*, 1956, p. 174.
202   GOC 4th DM, 5 December 1846, in AHG E⁵155.
203   Paris *Préfet* of Police, 28 September 1867, in *Papiers et correspondance de la famille impériale*, vol. 2, 1871, p. 273.
204   Point made in 1859 *Enquête*, p. 696, evidence of Darblay *jeune*, merchant and miller; president, *comice agricole*, Seine-et-Oise; deputy.
205   OC *gendarmerie* Oise, 4 March 1847, in AHG E⁵154.
206   See, for example, PG, Limoges, 14 February 1847, in AN BB¹⁹38.
207   GOC 1st DM, 30 May 1847, in AHG E⁵154.
208   11 July 1846, in AN F¹¹2758.
209   Ministère de l'Agriculture, internal memorandum, undated but probably autumn 1853, in AN F¹¹2752.
210   See Mayor of Caen to Minister of Interior, 2 July 1847, in AN F¹¹2758.
211   OC *gendarmerie* Charente, 18 August 1854, in AN BB³⁰432.
212   See, for example, OC *gendarmerie* Moselle, report on June 1846, in AN F⁷4099.
213   See, for example, OC *gendarmerie* Lot-et-Garonne, report on September 1855, in AN F⁷4064.
214   See, for example, PG, Rennes, 31 August 1853, in AN BB³⁰432, re bakers at Châteaubriant on 25 and 26 August, threatened with a 500-franc fine.
215   See, for example, PG, Bourges, 14 July 1854, in AN BB³⁰432, re events at Aubigny.
216   A. Boland, *Traité pratique de la boulangerie*, 1860, pp. 197–210, 235, for technical details.
217   See, for example, PG, Aix, 7 December 1854; PG, Besançon, 16 January 1854, for instructions to subordinates, in AN BB³⁰432.
218   See, for example, R. Mémain, 'La crise de 1845–47 dans la Vienne', *Bulletin de la société des antiquaires de l'Ouest*, 1961, p. 551.
219   PG, Poitiers, 5 September 1853, in AN BB³⁰432.
220   PG, Besançon, 10 January 1854, in AN BB³⁰432.
221   PG, Montpellier, 20 April 1847, in AN BB³⁰382.
222   1859 *Enquête*, p. 322, evidence of D. Lauth, retired miller and member of the municipal council of Strasbourg.
223   ibid., pp. 608–9, evidence of M. Jacob.
224   PG, Rennes, 28 May 1847, in AN BB¹⁹41.
225   GOC 3rd DM, 22 June 1847, in AHG E⁵154.
226   See, for example, PG, Limoges, 18 August 1854, in AN BB³⁰432.
227   GOC 18th DM, 9 and 10 August 1847, in AHG E⁵159; OC *gendarmerie* Aube on August 1847, in AN F⁷3933; *Gazette des Tribunaux*, 11 August 1847.
228   *Gendarmerie lieutenant* Lisieux (Calvados), 1 and 9 August 1847; Administration des postes: rapport des courriers, 1 August 1847, in AHG E⁵157; *Gazette des Tribunaux*, 12 December 1847.
229   Report on assizes of Ille-et-Vilaine, held on 18–19 March, in *Gazette des Tribunaux*, 22–23 March 1847.
230   PG, Douai, 15 May 1847, in AN BB¹⁹39.

231   1859 *Enquête*, p. 65, evidence of M. Bethmont.

232   *Gazette des Tribunaux*, 2, 3 and 31 October and 13 December 1846.

233   Appeal of Alex. Delapaul, *rattacheur*, against sentence of 19 May 1847 to five years' imprisonment for *excitation à l'émeute*, dated 16 December 1848, in AN BB²⁴327–47.

234   GOC 16 DM, 13 March, 12 and 17 May, 1847, OC *gendarmerie*, Nord, 13 May 1847, in AHG E⁵158; and report on May 1847 in AN F⁷4106; A. M. Gossez, *Le Département du Nord sous la 2ᵉ République*, Lille, 1904, p. 83.

235   GOC 5th DM, 27 June 1847; GOC Haut-Rhin, 3 July 1847, in AHG E⁵156; OC *gendarmerie*, Haut-Rhin, 7 July 1847 and 7 January 1848, in AN F⁷4142.

236   GOC Haut-Rhin, 30 June 1847, in AHG E⁵156.

237   *Préfet*, Meurthe, 11 July 1846, in AN F¹¹2758; A. Gueslin, 'La dernière grande crise fromentaire en Lorraine', *Annales de l'Est*, 1980, p. 97.

238   GOC 1st DM, 8 March 1847, in AHG E⁵154.

239   Appeal for pardon from five women of Château-Chinon, dated 11 November 1846, in AN BB²⁴286–326.

240   See, for example, OC *gendarmerie* Sarthe, 4 July 1847, in AHG E⁵155.

241   See, for example, OC *gendarmerie* Manche, report on January 1847, in AN F⁷4075.

242   17 March 1847, in AHG E⁵156.

243   Mayor of St-Agrève (Ardèche) to Minister of Justice, 21 April 1847, in AN BB²⁴286–326.

244   GOC 20th DM, 25 March 1847, in AHG E⁵159, re markets in the Landes.

245   See, for example, PG, Rennes, 18 November 1845, in AN BB¹⁸1436.

246   1859 *Enquête*, pp. 66–7, evidence of M. Bethmont, lawyer resident near Buzançais.

247   PG, Angers, 11 September 1846, in AHG E⁵157.

248   Tilly, 'How protest modernized in France', p. 206.

249   Cobb, *The Police and the People*, pp. 261–2.

250   See PG, Angers, 11 September 1846, in AHG E⁵157; GOC Mayenne, 24 January 1847, in AHG E⁵155.

251   *Préfet*, Côte-d'Or, 4 November 1846, in AN F¹¹2758.

252   *Préfet*, Deux-Sèvres, 5 January 1839, in AHG E⁵152; *Préfet*, Dordogne, 30 November 1846, in AN F¹¹2758; GOC 11th DM, 5 February 1847, in AHG E⁵156.

253   GOC 3rd DM, 19 February 1847, in AHG E⁵154.

254   PG, Riom, 1 February 1847, in AN BB¹⁹42.

255   GOC Finistère, 7 February 1847, in AHG E⁵157.

256   *Préfet*, Côtes-du-Nord, 21 January 1847, in AHG E⁵159.

257   PG, Angers, 11 September 1846, in AHG E⁵157; Suret-Canale, 'L'état économique', pp. 318–20.

258   PG, Limoges, 9 December 1846, in AN BB¹⁹38.

259   PG, Poitiers, 14 July 1856, in AN BB²⁴494–9.

260   Mayor of Commercy to *Préfet*, Allier, 20 November 1846, in AN F¹¹2758.

261   GOC 9th DM, 21 February 1847, in AHG E⁵156.

262   PG, Orléans, 20 August 1847, in AN BB¹⁹39.

263   PG, Angers, no date but probably January 1847, in AN BB¹⁹37.

264   GOC 12th DM, 21 August 1846, in AHG E⁵157.

265   *Gazette des Tribunaux*, 28 February 1847, report on assizes of Indre session of 25 February.

266   OC *gendarmerie* Saône-et-Loire, 30 November 1846, in AN F⁷4154.

267   PG, Angers, 11 January 1847, in AN BB¹⁹37.

268   *Gazette des Tribunaux*, 8 September 1846.

269   PG, Orléans, 2 February 1847, in AN BB¹⁹39; PG, Rennes, 22 January 1847, in AN BB¹⁹41, and 3 May 1847, in AN BB¹⁸1436.

270   PG, Rennes, 24 October 1846, in AN BB¹⁹41.

271   OC *gendarmerie* Côtes-du-Nord on November 1845, in AN F⁷3975.

272   *Préfet* Mayenne, 12 January 1847, in AN F¹¹2758.

273   PG, Dijon, 19 February 1847, in AN BB¹⁹42.

274   PG, Bourges, 31 October 1853, in AN BB³⁰432.

275   GOC 16th DM, 24 February 1847, in AHG E⁵158; PR, Lille, 24 February 1847, in AN BB¹⁹38.

276   *Gendarmerie lieutenant*, Béthune, 18 March 1847, in AHG E⁵158; *gendarmerie* Pas-de-Calais in AN F⁷4118.

277   PG, Toulouse, 22 March 1847, in AN BB¹⁹42.

278   *Préfet*, Loiret, 29 March 1847, in AHG E⁵154.

279   GOC 1st DM, 31 March 1847, in AHG E⁵154.

280   OC *gendarmerie* Loiret, two reports of 15 March 1847; GOC 1st DM, 18 March 1847, in AHG E⁵154.

281   *Sous-préfet* Montargis to GOC Loiret, 6 April 1847; GOC 1st DM, 19 March 1847, AHG E⁵154.

282   OC *gendarmerie* Ille-et-Vilaine, 10 January 1847, in AHG E⁵157.

283   PG, Rennes, 29 November 1845; président of tribunal of Dinan, to PG, Rennes, 17 March 1846, in AN BB¹⁸1436.

284   OC *gendarmerie* Saône-et-Loire, 30 November 1846, in AN F⁷4154.

285   PG, Rennes, 21 November 1847, in AN F¹¹2758.

286   See, for example, Minister of Finance to Justice, 23 January 1850, in AN BB³⁰361–368.

287   *Gendarmerie lieutenant* Dunkirk (Nord), 12 January 1847, in AHG E⁵158; PR, Dunkirk, 13 January 1847, in AN BB¹⁹38.

288   OC 24th Legion *gendarmerie*, 27 November 1846; *Préfet*, Pas-de-Calais, 2 December 1846, in AHG E⁵158.

289   *Gendarmerie lieutenant* Yvetot, 23 January 1847, in AHG E⁵157.

290   OC 3rd Legion *gendarmerie*, 24 January 1847, in AHG E⁵157.

291   OC *gendarmerie* Manche, 30 January 1847, in AHG E⁵157.

292   OC *gendarmerie* Finistère, 24 January 1847, in AHG E⁵159.

293   PG, Rennes, 30 October and 15 November 1860, in AN BB¹⁸1618.

294   PG, Angers, undated report (probably January 1847), in AN BB¹⁹37.

295   GOC 13th DM, 25 January 1847, in AHG E⁵157.

296   OC *gendarmerie* Morbihan, 15 March 1847, in AHG E⁵157.

297   See, for example, GOC Mayenne, 24 January 1847, in AHG E⁵155.

298   See, for example, Dupeux, 'Aspects agricoles de la crise: le département de Loir-et-Cher', in Labrousse (ed.), *Aspects de la crise*, p. 84.

299   See, for example, PG, Grenoble, 17 March 1847, in AN BB¹⁹38.

300   See, for example, 1859 *Enquête*, pp. 66–7, evidence of M. Bethmont.

301   8 February 1847, in AN BB¹⁹38.

302 See, for example, OC *gendarmerie* Ille-et-Vilaine, report on January 1847, in AN F⁷4022.

303 GOC 9th DM, 10 February 1847, in AHG E⁵156.

304 PG, Angers, 22 October 1853, in AN BB³⁰432.

305 OC *gendarmerie* Manche, 30 January 1847, in AHG E⁵157.

306 *Gendarmerie sous-lieutenant* Châteaulin, 6 February 1847, in AHG E⁵157.

307 OC *gendarmerie* Mayenne, 31 December 1846, in AHG E⁵155.

308 GOC 4th DM, 27 April 1847, in AHG E⁵155.

309 GOC 4th DM, 27 February 1846, in AHG E⁵155.

310 PG, Bordeaux, 13 April 1847, in AN BB¹⁹37.

311 For example, PI, Sedan, 3 September 1853, in AN BB³⁰432.

312 OC 7th Legion *gendarmerie*, 20 January 1847, in AHG E⁵155.

313 OC 7th Legion *gendarmerie*, 27 January 1847, in AHG E⁵158.

314 *Gendarmerie lieutenant* Nogent-le-Rotrou, 14 June 1847, in AHG E⁵154.

315 PG, Angers, 11 January 1847, in AN BB¹⁹32.

316 *Gendarmerie* Allier, report on August 1856, in AN F⁷3916.

317 OC 7th Legion *gendarmerie*, 18 December 1846, in AHG E⁵155.

318 *Préfet*, Dordogne, 1 March 1847, in AN F¹¹2758.

319 PG, Colmar, 26 November 1853, in AN BB³⁰376.

320 See, for example, PG, Rennes, 3 November 1846, in AN BB¹⁹41.

321 GOC 4th DM, 21 January 1847, in AHG E⁵155.

322 PG, Poitiers, 10 September 1846, in AN BB¹⁹40.

323 GOC 13th DM, 17 January 1847, in AHG E⁵157, re communes of Jenzé, Genezé, Liré (Ille-et-Vilaine) and Merdrignac (Côtes-du-Nord).

324 For example, GOC 4th DM, 11 January 1847, in AHG E⁵155.

325 See, for example, letter from a farmer called Renou to a baker at Moulins, copy enclosed with report from *Préfet*, Allier, 18 November 1846, in AN F¹¹2758.

326 GOC 4th DM, 22 March 1847, in AHG E⁵155.

327 *Gendarmerie sous-lieutenant* Lapalisse (Allier), 11 February 1847, in AHG E⁵159; report on assizes of Allier, 2ᵉ *trimestre*, 1847, session of 6–7 May, in AN BB²⁰141; petition for release by Oblette, in AN BB²⁴286–326.

328 GOC Saône-et-Loire to GOC 18th DM, 22 August 1846, in AHG E⁵159; *Avocat-général*, Dijon, 25 August, 15 September 1846, in AN BB¹⁹38.

329 *Avocat-général*, Dijon, 27 September and 20 October 1846, in AN BB¹⁹38.

330 *Gendarmerie lieutenant* Bellac (Haute-Vienne), 31 January 1847, in AHG E⁵158.

331 See, for example, GOC 1st DM, 19 March 1847, in AHG E⁵154, re fears of inhabitants of Courtenay (Loiret) and neighbouring areas of Yonne.

332 *Préfet*, Lozère, 26 February 1847; PG Nîmes, 11 February 1847, in AN F¹¹2758.

333 GOC 20th DM, 21 March 1858, report on Issoire, in AHG MR 2151.

334 OC *gendarmerie*, Vendée, 20 January 1847, in AHG E⁵157.

335 PG, Orléans, 22, 25, 26 November 1846, and PR, Tours, 22 November 1846, in AN BB¹⁹39; PR, Tours, 25 November 1846, in AHG E⁵157.

336 1ᵉʳ *avocat-général*, 22 January 1847, in AN BB¹⁹37; see also Y. Bionnier, *Les jacqueries de 1847 en Bas-Berry*, Châteauroux, 1979, *passim*.

337 'Affaire de Buzançais. Rapport sur la session extraordinaire des assizes de l'Indre', 25 February 1847, in AN BB²⁴327–47.

338   1er *avocat-général*, 22 January 1847; PG, Bourges, 15 January 1847, in AN BB^{19}37; *Cour d'Assises de l'Indre. Affaire des Troubles de Buzançais*, Châteauroux, 1847, p. 2, evidence of Baptiste Bienvenue, *journalier*.

339   *Gazette des Tribunaux*, 28 February 1847, report on assizes of the Indre, session of 25 February.

340   PG, Bourges, 15 January 1847, in AN BB^{19}37; OC 7th Legion *gendarmerie*, 15 January 1847, in AHG E^{5}158.

341   *Gazette des Tribunaux*, 27 February 1847.

342   ibid., 28 February 1847.

343   PG, Bourges, 17 and 18 January 1847, in AN BB^{19}37; GOC 4th DM, 17 January 1847, in AHG E^{5}158; OC 7th Legion *gendarmerie*, 17 January 1847, in AHG E^{5}155.

344   *Gazette des Tribunaux*, 22 January 1847; *gendarmerie lieutenant*, Blanc (Indre), 18 January 1847, in AHG E^{5}158; PG, Bourges, 17 January 1847, in AN BB^{19}37.

345   PG, Bourges, 18 January 1847, in AN BB^{19}37.

346   GOC Indre, 19 January 1847, in AHG E^{5}155; PG, Bourges, 18 January 1847, in AN BB^{19}37.

347   OC 7th Legion *gendarmerie*, 9 January 1847, in AHG E^{5}155; GOC 15th DM, 20 January 1847, in AHG E^{5}158.

348   OC 7th Legion *gendarmerie*, 20 January 1847, in AHG E^{5}155; *Gazette des Tribunaux*, 25 March 1847, report on assizes of Indre, session of 22 March.

349   GOC 15th DM, 16 January 1847, in AHG E^{5}155.

350   PG, Bourges, 20 January 1847, in AN BB^{19}37; *Gazette des Tribunaux*, 22 January 1847.

351   On Issoudun see OC 7th Legion *gendarmerie*, 19 January 1847, in AHG E^{5}155; on *arrondissement* La Châtre see OC 7th Legion *gendarmerie*, 19 January, and PG, Bourges, 27 January 1847, in AHG E^{5}158.

352   GOC 15th DM, 25 and 26 January 1847, in AHG E^{5}158.

353   *Gendarmerie lieutenant*, Blanc (Indre), 20 and 23 January 1847, in AHG E^{5}158.

354   *Gazette des Tribunaux*, 6 March and 21 May 1847.

355   OC 7th Legion *gendarmerie*, 22 January 1847, in AHG E^{5}155.

356   Proclamation by *Préfet*, Indre, 20 January 1847, in AHG E^{5}155; PG, Bourges, 19 January 1847, in AN BB^{19}37.

357   PG, Bourges, 7 April 1847, enclosing a copy of interrogation reports from the *juge d'instruction* of the *arrondissement* of Cosne, in AN BB^{24}286–326.

358   PG, Bourges, 18 January 1847, in AN BB^{19}37.

359   GOC 15th DM, 26 and 27 January 1847, in AHG E^{5}158.

360   GOC 15th DM, 14 and 16 January 1847, *Préfet*, Indre, 18 January 1847, in AHG E^{5}158.

361   PG, Bourges, 19 and 22 January 1847, in AN BB^{19}37.

362   Minister of Justice to PG, Bourges, 21 January 1847, in AN BB^{19}37.

363   GOC 4th DM, 17 January 1847, in AHG E^{5}158.

364   PG, Angers, 25 September 1855, in AN BB^{30}433.

365   H. J. Zehr, *Patterns of Crime in 19th Century Germany and France*, PhD thesis, Rutgers University, 1974, pp. 274–6.

366   OC *gendarmerie*, Côtes-du-Nord, report for March 1855, in AN F^{7}3975.

367 PG, Montpellier, 17 January 1854, in AN BB^{30}380.

368 See, for example, OC *gendarmerie*, Eure-et-Loir, report on April 1847, in AN F^{7}3996.

369 For example, OC *gendarmerie*, Pas-de-Calais, report on March 1847, in AN F^{7}4118; OC *gendarmerie*, Seine-et-Oise, report on May 1847, in AN F^{7}4197.

370 OC *gendarmerie* Finistère, 10 February 1847, in AHG E^{5}157.

371 GOC 1st DM, 21–5 April 1847, in AHG E^{5}154.

372 OC *gendarmerie*, Seine-et-Oise, reports on December 1846, February and May 1847, in AN F^{7}4197.

373 OC *gendarmerie*, Somme, report on November 1846, in AN F^{7}4204; GOC 16 DM, 13 February 1847, in AHG E^{5}158; PG, Douai, 20 January 1854, in AN BB^{30}377; PG, Amiens, 14 April 1854, in AN BB^{30}371, and 9 November 1855, in AN BB^{30}433.

374 AN C 961.

375 GOC 16th DM, 22 May 1847; OC *gendarmerie*, Nord, 7 May 1847, in AHG E^{5}158.

376 OC *gendarmerie*, Orne, report on January 1847, in AN F^{7}4114; GOC 14 DM, 27 April 1847, in AHG E^{5}157.

377 GOC 4th DM, 18 December 1846, in AHG E^{5}155.

378 AN C 965.

379 PG, Poitiers, 31 January 1854, in AN BB^{30}385.

380 Vigier, *La Seconde République*, vol. 1, p. 80; Corbin, *Archaïsme et modernité*, vol. 1, p. 489.

381 M. Chevalier, *La vie humaine dans les Pyrénées ariègeoises*, 1956, pp. 669–70.

382 OC *gendarmerie*, Nord, 7 May 1847, in AHG E^{5}158.

383 See, for example, Corbin, *Archaïsme et modernité*, vol. 1, p. 489; Chevalier, *La vie humaine*, pp. 669–70.

384 A. Jardin, A.-J. Tudesq, *La France des notables*, vol. 1, 1973, p. 236.

385 J. C. Farcy, *Agriculture et société rurale en Beauce pendant la première moitié du 19e siècle, thèse*, 3e cycle, Université de Paris, n.d., p.263.

386 GOC 12th DM, 16 April 1847, in AHG E^{5}157.

387 See, for example, Mayor, Lille, 1847, quoted by F. Lentacker, *La frontière Franco-Belge. Etude géographique des effets d'une frontière internationale sur la vie des relations*, Lille, 1976, p. 200.

388 GOC 4th DM, 20 March 1847, in AHG E^{5}155.

389 See, for example, PG, Amiens, 28 July 1855, in AN BB^{30}433.

390 See, for example, PG, Rouen, 12 January 1854, in AN BB^{30}387.

391 For statistics see *Annuaire statistique de la France. Résumé retrospectif*, 1966.

392 See, for example, OC *gendarmerie*, Moselle, report on January 1847, in AN F^{7}4099.

393 OC *gendarmerie*, Pas-de-Calais, report on June 1847, in AN F^{7}4118.

394 OC *gendarmerie*, Oise, report on April 1847, in AN F^{7}4110.

395 See Gonnet, 'Esquisse de la crise économique en France de 1827 à 1832', p. 271.

396 See, for example, OC *gendarmerie*, Maine-et-Loire, report on December 1846, in AN F^{7}4071.

397 PG, Poitiers, 22 May 1854, in AN BB^{30}434.

398   See OC *gendarmerie*, Maine-et-Loire, report on September 1847, in AN
      F⁷4071; OC *gendarmerie*, Eure-et-Loir, report on November 1846, in AN
      F⁷3996.
399   PG, Angers, 11 September 1846, in AHG E⁵157.
400   See, for example, PG, Amiens, 28 July 1858, in AN BB³⁰371.
401   See, for example, GOC 4th DM, 22 March 1847, in AHG E⁵155, re Vienne and
      Sarthe.
402   A. Thuillier, 'La crise des subsistances dans la Nièvre en 1846–47', *Actes du
      Congrès des sociétés savantes*, vol. 3, 1966, pp. 230–4.
403   *Gendarmerie*, Doubs, report on May 1846, in AN F⁷3985.
404   PG, Bourges, 17 January 1847, in AN BB³⁰374.
405   See, for example, report of *justice de paix* at Bourbonne (Côte-d'Or), 20 March
      1847, in AN BB¹⁹38.
406   Five-day report, 18th DM, 21–5 October 1853, in AHG G⁸9.
407   See, for example, OC *gendarmerie*, Côtes-du-Nord, report on June 1856, in
      AN F⁷3975.
408   G. Désert, 'Aperçus sur l'industrie française du bâtiment au 19ᵉ siècle', in J.-P.
      Bardet, *et al.*, *Le bâtiment. Enquête d'histoire économique*, 1971, pp. 42–3.
409   PG, Amiens, 4 August 1853, in AN BB³⁰371.
410   PG, Bourges, 17 January 1854, in AN BB³⁰374.
411   PG, Orléans, 24 July 1855, in AN BB³⁰382.
412   PG, Rouen, 14 August 1855, in AN BB³⁰387.
413   Labrousse (ed.), *Aspects de la crise*, pp. xxix–xxx.
414   GOC 16th DM, 1–5 September 1855, in AHG E⁵155.
415   J.-P. Aguet, *Les grèves sous la monarchie de juillet*, Geneva, 1954, pp. 368–9.
416   OC *gendarmerie* Nord, reports on February 1846 and April 1847, in AN
      F⁷4106.
417   GOC 5th DM, 1 and 2 July 1847, in AHG E⁵157.
418   OC *gendarmerie*, Haut-Rhin, report on June 1855, in AN F⁷4142.
419   PG, Rouen, 8 August 1856, in AN BB³⁰387.
420   For example, at Boisville on 6 August 1855, reported by OC *gendarmerie*,
      Eure-et-Loir, in AN F⁷3996.
421   OC *gendarmerie*, Loiret, report on January 1847, in AN F⁷4058.
422   GOC 7th DM, 15, 18 and 23 February 1847, in AHG E⁵156.
423   See, for example, OC *gendarmerie*, Haute-Garonne, report on June 1855, in
      AN F⁷4008.
424   See, for example, *Préfet*, Vosges, 1 September 1853, in AN F¹²4651; PG,
      Orléans, 24 July 1855, in AN BB³⁰380.
425   PG, Rouen, 14 August 1855, in AN BB³⁰387.
426   20 July 1855, in AN BB³⁰377.

Chapter 6   An end to dearth

1   *Journal des Chemins de Fer*, 28 August 1852.
2   See, for example, 1859 *Enquête*, p. 766, evidence of M. Boussingault.
3   See, for example, PG, Metz, 5 April 1862, in AN BB³⁰380.
4   *Commissaire royal* attached to the Orléans–Bordeaux Company to *Préfet*,
    Loiret, 5 June 1847, quoted by M. Blanchard, *Essais historiques sur les*

premiers chemins de fer du midi languedocien et de la vallée du Rhône, Montpellier, 1935, p. 190.

5   1859 *Enquête*, p. 619, evidence of M. Dumont, Mayor of Rouvilliers (Oise), as an example of contemporary awareness of this; see also PG, Limoges, 12 January 1857, in AN BB³⁰378.

6   See, for example, PG, Douai, October 1867, in AN BB³⁰377; PG, Riom, 11 January 1868, in AN BB³⁰386.

7   4 October 1859, in AN BB³⁰374.

8   *Journal d'agriculture pratique, chronique agricole 1ᵉʳ quinzaine*, August 1861.

9   12 October 1861, in AN BB³⁰387.

10   See, for example, 1859 *Enquête*, p. 248, evidence of I. Fould; p. 504, evidence of M. Boittelle.

11   Editorial of *Journal des Chemins de Fer*, 19 January 1850.

12   P. Froment, 'Les chemins de fer et l'agriculture', *L'année ferroviaire*, 1948, pp. 86–7.

13   *Journal des Chemins de Fer*, 14 October 1854, unsigned article, 'L'approvisionnement de Paris par les chemins de fer'.

14   PG, Riom, 11 January 1855, in AN BB³⁰386.

15   PG, Agen, 28 January 1855, in AN BB³⁰371.

16   See, for example, PG, Riom, 17 January 1854, in AN BB³⁰386; PG, Agen, 28 January 1855, in AN BB³⁰371.

17   PG, Paris, 21 February 1855, in AN BB³⁰383; PG, Bordeaux, 3 February 1854, in AN BB³⁰374.

18   See, for example, OC *gendarmerie*, Pas-de-Calais, report on September 1855, in AN F⁷4118; OC *gendarmerie*, Bas-Rhin, report on May 1855, in AN F⁷4137.

19   OC *gendarmerie*, Haut-Rhin, report on April 1855, in AN F⁷4142.

20   PG, Paris, ? August 1855, in AN BB³⁰383.

21   PG, Rouen, 2 February 1857, in AN BB³⁰387.

22   PG, Limoges, 12 January 1857, in AN BB³⁰378.

23   PG, Riom, 11 January 1855, in AN BB³⁰386.

24   OC *gendarmerie*, Indre, report on May 1856, in AN F⁷4025; PG, Bourges, 21 January 1854, in AN BB³⁰374.

25   See, for example, PG, Paris, 2 February 1855, in AN BB³⁰383.

26   PG, Rouen, 2 February 1857, in AN BB³⁰387.

27   PG, Poitiers, 30 August 1853, in AN BB³⁰432.

28   OC *gendarmerie*, Nord, reports on May, June, August and September 1856, in AN F⁷4106.

29   PG, Angers, 8 January 1854, in AN BB³⁰371.

30   See PG, Paris, 21 February 1855 and 1 September 1856, in AN BB³⁰383; PG, Orléans, 28 January 1854, in AN BB³⁰382.

31   G. Dupeux, *Aspects de l'histoire sociale et politique du Loir-et-Cher*, 1962, pp. 411–12.

32   See, for example, PG, Riom, 15 July 1860, in AN BB³⁰387.

33   *Préfet* of Police, Paris, 15 and 22 September 1867, in *Papiers et correspondance de la famille impériale*, vol. 2, 1870, pp. 264–9.

34   PG, Toulouse, in series of reports March–August 1868, in AN BB¹⁸1766, 1769, 1775.

35   PG, Paris, April 1868, in AN BB¹⁸1766.

36   PG, Nîmes, April 1868, in AN BB[18]1778.
37   PG, Colmar, 24 and 28 June 1868, in AN BB[18]1772.
38   M. Perrot, *Les ouvriers en grève. France 1871–90*, vol. 1, 1974, p. 76.
39   See, for example, PG, Bourges, 9 January 1868, in AN BB[30]368.
40   See, for example, PG, Bourges, 9 January 1868, in AN BB[30]368.
41   1866 *Enquête*, vol. 22, Gard.
42   A. Corbin, *Archaïsme et modernité en Limousin au 19ᵉ siècle*, vol. 1, 1975, pp. 514–16.
43   See, for example, PG, Rouen, 12 January 1854, in AN BB[30]387; PG, Montpellier, 17 January 1854, in AN BB[30]380; 1859 *Enquête*, p. 193, evidence of M. Fournier, Mayor of Meaux (Seine-et-Marne).
44   1859 *Enquête*, p. 65, M. Bethmont.
45   J.-C. Devos, 'Les conséquences du décret du 22 juin 1863 sur la liberté du commerce de la boulangerie', *Actes du 93ᵉ Congrès des sociétés savantes 1968*, 1971, pp. 352–3.
46   See, for example, PG, Angers, 19 June 1865, in AN BB[18]1715; PG, Orléans, 5 January 1867, in AN BB[30]382.
47   Devos, 'Les conséquences du décret du 22 juin'.
48   See, for example, PG, Paris, 20 May 1867 and 15 February 1868, in AN BB[30]383; PG, Amiens, 11 October 1867 and 9 April 1868, in AN BB[30]371.
49   See, for example, OC *gendarmerie*, Côtes-du-Nord, 31 July 1869, in AHG G[8]166; PG, Amiens, 9 April 1868, in AN BB[30]371.
50   See, for example, PG, Paris, 15 February 1864, in AN BB[30]383; PG, Orléans, 5 January 1867, in AN BB[30]382.
51   Ministère de l'Agriculture, Bureau des Subsistances, internal memorandum, 12 July 1878, in AN F[11]4854.
52   J. Gaillard, *Paris, la ville (1852–70)*, vol. 3, Doctorat d'état, Université de Paris, 1974, p. 257.
53   J. Singer-Kérel, *Le coût de la vie à Paris de 1840 à 1961*, 1961, p. 183.
54   1882 *Enquête*, Préfecture du département de la Seine, 'Rapport de M Morillon', in AN C 3373[2].
55   See, for example, R. Price, 'The onset of labour shortage in French agriculture', *Economic History Review*, 1975, *passim*.
56   See, for example, P. Estienne, 'L'étude de la dépopulation en Montagne', *Revue de géographie alpine*, 1947, pp. 373–5.
57   See, for example, PG, Limoges, 11 June 1854, in AN BB[30]378; PG, Lyon, 29 July 1855, in AN BB[30]379.

Chapter 7   The transport revolution: railways, roads, waterways

1   M. Chisholm, *Human Geography: Evolution or Revolution?*, 1975, p. 94.
2   'Les transports en France de 1830 à 1968', *Economie et société*, 1968, p. 252.
3   D. Renouard, *Les transports de marchandises par fer, route et eau depuis 1850*, 1963, p. 39.
4   C. Lavollée, 'Les chemins de fer français en 1866', *Revue des deux mondes*, January 1866, p. 5.
5   P. Toyne, *Organisation, Location and Behaviour*, 1974, p. 241.

6   For basic legislation see, for example, J.-P. Adam, *Instauration de la politique des chemins de fer en France*, 1972, *passim*.

7   A. Picard, *Les chemins de fer français*, vol. 1, 1884, p. 230.

8   In AN F¹⁴8508A.

9   ibid.

10 Conventions printed in Picard, *Les chemins de fer français*, vol. 2, p. 556.

11 *Recueils des conventions passées de 1883 à 1892 entre l'état et les compagnies de chemin de fer*, in AN AD XIX N 108.

12 See, for example, M. Martin, 'Presse, publicité et grandes affaires sous le Second Empire', *Revue historique*, 1976, p. 373.

13 In AN C 2854.

14 See, for example, *Chemin de fer de Paris à Mulhouse, Ville de Provins, Mémoire présenté par le conseil municipal*, Provins, 1854, pp. 1–2; Ville de Grenoble, *Chemin de fer d'embranchement de Grenoble sur les lignes de Lyon à Avignon*, Grenoble, n.d. but probably 1850.

15 For detailed statistics see the various volumes of the *Statistique des chemins de fer*.

16 Ministère des Travaux publics (Min. des TP), *Statistique des chemins de fer français au 31 Décembre 1906*, vol. 2, Meulun, 1908, p. 5.

17 Toutain, *Les transports en France*, p. 188.

18 Based on M. Lévy-Leboyer, 'Capital investment and economic growth in France 1820–1930', *Cambridge Economic History of Europe*, vol. 7, Part 1, Cambridge, 1978, pp. 250, 287.

19 Orléans–Bordeaux, *Rapport du Conseil d'administration*, 1850.

20 Ouest. *Assemblée générale des actionnaires du 30 Novembre 1850, rapport du conseil d'administration*; Min. des TP, internal memorandum, 'Le chemin de fer de Paris à Avignon sera-t-il achevé par l'état?', in AN C 987.

21 Est, *Rapport*, 1853, p. 4.

22 Nord, *Rapport*, 1853, p. 18.

23 Conseil général, Seine-Inférieure, *Session ordinaire de 1843. Procès-verbaux des délibérations*. Rouen, 1843, p. 34.

24 E. Charles, *Les chemins de fer en France pendant le règne de Louis-Philippe*, 1896, p. 227.

25 See, for example, Conseil municipal de Neufchâtel (Seine-Inférieure), *Chemin de fer de Rouen à St-Quentin*, Neufchâtel, 1843, p. 4.

26 See, for example, Conseil municipal de Lyon, *Rapport sur le projet d'un chemin de fer de Lyon à Genève par la vallée du Rhône*, Lyon, 1848, p. 5.

27 See, for example, Chemin de fer du Nord, *Compte d'exploitation pour l'exercice*, 1846, in AN 48 AQ 3660.

28 Renouard, *Les transports de marchandises*.

29 Min. des TP, Bureau de la Statistique des chemins de fer, *Documents relatifs à la construction et a l'exploitation*, 1872, pp. 56–7.

30 2ᵉ *Rapport*, in AN F¹⁴9239.

31 *Considérations sur le tracé du chemin de fer de Paris à Caen présentées . . . par une réunion des délégués et des propriétaires de plusieurs départements de l'Ouest, 26 Mars 1852*, in AN C 1028.

32 *Journal des chemins de fer départementaux*, no. 1, 7 June 1855; see also editorial of 30 June.

33   See, for example, M. Wolkowitsch, *L'économie régionale des transports dans le centre et le centre-ouest de la France*, n.d., p. 72.
34   Chemin de fer de l'Est, *Rapport du Conseil d'administration*, 1858, pp. 9–10.
35   In AN C 1156.
36   See, for example, Conseil d'Etat, session 1868, *Exposé des motifs d'un projet de loi relatif à l'exécution de plusieurs chemins de fer*, in AN C 1125.
37   Ministère de l'Agriculture, *Enquête agricole*, 1868, vol. 1, 'Rapport . . . par le Directeur de l'agriculture, commissaire général de l'enquête'.
38   See, for example, *1871 Enquête . . . Observations présentés par le conseil municipal d'Ambert sur le chemin de fer de Vichy à Thiers et de Thiers à Ambert, 28 June 1873*, in AN C 2855.
39   *Rapport fait au nom de la Commission d'enquête sur les chemins de fer et autres voies de transport concernant diverses petitions relatives à la concession d'une ligne directe de Calais à Marseille, 3 February 1873*, in AN C 2856.
40   Conseil général, Nord, session 1860, *Rapport sur les chemins de fer par M. Plichon*, p. 4.
41   See, for example, M. Noblemaire, *Les chemins de fer départementaux*, 1890, *passim*.
42   See, for example, Min. des TP, Direction générale des ponts-et-chaussées et des chemins de fer, to Min. des TP, 30 August 1873, in AN F^{14}9449.
43   See, for example, Min. des TP, *Inspection de l'exploitation commerciale des chemins de fer, Ouest. Rapport de l'inspecteur principal, 14 July 1874*, in AN F^{14}9449.
44   E. Lavasseur, *Histoire du commerce de la France*, vol 2, 1912, p. 378.
45   See, for example, Min. des TP, *Avis du directeur du contrôle commercial, 26 June 1903*, in AN F^{14}11295. The problem had been recognized much earlier. See, for example, Chambre des députés, *Commission relative à la constitution du réseau national des chemins de fer et leur régime d'exploitation, Séance 18 July 1883*, speeches by MM. Waddington and Wilson, in AN C 3308.
46   Chambre des députés, *Commission des travaux publics, des chemins de fer et des voies de communication, séance 10 March 1910*, in AN C 7353.
47   R. Bresson, *L'évolution de l'idée d'intérêt local dans la constitution du réseau ferré français*, 1913, pp. 79, 98.
48   C. de Freycinet, *Souvenirs*, 1914, pp. 11, 78–9.
49   *Journal officiel*, 2 and 16 January 1878.
50   Chambre des députés, *Commission des chemins de fer, Commission chargée de l'étude des projets et propositions tendant au classement ou à la déclaration d'utilité publique des chemins de fer, nommée 3 décembre 1881, 20 janvier 1883, 2 février 1884*, in AN C 3307.
51   Bresson, *L'évolution de l'idée*, p. 111.
52   Chambre des députés, *Commission relative à la construction du réseau national des chemins de fer et a leur exploitation, nommée 9 March 1882, séance 30 January 1883*, in AN C 3308.
53   ibid., session 18 July 1883.
54   Chambre des députés, *Commission relative à la constitution du réseau national des chemins de fer et a leur régime d'exploitation, nommée 9 March 1882, séance 8 May 1883*, in AN C 3308, evidence of M. Waddington.

55 Chambre des députés, *Commission des travaux publics* . . ., séance 23 February 1910, in AN C 7353.

56 1882 Commission, séance 19 June 1883, in AN C 3308.

57 M. Considère, 'Utilité des chemins de fer d'intérêt local', *Annales des ponts-et-chaussées*, 7ᵉ série, vol. 7, 1894.

58 On the need for such construction see e.g. Compagnie des chemins de fer de l'Est to Inspecteur général Est, 22 November 1873, in AN F¹⁴12161.

59 See, for example, reports in AN F¹⁴9239.

60 See, for example, Min. des TP, Direction générale des chemins de fer, *Commissions régionales instituées par décret du 2 janvier 1878, sous-commission du centre-ouest*, in AN F¹⁴9572.

61 Considère, 'Utilité'.

62 See also M. Gonjo, 'Le Plan Freycinet, 1878–82: un aspect de la grande dépression économique en France', *Revue historique*, 1972, *passim*.

63 Bresson, *L'évolution de l'idée*, pp. 103f.

64 Min. des TP, *Statistique des chemins de fer français au 31 décembre 1906*, vol. 2, p. 5.

65 Min. des TP, *Commission instituée par décret du 31 août 1907*, pp. 116–18.

66 Considère, 'Utilité', p. 307.

67 F. Caron, *Histoire de l'exploitation d'un grand réseau. La compagnie du Chemin de fer du Nord*, 1973, pp. 14, 113, 172, 328.

68 F. Crouzet, 'Essor, déclin et renaissance de l'industrie française des locomotives', *Revue d'histoire économique et sociale*, 1977, pp. 163–73.

69 F. Caron, 'Essai d'analyse historique d'une psychologie du travail. Les mécaniciens et chauffeurs de locomotives du réseau du Nord de 1850 à 1910', *Le Mouvement social*, 1965, *passim*.

70 F. Jacqmin, *De l'exploitation des chemins de fer. Leçons faites en 1867 à l'école impériale des ponts-et-chaussées*, vol. 2, 1868, pp. 16–17, 21.

71 Toutain, *Les transports en France*, p. 165.

72 See G. Marqfoy, *De l'abaissement des tarifs des chemins de fer en France*, 1863, p. 41; Considère, 'Utilité', p. 307; *Journal des chemins de fer*, 19 January 1878; PLM *Rapport*, 1883, p. 21.

73 Min. des TP, *Chemins de fer français d'intérêt général. Documents statistiques relatifs à l'année 1879*, p. 88.

74 Cost of establishment per metre, in francs, by 1865: Nord 2358; Est 3001; Ouest 3541; Paris–Orléans 3025; PLM 2541; Midi 1304. Min. des TP, Direction-générale des ponts-et-chaussées, *Bureau de statistiques Chemin de fer. Conditions techniques d'établissement*, 1865, p. xxviii, in AN AD XIX N 182.

75 See, for example, Cle. des chemins de fer de l'Est to Inspecteur général Est, 22 November 1873, in AN F¹⁴12161.

76 See, for example, P–O *Rapport*, 1893, p. 533.

77 3 September 1887.

78 See, for example, undated memorandum Nord (1847) in AN 48 AQ 3661; inspectors reports to Comité de Direction, Nord, 11 and 13 March 1847, in AN 48 AQ 3660.

79 See, for example, Min. des TP to Administration, Orléans, 13 November 1871, in AN 60 AQ 316; see also reports on disorganization of traffic, in AN F¹⁴9480.

80 Sous-secrétaire d'état to Min. des TP, 28 November 1846, in AN F¹⁴9451.

81   Cie. des chemins de fer de Rouen du Havre et de Dieppe to Min. des TP, 14 November 1850, in AN F¹⁴9436.

82   See, for example, Chef de la division des chemins de fer de l'Ouest to Min. des TP, 18 December 1850, in AN F¹⁴9437.

83   See, for example, *Réponse de la Compagnie des chemins de fer de l'Est au questionnaire de la commission d'enquête administrative sur les chemins de fer,* n.d. (1871), p. 49, in AN 109 AQ 95.

84   Jacqmin, *De l'exploitation des chemins de fer,* vol. 1, p. 54.

85   Min. des TP, Chemin de fer d'Orléans à Bordeaux, Commissariat royal to Min. des TP, 4 January 1848, in AN F¹⁴9452.

86   PLM, *Notes pour la commission parlementaire . . . 1871,* in AN C 3005.

87   Ouest, 'Rapport du Conseil d'administration', *Journal des chemins de fer,* 1899, p. 332.

88   See, for example, Chambre de Commerce Avignon, *Procès-verbaux,* session 23 November 1872, in AN C 3005.

89   Nord, *Rapport,* 1884, p. 23, on problems due to inadequate repair facilities in 1878–80.

90   PLM, *Rapport,* 1884, p. 21.

91   See Crouzet, 'Essor, déclin et renaissance', p. 118.

92   P. Léon *et al.,* *Histoire économique et sociale de la France* vol. 3 pt 1, 1976, p. 267.

93   Jacqmin, *De l'exploitation des chemins de fer,* vol. 1, p. 5.

94   1863 *Enquête,* p. 62.

95   Min. des TP, *Contrôle des chemins de fer du Nord. Rapport de l'inspecteur principal, 4 April 1905,* in AN F¹⁴11277.

96   Caron, *Histoire de l'exploitation,* p. 135.

97   See, for example, Min. des TP to Administration Cie d'Orléans, 6 December 1871, in AN 60 AQ 316.

98   See, for example, Président du Conseil d'administration Strasbourg–Bâle, 14 July 1845, *Note en réponse au rapport de M l'Inspecteur-en-chef du Bas-Rhin sur le nouveau tarif des marchandises,* in AN F¹⁴9388.

99   P–O *Rapport,* 1848, p. 21.

100   J. Gouhier, *Naissance d'une grande cité. Le Mans au milieu de 20ᵉ siècle,* 1953, p. 19.

101   Chemins de fer de Paris à Lyon et à la Méditerranée, *Note sur le service de la ligne de Lyon à St-Etienne,* 1869, p. 9, in AN 45 AP 24; Ville de Valence, *Chemin de fer Valence à Grenoble,* 1862, pp. 23–4.

102   1871 *Enquête,* PLM, *Notes pour la commission parlementaire* and evidence of Montpellier Chamber of Commerce, 30 May 1872; *Commission relative à l'enquête des chemins de fer,* sessions of 21 February 1872 and 1 February 1873, in AN C 3005.

103   *Rapport fait au nom de la commission d'enquête sur les chemins de fer,* 3 February 1873, in AN C 2856.

104   P–O *Rapport,* 1900, p. 33.

105   P–O *Rapport,* 1866, pp. 34–5.

106   Jacqmin, *De l'exploitation des chemins de fer,* vol. 1, p. 54; *Rapport fait au nom de la commission d'enquête sur les chemins de fer,* 3 February 1873, in AN C 2856; R. Clozier, *La gare du Nord,* 1940, pp. 74–7, 115, 138.

107 AN F¹⁴12152.

108 In AN C 3005.

109 See, for example, 1870 *Enquête* (transport), evidence of E. and I. Koechlin on behalf of the Mulhouse Chamber of Commerce, in AN C 1161.

110 See, for example, PI, Cherbourg, to PG, Caen, copy enclosed with latter's report of 6 July 1864, in AN BB³⁰375; Chamber of Commerce of Nîmes, *Les transports par chemins de fer*, 1872, *passim*.

111 See, for example, Jacqmin, *De l'exploitation des chemins de fer*, vol. 1, pp. 249f.; *Commission chargée d'étudier l'abbréviation des délais de transport en petite vitesse 1907–1912*, especially the evidence of M. Sartiau, representing the Nord, and the evidence of the Ouest, in AN F¹⁴12152.

112 P–O *Rapport*, 1899, p. 377.

113 Sous-secrétaire d'Etat to Min. des TP, 6 March 1847, in AN F¹⁴⁹435.

114 Chemin de fer du Nord, *Compte de l'exploitation pour l'exercice*, 1846, in AN 48 AQ 3660.

115 See, for example, Min des TP, *Commission chargée d'étudier des réformes à réaliser dans l'organisation du contrôle des chemins de fer*, 1912, p. 7; Caron, *Histoire de l'exploitation*, p. 122.

116 See *Commission chargée d'étudier l'abbréviation des délais de transport en petite vitesse 1907–1912/13*, in AN F¹⁴12152.

117 AN F¹⁴12161; J. Gaillard, *Paris, la ville (1852–70)*, Doctorat d'état, Université de Paris, 1974, vol. 3, p. 491.

118 See, for example, Min. des TP, *Contrôle et surveillance des chemins de fer, Réseau d'Orléans. Rapport Inspecteur général 26 May 1875*, in AN F¹⁴12161.

119 In AN C 1161.

120 1871 *Enquête*, evidence of the Syndicat des compagnies des chemins de fer d'intérêt général secondaire et d'intérêt départemental, 14 December 1875, in AN C 3008.

121 See, for example, PLM to Inspecteur général, 11 October 1873, in AN F¹⁴12161

122 See, for example, 30 April 1857, agreement between P–O and Ouest, in AN F¹⁴⁹459.

123 PLM, *Rapport*, 1865, p. 38.

124 See, for example, *Avis de l'Inspecteur général Ouest*, 14 July 1874, in AN F¹⁴⁹449.

125 Evidence of government efforts, in AN F¹⁴12162.

126 See, for example, Min. des TP to Cie des chemins de fer du Midi, 25 April 1898, in AN F¹⁴11272.

127 Jacqmin, *De l'exploitation des chemins de fer*, vol. 1, p. 53.

128 *Enquête sur les moyens d'assurer la régularité et la sûreté de l'exploitation sur les chemins de fer*, 1858, p. 89.

129 Caron, *Histoire de l'exploitation*, p. 333.

130 Wolkowitsch, *L'économie régionale*, p. 51.

131 1863 *Enquête*, p. xlvii, evidence of M. Denière, president of the Tribunal de Commerce of the Seine.

132 ibid, p. 40.

133 Toutain, *Les transports en France*, p. 279, but cf. Renouard, *Les transports de marchandises*, pp. 58, 75, for lower estimates. See also F. Jacqmin 'Notes sur

l'agriculture et les chemins de fer', Annales des ponts-et-chaussées, 4ᵉ série, vol. 10, 1865, *passim.*

134   See also Caron, *Histoire de l'exploitation*, pp. 131–41.

135   Cie du chemin de fer de Strasbourg à Bâle to Min. des TP, 13 February 1843, in AN F¹⁴9388.

136   Cie Paris–Rouen to sous-secrétaire d'Etat, 28 August 1843; Cie Paris–Rouen to Min. des TP, 20 February 1844, in AN F¹⁴9435.

137   Chemin de fer de Paris à Lyon, *Commission du contrôle, séance 11 April 1850*, in AN F¹⁴9466.

138   See, for example, Chemins de fer de l'Ouest to Min. des TP, 28 June 1865, in AN F¹⁴9449.

139   See note 74.

140   See Min. des TP, *Commission chargée d'étudier les réformes à réaliser dans l'organisation du contrôle des chemins de fer*, 1912, p. 7.

141   See, for example, Ingénieur en chef, Ponts-et-Chaussées, *Chemin de fer de Lille et de Valenciennes à la frontière de Belgique*, to Min. des TP, 11 April 1845, in AN F¹⁴9378; Min. des TP, *Comité consultatif séance 10 July 1903*; Chemin de fer de l'Etat, 2ᵉ Division, 'Bureau des tarifs', undated memorandum (1910), in AN F¹⁴11295.

142   See, for example, Min. des TP, *Rapport de l'inspecteur général chargé de la Direction du Contrôle des chemins de fer de l'Ouest*, 30 May 1890, in AN F¹⁴11295.

143   Cie de l'Est to Min. des TP, 23 August 1861, in AN F¹⁴9412.

144   Min. des TP, PLM, *Rapport de l'inspecteur principal*, 21 October 1893, in AN F¹⁴11305.

145   See also C. Baum, 'Note sur le prix de revient des transports par chemin de fer en France', *Annales des ponts-et-chaussées*, 1883 p. 453; Jacqmin, *De l'exploitation des chemins de fer*, vol. 2, 1867, p. 118.

146   See, for example, Chef de la Division des chemins de fer to Min. des TP, 31 October 1850, in AN F¹⁴9436.

147   AN 48 AQ 3661.

148   ibid.

149   *Agent commercial*, Amiens, to Administration, Nord, 17 June 1850, 2 May 1853, in AN 48 AQ 3702.

150   Caron, *Histoire de l'exploitation*, p. 136.

151   *Journal des chemins de fer*, 21 July 1888.

152   Min. des TP, *Rapport de l'inspecteur général chargé de la Direction du Contrôle des chemins de fer de l'Ouest*, 27 July 1889, 30 May 1890, in AN F¹⁴11295.

153   See, for example, Min. des TP, Division des chemins de fer, 8 November 1851, in AN F¹⁴9453.

154   See, for example, *Rapport de l'ingénieur en chef du service spécial du Rhône*, 27 February 1895, in AN F¹⁴11305.

155   See, for example, Min. des TP, internal note, 22 October 1850, in AN F¹⁴9555; Min. des TP, *Rapport de l'inspecteur . . . Ouest*, 27 July 1889, in AN F¹⁴11295.

156   Ministerial note, 'Le chemin de fer de Paris à Avignon sera-t-il achevé par l'état?', 1849, in AN C 987.

157   Min. des TP, *Comité consultatif . . . PLM*, 12 March 1891, in AN F¹⁴11305.

158 *Rapport de l'ingénieur en chef du service spécial du Rhône*, 27 February 1895, in AN F¹⁴11305.

159 1871 *Enquête*, response of Montpellier Chamber of Commerce, 30 May 1872, in AN C 3005.

160 See, for example, La Rochelle Chamber of Commerce to Min. des TP, 21 May 1896, in AN F¹⁴12153.

161 Min. of Marine to Min. des TP, 5 May 1898, and reply of 18 May, in AN F¹⁴12153.

162 See, for example, Min. des TP. *L'ingénieur en chef des mines chargé du contrôle . . . des chemins de fer*, 9 February 1857, in AN F¹⁴⁹440; *Chambre consultative des arts et manufactures de l'arrondissement d'Evreux, séance 17 July 1875*, in AN F¹⁴⁹449.

163 Min. des TP, Commissariat Central des chemins de fer, Sous-secrétaire d'état to Min. des TP, 6 March 1847, in AN F¹⁴⁹435.

164 Min. des TP, *Comité consultatif. . . 20 October 1897*, in AN F¹⁴11277.

165 Min. des TP, PLM, *Rapport de l'inspecteur principal 21 October 1893*, in AN F¹⁴11305.

166 See, for example, Letter to Min. des TP of 7 March 1843, in AN F¹⁴⁹388.

167 Société d'agriculture de Valenciennes to Min. des TP, 27 February 1850, in AN F¹⁴⁹382.

168 See, for example, *Journal des chemins de fer*, 14 May 1887, report by the Comité consultatif des chemins de fer on P–O tarrifs.

169 Toutain, *Les transports en France*, p. 279; Marqfoy, *De l'abaissement des tarifs des chemins de fer en France*, p. 7.

170 P. E. Lloyd, and P. Dickens, *Location in Space: A Theoretical Approach to Economic Geography*, New York, 1972, p. 78.

171 AN C 1161.

172 Caron, *Histoire de l'exploitation*, p. 136.

173 Min. des TP, *Enquête sur l'exploitation et la construction des chemins de fer*, 1863, pp. 44–5.

174 ibid.

175 AN C 1161.

176 Min. des TP, *Inspection . . . Ouest 27 July 1889*, in AN F¹⁴11295.

177 See, for example, Min. des TP, *Comité consultatif. . . 18 August 1890*, in AN F¹⁴11295; Chemin de fer du Nord, *Exploitation*, to Min. des TP, 25 June 1898, in AN F¹⁴11277.

178 Conseil d'Etat, *Enquête sur l'application des tarifs des chemins de fer*, 1850, p. x.

179 See, for example, *Préfet*, Seine-Inférieure, to Min. des TP, 25 August 1843, in AN F¹⁴⁹435; Tribunal de commerce of the *arrondissement* of Chartres to Min. des TP, 29 March 1849, in AN F¹⁴⁹437 Contrôle et surveillance des chemins de fer du Midi, service de l'ingénieur en chef, *Lignes du Gard et de Marseille à Avignon* to Min. des TP, 27 June 1852, re section Nîmes to Alais, in AN F¹⁴⁹463.

180 *Documents statistiques*.

181 See also Jacqmin, *De l'exploitation des chemins de fer*, vol. 2, p. 128; Lavollée, 'Les chemins de fer français', p. 26.

182 P–O *Rapport*, 1896, published in *Journal des chemins de fer*, 1896, p. 332.

183   Est, *Rapport*, 1899, p. 36.
184   D. Zolla, *Le blé et les céréales*, 1909, p. 239.
185   Ouest, *Rapport*, 1866, p. 51.
186   P–O, *Rapport*, 1891.
187   PLM, *Rapport*, 1896, in *Journal des chemins de fer*, 1896, p. 326.
188   ibid.
189   Ouest, *Rapport*, 1894, in ibid., p. 318.
190   Zolla, *Le blé et les céreales*, p. 237.
191   ibid., p. 268.
192   Préfecture du département de la Seine, *Rapport de M. Morillon, Chef de bureau, sur les consommations de Paris et sur la gestion des halles, marchés et abattoirs*, 1883, *passim*, in AN C 3373².
193   Chemin de fer de l'Ouest, report on section Paris–Chartres, 12 July 1849 to 30 November 1850, in AN C 987.
194   Ouest *Rapport*, 1880, pp. 38–9.
195   Midi *Rapport*, 1880, p. 39.
196   Midi *Rapport*, 1899, p. 333.
197   G. Désert, *Une société rurale au 19ᵉ siècle: les paysans du Calvados, 1815–95*, vol. 1, Lille, 1975, p. 396.
198   1871 *Enquête, Réponse de la compagnie des chemins de fer de l'Est*, pp. 39–40, in AN 109 AQ 95.
199   PLM, *Rapport*, 1883, p. 25.
200   1866 *Enquête*, vol. I, *Rapport général*, p. 96.
201   P–O, *Rapport*, 1857, p. 26, and 1866, p. 34.
202   See, for example, Chambre de Commerce de Rouen, *Observations sur les tarifs généraux, spéciaux et communs des Cies. de chemin de fer*, Rouen, 1862, p. 22; *Les tarifs des transports des vins par D. Aubry, Président Syndicat agricole de l'arrondissement de Muret (Haute-Garonne)*, Toulouse, 1907 p. 6.
203   Min. des TP, *Chemins de fer français d'intérêt général. Album des tarifs généraux et spéciaux actuels (petite vitesse)*, 1882, p. 1.
204   See, for example, Chambre de Commerce de Mulhouse, *Transport par chemin de fer*, Mulhouse, 1870, p. 7; Chambre de Commerce La Rochelle to Min. des TP, 21 May 1896, in AN F¹⁴12153.
205   AN C 1161.
206   Nord, chef d'exploitation, circular 15 January 1847, in AN 48 AQ 3661.
207   Préfecture, Loiret arrêt, . . . *Tarif spécial pour le transport des grains, farines et issues . . . 2 April 1853*, in AN 60 AQ 45.
208   AN 48 AQ 3661.
209   See also agreements signed 3 May, 30 June, 1 September 1847, in AN 60 AQ 316 and 48 AQ 3661.
210   Agreements of 5 March 1847 between Cie du Nord and milk merchants of Pontoise and St-Denis, in AN 48 AQ 3661.
211   See, for example, Min. des TP, *Commission de contrôle du chemin de fer de Lyon, séance December 1850*, in AN F¹⁴9466.
212   Chemin de fer du Nord, *Exploitation, 18 January 1905*, in AN F¹⁴11277.
213   See, for example, 1870 *Enquête* (transport), response from the town of Pithiviers (Loiret), in AN C 1161.
214   *Commission générale des chemins de fer, séance 18 May 1850*, in AN F¹⁴9389.

215 Chef de la Division des chemins de fer to Min. des TP, 24 July 1851, in AN F^{14}9466. See also similar case of millers at Corbeil, Inspecteur de l'exploitation commerciale des chemins de fer d'Orléans to Min. des TP, 5 March 1851, in AN F^{14}9450.

216 See, for example, Min. des TP, *Commission centrale des chemins de fer, séance 18 July 1849*, in AN F^{14}9555.

217 1870 *Enquête*, (transport), reply from Brive (Corrèze), in AN C 1161.

218 Nancy Chamber of Commerce to Min. of Agriculture, 19 September 1861, in AN F^{14}9412.

219 See, for example, Chamber of Commerce of Roanne, *Réponse au questionnaire de la commission d'enquête parlementaire sur le régime général des chemins de fer*, Roanne, 1872, p. 22.

220 See, for example, 1870 *Enquête*, (transport), response of the Chamber of Commerce of Vosges, in AN C 1161.

221 1866 *Enquête*, vol. 6, Seine-et-Marne, p. 130.

222 See, for example, Boulogne Chamber of Commerce, January 1850, quoted by M. Blanchard, *Essais historiques sur les premiers chemins de fer du Midi languedocien et de la vallée du Rhône*, Montpellier, 1935, p. 191; and 1890 petition from grain merchants of Gray (Haute-Saône), in AN F^{14}11305.

223 Orléans Chamber of Commerce to Min. of Agriculture, 11 October 1850, in AN F^{14}9555; *Syndicat des agriculteurs du Loiret, séance 9 December 1893*, in AN F^{14}11205.

224 See, for example, Cie du chemin de fer de Paris à Rouen to Min. des TP, 25 November 1843, in AN F^{14}9435.

225 *Journal des chemins de fer*, 24 May 1851.

226 Caron, *Histoire de l'exploitation*, pp. 135–40.

227 Min. des TP, *Comité consultatif . . . 15 May 1901*, in AN F^{14}11305.

228 See, for example, Rouen Chamber of Commerce to *Préfet*, Seine-Inférieure, 18 November 1845; Paris Chamber of Commerce to Min. des TP, 24 February; 1844, in AN F^{14}9435.

229 See Min. des Finances to Min. des TP, 6 May 1843, re Cie des chemins de fer d'Alsace, in AN F^{14}9388.

230 Min. des TP, *Commission centrale des chemins de fer, séance 1 December 1849*, in AN F^{14}9463.

231 Chambres de commerce et chambres consultatives des arts et des manufactures de la région du Nord, *Défense du commerce et de l'industrie contre ses compagnies de chemin de fer*, Boulogne, 1871.

232 See, for example, *Conseils généraux de l'agriculture, des manufactures et du commerce 1845–6*, vol. 3 pp. 290–304; Conseil d'Etat 1859, p. 497, evidence of Paris Chamber of Commerce.

233 Min. des TP, *Commission chargée d'étudier des réformes à réaliser dans l'organisation du contrôle des chemins de fer: Rapport général*, 1912.

234 ibid, p. 12.

235 See, for example, Cie du chemin de fer de Paris à Strasbourg to Min. des TP, 23 December 1850, in AN F^{14}9389; Cie du chemin de fer de Paris à Rouen to Min. des TP, 25 November 1843, in AN F^{14}9435.

236 Min. des TP, Section des chemins de fer et de la police du roulage, Chemin de Mulhouse à Thann to *Préfet*, Haut-Rhin, 13 August 1840; Président du Conseil

d'administration Strasbourg-Bâle, 'Note en réponse au rapport de M. l'ingénieur en chef du Bas-Rhin sur le nouveau tarif des marchandises', 4 July 1845, in AN F^{14}9388.

237   See, for example, *Préfet* Gard, to Min. des TP, 31 December 1850, in AN F^{14}9463; Paris *Préfet de police* to Min. des TP, 31 May 1867, in AN F^{14}9449.

238   See, for example, Secrétaire-général, Commissariat central des chemins de fer, to Min. des TP, 16 October 1847, in AN F^{14}9451.

239   See, for example, *Préfet de police* to Min. des TP, 4 February 1852, in AN F^{14}9555.

240   A. Vigarié, *Les grands ports de commerce de la Seine au Rhin*, n.d., pp. 329–30.

241   Min. des TP, *Commission centrale des chemins de fer, séance 1 December 1859*, in AN F^{14}9463.

242   Pointed out by, for example, Ingénieur en chef des Ponts-et-Chaussées, ligne de Bordeaux, to Min. des TP, 27 November 1851, in AN F^{14}9454; see also A. Picard, *Les chemins de fer français*, vol. 1, 1884, p. 571; C. Colson, *Abrégé de la législation des chemins de fer et tramways*, 1903, p. 24.

243   See, for example, Min. des TP, *Comité consultatif . . . 5 May 1903*, in AN F^{14}11295.

244   Article 42 of P–O *Cahier des charges*.

245   See, for example, Cie du Nord, *Ordre de service 155* in 1847, in AN 48 AQ 3661; P. C. Laurent de Villedeuill, *Oeuvres d'Emile et Isaac Pereire*, vol. 3, 1919–20, p. 2306.

246   *Journal des chemins de fer*, 17 September 1853.

247   1870 *Enquête*, (transport), evidence presented by E. and I. Koechlin on behalf of Mulhouse Chamber of Commerce, in AN C 1161.

248   Préfecture du Loiret, 2 April 1853, in AN 60 AQ 35.

249   Min. des TP, *Comité consultatif . . . 7 March 1898*, re ministerial circular of 28 August 1897, in AN F^{14}11272.

250   See, for example, Conseil d'Etat, *Enquête sur l'application des tarifs des chemins de fer de l'Est*, pp. 23–4, in AN 109 AQ 95.

251   Cie du Chemin de fer du Nord, *Séance de l'Assemblée générale extraordinaire du 24 May 1848*, in AN C 915.

252   Jacqmin, *De l'exploitation des chemins de fer*, vol. 1, p. 54.

253   *Journal des chemins de fer*, 15 March 1856.

254   See, for example, Min. des TP, Inspection de l'exploitation commerciale des chemins de fer, to Ingénieur en chef du contrôle des chemins de fer, 17 September 1861, in AN F^{14}9412.

255   Min. des TP, *Rapport de l'inspecteur général chargé de la direction du contrôle des chemins de fer de l'Ouest, 21 June 1890*, in AN F^{14}11295.

256   Chemins de fer de l'Etat, 2e Division, Bureau des Tarifs, n.d. (1912); see also Min. des TP, Direction des chemins de fer, 15 March and 19 August 1912, in AN F^{14}11295.

257   Secrétaire-général, Commissariat central des chemins de fer, to Min. des TP, 16 October 1847, in AN F^{14}9451.

258   See, for example, Min. des TP, *Avis du directeur du contrôle commercial, 26 June 1903*, in AN F^{14}11295; Min. des TP, Comité consultatif, Section pmnte, P–O, March 1914, in AN F^{14}11283.

259   See, for example, Rouen Chamber of Commerce to *Préfet*, Seine-Inférieure, 15 March 1840, in AN F¹⁴9435.

260   *Procès-verbal, séance 30 May 1894*, in AN F¹⁴11283.

261   See, for example, Min. des TP, Direction des chemins de fer, *Note du service chemins de fer de l'Ouest*, n.d. (1890?), in AN F¹⁴11295.

262   See Min. des TP, *Comité consultatif . . . section pmnte, P–O, 1 January 1896, in AN F¹⁴11283.*

263   Min. des TP, *Comité consultatif . . . section pmnte, P–O, 18 July 1892*; Min. des TP, *P–O, Rapport de l'inspecteur général des ponts-et-chaussées, 27 October 1896*, in AN F¹⁴11283.

264   Min. des TP, *Comité consultatif . . . section pmnte. Ouest, 15 May 1894*, in AN F¹⁴11295.

265   Min. des TP, *Avis de l'inspecteur principal, 18 January 1894*, in AN F¹⁴11272.

266   ibid., 20 December 1892.

267   Min. des TP, *PLM, Rapport de l'inspecteur principal, 21 October 1893*; Min. des TP, *Comité consultatif . . . section pmnte, PLM, 31 July 1895*, in AN F¹⁴11305.

268   See, for example, Min. des TP, Inspecteur général, Directeur du contrôle des chemins de fer, 28 June 1888, in AN F¹⁴11305; and 'La protection à l'intérieur par les tarifs de chemins de fer, *Journal des chemins de fer*, 19 December 1891.

269   Min. des TP, *Rapport de l'inspecteur particulier de l'exploitation commerciale Ouest, 26 August 1889*, in AN F¹⁴11295.

270   Chambre consultative des arts et manufactures de l'arrondissement d'Evreux, *Procès-verbal, 17 July 1875*, in AN F¹⁴9435.

271   Min. des TP, *Avis de l'inspecteur général, 29 July 1877*, in AN F¹⁴9449.

272   Min. des TP, *Avis de l'inspecteur général, 14 July 1874*, in AN F¹⁴9449.

273   V. Wright, 'Les directeurs et secrétaires généraux des administrations centrales sous le Second Empire', in F. de Baecque *et al.*, *Les Directeurs de Ministère en France*, Geneva, 1976, p. 42.

274   See, for example, Min. des TP, *Dépenses à faire pour l'achèvement et l'amélioration des routes nationales, 2 August 1878*, in AN F¹⁴1971.

275   See, for example, *Rapport du . . . Préfet du Rhône au conseil général*, session 1851–2, p. 8.

276   Lévy-Leboyer, 'Capital investment and economic growth', p. 250.

277   L. Girard, *La politique des travaux publics du Second Empire*, 1952.

278   Published in *Journal des chemins de fer*, 3 March 1860.

279   Min. des TP, 2 August 1878, *Dépenses à faire pour l'achèvement et l'amélioration des routes nationales*, p. 7, in AN F¹⁴1971.

280   Toutain, *Les transports en France*, p. 25.

281   See, for example, Min. des TP, *Direction des routes et de la navigation. Routes nationales. Situation au 1 Janvier 1881 des travaux en cours ou à entreprendre*, 1882.

282   *Rapport à l'Empereur* by Rouher as Min. des TP, 25 February 1860.

283   1870 *Enquête*, Chambre consultative d'agriculture, *arrondissement* Versailles (Seine-et-Oise), in AN C 1158.

284   Min. des TP, *Routes nationales. Situation au 1ᵉʳ Janvier 1881*, Loire-Inférieure.

285   H. Paulin, *La question des routes devant le parlement en 1891*, 1891, pp. 18–19.

286   See, for example, *sous-préfet*, Sceaux (Seine), July 1867, in AN F¹CIII Seine 31.

287   1866 *Enquête*, vol. 5, Pas-de-Calais, p. 122.

288   See, for example, G. Dupeux, *Aspects de l'histoire sociale et politique du Loir-et-Cher*, 1962, p. 218.

289   Paulin, *La question des routes*.

290   Min. des TP, *Direction des routes et ponts. Routes nationales. Situation au 1 Janvier 1888 des travaux en cours ou à entreprendre*, 1888, pp. 14–15.

291   Toutain, *Les transports en France*, p. 251.

292   1866 *Enquête*, vol. 24, Basses-Alpes, p. 8.

293   Min. de l'Intérieur, *Rapport au roi sur l'exécution pendant l'année 1839 de la loi du 21 Mai 1836 relative aux chemins vicinaux*, 1840, pp. vii–ix; for text of the 1836 law see G. Monsarrat, *Les chemins vicinaux*, n.d., pp. 556f.

294   See, for example, AHG MR 2259, *Mémoire topographique région de Paris*, an example of the detailed description of road conditions. AN AD XIX N 66–71 and AN F²I 1027f contain details of works carried out.

295   Min. de l'Intérieur, *Rapport à S.M. l'Empereur sur le service des chemins vicinaux pendant la période quinquennale de 1852 à 1856*, 1858, p. 4; A. de Foville, *La transformation des moyens de transport et ses conséquences économiques*, 1880, p. 108.

296   Conseil d'état, session 1868, *Exposé des motifs d'un projet de loi relatif à l'achèvement des chemins vicinaux . . .*, in AN C 1125.

297   Min. de l'Intérieur, *Rapport sur le service des chemins vicinaux pendant l'année 1879*, 1883, in AN AD XIX i 93.

298   1866 *Enquête*, vol. 1, *Rapport général*, p. 153.

299   See, for example, Corps législatif, *Proposition de loi tendant à modifier la loi de 1836 sur les chemins vicinaux. Exposé des motifs*, session 1870, in AN C 1142.

300   1866 *Enquête*, vol. 1, *Rapport général*, p. 158.

301   1866 *Enquête*, vol. 2, Mayenne, p. 123.

302   *Journal des chemins de fer*, 16 July 1870. Conseil d'Etat, session 1868, *Exposé des motifs d'un projet de loi relatif à l'achèvement des chemins vicinaux et à la création d'une caisse spéciale pour leur exécution*, in AN C 1125.

303   See especially Min. de l'Intérieur, *Instruction spéciale pour l'application de la loi du 12 Mars 1880*, 1888, p. 9, in AN AD XIX i 89.

304   Conseil général du Nord, *Rapport sur les chemins vicinaux par M. le Comte Martin*, Lille, 1862, p. 2.

305   PG, Nîmes, 18 January 1869, in AN BB³⁰389.

306   See Conseil général du Gard, *Rapport de la commission d'examen des projets de loi sur les réformes de la loi vicinale et du régime de prestations*, Nîmes, 1895, p. 4.

307   Min. de l'Intérieur, *Rapport à S.M. l'Empereur sur le service des chemins vicinaux pendant la période quinquennale de 1852 à 1856*, 1858 p. 8; 1866 *Enquête*, vol. 1, *Rapport général*, p. 15.

308   G. Garrier, *Paysans du Beaujolais et du Lyonnais*, Grenoble, 1973, p. 332.

309   In AN C 1157.

310   For a summary of the arguments for and against see Min. des TP, *Enquête sur la réforme de la prestation et des modifications à introduire dans le régime des routes et des chemins vicinaux*, 1889, pp. 12–13.

311   For example, *Observations relatives à la voirée rurale de la France*, par C. Guerrier, *propriétaire et cafetier* at Pont l'Evêque (Calvados), to Ministère de l'Intérieur, 16 January 1861, in AN F²I 1027.

312 J. Cambacère, 'De l'impôt pour les chemins vicinaux', *Annales des ponts-et-chaussées*, May 1848; see also Constituent Assembly, session 1–7 September 1848.

313 Min. of Finance to Interior, 8 August 1848, in AN C 915.

314 Quoted by Monsarrat, *Les chemins vicinaux*, p. 226.

315 M. Bourgnon de Layre, *Des voies de communication en France*, Poitiers, 1846 pp. 31–2.

316 *Agent-voyer directeur des Vosges* to Min. of Commerce, 2 August 1856, in AN F²I 1027.

317 *Enquête sur la réforme de la prestation*, p. 12.

318 Min. des TP, *Notes sur l'achèvement des chemins vicinaux, 31 July 1867*, in AN 45 AP 24; Monsarrat, *Les chemins vicinaux*, p. 2.

319 See, for example, report of the *agent-voyer directeur des Vosges*.

320 See, for example, 1866 *Enquête*, vol. 3, Morbihan, p. 40; ibid., vol. 26, Vosges, p. 43; ibid., vol. 2, Orne, pp. 51–2, Mayenne, p. 123, Maine-et-Loire, p. 269.

321 Conseil d'Etat, session 1868; Min. de l'Intérieur, *Rapport sur le service des chemins vicinaux pendant l'année 1879*.

322 Colonel Berthaut, *La carte de France, 1750–1898*, vol. 2, 1898, pp. 128–9.

323 Désert, *Une société rurale au 19ᵉ siècle*, vol. 1, pp. 381–2.

324 See, for example, 1866 *Enquête*, resumé of complaints re communications, in AN 45 AP 24.

325 See, for example, 1866 *Enquête*, vol. 6, Seine-et-Oise, p. 219.

326 Min. de l'Intérieur, *Rapport sur le service des chemins vicinaux pendant l'année 1881*, 1883, pp. 17–18

327 See, for example, PG, Grenoble, 5 July 1865, in AN BB³⁰378.

328 See, for example, 1848 *Enquête*, canton Morlaix (Finistère), in AN C 952.

329 Conseil général du Nord, *Rapport . . . par M. le Comte Martin*, p. 2.

330 1866 *Enquête*, vol. 5, Pas-de-Calais, pp. 127, 132.

331 See, for example, 1870 *Enquête*, canton Mabarleur (Tarn), in AN C 1157; 1866 *Enquête*, vol. 4, Seine-Inférieure, p. 89.

332 Conseil général du Nord, *Rapport . . . par M. le Comte Martin*.

333 M. Charté-Marsaines, 'Mémoire sur la comparaison des chaussées pavées et empierrées, et sur la force de traction du cheval', in *Annales des ponts-et-chaussées*, 3ᵉ série, vol. 13, 1857, p. 161.

334 1866 *Enquête*, vol. 27, Ain, p. 239.

335 P. Bozon, *La vie rurale en Vivarais*, 1963, p. 277; 1866 *Enquête*, vol. 5, Aisne, p. 55.

336 See, for example, PG, Paris, 8 February 1869, in AN BB³⁰389; Département de la Seine, *Rapport de l'agent-voyer en chef sur la situation des chemins vicinaux au 1 September 1872*, in AN AD XIX T134.

337 Garrier, *Paysans du Beaujolais et du Lyonnais*, pp. 331–2.

338 1870 Enquête, conseiller général for Dijon (Côte-d'Or), in AN C 1157.

339 Conseil d'Etat, session 1868, *Exposé des motifs d'un projet de loi relatif à l'achèvement des chemins vicinaux . . .* , in AN C 1125.

340 See, for example, 1870 *Enquête*, reply from D. S. Chopard, *propriétaire* resident at Vichy, in AN C 1161.

341 *Enquête sur la situation de l'agriculture en France en 1879*, vol. 2, pp. 57–9.

342 ATP, Côtes-du-Nord, p. 17.

343   See, for example, 1870 *Enquête*, conseiller général from Lannemezan (Hautes-Pyrénées), in AN C 1157.

344   For precise distinction between rural roads and private *chemins d'exploitation* and public rights of usage on latter see article 23 of 1881 law in Monsarrat, *Les chemins ruraux publics et privés*, n.d., pp. 282–7.

345   See, for example, 1866 *Enquête*, vol. 12, Meuse, p. 13; 1866 *Enquête*, vol. 2, Mayenne, pp. 127–8; 1848 *Enquête*, reply from Louis d'Andelarre, *cultivateur* and manufacturer at Tréveray (Meuse), in AN C 959.

346   1866 *Enquête*, vol. 1, Manche, p. 36; vol. 2, Orne, p. 56.

347   *Enquête sur la situation de l'agriculture*, p. 57; 1866 *Enquête*, vol. 6, Seine-et-Marne, p. 126.

348   Min. of Interior circular of 16 November 1839, printed in R. Falaize, *Des chemins et sentiers d'exploitation*, 1907, p. 14.

349   1866 *Enquête*, vol. 2, Orne, p. 56.

350   ibid., vol. 12, Moselle, p. 3; vol. 7, Deux-Sèvres, pp. 55–6; vol. 9 Allier, pp. 27–8.

351   Corps législatif, *Proposition de loi tendant à modifier la loi de 1836 sur les chemins vicinaux. Exposé des motifs*, session 1870, in AN C 1142.

352   See, for example, detailed reports in AN F^{10}2295; Monsarrat, *Les chemins ruraux*, pp. 113–15.

353   Désert, *Une société rurale au 19e siècle*, vol. 1, p. 392.

354   Toutain, *Les transports en France*, p. 56.

355   Examples from the 1870 *Enquête* into transport and agriculture and in particular cartons AN C 1156–7, C 1160–1.

356   1866 *Enquête*, vol. 5, Nord, p. 214.

357   Toutain, *Les transports en France*, p. 248.

358   Nord, Chef du service commercial, n.d. (1854) in AN 48 AQ 3710; Min. des TP, *Commission centrale des chemins de fer, séance 22 January 1850*, re agreement between Paris–Rouen Company and MM. Malcouronne and Delecluze, *commissionnaires de roulage* at Rouen, in AN F^{14}9436.

359   1871 *Enquête*, Réponse . . . de l'Est.

360   1870 *Enquête*, reply of a *conseiller d'arrondissement* at Metz, in AN C 1156.

361   ibid., *comice agricole* of Langres (Haute-Marne), in AN C 1160.

362   1863 *Enquête*, p. xlix, evidence of M. Denière, president of the Seine Tribunal de commerce.

363   See, for example, 1870 *Enquête*, reply from Tours Chamber of Commerce, in AN C 1161.

364   See, for example, 1870 *Enquête*, reply from commune of Borest (Oise), in AN C 1161.

365   Point also made Conseil d'Etat, *Enquête*, 1850, p. 14, evidence of M. Courpin, *chef de l'exploitation commerciale*, Chemin de fer de l'Ouest.

366   See, for example, 1870 *Enquête*, (transport), response from commune of Borest (Oise), in AN C 1161.

367   Min. des TP, *sous-commission des tarifs du chemin de fer de l'Ouest, séance 12 July 1850*; chef de la division des chemins de fer Ouest to Min. des TP, 17 August 1850, in AN F^{14}9437.

368   Toutain, *Les transports en France*, p. 248.

369   For a local example see MM. Pfluget et Cie, *commissionnaires de roulage* at Colmar, to Min. des TP, 10 May 1849, in AN F^{14}9388.

370 Renouard, *Les transports de marchandise*, pp. 72–3.

371 1866 *Enquête*, vol. 22, Hérault, p. 63.

372 See, for example, 1870 *Enquête*, (transport), reply from MM. Bride and Tetral, millers at Attichy (Oise), in AN C 1161.

373 1871 *Enquête*, Réponse de la Cie de l'Est, p. 29.

374 Min. des TP, *Routes nationales, recensement de la circulation en 1882*, 1883, p. 25.

375 See, for example, chef de l'exploitation, Nord, reports 1 March and 13 April 1847, in AN 48 AQ 3661.

376 M. Vallès, 'Des chemins de fer et des routes impériales au point de vue de l'importance de leurs transports respectifs', *Annales des ponts-et-chaussées* 3ᵉ série, vol. 16, 1858, pp. 79–80.

377 Conseil général . . . du Nord, session 1860, *Rapport sur les chemins de fer par M. Plichon*, p. 14.

378 1866 *Enquête*, vol. 2, Mayenne, p. 131.

379 AN C 1156.

380 Statistics were collected by the *bureaux de navigation* on the various waterways, which also collected tolls. A considerable number of users were believed to avoid payment, and the statistics were regarded by officials as grossly inaccurate. See, for example, Min. des TP, Chemin de fer d'Orléans à Bordeaux, report of Commissariat Royal, 19 February 1848, in AN F¹⁴9452.

381 See, for example, report of Commission on Waterways, established by decree of 16 June 1873, in Freycinet, *Souvenirs*, p. 12.

382 Lévy-Leboyer, 'Capital investment and economic growth in France', p. 25.

383 Toutain, *Les transports en France*, p. 79.

384 Léon, *Histoire économique et sociale*, p. 299.

385 See especially Girard, *La politique des travaux publics*, pp. 302–4; Léon, Histoire économique et sociale, p. 271; Renouard, *Les transports de marchandise*, pp. 12, 58; Vigarié, *Les grands ports*, p. 299.

386 1866 *Enquête*, vol. 6, Seine-et-Marne, p. 127; ibid., Seine, p. 131; Vigarié, *Les grands ports* p. 300; Léon, *Histoire économique et sociale*, p. 249; J. Bethmont, *Le thème de l'eau dans la vallée du Rhône. Essai sur la genèse d'un espace hydraulique*, St Etienne, 1972, pp. 131–48.

387 Min. des TP, *Notice sur les travaux compris dans un projet de loi déposé le 1ᵉʳ Mai 1901 et tendant à compléter l'outillage national par l'exécution d'un certain nombre de voies navigables nouvelles, l'améliorations des canaux, des rivières et des portes maritimes . . .* , p. 14.

388 ibid., p. 13.

389 ibid., pp. 29, 31; Min du Commerce, *Enquête sur les voies de communication 1900*, pp. 89–90 (expenditure on the Loire was estimated at 91,700,000 francs during the nineteenth century).

390 ibid., pp. 14, 18

391 1866 *Enquête*, vol. 14, Saône-et-Loire, p. 22.

392 1870 *Enquête*, (transport), evidence of E. and I. Koechlin representing Mulhouse Chamber of Commerce, in AN C 1161.

393 PG, Pau, 15 October 1859, in AN BB³⁰384.

394 See, for example, 1870 *Enquête*, (transport), reply from La Rochelle Chamber of Commerce, in AN C 1161; Conseil général Tarn to Min. des TP, 11 October

1905, in AN F¹⁴12153.

395   Min. du Commerce, *Enquête*, 1900, p. 103, evidence of Lyon Chamber of Commerce; ibid., p. 106, of Société pour la défense du commerce de Marseille.

396   'Observations sur les conditions dans lesquelles on doit mettre les canaux de navigation pour qu'ils puissent augmenter la fortune publique', in *Annales des ponts-et-chaussées*, 2ᵉ série, vol. 14, pp. 166–7.

397   1870 *Enquête*, (transport), reply of Tours Chamber of Commerce, in AN C 1161; Min. des TP, *Comité consultative . . . Procès verbal de la séance du . . . 31 mai 1894*, in AN F¹⁴11295.

398   1871 *Enquête*, evidence from Paris Chamber of Commerce, 10 December 1874, in AN C 3006.

399   1870 *Enquête*, (transport), reply of the *voituriers par eau* of Vertrieu (Isère), in AN C 1161.

400   1871 *Enquête*, PLM notes for parliamentary commission on difficulties faced at end of 1872 due to floods on Rhône and Saône, in AN C 3005.

401   Jacqmin, *De l'exploitation des chemins de fer*, vol. 1, p. 415.

402   1871 *Enquête*, *Commission, séance 29 December 1871*, evidence on delays due to low water on the canal at Commentry in AN C 3005.

403   Min. des TP, *Notice sur les travaux . . . 1901*, pp. 13–14; J. B. Jobard, *Les disparités régionales de croissance. Analyse économique des départements situés dans le centre-est de la France, 1801–1962*, 1971, p. 152.

404   Min. des TP, *Statistiques de la navigation intérieure. Recensement de la batellerie. Année 1888*, p. 488–9; ibid., *Année 1891*, pp. 8–9, 12, 13, 23, 59, 81.

405   See, for example, Conseil municipal de Paimboeuf, *Observations sur l'établissement d'un chemin de fer entre Napoléon-Vendée et St-Nazaire*, 1858, p. 12.

406   M. Vignon, 'Etude statistique sur la navigation de la rivière d'Yonne', in *Annales des ponts-et-chaussées*, 3ᵉ série, vol. 1, 1851, p. 364.

407   1870 *Enquête*, response of the *voituriers par eau* at Vertrieu (Isère), in AN C 1161.

408   Min. des TP, *Comité consultatif . . . séance 7 March 1895*, in AN F¹⁴11205.

409   C. Beuchot, *Navigation intérieure*, 1875.

410   Girard, *La politique des travaux publics*, pp. 215, 304.

411   1850 *Enquête*, Conseil d'Etat, p. 155, evidence of M. Dehaynin, *entrepreneur de transports par eau*: 1870 *Enquête*, (transport), reply from the commune of Montjean (Maine-et-Loire) (the signatories include a large number of barge owners), in AN C 1161; Caron, *Histoire de l'exploitation*, p. 67.

412   Girard, *La politique des travaux publics*, p. 217; Caron, *Histoire de l'exploitation*, pp. 127, 261; Renouard, *Les transports de marchandises*, p. 61.

413   *Journal des chemins de fer*, 21 October 1854; Ouest, *Rapport*, 1895.

414   Girard, *La politique des travaux publics*, p. 301.

415   Quoted in ibid., p. 155.

416   See, for example, Paris Prefect of Police to Min. des TP, 22 March 1844, in AN F¹⁴9451; Cie du Nord, Agence commerciale 2ᵉ section Valenciennes, 24 February 1847, in AN 48 AQ 3660; Nord, Agence commerciale Amiens to Administration, 17 June 1850, 2 May 1853, in AN 48 AQ 3702.

417   *Commission relative à l'enquête sur les chemins de fer 1871, séance 14 February 1872*, in AN C 3005; Girard, *La politique des travaux publics*, p. 18.

418 Min. des TP, Inspecteur-général, Directeur du contrôle de chemin de fer, 28 June 1888, in AN F¹⁴11305.

419 See, for example, *Préfet*, Seine-Inférieure to *sous-secrétaire d'Etat*, Min. des TP, 16 February 1844, 15 October 1845, in AN F¹⁴9435.

420 See, for example, Rouen Chamber of Commerce to *Préfet*, Seine-Inférieure, 18 November 1845, in AN F¹⁴9435; Amiens Chamber of Commerce to Min. des TP, 27 February 1850, in AN F¹⁴9382.

421 Min. des TP, *Comité consultatif des chemins de fer, Compagnie de l'Ouest*, 15 May 1894, in AN F¹⁴11295.

422 ibid., sessions of 15 May 1894, 31 July 1895; Min. des TP, *Rapport de l'ingénieur en chef du service du Rhône*, 27 February, 16 March 1895, in AN F¹⁴11295.

423 Min. des TP, *Comité consultative. . . 7 March 1895*, in AN F¹⁴11205.

424 Min. des TP, *Comité consultative . . . Ouest. 30 May 1894*, in AN F¹⁴11295.

425 See, for example, 1870 *Enquête*, comice agricole, canton St-Servan (Ille-et-Vilaine), in AN C 1161.

426 See, for example, Petition from the Toulon Chamber of Commerce of 16 March 1851, in AN C 987; F. Larget, *Les chemins de fer et la navigation*, Rouen, 1860; letters to the Min. des TP, from the Chambre syndicate professionnelle des mariniers, 15 September 1898, and Ministère de la Marine, 5 May 1898, criticizing rail tariff policies, in AN F¹⁴12153.

427 Vigarié, *Les grands ports*, p. 223.

428 F. N. Affleck, 'The beginnings of modern transport in France: the Seine Valley, 1820 to 1860', PhD thesis, London University, 1972, p. 270.

429 See, for example, J.-C. Renoul, *Rapport sur le mouvement maritime et commercial du port de Nantes*, Nantes, 1861; Chambre de Commerce de Marseille, *Rapport sur le mouvement du cabotage en France pendant l'année 1868*, Marseille, 1869.

430 Toutain, *Les transports en France*, p. 248.

431 *Direction générale des Douanes. Tableau général des mouvements du cabotage pendant l'année 1893*, 1894, p. xxi.

432 Min. des TP, Division de la navigation, *Relevé général du tonnage des marchandises transportées sur les fleuves, rivières et canaux pendant l'année 1881*, 1883, p. 10.

433 Min. des TP, *Statistique de la navigation intérieure. . . année 1887*, 1888, p. 50.

434 *Direction générale des contributions indirectes. Navigation intérieure . . . Relevé général du tonnage des marchandises . . . pendant l'année 1878*, 1879.

435 ibid., p. 11.

436 Min. des TP, *Statistique de la navigation intérieure. Recensement de la batellerie année 1891*.

437 Conseil d'état, 1850 *Enquête*, pp. 98–9, evidence of M. Thibeaudeau of Paris–Rouen Railway Company.

438 M. Chanoine, 'Mémoire sur le tonnage de la Haute-Seine', in *Annales des ponts-et-chaussées*, 3ᵉ série, vol. 8, 1854, p. 358.

439 Zolla, *Le blé et les céréales*, pp. 237–8.

440 Ouest. Rapports 1894–95.

441 Chanoine, *Mémoire*, p. 346.

442 Min. des TP, *Statistique de la navigation intérieure année 1887*, p. 65.

443 PG, Lyon, 4 January 1859, in AN BB³⁰379.

444 D. Faucher, *L'homme et le Rhône*, 1968, p. 230.

445 Y. Babonaux, 'L'évolution contemporaine d'une ville de la Loire: Blois', *Information historique*, 1956, p. 47.

446 See, for example, Orléans Chambre de Commerce to Min. de l'Agriculture et des TP, 11 October 1850, in AN F¹⁴9555.

447 R. Caralp-Landon, *Les chemins de fer dans le Massif Central*, 1959, p. 142.

448 Renouard, *Les transports de marchandises*, p. 60; J. J. Hannaway, 'The canal of Burgundy, 1720–1853', PhD thesis, Johns Hopkins University, 1971, pp. 197–8, 206.

449 Min. des TP. *Rapport de l'inspecteur général chargé de la direction du contrôle des chemins de fer de l'Ouest, 27 July 1889* in AN F¹⁴11295

450 1871 *Enquête, Commission, séance 20 December 1873*, in AN C 3005.

451 See, for example, 1870 *Enquête*, reply from a *conseiller général* at Dijon (Côte-d'Or), in AN C 1159.

452 Min. des TP, *Rapport de l'inspecteur particulier de l'exploitation commerciale. Réseau de l'Ouest, 12 May 1890*, in AN F¹⁴11295; M. Tearse, 'Problems of economic development in the area of Redon in Brittany, 1850–1900', PhD thesis, University of East Anglia, 1981, ch. 5, *passim.*

453 See, for example, Min. des TP, *Avis des ingénieurs du port de St-Nazaire, 15 May 1894*, in AN F¹⁴11295.

454 A. Moyen, 'Transport 1730–1900', in R. A. Dodgshon, and R. A. Butlin (eds.), *An Historical Geography of England and Wales*, 1978, p. 401.

455 Min. des TP, *Proposition de loi concernant les tarifs de chemins de fer. Rapport de M. Richard Waddington. Discussion au comité consultatif des chemins de fer*, 1891, p. 4.

456 L. Marchal, 'De l'utilité des chemins de fer français pour les transports agricoles', *Journal d'agriculture pratique*, 1855, p. 287.

457 7ᵉ série, vol. 12, 1896, p. 6.

458 See, for example, M. Minard, 'Notions élémentaires d'économie politique appliquée aux travaux publics', *Annales des ponts-et-chaussées*, 2ᵉ série, vol. 19, 1850, p. 12.

459 G. Gunderson, *A New Economic History of America*, New York, 1976, p. 325.

Chapter 8 Modernizing market structures

1 E. Labrousse, *Esquisse du mouvement des prix et des revenus en France au 18ᵉ siècle*, 2 vols., 1937; *La crise de l'économie française à la fin de l'Ancien Régime et au début de la Révolution*, 1944.

2 See especially E. Labrousse (ed.), *Aspects de la crise et de la dépression de l'économie française au milieu du 19ᵉ siècle, 1846–51*, 1956.

3 One exception is R. Laurent, 'Les variations départementales du prix du froment en France (1801–70)', in *Histoire, économies, sociétés*, Lyon, 1978.

4 1866 *Enquête*, vol. 6, Seine-et-Oise, p. 226.

5 See, for example, Orléans Chamber of Commerce to Min. de l'Agriculture et du Commerce, 11 October 1850, in AN F¹⁴9555; 1866 *Enquête*, vol. 6, Seine-et-Marne, p. 122; 1870 *Enquête*, reply from an *agriculteur* near Montdidier

(Somme), in AN C 1156; *Société des agriculteurs de France devant la commission parlementaire du tarif général des douanes*, 1879, p. 88.

6   G. Garrier, *Paysans du Beaujolais et du Lyonnais*, vol. 1, Grenoble, 1973, p. 430.

7   See, for example, P–O *Rapport*, 1895, in *Journal des chemins de fer*, 1895, p. 332.

8   Min. des TP, *Comité consultatif. . . 25 March 1896*, in AN F^{14}11205.

9   Min. de l'Agriculture, Office de renseignements agricoles, *Notes sur le commerce des produits agricoles*, vol 1, 1906, p. 89.

10   ibid., p. 108, Côtes-du-Nord; p. 202, Loiret.

11   See, for example, 1870 *Enquête*, reply from canton Penne (Lot-et-Garonne), in AN C 1157; ATP, Gers, p. 10.

12   See, for example, 1866 *Enquête*, vol. 19, Tarn, p. 44.

13   Session of 16 December 1896, in AN F^{14}11283.

14   F. Caron, *Histoire de l'exploitation d'un grand réseau*, 1973, p. 407.

15   1866 *Enquête*, vol. 10, Indre, p. 10.

16   1870 *Enquête*, reply from Beaulieu (Corrèze), in AN C 1157; Caralp-Landon, p. 144.

17   See, for example, Orléans Chamber of Commerce to Min. de l'Agriculture et des TP, 11 October 1850, complaining about this process, in AN F^{14}9555.

18   G. Désert, *Une société rurale au 19e siècle: les paysans du Calvados*, vol. 1, Lille, 1975, p. 397.

19   Min de l'Agriculture, *Notes sur le commerce*, vol. 1, p. 119, Jura; p. 158, Ille-et-Vilaine; p. 163, Indre-et-Loire; p. 174, Landes; p. 183, Loire; p. 202, Loiret; p. 209, Lot-et-Garonne; p. 225, Maine-et-Loire; p. 256, Nord; p. 309, Haute-Savoie; p. 338. Somme.

20   1866 *Enquête*, vol. 5, Pas-de-Calais, p. 126; R. Clozier, *La gare du Nord*, 1940, p. 115.

21   Min de l'Agriculture et des TP, internal memorandum, 22 October 1850, in response to Orléans Chamber of Commerce to Min. de l'Agriculture et des TP, 11 October 1850, in AN F^{14}9555.

22   PG, Dijon, 8 April 1859, in AN BB^{30}377; Conseil d'Etat 1859, evidence of Marquis d'Andelarre, pp. 5–6; Min. de l'Agriculture, *Notes sur le commerce des produits agricoles*, vol. 1, p. 99, Côte-d'Or.

23   See, for example, petitions from the mayor and council of Souillac (Lot), in AN C 1125; A. Chatelain, *Les migrants temporaires en France de 1800 à 1914*, Lille, 1977, vol. 1 p. 665.

24   P. Claval, *Régions, nations, grands espaces*, 1968, p. 346; G. Cholvy, *Religion et société au 19e siècle. Le diocèse de Montpellier*, vol. 2, Lille, 1973, p. 1517.

25   In AN 48 AQ 3915, also quoted by Caron, *Histoire de l'exploitation*, pp. 155–6.

26   PG, Rouen, 2 October 1855, in AN BB^{30}387.

27   Conseil d'Etat, 1859, vol. 2, p. 526.

28   PG, Paris, 26 September 1854, in AN BB^{30}432.

29   R. Bloch, 'Le commerce des bestiaux et de la viande et les transports par chemin de fer', *Revue politique et parlementaire*, 1908, *passim*.

30   J. Gaillard, *Paris, la ville (1852–70)*, vol. 2, Doctorat d'état. Université de Paris, 1974, pp. 509–12.

31 1870 *Enquête*, Lille Chamber of Commerce, in AN C 1157; Clozier, *La gare du Nord*, p. 112.

32 Conseil d'Etat, 1859, vol. 1, p. 417, evidence of M. Vachon, *négociant meunier*, member of Société d'agriculture, des arts et de l'industrie de Lyon.

33 Conseil municipal de Toulouse, *Chemin de fer de jonction entre Toulouse et le Grand-Central*, 1860.

34 Min. des TP, *Exploitation commerciale, Réseau du Midi. Rapport de l'inspecteur particulier de la 2ᵉ circonscription, 20 October 1897*, in AN F¹⁴11272; see also G. Jorré, 'Le commerce des grains et la minoterie à Toulouse', *Revue géographique des Pyrénées et du Sud-Ouest*, 1933, p. 55.

35 Quoted by Gaillard, *Paris, la ville*, vol. 3, p. 509.

36 Min. des TP, *Avis de l'inspecteur général Ouest*, 22 November and 21 December 1888, in AN F¹⁴11295.

37 See, for example, Société impériale et centrale d'agriculture, session 23 March 1859, in AN F¹¹2752.

38 D. Zolla, *Le blé et les céréales*, 1909, pp. 186–7.

39 Legislation reviewed in Min. de l'Agriculture, Bureau des subsistances internal memorandum, 27 July 1853, in AN F¹¹2752, and H. F. Rivière, *Précis historique et critique de la législation française sur le commerce des céréales . . . ,* 1859, pp. 157–160.

40 Conseil d'Etat, 1859, vol. 3, p. 5.

41 See, for example, PG, Agen, 7 January 1861, in AN BB³⁰370.

42 A. Léfèvre, *Sous le Second Empire: chemins de fer et politique*, 1951, p. 183.

43 Conseil d'Etat, 1859, vol. 1, p. 129, evidence of M. Pommier, editor of the *Echo agricole*; p. 417, evidence of M. Vachon, *négociant-meunier* at Lyon; 1859 *Enquête*, pp. 2–4, evidence of M. Doussaient-Péan, grain merchant at St-Mesmin (Loiret).

44 See, for example, Conseil d'Etat, 1859, vol 1 p. 481, evidence of M. Ligières, retired miller and former mayor of Toulouse; PG, Besançon, 9 April 1859, in AN BB³⁰373.

45 See, for example, *Annales de l'agriculture pratique*, Chronique agricole, 15 November 1861.

46 F. Jacqmin, 'Notes sur l'agriculture et les chemins de fer', *Annales des ponts-et-chaussées*, 4ᵉ série, vol. 10, 1865, p. 326.

47 1866 *Enquête*, vol. 1, pp. 186–7.

48 See, for example, PG, Amiens, 11 October 1867, in AN BB³⁰371.

49 *Journal des chemins de fer*, 6 October 1888.

50 PG, Metz, 8 January 1862, in AN BB³⁰380.

51 Min. de Commerce, *Annales du commerce extérieur . . . Situation comparative pour la période 1883–97*, p. 84.

52 J. Milhau, 'Etude du revenu de l'agriculture et des agriculteurs', *Revue de l'économie méridionale*, 1960, p. 212.

53 Min. de l'Agriculture, 'Question des subsistances. Note sur la situation et sur les mesures qui pourraient être prises', undated internal memorandum (1854), in AN F¹¹2752.

54 E. Levasseur, *Histoire du commerce de la France*, vol. 2, 1912, pp. 731–2.

55 A. Broder, 'Le commerce extérieur: l'échec de la conquête d'une position internationale', in P. Léon *et al.*, *Histoire économique et sociale de la France*, tome 3, vol. 2, 1976, p. 34.

56 Min. de l'Agriculture, *Statistique agricole de la France . . . 1882*, p. 58; ibid., 1892, p. 93; see also Min. de l'Agriculture, Bureau des subsistances, *Récoltes des céréales et des pommes de terre de 1815 à 1876*, 1878, pp. xxii–iv.

57 See, for example, 1866 *Enquête*, vol. 5, Pas-de-Calais, p. 134.

58 See, for example, 1866 *Enquête*, vol. 6, Seine-et-Marne p. 132; PG, Metz, 10 April 1866, in AN BB³⁰380; 1882 *Enquête, Comice agricole central*, Loire-Inférieure, in AN C 3358.

59 Chef de la division des chemins de fer to Min. des TP, 6 December 1848, in AN F¹⁴9451.

60 Secrétaire-général, Commissariat central des chemins de fer to Min. des TP, 30 March 1848, in AN F¹⁴9451.

61 F. Jacqmin, *De l'exploitation des chemins de fer*, vol. 2, 1868, p. 155.

62 Désert, *Une société rurale*. vol. 1, p. 292.

63 See, for example, 1870 *Enquête, comice agricole*, Issoudun (Indre), in AN C 1160; Chambre d'agricole, *arrondissement* Lapalisse (Allier), in AN C 1158.

64 See, for example, 1870 *Enquête*, Ville de Sarvallée (Moselle); ibid., Société d'agriculture et d'industrie, Lot, in AN C 1160; ibid., Société d'agriculture, Gard, in AN C 1157.

65 See, for example, Min. de l'Agriculture to Min. des TP, 17 May 1856, in AN F¹⁴9451, re request by poultry and egg merchants for reduced tariffs on P–O to Paris.

66 See, for example, Société agricole, Cannes et *arrondissement* Grasse (Alpes-Maritimes); *comice agricole*, canton Mortagne (Orne), in AN C 1156.

67 See, for example, *Préfet*, Loir-et-Cher, to Min. des TP, 21 May 1851, in AN F¹⁴9454; *Préfet*, Seine-et-Oise, 30 October 1884, in AN C 3371¹; PLM *Rapport*, 1884, p. 21, on movements from Midi to Paris.

68 See, for example, 1870 *Enquête*, Saône-et-Loire Chamber of Commerce, in AN C 1160.

69 D. Renouard, *Les transports de marchandises par fer, route et eau depuis 1850*, 1960, p. 44.

70 R. Dubuc, 'L'approvisionnement de Paris en lait', *Annales de géographie*, 1938, pp. 258–60.

71 See, for example, PG, Besançon, 30 January 1860, in AN BB³⁰373; G. P. Azémar, and M. de la Pradelle, 'Le marché-gare de Carpentras. Entre tradition et modernité', *Etudes rurales*, 1980, p. 297.

72 See, for example, 1871 *Enquête, Réponse . . . de l'Est*, pp. 39–40.

73 P. Goujon, 'Le temps des révolutions inachevées', in J.–P. Houssel (ed.), *Histoire des paysans français du 18ᵉ siècle à nos jours*, Roanne, 1976, p. 279.

74 Gaillard, *Paris la ville*, vol. 2, pp. 234–41. See also J. L'Homme, 'Le pouvoir d'achat de l'ouvrier français . . .', *Le mouvement social*, 1968, pp. 45f.

75 See, for example, 1870 *Enquête*, Chambre de Commerce La Rochelle (Charente-Inférieure), in AN C 1160.

76 See, for example, 1870 *Enquête, comice agricole* des cantons est et ouest de Dinan (Côtes-du-Nord) in AN C 1157; ibid., Société d'agriculture de Vire (Calvados), in AN C 1157.

77   Reply of L. Porteu, *négociant* at Rennes (Ille-et-Vilaine), in AN C 1159.
78   See reports in AN C 3370⁴.
79   See, for example, in ibid., Société des sciences, agriculture et arts du département du Bas-Rhin, re German tariff; Société centrale d'agriculture de l'Yonne, re English tariff, in AN C 1160.
80   Min. du Commerce, Conseil supérieur du commerce et de l'industrie, *1. Admission temporaire des céréales. 2. Entrepôts de céréales. 3. Projet de loi du Cadenas*, 1896, p. 46; Min. des TP, *Rapport de l'inspecteur principal, 21 October 1893*, in AN F¹⁴11305.
81   Chambre de commerce de Rouen, *Observations sur les tarifs généraux, spéciaux et communs des compagnies des chemins de fer*, 1863, p. 26.
82   Min. des TP, *Comité consultatif . . . séance 7 March 1895*, in AN F¹⁴11205.
83   Chemin de fer du Nord-Exploitation, 20 October 1897, in AN F¹⁴11277.
84   Min. des TP, *Rapport du contrôleur général, 12 October 1896*, in AN F¹⁴11283.
85   Min. des TP, *Midi. Avis de l'inspecteur général, 20 December 1892*, in AN F¹⁴11272.
86   Min. des TP, *Comité consultatif . . . PLM et Midi, 25 March 1896*, in AN F¹⁴11205.
87   Editorial, 'La protection à l'intérieur par les tarifs des chemins de fer', *Journal des chemins de fer*, 19 December 1861.
88   Min. des TP, *Comité consultatif . . . séance 7 July 1909*, in AN F¹⁴11283; Caron, *Histoire de l'exploitation*, p. 193, re Dietz–Morin Commission.
89   Min. des TP, *Comité consultatif . . . séance 30 May 1894*, in AN F¹⁴11295.
90   Report of the Commission des valeurs of Ministère du Commerce, de l'Agriculture et des TP, printed in *Journal des chemins de fer*, 19 September 1868.
91   See, for example, 1866 *Enquête*, vol. 2, Mayenne, p. 129; ibid., vol. 6, Seine-et-Marne, p. 228.
92   See, for example, *Journal d'agriculture pratique*, Revue commerciale, 1ʳᵉ quinzaine, January 1853; ibid., 1ʳᵉ quinzaine August 1861.
93   Désert, *Une société rurale*, vol. 1, p. 422.
94   Min. des TP, *Rapport de l'inspecteur général chargé de la Direction du contrôle des chemins de fer de l'Ouest, 27 July 1889*, in AN F¹⁴11295.
95   See, for example, PG, Rouen, 12 October 1861, in AN BB³⁰387; 1866 *Enquête*, vol. 6, Seine-et-Marne, p. 131; Min. des TP, *Rapport de l'inspecteur général chargé de la Direction du contrôle des chemins de fer de l'Ouest, 27 July 1889*, in AN F¹⁴11295.
96   M. Wolkowitsch, *L'économie régionale des transports dans le centre et le centre-ouest de la France*, n.d., p. 228.
97   1866 *Enquête*, vol. 22, Bouches-du-Rhône, p. 125, evidence of Marseille grain merchants.
98   ibid., vol. 19, Tarn p. 44.
99   See, for example, 1866 *Enquête*, vol. 22, Bouches-du-Rhône, p. 818, evidence of M. Gros, miller at Marseille.
100   See, for example, 1870 *Enquête*, evidence of Delarue *père et fils*, merchants and millers at Fougères (Ille-et-Vilaine), in AN C 1156.
101   G. Martin, 'L'évolution de l'agriculture en Auxois de 1840 à 1939', *Cahiers de l'association interuniversitaires de l'Est*, 1966, pp. 119–20.

102 See, for example, 1870, Chambre de commerce La Rochelle (Charente-Inférieure), in AN C 1160.

103 For example, 1866 *Enquête*, vol. 16, Lot-et-Garonne, pp. 35–6.

104 See, for example, PG, Nancy, 9 April 1859, in AN BB³⁰381;1866 *Enquête*, vol. 26, Haute-Saône, p. 60; 1870 *Enquête*, reply of F. Ferron, former mayor and vice-president of *comice agricole*, Gray (Haute-Saône), in AN C 1160.

105 1866 *Enquête*, vol. 27, Rhône, p. 180, evidence of Commission départementale d'enquête and of Chambre consultative d'agriculture de Lyon.

106 1866 *Enquête*, vol. 26, Vosges, p. 68; ibid., Haute-Saône, p. 30; ibid., vol. 14, Saône-et-Loire, p. 26; Conseil d'Etat 1859, vol. 1, p. 471, evidence of M. Bodin, *propriétaire-agriculteur*, president of *comice agricole, arrondissement de Trévoux (Ain)*.

107 1866 *Enquête*, vol. 25, Isère, p. 48; 1870 *Enquête*, mayor of Pont-Evêque (Isère), in AN C 1158.

108 1866 *Enquête*, vol. 22, Bouches-du-Rhône, p. 125; ibid., p. 814, evidence of M. Paul Rodocanachi, *négociant* at Marseille.

109 Comment made in Min. des TP, *Rapport de l'inspecteur-général chargé de la Direction du contrôle des chemins de fer de l'Ouest, 30 May 1890*, in AN F¹⁴11295.

110 Min. des TP, *Rapport de l'inspecteur particulier de l'exploitation commerciale, Ouest, 12 May 1890*, in AN F¹⁴11295.

111 *Avis de l'inspecteur-général Ouest*, 26 August 1889; *Comité consultatif . . . séance 25 February 1883*, in AN F¹⁴11295.

112 Min. des TP, *Avis de l'inspecteur-général, 20 December 1892*, in AN F¹⁴11295.

113 1866 *Enquête*, vol. 24, Basses-Alpes, pp. 22–3; vol. 21, Aude, pp. 27–8, 31; vol. 18, Gers, Tarn-et-Garonne, Haute-Garonne, p. 19; 1870 *Enquête*, Chambre consultative d'agriculture, Marmande (Lot-et-Garonne), in AN C 1160; ibid., from the *conseiller-général* for Marbarleur (Tarn); ibid., Sociéte d'encouragement pour l'agriculture et l'industrie de l'arrondissement de Bagnères de Bigorre (Hautes-Pyrénées), in AN C 1157; Chambre de commerce de Toulouse, *Rapport de la Commission chargée de l'examen des questions qui se rattachent au commerce des céréales*, Toulouse, n.d., p. 7.

114 1866 *Enquête*, vol. 21, Aude, pp. 28–9; Min. des TP, *Midi. Rapport de l'inspecteur principal de l'exploitation commerciale, 13 November 1897*, in AN F¹⁴11272.

115 1866 *Enquête*, vol. 13, Bas and Haut-Rhin, p. 134.

116 1870 *Enquête*, mayor of Athis (Marne), in AN C 1158.

117 See, for example, ibid., reply from canton Gueugnon (Saône-et-Loire), in AN C 1159.

118 PG, Dijon, 8 April 1859, in AN BB³⁰377.

119 Jacqmin, *De l'exploitation*, vol. 2, pp. 134–6.

120 Renouard, *Les transports de marchandise*, pp. 42–4.

121 Jacqmin, 'Notes sur l'agriculture et les chemins de fer', p. 330.

122 C. Lavollée, 'Les chemins de fer français en 1866' *Revue des Deux-Mondes*, 1866, p. 26.

123 PG, Poitiers, September 1853, in AN BB³⁰432, and especially a detailed report by PG, Caen, 26 November 1856, in AN BB³⁰433.

124   See, for example, 1870 *Enquête*, reply of G. de Puynode, secretary of Chambre consultative d'agriculture, *arrondissement* Blanc (Indre), and editor of *Journal des Economistes*.

125   25 January 1857, in AN BB^{30}370.

126   See, for example, PG, Paris, 4 March 1854, in AN BB^{30}432.

127   J. Pautard, *Les disparités régionales dans la croissance de l'agriculture française*, 1965, p. 151.

128   Wolkowitsch, *L'économie régionale*, p. 261.

129   See, for example, PG, Nancy, 10 October 1861, in AN BB^{30}381.

130   1866 *Enquête*, vol. 9, Allier, pp. 27–30.

131   Jacqmin, *De l'exploitation*, vol. 2, p. 352.

132   Min. des TP, *Comité consultatif. . . séance 18 July 1892*, in AN F^{14}11283.

133   See, for example, Conseil d'Etat, 1859, p. 118, president of the Commission commenting on the levelling of prices between the major markets of Gray and Marseille.

134   1866 *Enquête*, vol. 5, Aisne, p. 58.

135   Same stress in *sous-préfet*, Provins, report on September–October 1854, in AN F^1 CIII, Seine-et-Marne 7.

136   See especially *Chronique agricole*, 2e quinzaine, January 1856.

137   See especially R. Laurent, *Les vignerons de la Côte-d'Or au 19e siècle*, 1958, pp. 243–4.

138   See, for example, *Préfet*, Gers, 14 November 1884, in AN C 3350.

139   See, for example, D. Aubry, president of Syndicat agricole, *arrondissement* de Muret (Haute-Garonne), *Les tarifs de transport des vins*, Toulouse, 1907, in AN C 7392.

140   See, for example, 1882 *Enquête*, reply from a *salarié* at Eveux (Rhône), in AN C 3369^3.

141   See, for example, Chambre de Commerce de Gers, 25 April 1907, in AN C 7392.

142   Préfecture du département de la Seine, *Rapport de M. Morillon, chef de bureau, sur les consommations de Paris et sur la gestion des halles, marchés et abattoirs, 1883*, in AN C 3373^2.

143   Min. des TP, *Rapport du contrôleur-général, 19 October 1896*, in AN F^{14}11283.

144   Midi *Rapport*, 1894, p. 299; P–O *Rapport*, in *Journal des chemins de fer*, 1894, p. 309.

145   See, for example, 1870 *Enquête*, reply of Mayor of Prissac (Indre), in AN C 1156.

146   Conseil municipal de Lyon, *Rapport sur le projet d'un chemin de fer de Lyon à Genève par la vallée du Rhône*, Lyon, 1845, p. 5.

147   Désert, *Une société rurale*.

148   J.–P. Moreau, *La vie rurale dans le sud-est du bassin parisien, entre les vallées de l'Armançon et de la Loire*, 1958, p. 317.

149   Cholvy, *Religion et société*, vol 1, pp. 740–1; Jorré, 'Le commerce des grains', p. 54.

150   Gaillard, *Paris, la ville*, vol. 2, p. 243.

151   1870 *Enquête*, evidence from canton of Beaulieu (Puy-de-Dôme), in AN C 1161; from Beaulieu (Corrèze), in AN C 1157; from Vassely (Cher); from *comice agricole*, Thionville (Moselle), in AN C 1160; Société départementale d'agriculture, Haut-Rhin, in AN C 1161.

152   AN C 1156.

153   See, for example, D. Aubry, président, Syndicat agricole de l'arrondissement de Muret (Haute-Garonne), *Les tarifs du transport des vins*, Toulouse, 1907, *passim*.

154   See, for example, 1870 *Enquête, comice agricole*, Luneville (Meurthe), AN C 1160; ibid., mayor of Boigny (Loiret), in AN C 1157.

155   *Procès-verbal des délibérations du conseil général de l'Aveyron, 8 April 1907*, in AN C 7392.

156   O. Voillard, *Recherches sur une bourgeoisie urbaine: Nancy au 19ᵉ siècle*, Doctorat d'état, Université de Strasbourg, 1976, p. 72.

157   AN C 1157.

158   Société d'agriculture du Gard, in AN C 1157.

159   See, for example, PLM *Rapport*, 1860, p. 32.

160   See, for example, complaints of Chambre de commerce de Tarbes et des Hautes-Pyrénées, *séance* 14 April 1907, in AN C 7392.

161   Désert, *Une société rurale*.

162   *Préfet's* report to Manche *conseil-général*, 1849, AN C 987.

163   1870 *Enquête*, reply from the *justice de la paix*, canton Royère (Creuse), in AN C 1159.

164   See, for example, 1866 *Enquête*, vol. 20, Lozère, pp. 12–13.

165   1866 *Enquête*, vol. 19, Tarn, p. 44.

166   See, for example, Conseil général du département du Bas-Rhin, *Session extraordinaire du 21 Mars 1859, Extrait du procès-verbal des délibérations*, 1859, pp. 3–4.

167   AN C 1157.

168   Société nationale d'agriculture de France, *Enquête . . . 1879*, vol. 2 pp. 57–9.

169   Min. des TP, *Commission chargée d'étudier des réformes à réaliser dans l'organisation du contrôle des chemins de fer. Rapport général*, 1912, p. 3.

170   Quoted by *Préfet*, Manche, in report to Conseil général, 1849, in AN C 987.

171   See, for example, 1866 *Enquête*, vol. 24, Basses-Alpes, p. 19.

172   Nord, Services commerciaux, memo, 'Le port du Dunkerque et le chemin de fer du Nord', n.d. (1847), in AN 48 AQ 3661.

173   A. Corbin, *Archaïsme et modernité en Limousin au 19ᵉ siècle*, vol. 1, 1975, p. 143.

174   M. Philipponneau, *La vie rurale de la banlieue parisienne*, 1956, p. 75.

175   Conseil d'Etat, 1859, vol. 1 p. 157, evidence of M. Babille, *propriétaire* in Loiret; 1870 *Enquête, comice agricole*, Cambrai (Nord), in AN C 1156.

176   See Conseil d'Etat, *Enquête sur le régime de courtage*, 1869, p. 259, evidence of M. Banchais, member of Chambre syndicale des courtiers de Nantes; Min. de l'Agriculture, *Notes sur le commerce des produits agricoles . . .*, vol. 1, p. 139.

177   1859 *Enquête*, p. 404, evidence of M. Briaune, *propriétaire* at Eceuiele (Indre).

178   1870 *Enquête*, mayor of Salles-la Source (Aveyron), in AN C 1157; PG, Pau, 6 April 1859, in AN BB³⁰384.

179   Min. des Finances et Min. de l'Agriculture, du commerce et des TP, *Enquête*, sur les principes et les faits généraux qui régissent la circulation monétaire et fiduciaire, 1867, p. 743, evidence of M. Picard, président de la Chambre de commerce de St-Quentin; J. Labasse, *Les capitaux et la région*, 1955, pp. 10–11.

180 Conseil d'Etat, 1859, p. 588, evidence of Darblay *jeune, négociant*, miller, président du *comice agricole* de Seine-et-Oise, deputy.
181 See, for example, 1870 *Enquête*, mayor of Le Teilleul (Manche), in AN C 1157.
182 ibid., G. de Puynode (Indre) and editor of *Journal des économistes*.
183 Conseil d'Etat, 1859, p. 731, evidence of M. Lebeau, *négociant* and shipowner at Boulogne-sur-Mer; Jacqmin, *De l'exploitation*, vol. 2, p. 134.
184 1870 *Enquête, comice agricole*, Haut-Beaujolais, in AN C 1156.
185 See, for example, PI, Laon, to PG, Amiens, 25 June 1854, in AN BB^{30}432; ATP, Seine-Infèrieure; Min. de l'Agriculture, *Notes sur le commerce*, vol. 1., p. 63, Aude; p. 99, Côte-d'Or; pp. 131–2 Eure, re mills at Neubourg and Chartres; p. 162, Indre; p. 174, Landes; p. 269, Oise; p. 274, Orne; p. 299, Haute-Saône; p. 327, Seine-Infèrieure; p. 338, Somme.
186 Min. de l'Agriculture, *Notes sur le commerce*, vol. 1, p. 7.
187 ibid., p. 98.
188 For example, 1859 *Enquête*, p. 280, evidence of H. Barbet, *propriétaire-agriculteur* in Seine-Infèrieure, former mayor of Rouen, president of *conseil général* of Seine-Infèrieure.
189 P. Claval, *Géographie générale des marchés*, 1969, p. 121.
190 PI, Marseille, 17 February 1855, in AN BB^{30}433.
191 Letter of 6 June 1856; undated internal Ministry of Justice note (1856), in AN BB^{18}1553.
192 1870 *Enquête*, mayor of Athis (Marne), in AN C 1158; Min. de l'Agriculture, *Notes sur le commerce*, vol. 1, pp. 69–70, Bouches-du-Rhône; p. 239, Haute-Marne.
193 ibid., p. 158, Ille-et-Vilaine; p. 169, Jura; p. 275, Pas-de-Calais; p. 327, Seine-Infèrieure.
194 See, for example, 1882 *Enquête*, mayor of St-Christal-de-Rodières (Gard), in AN C 3349.
195 1866 *Enquête*, vol. 9, Allier, p. 30.
196 Conseil d'Etat, 1859, p. 92, evidence of Général Yvelin, aide-de-camp to the Empereur, *propriétaire-agriculteur* near Provins (Seine-et-Marne); 1870 *Enquête, comice agricole*, Epinal (Vosges), in AN C 1159.
197 1871 *Enquête, Réponse de la cie des chemins de fer de l'Est . . .*, p. 22.
198 See, for example, 1870 *Enquête*, reply from commune of Grignerville (Loiret); from thirteen *cultivateurs* meeting at Villeneuve l'Archevêque (Yonne), in AN C 1159.
199 See, for example, ibid., *conseillers généraux* of Forges-les-Eaux (Seine-Infèrieure).
200 Min. des TP, *Comité consultatif. . . Ouest, 1 October 1896*, in AN F^{14}11295.
201 See, for example, Min. de l'Agriculture, *Notes sur le commerce*, vol. 1, p. 63, Aude; p. 124 Doubs; M. Gervais *et al., Histoire de la France rurale*, vol. 4, 1977, p. 79.
202 AN BB^{20}633.
203 1870 *Enquête, Commission statistique agricole*, St-Loup (Deux-Sèvres), in AN C 1159.
204 AN C 957.
205 AN C 3349.

206 See, for example, 1882 *Enquête*, evidence of mayor of Curac (Charente), in AN C 3343.

207 1866 *Enquête*, vol. 6, Eure-et-Loir, p. 6.

208 1859 *Enquête*, p. 132, evidence of M. Lamarre, *syndic de la boulangerie*, *arrondissement* of St-Denis; 1870 *Enquête*, reply of M. Charpentier, *conseiller général* for the milling centre of Etampes (Seine-et-Oise), in AN C 1156.

209 See, for example, 1870 *Enquête*, evidence of MM. Delarue, *négociants* and millers at Antrain (Ille-et-Vilaine), in AN C 1156.

210 *Rapport du contrôleur général, 19 October 1896*, in AN F^{14}11283; *Comité consultatif, section permanente, 15 May 1901*, in AN F^{14}11305.

211 1859 *Enquête*, p. 129, evidence of M. Donan; ibid., p. 298, evidence of M. A. Dailly, secretary of *comice agricole* of Seine-et-Oise; Min. de l'Agriculture, *Notes sur le commerce*, vol. 1, p. 5, Ain.

212 1882 *Enquête*, deposition of M. H. A. Way, president of the Chambre syndicale des grains, graines, farines et huiles de Paris, in AN C 3368. See also evidence of A. Rousseau, miller at Craon (Mayenne), in AN C 3368.

213 Min. du Commerce, *La petite industrie* vol. 1 p. 18; Min. des TP, *Comité consultatif. . . séance, 1 October 1896*, in AN F^{14}9450.

214 Reply of *conseiller général* at Pontarlier (Doubs), in AN C 1158.

215 PG, Paris, 16 June 1862, in AN BB^{30}383; Inspecteur de l'exploitation commerciale des chemins de fer d'Orléans to Min. des TP, 2 and 5 March 1849, in AN F^{14}9450; *Comité consultatif . . . PLM et Midi, 25 March 1896*, in AN F^{14}11205.

216 Min. de l'Agriculture, *Notes sur le commerce*, vol. 1, p. 28.

217 Conseil d'Etat, 1859, p. 54, evidence of M. de Benoist, *propriétaire* in Meuse and deputy.

218 PG, Dijon, 1 October 1867, in AN BB^{30}377; Min. de l'Agriculture, *Notes sur le commerce*, p. 99, Côte-d'Or.

219 See, for example, Min. des TP, *Rapport de l'inspecteur particulier de l'exploitation commerciale, Ouest, 12 May 1890*, in AN F^{14}11295.

220 1882 *Enquête*, deposition of M. H. A. Way, president of the Chambre syndicale des grains, graines, farines et huiles de Paris, in AN C 3368.

221 *Comice agricole*, Albi (Tarn), in AN C 1159.

222 JP for the *canton sud* of Castelnaudary, in AN C 1159; PG, Toulouse, 8 October 1869, in AN BB^{30}389.

223 Min. des TP, *Comité consultatif. . . séance, 7 July 1909*, in AN F^{14}11283.

224 Min. des TP, *Comité consultatif . . . PLM et Midi, 25 March 1896. Rapport de l'inspecteur particulier de l'exploitation commerciale attaché à la 1re circonscription*, Midi, 3 February 1893, in AN F^{14}11272.

225 *Rapport du contrôleur général*, 19 October 1896, in AN F^{14}11283.

226 Min. de l'Agriculture, *Notes sur le commerce*, vol. 1, p. 269, Oise; p. 60, Aude; p. 99, Côte-d'Or. This source does not provide statistics for every department, and the classification of importance varies between departments.

227 PG, Rouen, 2 October 1855, in AN BB^{30}433.

228 1859 *Enquête*, p. 196, evidence of M. Darblay; ibid., p. 170, evidence of M. Boittelle.

229 See, for example, Min de l'Agriculture, *Notes sur le commerce*, vol. 1, p. 60, Aude; p. 80, Charente; p. 117, Dordogne.

230   29 June 1855, in AN BB³⁰373.

231   Min. du Commerce, *La petite industrie*, vol. 1, 1893, p. 18.

232   1870 *Enquête*, Société d'agriculture, *arrondissement* Bernay de l'Eure, in AN C 1160; Min. du Commerce, *La petite industrie*, vol. 1, p. 18.

233   Evidence of M. Picard, président de la Chambre de commerce de St-Quentin, pp. 241–2; see also *Préfet*, Cher, to Direction, Chemin de fer du Centre, 15 July 1850, in AN 60 AQ 320.

234   1870 *Enquête, comice agricole*, St Junien (Haute-Vienne), in AN C 1161.

235   1870 *Enquête, conseiller général* for Narbonne (Aude), in AN C 1161.

236   PG, Orléans, 1 July 1862, in AN BB³⁰382.

237   1870 *Enquête*, reply from Baron de Roury, in AN C 1156; see also A. Bonnet, *Enquête sur la situation et les besoins de l'agriculture*, Dijon, 1867 p. 46.

238   PG, Colmar, 20 January 1866, in AN BB³⁰376.

239   AN C 1156.

240   See, for example, 1870 *Enquête*, reply from commune of Benevent l'Abbaye (Creuse), in AN C 1159.

241   1870 *Enquête*, evidence of M. Combes, engineer and member of Société d'agriculture de l'Ardèche, in AN C 1156.

242   1870 *Enquête*, reply from commune of Villebourg (Indre-et-Loire), in AN C 1159.

243   See, for example, Min. de l'Agriculture, Bureau des subsistances, internal memorandum on the question of cereals, 20 January 1866, in AN 45 AP 23.

244   The gross product per hectare of wheat, however, remained substantially higher than that of other cereals.

245   M. Agulhon *et al.*, *Histoire de la France rurale*, vol. 3, 1976, pp. 394–6.

246   ibid., p. 398.

247   J. L'homme, 'La crise agricole à la fin du 19ᵉ siècle en France', *Revue économique*, 1970, pp. 527–8.

248   Agulhon *et al.*, *Histoire de la France rurale*, vol. 3, p. 403; Goujon, 'Le temps des révolutions inachevées' p. 319.

249   G. Postel-Vinay, *La rente foncière dans le capitalisme agricole*, 1974, p. 162; see also Désert *Une société rurale*, vol. 2, p. 969; Agulhon *et al.*, *Histoire de la France rurale*, p. 402.

250   See, for example, PG, Nancy, 15 January 1865, in AN BB³⁰381; Min. des TP, *Rapport du contrôleur général, 19 October 1896*, in AN F¹⁴11283.

251   Conseil d'Etat, 1859, vol. 2, p. 706.

252   1870 *Enquête, comice agricole*, Langres (Haute-Marne); F. Ferron, former mayor and ex-president of *comice agricole*, Gray (Haute-Saône), in AN C 1160.

253   PG, Nancy, 9 April 1859, in AN BB³⁰381; 1870 *Enquête*, mayor of Vigny (Saône-et-Loire), in AN C 1157; Société d'agriculture, Louhans (Saône-et-Loire), in AN C 1159.

254   Bonnet, *Enquête*, pp. 46–7.

255   1866 *Enquête*, vol. 27, p. 180, evidence of commission départementale d'enquête du Rhône and Chambre consultative d'agriculture de Lyon.

256   Conseil d'Etat, 1859, p. 480, evidence of M. Lignières, retired miller and former mayor of Toulouse; 1866 *Enquête*, vol. 22, Gard, p. 8; ibid., vol. 21, Aude, p. 28.

257 1866 *Enquête*, vol. 18, Gers, Tarn-et-Garonne, Haute-Garonne, p. 19; ibid., vol. 7, Vendée, p. 27.

258 1870 *Enquête*, Société d'agriculture du Gard, in AN C 1157; evidence of J. Durand, deputy for Pyrénées-Orientales, in AN C 1158.

259 PG. Aix, 14 April 1866, in AN BB[30]370; 1870 *Enquête*, by Beaumont de Lomagne, *conseiller général* for Laborde (Tarn-et-Garonne), in AN C 1156.

260 Conseil d'Etat, 1859, pp. 304–5, evidence of M. Cohen, retired grain merchant at Marseille; 1866 *Enquête*, vol. 22, Bouches-du-Rhône, p. 814, evidence of P. Rodocanachi, *négociant*, member of Marseille Chamber of Commerce.

261 1866 *Enquête*, vol. 13, Bas and Haut-Rhin, p. 136.

262 1866 *Enquête*, vol. 19, Tarn, p. 44.

263 See 1870 *Enquête*, piece no. 10, in AN C 1156, for complaints about effects in Beauce and Brie.

264 See, for example, PG, Paris, 30 July 1868, re wine producers of Champagne and Bourgogne, in AN BB[30]383; 1870 *Enquête comice agricole*, Melle (Deux-Sèvres), in AN C 1160.

265 See, for example, 1870 *Enquête, comice agricole, arrondissement* Argèles (Hautes-Pyrénées), in AN C 1156.

266 ibid., *comice agricole*, Pontarlier (Doubs), AN C 1157.

267 1866 *Enquête*, vol. 26, p. 67.

268 1870 *Enquête*, reply from Mézières (Ardennes); ibid., Société d'agriculture, Villefranche-sur-Saône, in AN C 1160.

269 1866 *Enquête*, vol. 22, Gard, p. 29.

270 1866 *Enquête*, vol. 22, Hérault, pp. 66, 72.

271 PI, Tours, to PG, Orléans, April 1866, in AN BB[30]382.

272 1870 *Enquête*, reply of M. Ragot, member of Chambre consultative d'agriculture du Rhône, in AN C 1157.

273 AN C 1156.

274 See, for example, PG, Nancy, 16 October 1865, in AN BB[30]381; and especially PG, Agen, 5 October 1865, in AN BB[30]370.

275 1866 *Enquête*, vol. 9, Allier, p. 30.

276 4 October 1859, in AN BB[30]374.

277 M. S. Smith, *Free Trade, Protection and Tariff Reform. Commerce and Industry in French Politics, 1868–82*, PhD thesis, Cornell University, 1972, p. 28.

278 See, for example, 1870 *Enquête*, reply of Beaumont de Lomagne, *conseiller général* for Laborde (Tarn-et-Garonne), in AN C 1156.

279 See especially PG, Colmar, 17 April 1867., in AN BB[30]380.

280 1882 *Enquête*, mayor of St-Germain-de-Azincay, in AN C 3373[1].

281 *Préfet*, Gers, to Min. d'Agriculture, 14 November 1884, in AN C 3350.

282 PG, Douai, 9 April 1859, in AN BB[30]377.

283 Smith, *Free Trade*, pp. 293–7.

284 AN C 3371[1].

285 For example, 1882 *Enquête*, reply from commune of Frémauville (Seine-Inférieure), in AN C 3370[3].

286 AN C 3371[1].

287 *Procès-verbal, séance extraordinaire, 7 October 1884*, in AN C 3365.

288 L. Martin, *propriétaire* and agronomist at Chartres, *L'agriculture en Beauce*, in AN C 3348.

289 *Préfet*, Gers, 14 November 1884, in AN C 3350.

290 See, for example, 1882 *Enquête*, mayor of Léon (Landes), in AN C 3356.

291 See, for example, ibid., mayors of Lacapelle (Lot) and Fumel (Lot-et-Garonne), in AN C 3359.

292 See, for example, *Préfet*, Vosges, 9 November 1884, in AN C 3371².

293 Point made by Conseil d'Etat, 1859, p. 670, evidence of M. Miquel, president, *comice agricole*, Tonnay-Charente.

294 See, for example, 1866 *Enquête*, vol. 14, Haute-Marne, p. 10.

295 PG, Douai, 9 April 1859, in AN BB³⁰377.

296 See, for example, 1870 *Enquête*, reply from *comice agricole, arrondissement* Epernay (Marne), in AN C 1156.

297 15 November 1884, in AN C 3368; 4 November 1884, in AN C 3364.

298 See, for example, 1866 *Enquête*, vol. 9, Allier, p. 30.

299 1870 *Enquête*, reply of Comte de Drée, *propriétaire* at Bargemans (Var), in AN C 1156.

300 PG, Amiens, 9 October 1866, in AN BB³⁰371.

301 Conseil général du Nord, *Rapport sur l'échelle mobile et la prohibition par M. Mimerel*, Lille, 1859, p. 2.

302 Smith, *Free Trade*, p. 324.

303 D. Salem, 'Sur quelques conséquences du retour de la France au protectionisme à la fin du 19ᵉ siècle', *Revue d'histoire économique et sociale*, 1967, pp. 331–2; P. Barral, *Les agrariens français de Méline à Pisani*, 1968, pp. 84–6.

304 Min. des TP, *Rapport de l'inspecteur général chargé de la direction du contrôle des chemins de fer de l'Ouest, 30 May 1890*, in AN F¹⁴11295.

305 Levasseur, *Histoire du commerce*, pp. 724–5.

306 Chambre de commerce de Marseille, *La question des blés devant le parlement*, Marseille, 1894, p. 7.

307 See, for example, PLM *Rapport*, 1896, in *Journal des chemins de fer*, 1896, p. 326.

308 1866 *Enquête*, vol. 22, Hérault, p. 66.

309 ibid., Gard, p. 8.

310 ibid., vol. 24, Var–Alpes Maritimes, p. 56.

311 PG, Agen, 7 October 1864, in AN BB³⁰370.

312 1866 *Enquête*, vol. 24, Basses-Alpes, pp. 9–10.

Chapter 9 Agriculture in a changing market

1 D. H. Penny, 'Growth of "economic mindedness" among small farmers in north Sumatra, Indonesia', in C. R. Wharton (ed.), *Subsistence Agriculture and Economic Development*, 1970, p. 156.

2 See R. Musset, 'Les statistiques agricoles officielles françaises: "étude critique"', *Annales d'histoire économique et sociale*, 1933, *passim*.

3 1882 *Enquête*, mayor of Gouttières to *Préfet*, Eure: 'the questionnaire is so complicated that I can't answer it', in AN C 3348.

4 See also 1882 *Enquête*, deposition of M. Sauvage, *maître de conférence*, Institut national agronomique, in AN C 3368.

5 Report of 4 November 1884, in AN C 3364.

6   See also *Préfet*, Somme, 30 April 1855, and enclosed letter from Baron de Morgan, président, *comice agricole*, Amiens, in AN F[11]2682.

7   See, for example, G. Garrier, 'Les enquêtes agricoles du 19e siècle. Une source contestée', *Cahiers d'histoire*, 1967, pp. 106–7; B. Gille, *Les sources statistiques de l'histoire de la France*, Geneva, 1964, p. 243.

8   M. Agulhon *et al.*, *Histoire de la France rurale*, vol. 3, 1976, pp. 221f. 395f.

9   J. C. Toutain, *Le produit de l'agriculture française de 1700 à 1958*, vol. 2, *La Croissance, Cahiers de l'Institut de Science Economique Appliquée*, 1961, table 118.

10 In F. Caron, *An Economic History of Modern France*, 1979, p. 24.

11 G. Désert, in Agulhon *et al.*, *Histoire de la France rurale*, pp. 243f.

12 Toutain, *Le produit de l'agriculture*, pp. 13–14.

13 See R. Laurent, 'Tradition et progrès: le secteur agricole', in E. Labrousse, and F. Braudel (eds.), *Histoire économique et sociale de la France*, tome 3, vol. 2, 1976, pp. 733–4; C. Matyja-Ochs, *Aspects de la croissance de l'agriculture française. Etude départementale 1852–82*, Doctorat du 3e cycle, Université Paul Valéry – Montpellier III, 1974, *passim*.

14 Min. de l'Agriculture, *Statistique agricole de la France, résultats généraux de l'enquête décennale de 1862*, Strasbourg, 1868; ibid., 1882, Nancy, 1887.

15 1870 *Enquête*, evidence of Comte de Cugnac, in AN C 1158.

16 G. W. Grantham, 'Scale and organisation in French farming, 1840–1880', in W. N. Parker, and E. L. Jones (eds.) *European Peasants and their Markets*, 1975, p. 296.

17 P. Goujon, 'Le temps des révolutions inachevées', in J.-P. Houssel (ed.), *Histoire des paysans français du 18e siècle à nos jours*, Roanne, 1976, p. 317.

18 R. Estier, 'La dépression agricole de la fin du 19e siècle', ibid., p. 318.

19 B. Supple, 'Thinking about economic development', in A. J. Youngson (ed.), *Economic Development in the Long Run*, 1972 p. 24.

20 *Statistique agricole*, 1862 and 1882.

21 *Statistique de la France: Territoire et population. Résultats généraux du dénombrement de 1852*, 1855; ibid., 1862, (1864).

22 See, for example, 1870 *Enquête*, reply of the *conseiller général*, canton of Pont-Audemer (Eure), in AN C 1160.

23 See, for example, Min. de l'Agriculture, *Notes sur le commerce*, vol. 1, 1906, pp. 79–80, Seine-Inférieure; 1882 *Enquête*, mayor of Garamac (Ariège), in AN C 3337; 1866 *Enquête*, vol. 5, Pas-de-Calais, p. 192.

24 See, for example, 1870 *Enquête*, reply of A. Petit, a *cultivateur* near Meaux (Seine-et-Marne), in AN C 1156; of *comice agricole*, Gray (Haute-Saône), in AN C 1160.

25 D. Faucher, 'Aspects sociologiques du travail agricole', *Etudes rurales*, 1964, pp. 126–7.

26 A. Chatelain, *Les migrants temporaires en France de 1800 à 1914*, vol. 1, Lille, 1977, p. 161.

27 See, for example, 1882 *Enquête*, replies of a *propriétaire-agriculteur* at Chézeaux (Haute-Marne), in AN C 3373[1].

28 See, for example, views of a labourer at St-Clou-Ternoir (Pas-de-Calais), in AN C 3367.

29 See, for example, 1882 *Enquête*, reply of mayor of Piré (Ille-et-Vilaine), in AN C 3354.

30 See, for example, 1882 *Enquête*, mayor of Lavignac (Lot-et-Garonne), re public works of the Second Empire, in AN C 3359.

31 See, for example, 1882 *Enquête*, reply of a *cultivateur* at Balazac (Ardèche), a commune affected by both diseased silkworms and phylloxera, in AN C 3332.

32 See, for example, 1882 *Enquête*, reply from the mayor of Aigleville (Eure), in AN C 3348.

33 1866 *Enquête*, vol. 27, Loire, p. 76.

34 See, for example, 1870 *Enquête*, *comice agricole*, Châtellerault (Vienne), in AN C 1160.

35 H. Hitier, 'La culture intensive et les conditions de la main-d'oeuvre agricole dans les fermes industrielles de l'Ile-de-France', *La Réforme Sociale*, 6ᵉ série, vol. 8, 1909, p. 321.

36 Distinction made by L. Malassis, *Economie des exploitations agricoles*, 1958, p. 210.

37 See, for example, Société nationale d'agriculture, *Enquête sur la situation de l'agriculture en France en 1879*, vol. 2, 1880, *passim*.

38 P. Brunet, *Structure agraire et économie rurale des plateaux tertiares entre la Seine et l'Oise*, Caen, 1960, p. 187.

39 J. Sion, *La France méditerranéenne*, n.d., p. 143; see also 1870 *Enquête*, reply of the Société d'agriculture du Gard, in AN C 1157.

40 Brunet, *Structure agraire*, p. 371; E. Constant, *Le département du Var sous le Second Empire et au début de la 3ᵉ République*, Doctorat ès lettres, Université de Provence, Aix, 1977, vol. 2, p. 458.

41 See, for example, 1882 *Enquête*, reply St-Montant (Ardèche), in AN C 3333; and mayor of St-Vincent-Puymanfrais (Vendée), in AN C 3372[1].

42 J. Renard, *Les évolutions contemporaines de la vie rurale dans la région nantaise*, Les Sables-d'Olonne, 1975, pp. 131–45.

43 AN C 3372[1].

44 See, for example, 1870 *Enquête*, reports from the Société d'agriculture de la Haute-Saône, in AN C 1159, and the *comice agricole*, Issoudun (Indre), in AN C 1160.

45 See B. Berg, 'Nutrition and national development', in Berg *et al.*, *Nutrition, National Development and Planning*, Cambridge, Mass., 1973, pp. 54–5.

46 For example, 1870 *Enquête*, response from Aurillé (Vendée), in AN C 1158.

47 For example, ibid., individual replies from Dampierre (Haute-Seine), in AN C 1158, and Châteaudun (Eure-et-Loir), in AN C 1157.

48 Process described, for example, by M. Petitbon-Gillonnière, a landowner in the Sarthe, in A. Pinet (ed.), *L'enseignement primaire en présence de l'enquête agricole*, 1873, p. 281.

49 AN C 3368.

50 R. Hubscher, 'Le livre de compte de la famille Flahaut (1811–77)', *Revue d'histoire économique et sociale*, 1969, pp. 54–5.

51 See, for example, 1882 *Enquête*, reply from the mayor of Hastingues (Landes), in AN C 3356.

52 Reply of D. Chopard, landowner of Vichy (Allier), to 1870 *Enquête*, in AN C 1161.

53 H. Mendras, 'Schémas d'analyse villageoise', in M. Jollivet (ed.), *Les collectivités rurales françaises*, 1974, pp. 54–5.

54 See, for example, rector, Académie Hautes-Alpes, April 1853, in AN F[17]9279; 1870 *Enquête*, reply from the Société d'agriculture des Pyrénées-Orientales re *école normale* at Perpignan, in AN C 1161.

55 See, for example, 1870 *Enquête, comice agricole*, Albi (Tarn), on unsuitability of texts originally written for northern France in AN C 1159; cf. *L'agriculture à l'école primaire en 42 leçons*, published at Ploërmal (Morbihan) (2nd edn 1894) by the Frères de l'instruction chrétienne for use in their schools. This work, awarded the gold medal of the Société des agriculteurs de France, was written specifically for Breton conditions. The *Bulletin de la Société Franklin, Journal des bibliothèques populaires* provided those responsible for setting up communal libraries from the 1860s with advice on the purchase of books of practical utility. In 1869, for example, it printed a review of A. Bobierre, *Simples notions sur l'achat et l'emploi des engrais commerciaux*.

56 See, for example, 1870 *Enquête, comice agricole*, Melle (Deux-Sèvres), in AN C 1160; Conseil d'Etat, 1859, p. 374, evidence of Marquis de Vogüe.

57 For statistics see *Annuaire statistique. Résumé retrospectif*, 1951, p. 67.

58 See, for example, 1882 *Enquête*, mayor, Bordes-sur-Arize (Ariège), in AN C 3337, and very similar views of *sous-préfet*, Provins (Seine-et-Marne), in AN C 3371[1].

59 See, for example, Rector, Académie Creuse May 1851; ibid., Corrèze, December 1852, in AN F[17]9279.

60 *Mémoire* of M. Jauras, *instituteur* at Carri-le-Rouet; and of M. Pettetier, *instituteur* at Thalouet (Bouches-du-Rhône), in AN F[17]10758.

61 *Inspecteur primaire*, Loiret, 31 December 1848, in AN F[17]9312.

62 *Inspecteur primaire*, Vendée, 15 November 1848, contrasts Luçon area (involved in cattle trade) with other areas of the department, in AN F[17]9312; see also mémoire by M. Gobinot, *instituteur* at Sauday (Marne), in AN F[17]10758.

63 See, for example, 1882 *Enquête*, reply from the commune of Gaillardbois-Cresserville (Eure), in AN C 3347.

64 See, for example, *Préfet*, Pas-de-Calais, 13 June 1855, in AN F[17]9373.

65 See, for example, 1870 *Enquête*, reply from canton of St-Vincent-de-Tyr (Landes), in AN C 1160.

66 1866 *Enquête*, vol. 24, Var, p. 345.

67 1870 *Enquête*, reply from commune of Cournans (Marne), for a conservative vision of an idyllic, harmonious past in AN C 1160.

68 Hitier, 'La culture intensive', pp. 316–17.

69 See, for example, 1870 *Enquête*, reply of Société agricole des Pyrénées-Orientales, in AN C 1161; of *comice agricole*, La Châtre-sur-Loire (Sarthe), in AN C 1156.

70 1870 *Enquête*, reply of *comice agricole*, Meslay (Mayenne), in AN C 1161.

71 1870 *Enquête*, reply of *comice agricole, arrondissement* Lille (Nord), in AN C 1161.

72 See, for example, 1870 *Enquête*, reply from the canton of Sarvallée (Moselle), in AN C 1160; F. Bourquelat, *Les salaires agricoles en France. Evolution de leurs conditions de vie et de travail*, Doctorat du 3ᵉ cycle, Ecole pratique des

hautes études, 1973, p. 85; G. Postel-Vinay, *La rente foncière dans le capitalisme agricole*, 1974, pp. 123, 169.

73 Compare, for example, 1870 *Enquête, comice agricole*, Matignon (Côtes-du-Nord), in AN C 1160, and Chambre d'agriculture, *arrondissement* Lapalisse (Allier), in AN C 1158.

74 See 1870 *Enquête, comice agricole, arrondissement* Châteaudun (Eure-et-Loir); president, *comice agricole*, Gray (Haute-Saône), in AN C 1160.

75 See, for example, Rector, Indre, circular to cantonal education committees, May 1854, in AN F^{17}9280; circular of Rector, Mayenne, 12 March 1854, in ibid.

76 Toutain, *Le produit*, pp. 98–9.

77 Laurent, 'Tradition et progrès', p. 742.

78 Postel-Vinay, *La rente foncière*, pp. 136–7.

79 Quoted by Brunet, *Structure agraire*, p. 367.

80 G. Calvet, C. Rivals, 'Notes sur la maison paysanne', *Homo*, 1970, pp. 118–19.

81 L. Martin, agronomist, MSS, 'L'agriculture en Beauce', p. 9, in AN C 3348.

82 See, for example, 1882 *Enquête*, mayor of Lavignac (Lot-et-Garonne), in AN C 3359.

83 J. W. Mellor, 'The subsistence farmer in traditional economics', in Wharton, *Subsistence Agriculture*, p. 210.

84 In AN C 3335 and C 3349 respectively.

85 See, for example, 1866 *Enquête*, vol. 24, Basses-Alpes, pp. 9–10; 1870 *Enquête*, Société d'agriculture, *arrondissement* St-Lô (Manche), in AN C 1161.

86 For example, 1870 *Enquête*, reply from St-Vincent-de-Grasse (Landes), in AN C 1160.

87 A. Deuvy, 'Capital, credit and saving in Javanese marketing', in R. Firth, and R. S. Yamey (eds.), *Capital, Saving and Credit in Peasant Societies*, 1964, p. 230.

88 See 1848 *Enquête*, canton Pont-de-Beauvoisin (Isère), on effects of low prices on capital accumulation and investment, in AD 162^{m}1–2; on reductions of rates of capital accumulation from the 1870s see 1882 *Enquête*, deposition of M. Armand Joigneault, *propriétaire et fermier* in the commune of Villy-le-Moutier (Côte-d'Or), in AN C 3340.

89 See, for example, G. Désert, 'L'agriculture et les paysans sarthois au 19e siècle', in M. Lévy-Leboyer (ed.), *Un siècle et demi d'économie sarthoise*, Rouen, 1969, p. 77; A. Fel, *Les hautes terres du Massif Central. Tradition paysanne et économie agricole*, 1962, p. 181.

90 See, for example, 1882 *Enquête*, reply of mayor of Mazières (Indre-et-Loire), in AN C 3355; mayor of Fauillet (Lot-et-Garonne), in AN C 3360.

91 See, for example, 1882 *Enquête*, reply of a *propriétaire* at Chézeaux (Haute-Marne), in AN C 3373^1.

92 J. Suret-Canale, 'L'état économique et social de la Mayenne au milieu du 19e siècle', *Revue d'histoire économique et sociale*, 1958, pp. 300–1; R. Laurent, 'Droite et gauche en Languedoc', in *Droit et gauche de 1789 à nos jours*, Montpellier, 1975, p. 18.

93 See, for example, 1870 *Enquête*, reply from *comice agricole*, Genlis (Côte-d'Or), in AN C 1160.

94 H. Mendras, *Sociétés paysannes*, 1976, p. 43.

95 Point made by Conseil d'Etat, 1859, vol. 1 p. 196, evidence of M. Guillaumin, *propriétaire-agriculteur*, president, *comice agricole*, Aubigny (Cher).

96 1862 *Enquête*, p. cix.

97 ibid., p. cxiii.

98 1870 *Enquête*, reply of the mayor of Montigny (Loiret), in AN C 1157.

99 See 1870 *Enquête*, replies from the secretary of the Chambre d'agriculture of Alençon (Orne), in AN C 1156, and the Société agricole des Pyrénées-Orientales, in AN C 1161.

100 See, for example, 1866 *Enquête*, vol. 1, Calvados, p. 62.

101 See, for example, L. Ogès, *L'agriculture dans le Finistère au milieu du 19ᵉ siècle*, Brest, 1949, p. 33; R. Hubscher, 'La rente foncière dans le département du Pas-de-Calais . . . (1846–1914)', *Revue Historique*, 1971, pp. 373–4.

102 AN C 3356.

103 Suret-Canale, 'L'état économique'.

104 M. Denis, *Les royalistes de la Mayenne et le monde moderne*, vol. 2, Doctorat d'état, Université de Paris, p. 646.

105 B. Jeannenay, *Tentative de rénovation rurale sous le Second Empire: la ferme d'Andelarre en Haute-Saône*, Mémoire de maîtrise, Institut d'études politiques de Paris, 1971, p. 6.

106 G. Désert, 'Les paysans du Calvados au 19ᵉ siècle', *Annales de Normandie*, 1971, p. 128.

107 J.-C. Farcy, *Agriculture et société rurale en Beauce pendant la 1ʳᵉ moitié du 19ᵉ siècle*, Doctorat du 3ᵉ cycle, Université de Paris X, p. 156.

108 AN C 3368.

109 1882 *Enquête, réponse collective des comices agricoles du département* (Seine-et-Marne), Melun, 1884, pp. 9–10, in AN C 3371[1].

110 A. Daumard, *Les fortunes françaises au 19ᵉ siècle*, 1973, p. 588.

111 See, for example, 1882 *Enquête*, reply of L. Martin, agronomist, in AN C 3360; *Préfet* of Somme, 6 November 1884, in AN C 3370[4].

112 PG, Nancy, 6 July 1861, in AN BB[30]381.

113 1882 *Enquête, Réponse collective*, p. 6.

114 See, for example, 1870 *Enquête*, reply of M. Cros, member of *comice agricole*, St-Pons (Hérault), in AN C 1158.

115 See, for example, R. Brunet, 'Les mutations du 19ᵉ siècle', in P. Woolff (ed.), *Histoire du Languedoc*, Toulouse, n.d., p. 497.

116 Désert, 'Les paysans du Calvados au 19ᵉ siècle', p. 132.

117 AN C 1160.

118 This was the figure most often quoted in replies to the 1870 *Enquête*.

119 See, for example, 1870 *Enquête, comice agricole*, canton of Rumilly (Haute-Savoie), in AN C 1158.

120 See especially Société nationale d'agriculture de France, *Enquête sur le Crédit agricole faite sur la demande de M. le Ministre de l'Agriculture*, vol. 1, 1884, p. 575; A. Gueslin, *Les origines du Crédit agricole*, Nancy, 1978, pp. 25f.

121 1882 *Enquête*, reply of mayor, Beaumont (Meurthe-et-Moselle), in AN C 3364; on the importance of reputations as a form of collateral see, for example, 1882 *Enquête*, the reply of a sharecropper at Mareuil (Vendée), in AN C 3372[1].

122 See, for example, ibid., mayor of Néac (Gironde), in AN C 3353.

123 *Annuaire Statistique, Résumé rétrospectif*, 1951, pp. 104f.

124 Matyja-Ochs, *Aspects*, pp. 165–7.

125 See, for example, G. Désert, *Une société rurale au 19ᵉ siècle: les paysans du Calvados*, Lille, 1975, pp. 555–6; Matyja-Ochs, *Aspects*, p. 92; Fel, *Les hautes terres*, p. 183; K. Sutton, 'Reclamation of wasteland during the 18th and 19th centuries', in H. D. Clout (ed.), *Themes in the Historical Geography of France*, 1977, pp. 165–7.

126 M. de Sauvage, *maître de conférence*, Institut national agronomique, in AN C 3368; see also response from L. Martin, agronomist, at Chartres in AN C 3348.

127 H. D. Clout, and A. D. M. Phillips, 'Sugar beet production in the Nord department of France during the 19th century', *Erkunde*, vol. 27, p. 117.

128 J. Pitié, *Exode rural et migrations intérieures en France. L'exemple de la Vienne et du Poitou-Charentes*, Poitiers, 1971, p. 294.

129 D. Faucher, *La vie rurale vue par un géographe*, Toulouse, 1962, pp. 12–15; Fel, *Les hautes terres*, p. 184.

130 See, for example, 1870 *Enquête*, mayor of St-Jean de Bournay (Isère), in AN C 1158; ATP, Gironde.

131 See, for example, 1870 *Enquête*, reply from Sarvallée (Moselle), in AN C 1160.

132 E. Juillard, *La vie rurale dans la plaine de Basse-Alsace. Essai de géographie sociale*, 1953, p. 13; A. Corbin, *Archaïsme et modernité en Limousin au 19ᵉ siècle*, vol. 1, 1975, pp. 460–1.

133 PG, Nancy, 16 October 1865, in AN BB³⁰381.

134 AN C 1160.

135 See 1866 *Enquête*, vol. 20, Haute-Loire, p. 9.

136 R. Laurent, 'Les mutations de la société rurale', in Labrousse and Braudel, *Histoire économique*, p. 742.

137 Process described e.g. by 1870 *Enquête*, reply of the Société centrale d'agriculture du département de la Savoie, in AN C 1160.

138 See, for example, 1866 *Enquête*, vol. 22, Hérault, p. 65; 1870 *Enquête*, reply of the Sociétés d'agriculture of Riberac and Périgueux (Dordogne), in AN C 1157 and 1160; P. Poutenson, *L'Evolution économique du Roussillon de 1848 à 1920*, Doctorat du 3ᵉ cycle, Université de Toulouse – Le Mirail, 1976, p. 38; R. Caralp-Landon, 'Le transport ferroviare des vins du Languedoc vers Paris', *Revue de géographie de Lyon*, 1951, p. 273; G. Galtier, *Le vignoble du Languedoc méditerranéen et du Roussillon*, Montpellier, n.d., p. 125; A. Perpillou, 'L'évolution de l'utilisation du sol par l'agriculture dans huit départements du Midi de la France', *Mémoires et documents du centre de documentation cartographique et géographique*, 1960, pp. 123f.; G. Gavignaud, 'La propriété en Roussillon', Doctorat d'état, Université de Paris I, 1980, vol. 2, pp. 513f.

139 See Constant, *Le département du Var*, vol. 1, p. 230.

140 PG, Montpellier, 5 July 1860, in AN BB³⁰380.

141 PG, Aix, 7 April 1861, in AN BB³⁰370; see also H. J. Smith, *Village Revolution: Agricultural Workers of Cruzy (Hérault), 1850–1910*, PhD thesis, University of Wisconsin, 1972, pp. 57f.

142 PG, Aix, 14 April 1866.

143 G. Cholvy, *Religion et société au 19ᵉ siècle. Le diocèse de Montpellier*, vol. 1, Lille, 1973, p. 158; M. Agulhon, 'L'agriculture et la société rurale du Var dans la première moitié du 19ᵉ siècle', in *Etudes d'histoire provençale*, Gap, 1971, p. 168.

144   See, for example, *Statistique agricole*, 1862, pp. 24–5.

145   Brunet, *Structure agraire*, pp. 497–8; P. V. Adams, *Economic and Geographic Change in Mediterranean France, 1850–1914* PhD thesis, University of New York at Buffalo, 1972, pp. 64, 72.

146   Désert, in Agulhon *et al.*, *Histoire de la France rurale*, p. 241.

147   R. Laurent, *Les vignerons de la Côte-d'Or au 19ᵉ siècle*, 1958, pp. 176f.

148   Adams, *Economic and Geographic Change*, p. 133.

149   See 1882 *Enquête*, reply of a *propriétaire-cultivateur* at Challignac (Charente), in AN C 3342.

150   AN C 3352.

151   See, for example, 1882 *Enquête*, reply of a labourer at Eveux (Rhône), in AN C 3369[3].

152   Min. de l'Agriculture, *Statistique agricole de la France. Résultats généraux de l'enquête décennale de 1892*, 1897, p. 93.

153   See, for example, D. Faucher, *L'homme et le Rhône*, 1968, p. 255.

154   See, for example, 1870 *Enquête*, Société d'agriculture de Riberac (Dordogne), in AN C 1157; and report of the *Procureur-impérial* at Orléans of April 1866, in AN BB[30]382.

155   See, for example, 1882 *Enquête*, reply from Marcilly (Haute-Marne), in AN C 3363.

156   For example, 1882 *Enquête*, reply from a *fermier* at Cossaye (Nièvre), in AN C 3369[4].

157   See also Désert, in Agulhon *et al.*, *Histoire de la France rurale*, pp. 429–30; J. Klatzmann, *La localisation des cultures et des productions animales en France*, 1955, p. 351.

158   Livestock (thousands):

Year	Horses	Bovines	Ovines
1840	2,818	11,762	32,131
1852	2,866	11,911	33,282
1862	2,914	11,813	29,530
1882	2,838	12,997	23,809

Source: Annuaire statistique, vol. 58, 1951, résumé rétrospectif, pp. 119–20. (These are among the least reliable of statistics.)

159   *Statistique*, 1882, p. 263.

160   Min. de l'Agriculture, *Notes sur le commerce*, vol. 2 pp. v–vi.

161   See, for example, 1882 *Enquête*, mayor of St-André-Goule d'Oie (Vendée), in AN C 3372; mayor of Petit-Mesnil (Aube), in AN C 3338.

162   PG, Caen, 11 January 1865, in AN BB[30]375.

163   Désert, *Une société rurale au 19ᵉ siècle: les paysans du Calvados*, vol. 2, Lille, 1975, pp. 565, 742.

164   See, for example, 1870 *Enquête*, reply of an *agriculteur* at Landéan (Ille-et-Vilaine), explaining his switch from wheat to cows and butter, in AN C 1159.

165   See, for example, Désert, *Une société rurale*, vol. 1, p. 401; G. Martin, 'L'évolution de l'agriculture en Auxois de 1840 à 1939', *Cahiers de l'association interuniversitaires de l'Est*, 1966, p. 109.

166 Average milk yields increased from around 9 hectolitres per annum in 1852 to 10–15 hectolitres by 1882.

167 1866 *Enquête*, vol. 24, Basses-Alpes, pp. 9–10; see also P. Arbos, 'Vie rurale des massifs volcaniques auvergnats', *Revue de géographie alpine*, 1947, pp. 125–6.

168 See Fel, *Les hautes terres*, p. 20.

169 See, for example, 1882 *Enquête*, *Réponse collective des comices agricoles du département* (Seine-et-Marne), in AN C 3371¹; R. Brunet, *Les campagnes toulousaines*, Toulouse, 1965, p. 405.

170 AN C 3368.

171 See, for example, 1880 *Enquête*, mayor of Jouy-sur-Eure (Eure), in AN C 3345; P. Vigier, *Essai sur la répartition de la propriété foncière dans la région alpine*, 1963, p. 221.

172 See, for example, 1866 *Enquête*, vol. 27, Rhône, p. 153; 1882 *Enquête*, reply from Authe (Ardennes), in AN C 3335.

173 J. Mulliez, 'Du blé "mal nécessaire": réflexions sur le progrès de l'agriculture de 1750 à 1850', *Revue d'histoire moderne et contemporaine*, 1979, p. 3.

174 Matyja-Ochs, *Aspects*, p. 171.

175 In AN C 3370³.

176 1870 *Enquête*, reply of *comice agricole*, Albi (Tarn), in AN C 1159.

177 Matyja-Ochs, *Aspects* pp. 170–73, and especially H. D. Clout, and A. D. M. Phillips, 'Fertilisants minéraux en France au 19ᵉ siècle', *Etudes rurales*, 1972, pp. 9f.

178 Point made to 1870 *Enquête*, by the secretary of the *comice central agricole*, Sologne (Loir-et-Cher), in AN C 1157.

179 See, for example, ATP, Aveyron.

180 AN C 1158.

181 G. Désert, 'L'agriculture et les paysans sarthois au 19ᵉ siècle', p. 73.

182 See 1870 *Enquête*, *comice agricole*, St-Maixent (Deux-Sèvres), in AN C 1159; 1882 *Enquête*, reply from Montaigu (Allier), in AN C 3330.

183 In AN F¹⁴12162.

184 See, for example, Min. de l'Agriculture to TP, 15 July 1850, asking for reduction. Letter from Min. des TP to Chemin de fer du centre, 20 July 1850, passing on request in AN F¹⁴9555.

185 P–O *Rapport*, 1898, p. 340; fertilizer carried increased by 85 per cent, 1887–97.

186 See, for example, 1882 *Enquête*, mayor of Bardenac (Aveyron), in AN C 3421, of a *fermier* at St-Izaire (Aveyron), in AN C 3339.

187 See, for example, 1870 *Enquête*, reply of *comice agricole*, Bergheim (Haut-Rhin), in AN C 1160.

188 See, for example, 1882 *Enquête*, reply of the mayor of Villez-sur-le-Neubourg (Eure), in AN C 3345 and from the Mayor of Régnie (Rhône), in AN C 3335.

189 Min. de l'Agriculture, *Commission des engrais*, 1864, p. 68.

190 Conseil d'Etat, 1859, vol. 2, p. 162, evidence of M. Lecouteux, *propriétaire-agriculteur* in Loir-et-Cher, former *chef des cultures*, Institut agronomique de Versailles.

191 See, for example, 1870 *Enquête*, *comice agricole*, Lille, in AN C 1161.

192 A. D. M. Phillips, and H. D. Clout, 'Underdraining in France during the second half of the 19th century', *Transactions of the Institute of British Geographers*, 1970, p. 79.

193 For example, E. Tamais, 'La situation de l'agriculture dans le département du Gard', MSS in AN C 3337.

194 See, for example, 1882 *Enquête*, report from M. Alix, civil engineer at Toulouse, in AN C 3350.

195 G. P. Azèmer, M. de la Pradelle, 'Le marché-gare de Carpentras. Entre tradition et modernité', *Etudes rurales*, 1980. p. 297.

196 Conseil d'Etat, 1859, vol. 1, p. 153, evidence of M. Lecouteux.

197 See, for example, 1870 *Enquête*, reply of D. S. Chopard, landowner at Vichy (Allier), in AN C 1161; J. Merley, *La Haute-Loire de la fin de l'Ancien Régime aux débuts de la 3e République*, Le Puy, 1975, p. 509.

198 See, for example, ATP, Haut-Rhin, Côte-d'Or, Marne, Meuse, Aube; also A. Chatelain, 'La lente progression de la faux', *Annales ESC*, 1956, pp. 495f; R. Price, 'The onset of labour shortage in French agriculture in the nineteenth century', *Economic History Review*, 1975, p. 274.

199 E. J. T. Collins, 'Labour supply and demand in European agriculture', in E. L. Jones and S. J. Woolf (eds.), *Agrarian Change and Economic Development*, 1969, p. 82.

200 See, for example, 1870 *Enquête*, replies from the *comice agricole*, Albi, in AN C 1159, and Justin Durand, deputy for Pyrénées-Orientales and vice-president of the Société départementale d'agriculture des Bouches-du-Rhône, in AN C 1156.

201 See, for example, 1870 *Enquête*, reply by the Société agricole des Pyrénées-Orientales, in AN C 1161.

202 A. G. Haudricourt, and J. B. Delamarre, *L'Homme et la charrue à travers le monde*, 1955, pp. 13–20, 113–4, 331–47.

203 M. Vielfaure, 'Etude d'une araire observée à Montselogoes (Ardèche)', *Ethnologie française*, 1972, p. 357.

204 Brunet, *Structure agraire*, p. 324.

205 Désert, *Une société rurale*, vol. 1, p. 596.

206 See, for example, 1870 *Enquête*, reply from the canton of Guize (Aisne), in AN C 1159; ATP, Seine-Inférieure.

207 E. Gautier, *Un siècle d'indigence (Côtes-du-Nord)*, 1950, p. 209.

208 See, for example, 1882 *Enquête*, reply from mayor of Beaumont (Meurthe-et-Moselle), in AN C 3364.

209 See, for example, ATP, Seine-et-Oise.

210 See, for example, 1870 *Enquête*, Société d'agriculture départementale de la Lozère, and mayor of Bargemon (Var), in AN C 1157; Chambre d'agriculture, *arrondissement* Argèles (Pyrénées-Orientales), in AN C 1160; ATP, Hautes-Alpes.

211 ATP, Aveyron.

212 ATP, Tarn-et-Garonne.

213 1870 *Enquête*, Société d'agriculture de Riberac (Dordogne), in AN C 1157.

214 R. Thabault, *Education and Change in a Village Community: Mazières-en-Gâtine, 1848–1914*, 1971, p. 83.

215 See, for example, 1870 *Enquête*, replies from Amboise (Indre-et-Loire), in AN C 1161, and the *comice agricole*, Pyrénées-Orientales, in AN C 1160.

216 See, for example, Conseil d'Etat, 1859, vol. 2 p. 351, evidence of M. Pagézy, mayor of Montpellier (Hérault).

217 Horse hoes: 1862, 26,000; 1882, 195,000; 1892, 252,000.
218 See, for example, 1870 *Enquête*, reply from the mayor of the commune of Fussy (Cher), in AN C 1158; 1882 *Enquête*, reply from La Garnache (Vendée), in AN C 3372[1].
219 Point made to 1870 *Enquête*, in a reply from Nantua (Ain), in AN C 1159.
220 See ibid., reply from the director of the farm school at Marseille-le-petit (Oise).
221 1870 *Enquête*, reply of *comice agricole*, Genlis (Côte-d'Or), in AN C 1160; ATP, Puy-de-Dôme.
222 See, for example, ATP, Morbihan.
223 M. Chevalier, *La vie humaine dans les Pyrénées ariègeoises*, 1956, p. 692.
224 AN C 3344.
225 See, for example, 1870 *Enquête*, replies from the *comices agricoles*, Perreux (Loire), in AN C 1157, and Ambert (Puy-de-Dôme), in AN C 1159.
226 See, for example, 1882 *Enquête*, mayor of Villez-sur-le-Neubourg (Eure), in AN C 3346.
227 Conseil d'Etat, 1859, vol. 2, p. 349; see ATP, Aube, on contrasts between plain, valley and uplands.
228 AN C 1156.
229 See, for example, 1882 *Enquête*, reply of mayor of Bouxières-aux-Dames (Meurthe-et-Moselle), in AN C 3352.
230 1882 *Enquête*, reply of a *cultivateur-propriétaire*, in AN C 3333.
231 On abandonment see Matyja-Ochs, *Aspects*, p. 158, and on motives 1870 *Enquête*, reply of the *instituteur* at Châteauneuf-les-Mouthiers (Basses-Alpes), in AN C 1158, and the mayor of Pont-de-Montvert (Lozère), in AN C 1157.
232 cf., for example 1870 *Enquête*, reply of Société d'agriculture des Pyrénées-Orientales, in AN C 1161, and from the canton of Sarvallée (Moselle), in AN C 1160, with reply from the *arrondissement* of Rocroy (Ardennes), in AN C 1156; Fel, *Les hautes terres*, p. 183.
233 Proceedings of a meeting of the Conseil supérieur de l'agriculture of 29 March 1883, in AN F[14]12162, and P. Richard, 'Les charges de transport dans les exploitations agricoles de divers types', *Economie rurale*, 1962, p. 14.
234 1870 *Enquête*, reply from the *comice agricole*, Montigny-le-Roi (Haute-Marne), in AN C 1157; Ogès, *L'agriculture*, p. 116.
235 ATP, Bouches-du-Rhône.
236 Matyja-Ochs, *Aspects*, pp. 175–6.
237 G. Grantham, *Technical and Organisational Change in French Agriculture between 1840 and 1880*, PhD thesis, Yale University, 1972, p. 65; D. Faucher, *Le paysan et la machine*, 1954, p. 65.
238 Klatzmann, *La localisation des cultures*. p. 408; J. Pautard, *Les disparités régionales dans la croissance de l'agriculture française*, 1965, p. 113.
239 Pitié, *L'exode rural*, p. 319.
240 Désert, *Une société rurale*, vol. 1, pp. 335–6.
241 ATP, Haut-Rhin.
242 See, for example, 1882 *Enquête*, deposition of MM. J. J. Demozet of Tarbes (Hautes-Pyrénées), in AN C 3368; reply of a *fermier* at La Folletière (Seine-Inférieure), in AN C 3378[2].
243 AN C 1157; see also 1866 *Enquête*, vol. 5, Pas-de-Calais, p. 95.
244 This paragraph follows Chatelain, *Les migrants*, vol. 1, pp. 211; vol. 2, p. 683.

245   Departments of Aisne (457), Marne (1311), Aube (614), Oise (637), Somme (628), Eure-et-Loir (528), Seine-Inférieure (491), Seine-et-Oise (447), Ardennes (442), Eure (422).

246   Thus Pas-de-Calais (378), Nord (233), Nièvre (181), Cher (210), Sarthe (57), Orne (30), Calvados (39).

247   Bouches-du-Rhône (398), Hérault (277), Gard (180) cf. with Var (14), Basses-Alpes (7), Drôme (48).

248   See also Brunet, *Les campagnes toulousaines*, p. 324; Matyja-Ochs, *Aspects*, p. 178.

249   ATP, Aude.

250   Laurent, *Tradition et progrès*, p. 681.

251   Désert, *Une société rurale*, vol. 1, p. 334.

252   ATP, Var, and Bouches-du-Rhône.

253   See, for example, 1870 *Enquête*, reply of the Société d'agriculture of the *arrondissement* of St-Lô (Manche), in AN C 1161. AN F¹²1389 contains proposals for their improvement.

254   1870 *Enquête, comice agricole*, communes of Noutrou and Bussière (Dordogne), in AN C 1160.

255   See, for example, 1866 *Enquête*, vol. 6, Seine-et-Oise, p. 179; the effort is well described in Emile Guillaumin, *La vie d'un simple; mémoires d'un métayer*, 1904, p. 56.

256   See, for example, 1870 *Enquête*, replies from the *comice agricole*, Ensisheim, Guebwiller, Glebwiller and Soultz (Haut-Rhin), and The *comice agricole* of the *arrondissement* of Châteaudun (Eure-et-Loir), in AN C 1160.

257   See, for example, 1870 *Enquête*, reply of *comice agricole*, canton Domfront (Orne), in AN C 1160; and mayor, Fresnes-en-Wavre (Nord), in AN C 1157.

258   See, for example, 1870 *Enquête*, replies of the *comices agricoles* of Ensisheim, Guebwiller, Glebwiller and Soultz (Haut-Rhin).

259   See, for example, 1870 *Enquête*, replies from Ch. Dehais, farmer at Fransières (Eure), and the Société des sciences, agriculture et arts, department of Bas-Rhin, in AN C 1160.

260   1870 *Enquête*, reply from the *comice agricole*, canton of Perreux (Loire), in AN C 1157.

261   See, for example, 1870 *Enquête, comice agricole*, St-Servan (Ille-et-Vilaine), in AN C 1161; and Price, 'The onset of labour shortage', *passim*.

262   See, for example, Jeannenay, *Tentative de rénovation*, p. 92; G. Dupeux, *Aspects de l'histoire sociale et politique du Loir-et-Cher*, 1962, p. 213.

263   See, for example, 1870 *Enquête*, reply from municipal commission of Montmirail (Sarthe), in AN C 1160.

264   PG, Riom, 6 April 1870, in AN BB³⁰390.

265   See, for example, PG, Nancy, 16 October 1865, in AN BB³⁰381; ATP, Savoie.

266   See, for example, Désert, *Une société rurale*, vol. 1, p. 353, on discussion in Chambre d'agriculture at Lisieux in 1855.

267   See, for example, 1866 *Enquête*, vol. 16, Gironde, p. 378; R. Fruit, *La croissance économique du pays de St-Amand (Nord)*, 1963 p. 149.

268   See, for example, 1866 *Enquête*, vol. 18, Tarn-et-Garonne; 1870 *Enquête*, reply from a *cultivateur* at Champigny (Marne), in AN C 1157.

269   ATP, Alpes-Maritimes.

270 Brunet, *Les campagnes toulousaines*, p. 497.
271 An 1823 law to encourage the exchange of dispersed plots by requiring only a 1-franc registration fee had no significant results.
272 See, for example, Goujon, *Le temps des révolutions*, pp. 281–2; Postel-Vinay, *La rente foncière*, pp. 99–100.
273 J. Bastié, 'Au temps de la révolution des chemins de fer et des transformations agricoles', in M. Mollat (ed.), *Histoire de l'Ile-de-France et de Paris*, Toulouse, 1971, pp. 450, 463–4.
274 As it was by, for example, 1866 *Enquête*, vol. 6, Seine-et-Oise, p. 227; ATP, Basses-Alpes.
275 Désert, *Une société rurale*, vol. 1, p. 249.
276 Matyja-Ochs, *Aspects*, p. 130.
277 M. Hechter, *Internal Colonialism: the Celtic Fringe in British National Development*, 1975, p. 132.
278 Société des agriculteurs de France, *Dépositions des délégués de la société des agriculteurs de France devant la commission parlementaire du tarif général des douanes*, 1879.
279 See, for example, déposition of MM. J. J. Domozier of Tarbes (Hautes-Pyrénées), in AN C 3368; 1882 *Enquête*, mayor of Chamblac (Eure), in AN C 3348; *Préfet*, Somme, 6 November 1884, in AN C 3370⁴.
280 4 November 1884, in AN C 3364.
281 See, for example, D. Salem, 'Sur quelques conséquences du retour de la France au protectionnisme à la fin du 19ᵉ siècle', *Revue d'histoire économique et sociale*, 1967, p. 364; Estier, 'La dépression agricole de la fin du 19ᵉ siècle', p. 324.

Bibliography

Primary sources

Archives

Archives nationales

SERIES C (Chamber of Deputies)
C 943   Rail tariffs, road works
C 943–69   *Enquête sur le travail agricole et industriel*
               Décret du 25 mai 1848
C 987   Compagnie du chemin de fer PLM, 1849–51
               Compagnie du chemin de fer Ouest
C 1028   Discussion of routes for railways
C 1072   Petitions requesting railways
C 1082   Proposals in favour of concessions to local railway companies
C 1088   Repurchase of canals by state, 1861–3
C 1125   Petitions requesting railways; legislation on *chemins vicinaux*
C 1142   *Proposition de loi tendant à modifier le loi de 1836 sur les chemins*
               vicinaux, 1870
C 1154   Consular reports on international transport and harvest conditions
C 1157–61   Agricultural inquiry, 1870
               Transport inquiry, 1870
C 1161   Discussions of proposals for new railway lines
C 2854   Complaints from various chambers of commerce about railway services
C 2855   Petitions requesting railways
C 2856   *Rapport fait au nom de la Commission d'enquête sur les chemins de fer et*
               autres voies de transport concernant diverses pétitions relatives à la
               concession d'une ligne directe de Calais à Marseille, 1873
C 3005   *Commission relative à l'enquête sur les chemins de fer*, 1871
C 3006   Waterways
C 3007   Complaints from chambers of commerce about railway services
C 3307–8   *Commission des chemins de fer*, 1881–5
C 3309   *Chemins de fer. Dispositions spéciales à diverses lignes*
C3330–73   *Enquête parlementaire sur la situation des ouvriers de l'industrie et de*
               l'agriculture, 1882
C 7353   *Commission des travaux publics, des chemins de fer et des voies de*
               communication, 1910

C 7392   *Commission chargée de faire une enquête sur la situation de la production, du transport et du commerce des vins*, 1907
C 7432   *Commission des travaux publics, chemins de fer et voies de communication*, 1910
C 7433   *Chemins de fer. Dispositions concernant les grandes compagnies*
C7455–68   *Enquête sur la situation du commerce en France et notamment sur la condition du petit commerce*, 1912

SERIES F¹ (Ministry of the Interior)
F¹CIII   Bouches-du-Rhône, 12–13
F¹CIII   Charente-Inférieure, 9
F¹CIII   Côtes-du-Nord, 11, 13
F¹CIII   Haute-Saône, 9, 12
F¹CIII   Indre, 8
F¹CIII   Indre-et-Loire, 10
F¹CIII   Nord, 8 14–16
F¹CIII   Saône-et-Loire, 8, 13
F¹CIII   Seine, 12, 30–2
F¹CIII   Seine-et-Marne, 7
F¹CIII   Finistère, 11
F¹CIII   Vienne, 9
F¹CIII   Somme, 10–11
F¹CIII   Isère, 9, 18
F¹CIII   Nièvre, 9
F¹CIII   Eure, 13
F¹CIII   Tarn-et-Garonne, 7
F¹CIII   Hérault, 15
F¹CIII   Yonne, 11
F¹CIII   Maine-et-Loire, 12
F¹CIII   Calvados, 14
F¹CIII   Bas-Rhin, 15

SERIES F²
F²I 1027–104   Departmental administration: *chemins vicinaux* (sampled)

SERIES F⁷ (*Gendarmerie* reports)
3909–4214

SERIES F¹⁰ (Agriculture)
1482   General
1488–9   Markets
1490   Forests
1526–9   Markets
1640   Cereals: cultivation and storage
2295   Expenditure on local roads

SERIES F¹¹ (Subsistence)
1408–10   Transport of cereals, 1816–17

2319	*Mercuriales*
2681	State of crops, 1848
2682–3	Correspondence with cantonal statistical commissions, 1853–60
2680	ibid., 1862
2689	ibid., 1864–5
2694	ibid., 1853–60
2694	State of crops, 1867
2695	State of crops, 1871
2713–22	1882 inquiry: statistical returns
2740–1	Subsistences, 1816–17
2749	Subsistences, 1820–35
2750	Subsistences, 1835–50
2751	International state of crops, 1846–59
2752	Trade in cereals and flour, 1848–59
2754	Imports and exports: grain and flour
2755	Subsistences, 1831
2756	Subsistences, 1850–1
2758	Subsistences, 1846–7
2760–6	Bread prices and effects of ending of restrictions on bakers in 1863
2768	Trade in cereals and prices, 1880–1900
2772–98	Regulation of bakers, bread prices, 1817–80
2801–2	Provisioning of Paris

SERIES F¹² (Commerce and industry)

2198	Proposals for the improvement of the efficiency of flour mills
2211	Agricultural machinery
2309	Agricultural machinery
2370–4	Wages
4651–2	Strikes: Second Empire
4841	Customs tariffs
4854	Petitions concerning customs

SERIES F¹⁴ (Public works)

1270	Inquiry into transport conditions, 1811–12
1674–756	Roads, 1840–95
1757–878	Roads, 1820–50
1971	*Routes nationales*
8508–88	*Statistique des chemins de fer* (construction, exploitation etc.)
8666–819	*Chemins de fer: études et concessions* (sampled)
8821–9188	*Chemins de fer: avant-projets et projets* (sampled)
9066–142	*Chemins de fer: tarifs*
9218–28	*Conventions et projets de convention entre l'état et les grandes compagnies pour l'exploitation et la concession des lignes secondaires*
9239	*Chemins de fer: études*, 1860
9240–377	*Chemins de fer: travaux, expropriation, adjudications . . . projets* (sampled)
9378–555	*Chemins de fer: tarifs* (sampled)
9572	*Chemins de fer: nouvelles lignes proposées*, 1875

11041	*Ponts-et-chaussées. Section des chemin de fer*
11205–305	Inspectors' reports on commercial exploitation
12141–64	*Comité consultatif des Chemins de fer*
12155	*Etat* network
12157	Tariffication
12161–2	Relationships between railway companies
12362–9	*Comité de l'exploitation technique des chemins de fer. Procès-verbal*
12374–8	ibid.

SERIES F[17] (Education)

2609	Patois
2649	*Rapports trimestriels de l'état politique, moral et religieux*, 1858–9
9109–14	Preparation and implementation of 1833 and 1850 laws
9146	Popular literature
9279–80	Reports of school inspectors, academic rectors, etc.
9373–4	ibid.
10758–85	*Instituteurs' mémoires* on needs of primary education in rural communes

SERIES F[20] (Statistics)

560–1	Crop statistics based on Ministry of Finance returns
633	Statistics on flour mills
714	Correspondence with cantonal statistical commissions
724	Inquiry into transport tariffs 1845
765	*Evaluation des revenus territoriaux de la France faite en exécution de l'article II de la loi de 7 août 1850. Rapport fait au Ministère par M. Vandal, Directeur-général des Contributions directes, le 18 juin 1854*

SERIES BB[18] (Ministry of Justice)

Information on subsistence disorders, 1186, 1188–93; 1319–20, 1436, 1438, 1440, 1444, 1447, 1448, 1448B, 1449, 1451, 1452, 1454, 1460–1, 1475–9, 1517, 1537, 1545, 1553, 1558, 1563, 1581, 1618, 1633, 1639, 1644, 1707, 1715, 1728, 1754A, 1757, 1766, 1765, 1769, 1772, 1785.

SERIES BB[19] (Ministry of Justice)

| 37–42 | *Procureurs-généraux*: reports on subsistence disorders, 1846–7 |

SERIES BB[20] (Ministry of Justice: reports on Assizes, 1846–56)

141
157
193

SERIES BB[24] (Ministry of Justice: appeals for pardon)

286–326	For involvement in subsistence disorders: 1846–7
327–47	ibid.
348–60	ibid., 1849
409–18	ibid., 1852–3
440–56	ibid., 1854

478–83   ibid., 1855
484–8   ibid., 1856
494–506   ibid.

SERIES BB³⁰ (Ministry of Justice)
369–89   *Procureurs-généraux*: general reports, 1849–70
432–3   Subsistence disorders, 1853–6
434–5   False news, 1853–6

SERIES AQ
18AQ20   Cereal price movements: market of Châteauroux (Indre)
            Railway company commercial papers
48AQ3659–706Compagnie du chemin de fer du Nord
60AQ270–345 Paris–Orléans
77AQ45–138 PLM

SERIES AP (Private papers)
45AP 23–4   Rouher papers

SERIES AB
AB XIX173–5 Tuileries papers confiscated in 1870

SERIES AD
AD XIXN 113   Railway transport of perishables
AD XIXN 146–82 Regulations for railway operation
AD XIX⁵ 1–7   Paris Préfecture of Police: administrative responsibilities. Subsistence 1858–60
AD XIX T 134   *Dépt. de la Seine. Rapport de l'agent-voyer en chef sur la situation des chemins vicinaux au 1 Sept. 1872*

SERIES AN
AN XIXN 108–9   *Recueils des conventions passées de 1883 à 1892 entre l'état et les cies. des chemins de fer*
160   *Cie du chemin de fer du Nord. Etat du matériel roulant 1 mars 1888*
161   *Documents officiels*
AN XIXN 175–82 Proposals for the connection of local lines

Archives historiques du Ministère de la Guerre
E⁵ 1   Correspondance générale, 1830–1
E⁵ 152   Correspondance générale, 1839–40
153–9   Correspondance générale, 1846–7
G⁸ 1–176   Correspondance générale, 1852–70
MR 2151   *Dispositions à prendre en cas d'émeutes et de troubles en Paris et en provinces*
2259   *Reconnaissance. Mémoires topographiques* (Paris region)

Archives départementales
Isère   162^m 1–2 *Enquête sur le travail agricole et industriel. Décret du 25 mai 1848*
Nord   m 547/1, ibid.

Musée des Arts et traditions populaires
Enquête. Ancienne agriculture. Manuscripts prepared for each department by departmental *directeur des services agricoles* in response to ministerial circular of 3 March 1937

Printed sources (place of publication Paris unless otherwise stated)

Population
Statistique de la France publiée par le Ministre de l'Agriculture, du Commerce et des Travaux Publics, 2e série, vol. 2, *Territoire et population*, 1855; 2e série, vol. 13, *Population*, Strasbourg, 1864
   Population. Résultats généraux du dénombrement de 1872, 1873
Ministère du Commerce, Service de la statistique générale, *Résultats statistiques du dénombrement de 1881–1883*
   Dénombrement général. Résultats statistiques du dénombrement de 1891–1894
   Statistique générale de la France. Résultats du recensement général de la population effectué le 24 mars 1901, 5 vols, 1902, 1907

Communications

Governmental
Conseil d'Etat, *Enquête sur l'application des tarifs des chemins de fer*, 1850
Conseil supérieur du commerce et de l'industrie, *Enquête sur les voies de communication*, 1900
Direction générale des contributions indirectes, *Navigation intérieure . . . Relevé général du tonnage des marchandises . . . pendant l'année 1878*, 1880
Direction générale des douanes, *Tableau général des mouvements du cabotage pendant l'année 1893*, 1894
Ministère de l'Agriculture, du Commerce et des Travaux Publics, *Statistique des routes royales de France*, 1824
   Tableau des routes royales divisées en trois classes, 1824
   Direction générale des ponts-et-chaussées. Situation des travaux au 31 décembre 1833, 1834
   Recueil de documents statistiques. Routes royales, routes départementales, 1837
   Procès-verbaux des séances de la commission chargée d'examiner les questions qui peuvent soulever les projets d'établissement de chemins de fer, 1837
   Mémoire sur le projet d'un chemin de fer de Lyon à Marseille par M. Kermaingout, 1837
   Chemins de fer français d'intérêt général. Documents statistiques relatifs à l'année . . ., (1866–87)
   Statistique des chemins de fer français, 2 vols. per annum, 1887–1906
   Statistique des chemins de fer français d'intérêt général (1906–13)

Enquête sur les moyens d'assurer la régularité et la sûreté de l'exploitation sur les chemins de fer, 1858

Enquête sur l'exploitation et la construction des chemins de fer, 1858

Chemins de fer du globe au 31 décembre 1857 et 31 décembre 1861, n.d.

Enquête sur l'exploitation et la construction des chemins de fer, 1863

Enquête sur la marine marchande, 2 vols., 1863

Chemins de fer. Conditions techniques d'établissement, 1865

Documents statistiques sur les chemins de fer 1823–70, n.d., n.p.

Chemins de fer de l'Europe. Résultats généraux de l'exploitation 1864–66, 1871

Bureau de la statistique des chemins de fer. Documents relatifs à la construction et à l'exploitation, 1872

Ministère de l'Intérieur, *Police du roulage. Rapport d'une commission . . .*, 1814

Rapport au Roi sur la situation, au 31 mars 1825, des canaux, n.d. (also for 1826–7, 1830)

Rapport au Roi sur l'exécution pendant l'année 1839, de la loi du 21 mai 1836 relative aux chemins vicinaux, 1840 (also volumes for 1840 and 1841)

Rapport à S. M. l'Empereur sur le service des chemins vicinaux pendant la période quinquenniale de 1852 à 1856, 1858

Publications relatives à l'achèvement des chemins vicinaux. Compte rendu général des opérations effectuées en . . ., annually from 1869

Documents relatifs à la répartition de la 12ᵉ annuité des subventions accordées, en vertu de la loi du 11 juillet 1868 pour l'achèvement des chemins vicinaux, 1879

Documents relatifs au déclassement des routes départementales et à l'unification des services de voies, 1887

Statistique de la navigation intérieure. Recensement de la batellerie année 1887, 1888 (also for 1891)

Instruction spéciale pour l'application de la loi du 12 mars 1880, 1888

Enquête sur la réforme de la prestation et les modifications à introduire dans le régime des routes et des chemins vicinaux, 1889

Ministère des Travaux Publics, *Routes nationales. Tableaux de classement des travaux d'achèvement et d'amélioration*, 1880

Routes nationales. Situation au 1 janvier 1881 des travaux en cours ou à entreprendre, 1882

Chemins de fer français d'intérêt général. Album des tarifs généraux et spéciaux actuels (petite vitesse), 1882

Routes nationales. Recensement de la circulation en 1882, 1883

Relevé général du tonnage des marchandises transportées sur les fleuves, rivières et canaux pendant l'année 1881, 1883

Proposition de loi concernant les tarifs de chemins de fer. Rapport de M. Richard Waddington. Discussion au Comité consultatif des chemins de fer, 1891

Album de statistique graphique de 1897–99, 1900

Répertoire de la législation des chemins de fer français, 1901

Notices sur les travaux compris au projet de loi déposé le 1ᵉʳ mai 1901 et tendant à compléter l'outillage national par l'exécution d'un certain nombre de voies navigables nouvelles, l'amélioration des canaux, des rivières et des ports maritimes, n.d.

Comité consultatif des chemins de fer. Frais accessoires et conditions générales d'application des tarifs spéciaux 1900, 1902

Commission instituée par décret du 31 avril 1907 pour l'étude de la révision de la loi du 11 juin 1880 sur les chemins de fer d'intérêt local et les tramways, 1908

Commission chargée d'étudier les réformes à réaliser dans l'organisation du contrôle des chemins de fer. Rapport général, 1912

Senate, *Enquête parlementaire sur le régime des chemins de fer d'intérêt général. Dépositions des représentants des compagnies de chemin de fer*, 1878

RAILWAY COMPANIES

Assemblée générale annuelle des actionnaires, *Rapport du conseil d'administration* . . .

Compagnies du chemin de fer Est, Midi, Nord, Ouest, PLM, P–O, annual publications

Est, *Réponse* . . . *au questionnaire de la commission d'enquête administrative sur les chemins de fer*, n.d. (1870)

OTHER

Publications of conseils généraux, conseils d'arrondissement, municipal councils and chambers of commerce and agricultural societies (Bibliothèque nationale)

PRIVATE PUBLICATIONS (selected titles)

Audiganne, A., *Les chemins de fer aujourd'hui et dans cent ans*, 2 vols., 1858

Beuchot, C., *Navigation intérieure*, 1875

Bloch, R., 'Les chemins de fer français et les transports de céréales', *Revue générale des chemins de fer et tramways*, 1901

Bloch, R., *Questions de chemin de fer. Etudes commerciales*, 1921

Bonnal, A., *Exploitation commerciale des chemins de fer*, 1909

Bourgnon de Layre, M., *Des voies de communication en France*, Poitiers, 1846

Bresson, R., *L'évolution de l'idée d'intérêt local dans la constitution du réseau ferré français*, 1913

Campredon, E., *Rôle économique et social des voies de communication*, 1899

Colson, C., *Transports et tarifs*, 1898

Coursac, M. de, *Les transports agricoles en France*, 1907

Dictionnaire général des villes, bourgs, villages, hameaux et fermes de la France, 5th edn, 1853

Dubel, G., *Le transport des denrées périssables par chemin de fer*, Laval, 1914

Edleston, T. H., *Des chemins et sentiers d'exploitation*, 1907

Flachat, I., *Chemin de fer de Paris à Toulouse*, 1863

Foville, A. de, *La transformation des moyens de transport et ses conséquences économiques et sociales*, 1880

Freycinet, C. de, *Souvenirs*, 1914

Jacqmin, F., *De l'exploitation des chemins de fer. Leçons faites en 1867 à l'école impériale des ponts-et-chaussées*, 2 vols., 1868

Jacqmin, F., *M. de Franqueville. Directeur-général des ponts-et-chaussées et des chemins de fer. Sa vie et ses travaux*, 1877

Lafitte, L., *L'expansion économique de la France par l'amélioration et le développement de ses moyens de transport*, 1904

Lalanne, L., 'Essai d'une théorie de réseaux des chemins de fer', *Comptes rendus hebdomadaires des séances de l'Académie des sciences*, 1863

Lamé Fleury, E., *Code annoté des chemins de fer en exploitation ou Recueil méthodique et chronologique des lois, décrets, ordonnances, arrêtés, circulaires, etc., concernant l'exploitation technique et commerciale des chemins de fer*, 1868

Larget, F., *Les tarifs des chemins de fer. Le cabotage et la navigation intérieure*, Rouen, 1872

Laurent de Villedeuill, P. C., *Oeuvres de Emile et Isaac Pereire*, 4 vols., 1919–20

Leroy-Beaulieu, P., 'L'accroissement du mouvement maritime depuis un demi-siècle et les constructions navales', *L'économiste français*, 1889

Lillet, P., *Considérations économiques sur la tarification française des transports de marchandises par chemins de fer*, Bordeaux, 1903

Lucas, F., *Etude historique et statistique sur les voies de communication de la France*, 1873

Marcillaud de Goursac, M., *Les transports agricoles en France*, 1907

Marqfoy, G., *De l'abaissement des tarifs des chemins de fer en France*, 1863

Médeau, G., *De la concurrence entre la navigation intérieure et les chemins de fer*, Bordeaux, 1909

Michel, G., 'Variations des cours des frets maritimes, depuis 1850', *L'économiste français*, 1894

Monsarrat, G., *Les chemins vicinaux*, n.d.

Monsarrat, G., *Les chemins ruraux publics et privés* n.d.

Noblemaire, M., *Les chemins de fer départementaux*, 1890

Paulin, H., *La question des routes devant le parlement en 1891*, 1891

Pélicier, E., *Statistique du télégraphe privé depuis son origine en France*, 1858

Peut, H., *Des chemins de fer et des tarifs différentiels*, 1858

Picard, A., *Les chemins de fer français*, 4 vols., 1884

Picard, A., *Les chemins de fer. Aperçu historique*, 1918

Piot, G., *De l'application des prix des tarifs des chemins de fer*, 1913

Renoul, J.-C., *Rapport sur le mouvement maritime et commercial du port de Nantes*, 1861

Schlemmer, G., Bonneau, H., *Histoire parlementaire des chemins de fer français, contenant les principaux discours aux chambres, exposés des motifs des projets de lois, rapports, etc.*, 1897

Vallès, M. F., *Des chemins de fer et des routes impériales au point de vue de l'importance de leurs transports respectifs*, 1857

Vitard, A., *Rapport intime des progrès agricoles avec l'organisation du service vicinal*, Beauvais, 1857

Commerce

GOVERNMENTAL

Conseil d'Etat, *Enquête sur la révision de la législation des céréales*, 3 vols., 1859

Enquête sur la boulangerie du département de la Seine ou Recueil des dépositions concernant les commerçants du blé, de la farine et du pain, faites en 1859 devant une commission présidée par M. Boinvillier, Président de la Section de l'Intérieur . . ., 1859

Enquête sur le régime du courtage, 1864

Conseils généraux de l'agriculture, de la manufacture et du commerce, *Procès-verbaux*, vols. 1–3, 1845–6

Direction générale des Douanes et des contributions indirectes, *Tableau décennal du commerce de la France* (every decade from 1838)

Documents pour servir à l'étude des questions relatives au régime des ventes en gros dans les marchés de Paris, 1869

Ministère de l'Agriculture, *Le prix du froment en France, 1726–1913*, 1970

Descriptions des espèces bovines, ovines et porcines de la France par MM. les inspecteurs de l'agriculture, 1862

Notice sur le commerce des produits agricoles, 2 vols., 1906–8

Tableaux de prix moyens mensuels et annuels de l'hectolitre de froment en France, 1800–1872, corrected and supplemented by E. Labrousse *et al.*

Ministère de l'Agriculture et du Commerce, *Admissions temporaires*, 1877

Ministère de l'Agriculture et Ministère des Finances, *Enquête sur les principes des faits généraux qui régissent la circulation monétaire et fiduciaire*, 1867

Ministère du Commerce, *Enquête sur le régime douanier*, 1893

La petite industrie, 2 vols., 1893

'Admissions temporaires des céréales', 'Entrepôts de céréales', 'Projet de loi dit du Cadenas', 1896

Paris Préfecture de Police, *Des moyens de prévenir des fluctuations excessives du prix des blés en France*, 1854

De l'organisation de la boulangerie comme moyen de prévenir la fluctuation excessive du prix des blés en France, 1854

Commission des subsistances. Taxe du pain. Rapport présenté au nom de la sous-commission par V. Foucher, 1855

Documents pour servir à l'étude des questions rélative au régime des ventes en gros dans les marchés de Paris, 1869

PRIVATE PUBLICATIONS

Boland, A., *Traité pratique de boulangerie*, 1860

Drouet, H., *Notes et souvenirs sur la boulangerie de la Sarthe*, Le Mans, 1905

Husson, A., *Les consommations de Paris*, 1856

Marchal, L., *Question des subsistances. Mémoire qui a obtenu la médaille d'or de M. Cormenin dans le concours ouvert par la société d'économie charitable*, 1849

du Maroussern, P., and Guérce, C., *La question ouvrière. Halles centrales de Paris et commerce de l'alimentation*, 1894

Minard, C. J., *Carte du mouvement des céréales en 1853 sur les voies d'eau et de fer de l'Empire français*, 1855

Molinari, G. de, *Conversations sur le commerce des grains et la protection de l'agriculture*, 1886

Perrier, G., *Observations sur la production et les prix des blés étrangers*, 1885

Rivière, H.-F., *Précis historique et critique de la législation française sur le commerce des céréales et des mesures d'administration prises dans les temps de cherté*, 1859

Société des agriculteurs de France, *Dépositions des délégués de la société . . . devant la commission parlementaire du tarif général des douanes*, 1879

Zolla, D., *La crise agricole dans ses rapports avec la baisse des prix et la question monétaire*, 1903

Zolla, D., *Le blé et les céréales*, 1909

Agriculture

GOVERNMENTAL

Conseil d'Etat, *Enquête sur le crédit foncier*, 1850
Enquête sur la production et la consommation de la boucherie, 1851
Ministère de l'Agriculture, du Commerce et des Travaux Publics, *Statistique de la France*:
Agriculture, 4 vols., 1840–1
Statistique agricole, 2ᵉ série, vols. vii, viii, 1858–60
Résultats généraux de l'enquête décennale de 1862, Strasbourg, 1868
Résultats généraux de l'enquête décennale de 1882, Nancy, 1887
Résultats généraux de l'enquête décennale de 1892, 1897
Agriculture française par MM. les inspecteurs de l'agriculture, Département l'Aude, 1847; Hautes-Pyrénées, 1843; Tarn 1845; Haute-Garonne, 1843
Documents statistiques relatifs à la question de la boucherie, 1856
Enquête sur les engrais industriels, 1864
Enquête agricole, 37 vols., 1867–72
Récoltes des céréales et des pommes de terre de 1815 à 1876, 1878
La petite propriété rurale en France. Enquêtes monographiques, 1909
Dix ans de crédit agricole, 1911
Enquête sur les salaires agricoles, 1912
Le crédit agricole. Encouragement à la petite propriété rurale, 1912
Culture, production et commerce du blé dans le monde, 1912

PUBLIC

Congrès central d'agriculture, *Compte-rendu et procès-verbaux des séances*, 2 vols., 1844–5
Conseil général, Hérault, *Rapport présenté au nom de la commission de l'agriculture et du commerce par M. Chambon*, 1850
Société nationale d'agriculture de France, *Enquête sur la situation de l'agriculture en France en 1879*, 2 vols., 1880
Enquête sur le crédit agricole faite sur la demande de M. le Ministre de l'agriculture, 2 vols., 1884

PRIVATE

André-Gabriel Roche, J.-C., *Les subsistances et les moyens de remédier à leur insuffisance* 1855
Anon., *Agriculture et l'enquête*, Villeneuve-sur-Lot, 1867
Baudrillart, H., *Les populations agricoles de la France. Normandie et Bretagne*, 1885
Bonnet, A., *Enquête sur la situation et les besoins de l'agriculture*, Dijon, 1867
Imbart-Latour, I., *Réponse au questionnaire de la grande enquête agricole de 1888 notamment en ce qui concerne le Nivernais*, 1888
Léonce de Lavergne, *L'agriculture et la population*, 1865
Léonce de Lavergne, *L'économie rurale de la France depuis 1789*, 1877
Levasseur, E., 'L'organisation, les travaux et les publications de la statistique officielle en France', *J. de la société statistique de Paris*, 1885
Lullin de Châteauvieux, F., *Voyages agronomiques en France*, 2 vols., 1843

Economic crises

GOVERNMENTAL

Ministère des Travaux Publics, *Notice sur la périodicité des crises économiques et ses rapports avec l'exploitation des chemins de fer français*, n.d.

PRIVATE

Briaune, M., *Des crises commerciales, de leurs causes et de leurs remèdes*, 1840
Chevalier, M., *Des forces alimentaires des états et des devoirs du gouvernement dans la crise actuelle*, 1847
Puynode, G. du, *Les grandes crises financières de la France*, 1876

Social conditions

GOVERNMENTAL

Ministère de l'Agriculture, du Commerce et des Travaux Publics, *Documents statistiques et administratifs concernant l'épidémie de choléra de 1854 comparée aux précédentes épidémies cholériques qui ont sévi en France*, 1862
Statistique de la France, 2ᵉ série, vol. 12, *Prix et salaires à diverses époques*, Strasbourg, 1864

PUBLIC

Paris Chambre de commerce, *Statistique de l'industrie à Paris résultant de l'enquête faite pour les années 1847–48*, 1851; . . . *pour l'annee 1860*, 1864
   Enquête sur les conditions du travail en France, 1872

PRIVATE

Audiganne, A., *Les populations ouvrières et les industries de la France dans le mouvement social du 19ᵉ siècle*, 2 vols., 1854
Benoît, J., *Confessions d'un prolétaire*, 1871 (1968)
Blanqui, A., 'Les populations rurales de la France en 1850', *Annales provençales d'agriculture*, 1851
Blanqui, A., 'Tableau des populations rurales de la France en 1850', *J. des économistes*, 1851
Brame, J., *De l'émigration des campagnes*, Lille, 1859
Dumay, J. B., *Mémoires d'un militant ouvrier du Creusot* (1841–1905), Grenoble, 1976
Dutouquet, H. E., *De la condition des classes pauvres à la campagne, des moyens les plus efficaces de l'améliorer*, 1846
Forestier, H., *L'Yonne au 19ᵉ siècle*, 2 vols., Auxerre, 1959
Foville, A. de, *Enquête sur les conditions de l'habitation en France*, 1894
Guillaume, H., *La vie d'un simple*, 1904
Kahan-Rabecq, M.-M. (ed.), *Réponses du dépt. du Haut-Rhin à l'enquête faite en 1848 par l'Assemblée nationale sur les conditions du travail industriel et agricole*, 1939
Le Roy, E., *Le moulin du Frau*, n.d.
Lavasseur, E., *Histoire des classes ouvrières*, vol. 2, 1864
Nadaud, M., *Mémoires de Léonard*, 1948

Rémusat, C. de, *Mémoires de ma vie*, vol. 4, 1962
Tocqueville, A. de, *Oeuvres complètes*, vols. 5–7, 1967

Mentalities

GOVERNMENTAL
Ministère de l'Instruction Publique, *Rapport au roi par le ministre secrétaire d'Etat . . . sur l'exécution de la loi du 28 juin 1833 relative à l'instruction primaire*, 1834
　Rapport au roi . . . sur la situation de l'instruction primaire . . . 1840, 1841 (also reports on years 1843, 1848, 1863)
　Etat de l'instruction primaire en 1864 après les rapports des Inspecteurs d'Académie, 2 vols., 1866
　Statistique comparée de l'enseignement primaire, 1829–77, 1880

PRIVATE
Frères de l'instruction chrétienne, *L'agriculture à l'école primaire en 42 leçons*, 2nd edn., Ploermel, 1894
Pinet, A., *L'enseignement primaire en présence de l'enquête agricole*, 1873
Robert, C., *De l'ignorance des populations ouvrières et rurales de la France et des causes qui tendent à la perpétuer*, Montbeliard, 1862

Protest
Anon., *Le socialisme c'est la famine!*, Bordeaux, 1849
Anon., *L'Armée et le socialisme, simples réflexions sur la question du moment par un paysan qui a été soldat*, 1849
Boucher de Perthes, J., *Misère, émeute, choléra*, Abbeville, 1849
Castellane, Maréchal de, *Journal*, vols. 3 and 4, 1849
Chesseneau, G. (ed.), *La Commission extra-parlementaire de 1849* 1937
Cour d'assises de l'Indre, *Affaire des troubles de Buzançais*, Châteauroux, 1847
Documents pour servir à l'histoire du Second Empire: circulaires, rapports, notes et instructions confidentielles, 1872
Guiral, P., and Brunon, R., *Aspects de la vie politique et militaire en France au milieu du 19ᵉ siècle à travers la correspondance reçue par le Maréchal Pelissier (1828–64)*, 1968
Holt, R. (ed.), *Papiers sauvé des Tuileries*, 1871
Modeste, V., *De la cherté des grains et des préjuges populaires*, 3rd edn, 1862
Papiers et correspondance de la famille impériale, 2 vols, 1871.
Ténot, E., *Le suffrage universel et les paysans*, 1865
Ténot, E., *La province en décembre 1852*, 1868
Vallès, J., *Les Blouses*, 1957
Watelet, E., *Les récents troubles du Nord de la France*, 1912

Contemporary journals

Annales de l'agriculture française
Annales des ponts-et-chaussées
Bulletin officiel des chemins de fer
Bulletin des séances de la société d'agriculture

Bulletin de la Société Franklin
Gazette des Tribunaux
Journal d'agriculture pratique
Journal des chemins de fer
Journal des chemins de fer départementaux
Journal des économistes
Réforme sociale
Revue des Deux Mondes
Revue générale des chemins de fer

Secondary sources

Selected titles; see also Notes and references. For a complete bibliography, please contact the author.

Agulhon, M., Désert, G., and Specklin, R., *Histoire de la France rurale*, vol. 3, 1976
Armengaud, A., *Les populations de l'Est-Aquitain au début de l'époque contemporaine*, 1961
Bédarida, F., *et al.*, *Pour une histoire de la statistique*, 2 vols. 1976
Braudel, F., and Labrousse, E. (eds), *Histoire économique et sociale de la France*, vols. 3/2, 4, 1976–9
Brunet, P., *Structures agraires et l'économie rurale des plateaux tertiaires entre la Seine et l'Oise*, Caen, 1960
Caralp-Landon, R., *Les chemins de fer dans le Massif Central*, 1959
Caron, F. *Histoire de l'exploitation d'un grand réseau. La compagnie du chemin de fer du Nord, 1846–1937*, 1973
Claval, P., *Géographie générale des marchés*, 1965
Claverie, J.-C., 'Les cadres spatiaux de la vie de relation dans le sud-ouest de la France pendant la première moitié du 19ᵉ siècle', *Revue géographique de l'Est*, 1973
Chevalier, M., *La vie humaine dans les Pyrénées ariègeoises*, 1956
Clout, H. D. (ed.), *Themes in the Historical Geography of France*, 1977
Clout, H. D., *Agriculture in France on the Eve of the Railway Age*, 1980
Clozier, R., *La gare du Nord*, 1940
Corbin, A., *Archaïsme et modernité en Limousin au 19ᵉ siècle*, 2 vols., 1975
Désert, G., *Une société rurale au 19ᵉ siècle: les paysans du Calvados, 1815–95*, 3 vols., Lille, 1975
Dupeux, G. *Aspects de l'histoire sociale et politique du Loir-et-Cher*, 1962
Faucher, D., *La vie rurale vue par un géographe*, Toulouse, 1962
Faucher, D., *L'homme et le Rhône*, 1968
Fel, A., *Les hautes terres du Massif Central. Tradition paysanne et économie agricole*, 1962
Froment, P., 'Les chemins de fer et l'agriculture', *L'Année ferroviaire*, 1948
Garrier, G., *Paysans du Beaujolais et du Lyonnais, 1800–1970*, 2 vols., Grenoble, 1973
Garrier, G., 'Les enquêtes agricoles du 19ᵉ siècle. Une source contestée', *Cahiers d'histoire*, 1967
Gautier, M., *Chemins et véhicules de nos campagnes*, St-Brieuc, 1971

Gille, B., 'Les archives des compagnies de chemins de fer', *Histoire des entreprises*, 1958

Gille, B. *Les sources statistiques de l'histoire de France*, Geneva 1964

Gille, B., 'Bibliographie analytique des enquêtes effectuées par ordre du Ministre du Commerce et de l'Agriculture de 1800 à 1918', *Histoire des entreprises*, no. 11

Girard, L., *La politique des travaux publics du Second Empire*, 1952

Gonnet, P., 'Esquisse de la crise économique en France de 1827 à 1832', *Revue d'histoire économique et sociale*, 1955

Gonnet, P., 'Dijon, pôle d'organisation régionale au 19e siècle', *Annales de Bourgogne*, 1977

Grantham, G., 'Scale and organization in French farming 1840–80', in W. N. Parker, *European Peasants and their Markets*, 1975

Hohenberg, P., 'Change in rural France in the period of industrialization', *Journal of Economic History*, 1972

Houssel, J. P. (ed.), *Histoire des paysans français*, Roanne, 1976

Hubscher, R. H., *L'agriculture et la société rurale dans le Pas-de-Calais du milieu du 19e siècle à 1914*, Doctorat d'état, Université de Paris, 1978

Jouffrey, L. M., *Une étape de la construction des grandes lignes de chemins de fer en France. La ligne de Paris à la frontière d'Allemagne*, 4 vols., n.d.

Juillard, F., *La vie rurale dans les plaines de Basse-Alsace: essai de géographie sociale*, 1953

Labrousse, E. (ed.), *Aspects de la crise et de la dépression de l'économie française au milieu du 19e siècle*, 1956

L'homme, J., 'La crise agricole à la fin du 19e siècle en France – essai d'interprétation économique et sociale', *Revue économique*, 1970

Livet, R., *Habitat rural et structures agraires en Basse-Provence*, Aix, 1962

Marcilhacy, C., *Le diocèse d'Orléans au milieu du 19e siècle. Les hommes et leurs mentalités*, 1964

Matyja-Ochs, C., *Aspects de la croissance française. Etude départementale 1852–82*, Doctorat du 3e cycle, Université Paul-Valéry, Montpellier III, 1974

Mulliez, J., 'Du blé "mal nécessaire", réflexions sur les progrès de l'agriculture de 1750–1850', *Revue d'histoire moderne et contemporaine*, 1979

Musset, R., 'Les statistiques agricoles officielles françaises. Etude critique', *Annales d'histoire économique et sociale*, 1933

Newell, W. H., 'The agricultural revolution in 19th century France', *Journal of Economic History*, 1973

O'Brien, P., and Keyder, C., *Economic Growth in Britain and France (1780–1914)*, 1978

Pautard, J., *Les disparités régionales dans la croissance de l'agriculture française*, 1965

Pech, R., *Entreprise viticole et capitalisme en Languedoc–Roussillon du phylloxera aux crises de mévente*, Toulouse, 1976

Philopponneau, M., *La vie rurale de la banlieue parisienne. Etude de géographie humaine*, 1956

Pitié, J., *Exode rural et migrations intérieures en France. L'exemple de la Vienne et du Poitou-Charentes*, Poitiers, 1971

Postel-Vinay, G., *La rente foncière dans le capitalisme agricole*, 1974

Renard, J., *Les évolutions contemporaines de la vie rurale dans la région nantaise*, Les Sables-d'Olonne, 1975

Renouard, D., *Les transports de marchandises par fer, route et eau depuis 1850*, 1960

Rivals, C., *Le moulin à vent et le meunier dans la société traditionelle française*, 1976

Rivet, F., *La navigation à vapeur sur la Saône et le Rhône*, 1962

Ruttan, V. W., 'Structural retardation and the modernisation of French agriculture: a sceptical view', *Journal of Economic History*, 1978

Suret-Canale, J., 'L'état économique et social de la Mayenne au milieu du 19ᵉ siècle', *Revue d'histoire économique et sociale*, 1958

Thabault, R., *Education and Change in a Village Community: Mazières-en-Gâtine*, 1971

Thuillier, A., *Economie et société nivernaises au début du 19ᵉ siècle*, 1976

Thuillier, G., *Aspects de l'économie nivernaise au 19ᵉ siècle*, 1966

Toutain, J.-C., *Le produit de l'agriculture française de 1700 à 1958*, 1961

Toutain, J.-C., 'Les transports en France de 1830 à 1908', *Economie et société*, 1967

Toutain, J.-C., 'La consommation alimentaire en France de 1789 à 1964', ibid., 1971

Viallon, 'L'agriculture bourguignonne a-t-elle manqué sa modernisation?', *Annales de Bourgogne*, 1977

Vigier, P., *La Seconde République dans la région alpine*, 2 vols, 1963

Wolkowitsch, M., *L'économie régionale des transports dans le centre et le centre-ouest de la France*, n.d.

Index